**OLD BAILEY PRESS**

OLD BAILEY PRESS
at Holborn College, Woolwich Road,
Charlton, London SE7 8LN

First published 1997
Fourth edition 2003

© The HLT Group Ltd 2003

ISBN 1 85836 497 3

*British Library Cataloguing-in-Publication.*
A CIP Catalogue record for this book is
available from the British Library.

*Acknowledgement*
The publishers and author would
like to thank the Incorporated
Council of Law Reporting for
England and Wales for kind
permission to reproduce extracts
from the Weekly Law Reports, and
Butterworths for their kind
permission to reproduce extracts
from the All England Law Reports.

Printed and bound in Great Britain

# Contents

# Preface

Old Bailey Press textbooks are written specifically for students. They will find that the books provide comprehensive and up-to-date coverage which should enable them to secure a sound grasp of the basic principles and their practical application.

Family law continues to be a dynamic area in a constant state of change. The Human Rights Act 1998, which incorporated the European Convention on Human Rights into English law, continues to make a significant impact on family law. This fourth edition of the *Family Law* textbook makes reference to the Convention and decisions of the European Court of Human Rights throughout. Particular areas of development include the changing law on the status of transsexuals, highlighting the ECHR judgment in *Goodwin* v *United Kingdom*; *I* v *United Kingdom*. Also included in the ancillary relief chapter is the development of case law since the landmark decision in *White* v *White*. The courts continue to strive to avoid discrimination between the breadwinner and the homemaker. Decisions reported in this edition include the important case of *Lambert* v *Lambert*. The Adoption and Children Act 2002 has been passed though not yet brought into force. The radical changes the Act brings to adoption law are included, as well as the important changes for parental responsibility.

Account has been taken of changes in the law up to 1 March 2003.

# Table of Cases

vii

# Table of Statutes and Other Materials

# 1

# Introduction

1.1 History

1.2 Human Rights Act 1998

## 1.1 History

A brief outline of the history of family law helps put the present law into context.

Up until the nineteenth century the Church's ecclesiastical courts dominated family law. The state then transferred jurisdiction to the High Court (a new divorce court was created in 1857). In 1886 the county court then assumed jurisdiction to make orders concerning children. Magistrates' courts long had jurisdiction to deal with particular family law matters, such as the maintenance of illegitimate children. The result of this somewhat haphazard evolution were three levels of court – the Family Division of the High Court, the county court and the magistrates' court – each dealing with different aspects of parts of family law and having overlapping jurisdiction in other parts. Some aspects of family law were dealt with by the criminal courts (eg care proceedings were heard in juvenile crime courts and in the Crown Court). There were proposals to create a unified family court (eg through the Finer Report in 1974), and something of a unified system was achieved in 1991 when the Children Act 1989 came into force. The 1989 Act codified much of the law relating to disputes between parents about their children and the law relating to local authorities taking action to protect children at risk of harm. The law applied more or less equally to each of the three courts and work could be transferred between the three levels depending on complexity, speed of hearing and convenience.

In the nineteenth century family law was largely concerned with marriage and the consequences of a failed marriage. The principal remedy was nullity. A divorce could only be obtained at great cost and with considerable difficulty. Courts were then given greater powers to grant divorces using the concept of the 'matrimonial offence'. The present divorce law was established through the Divorce Reform Act 1969 which considerably reduced the need to find fault (or an 'offence') in order to gain a divorce. These provisions are now contained in the Matrimonial Causes Act 1973. There was an attempt to eliminate the concept of fault altogether in divorce through the Family Law Act 1996, but the relevant parts of the Act have never been brought into force. Contested divorces are rare and attention is largely focused on the court's wide-ranging powers to settle the financial arrangements of the parties following the divorce. In 1993 the Child Support Act 1991 came into force creating a special government agency, the Child Support Agency, to deal with almost all applications for the financial support of children. As a result many applications for financial support within families are dealt with by two bodies – the courts and the Child Support Agency – who operate independently of each other.

As far as the upbringing of children was concerned the law used to treat children as the property of their fathers. The rights of mothers became more important until the rights of parents largely became equal. The law then moved towards recognising the rights of the child whose welfare is now the paramount consideration in many applications concerning the child's upbringing. The Children Act 1989 is now the dominating statute in this respect.

English and Welsh family law has to be interpreted in light of the European Convention on Human Rights following the enactment of the Human Rights Act 1998 (which came into force in October 2000). The future shape of family law is likely to be significantly influenced by the Convention and other international agreements.

## 1.2 Human Rights Act 1998

The Human Rights Act (HRA) 1998 provides for the following:

1. Courts must have regard to particular articles in the European Convention on Human Rights in interpreting English and Welsh law and must interpret the law, so far as is possible, to give effect to those Convention rights: s3(1) HRA 1998.
2. The court must have regard to the decisions of the European Court of Human Rights in interpeting and applying the Convention: s2(1) HRA 1998.
3. If a provision in English and Welsh law is incompatible with the Convention then the court has the following options under ss3(2) and 4 HRA 1998:

   a) in the case of primary legislation the court must give effect to the primary legislation even if it is incompatible with the Convention (but the High Court, the Court of Appeal or the House of Lords can make a declaration of incompatibility which will enable the Government to speedily amend the primary legislation so as to make it compatible with the Convention);
   b) in the case of secondary legislation the court can give effect to the Convention and ignore the secondary legislation if it is incompatible with the secondary legislation (unless the secondary legislation is inextricably linked with primary legislation whereby the primary legislation forces the incompatibility whereupon the court must give effect to the secondary legislation);
   c) in the case of case law the court must give effect to the Convention and ignore the case law if the case law is incompatible with the Convention.

4. All public authorities must act in accordance with the Convention, unless required to do so by statute ('public authority' has a wide definition and will include local authorities): s6 HRA 998.
5. Individuals who believe that their Convention rights have been infringed by a public authority may either bring proceedings against that public authority or rely on their Convention rights in proceedings brought by other: ss7 and 8 HRA 1998. The remedies for breach of Convention rights are wide and include damages.

## The Convention rights applied by the Human Rights Act 1998

The main parts of the Convention which are applied by the Human Rights Act 1998 (s1(1)) are:

| | |
|---|---|
| Article 2 | Right to life |
| Article 3 | Prohibition on torture and inhuman or degrading treatment (see *A v United Kingdom* [1998] 2 FLR 959 which considered the failure of the UK courts to protect a child from degrading treatment from his step-father; see also *Costello–Roberts* v *United Kingdom* (1995) 19 EHRR 112) |
| Article 4 | Prohibition on slaveryand forced labour |
| Article 5 | Right to liberty and security |
| Article 6 | Right to a fair trial |
| Article 7 | No punishment without law (protection from retrospective criminal offences) (considered in *CR* v *United Kingdom* [1996] 1 FLR 434 in which the UK was not held to have breached art 7 in relation to a husband convicted of raping his wife following developments in the common law) |
| Article 8 | Right to private and family life |
| Article 9 | Right to freedom of thought, conscience and religion |
| Article 10 | Freedom of expression |
| Article 11 | Freedom of assembly and association |
| Article 12 | Right to marry and found a family |
| Article 14 | Prohibition on discrimination |
| First Protocol | |
| Article 2 | Right to education |

These rights can be classified in three kinds of right:

## Absolute rights
These rights cannot be infringed and must be safeguarded by national law. Articles 2, 3, 4 and 7 are absolute rights.

**Limited rights**
These rights are subject to limitations contained in the articles. Articles 5 and 6 are limited rights.

**Qualified rights**
These rights may be restricted if it is necessary in a democratic society to restrict the right and the restriction is proportionate to the harm being avoided. Articles 8, 9, 10 and 11 are qualified rights.

## Words and phrases used in Convention law

Family law practitioners will need to be familiar with certain words and phrases used in Convention law. These include:

*Autonomous terms* ie terms in the Convention have an autonomous meaning which may differ from a similar term in national law. For example, criminal proceedings in Convention law can include proceedings to enforce local authority taxes which would be classified as civil proceedings in English law.

*Derogation* ie the right of a national state to ask that a Convention right not apply or apply in a restricted way because of war or emergency (see art 15 – the UK has one derogation in place concerning pre-trial detention under prevention of terrorism legislation).

*Equality of arms* ie the concept that an individual is less strong than a public authority and the Convention should be interpreted to protect the rights of the individual and insofar as is possible given the individual equality of arms with the public authority.

*Living instrument* ie recognition that the Convention is a living instrument and interpretation of it will develop over time. This is perhaps best illustrated by the series of cases dealing with the rights of transsexuals which go from *Rees* v *United Kingdom* [1987] Fam Law 157 (no violation under arts 8 and 12) to *Goodwin* v *United Kingdom; I* v *United Kingdom* [2002] 2 FLR 487 and 518 (violation of arts 8 and 12 found).

*Margin of appreciation* ie the acknowledgement of the European Court that in some matters, such as morality, national courts may have greater knowledge or expertise, whereby the European Court gives a margin of appreciation to the national court in interpreting how a Convention right should apply in a nation state.

*Positive obligation* ie the obligation on the national state to actively safeguard and secure Convention rights. The national state must take positive steps to apply the

Convention and not pay lip service to it (eg the positive obligation to enforce court orders giving effect to Convention rights as in *Hokkanen* v *Finland* (1995) 19 EHRR 139).

*Purposive approach* ie the courts should not just look at the words of the Convention but look at the purpose behind the articles and develop the law accordingly. This means that all sorts of rights and obligations not mentioned in the Convention are protected because they are deemed to be protected by the purpose behind the relevant article.

*Quality of law* ie national law must be sufficiently precise and accessible to predict whether an act is or is not unlawful.

*Reservation* ie before signing the Convention a national state can enter a reservation confirming that national law is not in accordance with the Convention: art 64. The UK has entered a reservation with respect to art 2 of the First Protocol with respect to education. It remains to be seen whether this reservation will withstand challenge in the European Court.

# 2

# Nullity

2.1 Introduction

2.2 Void marriages

2.3 Voidable marriages

2.4 Bars where marriage voidable

## 2.1 Introduction

A considerable body of law built up on the annulment of marriage during the period when there was difficulty in obtaining a divorce. As divorce became much easier to obtain, petitions for nullity declined. In 2001 the number of nullity petitions was 657, compared with 161,580 divorce petitions. Nevertheless, nullity remains an important remedy for those who do not wish to end marriage through divorce for religious reasons. Anecdotal evidence also suggests an increased use of nullity based on the ground of wilful refusal to consummate arranged marriages.

Null marriages fall into two categories: *void* and *voidable* marriages. The distinctions between void and voidable marriages are as follows:

### Void

If *void* the marriage is so defective on social and public policy grounds that it does not exist – this takes priority over anything the parties to the void marriages may wish themselves. Thus:

1. There is no need for a decree which is purely declaratory (but either party may want a decree in order to claim ancillary relief).
2. Children are illegitimate, unless both or either the parents reasonably believed at the time of the artificial insemination or conception or marriage, whichever was later, that the marriage was valid, and the father was domiciled in England and Wales at the date of the birth, or, if the father died beforehand, at the date of his death (see s1 Legitimacy Act 1976 which has been amended by the Family Law Reform Act 1987 from 4 April 1988 for children born after that date so that it is presumed that one of the parties reasonably believed that the marriage was valid, so that the children are legitimate, unless the contrary is shown).

3. A third party can challenge the validity of the marriage (eg the trustee of a marriage settlement).
4. A petition is possible even after the death of one spouse.
5. There are no special defences.

## *Voidable*

If *voidable* the marriage is defective but it is left to the parties whether or not they take advantage of their right to end the marriage. There is a valid subsisting marriage until decree. Thus:

1. The decree is necessary to prove that the marriage is a nullity.
2. Children are legitimate both before and after decree.
3. Only the spouse can challenge its validity.
4. No petition is possible after the death of one spouse.
5. There may be defences to a petition (s13 MCA 1973).

In *De Reneville* v *De Reneville* [1948] 1 All ER 56 Lord Greene MR expressed the distinction as follows:

'A void marriage is one that will be regarded by every court in any case in which the existence of the marriage is in issue as never having taken place and can be so treated by both parties to it without the necessity of any decree annulling it; a voidable marriage is one that will be regarded by every court as a valid subsisting marriage until a decree annulling it has been pronounced by a court of competent jurisdiction.'

Section 16 MCA 1973 reflects the distinction between void and voidable marriages by the following provision:

A decree of nullity granted after 31 July 1971, on the ground that a marriage is voidable, will only annul the marriage as respects any time after the decree has been made absolute and the marriage will be treated as if it had existed up to that time, notwithstanding the decree.

For example, in *Re Roberts (dec'd)* [1978] 3 All ER 225, H made a will giving property to B. He then married her. The marriage revoked the gift to B in the will. H died. B argued that the marriage was in fact a nullity by reason of H's insanity under s12(c) Matrimonial Causes Act 1973 so that she was entitled to the property.

HELD: B's argument was irrelevant. Even if she was correct the marriage was voidable and by s16 the marriage remained valid for all purposes until decree absolute so that the gift remained revoked.

Another example is *Ward* v *Secretary of State for Social Services* [1990] Fam Law 58. W married a naval officer. He died in 1982 and W obtained a pension as his widow. One of the regulations governing her pension stated that her pension would cease if she remarried. W did remarry in 1986 but she found that her second husband was a manic-depressive. The marriage lasted only a week and was never consummated. W obtained a decree of nullity under s12(a) MCA 1973. Her pension was stopped. W argued that her remarriage had been avoided so that the regulation did not apply.

HELD: Applying s16 MCA 1973 a decree of nullity in respect of a voidable marriage operated only with respect to any time *after* the decree had been made absolute. Since the marriage was valid up to that time the regulation came into effect and W was not entitled to the pension.

In *P v P (Ouster: Decree Nisi of Nullity)* [1994] 2 FLR 400 H petitioned for nullity on the basis that his marriage to W was voidable. He obtained a decree nisi of nullity. Before the decree was made absolute W applied for an order under the Matrimonial Homes Act (MHA) 1983 to oust H from the matrimonial home. She could only apply under the MHA 1983 if she was still married to H. The judge said that the marriage no longer subsisted and that W's application could not be considered. W appealed.

HELD: By s16 Matrimonial Causes Act (MCA) 1973 a voidable marriage was subsisting up to the time of decree absolute. The court did have jurisdiction to consider W's application. A rehearing was ordered before a different judge.

The form of petition for nullity is the same as that for divorce, and these decrees can be petitioned in the alternative. When petitioning for both decrees in the alternative, it is correct to petition first for dissolution of the marriage on the ground of nullity, for there can be no divorce from a marriage which does not exist.

It is possible to obtain ancillary financial relief even in circumstances where there has been a void marriage (see ss21–26 MCA 1973).

Therefore nullity petitions have been assimilated to the law of divorce in this respect. If a void or voidable marriage is terminated not by a nullity decree but by the death of one of the parties, then the survivor may ask for financial provision from the estate of the deceased partner provided that the survivor entered into the marriage in good faith (see s25(4) Inheritance (Provision for Family and Dependants) Act 1975).

## 2.2 Void marriages

Under the Matrimonial Causes Act 1973 a marriage celebrated after 31 July 1971 shall be void on the following grounds only:

*That it is not a valid marriage under the provisions of the Marriage Acts 1949 and 1970 (see s11(a))*

**The parties to the marriage are within the prohibited degrees of relationships**
Section 11(a)(i) Matrimonial Causes Act 1973, s1(1) and Schedule 1 Marriage Act 1949 – if such relations marry the marriage is void:

*Blood relations* prohibited because there are socially unacceptable and physical defects in children born of parents who share the same genes.

THE IMMEDIATE FAMILY. Mother cannot marry son and vice versa. Father cannot marry daughter and vice versa. Sister cannot marry brother and vice versa. NOTE: Adopted children cannot marry their adoptive parents but can marry adoptive brothers and sisters.

GRANDPARENTS. Grandfather cannot marry granddaughter and vice versa. Grandmother cannot marry grandson and vice versa.

AUNTS AND UNCLES (ie brother or sister of parent). An uncle cannot marry his niece or vice versa. An aunt cannot marry her nephew or vice versa. NOTE: First cousins can marry.

*Non-blood relations* referred to as being related by affinity; prohibited because socially unacceptable

STEP-PARENTS. A stepfather cannot marry his stepdaughter or vice versa. A stepmother cannot marry her stepson or vice versa. BUT the above can marry if both over twenty-one years and stepchild never actually lived with the step-parent as a child of the family (see s1(1) Marriage (Prohibited Degrees of Relationship) Act 1986).

MOTHERS-IN-LAW AND FATHERS-IN-LAW. A man cannot marry his mother-in-law or vice versa. A woman cannot marry her father-in-law or vice versa. BUT s1(3) and (4) Marriage (Prohibited Degrees of Relationship) Act 1986, which relates to marriages solemnised after 1 November 1986, allows such a marriage if both parties are over twenty-one years and both other spouses have died (eg a man may marry his mother-in-law if both over twenty-one and the man's wife (daughter of mother-in-law) and mother-in-law's husband (father of daughter) have both died). NOTE: A man may marry his sister-in-law and a woman may marry her brother-in-law under the Marriage (Enabling) Act 1960 as long as the existing marriage has been terminated by death or divorce.

ADOPTED CHILDREN. If a child is adopted then:

1. Members of the child's natural family remain within the prohibited degrees as if the child had not been adopted (see ss39(1) and 47(1) Adoption Act 1976).
2. The adoptive parents become within the prohibited degrees (see s39(1) Adoption Act 1976). BUT other members of the adoptive family are not so a man may marry his adoptive sister.

**Either party is under the age of sixteen**

Section 11(a)(ii) Matrimonial Causes Act 1973 and s2 Marriage Act 1949. A foreign marriage to a person under age will be recognised as valid if both parties are domiciled abroad and the marriage is recognised as valid by the law of the country in which it was celebrated.

In *Alhaji Mohamed* v *Knott* [1968] 2 WLR 1446; [1968] 2 All ER 563 a Nigerian man married a thirteen-year-old Nigerian girl. Both were domiciled in Nigeria at the time of the marriage. Nigerian law recognised the marriage, therefore, it was valid when they both came to live in England. However, this would not be so where either party is domiciled in this country. In *Pugh* v *Pugh* [1951] 2 All ER 680 a British soldier, domiciled in England, married a fifteen-year-old Hungarian girl in Austria. Both Hungarian and Austrian law recognised the marriage but, since the soldier was domiciled in England whose law does not permit such a marriage, the marriage was void.

NOTE: If either person is over the age of sixteen but under the age of eighteen (and not a widow or widower), then certain persons are normally required to give their consent to the marriage:

1. Each parent who has parental responsibility for the child (this would not include an unmarried father unless he has acquired parental responsibility under the Children Act 1989) and each guardian (if any) for the child.
2. A person in whose favour there is a residence order for the child (this replaces the consent of the parents and guardians).
3. If a care order is in force the consent of the local authority (this is in addition to the consent of the parents and guardians).

(See s3 MA 1949 as amended by Children Act 1989.)

However, if consent is not given, then the marriage may still take place. If consent cannot be given because a parent is absent or inaccessible or disabled, then consent may be given by a superintendent registrar or by a court. If a parent refuses to give consent application may be made to a court for the court to give its consent to allow the marriage to take place (see s3(1)(a) and (b) Marriage Act 1949). The High Court, county court or magistrates' court may hear such an application. However, if the marriage is solemnised without parental consent (and there has been no application to a court) the lack of consent does not void the marriage (see s48(1)(b) Marriage Act 1949). Only if the parent has publicly objected to the banns (thereby voiding the banns) or if the parent has lodged a caveat with the superintendent registrar (thereby preventing the issue of a certificate) will the validity of the marriage be affected (see ss3(3), 29 and 30 Marriage Act 1949).

**The parties have intermarried in disregard to certain requirements as to the formation of marriage**

Section 11(a)(iii) Matrimonial Causes Act 1973 and ss25 and 49 Marriage Act 1949. If parties disregard certain requirements in getting married then the marriage is void. Defects in the formalities only void a marriage if they are done 'knowingly and wilfully' by *both* parties (see ss25 and 49 Marriage Act 1949).

Marriages under the Marriage Act 1949 are divided into two kinds:

1. marriages according to the rites of the Church of England (Part II of the Act);
2. marriages under superintendent registrar's certificate – which covers all other kinds of marriage including religious marriages pursuant to other Christian and non-Christian faiths (Part III of the Act).

The grounds for voiding a marriage are different depending on which type of marriage is used.

*According to the rites of the Church of England.* A Church of England marriage may be solemnised:

1. after the publication of banns;
2. under the authority of a special licence of marriage granted by the Archbishop of Canterbury;
3. under the authority of a common licence;
4. on the authority of a superintendent registrar's certificate under Part III of the Act.

All marriage solemnised according to the rites of the Church of England must be solemnised in the presence of two or more witnesses in addition to the clergyman (s22).

The publication of banns is dealt with by ss6–12 of the Act. Generally the persons to be married must give at least seven days' notice before the publication of the banns to the relevant clergymen. The banns must be read out loud in the church in the parish or parishes in which they reside and in the church in which they are to be married on the three Sundays before the marriage service. The banns are recorded in a register held at each of the relevant churches and a certificate of banns is issued to the clergyman celebrating the marriage. The marriage must take place within three months of the completion of the publication of the banns. If a person wishes to object to the banns he or she must publicly object in the church after the banns have been read. Such objection can void the banns.

A common licence may be granted by a bishop to dispense with banns. It cannot be granted for the solemnisation of a marriage unless one of the persons to be married has had his or her usual place of residence for 15 days in the relevant parish before the grant of the licence or the parish is his or her usual place of worship (s15). One of the persons to be married must make a sworn declaration that there is no impediment to the marriage and that certain requirements (eg as to residence are satisfied). The marriage must be solemnised within three months of the grant of the common licence.

A special licence granted by the Archbishop of Canterbury allows the marriage to take place at any time or place.

For details of the superintendent registrar's certificate see below.

A Church of England marriage (other than by special licence) is void if both parties knowingly and wilfully intermarry:

1. in a place other than a church in which banns may be published (with certain exceptions) (s25(a));
2. without banns having been duly published or a common licence having been obtained or without a superintendent registrar's licence (s25(b));
3. on the authority of banns which have been voided by valid public objection being made in the relevant church or on the authority of banns completed more than three months before the marriage or on the authority of a void common licence or a void superintendent registrar's certificate (s25(c));
4. in the case of a marriage on the authority of a superintendent registrar's certificate, in a church or other place not specified in the notice of marriage and certificate (s25(d)).

Case law has considered the phrase 'without banns having been duly published'. In *Dancer* v *Dancer* [1948] 2 All ER 731 the wife was the legitimate daughter of Mr and Mrs Knight. When she was aged three her mother went to live with a Mr Roberts by whom she had five children. The wife thought that Mr Roberts was her father and used his surname. After Mr Roberts died the wife discovered that he was not her father but she continued to use the surname Roberts. When she got married the banns were published in the name of Roberts. It was held that the banns had been duly published. The wife was generally known as Roberts and there was no attempt to conceal her identity. By contrast in *Small* v *Small* (1923) 67 SJ 277 a deserter from the army used a false name in the banns to avoid detection and prosecution. It was held that the banns were not duly published so there was a deliberate intent to conceal his identity. In *Chipchase* v *Chipchase* [1939] 3 All ER 895 the wife's maiden name was Matthews. She married Mr Leetch who deserted her. Some years afterwards she began to re-use her maiden name. Banns were published in her maiden name. Magistrates held that her marriage was invalid. On appeal, the appeal was allowed and the case remitted back to the magistrates to determine whether she had 'knowingly and wilfully' concealed her identity (following *Dancer*).

*Marriages under a Superintendent Registrar's Certificate under Part III of the Act.* The following marriages may be solemnised under the authority of a superintendent registrar's certificate:

1. a marriage in a registered building with such form and ceremony as the persons to be married see fit to adopt;
2. a marriage in the office of a superintendent registrar;

3. a marriage according to the use of the Quakers;
4. a marriage according to the use of the Jews;
5. a marriage in a house for a housebound person or in a prison for a detained person;
6. a Church of England marriage.

Fifteen days' notice of the marriage must be given to the superintendent registrars in the districts where the parties have resided for the last seven days by each party in person. The notice is in a prescribed format and is accompanied by a solemn declaration that there are no lawful impediments to the marriage, that the residential requirements have been satisfied and that any required parental consent has been given (s27 Marriage Act 1949 as amended from 1 January 2001 by the Immigration and Asylum Act 1999). A notice must be entered in the marriage notice book which is open to public inspection. Public notice is also displayed. A certificate is then issued which authorises the marriage to be solemnised. The marriage must be solemnised within 12 months from the day in which notice of the marriage was entered in the marriage book, otherwise the marriage will be void (s33). Any person who wishes to object to the marriage may enter a caveat at the superintendent registrar's office and such objection must either be ruled invalid or withdrawn before the certificate can be issued.

After the issue of the marriage licence the parties can marry in accordance with their chosen ceremony. There are rules which apply to particular kinds of ceremony. For example, a civil marriage in a register office must be public and in the presence of a superintendent registrar or registrar. Local authorities can approve premises other than register offices for wedding ceremonies, provided such places are open to the public. Religious weddings must take place in places registered by the Registrar General and be conducted by a minister of the religion concerned (with the exception of Quaker or Jewish weddings which have their own rules).

A marriage under the authority of a superintendent registrar's certificate is void if both parties knowingly and wilfully intermarry:

1. without having given due notice of marriage to the superintendent registrar (s49(a));
2. without a certificate for marriage having been duly issued (s49(b));
3. on the authority of a certificate void under s33 (s49(d));
4. in a place other than the place specified in the notice of marriage and the superintendent registrar's certificate (s49(e));
5. in the absence of a registrar or superintendent registrar or authorised person (s49(f), (g) and (h)).

Case law has considered the following grounds:

WITHOUT HAVING GIVEN DUE NOTICE OF THE MARRIAGE. Unlike the banns procedure the giving of false information does not invalidate the marriage. See *Puttick* v *Attorney-*

*General* [1979] 3 WLR 542; [1979] 3 All ER 463 in which a woman wanted in Germany for terrorist offences escaped to England using a false passport. She met and married her husband in England using a false name and false particulars. The marriage was not held to be void by virtue of the false information given.

KNOWINGLY GETTING MARRIED IN A PLACE OTHER THAN THE PLACE SPECIFIED IN THE NOTICE OR CERTIFICATE. See *Chief Adjudication Officer* v *Bath* [2000] 1 FLR 8 where H and W got married in a Sikh temple in England in 1956. They lived together for 37 years and had two sons. H then died. W applied for a widow's pension but this was refused since there was no evidence that the Sikh temple had been registered for marriages. W successfully appealed and the Benefits Agency appealed to the Court of the Appeal. It was held, dismissing the appeal, that when a man and woman had lived together for a long period there is a strong presumption that there was a valid marriage. This presumption can only be displaced by positive evidence. How positive that evidence needs to be depends on the strength of the evidence giving rise to the presumption, primarily the length of the cohabitation and evidence that the parties regarded themselves, and were regarded by others, as married. The marriage could not be invalid merely on the basis that building took place in an unregistered building. Guilty knowledge by both parties is necessary for s49(e) to apply. A similar conclusion was reached in *Pazpena de Vire* v *Pazpena de Vire* [2001] 1 FLR 460 in which the couple married in Uruguary and lived together as husband and wife for 35 years. The court relied on the strong presumption that they had been validly married. The presumption was also applied in *A–M* v *A–M (Divorce: Jurisdiction: Validity of Marriage)* [2001] 2 FLR 6.

## Foreign marriages

United Kingdom law recognises that provision should be made for couples who are obliged to marry in difficult circumstances in which they are unable to comply with the normal formalities. This is best illustrated by cases dealing with soldiers marrying abroad during wartime or other emergencies. The UK courts may recognise the marriage as valid if a recognised form of marriage ceremony took place before a priest or other person able to conduct marriages, even though important formalities were not complied with: see *Taczanowska* v *Taczanowska* [1957] 2 All ER 563 and *Preston* v *Preston* [1963] 2 All ER 405.

NOTE:

1. Not every defect in the formalities will render a marriage void (eg where the necessary consents have not been given in the case of a marriage of a minor by a common licence or Superintendent Registrar's certificate, the marriage is still valid).
2. *Both* parties must be aware of the defect in the formalities for the marriage to be void.

## That at the time of marriage either party was already lawfully married (s11(b))

Lord Penzance provided the classical definition of marriage in *Hyde* v *Hyde* (1866) LR 1 P & D 130 – 'the voluntary union for life of one man and one woman to the exclusion of all others'.

In *Baindall* v *Baindall* [1946] 1 All ER 342 a woman domiciled in England went through a ceremony of marriage in England with a Hindu domiciled in India. She later discovered he already had a wife in India and petitioned for nullity on the ground the marriage was bigamous, and therefore void. The respondent was permitted by his lex domicilii to practise polygamy and the first marriage was therefore clearly polygamous.

HELD: The husband's first marriage was valid by the law of the husband's domicile, and so it must be recognised as valid here. The second marriage was therefore void.

In *Padolecchia* v *Padolecchia* [1967] 3 All ER 863 the husband married an Italian wife. He then purported to divorce her using a Mexican divorce which was not recognised in Italy. He then tried to marry a second wife in London.

HELD: The second marriage was void since the husband was already married.

In *Maples* v *Maples* [1987] 3 All ER 188 the wife married her first husband in Israel. They settled in England. They got divorced by a religious ceremony not recognised in England. She then tried to marry a second husband.

HELD: The second marriage was void since she was still married to her first husband.

NOTE: Contravening s11(b) does not necessarily mean that a person is also guilty of the offence of bigamy under s57 Offences Against the Person Act 1861. For instance, it may be a defence to bigamy to show that at the time of the second marriage the accused reasonably and honestly believed that his first marriage was void or had been dissolved (see *R* v *Gould* [1968] 1 All ER 849). It may also be a defence if the first marriage was a polygamous one (see *R* v *Sagoo* [1975] 2 All ER 926).

## That the parties are not respectively male and female (s11(c))

United Kingdom law does not at present allow two persons of the same sex to marry. 'Marriages' involving homosexual partners are therefore void.

The position of transsexuals, namely persons registered at birth as being of one sex who then undergo a process of transformation to the opposite sex, is in a state of flux. Can a person born a male who becomes a female marry a man? Can a person born a female who becomes a male marry a woman? The answer is probably yes because of a decison of the European Court of Human Rights, the likely outcome of an appeal presently before the House of Lords and proposals by the government to change United Kingdom law. However existing United Kingdom case law says no. The leading case was *Corbett* v *Corbett* [1970] 2 WLR 1306; [1970] 2 All ER 33 in which C, born a male, became a woman and married a man. The marriage was held to be void under s11(c) since C's biological sex was fixed at birth and could not be subsequently changed. The United Kingdom courts have consistently followed *Corbett* (eg *Re P and G (Transsexuals)* [1996] 2 FLR 90). There have been a series of unsuccessful challenges to the European Court of Human Rights alleging violations of art 8 (the right to family life) and art 12 (the right to marry). See *Rees* v *United Kingdom* [1987] Fam Law 157; *Cossey* v *United Kingdom* [1991] Fam Law 362; *X, Y and Z* v *United Kingdom* [1997] 2 FLR 892; and *Sheffield and Horsham* v *United Kingdom* [1998] 2 FLR 928.

The most recent decisions of the European Court of Human Rights are *Goodwin* v *United Kingdom*; *I* v *United Kingdom* [2002] 2 FLR 487 and 518. In the case of *Goodwin*, Miss Goodwin (G) was born a male and fathered four children. She went from male to female and lived full time as a woman from 1984 and had irreversible gender re-assignment surgery in 1990. Under English law she was still male. She claimed that she could not claim a pension at 60, like other women. She faced sexual harassment at work but was unable to sue her employer under English law. She was dismissed on health grounds but insisted that the real reason was because she was a transsexual. When she started work with a new employer she asked for a different NI number so that her new employers could not find out from her previous employers that she had been born male. This request was refused. Her new employers discovered her past and this led to problems at work She was written to by the DSS as a man. She also complained about her inability of marry. The UK government submitted that the degree of recognition of G as a female was within the margin of appreciation left to members states under the European Convention on Human Rights. In the case of *I*, she was a post-operative male to female transsexual. She complained that she could not work because she refused to present her birth certificate to a potential employer. She also complained about her inability to marry.

The European Court held that the unsatisfactory situation in which post-operative transsexuals lived in an intermediate zone as not quite one gender or the other was no longer sustainable. That was not to underestimate the difficulties posed and the repercussions which any major change in the law would have, not only in the field of birth registration but also for access to records, family law, inheritance, criminal justice, employment and social security. However, these problems were far from insuperable. Society might reasonably be expected to tolerate a certain inconvenience to enable individuals to live in dignity and worth in accordance with the sexual identity chosen by them at great personal cost. There was clear and contested evidence of a continuing international trend in favour of not only increased social acceptance of transsexuals but also of legal recognition of the new sexual identity of post-operative transsexuals. Third parties would not would not suffer any material prejudice from any possible changes to the birth register system that might flow from gender re-assignment. The UK government was currently discussing proposals for reform of the registration system in order to allow amendment of civil status data. However, art 8 of the European Convention on Human Rights emphasised the personal automony of the individual. In the twenty-first century the rights of transsexuals to personal development and to physical and moral security in the full sense judged by others in society could no longer be regarded as a matter of controversy requiring the lapse of time to cast clearer light on the issues involved. Domestic recognition of that evaluation could be found in the report on the Interdepartmental Working Group on Transsexual People. Despite the European Court's reiteration since 1986 and most recently in 1998 of the importance of keeping the need for appropriate legal measures under review having regard to scientific and societal developments, nothing had effectively been done by the UK government. The Court found that the UK government could no longer claim that the matter fell within their margin of appreciation. The fair balance that was inherent in the Convention now tilted decisively in favour of the applicants. There had been a failure to respect G and I's private lives pursuant to art 8. While art 12 referred in express terms to the right of a man and a woman to marry, the Court was not persuaded that those terms restricted the determination of gender to purely biological criteria. There had been major social changes in the institution of marriage since the adoption of the Convention, as well as dramatic changes brought about by developments in medicine and science in the field of transsexuality. A test of congruent biological factors could no longer be decisive in denying legal recognition to the change of gender of a post-operative transsexual. There were other important factors: the acceptance of the condition of gender identity disorder by the medical professions and health authorities within the contracting states; the provision of treatment, including surgery, to assimilate the individual as closely as possible to the gender in which they perceived that they properly belonged; and the assumption by the transsexual of the social role of the assigned gender. In these cases the applicants lived as women and would only marry men. While it was for the contracting states to determine the conditions under which a person claiming legal recognition as a transsexual established that gender re-assignment had been effected and the form of marriage, the Court found no justification for barring the transsexual from enjoying the right to marry under any circumstances. There had been a breach of art 12.

The most recent UK case is the Court of Appeal's decision in *Bellinger* v *Bellinger* [2002] WLR 411 which again upheld *Corbett*. However, there was a powerful dissenting judgement from Thorpe LJ, and all the judges said that the law was in a profoundly unsatisfactory state and that the lack of action by the UK government was disappointing. In January 2002 leave to appeal to the House of Lords was granted in the case of *Bellinger* v *Bellinger* and judgment is expected in 2003. In *A* v *Chief Constable of West Yorkshire Police* [2003] 1 FLR 223 a male-to-female transsexual was recognised as female for the purpoe of tribunal proceedings.

The Interdepartmental Working Group on Trannsexual People, set up by the Home Secretary in April 1999, was reconvened to give further consideration to the rights of transsexuals. The Working Group originally reported in July 2000 and identified three possible options: retain the status quo; issue birth certificates showing a transsexual's new name and possibly sex; and grant full recognition of the acquired gender. It made no firm recommendation. In December 2002 the government announced that it will change the law to allow transsexuals to change their birth certificates and to marry in their adopted gender. Such a change in the law is unlikely to come into force until 2004.

## In the case of a polygamous marriage entered into outside England and Wales, that either party was at the time of the marriage domiciled in England and Wales (s11(d))

Section 11(d) MCA 1973 now has to be read in conjunction with the Private International Law (Miscellaneous Provisions) Act 1995 (the relevant parts of which came into force on 8 January, 1996).

For the purposes of s11(d) a marriage is not polygamous if at its inception neither party has any spouse additional to the other (see s11 MCA 1973 as amended by the Schedule to the Private International Law (Miscellaneous Provisions) Act 1995 with effect from 8 January 1996). As a result s11(d) MCA 1973 only applies if a marriage is actually polygamous. If the marriage is potentially polygamous (ie the parties have the capacity to take more than one spouse) but neither spouse has an additional spouse at the time of the marriage then s11(d) will not make the marriage void. This interpretation of s11(d) is further underlined by s5(1) Private International Law (Miscellaneous Provisions) Act 1995 which states that a marriage entered into outside England and Wales between parties neither of whom is already married is not void under the law of England and Wales on the ground that it is entered into under a law which permits polygamy and that either party is domiciled in England and Wales.

Before the 1995 Act, s11(d) was capable of rendering void many marriages by British people who chose to go abroad to marry and used a form of marriage which permitted polygamy (though they had no intention of making the marriage actually polygamous). Section 6 Private International Law (Miscelleneous Provisions) Act 1995 applies s5 of the 1995 Act even to marriages entered into before 8 January 1996 (unless previously annulled or the marriage has become actually polygamous). This provides protection for many marriages which could have been the subject of a s11(d) petition.

Before the 1995 Act, came into force a number of cases tried to avoid the consequences of s11(d).

In *R* v *Immigration Appeal Tribunal, ex parte Asfar Jan* [1995] Imm 440, W was a Pakistani national. She had been married to her second husband (H2) who already had one wife. He then divorced her by talaq which was pronounced in the United Kingdom. She then married her third husband (H3) who was a British citizen. She was refused entry into the United Kingdom on the ground that her marriage to H3 was void and she would be dependent on public funding for maintenance. W sought judicial review of the refusal on the grounds that her marriage to H3 was valid.

HELD: The talaq divorce was not recognised under United Kingdom law (see Chapter 6) so the second marriage had not been ended. The second marriage was valid under s11(d) MCA 1973 as the marriage had taken place outside England and Wales, and neither H2 nor W had been domiciled in the United Kingdom at the time of the marriage. The polygamous marriage was therefore valid and W did not have capacity to marry H3 under United Kingdom law.

In relation to a potentially polygamous marriage see *Hussain* v *Hussain* (1983) 4 FLR 339; [1982] 3 All ER 369, where an English domiciled man married a Pakistani domiciled woman in Pakistan. The marriage permitted the husband to take a second wife but did not allow the wife to take a second husband. They settled in London. The wife petitioned for judicial separation. The husband cross-petitioned for nullity on the basis that the marriage was void under s11(d).

HELD: The marriage was potentially polygamous but could never become actually polygamous. The husband was an English domicile and English law prevented him from taking a second wife. The wife was a Pakistani domicile and Pakistani law prevented her from taking a second husband. Since neither party had the capacity to marry again s11(d) did not apply and the marriage was not void.

In relation to what was an actually polygamous marriage see *Radwan* v *Radwan (No 2)* [1972] 3 WLR 939; [1972] 3 All ER 1026 an Egyptian domiciled man married an Egyptian domiciled woman in Egypt under Egyptian law which permitted polygamy. He then married a second wife who was an English domicile. They married at the Egyptian consulate in Paris intending to enter into a polygamous marriage according to Egyptian law and intending to live in Egypt. They did live in Egypt but then moved to England and became domiciled there. The second wife petitioned for divorce and the question of the validity of the second marriage arose.

HELD: The second marriage was valid in Egyptian law which gave the second wife the capacity to contract a polygamous marriage (despite s11(d)). The parties had intended to live in Egypt when they married. English law recognised that the marriage was valid by the law of the parties' intended matrimonial home. Section 11(d) did not apply.

NOTE: See also *Lawrence* v *Lawrence* [1985] 1 All ER 506 and on appeal [1985] 2 All ER 733 which considered *Radwan* v *Radwan (No 2)* (see Chapter 6, section 6.3, 'The intended matrimonial home test', below).

## 2.3 Voidable marriages

Under s12 Matrimonial Causes Act 1973 a marriage celebrated after 31 July 1971 shall be voidable on the following grounds only:

### That the marriage has not been consummated owing to the incapacity of either party to consummate it (s12(a))

A party may petition on his or her own incapacity (see *Harthan* v *Harthan* [1948] 2 All ER 639).

### That the marriage has not been consummated owing to the wilful refusal of the respondent to consummate it (s12(b)).

A party cannot petition on his or her own refusal.

## Meaning of consummation

A marriage is held to be consummated as soon as the parties have sexual intercourse after the celebration of the marriage. Sexual intercourse before the marriage does not prevent a petition – there must be intercourse after the marriage (see *Dredge* v *Dredge* [1947] 1 All ER 29).

The standard of sexual intercourse necessary to establish consummation was considered in *D* v *A* (1845) 1 Rob Eccl 279, where the husband could not achieve full penetration because of a deformity of the wife's vagina.

Dr Lushington said:

'Sexual intercourse in the proper meaning of the term is ordinary and complete intercourse; it does not mean partial and imperfect intercourse.'

It requires ability to achieve full penetration which must be more than transient in nature. In *W* v *W* [1967] 1 WLR 1554; [1967] 3 All ER 178 the erection quickly collapsed. There was some penetration but not ordinary and complete intercourse. Therefore there was no consummation.

The sterility of either party or the inability of the husband to ejaculate are not relevant. *R* v *R* [1952] 1 All ER 1194 – no ejaculation, but still consummation. *S* v *S* [1962] 3 All ER 55 – wife unable to have children since she had no uterus – marriage not voidable.

Lack of satisfaction in intercourse is not relevant – *S* v *S* (above) – wife did not achieve satisfaction in intercourse because had to have surgery to create an artificial vagina. *P* v *P* [1964] 3 All ER 919 – intercourse only eight times in 18 years of marriage – marriage not voidable.

The birth of a child as a result of fecundatio ab extra (ie fertilisation achieved by ejaculation outside the vagina) or artificial insemination will not amount to consummation (see *Clarke* v *Clarke* [1943] 2 All ER 540).

*Effect of use of contraceptives.* In *Cowen* v *Cowen* [1945] 2 All ER 197 the Court of Appeal held that there had been no consummation where the husband had invariably worn a contraceptive sheath, or practised coitus interruptus, but in *Baxter* v *Baxter* [1947] 2 All ER 886 the House of Lords overruled the first part of the decision in

*Cowen* by holding that the marriage had been consummated notwithstanding husband's use of a sheath.

In *Cackett* v *Cackett* [1950] 1 All ER 677 Hodson J held that the marriage was consummated by coitus interruptus. The court would otherwise be driven into an impossible position if it tried further to define what normal sexual intercourse was.

## Incapacity

In order for a petition to succeed on this ground the defect must be incurable, which arises not only if it is incapable of remedy but also if it can only be cured by an operation which is attended by danger; or in any event, the chances of success are small; or the respondent refuses to undergo treatment.

In *S* v *S* [1962] 3 All ER 55 the wife had a malformed vagina which prevented consummation. This could be cured by an operation. A petition based on incapacity to consummate was refused.

AND the petitioner must also probably show that the incapacity to consummate is in existence at the time of the marriage and there is no practical possibility of the marriage being consummated at the date of the hearing.

See *Napier* v *Napier* [1915] P 184 and *S* v *S* [1954] 3 All ER 736 where after 16 years of frequent but unsuccessful attempts to have intercourse the husband petitioned for nullity. The wife underwent an operation six days before the hearing. The hearing was adjourned to see if there was then a possibility of consummation. The case was ultimately dismissed since the incapacity was curable.

Incapacity to consummate the marriage may include a psychological inability to consummate the marriage. There must be an invincible repugnance to the act of intercourse because of some psychiatric or sexual aversion. See *Singh* v *Singh* [1971] 2 All ER 828 where the wife met her husband for the first time at an arranged marriage and did not like what she saw. Her dislike of her husband did not amount to an invincible repugnance and her petition based on her incapacity to consummate the marriage was dismissed.

## Impotence

It has been argued that impotence was a ground for avoiding a marriage at common law only if it existed at the time of the ceremony and if there was no possibility of consummation at the date of the hearing. Therefore, if a party, although capable of consummating the marriage at the time of the ceremony, subsequently became impotent before consummation could take place, a petition would fail. However, the Matrimonial Causes Act 1973 is silent on this point, and it may be, therefore, that a petition would now succeed in such circumstances.

If the ground petitioned on is incapacity, either party may petition but subject to the defence in s13 (below). If, however, the ground is wilful refusal, a spouse cannot petition on his own wilful refusal.

See *Harthan* v *Harthan* [1948] 2 All ER 639 where the husband was granted a decree of nullity on the basis of his incapacity to consummate the marriage. It was pointed out that it was incorrect for the husband to petition on this ground and at the same time on the ground of his wife's wilful refusal to consummate the marriage, since if he could not consummate the marriage it could not be said that his wife could refuse to do something which was impossible in the first place.

Under r2.22 Family Proceedings Rules 1991 the petitioner must apply to the district judge to determine whether medical inspectors should be appointed to examine the parties in proceedings for nullity on the ground of incapacity to consummate. This is not normally required in undefended cases.

## Wilful refusal

This subject raises questions of psychological problems relating to sexual intercourse and the reason for the refusal.

*In Horton* v *Horton* [1947] 2 All ER 871 Lord Jowitt LC said that wilful refusal was:

> '... a settled and definite decision come to without just excuse'.

A just excuse may include religious reasons (as in *Jodla* v *Jodla* and *Kaur* v *Singh* below) or an agreement not to have intercourse so that the marriage is for companionship only (see *Morgan* v *Morgan* [1959] 2 WLR 487; [1959] 1 All ER 539 and *Scott* v *Scott* [1959] 2 WLR 447; [1959] 1 All ER 531 in cases on approbation).

A refusal to undergo an operation to cure a physical incapacity to consummate may amount to wilful refusal (see *D* v *D* [1979] 3 All ER 337), *but* not if the person has yet to come to a settled decision concerning the operation (see *S* v *S* [1954] 3 All ER 736).

Mere loss of sexual ardour is not sufficient. See *Potter* v *Potter* (1975) 5 Fam Law 161 where the wife had a physical defect which was cured by surgery. The husband attempted to consummate the marriage but he failed because his wife was still in an emotional state after the operation. The husband refused to try again. The wife failed in her petition since the husband's loss of ardour was natural and not deliberate.

If one spouse refuses to consummate the marriage the other spouse should first use appropriate tact, persuasion and encouragement to achieve consummation, otherwise the petition might fail (see *Baxter* v *Baxter* [1947] 1 All ER 387).

See *Ford* v *Ford* [1987] Fam Law 232 where the husband and wife did not live together before their marriage but they did have a casual relationship and had sexual intercourse. The husband was sentenced to five years' imprisonment. He got married to the wife in prison. After the marriage the parties were left alone and the wife tried to persuade the husband to consummate the marriage. The husband refused and said that he did not want her visits and did not wish to live with her on his release. He was allowed out of a prison on a home visit when he stayed with a former girlfriend. The wife sought a petition based on the husband's wilful refusal to consummate.

HELD: There was no right to conjugal visits in prison, therefore the husband's refusal to have intercourse on a prison visit could not amount to a wilful refusal. However, though there was no reasonable opportunity for consummation while the husband was in prison, his conduct showed a determination not to consummate the marriage in the future. The wife's petition was granted.

### Indirect refusal to consummate

In *Jodla* v *Jodla* [1960] 1 All ER 625 two Roman Catholics married in a Register Office on the understanding that a Catholic church wedding would take place afterwards. They agreed that they would not live together until after the church service. The respondent refused to take part in the church service. He was deemed to be wilfully refusing to consummate the marriage.

In *Kaur* v *Singh* [1972] 1 All ER 292 two Sikhs married in a civil ceremony. Both parties knew that by their religion and social custom a religious ceremony was necessary before they were fully married. The husband had the duty to arrange the religious ceremony. He refused to do so. He was deemed to be wilfully refusing to consummate the marriage.

In *A* v *J (Nullity)* [1989] Fam Law 63 a marriage was arranged by the respective families of two Indians. It was agreed that they should be married at a Register Office followed by a religious ceremony four months later, the religious ceremony being an essential condition of cohabitation. After the Register Office wedding the husband went abroad for business reasons. He returned for the religious ceremony. The wife refused to go ahead with the ceremony because she believed that the husband had shown a lack of concern for her during the short time they were together and by going abroad. The husband apologised saying that he thought he was supposed to treat her 'formally' until after the religious ceremony. The wife refused to accept his apology and refused to go ahead with the religious ceremony. The husband petitioned for nullity on the basis of the wife's refusal to consummate the marriage.

HELD: The husband had been wrong in the way he treated his wife. He should have found out what she wanted. The wife was no less at fault by not making her feelings known until the last moment. However, the husband was sincere in his apologies and his desire to share his life with the wife. The wife had adopted an uncompromising refusal to accept his apologies and to see whether he would change his behaviour towards her. Her adamant refusal to go through with the religious ceremony amounted to a wilful refusal to consummate since a religious ceremony for that couple was essential to cohabitation.

## Lack of consent

That either party to the marriage did not validly consent to it, whether in consequence of duress, mistake, unsoundness of mind or otherwise (s12(c)).

### Mistake

A mistake as the nature of the ceremony of marriage can invalidate the marriage because a spouse was not in a position to consent to the marriage. For example, in *Mehta* v *Mehta* [1945] 2 All ER 690 one party to a marriage thought that the ceremony was a conversion to the Hindu religion. The marriage was held to be void. Similarly in *Valier* v *Valier* (1925) 133 LT 830 a non-English-speaking Italian attended a Register Office wedding. In Italy there are many formalities before marriage, and he did not appreciate that the ceremony was a full marriage ceremony. The marriage was held to be void.

If a spouse knows that the ceremony is a marriage ceremony and in that ceremony consents to being married, but then finds that he or she is mistaken about the consequences of the marriage, the marriage will be valid since this is a mistake as to the consequences of the marriage, not as to the nature of the ceremony itself. For example, in *Kassim* v *Kassim* [1962] 3 WLR 865; [1962] 3 All ER 426 a spouse thought that the marriage was polygamous. This was a mistake, but only as to the consequences of the marriage, so the marriage was valid. Similarly in *Way* v *Way* [1949] 2 All ER 959 an English man thought that his marriage to a Russian woman would enable his wife to leave Russia and live with him in England. The Russian authorities refused to allow her to leave. The marriage was held to be valid since the husband had made a mistake about the consequences of the marriage, not about the nature of the marriage ceremony. In *Vervaeke* v *Smith* [1982] 2 All ER 144 a wife mistakenly thought that her marriage would protect her from deportation. The fact that it did not did not make the marriage invalid.

A mistake as to the quality of the person whom one is marrying would not make the marriage invalid. In *Moss* v *Moss (Otherwise Archer)* [1897] P 263 a woman concealed from her husband at the time of her marriage that she was pregnant by another man. This did not make the marriage void on the ground of a lack of consent (though see s12(f) later). In *Puttick* v *Attorney-General* [1979] 3 All ER 463 a man married a woman who gave a false name. It was clear that he wanted to marry that woman; the mistake as to her name went only as to the quality of the spouse, and the marriage was valid.

## Unsoundness of mind

The question is whether a party to the marriage could understand the nature of the ceremony.

*Durham* v *Durham* (1885) 10 PD 80 – marriage is a simple concept – no high degree of understanding needed.

*In the Estate of Park* [1953] 3 WLR 1012; [1953] 2 All ER 1411. When considering whether or not a marriage is to be annulled on the ground that one of the parties was of unsound mind at the time that it was celebrated, the correct test is whether he or she was capable of understanding the nature of the contract into which he or she was entering (ie capable of appreciating that it involved the duties and responsibilities attached to marriage).

Once the ceremony of marriage has been performed there is a presumption that each party has validly consented to it.

It is rare for this ground to succeed. *In the Estate of Park* involved an man aged 77 years who was mentally and physically weak. He became forgetful and untidy and was sometimes lucid and sometimes confused. He married and by doing so the will, which left his property to his relatives, was revoked and his property went to his new wife. The relatives challenged the validity of the marriage on the basis of lack of consent based on unsoundness of mind. They failed.

For a more recent case with similar facts see *Re Roberts (deceased)* [1978] 3 All ER 225.

**Duress**

Normally duress means fear which is so overbearing that the element of free consent is absent.

In *Szechter* v *Szechter* [1971] 2 WLR 170; [1970] 3 All ER 905 Sir Jocelyn Simon P summarised the law in a statement unanimously approved in *Singh* v *Singh* [1971] 2 WLR 963; [1971] 2 All ER 828 as follows:

> 'It must ... be proved that the will of one of the parties thereto has been overborne by genuine and reasonably held fear caused by threat of immediate danger (for which the party himself is not responsible) to life, limb or liberty, so that the constraint destroys the reality of consent.'

Polish woman in prison in Poland following arrest by security forces – married so could leave prison and Poland – health poor and life in danger if remained in prison – duress – decree granted.

*Parojcic* v *Parojcic* [1958] 1 WLR 1280; [1959] 1 All ER 1 – daughter who had just contrived to leave Yugoslavia and reach England was threatened by her father on arrival that unless she married the man who accompanied him, whom she had never met before, she would be sent back to Yugoslavia – decree granted.

*H* v *H* [1953] 2 All ER 1229 – married in order to escape from a totalitarian regime (Hungary) – married under duress – decree granted.

*Hussein* v *Hussein* [1938] 2 All ER 344 – marriage under threat of being killed by husband – decree granted.

*Scott* v *Sebright* (1886) 12 PD 21 – marriage under threat of being made bankrupt and being shot! – decree granted.

In *Singh* v *Singh* (above) a marriage arranged by the parents of two young Sikhs, where the petitioner had never seen her husband before the ceremony and had gone through with it only out of respect for her parents and the traditions of her people, was held to be valid as there was no evidence of fear.

However, note in *Hirani* v *Hirani* (1982) 4 FLR 232 a Hindu girl was friendly with a Muslim boy. Her parents opposed the relationship so they arranged a marriage with a Hindu man, Mr Hirani. She was nineteen years old and lived with her parents. They threatened to withdraw all support from her and oust her from their home if she did not go through with the arranged marriage. It was held that it was not necessary literally to find a threat to life, limb or liberty in order to find duress.

Ormrod LJ:

'The crucial question in these cases ... is whether the threats, pressure, or whatever it is, is such as to destroy the reality of consent and overbears the will of the individual'.

*'For which the party is not himself responsible'.* For example, ***Buckland*** v ***Buckland*** [1967] 2 WLR 1506; [1967] 2 All ER 300. The husband, 20 years old, was falsely charged with corrupting a 15-year-old girl. He was advised he would be inevitably convicted and sentenced to a long term of imprisonment unless he married her, which he did. The decree was granted. But the decree would not have been granted had he been guilty of the offence.

See the Irish case of *Griffith* v *Griffith* [1944] IR 35 where a man was forced to marry a girl under the false threat of prosecution for unlawful sexual intercourse with a girl under seventeen years of age. The court suggested that the approach should be whether the fear was justly imposed. If fear is justly imposed the marriage is valid and binding. A fear could not be justly imposed if the party was not responsible for it. A decree was granted in the case.

Is this approach necessarily fair? Does it matter whether or not the party is responsible? Is it not important to ascertain whether or not the party's will was overborne by fear?

***Does the fear have to be reasonably entertained or not?*** There are conflicting dicta: *Scott* v *Sebright* (1886) 12 PD 21 and the Law Commission (Law Com No 33) support a subjective approach, whereas *Buckland* (above) and *Szechter* (above) favour an objective approach. Is this fair?

***In the absence of fear or coercion, a mere ulterior motive is not enough.*** *Silver* v *Silver* [1955] 2 All ER 614 – marriage of German girl to Englishman in order to come to England to live with another Englishman – no duress – marriage valid.

## Mental disorder

That at the time of the marriage either party, though capable of giving a valid consent, was suffering (whether continuously or intermittently) from mental disorder within the meaning of the Mental Health Act 1983 of such a kind or to such an extent as to be unfitted for marriage (s12(d)).

In this case a party can give a valid consent and is, therefore, not within s12(c), but is unfitted to marriage by virtue of mental disorder.

*Bennett* v *Bennett* [1969] 1 WLR 430; [1969] 1 All ER 539 – is the party 'incapable of carrying out the ordinary duties and obligations of marriage'? In this case the wife suffered from a temporary hysterical neurosis. It meant that her behaviour was likely to be difficult and trying over a short period. The marriage was valid.

## *Venereal disease*

That at the time of marriage the respondent was suffering from venereal disease in a communicable form (s12(e)).

## *Pregnancy per alium*

That at the time of the marriage the respondent was pregnant by some person other than the petitioner (s12(f)).

This ground gets round the decision in *Moss* v *Moss* (above) referred to in relation to lack of consent, due to a mistaken belief that the woman the husband was marrying was carrying his child, when in fact it was another man's.

## 2.4 Bars where marriage voidable

### *Approbation bar*

Section 13(1) Matrimonial Causes Act 1973 provides that:

'The court shall not ... grant a decree of nullity on the ground that a marriage is voidable if the respondent satisfies the court –
(a) that the petitioner, with knowledge that it was open to him to have the marriage avoided, so conducted himself in relation to the respondent as to lead the respondent reasonably to believe that he would not seek to do so; and
(b) that it would be unjust to the respondent to grant the decree.'

This section is an enactment of the bar of approbation.

In *G* v *M* (1885) 10 App Cas 171 Lord Watson said that there could be circumstances 'as to render it most inequitable and contrary to public policy' that a complaining spouse should be able to challenge a marriage when he has implied recognition of the existence and validity of the marriage.

The respondent therefore has to satisfy the court on three points:

1.  That the petitioner knew it was open to him to have the marriage avoided (ie proof of actual knowledge of legal right to seek a decree of nullity).
2.  That with that knowledge, he so conducted himself in relation to the respondent as to lead the respondent reasonably to believe that he would not seek to do so. This is a question of fact in each case:

    An agreement between the parties not to have the marriage annulled would be an absolute bar (see *Aldridge* v *Aldridge* (1888) 13 PD 210).

    Institution of other proceedings such as possibly the adoption of a child (see *W* v *W* [1952] 1 All ER 858) or application to a magistrates' court for maintenance (see *Tindall* v *Tindall* [1953] 2 WLR 158; [1953] 1 All ER 139) may indicate that the petitioner is behaving as if the marriage is to be treated as valid and should not be allowed to petition for nullity.

BUT see *D* v *D* [1979] 3 All ER 337 which on similar facts to *W* v *W* (adoption application made by parties) came to a different conclusion. The court in *W* v *W* held that an adoption application involved a representation to a court that the joint adopters were husband and wife, so that it would be contrary to public policy to allow either to then claim the marriage to be a nullity.

In *D* v *D* public policy was held to be irrelevant. The marriage was never consummated because of a physical defect in the wife. The defect could be cured by an operation but the wife refused to undergo one. The husband and wife adopted two children. One year later the husband left the wife to live with another woman. He petitioned for nullity on the ground of the wife's wilful refusal to consummate. The court considered whether he had so conducted himself as to lead his wife to reasonably believe that he would not seek to avoid the marriage and whether it would be unjust to the wife to grant the decree and whether the court should have regard to public policy.

HELD: Public policy was not relevant under s13. The bar in s13(1) was absolute and not discretionary. It related wholly to conduct between parties. The only relevant considerations were the conduct of one party towards the other and the possibility of injustice to the respondent. These considerations were conjunctive. Therefore, although the husband's conduct in agreeing to the adoption while knowing that he could have avoided the marriage would otherwise have been a bar, there was no injustice to the wife. A decree of nullity was pronounced.

3. That it would be unjust to respondent to grant a decree. For example, in *Pettit* v *Pettit* [1962] 3 WLR 919; [1962] 3 All ER 37 the husband had always been impotent. The wife had borne him a child by artificial insemination and had kept the house going during the war years by paying bills and mortgage instalments. After twenty years he sought to obtain a decree of nullity, having fallen in love with another woman. The petition failed.

NOTE:

1. If the petitioner gives consent to adoption or artificial insemination, but at the same time *makes it clear to the respondent* that he will still be able to petition if his purpose fails and the marriage remains unconsummated, nothing he has done will have led the respondent to believe that he will not seek to have the marriage annulled.

2. A pre-marital agreement not to have sexual intercourse is contrary to public policy and, therefore, not binding on the parties (see *Brodie* v *Brodie* [1917] P 271). However, it may preclude a party from obtaining a decree where there has never been consummation, and because of the agreement the respondent has been led to believe that the petitioner would not bring such proceedings. See *Morgan* v *Morgan* [1959] 2 WLR 487; [1959] 1 All ER 539 where the husband and wife married when they were seventy-two and fifty-nine respectively on the basis of companionship only. They had no physical relationship. The husband

petitioned for nullity on the ground of his own inability to consummate the marriage. The petition was dismissed having regard to the companionship agreement which was reasonable having regard to the ages of the parties.

See also *Scott* v *Scott* [1959] 2 WLR 447; [1959] 1 All ER 531 where a husband, aged forty-three, married his wife, aged forty, on the understanding that she found intercourse distasteful and the marriage should not be consummated. The husband accepted this for three years but then he met another woman whom he wished to marry. He petitioned for nullity based on the wife's wilful refusal to consummate. His petition was refused since her refusal was not wilful in such circumstances and that he had accepted the marriage as understood by both parties.

3. The petitioner must be shown to have been aware both of the ground relied on itself under s12 and of the fact that it could *annul* the marriage. See *Slater* v *Slater* [1953] 2 WLR 170; [1953] 1 All ER 246 where the wife petitioned on the basis of the husband's inability to consummate the marriage. The husband argued that the wife had behaved as if the marriage was valid by, first, being artificially inseminated so that she could have a child and, secondly, by adopting a child. However, the wife had not known of her legal right to bring nullity proceedings when she had acted in this way, so that her acts could not amount to approbation. If she had known of her legal right her actions could well have amounted to approbation, but as she had not had the required knowledge so her decree was granted.

## Other bars

Section 13(2) Matrimonial Causes Act 1973 states:

'(2) Without prejudice to subsection (1) above, the Court shall not grant a degree of nullity by virtue of section 12 above on the grounds mentioned in paragraphs (c), (d) (e) or (f) of that section unless:
(a) it is satisfied that proceedings were instituted within the period of three years from the date of the marriage, or
(b) leave for the institution of proceedings after the expiration of that period has been granted under subsection (4) below.'

Section 13(4) MCA 1973 provides:

'(4) In the case of proceedings for the grant of a decree of nullity by virtue of section 12 above on the grounds mentioned in paragraph (c), (d), (e), or (f) of that section, a judge of the court may, on an application made to him, grant leave for the institution of proceedings after the expiration of the period of three years from the date of the marriage if:
(a) he is satisfied that the *petitioner* has at some time during that period suffered from mental disorder within the meaning of the Mental Health Act 1983, and
(b) he considers that in all the circumstances of the case it would be just to grant leave for the institution of proceedings.'

Section 13(5) MCA 1973 provides that an application for leave under s13(4) MCA 1973 may be made after the expiration of the period of three years from the date of the marriage.

Section 13(3) MCA 1973 remains unchanged and provides that the court shall not grant a decree of nullity by virtue of s12 above on the grounds mentioned in paragraphs (e) or (f) of that section unless it is satisfied that the petitioner was at the time of the marriage ignorant of the facts alleged.

See *Stocker* v *Stocker* [1966] 2 All ER 147 where, in relation to the wife being pregnant by another man at the time of the marriage, the husband knew his wife was pregnant but was ignorant that it was by another man – his petition was granted.

# 3

# Divorce

## 3.1 Introduction

The grounds for divorce are currently contained in ss1–7 of the Matrimonial Causes Act 1973. There was an attempt to radically reform divorce law in the Family Law Act 1996. Part I of the 1996 Act (objectives of divorce law) came into force in March 1997, but Parts II and III of the Act (which contain the radical reforms) have not been brought into force and may be repealed (see the announcement of the Lord Chancellor in January 2001). This Chapter therefore deals mainly with the grounds of divorce under the MCA 1973 but with an outline of the FLA 1996 to assist the student in understanding the pressure for reform of divorce law and what the FLA 1996 intended to achieve.

Part I of the FLA 1996 sets out the following objectives of divorce law:

1. to support the institution of marriage;
2. to include practical steps to prevent the irretrievable breakdown of marriage;
3. to ensure that spouses understand the practical consequences of divorce before taking any irretrievable decisions;
4. where divorce is unavoidable, to minimise the bitterness and hostility between the parties and to reduce the trauma for children;
5. to keep to the minimum the cost to the parties and to the taxpayer.

It is interesting to compare how well the the MCA 1973 achieves the above and how the FLA 1996 might have achieved them had it been fully brought into force.

In 2000 141,135 divorces were granted (the lowest number since 1979). Divorces were highest amongst men and women in the 25–29 age group. Seventy per cent of divorces were for couples married for the first time. A total of 142,457 children under 16 were in families where the parents divorced in 2000, a quarter of whom were under five.

## 3.2 One year bar on petitions

Section 3 Matrimonial Causes Act 1973 originally provided that no petition for divorce could be presented to the court before the expiration of the period of three years from the date of the marriage unless the case was one of exceptional hardship suffered by the petitioner or of exceptional depravity on the part of the respondent.

These provisions gave rise to a considerable amount of case law on applications to present a petition within three years of marriage, usually on the ground of exceptional hardship to the petitioner. However, the provisions came under increasing criticism and the Matrimonial and Family Proceedings Act 1984 abolished the discretionary three year bar and replaced it with an absolute bar on petitions for divorce within one year of marriage.

Section 1 Matrimonial and Family Proceedings Act 1984 provided for the substitution of the then s3 Matrimonial Causes Act 1973 with the following section:

'(1) No petition for divorce shall be presented to the court before the expiration of the period of one year from the date of the marriage.
(2) Nothing in this section shall prohibit the presentation of a petition based on matters which occurred before the expiration of that period.'

The absolute bar in s3(1) was considered in *Butler* v *Butler* [1990] Fam Law 21 where H and W married in October 1986. W filed for a petition for judicial separation in September 1987. In January 1988 W amended the petition to one of divorce. A divorce was granted. It was then discovered that the petition contravened s3(1) MCA 1973. The Queen's Proctor intervened and asked that the petition and divorce be declared null and void.

HELD: The one year rule was an inescapable statutory bar. There was no discretion to avoid it due to a genuine and honest mistake. The petition and divorce was null and void. The solicitors should have presented a fresh petition instead of trying to amend the judicial separation petition.

## 3.3 The ground for divorce

A petition for divorce may be presented to the court on one ground, namely that the marriage has broken down irretrievably (s1(1) MCA 1973).

The court cannot hold that the marriage has broken down irretrievably unless the petitioner satisfies the court of one or more of five facts (s1(2) with the facts set out in s1(2)(a) to (e) MCA 1973).

Section 1(1) and (2) are two separate requirements. The court must be satisfied on the evidence that any such fact has been made out and consider whether on all the evidence that the marriage has broken down irretrievably (see *Buffery* v *Buffery* [1988] 2 FLR 365). If it is satisfied as to the relevant fact(s) it must grant a decree nisi of divorce, unless it is satisfied on all the evidence that the marriage has not broken down irretrievably (s1(4) MCA 1973). For example, in *Richards* v *Richards* [1972] 1 WLR 1073; [1972] 3 All ER 695 the petitioner satisfied the court that the marriage had broken down irretrievably but not one of the facts (in that case 'behaviour'). The petition was dismissed. The same decision was reached in *Buffery* v *Buffery* in similar circumstances. In *Biggs* v *Biggs* [1977] 1 All ER 20 the court was satisfied that adultery had been proved but was not satisfied that the marriage had broken down irretrievably. Again the petition was dismissed.

The court has a duty to inquire, so far as it can, into the facts alleged by the petitioner and into any facts alleged by the respondent (see s1(3)). It should not 'rubber stamp' a divorce petition. For example in *Butterworth* v *Butterworth* [1998] 1 FCR 159 W issued a divorce petition on the ground that H had behaved in such a way that she could not reasonably be expected to continue to live with him pursuant to s1(2)(b) Matrimonial Causes Act 1973. In her petition W alleged that H was a heavy drinker, violent and extremely possessive and jealous, had accused her of having affairs, was sexually demanding and stopped W from going to church. In his answer H denied the allegations. A recorder heard the evidence of the parties and granted a decree nisi to W but did not make complete findings on W's allegations. H appealed. It was held, allowing the appeal, that all respondents to a divorce were entitled to proper pleadings and, if it was a defended divorce, to have their cases properly tried by a judge. In this case the allegations in W's petition were brief and lacked particulars. The case had not been dealt with justly, the decree would be set aside and remitted to be heard by a judge.

The court will limit its enquiries within reasonable boundaries. Modern divorce law seeks to avoid pointless or excessive inquiries into conduct and fault (see *Grenfell* v *Grenfell* [1977] 3 WLR 738; [1978] 1 All ER 561).

The five facts in s1(2) MCA 1973 are dealt with below.

## 3.4 Adultery plus intolerability

That the respondent has committed adultery and the petitioner finds it intolerable to live with the respondent (s1(2)(a) MCA 1973).

### *Defintion of adultery*

'Adultery' consists for the purposes of s1(2)(a) of voluntary sexual intercourse between a married person and a person of the opposite sex (who may or may not be married) and who is not the other person's spouse. It is not possible to commit adultery with a person of the same sex or with a sex-changed person (see *Corbett* v *Corbett* [1970] 2 All ER 33).

### Voluntary

A person cannot commit adultery if insane or (in the case of a wife) she has been raped (see *S* v *S* [1962] 3 All ER 816). Once intercourse has been proved the burden is on the respondent to show that the intercourse was involuntary. In *Redpath* v *Redpath* [1950] 1 All ER 600 the respondent W alleged that she had been raped by D. D was acquitted when tried for the offence of rape. She failed to show that the intercourse was involuntary and the decree based on her adultery with D was granted. A person may not be acting voluntarily if very drunk but generally drink is an aggravating feature since it more likely to inflame the passions and make adultery more likely (see *Goshawk* v *Goshawk* (1965) 109 SJ 290).

### Sexual intercourse

There must be some penetration, though it is not necessary that the complete act of intercourse take place. In *Dennis* v *Dennis* [1955] 2 WLR 187; [1955] 2 All ER 51 the respondent was impotent. He spent the night in bed with another woman giving rise to an inference that adultery had taken place. Since he was unable to penetrate the woman to any degree adultery could not be proved. Sexual familiarities short of intercourse are not sufficient (see *Sapsford* v *Sapsford* [1954] 2 All ER 373).

### *Proof of adultery*

Proof of adultery is treated by the courts as a serious matter. Generally the civil standard of proof is on a balance of probabilities, but the standard for proving adultery is higher on the principle that 'in proportion as the offence is grave so ought the proof to be clear'. For example, in *Bastable* v *Bastable* [1968] 3 All ER

701 the husband petitioned on his wife's adultery on the basis of her persistent association with another man. There was no evidence of her having intercourse with him. His petition was based on suspicion and inference which was insufficient. His petition was dismissed. There is no longer a requirement to name the co-respondent (see r2.7(1) Family Proceedings Rules 1991). If the person is named he or she has to be joined as a co-respondent unless the court otherwise directs.

Examples of how adultery can be proved include:

### Circumstantial evidence
If the parties spend the night in the same room this raises a rebuttable presumption that adultery has taken place (see *Woolf* v *Woolf* [1931] P 134 and *Dennis* v *Dennis* (above)). The contracting of VD from a person other than the petitioner would raise a similar presumption.

### Confession statement
A respondent can be asked to provide a confession statement admitting adultery at a specific time and place with a person of the opposite sex. That person's name and address should be disclosed or the respondent should state that he/she refuses to disclose the person's identity. The statement must be signed by the respondent even if his/her solicitor has also signed it. The statement can be admitted in evidence, although the petitioner normally has to swear an affidavit verifying that the confession statement is from the respondent.

### Birth of a child
If a child is born to a married couple it is presumed at common law that the child is the legitimate child of that couple. That presumption can be rebutted on the balance of probabilities (see s26 Family Law Reform Act 1969). However, the courts consider rebutting the presumption to be a serious matter and the standard of proof is accordingly higher than a narrow balance of probabilities (see *Serio* v *Serio* (1983) 4 FLR 756; *W* v *K (Proof of Paternity)* [1988] 1 FLR 86 and *Avon County Council* v *G* (1987) 152 JPN 78. For example, in *Preston-Jones* v *Preston-Jones* [1951] AC 391; [1951] 1 All ER 124 the husband went away abroad between six and 12 months before his wife gave birth to a child. Applying the accepted standards of medical science it was not possible that the husband could be the father. There was no evidence that the wife had any suspicious relationships with any other man. She seemed a respectable and hard-working wife. Nevertheless it was held that adultery was established.

A wife's refusal to enter the name of her husband on the birth certificate (see *Mayo* v *Mayo* [1948] 2 All ER 869) or to enter the name of the co-respondent (see *Jackson* v *Jackson and Pavan* [1961] 2 WLR 58; [1960] 3 All ER 621) can be used to show adultery.

Nowadays the status of a child can be established by DNA tests. Such tests cannot be ordered to prove adultery (see *Hodgkiss* v *Hodgkiss* [1985] Fam Law 87) but can be ordered to establish the parentage of a child (see Chapter 15, section 15.12). The results could then be used to establish adultery. Findings in other court proceedings in relation to adultery or to parentage of a child can be used in divorce proceedings (see s12 Civil Evidence Act 1968). In addition to findings in relation to the parentage of a child (for example in Children Act 1989 proceedings or a declaration of parentage under s55A Family Law Act 1986) this could include findings of adultery in other matrimonial proceedings. Particulars of the relevant proceedings must be included in the petition (see r2.4 Family Proceedings Rules 1991).

## *Intolerability*

Section 1(2)(a) MCA 1973 is silent on the question of whether the intolerability must result from the adultery.

In *Goodrich* v *Goodrich* [1971] 1 WLR 1142; [1971] 2 All ER 1340 the husband did not find it intolerable to live with his wife because of the adultery but because of her adamant refusal to consider a reconciliation. It was held that adultery and intolerability were independent of each other and his decree was granted. In *Roper* v *Roper* [1972] 1 WLR 1314; [1972] 3 All ER 668 it was held that the meaning of the section was 'in consequence of the adultery the petitioner finds it intolerable to live with the respondent'. In *Cleary* v *Cleary* [1974] 1 WLR 73; [1974] 1 All ER 498 the Court of Appeal held that it was not permissible to read such words into s1(2)(a). In that case the husband forgave the adultery and took his wife back. She then behaved 'intolerably' by corresponding with another man and going out at night leaving the husband with the children. The intolerability was not linked with the previous adultery. The decree was granted. This decision was followed (although with some reluctance) in *Carr* v *Carr* [1974] 1 WLR 1534; [1974] 1 All ER 1193 where the intolerability was based on the respondent's treatment of the children rather than the adultery.

The test of intolerability is subjective, not objective. It is what the particular petitioner finds intolerable, not what a reasonable petitioner would have found intolerable.

## *Reconciliation provisions*

These are designed to prevent reliance on adultery which occured some time ago and also to encourage attempts at reconciliation.

A spouse cannot rely on adultery committed by the other spouse if, after the adultery became known to him/her, the parties lived with each other for a period exceeding six months or for periods together exceeding six months (s2(1) MCA 1973). In *Biggs* v *Biggs* [1977] 1 All ER 20 a wife obtained a decree nisi of divorce on the basis of her husband's adultery. She was barred from having the decree made absolute because the parties lived together for six months after the decree nisi.

Where s2(1) does not apply and the spouse learns that the other spouse has committed adultery but the parties then live together, that period of living together must be disregarded in determining for the purposes of s1(2)(a) whether the petitioner finds it intolerable to live with the respondent (s2(2) MCA 1973). This allows a potential petitioner to attempt a reconciliation with the other spouse without prejuding his/her case in relation to 'intolerability'.

## 3.5 Behaviour

Section 1(2)(b) MCA 1973 provides 'that the respondent has behaved in such a way that the petitioner cannot reasonably be expected to live with the respondent'. This ground is often referred to as 'unreasonable behaviour', but the test applied is not whether the respondent has behaved unreasonably but whether the respondent has behaved in such a way that the petitioner could not reasonably be expected to live with him or her – a 'significantly different concept' according to the Court of Appeal in *Bannister* v *Bannister* (1980) 10 Fam Law 240. In *Carew-Hunt* v *Carew-Hunt* (1972) The Times 28 June Ormrod J made a similar point:

'The question is not whether the respondent has behaved unreasonably and the court is no longer required, except marginally, to pass judgment on whether a person's behaviour is right or wrong, good or bad.'

It is, therefore, inaccurate to refer to the ground of 'unreasonable behaviour' and wiser to simply refer to the 'behaviour' ground.

The behaviour ground is perhaps the most controversial of all the grounds and has produced much case law on how the ground should be applied.

In *Andrews* v *Andrews* [1974] 3 All ER 643 and *Balraj* v *Balraj* (1981) 11 Fam Law 110 it was held that in order to decide whether a respondent had behaved in such a way that it was unreasonable to expect the petitioner to live with him or her, it was necessary to first make findings of fact of what the respondent actually did and then findings of fact of the impact of the conduct on the petitioner. The court had to look at the particular husband and the particular wife whose conduct and suffering were under scrutiny. There was a subjective element in the totality of the facts but once the subjective element had been evaluated the question of whether s1(2)(b) was satisfied involved the court in applying an objective test.

The question asked was: 'can the particular petitioner in the case of question be reasonably expected to live with the respondent bearing in mind the character, personality, disposition and behaviour of each of the parties?' (restated in *Buffery* v *Buffery* [1988] 2 FLR 365).

In *Ash* v *Ash* [1972] 2 WLR 347; [1972] 1 All ER 582 Bagnall J asked:

'... can this petitioner with his or her character and personality, with his or her faults and other attributes, good or bad, and having regard to his or her behaviour during the marriage, reasonably be expected to live with this respondent?

... Then, if I may give a few examples, it seems to me that a violent petitioner can reasonably be expected to live with a violent respondent; a petitioner who is addicted to drink can reasonably be expected to live with a respondent similarly addicted; a taciturn and morose spouse can reasonably be expected to live with a taciturn and morose partner; a flirtatious husband can reasonably be expected to live with a wife who is equally susceptible to the attractions of the opposite sex; and if each is equally bad, at any rate in similar respects, each can reasonably be expected to live with the other.'

In *Livingstone-Stallard* v *Livingstone-Stallard* [1974] 3 WLR 302; [1974] 2 All ER 776 Dunn J suggested the 'jury approach':

'Assume that the case was being tried by a jury and consider what a proper direction to the jury would be, then decide the facts as a properly directed jury would.'

The direction to the jury was: 'Would any right thinking person come to the conclusion that this husband has behaved in such a way that this wife cannot reasonably be expected to live with him, taking into account the whole of the circumstances and the characteristics and personalities of the parties?'

This dictum was applied in *O'Neill* v *O'Neill* [1975] 1 WLR 1118; [1975] 3 All ER 289 and in *Buffery* v *Buffery* (above) where it was added that no glosses should be added to the test such as the respondent's behaviour having to be 'grave and weighty'.

One way of seeing how the test is applied is to look at the different kinds of marital behaviour which have been considered under s1(2)(b).

## The violent respondent

In *Ash* v *Ash* (above) the husband was violent and an alcoholic. The decree was granted. In *Bergin* v *Bergin* [1983] 1 All ER 905 (a magistrates' courts case dealing with an identical provision to s1(2)(b)) the husband assaulted his wife causing her a black eye and cuts to her face. She did not report the assaults to the police or to her doctor. The court considered that she had accepted and tolerated the violence as part of normal married life and had not been put in fear because she had not done anything about the assaults. Her application was dismissed. She appealed.

HELD: The fact that the wife had put up with the violence was no reason to dismiss her application. On the facts any right thinking person would have found that the husband had behaved in such a way that the wife could not reasonably have been expected to live with him taking into account all the circumstances and in particular the characteristics and personalities of the parties.

## The emotionally/sexually unsatisfactory spouse

In *Pheasant* v *Pheasant* [1972] 2 WLR 353; [1972] 1 All ER 587 the wife was unable to give the husband the spontaneous and demonstrative affection for which his nature craved. It was held on the facts that the behaviour test was not satisfied.

There was no breach of the obligations of marriage on the wife's part. She did not effectively contribute to the break-up of the marriage and would have welcomed the husband back.

In *Dowden* v *Dowden* (1977) 8 Fam Law 106 the wife presented an undefended petition under s1(2)(b) alleging that the respondent husband was uninterested in sexual intercourse. Her sex life was therefore unsatisfactory causing her physical frustration and tension. Her decree was refused and her petition was dismissed because the petitioner had failed to establish the ground upon which the petition was based. The wife appealed to the Court of Appeal which dismissed her appeal and affirmed the judge's decision.

## The couple who drift apart

In *Morgan* v *Morgan* (1973) 117 SJ 223 the husband was in his 60s. His wife was bored with the marriage. The house was sold and the wife found the husband a room. The court held that this was a case of simple desertion which could not fall within s1(2)(b).

In *Stringfellow* v *Stringfellow* [1976] 1 WLR 645; [1976] 2 All ER 539 the husband and wife were married for six or seven years. The husband then ceased to love his wife and said he wanted the freedom he had lost by marrying at nineteen. He refused to have sexual intercourse with her because he was not in the mood and was depressed. He went out without her and told her he could not stand being near her. He showed more interest in his sporting hobbies than he did in his wife and children. He then left. The wife petitioned for divorce under s1(2)(b).

HELD: Section 1(2)(b) was not the same as desertion in s1(2)(c). It meant something else, namely, something which justified the court in finding that the marriage had irretrievably broken down before the two year period had elapsed after the separation (when s1(2)(c) or (d) could have been used as grounds for divorce). There had to be conduct by the respondent which went beyond simple desertion or the steps leading up to simple desertion. The wife's petition was dismissed. She would have to have waited for two years to pass and then use either s1(2)(c) or (d).

In *Buffery* v *Buffery* [1988] 2 FLR 365 the spouses were married for over twenty years and had three grown up children. While the children lived with them they did not go out together, though they shared in the children's upbringing. Over the years they grew apart. The wife complained that her husband was insensitive and never took her out. Once the children had left home the spouses found that they had lost the ability to talk to each other and had nothing in common. Neither spouse bore any greater blame than the other.

HELD: The wife's petition for divorce under s1(2)(b) was dismissed since there was insufficient behaviour to satisfy the ground.

Contrast *Bannister* v *Bannister* (above) where the husband had not taken the wife out for two years. He did not speak to her unless it was unavoidable. He stayed out at night without telling his wife where he was going. He led an entirely independent life ignoring his wife. A decree was granted under s1(2)(b).

## Lots of little incidents

There could have been a course of conduct rather than a series of dramatic incidents which taken with the character of the other spouse was none the less serious in the long run, even though the petitioner could not point to specific incidents in their own right. In *Livingstone-Stallard* v *Livingstone-Stallard* (above) a wife married a husband who was more than twice her age. He was abusive, critical and boorish and treated his wife like a child. There were many small incidents and arguments.

HELD: There was sufficient behaviour for a decree to be granted. Dunn J said:

'I accept that many of the incidents were, or might appear to be, trivial in themselves ... But taking the facts as I have found them in the round in relation to the husband's character, in my judgment, they amount to a situation in which this young wife was subjected to a constant atmosphere of criticism, disapproval and boorish behaviour on the part of her husband. Applying the test which I have formulated, I think that any right thinking person would come to the conclusion that this husband has behaved in such a way that this wife could not reasonably be expected to live with him.'

In *O'Neill* v *O'Neill* (above) the wife said that the husband had a withdrawn personality. He cast doubt on the paternity of the children. He worked about the flat. He removed the floorboards. He mixed cement in the living room. He removed the lavatory door which remained off for about eight months. He put rubble in the garden. He spent two years 'improving' the flat. All of this led to discomfort.

HELD: On appeal, decree should be granted. The court made allowances for the ordinary wear and tear and give and take of married life. However, it did not expect either heroic virtue or selfless abnegation.

See also *Stevens* v *Stevens* [1979] 1 WLR 885 where the petitioner failed in her first divorce petition since she had caused the breakdown of the marriage. The respondent then decided to make her life so unpleasant that she would be forced to leave the house. He refused to pay the electricity bill, and so it was cut off. He prevented her from cooking. He experimented with paraffin which aggravated her asthma. He constantly invaded her privacy by searching her room and clothes. He insulted her. Her second petition was successful.

In *Birch* v *Birch* [1992] 1 FLR 564; [1992] Fam Law 290 H and W married in 1961. After 27 years of marriage all the children had grown up. W petitioned for divorce under s1(2)(b) MCA 1973. She alleged that H was dogmatic and dictatorial towards her. She had been born in Ireland and H made pointless and bigoted remarks about W being Irish whenever Ireland or Northern Ireland were in the news. He belittled her opinions. He insulted her and drank to excess. This behaviour caused W tension and anxiety. She endured his behaviour until after the children had left home. H denied her allegations.

At the hearing the court had to rely on the unsupported evidence of each spouse. It was satisfied that the marriage had broken down irretrievably but dismissed the petition because the husband's evidence was preferred and the evidence did not satisfy an objective test of whether H had behaved in such a way that W could not reasonably have been expected to live with him. W appealed.

HELD: Allowing the appeal, the wrong test had been applied. Following *Ash* v *Ash*, *O'Neill* v *O'Neill* and *Livingstone-Stallard* v *Livingstone-Stallard* the court had to consider the character, personality, disposition and behaviour of the petitioner. In this case W was passive and sensitive while H was strong minded, outspoken, dogmatic and chauvinistic. His behaviour began as an irritation but when repeated became intolerable.

## Financial irresponsibility

In *Carter-Fea* v *Carter-Fea* [1987] Fam Law 131 the husband's financial irresponsibility affected the family and caused the wife stress. The decree was granted.

## Illness

Behaviour arising out of the respondent's illness and for which, therefore, the respondent may not have been responsible, can be the basis of a s1(2)(b) petition having taken into account all the circumstances of the case including the responsibilities of marriage and having made allowances for the respondent's disabilities.

In *Katz* v *Katz* [1972] 1 WLR 955; [1972] 3 All ER 219 the parties married in 1954. In 1967 the husband began to show signs of mental illness. He was committed to hospital in 1968 for four weeks. He constantly criticised his wife and made objectionable remarks about her. His condition began to improve, but he still visited his doctor and was taking drugs on prescription. In 1971 he showed signs of being disturbed again. He made frequent accusations about his wife's alleged 'misdoings', calling her a tramp and a slut. This behaviour had a serious effect on the wife who at one stage attempted suicide.

HELD: 'Behaviour' was more than a mere state of affairs or state of mind, being action or conduct by one spouse which affects the other and which had some reference to the marriage. The test applied was whether after making all allowances for the respondent's disabilities and the temperament of both parties, the character and gravity of his behaviour was such that the petitioner could not reasonably have been expected to live with him. The wife was entitled to a decree nisi.

In *Richards* v *Richards* [1972] 1 WLR 1073; [1972] 3 All ER 695 the parties married in 1963. In early 1970 the husband became mentally ill and began to suffer from moodiness, taciturnity and insomnia. Because of insomnia, he used to get up at night and go downstairs, which disturbed the wife. In June 1970, he hit her on the head with his hands, and in December slapped her once on the face. After the first assault, the parties realised the husband was suffering from mental illness, and thereafter he received medical treatment. The wife left.

HELD: Petition dismissed. The court was required to make a value judgment about the respondent's behaviour, and the effect of that behaviour upon the petitioner and at the same time to take into account the temperament of both parties and the mental illness of the respondent.

Although the marriage had irretrievably broken down, the wife had failed to establish s1(2)(b).

See *Thurlow* v *Thurlow* [1975] 3 WLR 161; [1975] 2 All ER 979 where the wife was an epileptic whose condition got progressively worse. The wife became incontinent. She was also bad-tempered and threw objects about. She wandered about the streets causing the husband alarm and distress. He was in full-time work and found trying to care for his wife and run the household very stressful. The strain had a significant effect on his health. His wife really required indefinite institutional care.

HELD (by Rees J): When considering whether to grant a decree under s1(2)(b), the behaviour of the respondent could be positive or negative in character, or both and could include cases where the behaviour was caused by mental or physical illness or injury and might be involuntary. It was for the judge to decide whether the behaviour was sufficiently grave to make it unreasonable to expect the petitioner to endure it.

'If the behaviour stemmed from misfortune such as onset of a mental illness or from disease of the body or from accidental physical injury the court would take full account of all the obligations of the married state. Those would include the normal duty to accept and to share the burdens imposed upon the family as a result of the mental or physical ill-health of one member. It would also consider the capacity of the petitioner to withstand the stress imposed by the behaviour, the steps taken to cope with it, the length of time during which the petitioner has been called upon to bear it, and the actual or potential effect upon his or her health.'

A decree nisi was granted to the husband relying mainly upon the wife's behaviour during the gradual deterioration of her mental and physical condition due to severe physical neurological disorder.

## Summary

Each case was a question largely of fact, but note that a non-adulterous association, which might have been more destructive than a casual act of adultery, could have been sufficient behaviour (see *Wachtel* v *Wachtel* [1973] 2 WLR 366; [1973] 1 All ER 829 (CA)), as could obtaining artificial insemination without the husband's consent, although that was not held to amount to adultery.

## *Reconciliation provisions*

Section 2(3):

> 'Where in any proceedings for divorce the petitioner alleges that the respondent has behaved in such a way that the petitioner cannot reasonably be expected to live with him, but the parties to the marriage have lived with each other for a period or periods after the date of the occurrence of the final incident relied on by the petitioner and held by the court to support his allegation, that fact shall be disregarded in determining for the purposes of section 1(2)(b) above whether the petitioner cannot reasonably be expected to live with the respondent if the length of that period or of those periods together was six months or less.'

That is, if the parties live together for less than six months since the date of the final incident relied upon, the fact of the cohabitation should be disregarded in determining whether the petitioner could not reasonably be expected to live with the respondent.

If the cohabitation is for a period in excess of six months, there is no absolute bar, but it will be taken into account in considering the question of 'reasonably expected'.

In *Bradley* v *Bradley* [1973] 1 WLR 1291; [1973] 3 All ER 750 the wife petitioned for divorce on the ground of her husband's violent behaviour. She obtained magistrates' separation and maintenance orders in 1969 and 1970 on the basis of his violence. The husband returned to live with the wife despite these orders because the wife felt obliged to let him back. In June 1972 she petitioned for divorce. The last incidence of violence she referred to was in February 1972. The court dismissed her petition because she had lived with her husband more or less continuously since the magistrates' orders. Her appeal was allowed. The fact that she lived with her husband did not prevent her from relying on s1(2)(b) as she had no alternative open to her and no place to go. It was open to the court to grant a divorce decree.

In *Savage* v *Savage* [1982] 3 WLR 418; [1982] 3 All ER 49 the parties resumed cohabitation for three and a half years, three months after the wife was granted a decree nisi. It was accepted that the marriage had irretrievably broken down, but that the petitioner did not present a very strong case. Having examined the quality of the cohabitation and all the circumstances, the court refused to make the decree absolute.

In *Court* v *Court* [1982] 3 WLR 199; [1982] 2 All ER 531 the wife was granted a decree nisi in June 1979. From October 1979 to June 1980 the parties resumed cohabitation. From June 1980 to December 1980 when the husband left they lived separately under the same roof. In May 1981 the wife applied for the decree absolute. It was held in the light of the circumstances prior to the decree nisi that the wife had demonstrated that it was unreasonable to expect her to live with the respondent. The delay did not stand in her way and the decree absolute would be granted.

## 3.6 Desertion

Section 1(2)(c):

'That the respondent had deserted the petitioner for a continuous period of at least two years immediately proceeding the presentation of the petition.'

Desertion involves:

1. the fact of separation; and
2. an intention to desert by the respondent; and
3. a lack of consent by the petitioner; and
4. that the separation was without just cause.

The petitioner needs to establish all these elements; as a result of the ensuing complications desertion is difficult to prove.

### *The fact of separation*

Separation involves withdrawal from married life, which normally means that the respondent has left the matrimonial home and so deserted the petitioner. However, there does not need to be a withdrawal from a place. For example, in *Bradshaw* v *Bradshaw* [1897] P 24 the husband was a domestic servant. His wife visited him and had children by him. They did not have a matrimonial home together. The husband then refused to see the wife or receive her at the house where he lived and worked. He refused to contribute to the children. He was held to be in desertion from his wife. In *Milligan* v *Milligan* [1941] 2 All ER 62 the husband was an army officer. He and his wife did have a permanent matrimonial home. They lived in hotels and rented accommodation. The husband then went to live in the officers' mess and refused to live with his wife. He was held to be in desertion.

In *Dunn* v *Dunn* [1948] 2 All ER 822 the spouses quarrelled as to where the matrimonial home should be. The wife was acutely deaf and very shy, and she wanted to stay where they had first set up home. The husband wanted to move to where he worked, and moved there without his wife. He alleged that she was in desertion by refusing to move there with him. It was held that she was not in desertion since she had reasonable cause for not moving, and that the husband was in desertion by unreasonably refusing to discuss where the matrimonial home should be. Denning LJ said:

'The decision where the home should be is a decision which affects both the parties and their children. It is their duty to decide it by agreement, by give and take, and not by the imposition of the will of one over the other. Each is entitled to an equal voice in the ordering of affairs which are their common concern. Neither has a casting vote.'

It was possible to have desertion even where the parties are still living in the same house. The petitioner is required to show that there are two separate household and that there is no sharing of communal or family life. This was the case in *Naylor* v *Naylor* [1961] 2 WLR 751; [1961] 2 All ER 129 where the wife said that she would no longer be a wife to the husband. She removed her wedding ring, lived separately from the husband and did not provide any services for him. He did not pay her any housekeeping. She was held to be in desertion.

If there is any element of sharing of family life while the spouses are living under the same roof there may not be 'desertion'. For example, in *Hopes* v *Hopes* [1948] 2 All ER 920 the spouses slept in separate bedrooms. The wife did no mending or washing for the husband, but he continued to have his meals with the family and shared the rest of the house with them. It was held that there was insufficient separation of household for there to be desertion. Lord Denning explained as follows:

> 'The husband who shuts himself up in one or two rooms of his house, and ceases to have anything to do with his wife, is living separately and apart from her as effectively as if they were separated by the outer door of a flat. They may meet on the stairs or in the passageway, but so they might if they had separate flats in the same building. If that separation is brought about by his fault, why is that not desertion? He has forsaken and abandoned effectively as if he had gone into lodgings.
>
> ... It is most important to draw a clear line between desertion ... and gross neglect or chronic discord ... That line is drawn at the point where the parties are living separately and apart. In cases where they are living under the same roof that point is reached when they cease to be one household and become two households.'

The same result was reached in *Le Brocq* v *Le Brocq* [1964] 2 All ER 464, where the wife excluded the husband from the matrimonial bedroom by putting a bolt on the door. They did not communicate unless they had to, but the wife continued to cook the husband's meals, and he paid her housekeeping. There was a separation of bedrooms and a separation of hearts, but one household was carried on and so there was no desertion. A similar conclusion was reached in *Bull* v *Bull* [1953] 2 All ER 601 where a wife deserted her husband. She then returned to live with him. Though she refused to have sexual intercourse with him she cooked his meals and occasionally mended his clothes.

By contrast in *Bertram* v *Bertram* [1949] 2 All ER 270 the wife deserted the husband but had accommodation difficulties whereby she was forced to return to live in the matrimonial home. She did no cooking or mending for the husband, and though she ate at the same table she treated him as a lodger whom she cordially disliked. It was held that in these circumstances her desertion continued.

## The intention to desert (or 'animus deserendi')

The respondent must intend to desert the petitioner permanently.

Provided that there is the required intention, it does not matter if the parties were forced to live apart by circumstances outside their control. For example, in *Beeken* v *Beeken* [1948] P 302 the husband and wife were interned by the Japanese in

1941. Initially they were interned together. The wife formed a relationship with another internee. They were then interned in different camps in 1944, and the wife told the husband that she never intended to return to him. She was held to be in desertion from 1944 even though she had no choice but to live apart from her husband. Similarly in *Drew* v *Drew* (1888) 13 PD 97 a husband deserted his wife and was then sentenced to imprisonment. His desertion was held to continue. The court took the view that he would not have returned to his wife even if free to do so.

The respondent is required to have the mental capacity to form the intention to permanently desert the petitioner. If the respondent is insane he or she may not have been able to form the required intention. For example, in *Perry* v *Perry* [1963] 3 All ER 766 the wife left the husband because she had an insane delusion that he was trying to murder her. The court judged her conduct on the basis that she believed the delusion to be true and held that she was not in desertion. By contrast in *Kacmarz* v *Kacmarz* [1967] 1 WLR 317; [1967] 1 All ER 416 the wife had a delusion that her husband had committed a grave sin by having sexual intercourse with her, and she left him. She was held to be in desertion because her delusion was vague. Even if she believed it to be true it did not justify her leaving her husband. She was capable of forming a rational decision to leave him, albeit for strange reasons.

The onus is on the petitioner to prove that the respondent is capable of forming the required intention and that he or she did form the required intention. In *Crowther* v *Crowther* [1951] 1 All ER 1131 a wife petitioned for divorce on the basis of three years' continuous desertion. The husband had been in a mental hospital for two and a half months of that period. She failed to show that he had the capacity to form the required intention during that period, so she failed to show a continuous period of three years' desertion, and her petition failed. The effect of this decision had been overcome by s2(4) MCA 1973 which provides:

> 'The Court may still treat a period of desertion as having continued at a time when the deserting party was incapable of continuing the necessary intention if the evidence before the court is such that, had that party not been so incapable, the court would have inferred that his desertion continued at that time.'

## The petitioner must not consent to the desertion

If the petitioner agrees to the respondent leaving, then the petitioner is required to rely on the living apart grounds in s1(2)(d) and (e) MCA 1973. There cannot be desertion since there is an agreement to live apart (see *Lord* v *Lord* [1940] 4 All ER 230). In *Joseph* v *Joseph* [1953] 2 All ER 710 the husband deserted the wife, who then obtained a Jewish divorce from him which was ineffective under English law. She then tried to obtain a divorce decree on the basis of desertion. However, the Jewish decree showed that she wanted to live apart from him, so he could no longer be in desertion.

The petitioner is allowed to rely on the fact that the respondent has left provided that he or she had not agreed to the departure (see *Pizey* v *Pizey* [1961] 2 All ER 658).

Certain agreements about the respondent leaving may not affect the desertion; for example, an agreement to provide financial support would not have prevented desertion, provided that the agreement did not bind the parties to live apart (see *Crabtree* v *Crabtree* [1953] 1 WLR 708; [1953] 2 All ER 56).

Exclusion orders and injunctions do not prevent a violent spouse from being in desertion (s4(4) MCA 1973).

A decree of judicial separation ends desertion since it ends the duty to cohabit. However, if the judicial separation was obtained on the ground of desertion the petitioner can obtain a divorce using the same period of desertion provided that the decree of judicial separation had continually been in force and the parties have not resumed cohabitation (s4(3) MCA 1973).

The petitioner is required to be aware of the desertion, otherwise he or she will be treated as consenting to the separation. If, for example, the spouses had agreed to live apart but one spouse then formed an intention to desert, there could not be desertion until the other spouse is aware of the intention to desert and no longer agrees to the separation. This was the case in *Nutley* v *Nutley* [1970] 1 WLR 217; [1970] 1 All ER 410 where a husband and wife agreed to live apart so that the wife could look after her parents. While living with them she formed the intention not to return to her husband. The husband only became aware of this after the parents died. It was held that the wife's desertion only ran from the moment he became aware of her decision, since before that time he had consented to the separation.

## The petitioner must not have refused a reasonable offer of reconciliation

Where a respondent had deserted the petitioner but the respondent subsequently makes a reasonable offer of reconciliation which the petitioner unreasonably rejects, the respondent's desertion will end. Such an unreasonable rejection can put the petitioner in the position of desertion. A petitioner is required to give due consideration to a reasonable offer (see *Fraser* v *Fraser* [1969] 3 All ER 654). For example in *Gallagher* v *Gallagher* [1965] 1 WLR 1110; [1965] 2 All ER 967 the husband and wife separated by agreement. The husband then made a bona fide offer to return which the wife rejected out of hand. She later said she never wanted to live with him again. It was held that this put to an end the agreed separation and put the wife in desertion.

If the offer of reconciliation is unreasonable in all the circumstances the petitioner is entitled to reject it. For example, in *Fletcher* v *Fletcher* [1945] 1 All ER 582 the husband asked his wife to return to him on condition that she joined a religious commune. This was not a reasonable offer and did not end his desertion. In *Everitt* v *Everitt* [1949] 1 All ER 908 the husband offered reconciliation, but the wife refused his offer because she reasonably believed that he was committing adultery, which had caused the separation in the first place. It was held that the husband's desertion continued since the wife's refusal of his offer of reconciliation was reasonable.

The situation would have been different if the husband's adultery played no part in the wife's refusal. This was the case in *Day* v *Day* [1957] 1 All ER 848 where the husband committed adultery after he had left his wife. He then made an offer of reconciliation. The wife refused his offer. It was held that she had made no reference to his adultery in her refusal, and that the husband's offer was genuine. She had therefore unreasonably refused his offer. This showed that she had formed the intention to desert him, independently of his desertion, and this meant that she was in desertion.

### The petitioner must not have given the respondent just cause to leave – 'constructive desertion'

If one spouse behaves so badly that this forces the other spouse to leave, then the other spouse will not be held to be in desertion; indeed, the bad behaviour of the remaining spouse could put that spouse in what is termed 'constructive desertion' by reason of forcing the other spouse to leave. Whether there is constructive desertion depends on the court's view of the behaviour of the remaining spouse and if this gave good cause for the other spouse to leave. Examples of behaviour which justified a spouse in leaving and put the remaining spouse in constructive desertion include:

1. a respondent who kept 30 cats which made such a mess that the petitioner was forced to leave – the respondent was in constructive desertion (see *Winnans* v *Winnans* [1948] 2 All ER 862);
2. an overbearing, domineering and dictatorial husband who had a hasty temper and assaulted his wife – this justified her leaving him (*Timmins* v *Timmins* [1953] 2 All ER 187);
3. an extremely lazy husband whose slovenly conduct drove his wife away – he was in constructive desertion (even though he did not intend to drive his wife away) (see *Gollins* v *Gollins* [1963] 2 All ER 966);
4. a husband who unreasonably believed that his wife was committing adultery and made her life miserable – this justified her leaving him and put him in constructive desertion (see *Marsden* v *Marsden* [1967] 1 All ER 967);
5. a husband who was mentally ill, and whose behaviour frightened his daughter; when he left on a trip his wife refused to allow him back home – she was not in desertion (see *G* v *G* [1964] 1 All ER 129);
6. a husband who unreasonably took a second wife in a polygamous marriage without the consent of his first wife, and the first wife left him. Although according to Muslim law she could not prevent the second marriage, in the circumstances she had just cause for leaving her husband and was not in desertion (see *Quoraishi* v *Quoraishi* [1985] FLR 780).

In *Buchler* v *Buchler* [1947] 1 All ER 319 the husband formed a close relationship with one of his male farm hands. It was not a homosexual relationship, but the wife felt 'left out' and was upset by local gossip, so she left. It was held that the husband's behaviour was not sufficiently bad to justify her leaving, and she was in desertion. In *Kacmarz* v *Kacmarz* (above) the wife left because she believed that sexual intercourse with her husband was a grave sin. This was not held to be a good reason to justify her leaving, and she was in desertion.

There were conflicting decisions as to whether the refusal by one spouse to have sexual intercourse with the other gives just cause for the other spouse to leave. In *Weatherley* v *Weatherley* [1947] 1 All ER 563 a wife was held not to be in desertion for refusing sexual intercourse (though the parties remained in the same house, albeit in separate households). By contrast, in *Hutchinson* v *Hutchinson* [1963] 1 All ER 1 a husband's refusal to have intercourse with his wife was just cause for her to leave him, and the husband was in constructive desertion. The same conclusion was reached in *Slon* v *Slon* [1969] 1 All ER 759 where a wife refused to have intercourse in order to punish the husband for non-existent adultery. The husband left, and the wife was held to be in constructive desertion.

## For two years preceding the filing of the petition

Where the petitioner had obtained *either* a judicial separation *or* a maintenance order under the Domestic Proceedings and Magistrates' Courts Act 1978 using the ground of desertion, *and* the decree or order had been continuously in force and the parties had not resumed living with each other, then the petitioner can rely on a period of desertion before the decree or order (s4(1) and (3) MCA 1973).

The court can find that any period during which an exclusion order or injunction prohibiting one spouse from occupying the matrimonial home was in force is a period during which the respondent deserted the petitioner. Such an order would not have terminated an already subsisting desertion (s4(4) MCA 1973).

## Reconciliation provisions

No account can be taken of any one period not exceeding six months, or any two or more periods not exceeding six months in all, during which the parties resumed living with each other in considering whether the respondent had deserted the petitioner over a continuous period. However, any such period when the parties lived together cannot count towards the two-year period of desertion required under s1(2)(c) MCA 1973 (s2(5) MCA 1973).

If the parties resumed cohabitation on a frequent basis the courts will conclude that there never was any real desertion. In *France* v *France* [1969] 2 All ER 870 the wife told the husband to leave because she loved another man. The husband left but then returned on a number of occasions and had sexual intercourse with the wife. The court concluded that there could not be constructive desertion by the wife since the separation had become consensual and the parties regularly got back together.

## 3.7 Living apart for two years with consent (otherwise referred to as two years' separation)

Section 1(2)(d) MCA 1973:

'That the parties have lived apart for a continuous period of at least two years immediately preceding the presentation of the petition and the respondent consents to a decree being granted.'

### *That the parties had lived apart ...*

Section 2(6):

'A husband and wife shall be treated as living apart unless they are living with each other in the same household.'

Living apart means more than the physical separation of the parties. There must be a recognition by at least one of the parties that the marriage is at an end. See *Santos* v *Santos* [1972] 2 WLR 889; [1972] 2 All ER 246 where the husband lived in Spain and the wife lived apart from him in England. She visited him on a number of occasions and it was not clear whether they were living apart.

HELD: 'Living apart' means that the parties live apart and at the same time one or both of the parties recognise that the marriage is at an end. The decision to end the marriage could be made unilaterally without the other party being informed or accepting the decision.

The court recognised that this might cause hardship to a party who did not agree that the marriage was at an end and had not been told of the other party's decision about the marriage. An example of such a case would be a husband going abroad on business for over two years. Even though he and his wife had been on excellent terms for virtually all of that time, either might unilaterally decide that the marriage was finished just before the husband's return home and seek to rely on s1(2)(d) as a ground for divorce. As a result, the petitioner is required to establish when he or she decided that the marriage was at an end and when the parties actually commenced 'living apart'. Such evidence could be in the form of a letter or a cessation of visits to a spouse in prison or by cohabitation with a third party.

Where there is only oral evidence from the petitioner, special caution may be required. If the respondent's conduct is consistent with a continuing recognition that the marriage is 'alive and well', then a court will not automatically accept the petitioner's uncorroborated evidence that he decided that the marriage was at end when that is inconsistent with the respondent's conduct.

The court would look at all the circumstances: how the separation of the parties came about; what the petitioner's attitude to the marriage was at that time; and when had the petitioner changed his mind about the marriage and what led to that change of mind?

## Living apart in the same household

See *Fuller* v *Fuller* [1973] 2 All ER 650 where the wife left her husband to live with another man, taking the children with her. The husband became ill. His doctor told the wife that the husband only had a year to live and should not be left on his own. She allowed him to live in her new household but as a lodger paying a weekly rent. He had a separate bedroom. The wife got his meals which he ate with the rest of the family. The wife did his washing. Both the husband and the wife clearly treated their marriage as at an end. Four years later the husband was still alive and still living at the wife's house.

HELD: The husband and wife were living apart. They were not living with each other in the same household. Decree granted.

But contrast *Mouncer* v *Mouncer* [1972] 1 All ER 289 where the husband and wife were on bad terms. They slept in separate bedrooms. They ate their meals together with the children, the meals being prepared by the wife. They shared the cleaning of the house though the wife did not do any of the husband's washing. The husband did not want to live with the wife but did want to stay in the matrimonial home to live with and help look after the children. He then left and petitioned for divorce on the basis of two years living apart with the wife's consent.

HELD: The spouses had not been living apart. They had shared the same household. A rejection of the normal physical relationship between husband and wife coupled with the absence of normal affection was not sufficient to constitute living apart.

## Consent

The petitioner is required to provide the respondent with information enabling him or her to consent to the decree and the steps he or she would take to indicate consent (s2(7) MCA 1973, and the Notice of Proceedings and the Acknowledgement of Service sent to the respondent along with the petition).

The respondent is required to give a positive indication of consent by sending to the court a notice to the effect that he or she consents to the decree. This is normally the acknowledgement of service of the petition signed by the respondent (if unrepresented) and by both the respondent *and* his solicitor (if represented) (r2.10 Family Proceedings Rules 1991).

The burden of showing that the respondent has consented is on the petitioner.

The court will not imply consent if the correct procedure has not been followed. See *McGill* v *Robson* [1972] 1 All ER 362 where the husband lived in Africa and the wife lived in England. The wife's solicitors sent an acknowledgement of service form to the husband which did not have anything on it enabling the husband to signify his consent to the decree. He acknowledged service but did not give any specific consent to the decree. He did write to say that he wanted the proceedings finalised as soon as possible.

HELD: In the absence of any specific consent from the husband the court refused to imply his consent and the decree was refused.

The respondent is required to have the necessary capacity to give consent. See *Mason* v *Mason* [1972] 3 All ER 315 where the husband went into a mental hospital and lived apart from the wife for over two years either in the hospital or in local authority homes. When the wife petitioned for divorce on the ground of two years' living apart he sent her a typed consent form which he had signed. His doctor considered him to be rational enough to give a valid consent.

HELD: The test for the capacity of the respondent to give a valid consent was the same as the test for the validity of the contract of marriage propounded in *In the Estate of Park* [1953] 2 All ER 1411, namely, was the respondent capable of understanding the nature of the contract which he or she was entering? In this case the husband was capable of understanding what was involved in giving his consent and the decree was granted.

If there was any doubt as to the capacity of a respondent to give valid consent the burden is on the petitioner to satisfy the court that the respondent had the necessary understanding.

A consent can be withdrawn at any time before the pronouncement of decree nisi (see r2.10(2) Family Proceedings Rules 1991).

A respondent can apply to the court at any time before decree absolute for the decree nisi to be rescinded if the court is satisfied that the petitioner misled the respondent (whether intentionally or unintentionally) about any matter which the respondent had taken into account in deciding to consent to the grant of a decree (s10(1) MCA 1973).

## A continuous period of at least two years

The period of two years was construed strictly and excluded the day when the parties separated. See *Warr* v *Warr* [1975] 1 All ER 85 where the parties separated at noon on 6 February 1972. The wife petitioned for divorce on the afternoon of 6 February 1974.

HELD: The two years did not end until 7 February 1974 since the day of separation is excluded. A fresh petition had to be served in order for the decree to be granted.

## Reconciliation provisions

In calculating the period for which the parties had lived apart no account is taken of any one period not exceeding six months, or of any two or more periods not exceeding six months in all, during which the parties resumed living with each other (see s2(5) MCA 1973).

See *Santos* v *Santos* (above) where the wife returned to live with the husband for short periods and these were ignored in the calculation of the two years living apart.

## 3.8 Living apart for five years (otherwise referred to as five years' separation)

Section 1(2)(e) MCA 1973:

> 'That the parties have lived apart for a continuous period of at least five years immediately preceding the presentation of the petition.'

Section 2(6) MCA 1973 on the meaning of 'living apart' applies. The interpretation of the phrase in *Santos* v *Santos* is equally applicable as is the construction of the phrase 'a continous period' in *Warr* v *Warr*. The reconciliation provisions in s2(5) also apply.

## 3.9 Protecting the financial position in living apart cases

The court has power to in two-year and five-year living apart cases to delay or prevent the decree absolute in certain circumstances. Once the court has granted a decree nisi on either fact (and no other fact) the respondent can apply to the court for consideration of his/her financial position after the divorce (see s10(2) MCA 1973).

The court must then consider all the circumstances, including the age, health, conduct, earning capacity, financial resources and financial obligations of each of the parties, and the financial position of the respondent (if the decree is made absolute) if the petitioner should die first.

The court cannot then make the decree absolute unless it is satisfied:

1. that the petitioner should not be required to make any financial provision for the respondent; or
2. that the financial provision made by the petitioner for the respondent is reasonable and fair or the best that can be made in the circumstances; or
3. notwithstanding the above there are circumstances making it desirable that the decree should be made absolute without delay and the court has obtained a satisfactory undertaking from the petitioner that he/she will make financial provision for the respondent as the court may approve (s10(3), (4) MCA 1973).

The idea of the provisions is to enable the respondent to ask the court to protect his/her financial position by asking the court not to finalise the divorce until reasonable financial provision has been made or promised by the petitioner.

Examples of how the court has applied s10(2)–(4) include:

1. *Krystmann* v *Krystmann* [1973] 3 All ER 247 where the spouses married in Italy during the war but only cohabited for two weeks before the husband petitioner returned to England. There was no contact between them for 26 years. The husband petitioned for divorce on the fact of five years living apart. The

respondent wife applied under s10 for her financial position to be considered. It was held that taking into account the short period of cohabitation and the long separation, and the fact that the wife was better off than the husband, that he need not make any financial provision for her.

2. *Lombardi* v *Lombardi* [1973] 3 All ER 625 where the spouses were married for five years. They were separated for ten years. The husband petitioned for divorce on the fact of five years living apart. He was a successful businessman with a comfortable lifestyle. The respondent wife lived in a one bedroom flat and had a modest salary. It was held that the husband had made a reasonable offer of maintenance to the wife and the decree was made absolute.

3. *Parkes* v *Parkes* [1971] 3 All ER 870 where the petitioner husband agreed financial arrangements with the respondent wife so that she would not oppose the grant of the decree nisi under s5 MCA 1973 (see below). The decree nisi was granted. The husband was able to exploit ambiguities in the agreement to in effect rob the wife of the benefits she would otherwise have received. She was able to prevent the decree from being made absolute under s10 and force the husband to revise the agreement to provide her with fair and reasonable financial support.

4. *Garcia* v *Garcia* [1992] 2 WLR 347 where the parties married in 1974. They adopted the wife's illegitimate son. In 1982 they separated while living in Spain. They made an agreement under Spanish law that the husband pay maintenance and education costs for the child for ten years. In 1987 the husband broke the agreement and stopped payments. He moved to England and petitioned for divorce on the fact of five years living apart. He obtained decree nisi. The wife applied under s10 to delay the decree absolute until the husband fulfilled his obligations to her son under the agreement and paid the £4,000 of arrears owing. She did not want financial provision for herself. The decree was delayed. The husband appealed, arguing that s10 was not applicable. It was held on appeal that s10(3) covered 'any financial provision' and was not confined to future financial provision. It included past financial injustice and unfulfilled obligations. This was also part of 'all the circumstances' and the conduct and financial obligations of the parties.

5. *Grigson* v *Grigson* [1974] 1 All ER 478 where the husband petitioned for divorce on the fact of five years living apart. He wanted the decree made absolute without delay because he was living with another woman who had given birth to a daughter whom he wished to make legitimate. The wife was in her sixties and wanted security in her declining years. The husband was obliged to provide a formulated proposal as to the kind and amount of financial provision he intended to make for the wife. His proposal had to have enough content for it to be enforceable. A vague or blanket undertaking (eg such financial provision as the court may approve) would not suffice.

6. *Cumbers* v *Cumbers* [1975] 1 All ER 1 illustrates the problems caused by vague proposals in which all sorts of confusion resulted. The court had to decide on an

appropriate order in the absence of specific proposals from the petitioner husband.

## Special provision for Jewish marriages

The Divorce (Religious Marriages) Act 2002 came into force on 24 February 2003. It inserts s10A in to the Matrimonial Causes Act 1973 and applies to Jewish marriages which can only be properly ended by both a divorce under the MCA 1973 and a religious divorce according to the usages of Jewish law. Either party petitioning for divorce in such circumstances can ask the court to order that the divorce decree cannot be made absolute until a declaration is produced to the court, made by both parties, that the religious divorce has been obtained. The court can only make such an order if it is satisfied that in all the circumstances of the case it is just and reasonable to do so. The order can be revoked at any time. This provides special protection to Jewish spouses who cannot be treated as properly divorced in their communities until both the civil and religious divorces have been obtained.

## 3.10 Special defence in cases of living apart for five years

Section 5 MCA 1973 provides a special defence for petitions brought under s1(2)(e) MCA 1973 (the five years living apart ground). This defence does not apply to petitions brought under other grounds, for example s1(2)(d).

The respondent may oppose the grant of the decree if the divorce will result in grave financial or other hardship and that it would in all the circumstances be wrong to dissolve the marriage (s5(1) MCA 1973). The defence, if successful, prevents a decree nisi being granted, since the court must dismiss the petition if satisfied as to the above (s5(2) MCA 1973). This is in contrast to s10 MCA 1973 which only comes into play after the grant of the decree nisi and prevents or delays the decree being made absolute.

The court must consider all the circumstances, including the conduct of the parties to the marriage and the interests of those parties and of any children or other persons concerned (s5(2) MCA 1973).

The respondent must satisfy the court of two factors:

1. that the divorce will result in grave financial or other hardship to the respondent; and
2. that it would be all the circumstances be wrong to dissolve the marriage.

The test is objective, namely not what the particular respondent considers to be grave hardship but what a reasonable person would think was grave hardship.

## What is 'grave' financial hardship ?

Financial hardship includes the loss of the chance of acquiring any benefit which the respondent might acquire if the marriage were not dissolved (s5(3) MCA 1973). This normally refers to pension rights. On divorce a spouse (often the wife) loses her share of the other spouse's pension (often the husband's pension). She also loses her right to a widow's pension she would have received had her husband predeceased her. These can be significant losses if a husband has built up substantial pension rights while the wife has remained at home looking after the children with no independent income or only a limited income and as a result with little or no pension provision. A divorce when the parties are nearing retirement age can leave the husband significantly better off than his former wife who may become dependant on state benefits.

Generally, only older spouses are able to successfully argue a s5 defence. For younger wives the loss of pension rights may be too remote and the opportunity to build up an independent pension provision such that s5 cannot be satisfied. This is illustrated by the following cases:

1. *Talbot* v *Talbot* (1971) 115 SJ 870 in which the husband left the wife in 1966. The wife obtained a decree of judicial separation. Five years later the husband petitioned for divorce under s1(2)(e) and the wife opposed the petition under s5. Her defence failed because there were no pension rights to be lost. She was young, competent and capable to earn. A balance had to be maintained between upholding the sanctity of marriage and the desirability of ending empty ties. The decree was granted.

2. *Mathias* v *Mathias* [1972] 3 WLR 201; [1972] 3 All ER 1 in which a husband (who was a soldier) aged 35 petitioned for divorce under s1(2)(e). The respondent wife was aged 32. They had a nine-year-old daughter who lived with the wife and had been living apart for eight years. The wife opposed the petition because she would lose her right to a discretionary army pension and to a state widow's pension, and their daughter would lose her interest under her paternal grandmother's will. Her defence failed because the wife was a healthy, young woman who could go out to work. Given that the spouses were young and had new lives to make, it was right to end the marriage. The wife had not established grave financial hardship and public interest required the marriage be dissolved. Pension rights were rights which might accrue in the foreseeable future and were too remote a prospect for young wives.

3. *Grenfell* v *Grenfell* [1978] 1 All ER 561 in which the wife filed a petition on the ground of behaviour. The husband filed a petition on the ground of five years living apart. The wife opposed his petition under s5 but her defence was struck out. She could hardly oppose the husband's petition on the ground that it would cause her grave hardship when she had petitioned for divorce herself.

4. *Archer* v *Archer* [1999] 1 FLR 327 in which the husband (aged 55) petitioned for divorce against the wife (aged 53) on the basis of five years living apart. She

raised the s5(1) defence. The husband earned a good income but had little capital. The wife did not work but had capital assets of £500,000 which gave her an income of up to £14,000 a year. The husband paid her maintenance of £12,000 a year. On divorce she would potentially lose a widow's pension worth £11,000 a year. The judge ruled that while the loss of the pension entitlement was substantial, and would cause some hardship, the wife's assets were such that it could not be said that she would suffer grave hardship. She appealed. It was held, dismissing the appeal, that the judge's conclusion was not plainly wrong on the evidence and her decision should stand. The wife would not be expected to have to use her capital while the maintenance was paid. She would normally be expected to outlive the husband but not by all that much. She could then reasonably be expected to dip into her capital to make up her ordinary living expenses.

Cases in which the s5 defence was more successful include:

1. *Parker* v *Parker* [1972] 2 WLR 21; [1972] 1 All ER 410 in which the wife defended the husband's s1(2)(e) petition under s5 by arguing the loss of her right to a police widow's pension. She was nearing retirement and would face financial stringency after the age of 60. It was held that the loss of the right to a police widow's pension, albeit contingent on her surviving the husband, was a loss of future possible security at a time when she most needed it and amounted to grave financial hardship. The husband was able to offset this loss by buying an annuity for the wife secured by a second mortgage. On this basis the decree was granted. In addition, the husband had a child from the woman he now lived with and it is was right to allow him to start a new married life.

2. *Le Marchant* v *Le Marchant* [1977] 1 WLR 559; [1977] 3 All ER 610 in which the husband was about to retire from the Post Office. He petitioned for divorce under s1(2)(e). His wife opposed the divorce under s5 since she would lose her entitlement to a Post Office widow's pension which was index-linked. The husband made inadequate proposals to mitigate this hardship. It was held that the wife had established grave financial hardship and that the husband had to produce an improved offer otherwise his petition would be dismissed. This the husband did by proposing the transfer of the matrimonial home to the wife, the payment to her of a lump sum and the taking out of an insurance policy to give her security. The decree nisi was granted but the decree absolute delayed until the husband's proposals were carried out.

3. *Julian* v *Julian* (1972) 116 SJ 763 in which the husband was aged 61 and the wife aged 58. He petitioned for divorce under s1(2)(e). The wife defended the divorce under s5 because she would lose her entitlement to a substantial police widow's pension. The husband offered increased maintenance and an annuity. It was held that his offer was inadequate to offset the grave financial hardship to the wife. Even though the husband wished to remarry it was wrong to dissolve the marriage and his petition was dismissed.

4. *K* v *K* [1997] 1 FLR 35 in which the husband was aged 47 and earned £20,000 a year and lived in a house with negative equity with another woman. The wife was aged 50 and earning £11,279 a year. She was legally aided and had already incurred £9,000 in costs which would swallow up any lump sum order. The only sizeable asset was the husband's pension fund whereby in 1998 he could retire with an index-linked pension of £15,674 a year or a capital sum of £57,877 and a reduced pension of £11,755 a year. He was likely to carry on working until 2003. The wife was entitled to a widow's pension of half of the husband's pension. W's own pension at 65 would have been £3,388 a year plus state benefits. The husband petitioned for divorce under s1(2)(e) and the wife defended under s5. It was held that the law (as it was then) was inadequate in dealing with pensions and in particular with transferring some of the husband's pension rights to the wife. She would suffer grave financial hardship. The husband had made inadequate proposals. It was not suitable to use s10 MCA 1973 since the wife would be left in grave financial hardship given the limited resources available to the parties. The husband's petition was dismissed.

5. *Dorrell* v *Dorrell* [1972] 1 WLR 1087; [1972] 3 All ER 343 where the wife was aged 60 and the husband over 60. The wife depended on state benefits and stood to lose a local government widow's pension of £2 a week. It was held that there was grave financial hardship since the loss of the pension, albeit small, was in the wife's reduced circumstances a significant part of her income. The petition was adjourned for the husband to put proposals forward to offset the loss to the wife.

In *Dorrell* the husband argued that any loss of pension rights would be made up by state benefits. This was held not be relevant. However in *Reiterbund* v *Reiterbund* [1975] 2 WLR 375; [1975] 1 All ER 280 a different conclusion was reached. In that case the husband was 54 and the wife aged 52. The wife argued the s5 defence to the husband's s1(2)(e) petition on the basis of the loss of the state retirement pension which was based on her husband's national insurance contributions. It was held that the chances of his death before she reached the age of 60 and became entitled to her retirement pension were remote. The 'contingent' loss of pension rights would probably never arise. In contrast to *Dorrell* it was held that state benefits were a most relevant factor. Even if there was a loss of pension rights, any shortfall would be made up by state benefits paid to the wife. The argument that there was grave financial hardship because payment would come from state benefits as opposed to the state pension was described as 'unreal'. In *Reiterbund* the court also found that the wife had failed to show that it was wrong to dissolve the marriage. Even if there was no prospect of remarriage the court wished to pursue the policy of divorce law which aims to crush the shell of empty marriage unless there were exceptional circumstances.

*Reiterbund* was followed by *Jackson* v *Jackson* [1993] 2 FLR 851 in which the husband aged 71 petitioned for divorce under s1(2)(e) against his wife aged 62. The wife opposed the divorce under s5 because she would lose her right to a British Rail widow's pension. Both parties largely depended on state benefits. The s5 defence failed because the wife might never receive the widow's pension. Even if she gained the pension this would be deducted from her state benefits. As a result she would gain nothing from the pension.

Even if a respondent wife can show grave financial hardship she must also show that it is wrong to dissolve the marriage. In *Brickell* v *Brickell* [1973] 3 All ER 508 the wife defended the husband's s1(2)(e) petition under s5 because she would lose a widow's pension derived from her husband's previous employment with the Ministry of Defence. However, she became obsessed with the idea that her husband was having an affair with another woman who worked with him in running a nursing home. She kept spying on her husband and conducted herself in such a way that the home had to close down. Though the court was satisfied that the wife would suffer grave financial hardship by the loss of the pension, her conduct was such that it would not be wrong to dissolve the marriage. The petition was granted.

## What is other grave hardship?

There are few examples of cases in which a respondent successfully argued grave hardship other than grave financial hardship.

One form of hardship which results from divorce is social or religious stigma. The first examples relate to Hindu wives who married in India and the consequences for them and their daughters of divorce. In *Parghi* v *Parghi* (1973) 117 SJ 582 the husband and wife, who were Hindus, married in India. After 15 years of marriage the husband left his wife and came to England. He petitioned for divorce under s1(2)(e). The wife opposed the petition under s5 by arguing that the social conditions in India were such that a divorced wife would be ostracised and the marriage prospects of their children harmed. It was held that since the parties came from a section of Hindu society in which divorce was more accepted and because the wife had already suffered from the breakdown of the marriage the divorce would not add to that hardship. She failed to show grave hardship and the decree was granted. In *Balraj* v *Balraj* (1981) 11 Fam Law 110 there were similar facts. The parties had lived apart for 17 years. Since the wife had already suffered the stigma of being a deserted wife it was held that no greater hardship would result from the divorce. The position of the daughter of the marriage could be alleviated by the payment of compensation to a fiancé for such loss of reputation. The wife could make use of s10 to protect her financial position. The decree was granted. By contrast in *Banik* v *Banik* [1973] 3 All ER 45 there was greater sympathy for this line of argument. At first instance the court rejected the wife's argument that the divorce would make her a social outcast in the society in which she lived. On appeal it was held that the wife's case required investigation. The decree nisi was set aside and the case remitted for rehearing before a different judge.

In *Rukat* v *Rukat* [1975] 1 All ER 343 the spouses were Roman Catholics. The parties lived apart for 20 years with the wife returning to her home, Sicily. The husband then petitioned for divorce under s1(2)(e). The wife opposed the divorce under s5 arguing that the hostile attitude towards divorced women in Sicily and the serious repurcussions for the daughter of the marriage amounted to grave hardship. It was held that the wife had already suffered hardship as a result of the long period of living apart. If she had successfully lived in Sicily for all that time she could do so after the divorce.

In *Lee* v *Lee* (1973) 117 SJ 616 the spouses had a seriously ill son who required constant attention. The spouses separated. The husband petitioned for divorce under s1(2)(e). He offered the wife maintenance, a lump sum to compensate her for the loss of a widow's pension and a half share of the proceeds of the matrimonial home. The son lived in a small house of his own nearby. The wife opposed the petition under s5 because of the need to remain living near the son. His house was too small for her to live there as well. The husband's offer was not sufficient for her to be able to buy a house or flat nearby. It was held that there was grave hardship because of the need to care for the son and the difficulties which would result from the divorce if the wife had to leave the matrimonial home. The husband's offer had not compensated for the hardship. His petition was dismissed.

## Procedure

The respondent must file an answer if he or she wishes to oppose the decree nisi. The suit then becomes defended and is transferred to the High Court.

## 3.11 Encouraging reconciliation

A solicitor acting for a petitioner had to certify whether he has discussed with the petitioner the possibility of a reconciliation (s6(1) MCA 1973).

The solicitor would give the petitioner names and addresses of persons qualified to help effect a reconciliation between parties to a marriage who had become estranged (s6(1) MCA 1973).

The court would adjourn proceedings, for such period as it thought fit, if it thought there was a reasonable possibility of reconciliation (s6(2) MCA 1973).

Note also the cohabitation provisions (s2).

See *Practice Direction* [1971] 1 All ER 63 where it was stated that solicitors do not always need to give names of organisations to the petitioner. The object of the section was to ensure that parties knew where to seek guidance where there was a sincere desire for reconciliation. Reference to the relevant organisations was not a formal step which had to be taken in all cases irrespective of whether or not there was a prospect of reconciliation. The following organisations were suggested where there was a sincere desire for reconciliation: any marriage guidance council affiliated to the National Marriage Guidance Council (now called RELATE); any centre of the Catholic Advisory Council; the Jewish Marriage Education Council; and any probation officer (probation officers make up the court welfare service).

## 3.12  Opposing the decree absolute

Under s1(5) MCA 1973 there is a limit of six weeks before application can be made for a decree nisi of divorce to be made into a decree absolute. The court can fix a shorter period by 'special order'. Section 41 MCA 1973 requires that arrangements for any children of the family have to be considered before the decree can be made absolute (see Chapter 15).

The decree nisi does not terminate the marriage. Between decree nisi and decree absolute a number of things can happen:

1. The court can adjourn the proceedings if there is a chance of reconciliation.
2. The court can ask the Queen's Proctor to intervene and investigate matters, or any person can give information to the Queen's Proctor which might affect the decree (eg evidence of fraud) (s8(1) MCA 1973).
3. A third party may show cause why the decree should not be made absolute by reason of material facts not having been brought to the attention of the court (s9(1) MCA 1973).
4. The court has a general power not to make a decree absolute where, for example, there is a real risk that one party would prejudice the other party's position. For example, in *Wickler* v *Wickler* [1998] 2 FLR 326 there was a real risk that the husband would wash his hands of financially supporting the wife. The court delayed decree absolute (and therefore the husband's ability to remarry) to protect the wife's position. It was held that this power was independent of s10 MCA 1973. In *O* v *O (Jurisdiction: Jewish Divorce)* [2000] 2 FLR 147 an Orthodox Jewish husband refused to arrange a Jewish divorce which prevented the Orthodox Jewish wife from remarrying in a synagogue. The husband's application to have the decree nisi of divorce was refused until he obtained the Jewish divorce.

Once decree absolute has been granted it is difficult to set the decree aside. For example, in *Callaghan* v *Andrew-Hanson* [1992] 1 All ER 56; [1991] 2 FLR 519 the wife petitioned for divorce in February 1997 on the ground of two years living apart with consent in s1(2)(d) MCA 1973. In March 1997 the husband gave his consent. Decree nisi was granted and the decree made absolute in May 1997. The parties had in fact been living together and carried on living together until the wife died in 1986. She died intestate and her estate passed to her two children. The husband wished to have a share of the estate (which he would be entitled to on intestacy if he were still married to his wife when she died). He asked the court to set aside the decree absolute because it was obtained by fraud. His application was refused. The court which granted the decree had the jurisdiction to do so. There was no procedural irregularity. The husband had agreed to it and had recognised it until his wife's death. He could not now challenge its validity.

Normally, once the six weeks have elapsed, the petitioner applies to have the decree made absolute. If no application is made after three months and six weeks have elapsed then the respondent can apply for the decree to be rescinded or made absolute or for further enquiries to be made or for the court to otherwise deal with the decree as it thinks fit (s9(2) MCA 1973). If the petitioner allows more than 12 months to elapse before applying to make the decree absolute he or she must lodge an explanation in writing for the delay and in particular explain if the parties have lived together during this period (r2.49 Family Proceedings Rules 1991).

## 3.13 The procedure for obtaining a divorce

The usual procedure for obtaining a divorce is called the 'special procedure'. This is an out-of-date term from the period when 'special procedure' divorces were introduced, but is still used even though the vast majority of divorces are dealt with this way.

Some 90 per cent of divorces are dealt with by the special procedure. The procedure is largely administrative rather than judicial and no legal aid is available. It deals with with uncontested divorces.

The application is made by sending the divorce petition together with a fee (in 2002 £150) or an exclusion certificate (if the petitioner is in receipt of Legal Help or is on a low income or certain state benefits) and an affidavit in support of the petition (which may also attract a fee) to the county court.

There is no legal aid to employ a solicitor to obtain a divorce, though legal aid is available for ancillary relief proceedings. The petitioner may be able to get some funding (called Legal Help) to get advice on drafting the petition and completing the formalities.

There is also a requirement for a copy of the petition for each party to be served (one for the respondent; one for the co-respondent in adultery petitions); a statement of arrangements for the children signed by the petitioner in person, with a copy for the respondent; the original marriage certificate; and a reconciliation statement, namely, a statement relating to whether the petitioner has considered reconciliation.

Once the documents are sent to the court office of the appropriate county court the court will seal the originals (ie stamp them with the court seal) and keep them on the court file. The copies are also sealed and a copy sealed petition, the acknowledgement of service, the copy statement of arrangements and a notice of proceedings (guidelines on the proceedings) are sent to the respondent. A copy of the sealed petition, a copy of the acknowledgement of service and a notice of proceedings are sent to the co-respondent where appropriate.

The petitioner is then informed of the file number of the petition. This confirms that the court has issued the documents to the respondent and the co-respondent.

The court can be requested to return the documents direct to the petitioner for personal service if that was required.

The respondent and the co-respondent then respond in one of three ways:

1. The acknowledgement of service can be returned to the court admitting the allegations and stating that there is no intention to defend the petition (this should be done within eight days of receipt of the notice). The court will send to the petitioner a copy of the completed acknowledgement. The petitioner can then apply to the district judge for Directions supported by an affidavit supporting the truth of the petition and verifying the acknowledgement.

2. The acknowledgement of service can be returned to the court denying the allegations and giving notice to defend (this should again be done within eight days of receipt of the notice). The respondent will then follow it by filing an answer to the petition within 29 days of the receipt of the notice. If no answer is filed, then the district judge can be asked for Directions and the petition treated as undefended (see *Day* v *Day* [1979] 2 All ER 187, considered below). If an answer is filed, then the petition is transferred to the High Court for a trial of the issues as a defended petition. The petitioner can file a reply within 14 days of receiving the respondent's answer if the petitioner disputes any allegations made in the reply. In practice much is done to avoid a contested hearing and a compromise reached to avoid hurtful allegations. Defended divorces are rare – approximately 50 a year compared with 180,000 petitions.

3. The respondent does nothing (or the co-respondent does not acknowledge). The petitioner is required to obtain further copies sealed by the court and attempt personal service upon the respondent (or co-respondent). If the petition and documents are successfully served and there is still no reply, then the petitioner can then file an affidavit of service and a notice of application with the district judge for leave to proceed without an acknowledgement of service. If leave is granted, then the petitioner can apply for Directions.

## Directions

This is done in the absence of both parties. The respondent is not informed of when the district judge is considering making directions (see *Day* v *Day* (below)).

The district judge has with him the petition, the statement of arrangements, the acknowledgement of service (of affidavit of service) and the petitioner's affidavit in support of the petition. The district judge then determines whether the petition establishes a sufficiently proven case so that the petitioner is entitled to a divorce. If the petition does establish a case then the petition is entered on the special procedure list. The petition is entered on the decree nisi list and the petitioner is notified of the date and time when the decree nisi is to be announced as is the respondent (and the co-respondent).

On that date the decree nisi is announced 'en masse'. The petitioner can then apply for the decree to be absolute some six weeks and one day later. The decree absolute simply arrives in the post. There is a fee to obtain the decree absolute (in 2002 £30).

If the district judge is not satisfied with the petition then an application can be made for the petition to be dismissed by either party. As with the petition, the party applying for the petition to be dismissed sends a notice and a copy to the court to be sealed and served on the other party. The district judge can then end the proceedings.

Alternatively, the petitioner can appeal against the district judge's decision to a judge.

The procedure is strictly followed. See *Day* v *Day* [1979] 2 All ER 187 where the husband and wife lived in the same house. The wife wanted a divorce. The husband did not. The wife filed a divorce petition. The petition was served on the husband. He did not return the acknowledgement of service. He did consult the solicitors and indicated that he wished to defend the petition. The wife's solicitors re-served the petition and accompanying documents personally. The husband gave notice of intention to defend but he did not file an answer. The wife applied for directions to the Registrar (now 'district judge'). He gave directions on the basis that the petition was undefended. He entered the petition on the special procedure list. He considered the wife's evidence in her affidavit and decided that she was entitled to a decree. He fixed a day for the pronouncement of the decree nisi and sent notice to the husband. The husband attended on the day and applied for leave to file an answer out of time. The judge granted leave and took the case out of the special procedure list. The wife appealed.

HELD: The judge was wrong. Once the Registrar had made his decision and decided that the wife had proved the petition so that she was entitled to a petition the court was bound to grant a decree nisi. The husband could only apply after that decision had been made if he showed substantial grounds that the decree had been obtained contrary to the justice of the case. Since he had had ample time to file an answer and there was no injustice, the wife was entitled to her decree nisi and there was no need for a rehearing of the petition.

A more recent case suggests a more flexible approach. In *Lawlor* v *Lawlor* [1995] 1 FLR 269, H petitioned for divorce and W's solicitors failed to file an answer on her behalf within 21 days (as required by r21.12 Family Proceedings Rules 1991). An attempt was made to file the answer eight or nine days late. The district judge refused leave to file a late answer. W appealed to a judge who also refused leave. The decree was treated as uncontested and decree nisi was declared. Decree absolute was pronounced. W appealed.

HELD: The refusal to grant leave to file an answer out of time was a denial of justice. Leave should be given unless there was good reason. The decree nisi and absolute should not have been granted. The law was not in the position of 'no fault' divorce and W's case should be heard.

In relation to the statement of arrangements, if the district judge is satisfied that no orders needs to be made concerning the children then no court attendance is required and a certificate of satisfaction is issued. If the district judge is not so satisfied then the court can ask for a report or further evidence or for a hearing. The parties may then have to attend court for consideration as to what orders for the children should be made. The decree nisi is postponed until the court is satisfied as to the children's circumstances.

Please note the Law Society's *Family Law Protocol*, published in March 2002, which provides for how solicitors should advise clients in the interests of avoiding unnecessary conflict. It advises that petitioners should be encouraged not to name co-respondents in cases of adultery, and that respondents should be discouraged from defending divorce petitions or cross-petitioning unless there is good reason to do so.

## 3.14 The abandoned reforms of divorce law in the Family Law Act 1996

### Background

In 1988 the Law Commission published a discussion paper concerning the possible reform of divorce law, followed in 1990 by its report *The Ground for Divorce* (Law Com No 192). In 1993 the Lord Chancellor published a Green Paper, *Facing the Future: Mediation and the Ground for Divorce*, followed in 1995 by a White Paper called *Looking to the Future: Mediation and the Ground for Divorce*. This drew much from the Law Commission's proposals and was also based on responses to the Green Paper in addition to research commissioned by the Lord Chancellor's Department.

This action was taken against a background of public concern about divorce and the numbers of divorcing couples – the United Kingdom has the highest rate of divorce in Europe. Criticisms were made of the existing law. As has been, seen most petitioners make use of the fault-based facts in order to obtain a divorce (since this enables them to obtain a speedier divorce). It was said that the present law encourages petitioners to make allegations (sometimes exaggerated) against their spouses in order to order to obtain a quick divorce. This can result in needless conflict, unfairness and a sense of injustice which does nothing to save marriages.

The Government therefore introduced proposals with the following objectives:

1. to support the institution of marriage;
2. to include practical steps to prevent the irretrievable breakdown of marriage;
3. to ensure that spouses understand the practical consequences of divorce before taking any irreversible decision;
4. where divorce is unavoidable, to minimise the bitterness and hostility between the parties and reduce the trauma for the children;
5. to keep to the minimum the cost to the parties and the taxpayer.

The proposals are that the single ground for divorce should remain that of the marriage having broken down irretrievably. After one or both parties have applied for a divorce this ground will be demonstrated by the passing of a period for reflection and consideration. During this period couples will be required to settle arrangements for their children, property and finances (unless the court dispenses with this requirement, for example in the interests of the children). The spouse applying for the divorce will be obliged to attend an information-giving session which will inform him or her of the various options available (eg marriage guidance, counselling, family mediation) and the legal consequences of divorce. The other spouse will be encouraged to attend. The Government proposes to limit legal aid to specific legal advice during this process so that it should no longer be necessary for parties to be legally represented to the extent to which they currently are now. The Government wishes to make mediation available through the block funding of contracts for mediation services. Though mediation is not to be made compulsory, it is hoped that divorcing couples will keep control of their own affairs through mediation rather than be steered by lawyers.

The end result of this process is the Family Law Act 1996 which received Royal Assent on 4 July 1996. Various aspects of the new law have been piloted. In January 2001 the Lord Chancellor announced that Part II will not be brought into force and is likely to be repealed. The reasons given were that Part II was unworkable and difficult to implement.

Research on the implementation of Part II FLA 1996 (in particular the effectiveness of a variety of models of information meetings) was carried out by Professor Janet Walker from the Newcastle Centre for Family Studies. Between June 1997 and June 1999 14 information meeting pilots were established covering 11 different areas of England and Wales and testing six different models of information delivery. During the pilots nearly 6,000 people attended an individual information meeting, nearly 2,500 people attended a group presentation and nearly 1,500 people were sent postal packs. Just over 500 people attended a meeting with a marriage guidance counsellor. The research carried out on the results of the pilots highlighted the variety of expectations of those who attended. Some did not know what to do next. Some had taken decisions about the future but did not know how to proceed. Others had taken definite decisions and wanted information about specific issues. These persons required a mixture of support, advice and counselling. The standardised nature of information meetings meant that they could not meet such a variety of needs.

However, the initial findings indicated that most parties found the information meetings valuable. They increased knowledge and empowered people to make informed decisions. Individual meetings appeared to be more popular than group meetings since the former could be tailored to meet individual needs. In 2001 'Family Advice and Information Networks' (FAINs) were piloted. The networks are meant to provide information and advice to resolve disputes. There is some resemblance between FAINs and information meetings under the FLA 1996.

Attending FAINs is not compulsory (unlike the plans for information meetings). Information and advice will be tailored to the client rather than the general information provided in information meetings.

The provisions of Part II are summarised below for information and in case there is any change of heart before any repealing legislation is passed.

## Summary of provisions

### The general principles of divorce (s1 FLA 1996)

Section 1 Family Law Act 1996 came into force on 21 March 1997. It provides:

> 'The court and any person, in exercising functions under or in consequence of Parts II and III FLA 1996, shall have regard to the following general principles –
> (a) that the institution of marriage is to be supported;
> (b) that the parties to a marriage which may have broken down are to be encouraged to take all practicable steps, whether by marriage counselling or otherwise, to save the marriage;
> (c) that a marriage which has irretrievably broken down and is being brought to an end should be brought to an end –
> (i) with minimum distress to the parties and to the children affected;
> (ii) with questions dealt with in a manner designed to promote as good a continuing relationship between the parties and any children affected as is possible in the circumstances; and
> (iii) without costs being unreasonably incurred in connection with the procedures to be followed in bringing the marriage to an end; and
> (d) that any risk to one of the parties to a marriage, and to any children, of violence from the other party should, so far as reasonably practicable, be removed or diminished.'

### Divorce order

An order dissolving a marriage was to be called a divorce order (s2(1)(a)). Before the court could make this order (s3(1)) the following conditions were to be satisfied:

1. There had been the required attendance at an information meeting (s8), followed by a statement of marital breakdown (ss5 and 6).
2. The period for reflection and consideration had passed (s7), indicating that the marriage had broken down irretrievably.
3. Adequate financial arrangements for the future had been made.
4. The welfare of any child had been properly provided for (s11).
5. The application had not been withdrawn.

There are, however, four exemptions which could be invoked in special circumstances (s9), under which a divorce order could be made even if the above conditions had not been satisfied. It was also possible to put forward a special defence to a divorce order (s10) which, if accepted by the court, could prevent a divorce.

The court had power under s14 to adjourn any proceedings, either to allow the parties to comply with a mediation direction or for the purpose of enabling disputes to be resolved amicably.

## Attendance at information meetings

There have been a number of pilot projects on information meetings to enable decisions to be taken as to how these will be arranged.

The process of obtaining a divorce order would have begun with the provision of a statement of marital breakdown (see below). A party could not make a statement of marital breakdown until at least three months after he/she had attended an information meeting (see 8(2) FLA 1996).

An information meeting meant a meeting organised for the purpose of providing relevant information about matters which might arise in connection with the divorce or with property or financial matters. The information meeting might also have given the parties the opportunity to meet a marriage guidance counsellor and of encouraging the parties to attend that meeting (see s8(6) FLA 1996). An information meeting had to be conducted by a suitably qualified person with no financial or other interest in any marital proceedings between the parties (see s8(7) FLA 1996).

In the case of a statement of marital breakdown made by both parties the parties could attend separate meetings or the same meeting (see s8(4) FLA 1996).

Where one party had made a statement the other party (except in certain circumstances) had to attend an information meeting before:

1. making any application to the court with respect to a child of the family or certain applications relating to property or financial matters; or
2. contesting any such application (see s8(5) FLA 1996).

Regulations would have dealt with the details of how information meetings would have operated. In particular such regulations would have dealt with the importance to be attached to the welfare, wishes and feelings of children and how the parties might acquire a better understanding of the ways in which children could be helped to cope with the breakdown of a marriage.

## The statement of marital breakdown (ss5 and 6 FLA 1996)

Assuming there has been the required attendance at an information meeting the process of obtaining a divorce order would have begun with one or both parties providing a statement of marital breakdown that:

1. the maker of the statement (or each of them) believed that the marriage had broken down; and
2. the maker of the statement (or each of them) understood the purpose of the period for reflection and consideration; and
3. the maker of the statement (or each of them) wished to make arrangements for the future.

After the court had received a statement it could give direction requiring each party to attend a meeting for the purpose of explaining how to resolve any disputes between them through mediation, and to provide an opportunity to each party to agree to take advantage of mediation (see s13(1) FLA 1996). Such a direction could have been given at any time on the application of either party or on the court's initiative.

Note that a statement as to marital breakdown made within the first year of the marriage would have been ineffective for the purposes of any application for a divorce order (s7(6) FLA 1996).

## The period of reflection and consideration (s7 FLA 1996)

Where a statement of marital breakdown had been made then a period for the parties to reflect on whether the marriage can be saved and to have an opportunity to effect a reconciliation, and to consider what arrangement must be made for the future, had to pass before an application for a divorce order could be made by reference to that statement (see s7(1) FLA 1996). The period was nine months beginning with the fourteenth day after on which the statement of marital breakdown was received by the court (see s7(3) FLA 1996). Together with the three months minimum period between attendance at an information meeting and the filing of the statement of marital breakdown, this meant an overall minimum time of one year before a party could apply for a divorce order. This minimum time became 18 months where there were children of the family aged 16 years or under.

The period of reflection and consideration could be extended on the application of either party where there was an inordinate delay in the service of a copy of the statement on the other party where the statement has been made by one party. The period could be extended for any period not exceeding the time between the beginning of the period for reflection and consideration and the time when service was effected (see s7(4), (5) FLA 1996).

The period stopped running if, during the period, the parties jointly gave notice to the court that they were attempting a reconciliation but required additional time. The period stopped running on the day on which the notice was served on the court and resumed on the day on which either party gave notice to the court that the attempted reconciliation had been unsuccessful (see s7(7) and (8) FLA 1996). If the period was interrupted under s7(8) by a continuous period of more than 18 months any application by either of the parties for a divorce order had to be by reference to a new statement received by the court at any time after the end of the 18 months (s7(9) FLA 1996).

The period was extended by a further six months where there was a child of the family who was under the age of 16 when the application for a divorce order was made (see s7(11) and (13) FLA 1996). The six months' extension did not apply when the application for a divorce order was subject to an occupation order or a non-molestation order in force in favour of the applicant or a child of the family against the other party, or where the court was satisfied that delaying the making of a divorce order would be significantly detrimental to the welfare of any child of the family (see s7(12) FLA 1996).

The six months' extension also applied where an application was made for a divorce order by one party and the other party applied to the court for time for further reflection, and the requirements of s9 (arrangements for the future) were satisfied (see s7(10) and (13) FLA 1996). Again there could be no such extension if, at the time when the application for a divorce order was made, there was an occupation order or a non-molestation order in force in favour of the applicant or a child of the family, made against the other party, or the court was satisfied that delaying the making of a divorce order would be significantly detrimental to the welfare of any child of the family (see s7(12) FLA 1996).

### The one year period (called the 'specified period')

An application could *not* be made for a divorce order by reference to a particular statement if either:

1. the parties had jointly given notice withdrawing the agreement; or
2. a period of one year had passed since the end of the period for reflection and consideration (s5(3) FLA 1996).

This meant that an application for a divorce order had normally to be made within the 12 months following the end of the period for reflection and consideration. Any period during which an order preventing divorce was in force did not count towards the one year period (s5(4) FLA 1996).

If the parties jointly gave notice to the court that they were attempting reconciliation but required additional time, then the one year period stopped running on the day on which the notice was received by the court. The one year period resumed on the day on which either of the parties gave notice to the court that the attempted reconciliation had been unsuccessful (s5(6) FLA 1996). If the one year period was interrupted by a continuous period of more than 18 months any application by either of the parties for a divorce order had to be by reference to a new statement received by the court at any time after the end of the 18 months (s5(7) FLA 1996). This meant that the parties could suspend both the period for reflection and consideration and the 'specified period' could be up to 18 months in order to attempt a reconciliation.

### Arrangements for the future

A divorce order could not be made unless one of the following was produced to the court:

1. a court order (made by consent or otherwise) dealing with the financial arrangements; or
2. a negotiated agreement as to their financial arrangements; or
3. a declaration by both parties that they had made their financial arrangements; or
4. a declaration by one of the parties (to which no objection has been notified to the court by that other party) that he/she had no significant assets and did not intend to make any application for financial provision; and he/she believed that the other party had no significant assets and did not intend to make an

application for financial provision; and there were therefore no financial arrangements to be made (see s9(2) FLA 1996).

'Negotiated agreement' meant a written agreement between the parties as to future arrangements which had been reached as the result of mediation or any other form of negotiation involving a third party and which satisfied such requirements as would have been imposed by rules of court (see para 7, Sch 1 FLA 1996). A 'declaration' had to be in prescribed form and satisfy requirements specified in rules (see para 8, Sch 1 FLA 1996).

It would have been possible to make a divorce order even though s9(2) has not been satisfied. There were four exemptions:

1.  Where the requirements of s11 had been satisfied; and

    a)  the applicant had, during the period for reflection and consideration, taken such steps as were reasonably practicable to try to reach agreement about the parties' financial arrangements; and
    b)  the applicant had made an application to the court for financial relief and had complied with all requirements of the court in relation to proceedings for financial relief but –

        •   the other party had delayed in complying with requirements of the court or had otherwise been obstructive; or
        •   for reasons which were beyond the control of the applicant, or of the other party, the court had been prevented from obtaining the information which it required to determine the financial position of the parties.

    (See s9(7)(a) and para 1, Sch 1 FLA 1996.)

2.  Where the requirements of s11 had been satisfied; and

    a)  the applicant had, during the period for reflection and consideration, taken such steps as were reasonably practicable to try to reach agreement about the parties' financial arrangements; and
    b)  the applicant had not been able to reach agreement with the other party about those arrangements and was unlikely to be able to do so in the foreseeable future because of –

        •   the ill health or disability of the applicant, the other party or a child of the family (whether physical or mental), or
        •   an injury suffered by the applicant, the other party or a child of the family, and

    c)  a delay in making the order –

        •   would be significantly detrimental to the welfare of any child of the family; or

- would be seriously prejudicial to the applicant.

(See s9(7)(b) and para 2, Sch 1 FLA 1996.)

3. The requirements of s11 had been satisfied and the applicant had found it impossible to contact the other party, and as a result it had been impossible for the applicant to reach agreement with the other party about their financial arrangements (see s9(7)(c) and para 3, Sch 1 FLA 1996).

4. Where the requirements of s11 had been satisfied; and

a) an occupation order or a non-molestation order was in force in favour of the applicant or a child of the family, made against the other party; and

b) the applicant had, during the period for reflection and consideration, taken such steps as were reasonably practicable to try to reach agreement about the parties' financial arrangements; and

c) the applicant had not been able to reach agreement with the other party about those arrangements and was unlikely to be able to do so in the foreseeable future; and

d) a delay in making the order –

- would be significantly detrimental to the welfare of any child of the family; or
- would be seriously prejudicial to the applicant.

(See s9(7)(d) and para 4 Sch 1 FLA 1996.)

Section 9 did not require any order or agreement to have been carried into effect at the time when the court was considering whether arrangements for the future had been made by the parties. Also the fact that an appeal was pending against an order was to be disregarded (see para 5, Sch 1 FLA 1996).

## Special defence to a divorce order (s10 FLA 1996)

If an application had been made by one party to the marriage the court could, on the application of the other party, have ordered that the marriage was not to be dissolved. The court could only so order where it was satisfied that:

1. the dissolution of the marriage would have resulted in substantial financial or other hardship to the other party or to a child of the family; and

2. it would have been wrong in all the circumstances (including the conduct of the parties and the interests of any child of the family) for the marriage to be dissolved (see s10(1) and (2) FLA 1996).

For these purposes 'hardship' included the loss of a chance to obtain a future benefit (as well as the loss of an existing benefit) (see s10(6) FLA 1996).

An order preventing divorce could have included conditions which had to be satisfied before an application for cancellation could be made under s10(3) (see s10(5) FLA 1996). One or both parties could apply to cancel an order preventing the divorce and the court would be obliged to cancel the order unless it was satisfied that the above two conditions remained (see s10(3) FLA 1996). If an order preventing a divorce was cancelled the court could make a divorce order only if an application was made under s3 or s4(3) after the cancellation (see s10(4) FLA 1996).

### Welfare of children (s11 FLA 1996)

In any proceedings for a divorce order the court would have had to consider whether there were any children of the family to whom s11 applied and, where there were such children, whether in the light of the arrangements which had been made or were proposed to be made for their upbringing and welfare it should exercise any of its powers under the Children Act 1989 with respect to any of them (see s11(1) FLA 1996).

Section 11 applied to any child of the family who had not reached the age of 16 at the date when the court considered the case in accordance with s11, and any child who had reached that age at that date and in relation to whom the court directed that s11 should apply (see s11(5) FLA 1996).

Where it appeared to the court that the circumstances required it, or were likely to require it, to exercise any of its powers under the Children Act 1989 with respect to any child; and it was not in a position to exercise the power(s) without giving further consideration to the case; and there were exceptional circumstances which made it desirable in the interests of the child that the court should give a direction, then the court could direct that the divorce order not be made until the court ordered otherwise (see s11(2) FLA 1996).

The court was obliged to treat the welfare of the child as paramount in considering whether the circumstances of the case required the court or were likely to require it to exercise any of its powers under the Children Act 1989 with respect to that child (see s11(3) FLA 1996).

In making that decision the court had to have particular regard to:

1. the wishes and feelings of the child considered in the light of his/her age and understanding and the circumstances in which those wishes were expressed;
2. the conduct of the parties in relation to the upbringing of the child;
3. the general principle that in the absence of evidence to the contrary the welfare of the child will be best served by his having regular contact with those who have parental responsibility for him and with other members of his/her family and the maintenance of as good a continuing relationship with his parents as is possible; and
4. any risk to the child attributable to –

    a) where the person with whom the child will reside is living or proposes or reside;
    b) any person with whom that person is living or with whom he/she proposes to live; or

c) any other arrangements for his care and upbringing.

(See s11(4) FLA 1996.)

## Mediation and adjournments

There have been pilot projects involving mediation to explore how parties can reach agreement on ancillary relief.

The court's power to adjourn any proceedings connected with the breakdown of a marriage included power to adjourn for the purpose of allowing the parties to comply with a mediation direction or for the purpose of enabling disputes to be resolved amicably (s14(1) FLA 1996). In determining whether to adjourn for either purpose the court had to have regard in particular to the need to protect the interests of any child of the family (see s14(2) FLA 1996). A maximum period for any such adjournment would have been laid down in regulations (see s14(3) FLA 1996).

Where the adjournment was to allow the parties to resolve their dispute(s) amicably, the court would have been obliged to order one or both parties to produce to the court a report as to whether they had taken part in mediation during the adjournment, and whether as a result, any agreement had been reached between them. The report should also have included the extent to which any dispute between them had been resolved as a result of any such agreement, the need for further mediation, and how likely it was that such further mediation would be successful (see s14(4) FLA 1996).

## Section 29 of the Family Law Act 1996

Section 29 FLA 1996 came into force area by area in the period 1997–1999. By April 1999 all areas were covered by s29. The section requires those seeking civil legal aid for legal representation in family matters to firstly attend a meeting with a mediator to assess the suitability of mediation for their case. There is no requirement to attend for mediation if there is fear or harm of violence. An applicant for legal aid must complete a form showing that mediation has been tried before he/she can obtain civil legal aid. This is perhaps more relevant to applicants for ancillary relief, but any meeting with a mediator is likely to be at the divorce petition stage.

# 4

# Judicial Separation

4.2 Grounds

4.2 Defences and bars

4.3 Effect

4.4 Ancillary orders

4.5 Use

4.6 The Family Law Act 1996 – separation order

## 4.1 Grounds

Any ground for presenting a petition for divorce mentioned in s1(2) MCA 1973 shall be a ground for presenting a petition for judicial separation. There is no need to establish irretrievable breakdown (see s17(1) MCA 1973) and there is no one year bar to presenting a petition (s3 MCA 1973 only applies to divorce petitions).

## 4.2 Defences and bars

Sections 2, 6 and 7 apply equally to petitions for judicial separation as to divorce. Equally s41 applies whereby the court can refuse to make the decree if it considers orders under the Children Act 1989 need to be made about the children. Sections 5 and 10 do not apply. There is one final decree and not a decree nisi as for divorce.

## 4.3 Effect

It does not end the marriage, but it ends the duty to co-habit (see s18(1) MCA 1973). Thus it ends desertion; the wife's implied consent to sexual intercourse is revoked, the husband can be found guilty of raping the wife (*R* v *Clarke* [1949] 2 All ER 448); and there is a presumption of non-access (which helps to establish adultery).

If, while a decree of judicial separation is in force and the separation is continuing, either of the parties to the marriage dies intestate, his or her real property shall devolve as if the other party to the marriage had then been dead (see s18(2) MCA 1973 (compare with magistrates' court separation order below)).

## 4.4 Ancillary orders

The court's powers are exactly the same as in divorce proceedings (see below).

## 4.5 Use

Judicial separations are used by:

1. parties who do not yet accept that the marriage has irretrievably broken down;
2. parties who object to divorce on religious or other grounds; and
3. parties who wish to preserve widow/widower's pension rights which would otherwise be ended by divorce

In 2001 there were only 925 judicial separations, compared to 147,000 divorces.

## 4.6 The Family Law Act 1996 – separation order

The Family Law Act 1996 renames judicial separation as a 'separation order' (s2(1)(b) FLA 1996). It makes irretrievable breakdown of the marriage the sole ground for obtaining a separation order. This will be proved by the expiry of a one-year period for reflection and consideration, as for a divorce order (s3 FLA 1996: see Chapter 3, section 3.14). The separation order remains in force while the marriage continues or until it is cancelled by the court on the joint application of the parties (s2(3) FLA 1996). Application for a separation and a divorce order in respect of the same marriage is covered by s3(3) and the conversion of a separation order into a divorce order by s4 FLA 1996. These provisions are not yet in force.

# 5

# Presumption of Death and Dissolution of Marriage: s19 MCA 1973

5.1 Ground

5.2 Section 19(3) MCA 1973

---

## 5.1 Ground

Section 19(1):

> 'Any married person who alleges that reasonable grounds exist for supposing that the other party to the marriage is dead may ... present a petition to the court to have it presumed that the other party is dead and to have the marriage dissolved, and the court may, if satisfied that such reasonable grounds exist, grant a decree of presumption of death and dissolution of the marriage.'

## 5.2 Section 19(3) MCA 1973

> 'In any proceedings under this section the fact that for a period of seven years or more the other party to the marriage has been continually absent from the petitioner and the petitioner has no reason to believe that the other party has been living within that time shall be evidence that the other party is dead, until the contrary is proved.'

If there is less than seven years' absence, then the petitioner has to positively adduce evidence of valid reasons for assuming that death has occurred. In other words, when the seven-year period has elapsed, even though the matter may be one of speculation, the petition will succeed 'if nothing has happened within that time to give the petitioner reason to believe that the other party was living'.

See *Thompson* v *Thompson* [1956] 2 WLR 814; [1956] 1 All ER 603 where the husband was liable to maintain his wife under a court order. She became a tramp with no fixed address. She used to call into the court to collect her maintenance. Then she stopped calling for her money. No one saw her for many years. The husband continued paying maintenance until a considerable sum had accrued which had not been collected and he was advised to stop making payments. There were extensive enquiries which failed to locate her. Seven years and seven days from the date when she was last seen the husband filed a petition. The decree was granted.

Even then the failure to make reasonable enquiries will usually result in the court's refusal to exercise its discretion to grant a decree.

See *Bullock* v *Bullock* [1960] 2 All ER 307 where a wife obtained a magistrates' court's maintenance order against her husband. He fell into arrears. The court issued a warrant to enforce the order. The police were unable to execute the warrant because they could not find the husband. The wife made no further enquiries and did not hear from him again. Fourteen years later she tried to remarry. She married a second husband who knew about the disappearance of her first husband. After fifteen years of marriage to her second husband and some twenty-nine years after her first husband's disappearance, she sought a court order for maintenance against her second husband. He argued that the marriage was bigamous and void because the marriage to the first husband had never been dissolved.

HELD: If the wife had made no enquiries about the whereabouts of her first husband she would not be entitled to a decree of presumption of death and dissolution of her first marriage even after his absence for so many years. However, enquiries had been made through the court issuing the maintenance warrant and the police being unable to execute it. In those circumstances the wife had rightly inferred that her first husband was dead and she did not need to make further enquiries. She was entitled to a decree so that her second marriage was valid and she could obtain a court order against her second husband.

Note that even where a party has been continuously absent for a period of seven years or more, a petition under s19 must be sought to dissolve the marriage on this basis. See *Bullock* v *Bullock* (above) where the wife had the validity of her second marriage challenged since she failed to get a petition in relation to her first.

NOTE: Consider whether the petitioner might stand a greater chance of success under s1(2)(e) for divorce on the basis of five years' separation.

If the respondent is found to be alive after decree nisi, it will be rescinded, as happened in *Manser* v *Manser* [1940] 4 All ER 238.

If the respondent is found after decree absolute, the marriage remains dissolved, and consider applying for financial provision as in divorce proceedings (see below).

# 6

# Jurisdiction and Recognition of Foreign Decrees

6.1 Domicile and habitual residence

6.2 Jurisdiction

6.3 Recognition of foreign marriages and decrees

6.4 Declarations as to the validity of a foreign decree

6.5 Applications for financial relief after overseas divorce

## 6.1 Domicile and habitual residence

### Introduction

As will be seen English and Welsh courts will recognise decrees obtained abroad generally on the basis of either domicile or habitual residence. It is important therefore to define these terms.

### Definition of domicile

Everyone must have a domicile, namely, a permanent home in a place governed by one system of law. This includes states within a country with their own legal systems. Therefore, one is domiciled in the state of Texas, rather than in the United States of America, or in the province of Quebec rather than Canada. Domicile is used rather than other descriptions such as nationality. A person may have more than one nationality. A person may have no nationality. Nationality is also subject to political change and control. Domicile is not subject to those variables. A person must have a domicile. He can only have one domicile. Domicile is a matter of legal definition and is not subject to the uncertainties of politics.

Domicile is made up of three sorts of domicile. A person starts with a domicile of origin. He may then acquire a domicile of dependence. That domicile stays with that person for the rest of his life until and unless he chooses a new domicile – a domicile of choice.

## Domicile of origin

The domicile of origin is essentially the domicile of a person's parents at the time that person is born.

1. A legitimate child takes his father's domicile at the date of birth. This is not necessarily the country in which the child is born. See *Henderson* v *Henderson* [1965] 1 All ER 179 where a child was born in England. His father was domiciled in Scotland at the time of his birth. The child's domicile of origin was Scotland.
2. A child of unmarried parents takes his mother's domicile at the date of his birth.
3. In the case of an orphan the domicile of origin is where the child is found.

## Domicile of dependence

The domicile of origin will change if a child's parents change their domicile. Since the child is dependent on his parents his domicile is one of dependence on theirs.

In the case of a legitimate child, if his father and mother are alive but living apart, the child's domicile will be that of his mother if:

1. he then has his home with her and has no home with his father (see s4(2)(a) Domicile and Matrimonial Proceedings Act 1973); or
2. he has at any time had her domicile and has not since had a home with his father (see s4(2)(b) 1973 Act – this covers the situation where the child lives, for example, with relatives rather than his mother or father).

The domicile of a child whose mother is dead shall be the last domicile she had before her death, provided he has not since had a home with his father (s4(3)).

Otherwise the child's domicile of dependence is with the father.

Before 1 January 1974 a wife was treated as being dependent on her husband and, therefore, on marrying him she acquired his domicile as her domicile of dependency. After that date she had the ability to acquire her own independent domicile of choice (see below).

## Domicile of choice

A person may acquire his own independent domicile of choice once he is sixteen (see s3(1) Domicile and Matrimonial Proceedings Act 1973).

A married woman before 1 January 1974 could only have the domicile of her husband. After 1 January 1974 (when the Domicile and Matrimonial Proceedings Act 1973 came into force) she acquired the ability to acquire her own independent domicile of choice and was no longer tied to her husband's domicile (s1(1)). However, until she acquires a new domicile she retains her original domicile of dependency (s1(2)). See *IRC* v *Duchess of Portland* [1982] 1 All ER 784 where P's parents lived in Quebec, Canada, when she was born, so she had a domicile of origin in Quebec. She remained a Canadian citizen throughout her life. She married D, an English domiciled man. She thereby acquired an English domicile of dependency through her husband. She maintained her links with Canada. After 1 January 1974 she had the ability to acquire her own independent domicile of choice. She claimed to have acquired a Canadian domicile of choice because of her strong links with Quebec though she continued to live in England.

HELD: P started with a domicile of dependency in England which by s1(2) of the 1973 Act became an imposed domicile of choice after 1 January 1974. She had to show that she had changed that domicile by acquiring a new domicile of choice. She had ceased to intend to permanently or indefinitely reside in England but she had not ceased actual residence in England. Her limited visits to Quebec were not enough to make her an inhabitant of Quebec. She could not be said to have abandoned her imposed domicile of choice. She remained domiciled in England.

## Acquiring a domicile of choice

This requires residence in the particular place; and an intention to reside there permanently or indefinitely. See *Udny* v *Udny* (1869) LR 1 Sc & Div 44 applied in *IRC* v *Duchess of Portland* and more recently in *Plummer* v *IRC* [1988] 1 All ER 27:

'Domicile of choice is a conclusion or inference which the law derives from the fact of a man fixing voluntarily his sole or chief residence in a particular place, with an intention of continuing to reside there for an unlimited time.'

An alternative definition was given in *Lord* v *Colvin* (1859) 4 Drew 336:

'That place is properly the domicile of a person in which he has voluntarily fixed the habitation of himself and his family, not for a mere special and temporary purpose but with a present intention of making it his permanent home unless and until something (which is unexpected or the happening of which is uncertain) shall occur to induce him to adopt some other permanent home.'

A domicile of choice is lost where the person ceases to reside in the particular place; and ceases to intend to reside there permanently or indefinitely (see *IRC* v *Duchess of Portland* (above)).

The standard of proof of acquisition of a domicile of choice is on the balance of probabilities but the courts consider acquiring a domicile of choice a serious matter and accordingly the standard of proof is higher than a narrow balance of probabilities.

There is a presumption in favour of the existing domicile. The burden is on the applicant to prove that a change in domicile has taken place. If there is any doubt as to the matter, the court will decide in favour of the existing domicile (as in *IRC* v *Duchess of Portland*).

This means that the courts put great emphasis on the domicile of origin or dependence which may follow a person throughout his life if he is unable to show that he has ever acquired a domicile of choice.

For example, *In the Estate of Fuld (No 3)* [1965] 3 All ER 776 Mr Fuld was born of parents domiciled in Germany. His domicile of origin was Germany. He was a student in England for a year. He then spent six years in Canada and became a Canadian national. He went to live in England again for sixteen years. He kept contact with Germany. He built a house in Germany, got divorced there and died there. Where was he domiciled when he died?

HELD: He never really settled anywhere. His domicile of origin remained with him all his life since he never acquired a domicile of choice. He was a German domiciled man when he died.

In *Ramsay* v *Liverpool Infirmary* [1930] AC 558 Mr Ramsay had a domicile of origin in Scotland. He lived in England for the last thirty-six years of his life. That was insufficient to give him a domicile of choice since he had only lived in England while his relatives there were prepared to keep him. If they had ceased to keep him he would have returned to Scotland. He lacked the necessary intention to acquire a domicile of choice in England. He retained his domicile of origin in Scotland until he died.

In *Winans* v *A-G* [1904] AC 287 Mr Winans had a domicile of dependency as a child in Maryland, USA. He spent the last thirty-seven years of his life in England yet again that was insufficient to give him a domicile of choice in England. He had only lived in a hotel in England and had mixed very little with English people. He lacked the necessary intention. He retained his domicile of dependency until he died.

In *IRC* v *Bullock* [1976] 3 All ER 353 Mr Bullock's domicile of origin was Nova Scotia, Canada. He lived for forty years in England but never really intended to settle in England. His domicile of origin prevailed.

See a case where a person divided her time between two countries – *Plummer* v *IRC* [1988] 1 All ER 27. Miss Plummer was born in England of English parents and had a domicile of origin in England. Most of her family moved to Guernsey. She stayed in London to continue her education but often visited Guernsey and stayed there for considerable periods with her family during holidays. She said she ultimately intended to live and work there. She claimed a domicile of choice in Guernsey.

HELD: A person could only acquire a domicile of choice in a new country at the same time as retaining residence in the domicile of origin by establishing that her chief residence was in the new country. She had failed to show that she had settled in Guernsey and so she retained her domicile of origin in England.

If a domicile of choice is lost and no new domicile of choice is acquired, then the domicile of origin may revive even if the person has not returned to reside in the domicile of origin.

See *Tee* v *Tee* [1974] 1 WLR 213; [1973] 3 All ER 1105 where the husband was a domiciled Englishman. He married a domiciled American and they moved to the USA and the husband acquired a domicile of choice in the USA. They then moved to Germany. The husband had an affair there. He left his wife for the other woman. He wished to set up home in England with his mistress. While still living in

Germany he petitioned for divorce in England. He had bought a house in England before the petition but he and his mistress did not move to England until after the petition. The wife challenged the English court's jurisdiction to hear the petition since she maintained that the husband remained domiciled in the USA.

HELD: The husband had intended to abandon his domicile of choice in the USA and had in fact done so. He had, therefore, lost his domicile of choice. He had not started to live in England when the petition was issued and so had not acquired a new domicile of choice there. However, in such circumstances his domicile of origin automatically revived. It was not necessary to show that he in fact intended to reside in England. The English court, therefore, had jurisdiction to hear the petition.

In *Cramer* v *Cramer* [1987] 1 FLR 116 both parties were French nationals. The wife had a relationship with an Englishman. The wife was sent to England for a year by her employers. Two weeks after her arrival in England she presented a divorce petition. She claimed that she had a domicile of choice in England because of her clear intention to marry an Englishman.

HELD: A domicile of choice could only be acquired if there was a clear and settled intention to reside in England indefinitely. The wife's intention had not crystallised. She was uncertain. Matters in France remained unresolved (eg employment, children and schooling). She, therefore, had no domicile of choice in England. There was, therefore, no jurisdiction to hear the divorce petition.

NOTE: Domicile is an important feature of the Family Law Act 1986 which deals with jurisdiction and recognition of foreign decrees. Under the 1986 Act domicile means either domicile according to the law of the United Kingdom or according to the law of that country in family matters in which the question of recognition arises (s46(5)). Therefore, two alternative concepts of domicile may apply.

## Habitual residence

Habitual residence is another concept used in deciding on jurisdiction and is more a question of fact rather than of law. It was defined in *Cruse* v *Chittum* [1974] 2 All ER 940 as involving an intention to reside in a particular place coupled with a physical presence enduring for some time and involving more than ordinary residence. Habitual residence cannot be merely temporary or secondary. It is similar to the residence requirement necessary for a person to acquire a domicile of choice although there is no need for the same degree of intention to be shown.

In the case of *Cruse* v *Chittum* H was a domiciled Englishman married to W. W left him and went to the USA in the company of an American soldier. She obtained a divorce from H from a court in Mississippi. H wished to remarry. He asked for a declaration that his marriage to W had been validly dissolved. This turned on whether the Mississippi divorce would be recognised in the UK under s3(1) of the Recognition of Divorces and Legal Separations Act 1971 which allowed a foreign decree to be recognised if either spouse was habitually resident in the country (or state) where the proceedings were commenced. It was held that W had been habitually resident in Mississippi. She had a regular physical presence there which had endured for some time, namely she had been an actual and bona fide resident for more than one year. The declaration was granted so that H could remarry.

The habitual residence of a child is likely to depend on the child's parents. If both parents have parental responsibility and live together then the habitual residence of the child is that of the parents unless there was a contrary agreement. One parent cannot unilaterally change the habitual residence of the child. Whilst parents could agree to change the child's habitual residence without changing their own habitual residence, an agreement to send a child abroad for schooling was not sufficient to change his or her habitual residence (see *Re A (Wardship: Jurisdiction)* [1995] 1 FLR 767).

See *Ikimi* v *Ikimi* [2001] 2 FCR 385 in which H and W were Nigerian. They had a second home in England and spent their time between Nigeria and England. They had four children who were educated in England. Between 1995 and 1998 they could not come to England due to sanctions. During that time they separated. As soon as sanctions ended W came to England, though she returned to Nigeria for various periods. H petitioned for divorce in Nigeria. W petitioned for divorce in England, arguing that she had been habitually resident in England for the last 12 months (as required by s5(2) Domicile and Matrimonial Proceedings Act 1973). H challenged the jurisdiction because W had only been in England for 44 per cent of the 12-month period. The Court of Appeal held that a person could have more than one habitual residence at any one time, that W had adopted a voluntary and settled habitual residence in both countries and that the 12 months' statutory period did not require W to spend the whole of the period in the jurisdiction. She had to demonstrate a voluntary and settled intention for the whole of the period and to have spent an appreciable part of the period within the jurisdiction (which W had).

The law was restated in *Re H (Abduction: Habitual Residence)* [1996] 1 FLR 887 where it was again said that habitual residence was a question of fact and not a legal concept. Before a person could have habitual residence he or she must reside in the country concerned (although this did not require physical presence at all times). It was repeated that where both parents had parental responsibility neither parent could unilaterally change a child's habitual residence. On the facts of the case the child had gone to live in India and remained there. One parent returned to England and tried to argue that the child's habitual residence could be unilaterally changed, but the habitual residence remained in India.

Where only one parent has parental responsibility then that parent will largely determine a child's habitual residence. In *Re M (Minors)(Residence Order: Jurisdiction)* [1993] Fam Law 285 an unmarried couple living in England had two children. They separated, with the children staying with their mother. In September 1991 the children went to live with their paternal grandparents in Scotland, and both parents had contact with the children. In July 1992 the children went to stay with their mother in England. She decided not to return the children to the grandparents in Scotland and applied under s8 CA 1989 for residence and prohibited steps orders. The grandparents argued that there was no jurisdiction to hear the mother's applications. Orders were made in her favour. The grandparents appealed.

HELD: Dismissing the appeal, under s3 Family Law Act 1986 a court in England and Wales only had jurisdiction to make a s8 CA 1989 order if the child was habitually resident in England and Wales or was present in England and Wales and not habitually resident elsewhere. Under s2(2)(a) CA 1989 the mother had sole parental responsibility for the children. Parental responsibility included determining where a child should live (see s3(1) CA 1989). There was no statutory definition of habitual residence. Normally when a child was in the physical care of his or her mother who had sole parental responsibility then the child's habitual residence was the same as that of the mother. While the children were in Scotland they were habitually resident there. It was easy to lose habitual residence (even in a single day), but it was more difficult to acquire it (since an appreciable period of time and a settled intention may be necessary). Since the children had lost habitual residence in Scotland, even though there were doubts as to whether they had habitual residence in England, their presence in England was sufficient to give jurisdiction under s3(1)(b) Family Law Act 1986.

NOTE: Hoffmann LJ considered that the children had regained their habitual residence in England as soon as their mother changed her mind and they were living at her home.

## 6.2 Jurisdiction

Jurisdiction of the English courts in respect of the principal decrees and under s27 MCA 1973:

### *Divorce, judicial separation and presumption of death and dissolution of marriage*

The court has jurisdiction according to s5(2) DMPA 1973 if *either* of the parties is domiciled in England and Wales on date when proceedings are begun; or was habitually resident in England and Wales throughout the period of one year ending with that date.

In cases of presumption of death, the same conditions apply but in respect of the petitioner only (s5(4)).

### *Nullity*

The court has jurisdiction according to s5(3) DMPA 1973 if *either* of the parties is domiciled in England and Wales on the date when proceedings are begun; or was habitually resident in England and Wales throughout period of one year ending with that date; or in the case of void grounds, died before that date and either was at death so domiciled; or was so habitually resident for one year period prior to date of death.

In addition, once proceedings for divorce, nullity or judicial separation have begun for which the court has jurisdiction the court may hear a second application for divorce, nullity or judicial separation even though it may not then have the jurisdiction to hear the second application (s5(5)).

For example, a wife commences proceedings for judicial separation based on one year's habitual residence. She then goes abroad. Her husband is already living abroad. She can then petition for divorce even though neither she nor her husband complies with the jurisdiction requirements since proceedings were validly started in the first application.

## Failure to maintain (s27 MCA 1973)

The court has jurisdiction according to s6(1) DMPA 1973 where the applicant or respondent is domiciled in England and Wales on the date of the application; or the applicant has been habitually resident there throughout a one-year period ending with that date; or the respondent is resident there on that date.

## Applications for orders under s8 CA 1989

Jurisdiction to apply for orders under s8 CA 1989 is based on the habitual residence of the child (see s3 Family Law Act 1986). If the child is habitually resident in England and Wales then the courts in England and Wales have jurisdiction (unless divorce, nullity or judicial separation proceedings have already been started in Scotland or Northern Ireland with respect to the parents of the child) (see *Re M (Minors) (Residence Order: Jurisdiction)* above for an illustration of how the law operates). If the child is not habitually resident in any part of the United Kingdom then the simple presence of the child in England and Wales gives jurisdiction.

Another illustration of the jurisdictional rules is *D v D (Custody: Jurisdiction)* [1996] 1 FLR 574 where married parents lived in Scotland and had two children. In 1992 they moved to Spain and in 1994 they returned to Scotland. The marriage deteriorated, and in 1995 the mother and children left and went to live in England. The father started proceedings in Scotland, and the mother started proceedings in England. The English court applied ss2(2) and 3 Family Law Act 1986 whereby an English court only had jurisdiction if the children were habitually resident in England and Wales or present in England and Wales and not habitually resident in any other part of the United Kingdom. In this case the family had intended to settle in Scotland after leaving Spain. They had lived in Scotland for over a year, so s41 FLA 1986 (which deals with the habitual residence of a child removed without consent) meant that their habitual residence was in Scotland. The move by the mother and children to England did not change the children's habitual residence, since one parent could not unilaterally determine habitual residence when he or she shared parental responsibility with the other parent.

An English court may decline to hear a case where a child is simply present in England and Wales but is habitually resident elsewhere, because the issues in the case may be better determined by the foreign jurisdiction (for example, *Re F (Residence Order: Jurisdiction)* [1995] 2 FLR 518, where the court declined to hear a case concerning a child habitually resident in Spain, and *Re M (Jurisdiction: Forum Conveniens)* [1995] 2 FLR 224, where the court declined to make s8 orders concerning children habitually resident in Malta).

## Applications for care orders under CA 1989

A gap in the law was considered in *Re M (Care Orders: Jurisdiction)* [1997] 1 FLR 456; [1997] 2 WLR 314 which dealt with the jurisdiction of courts in England and Wales to deal with care proceedings under the Children Act 1989. The court decided that jurisdiction is based on the presence of the child in England and Wales, irrespective of whether the child is habitually resident either abroad or in another part of the UK. It was accepted that the Children Act 1989 is silent on jurisdiction in public law cases and the Family Law Act 1986 has no application. However as a matter of public policy it was considered that jurisdiction should be as extensive as the jurisdiction to deal with private law cases. Jurisdiction in public law cases may also be based on the child's ordinary or habitual residence even if he is not physically present at the time of the first application. The prohibition in s3(1)(b) Family Law Act 1986 does not apply. In this particular case there was jurisdiction to apply for a care order in England for a child present in England though he was habitually resident in Scotland.

## Applications for parental responsibility under s4 CA 1989

There is jurisdiction to entertain an application for a parental responsibility order under s4 Children Act 1989 in respect of a child who is permanently out of the jurisdiction even if the child was born out of the jurisdiction, though the court had a discretion whether or not to exercise that jurisdiction (see *Re S (Parental Responsibility: Jurisdiction)* [1998] 2 FLR 921; [1998] 1 WLR 1701).

## Staying proceedings

Matrimonial proceedings may be brought in England and in a foreign country at the same time. To prevent the embarrassment of contradictory decisions being reached by courts in different countries, the English court has a discretionary power to stay any matrimonial proceedings in this country if, before the beginning of the trial, it appears that any proceedings with respect to the marriage in question or capable of affecting its validity or subsistence are continuing in any country outside England and Wales.

For example, see *Re S (A Minor)* [1993] 2 FLR 915; [1993] Fam Law 674 where M and F lived in London. They had a son born in May 1992. M then took the boy with her to Scotland to live with her parents. She decided that her relationship with F was over and telephoned him to tell him this and that she was taking the child to Iceland. F applied in England for orders for residence, contact and parental responsibility. He obtained an ex parte order prohibiting M from removing the child from the United Kingdom. Meanwhile M began proceedings in Scotland and obtained an order that F be prohibited from removing the child from Scotland without M's written consent. In England the district judged stayed the proceedings pursuant to s5(2) Family Law Act 1986, pending the decision of the Scottish court on contact, upon M undertaking to allow F weekly supervised contact. F appealed. The judge dismissed the appeal holding that M had satisfied the English court that Scotland was the more appropriate venue for litigation. However he only stayed F's residence and contact applications. He allowed the parental responsibility application to be heard. F further appealed and M appealed against the refusal to stay F's parental responsibility application.

HELD: Dismissing the appeals of both F and M, it would be the worst of all worlds for proceedings relating to contact and residence to be pursued in different jurisdictions at the same time. All matters of dispute should be dealt with in the same forum. However, there was nothing illogical in making a parental responsibility order even though F had no immediate prospects of exercising parental rights. There was nothing illogical in staying his residence and contact applications while refusing a stay in his parental responsibility application.

## Obligatory stays

An English or Welsh court must stay proceedings if there are divorce or nullity proceedings in Scotland, Northern Ireland, the Channel Islands or the Isle of Man, on the application of either party, provided that they last resided together in the other jurisdiction and at least one of the parties was habitually resident in the other jurisdiction throughout the year ending with the date on which they last resided together (see s5 and Sch 1 DMPA 1973).

An example of the court applying an obligatory stay can be found in In *M* v *M (Abduction: England and Scotland)* [1997] 2 FLR 263 in which H and W married in 1986 in England. They had two children, born in 1987 and 1990. The parties lived in England until 1988 then in Germany from 1988 until 1991. In 1991 they returned to England but moved to Scotland in 1994. There H had a job, the family had a council flat and the children went to school. In June 1996 W and the children left H and returned to England. In June and July, 1996 W applied for ex parte residence and prohibited steps orders and petitioned for divorce in England. H decided to commence divorce proceedings in Scotland. W applied for an order preventing H from commencing Scottish proceedings. The court held that the children had no habitual residence so the English court had jurisdiction to make the orders W sought. H appealed. It was held, allowing the appeal, the family was living and settled in Scotland from 1994 to 1996. As a result they had an habitual residence in Scotland (applying *R* v *Barnet London Borough Council, ex parte Shah* [1983] 2 AC 309). The Domicile and Matrimonial Proceedings Act 1973 had the effect of giving Scotland jurisdiction to deal with divorce proceedings since this is where the parties had habitually resided before they separated. The Act also obliged proceedings elsewhere in the UK to be stayed pending the outcome of those proceedings. Sections 2A and 5 Family Law Act 1986 did allow an English court to stay proceedings if it were appropriate for a court outside England and Wales to deal with the proceedings. Such an order should have been made. The English proceedings should be stayed until the Scottish proceedings were finalised.

## Discretionary stays

The court may stay English or Welsh proceedings if there are proceedings in other countries. The court may only stay the English or Welsh proceedings if the balance of fairness is such that it is appropriate that the other proceedings should be disposed of first. The court must consider all the relevant facts, including the convenience of the parties and witnesses and any delay or expense that might otherwise result (see s5(6) and Sch 1 DMPA 1973).

See *de Dampierre* v *de Dampierre* [1987] 2 WLR 1006; [1987] 2 All ER 1 where the husband was resident in London. His wife left him and went to live in New York. Both parties were French nationals. The husband petitioned for divorce in France. The wife petitioned for divorce in England. She applied in England because she considered that she would get more maintenance in England. She feared that under French law she would be denied maintenance if the French court found her exclusively responsible for the breakdown of the marriage, whereas under English law she was likely to obtain substantial financial relief even taking into account her behaviour.

HELD: Whether proceedings should be stayed did not depend on whether one spouse might be deprived of a personal or legal advantage. The question was whether the foreign tribunal with competent jurisdiction could try the case in the interests of the parties and of justice. Both the husband and wife were French nationals. The wife had severed her tenuous links with England by going to the USA. The case was more closely linked with France than England and the French court was the natural and appropriate forum. The wife would not suffer injustice if the English proceedings were stayed though she might get a less generous order in France. English proceedings stayed.

In *Otobo* v *Otobo* [2003] 1 FLR 192 it was said that greater weight should be attached to where proceedings were first issued. In the case the wife started divorce proceedings in England and the husband then brought divorce proceedings in Nigeria. The court refused to stay the English proceedings.

## 6.3 Recognition of foreign marriages and decrees

### Foreign marriages

Foreign marriages may be recognised in this country even though one or both of the parties to the marriage did not have the capacity to marry in English law.

### The dual domicile test

Foreign marriages may be recognised if the parties had the capacity to marry as governed by the law of their country of domicile at the time they got married. If the parties have different domiciles, then the law of each domicile must be considered and each party must have the capacity to marry according to the law of their own domicile – the dual domicile test. If one party does not have the capacity to marry the marriage may not be recognised even if the other party had capacity.

See the cases discussed in Chapter 2 – especially *Alhaji Mohamed* v *Knott* where both parties were domiciled in Nigeria. The marriage was potentially polygamous and the bride was only thirteen years of age. Nigerian law permitted the marriage. Accordingly, English law recognised the marriage even though under English law there was no capacity for a girl of such an age to marry.

Contrast *Pugh* v *Pugh* (Chapter 2, above) where the husband was a domiciled Englishman. He married a fifteen-year-old, Hungarian-domiciled girl in Austria. Hungarian and Austrian law recognised such a marriage. However English law does not allow a marriage to any person under sixteen, and so under the dual domicile test the husband had no capacity to marry, and so the marriage was not recognised in this country.

See also *Cheni* v *Cheni* [1963] 2 WLR 17; [1962] 3 All ER 873 where both parties were domiciled in Egypt. They were uncle and niece. The marriage was potentially polygamous. Egyptian law allowed such a marriage and permitted an uncle and niece to marry. Accordingly, English law recognised the marriage even though an uncle and niece do not have the capacity to marry in English law.

See also *Baindall* v *Baindall* (Chapter 2, above) in relation to the recognition of a polygamous marriage where both parties were domiciled in India which permitted polygamy.

### The intended matrimonial home test

An alternative to the dual domicile test has been put forward. The foreign marriage will be recognised in England and Wales if it is valid according to the law of the country where the parties intend to set up their matrimonial home.

In *De Reneville* v *De Reneville* [1948] 1 All ER 56 the wife was domiciled in England. The husband was domiciled in France. They married in France. The wife challenged the marriage on the ground of non-consummation. The parties had lived for the first four years of their marriage in France. It was decided that the question of the validity of the marriage had to be determined according to French law, the law of the country where the parties had intended to make their matrimonial home.

See *Radwan* v *Radwan (No 2)* discussed in Chapter 2 where an English-domiciled woman married an Egyptian-domiciled man. The marriage was polygamous. Under the dual domicile test the marriage would not have been recognised because English law does not recognise such a marriage. However, the court applied the intended matrimonial home test (the intended matrimonial home being Egypt which allowed such a marriage) and treated the marriage as valid.

See also *Lawrence* v *Lawrence* at first instance ([1985] 1 All ER 506) where a Brazilian-domiciled woman married an English-domiciled man. The woman had been married before and had divorced her first husband in Nevada, USA. Brazilian law did not recognise such a decree. Under the dual domicile test she, therefore, had no capacity to marry since she was still married under Brazilian law. The court applied the intended matrimonial home test, namely, England which did recognise the Nevada decree, so that she could marry her second husband. The Court of Appeal affirmed the decision at [1985] 2 All ER 733 but on a different basis.

A further exception to the dual domicile test can be found in *Hussain* v *Hussain*, discussed in Chapter 2.

NOTE: A marriage which may be recognised under the dual domicile or intended matrimonial home tests must also be conducted according to the laws of the country in which the marriage is contracted if that is different to the domicile of the parties or their intended matrimonial home. See *Radwan* v *Radwan (No 2)* where the marriage took place in the Egyptian Consulate General in Paris and was validly conducted according to French law. If it had not been, the marriage would not have been recognised in England.

## Recognition of foreign decrees

This is governed by the Family Law Act 1986 which came into force on 4 April 1988. It replaced the complicated provisions of the Recognition of Divorces and Legal Separations Act 1971 which is now repealed.

Recognition of decrees granted in Scotland and Northern Ireland in England and Wales and vice versa:

A decree of divorce, annulment or judicial separation pronounced in any part of the British Islands shall be recognised throughout the United Kingdom (see s44(2) Family Law Act 1986).

NOTE: Channel Islands decrees are recognised in England and Wales, Scotland and Northern Ireland (though not vice versa).

Any form of divorce or annulment granted in England and Wales, Scotland or Northern Ireland or in the Channel Islands is only effective if obtained in a court of civil jurisdiction (see s44(1) of the Family Law Act 1986).

That is, any form of divorce obtained outside a court (eg a Muslim talaq or a

Jewish get form of religious divorce) *in this country* will not be recognised: for example, *Maples* v *Maples* [1987] 3 All ER 188 where a Jewish couple obtained a divorce in England by way of a get obtained from a Jewish religious court. The wife then tried to remarry.

HELD: A divorce obtained outside a court by way of extra judicial proceedings in this country was not recognised in this country since it was excluded by s16(1) Domicile and Matrimonial Proceedings Act 1973 (the predecessor of s44(1) Family Law Act 1986). The wife's first marriage had not been dissolved. Her second marriage was void because she was already married.

In *Sulaiman* v *Juffali* [2002] 2 FCR 427; [2002] Fam Law 97 H and W were nationals of, and domiciled in, Saudia Arabia. They were both Muslim and married there in accordance with Sharia law in 1980. In 2001 H pronounced a bare talaq pronounced in England which was then registered in Saudi Arabia. The bare talaq fell foul of s44(1) Family Law Act 1986 because it was divorce not obtained through a court. Since the talaq was pronounced in England it could not be an overseas divorce which could otherwise have been recognised under s46 FLA 1986. *Radwan* v *Radwan (No 2)* [1973] Fam Law 35 and *R* v *Secretary of State for the Home Department, ex parte Ghulam Fatima* [1986] AC 527 followed.

### Recognising a decree obtained overseas

An overseas divorce, annulment or legal separation obtained by means of proceedings will be recognised where (s46(1)):

'(a) the divorce, annulment or legal separation is effective under the law of the country in which it was obtained; and
(b) at the relevant date either party to the marriage –
(i) was habitually resident in the country in which the divorce, annulment or legal separation was obtained; or
(ii) was domiciled in that country; or
(iii) was a national of that country.'

Under s46(2) a divorce, annulment or legal separation obtained otherwise than by means of proceedings shall be recognised if:

'(a) the divorce, annulment or legal separation is effective under the law of the country in which it was obtained;
(b) at the relevant date –
(i) each party to the marriage was domiciled in that country; or
(ii) either party to the marriage was domiciled in that country and the other party was domiciled in a country under whose law the divorce, annulment or legal separation is recognised as valid; and
(iii) neither party to the marriage was habitually resident in the United Kingdom throughout the period of one year immediately preceding that date.'

(This means that parties habitually resident in the United Kingdom for at least one year can only obtain a decree through judicial or other formal proceedings.)

The 'relevant date' means:

1. in the case of an overseas divorce, annulment or legal separation obtained by means of proceedings, the date of the commencement of the proceedings;
2. in the case of an overseas divorce, annulment or legal separation obtained otherwise than by means of proceedings, the date on which it was obtained (s46(3)).

A key distinction is between foreign decrees obtained 'by means of proceedings' and those obtained 'otherwise than by means of proceedings'. An illustration of how this distinction works is how English courts have regarded divorce by the Muslim talaq.

A 'talaq' was treated as being obtained by means of proceedings in *Quazi* v *Quazi* [1979] 3 All ER 897. In that case a husband obtained a talaq divorce in Pakistan by pronouncing the talaq (the words 'I divorce you' said three times in the presence of witnesses) and then following various administrative procedures laid down by in the Pakistan Muslim Family Laws Ordinance which had been overseen by a religious court. See also *El Fadl* v *El Fadl* [2000] Fam Law 84 in which H and W underwent a polygamous Islamic marriage as permitted by local law in Lebanon in April 1981. In December 1981 a talaq divorce was pronounced in Lebanon by H in the presence of two witnesses and registered with the Sharia court in Lebanon. W was not notified of the divorce but became aware of it. They lived largely separate lives with H living in Lebanon and W in Europe and the USA. Sixteen years later H withdrew financial support and W petitioned for divorce. H defended the English divorce petition on the basis that the marriage had already been dissolved. The English court dismissed W's petition. It recognised that a talaq divorce was a unilateral act which did not require W's consent. She did not need to have notice for the talaq divorce to have effect. Under s46(1) and (2) Family Law Act 1986 a talaq divorce could be recognised as a divorce which was the result of judicial or other proceedings if either party was domiciled in the country in which the divorce was pronounced. Ordinarily a talaq divorce was not the product of judicial or other proceedings but was a simple pronouncement. Lebanese law required a talaq to be recorded with the Sharia court. Even though no judicial decision was required the registration was 'proceedings' for the purpose of s46(1) FLA 1986. The court had a discretion to decline recognition pursuant to s51 FLA 1986. It was not appropriate to decline recognition in this case since the divorce was valid by the personal law of both parties at the time it was pronounced and had been known by them for many years. It was not contrary to public policy even though it was obtained by a procedure which might offend English sensibilities. W was not financially prejudiced and could seek financial relief under Part III Matrimonial and Family Proceedings Act 1984.

By contrast in *Chaudhary* v *Chaudhary* [1984] 3 All ER 1017 a husband had first tried to divorce his wife by pronouncing talaq in England. That was invalid by virtue of what is now s44(1) Family Law Act 1986. He then tried to divorce her by pronouncing talaq in Kashmir. He simply said the words 'I divorce you' three times in the presence of witnesses. He followed no other procedures since this not required in Kashmir (unlike the position in the rest of Pakistan as in *Quazi*). Such a 'bare talaq' was a mere pronouncement of words and was a unilateral and private act. For there to be 'proceedings' there had to be a degree of formality and at least the involvement of some religious or civil agency or court or body recognised by the state which had some function which was more than a mere rubber stamp. The decree was obtained 'otherwise than by means of proceedings' and could not be recognised.

In *R* v *Immigration Appeal Tribunal, ex parte Asfar Jan* [1995] Imm 440, W was a Pakistani national. She had been married to her second husband (H2) who already had one wife. He then divorced her by talaq which was pronounced in the United Kingdom. She then married her third husband (H3) who was a British citizen. She was refused entry into the United Kingdom on the ground that her marriage to H3 was void and she would be dependent on public funding for maintenance. W sought judicial review of the refusal on the grounds that her marriage to H3 was valid. It was held that the talaq divorce was an overseas divorce 'obtained otherwise than by way of proceedings' under the Family Law Act 1986. It was not recognised under English law as H2 had been habitually resident in the United Kingdom prior to the divorce, so the second marriage had not been ended. The second marriage was valid under s11(d) MCA 1973 as the marriage had taken place outside England and Wales and neither H2 nor W had been domiciled in the United Kingdom at the time of the marriage. The polygamous marriage was therefore valid, and W did not have capacity to marry H3 under English law. See also *Wicken* v *Wicken* [1999] Fam Law 16 in which W and H1 were Muslims validly married in the Gambia by a Muslim ceremony in 1989. H1 signed a divorce letter in 1990 which was delivered to her and was effective under Gambian law. W married H2, who was British born, in 1992 in an English registry office. Some years later W petitioned for divorce and H2 petitioned for nullity. The question was whether W was validly divorced from H1. It was held that the divorce had been obtained otherwise than by divorce proceedings and would be recognised under s46(2) FLA 1986 if effective under Gambian law. It was effective so W's marriage to H2 was valid. Her petition for divorce was granted.

Difficulties arise with transnational decrees where proceedings take place both abroad and in the United Kingdom and so attract problems of jurisdictional rules having to take account of two countries/states. In *Fatima* v *Secretary of State for the Home Department* [1986] 2 WLR 643; [1986] 2 All ER 32 the husband pronounced talaq in England. The procedures then switched to Pakistan where the talaq was confirmed and the marriage dissolved. Such a 'transnational' divorce contravened rules relating to residence as well as the rule that any divorce obtained in England other than by way of court proceedings would not be recognised. Pakistani nationals resident in England were not permitted to obtain a divorce by post using the talaq procedure. *Fatima* was decided under the predecessor to the Family Law Act 1986.

The position seems to be the same under FLA 1986. In *Berkovits* v *Cornberg, Attorney-General Intervening* [1995] 2 WLR 553; [1995] 2 All ER 681 a divorce by way of a Jewish 'get' was obtained in writing by a husband in London and then sent to a Rabbinical Court in Israel where it was to be delivered to the wife. The decree was not recognised under s46(1) because 'proceedings' could only take place in one country.

Under s51 Family Law Act 1986 a decree obtained in any part of the British Isles or overseas will not be recognised where the divorce was granted or obtained at a time when it was irreconcilable with a decision determining the subsistence or validity of the marriage by a court in that part of the United Kingdom or by a foreign court whose decision is recognised in that part of the United Kingdom. For example in *Vervaeke* v *Smith* [1982] 2 All ER 144 the wife married her first husband. She then purported to marry a second husband who then died leaving property to his wife. Her claim to the property was only valid if her second marriage was valid. She asked an English court to declare that her first marriage was void so that her second marriage was not bigamous. The English court refused to declare the first marriage void. Having been born in Belgium, she then sought the same declaration from a Belgian court. When the Belgium court granted her decree the English court refused to recognise it since an English court had already ruled on the same issue.

Further, a decree may not be recognised if:

1. in the case of a divorce or legal separation, there was no subsisting marriage between the parties (s51(2);
2. in the case of a divorce, annulment or legal separation obtained by means of proceedings, reasonable steps were not taken to give notice of the proceedings to the other party or the other party was not given a reasonable opportunity of taking part in the proceedings (s51(3));
3. in the case of a divorce etc obtained otherwise than by means of proceedings, there is no official document certifying that the divorce etc is effective under the law of the country in which it was obtained, or, where either party was domiciled in another country at the relevant date, there is no official document certifying that the divorce etc is recognised as valid in that country (s51(3)); or
4. in either case, its recognition would be manifestly contrary to public policy (s51(3)).

For an example of a court considering the recognition of an overseas divorce on the grounds of public policy see *Eroglu* v *Eroglu* [1994] 2 FLR 287 where in 1974 a Turkish man, H, married a British woman, W, in Turkey. H was a university graduate, and under Turkish law he was only obliged to serve a shortened period of national service in the armed services. However, when he married a foreign national he lost that privilege and could be obliged to do full national service. H and W agreed to a divorce so that H could serve the shortened national service and then remarry as soon as that period was over. The parties obtained a divorce in Turkey in 1976 on the ground of extreme incompatibility but continued to live together and had two children. H did his shortened national service in 1981-82. They did not remarry. In 1992 W petitioned for divorce in England. H argued that her petition should be dismissed since the marriage had already been dissolved by the Turkish divorce.

HELD: The Turkish divorce satisfied the grounds for recognition under s46 Family Law Act 1986. Under s51(3)(c) recognition of the divorce could be refused on the grounds of public policy. The Turkish divorce was a deception. W had participated in that deception. The Turkish divorce was pronounced in good faith and would be recognised. W did not lose her right to apply for financial provision in that she was granted leave to make application under the Matrimonial and Family Proceedings Act 1984.

In *Kellman* v *Kellman* [2000] Fam Law 315 H and W obtained a 'mail order' divorce in the US territory of Guam in 1989. Neither lived in Guam or had ever visited it. In 1999 W tried to question the validity of the divorce but the court in Guam dismissed her application. W issued divorce proceedings in England. Her petition was dismissed since the Guam divorce was valid in English law under the Family Law Act 1986. The divorce was effective in the USA within the meaning of ss46-49, particularly in light of the 1999 decision confirming its validity. Recognition was not manifestly contrary to public policy under s51. There was a high threshold under s51 and there was nothing about the Guam divorce to reach that threshold other than the easily satisfied jurisdictional qualification.

In *Wicken* v *Wicken* (above) there was no basis for the court exercising its discretion under s51(3) FLA 1986 not to recognise the foreign decree of divorce.

Another example (decided under the predecessor to the 1986 Act) is *Kendall* v *Kendall* [1977] 3 All ER 471 where a foreign divorce was obtained by fraud. The wife had signed documents in Spanish which she thought related to taking the children out of the country but which probably related to a power of attorney. The decree also contained false details (for example, that there were no children of the marriage, that the wife had worked, and that there was no property involved). It was manifestly contrary to public policy to recognise the decree.

In *Mamdini* v *Mamdini* [1984] FLR 699 the spouses came from Tanzania. They became British nationals and married and lived in England. The wife commenced divorce proceedings in England. The husband went to the USA and began divorce proceedings in the state of Nevada. The wife was given notice of the proceedings but could not afford to travel to the USA to defend them. The Nevada court granted a divorce decree. The decree was not recognised under the predecessor to the 1986 Act since the wife had not been able to take part in the proceedings for sound financial reasons. The husband had known that. She was allowed to continue with the English divorce proceedings.

NOTE: If a country comprises territories with different systems of law (eg the states of the USA), s46 applies as if each territory were a country (s49). If there have been cross-proceedings then it is sufficient if the requirements under s46 are met when either the main proceedings or the cross-proceedings are initiated (s47). Where a divorce or annulment has been granted or recognised in the United Kingdom, the fact that such a decree is not recognised in a foreign country does not prevent the parties from remarrying in the United Kingdom or cause the remarriage to be treated as invalid in the United Kingdom (wherever the remarriage takes place) (s50).

## Brussells II

The Convention on Jurisdiction and the Recognition and Enforcement of Judgements in Matrimonial Matters and in Matters of Parental Responsibility for the Children of Both Spouses (Brussels II) was implemented in March 2001. The Convention deals with jurisdiction and with recognition and enforcement of certain proceedings. These are proceedings relating to divorce, legal separation and annulment and civil proceedings relating to parental responsibility for the children of both spouses on the occasion of divorce, legal separation or annulment. It was signed by all the EU countries apart from Denmark.

In particular Chapter II, art 2 gives uniform jurisdictional rules for the authomatic recognition of matrimonial judgments. Jurisdiction is based on the grounds of habitual residence, nationality or domicile in the UK in respect of divorce, legal separation or nullity. Jurisdiction in matters of parental responsibility arises where the child is habitually resident in the UK (art 3). Generally speaking the country in which proceedings first start has exclusive jurisdiction. If later proceedings are started in another Convention country then that country will refuse jurisdiction. For example, in *A v L (Jurisdiction: Brussels II)* [2002] 1 FLR 1042 F brought proceedings in Spain to appeal against a Spanish order. M brought the child to England and sought to bring fresh proceedings in England. It was held that the English court had no jurisdiction under art 11 of Brussels II (which provides that a second court cannot be seised of an application until the first court's proceedings have been finished). See also *Wermuth* v *Wermuth* [2003] 1 FCR 289 where German divorce proceedings started before English divorce proceedings meant that the Englishproceedings had to be stayed.

Chapter III of the Convention deals with recognition and enforcement. Generally UK courts must recognise orders made by other countries who are subject to the Convention.

## 6.4 Declarations as to the validity of a foreign decree

Section 55 Family Law Act 1986 provides that the High Court and the county court have a statutory power to make a declaration concerning the validity of a foreign decree, namely, a declaration:

1. that a marriage was at its inception a valid marriage;
2. that a marriage subsisted, or did not subsist, on a given date;
3. that a divorce, annulment or legal separation obtained outside England and Wales is, or is not, entitled to recognition in this country.

A third party may apply for a declaration but only if he has a sufficient interest in the outcome of the proceedings (s55(3)).

A declaration may be refused if it would be contrary to public policy (s58(1)) following *Puttick* v *Attorney-General* discussed in Chapter 2).

There is jurisdiction to make a declaration only if one of the parties to the marriage is domiciled in England and Wales at the time of the application or has been habitually resident in this country for one year before that date, or alternatively one party is dead and he or she satisfied one of the conditions at the time of his or her death (s55(2)).

## 6.5 Applications for financial relief after overseas divorce

Where a marriage has been dissolved or annulled or the parties to a marriage have been legally separated by means of judicial or other proceedings in an overseas country and the divorce, annulment or legal separation is recognised as valid in England and Wales, either party to the marriage can apply for financial relief in England or Wales (as long as that party has not remarried) (Part III, s12 Matrimonial and Family Proceedings Act 1984).

Leave must be obtained before an application can be made. The court must consider that there is a substantial ground for the application and may give leave even if a foreign court has already made payment or property transfer orders to the applicant or to a child of the family (s13).

There must be jurisdiction to make the application, namely:

1. either party to the marriage was domiciled in England and Wales either when he or she applied for leave or when the foreign divorce, annulment or legal separation took effect in that country; or
2. either party to the marriage was habitually resident in England or Wales for one year before he or she applied for leave or after the foreign divorce, annulment or legal separation took effect in that country; or
3. either party had a beneficial interest in a matrimonial home in England and Wales when applying for leave (s15).

England and Wales must be considered to be the appropriate forum for such an application. The court is directed to consider certain matters such as the parties connection with England and Wales as opposed to their connection with the foreign country which granted the decree, what financial benefits a party would gain by making application in England and Wales as opposed to the foreign country, the extent to which any order made in a foreign country has been complied with and how enforceable an order made in England and Wales would likely to be (s16).

For an example of a court considering ss13 and 16 see *Holmes* v *Holmes* [1989] 3 All ER 786 where a wife who had been divorced by her American husband was dissatisfied with the financial orders of the American divorce court in relation to a cottage in England. She sought leave to apply for an order under MFPA 1984 to obtain the transfer of the cottage to herself for her and the child of the family to live in. The court refused to give leave holding that the American court was the natural forum for the resolution of the dispute between the parties.

If leave is granted the court can then make similar orders as those under ss23, 24 and 24A MCA 1973 following considerations similar to those in ss25 and 25A MCA 1973 (ss17 and 18 MFPA 1984).

# 7

# Ancillary Relief in Divorce, Nullity and Judicial Separation Proceedings

## 7.1 Introduction

The breakdown of a marriage results in most cases in divorce. As a result the majority of disputes concerning finance and property between spouses are dealt with by the divorce courts under the Matrimonial Causes Act 1973. Unlike the strict rules of property ownership to be considered in Chapter 10, the courts are given a wide discretion as to the financial and property arrangements between the parties. The question is 'to whom shall this be given', as opposed to 'who is the legal owner of this property'. The courts will prevent any attempt to use a different form of litigation to avoid its powers.

Most ancillary relief orders are made by consent (75 per cent in 1998). Many divorces (which have gradually declined between 1985 and 1998 from 157,000 to 137,000) do not lead to any ancillary relief orders. There has been a dramatic decline in spousal periodical payments orders (1985–1998: 29,617–9,051). This is presumably because of the clean break provisions (see section 7.8). There has been a more dramatic decline in child periodical payment orders (1985–1998: 42,000–9,096) because of the introduction of the Child Support Agency (see section 7.17). Lump sum and property orders have been stable (1985–1998: 27,216–32,257)

It is important to appreciate the procedure used by the court to determine ancillary relief. From June 2000 what was called the 'ancillary relief pilot project' was extended nationwide. The 'pilot scheme' gives the judiciary powers to case manage to determine the speed and the route of the case. These tie in with the Woolf reforms of civil justice procedure contained in the Civil Procedure Rules 1998 (which do not apply to most family proceedings). Comment was made in a case, *Tee* v *Tee and Hillman* [1999] 2 FLR 613; [1999] Fam Law 534, about unnecessary adversarial litigation. This case involved a claim for ancillary relief under the MCA 1973 being complicated by proceedings being brought under Trusts of Land and Appointment of Trustees Act 1996. The proceedings resulted in costs of over £100,000, money largely wasted on irrelevant arguments. The case was held to be a prime example of the potential for the pilot procedures to curtail unnecessary adversarial litigation. In *Piglowska* v *Piglowski* [1999] 2 FLR 763, heard by the House of Lords, the assets were wholly swallowed up by legal costs. Lord Hoffmann referred to the pilot scheme and how it emphasised judicial control of the application, particularly in relation to costs.

The courts now expect:

1. parties to make offers and proposals;
2. recipients of offers and proposals to give them proper consideration at every stage of the court proceedings.

The court procedure is found in the Family Proceedings (Amendment No 2) Rules 1991, amending the Family Proceedings Rules 1991 which apply to proceedings commenced on or after 5 June 2000. The rules seek to ensure so far as is practicable that:

1. the parties are on an equal footing;
2. expense is saved;
3. cases are dealt with proportionate to the amount of money involved, the

importance of the case, its complexity and the financial position of each party;

4. cases are dealt with expeditiously and fairly;
5. cases are allotted an appropriate share of court resources.

There is an emphasis on full and frank disclosure at an early stage and disincentives to delay or inflated costs. The court must actively manage cases, including:

1. encouraging the parties to co-operate with each other in the conduct of the case;
2. encouraging the parties to settle through mediation where appropriate;
3. identifying the issues at an early stage;
4. regulating the extent of disclosure of documents and expert evidence so they are proportionate to the issues in question;
5. helping the parties to settle the whole or part of the case;
6. fixing timetables or otherwise controlling the progress of the case;
7. making use of technology;
8. giving directions to ensure that the trial of a case proceeds quickly and efficiently.

Ancillary relief now has four stages:

## *Making the application and fixing the first appointment*

There is an issue fee of £60. Application is made by Form A being filed with the court and being served on the other party within four days of filing with the court. A first appointment is fixed 12–16 weeks ahead. Within that time financial information must be gathered, drafting undertaken and consideration and service made on the other party. Various documents have to be produced:

1. statement of property and income (Form E);
2. questionnaire;
3. schedule of documents (which includes property valuation(s) obtained in last six months, mortgage statements, last 12 months' bank statements, surrender values of insurance policies, valuation of pension rights, last three payslips and most recent P60 and last two years of business accounts);
4. statement of apparent issues;
5. first costs estimate.

Parties are not allowed to submit documents other than those specified in the rules (without good reason). If a party fails to submit a document specified in the rules he/she may be penalised in costs. There is simultaneous exchange of Form E and accompanying documents (preventing one party having advance notice of the other party's means and 'massaging' his/her financial statement accordingly). There is an incentive to meet the deadline since the other party's case will not be forthcoming until both parties are ready to exchange.

In *W* v *W (Ancillary Relief: Practice)* [2000] Fam Law 473 Wilson J pointed out that Form E seeks to substantially limit the evidence to current circumstances and to avoid allegations which might reduce the chance of settlement.

Certain documents must be filed at least 14 days before the first appointment. These include a concise statement of the issues between the parties, a chronology, any request for further information and whether a party is ready to proceed to a financial dispute resolution (FDR) appointment. The information requested must be relevant and disclosure kept within reasonable bounds.

## The first appointment

The object of the first appointment is to define issues and to save costs. The court will consider what questions need answering and what further documents are needed. Any expert is expected to be jointly instructed (to avoid any proliferation in expert evidence). Both parties must attend the first appointment in person (unless their attendance is excused by the court).

The district judge will refer most cases to an FDR appointment and make directions as to the conduct of the case. He or she can make an interim order. For cases which are not ready, or are more complicated, a further directions appointment may be fixed or consideration be given to interim orders or an FDR appointment fixed at a later stage. Where an FDR appointment is not fixed the district judge must set a final hearing and determine the judicial level at which the case must be heard. Alternatively, the district judge can adjourn for an out-of-court mediation or negiotation or in exceptional cases adjourn without fixing another date. If the matters are agreed he/she can alter the first appointment to an FDR appointment (which leads the parties to a settlement). The district judge will ask for information on costs incurred and can make costs orders in the light of any compliance or non-compliance with the rules.

## The financial dispute resolution (FDR) appointment

The FDR appointment is designed to lead the parties to a settlement by exploring the common ground between them. The court will also warn the parties against unrealistic expectations. Offers may be open to debate and be without prejudice. Offers can also be *Calderbank* offers, ie definite proposals which if they reflect the final order are likely to lead to the opposing party having to pay any costs incurred after the making of the *Calderbank* offer. All offers must be filed with the court at least seven days before the FDR appointment. A second costs estimate must be filed. If the FDR is unsuccessful the district judge will give further directions towards a final, contested hearing. That district judge cannot deal with the final hearing since he/she will have been made aware of without prejudice offers. A new district judge will be allocated. The FDR may be adjourned from time to time. At the end of the FDR appointment the court can make a consent order. An interim order could be made. In *W* v *W* (above) Wilson J said that, in the absence of agreement at the FDR, broader evidence to that asked for in Form E is required to enable the court to perform its duty under s25 MCA 1973. This included some historical information as to the financial circumstances of the parties at the time of the marriage.

The FDR appointment was discussed by the Court of Appeal in *Rose* v *Rose* [2002] 1 FLR 978. The Court held that an FDR appointment could narrow the issues and dispel unrealistic expectations but could not be a substitute for a contested trial. The only possible results from an FDR would be an adjournment of the FDR, a consent order or directions to progress the case to a final hearing. In *Rose* v *Rose* the parties disputed the terms of a clean break settlement. At the FDR lengthy submissions were made and the judge indicated what the broad outcome would be if the case was listed for trial. The parties then agreed on an order. Before the order was drawn up H indicated that he was not happy with it and did not consider the agreement to be a final court order. The judge agreed with H. W appealed. The appeal was allowed since the whole purpose and effect of an FDR would be lost or compromised if parties were free to analyse and re-evaluate a crucial decision. The order agreed at the FDR was confirmed.

## The final hearing

Fourteen days before the final hearing the applicant must set out his/her final open proposals of the order he/she proposes should be made. The respondent must do the same seven days before the final hearing. The parties are therefore obliged to put their cards on the table. A written statement of costs must be filed by each party.

## Costs estimates and costs orders

As outlined above cost estimates are required at three stages: for the first appointment, the FDR hearing and the final hearing. The idea is to keep costs at the forefront of the parties' minds and to avoid any surprises as to the amount of legal costs incurred. It also allows the court to ensure that the costs do not outweight the issues/property at stake.

There are provisions whereby a party who has rejected an offer which is the same as, or better than, the resulting court order may be required to bear the costs incurred after the offer was rejected. It is also possible to award interest to the successful party. In other words, a party who fails to accept reasonable offers put forward by the other party is likely to be penalised very heavily unless it is unjust to make such an order.

## Practice Direction (Ancillary Relief Procedure) *[2000] Fam Law 509*

The President of the Family Division issued a *Practice Direction* on the new ancillary relief procedure which has effect from 5 June 2000. It included a 'pre-application protocol' outlining the steps the parties should seek and the information to be provided. It also sets out the expectations on the parties in the FDR. It emphasised that whatever is said in the FDR it cannot normally be used as evidence in subsequent proceedings. This should encourage flexible offers or proposals and proper consideration of them. The *Practice Direction*, where expert evidence is required, encourages the use of a single joint expert. In the absence of agreement the court can direct that only a single expert may give evidence.

The 'pre-application protocol' obliges solicitors to consider suggesting mediation to clients as an alternative to solicitor negotiation or court-based litigation. It also emphasises that the tone of the first letter from the applicant is important and sets out guidelines to be followed. Correspondence which raises irrelevant issues or which might cause the other party to adopt an entrenched, polarised or hostile position is to be discouraged. The duty of full and frank disclosure of all material facts is emphasised. Documents should only be disclosed to the extent that they are required by Form E.

## 7.2 Maintenance pending suit

Section 22 Matrimonial Causes Act 1973 provides:

> 'On a petition for divorce, nullity of marriage, or judicial separation, the court may make an order for maintenance pending suit, that is to say, an order requiring either party to the marriage to make to the other such periodical payments for his or her maintenance and for such term, being a term beginning not earlier than the date of the presentation of the petition and ending with the date of the determination of the suit, as the court thinks reasonable.'

The basis on which maintenance pending suit will be granted is the same (as far as is practicable) as that which determines a periodical payments order. The court is not directed to follow the considerations in s25 (discussed below), but they are used as a guideline in assessing what is reasonable (see *Peacock* v *Peacock* [1984] 1 WLR 532; [1984] 1 All ER 1069).

NOTE: It can be easier and cheaper to obtain an order in the magistrates' court as a preliminary to a divorce petition rather than maintenance pending suit (see for example *Lanitis* v *Lanitis* [1970] 1 WLR 506; [1970] 1 All ER 466). Maintenance pending suit is wide enough to cover an order to help fund the payee's legal fees during the divorce proceedings (see *A* v *A (Maintenance Pending Suit: Provision for Legal Fees)* [2001] 1 FLR 377).

## 7.3 Financial provision

Section 23 Matrimonial Causes Act 1973:

'(1) On granting a decree of divorce, a decree of nullity of marriage or a decree of judicial separation or at any time thereafter (whether, in the case of a decree of divorce or of nullity of marriage, before or after the decree is made absolute), the court may make any one or more of the following orders, that is to say –

(a) an order that either party to the marriage shall make to the other such periodical payments, for such term, as may be specified in the order;

(b) an order that either party to the marriage shall secure to the other to the satisfaction of the court such periodical payments, for such term, as may be so specified;

(c) an order that either party to the marriage shall pay to the other such lump sum or sums as may be so specified [which may be paid by instalments and can be used to enable a spouse to meet liabilities or expenses incurred before the making of the application – s23(3)];

(d) an order that a party to the marriage shall make to such person as may be specified in the order for the benefit of a child of the family, or to such a child, such periodical payments, for such term, as may be so specified;

(e) an order that a party to the marriage shall secure to such person as may be so specified for the benefit of such a child, or to such a child, to the satisfaction of the court, such periodical payments, for such term, as may be so specified;

(f) an order that a party to the marriage shall secure to such person as may be so specified for the benefit of such a child, or to such a child, such lump sum as may be so specified [which may be paid by instalments];

subject, however, in the case of an order under paragraph (d), (e) or (f) above, to the restrictions imposed by section 29(1) and (3) below on the making of financial provision orders in favour of children who have attained the age of eighteen.

(2) The court may also, subject to those restrictions, make any one or more of the orders mentioned in subsection 1(d), (e) and (f) above –

(a) in any proceedings for divorce, nullity of marriage or judicial separation, before granting a decree; and

(b) where any such proceedings are dismissed after the beginning of the trial, either forthwith or within a reasonable period after the dismissal [ie can make provision for the children even if the petition is dismissed].'

NOTE: In the majority of cases the court has no jurisdiction to make any maintenance orders for children since the Child Support Agency now deals with this in the form of child support. See section 7.17, Child Support Act 1991.

### *Secured and unsecured periodical payments*

If there is reason to believe that a spouse ordered to make periodical payments is likely to default in his payments he can be required to provide a security to secure his payments. If he defaults he can then lose the security to make up for the loss of payments. For example in *W v W (Periodical Payments: Pensions)* [1996] 2 FLR 480 the former husband was described as devious and obstructive. The maintenance order for his former wife was secured by way of an attachment of earnings order addressed to the company which held money for the former husband's life insurance. In *Aggett* v *Aggett* [1962] 1 WLR 183; [1962] 1 All ER 190 a wife's periodical payments were secured on the husband's house because there was a risk he would go to the USA and leave his wife without any means of support.

Secured periodical payments can only be ordered if the spouse has sufficient assets to provide a security. Securities have included stocks and shares or a mortgage on a spouse's house (eg *Parker* v *Parker* [1972] 2 WLR 21; [1972] 1 All ER 410).

While unsecured periodical payments cease on the payer's death (unless the payee has died or remarried before then), secured periodical payments will continue until the payee's death or remarriage even if the payer has died (with payments being made from the payer's estate). See *C* v *C (Financial Provision)* [1995] 2 FLR 171 where a husband (who had been severely injured in a road traffic accident) was ordered to pay maintenance to his child (who suffered from a separate medical problem). The husband had £5 million in damages in a structured settlement meant to provide for him over his expected lifespan. The child's maintenance was secured so that if the husband died prematurely the payments would continue to be paid by his estate.

## 7.4 Property adjustment orders

Section 24 Matrimonial Causes Act 1973:

'(1) On granting a decree of divorce, a decree of nullity of marriage or a decree of judicial separation or at any time thereafter (whether, in the case of a decree of divorce or of nullity of marriage, before or after the decree is made absolute), the court may make any one or more of the following orders, that is to say:

(a) an order that a party to the marriage shall transfer to the other party, to any child of the family or to such person as may be specified in the order for the benefit of such a child, such property as may be so specified, being property to which the first-mentioned party is entitled either in possession or reversion;

(b) an order that a settlement of such property as may be so specified, being property to which a party to the marriage is so entitled, be made to the satisfaction of the court for the benefit of the other party to the marriage and of the children of the family or either or any of them;

(c) an order varying for the benefit of the parties to the marriage and of the children of the family or either or any of them any ante-nuptial or post-nuptial settlement (including such a settlement made by will or codicil) made on the parties to the marriage;

(d) an order extinguishing or reducing the interest of either of the parties to the marriage under any such settlement;

subject, however, in the case of an order under paragraph (a) above to the restrictions imposed by section 29(1) and (3) below on the making of orders for a transfer of property in favour of children who have attained the age of eighteen.

(2) The court may make an order under subsection (1)(c) above notwithstanding that there are no children of the family.'

Section 24A gives the court express power to order the sale of any property (not just the home) in which 'either or both spouses has an interest'. The power can be exercised whenever the court makes a secured maintenance order, a lump sum or a property adjustment order.

## 7.5 Matters to be regarded when considering orders under ss23, 24 and 24A MCA 1973

The powers under ss23, 24 and 24A are wide. Sections 25 and 25A provide a list of considerations to assist the court in approaching cases in a fair and consistent way. Section 25 of the Matrimonial Causes Act 1973 provides:

'(1) It shall be the duty of the court in deciding whether to exercise its powers under sections 23, 24 and 24A above and, if so, in what manner, to have regard to all the circumstances of the case, first consideration being given to the welfare while a minor of any child of the family who has not attained the age of eighteen.

(2) As regards the exercise of the powers of the court under sections 23(1)(a), (b) or (c), 24 or 24A above in relation to a party to the marriage, the court shall in particular have regard to the following matters:

(a) the income, earning capacity, property and other financial resources which each of the parties to the marriage has or is likely to have in the foreseeable future, including in the case of earning capacity any increase in that capacity which it would in the opinion of the court be reasonable to expect a party to the marriage to take steps to acquire;

(b) the financial needs, obligations and responsibilities which each of the parties to the marriage has or is likely to have in the foreseeable future;

(c) the standard of living enjoyed by the family before the breakdown of the marriage;

(d) the age of each party to the marriage and the duration of the marriage;

(e) any physical or mental disability of either of the parties to the marriage;

(f) the contributions made by each of the parties to the welfare of the family, including any contribution made by looking after the home or caring for the family;

(g) the conduct of each of the parties, if that conduct is such that it would in the opinion of the court be inequitable to disregard it; ...'

Section 25A provides:

'(1) Where on or after the grant of a decree of divorce or nullity of marriage the court decides to exercise its powers under sections 23(1)(a), (b) or (c), 24 or 24A above in favour of a party to the marriage, it shall be the duty of the court to consider whether it would be appropriate so to exercise those powers that the financial obligations of each party towards the other will be terminated as soon after the grant of the decree as the court considers just and reasonable.

(2) Where the court decides in such a case to make a periodical payments or secured periodical payments order in favour of a party to the marriage, the court shall in particular consider whether it would be appropriate to require those payments to be made or secured only for such term as would in the opinion of the court be sufficient to enable a party in whose favour the order is made to adjust without undue hardship to the termination of his or her financial dependence on the other party.

(3) Where on or after the grant of a decree of divorce or nullity of marriage an application is made by a party to the marriage for a periodical payments or secured periodical payments order in his or her favour, then, if the court considers that no continuing obligation should be imposed on either party to make or secure periodical payments in favour of the other, the court may dismiss the application with a direction that the applicant shall not be entitled to make any further application in relation to that marriage for an order under section 23(1)(a) or (b) above.'

Section 25A is followed by ss25B–25D which oblige the court to look at the parties' pension provision. These sections are described in section 7.9.

## 7.6 Application of s25 MCA 1973

*Section 25(1) – having regard to all the circumstances – the yardstick of equal division*

In *White* v *White* [2000] 2 FLR 981 31 the House of Lords emphasised that the court had to be fair to both parties. The circumstances in which the statutory powers have to be exercised vary widely from the poverty stricken to the millionaire. Sometimes the conclusion was to divide the assets more or less equally. More often that was not so and one party would receive a bigger share than the other. The court is advised, before reaching a firm conclusion and making an order, to check its tentative view against the yardstick of equal division. As a general guide equality should be departed from only if and to the extent that there was good reason to do so. The need to consider and articulate reasons for departing from equality would help the parties and the court to focus on the need to ensure the absence of discrimination. The House of Lords emphasised that it was not trying to introduce a presumption of equal division. That was a matter for Parliament. Rather the courts should use equality as a form of check rather than a legal presumption of equal division.

The effect of *White* v *White* can be explained as follows:

1.  Where a divorced couple have limited means there are usually insufficient assets for there to be an equal division. Ancillary relief orders may concentrate on housing the children (who are the first consideration) and the primary carer and providing limited financial relief within the means of the spouses.
2.  Where a divorced couple are in the middle income bracket then again an equal division may leave both spouses with insufficient assets. Ancillary relief orders may again concentrate on housing the children and primary carer but providing more generous financial relief than in the past to the non-earning spouse who looked after the children and looked after the matrimonial home.
3.  Where a divorced couple are in the high income bracket there should be sufficient assets for there to be an equal division and *White* v *White* will be directly relevant.

Authority for the above can be found in *Cordle* v *Cordle* [2002] 1 FLR 207 where the Court of Appeal explained that there is no rule in *White* v *White* that equality must be achieved unless there are good reasons to justify otherwise. The cross check of equality of outcome is intended to be a safeguard against discrimination. The first duty of the court is to apply the s25 criteria in search of a fair outcome. Courts will look first to the housing needs of the parties. Homes are of fundamental importance and there is nothing more awful than homelessness. In the ordinary case the court's first concern will be to provide a home for the primary carer and the children (whose welfare is the first consideration). This may absorb all that is immediately available. Where there is sufficient to go beyond that, the court's concern will be to provide the means for the absent parent to rehouse. Another factor will be butressing the ability and opportunity to work. One party may need capital provision to enable him or her to get back into the labour market or to retrain or to modernise a skill which, through the years of the marriage, has grown rusty. In the case W received £125,000 of the proceeds of sale of the family home and H £55,000. A similar decision was reached in *B* v *B* [2002] Fam Law 173 in which the only available asset to H and W were the proceeds of sale of the former family home of £124,000. The eight-year-old daughter lived with W. All the proceeds were transferred to W. W was in receipt of state benefits. H appealed, arguing that applying *White* v *White* he should receive a share of the proceeds either immediately or via a *Mesher* order. The appeal was dismissed. First consideration has to be given to the welfare of the child. There was only just enough to house W and the child. Considering all the factors in s25(2), the overriding features were s25(2)(f) (the care of the child) and (g) (H's conduct in not disclosing his assets and failing to support his child). There were plainly good reasons for departing from equity. In *N* v *N* *(Financial Provision: Sale of Company)* [2001] 2 FLR 69 W got 39 per cent of the assets since a larger award would have endangered H's business.

In high income cases the yardstick of equal division is more directly applicable. A recent leading Court of Appeal case is *Lambert* v *Lambert* [2003] 1 FLR 139 in which a 50 per cent division was ordered. H and W had been married for 23 years and had two financially independent children. The family wealth amounted to £20.2 million. H offered W a 30 per cent share of the family wealth on the basis that he had made a special contribution to the company which provided the family wealth. W claimed a 50 per cent share because of her contribution as a wife and mother and as a director of the company. The court awarded a 63 per cent/37 per cent split in favour of H. W appealed. The Court of Appeal allowed her appeal, holding that it was unacceptable to place greater value on the contribution of the breadwinner than that of the homemaker. The Court criticised disputed and often futile evaluations of the contributions each had made to the family wealth. There was a distaste for 'special contributions'. The danger of gender discrimination resulting from special financial contributions was plain since there would no equal opportunity for the homemaker to demonstrate the scale of her comparable success. 'Special contribution' remained a legitimate possibility in only exceptional cases. A similar decision was reached in *HJ* v *HJ* [2002] Fam Law 176, in which an equal division was ordered. H's role as breadwinner and W's role as homemaker and parent were of equal standing. There was nothing special or exceptional about H's contribution. There were sufficient resources for an equal division. No account was taken of H's child from his new relationship since that was his choice and his responsibility. In *G* v *G (Financial Provision: Equal Division)* [2002] 2 FLR 1143 the wife was awarded £4 million from assets of £8.5 million. Again the concept of 'special contribution' was rejected. The contributions of the hard working and dedicated husband as father, spouse and provider were the same as those of the hard working and dedicated wife as mother, spouse and homemaker over 30 years of marriage.

In earlier cases the earning spouse argued that his 'special contribution' justified a departure from an equal division. In *Cowan* v *Cowan* [2001] 2 FLR 192 W received 38 per cent of the assets of over £11 million. This was said to reflect H's exceptional business talents which had generated the family wealth. See also *L* v *L (Financial Provision: Contributions)* [2002] 2 FCR 413 in which W received 37.5 per cent of the assets. This was held to be a fair outcome, which departed from the yardstick of equality in deference to the special contribution of H to the family's wealth. It also recognised in full W's contribution whose help and support allowed H the freedom to make the most of his skills. After *Lambert* the wealth-generating spouse may find it more difficult to argue 'special contribution' to justify departing from equal division.

## Section 25(1) – the first consideration is the welfare of the dependant children

The court has a duty to give first consideration to the welfare of the children of the family under the age of eighteen. 'Child of the family' is defined in s52(1) MCA 1973 and includes a child of both parties and any other child who has been treated by both parties as a child of their family (eg a step-child). This does not mean that the child's welfare is the paramount consideration overriding all other considerations. The court must still consider all the circumstances, bearing in mind the important consideration of the welfare of the children, and then attempt to reach a just financial decision.

In *Suter* v *Suter and Jones* [1987] 2 All ER 336 the welfare of the children did not prevent the court from considering the conduct of the wife (with whom the children resided). She was co-habiting with the co-respondent who was able to make a financial contribution to the household. Accordingly, her maintenance was reduced.

However, the welfare of the children is ofen the first call on the matrimonial assets. In *Harman* v *Glenross* [1986] 2 FLR 241 the first consideration meant that the former matrimonial home was transferred to the wife with whom the children resided since this preserved the home for the children. In cases in which there are limited matrimonial assets the needs of the children may determine what orders the court makes, leaving little surplus to be split between the spouses.

## Section 25(2) – general comment

Section 25(2) lays down a list of particular considerations. In *Piglowska* v *Piglowski* [1999] 1 WLR 1360; [1999] 3 All ER 632 and in *White* v *White* (above) the House of Lords made it clear that there was no priority in the s25(2) factors. The relative weight to be given to each depended on the facts of the particular case. In *Piglowska* v *Piglowski* it was stated that the weight to be given to factors could depend on value judgements on which reasonable people may differ. Some degree of diversity in the application of s25(2) was inevitable and, within limits, was an acceptable price to pay for the flexibility of the discretion conferred.

## Section 25(2)(a)

### A spouse's true income/wealth

The court will look at the reality of the situation. It may go behind what a party says he/she earns or owns. It will look at what income or property could reasonably be available to a party if he/she so wished. Parties may seek to conceal their wealth. The court may then look at the party's lifestyle and make a reasonable assumption of income based on that lifestyle (as opposed to the declared income) (see *J* v *J* [1955] 3 WLR 72; [1955] 2 All ER 617; *Wachtel* v *Wachtel* [1973] 2 WLR 366; [1973] 1 All ER 829; *Newton* v *Newton* [1990] 1 FLR 33).

See *Al Khatid* v *Masry* [2002] Fam Law 420 in which the court drew inferences on compelling evidence to judge what the assets of the husband were. The husband was guilty of substantial concealment and deceit. This was also relevant under s25(2)(g) MCA 1973 in determining W's award of ancillary relief. Applying *White* v *White* W was given an award totalling £26 million.

### A spouse's earning capacity

Pursuant to s25A (see section 7.8) the court will consider promoting the financial independence of the parties, insofar as this is consistent with the welfare of the children and fair in all the circumstances. Section 25(2)(a) makes specific reference to the parties' earning capacity and any increase in that capacity it might be reasonable for a party to take steps to acquire. For example, a non-working spouse might be expected to find suitable employment. This might be impractical if that spouse is looking after young children. Alternatively, the work may be part-time to fit in with school hours. Such a spouse may have no or limited work experience which might make it difficult to find well paid employment.

In *McEwan* v *McEwan* [1972] 1 WLR 1217; [1972] 2 All ER 708 the court expected a retired husband aged 59 to go out to work to supplement his pension. In *Mitchell* v *Mitchell* [1984] 1 WLR 387 the court expected a wife, aged 39, who was a qualified secretary, to make the most of her earning capacity once the youngest child, aged 13, had left school. The wife could then raise a small mortgage. This entitled the husband to a larger share when the former matrimonial home was sold (which was when the youngest child finished full time education) and enabled both parties to then buy their own accommodation. However, the court cannot take earning capacity too far. In *Williams* v *Williams* [1974] 3 WLR 379; [1974] 3 All ER 377 the husband was made redundant and could not find work. He claimed benefit. The court made a maintenance order on the basis that he should have been working. On appeal that approach was held to be wrong. The husband was genuinely unable to find work and could not pay maintenance. A similar conclusion was reached in *Girvan* v *Girvan* (1983) 13 Fam Law 213.

### A spouse's interest in a will
The court will take into account a spouse's interest under a will where the inheritance is likely to occur in the foreseeable future (see *B* v *B* [1988] 2 FLR 490; *B* v *B (Financial Provision)* [1990] 1 FLR 20). In some cases the court will adjourn the proceedings to await the inheritance. It seems that the maximum period a court would adjourn for is four or five years. See *MT* v *MT (Financial Provision: Lump Sum)* [1992] 1 FLR 362 in which the husband expected to inherit substantial capital from his 83-year-old father and the proceedings were adjourned pending the death of the father. The father had undergone a serious operation and had a heart condition and was likely to die within a few years. The court considered that this was the only way to do justice to the wife. The couple had been married for 20 years and had lived beyond their means with the help of the husband's father. The husband had no capital and sought to leave the wife with very little when he had a real prospect of considerable wealth.

If the inheritance is uncertain and the death of the testator unlikely in the foreseeable future then the interest in the will is unlikely to be considered as part of the spouse's income or property. In *Michael* v *Michael* [1986] 2 FLR 389 the wife had an interest under her mother's will. The mother was aged 64 and had high blood pressure. The court refused to consider the wife's prospect of an inheritance as part of her property and refused to adjourn the case. Nourse LJ said that 'the world is full of women in their eighties who had high blood pressure in their sixties'. In *K* v *K* [1990] 2 FLR 225 the interest of a wife in her 79-year old mother's will was not considered since the mother was in good health and the inheritance was not in the forseeeable future.

### Compensation or damages
Compensation or damages awarded to one spouse can be considered as part of that spouse's income or property. In *Wagstaff* v *Wagstaff* [1992] 1 WLR 320; [1992] 1 All ER 275; [1992] 1 FLR 333 the husband was seriously injured in a road traffic accident. He was confined to a wheelchair. His wife looked after him. They then separated. The wife and the child of the family remained in the matrimonial home, a

rented council house. The husband then recieved £418,000 damages for the accident. He bought a house specially adapted for his needs for £137,000 and lived there with a woman and her children. He invested in a business which was not likely to be profitable for up to five years. He was left with £291,000 (made up of the equity of his house, his business interests and deposit accounts). He received state benefits and interest from his deposit accounts which covered his outgoings. The wife applied for financial provision. She was awarded £32,000 as a clean break settlement. She had no immediate need for the lump sum. The husband appealed on the basis that he would have to sell his house or his business to raise the sum. The lump sum was set aside. The wife appealed to the Court of Appeal.

HELD: Allowing the appeal, damages awarded to a spouse for loss of amenity and for pain and suffering were part of that spouse's financial resources under s25(2)(a). The reason for the damages and the size of the award were relevant. After allowing for the husband's disabilities there was a disparity between the parties. The lump sum of £32,000 was restored. Each case had to be taken on its merits. In this case the wife had contributed to a twelve year marriage and had a child to support. Though she was able to meet her modest lifestyle she needed a cushion or security against unforeseen circumstances.

In some cases of small awards specifically for pain and suffering or where the needs of the disabled spouse absorbed all the capital it might be unsuitable to take damages into account. In *Jones* v *Jones* [1983] 1 WLR 901; [1983] 1 All ER 1039 damages of £167,100 to provide for the costs of nursing a husband seriously injured in a motorcycle accident were not considered. In another case *Jones* v *Jones* [1975] 2 WLR 606; [1975] 2 All ER 12 an award of £1,800 to a wife for an injury sustained during a knife attack were disregarded since it was the husband who had attacked the wife. In *C* v *C (Financial Provision)* [1995] 2 FLR 171 a husband who was severely injured in a road traffic accident received damages of £5 million in a structured settlement to last over his expected lifespan of forty years. Following divorce his wife claimed a lump sum. This was refused since all of the settlement was absorbed in meeting the husband's needs.

An earlier view in *Daubney* v *Daubney* [1976] 2 WLR 959; [1976] 2 All ER 453 that damages for pain and suffering and for loss of amenity should not be considered under s25 was disapproved in *Wagstaff*. In *Daubney* the flat a wife had bought using damages she had received in a road traffic accident was taken into account.

## State benefits

The fact that one party can claim state benefits does not entitle the other party to cast the burden of supporting that party on to the state. However in the case of low income families where a maintenance order set out at a reasonable level would reduce the payer to below subsistence level the court will reduce the amount payable and allow the state to make up the difference through payment of benefit (see Chapter 12, section 12.4).

**Wealth available to a spouse from his or her family or from a third party**
A spouse may have limited means but have the potential to acquire greater means because he or she has a wealthy family. The court may have regard to the potential availability of wealth from sources administered by others. The court may make financial provision orders which encourage third parties to enhance the means of the spouse without putting undue pressure on the third party.

In *Thomas* v *Thomas* [1995] 2 FLR 668 the husband was a joint manager of a successful family business owned by his family. The company's policy was to pay the husband a modest salary and plough profits back into the business. He was a name at Lloyds and had liabilities as a result of the losses in the insurance market. The wife had no assets and no independent income though she was training to be a nursery nurse. The judge made a clean break order whereby the husband paid the wife a lump sum of £158,000. There was also provision for child maintenance and the payment of school fees. The husband appealed arguing that the lump sum was improper and placed unfair pressure on him to throw himself on the charity of other members of his family.

HELD: Dismissing the appeal, the courts were not limited to the resources of capital or income the parties actually had. Where a spouse enjoyed access to wealth but no absolute entitlement to it the court would not act in direct invasion of the rights or usurp the discretion of a third party. The court would not put upon a third party undue pressure to act in a way which would enhance the means of the maintaining spouse. However the court could not ignore potential wealth owned or administered by others. It could make orders which encouraged third parties to provide the maintaining spouse with the means to comply with the court's view of the justice of the case. In this case the husband had immediate liquidity problems but had substantial means. The lump sum order was a powerful inducement to the extended family to come to his help but fell within the bounds of judicial encouragement and well short of placing improper pressure on third parties.

Other examples of cases where family assets were considered include:

1. *O'Donnell* v *O'Donnell* [1975] 3 WLR 308; [1975] 2 All ER 993 where the husband's family made large investments into his hotel business and this led to increased orders for the wife;
2. *Hardy* v *Hardy* (1981) 11 Fam Law 153 where a husband worked for his wealthy father on a low income of £70 a week and had no capital assets. He expected a large settlement from his wealthy father. The mother lived in a rented house on social security with the two children of the marriage. The court decided that she was entitled to both a maintenance order and a lump sum. The court could see no reason why the husband should enjoy the privilege of working for his father at a low wage at the expense of his wife and children. It made a maintenance order of £50 a week. It adjourned the matter of the lump sum until the husband has assets settled on him;
3. *B* v *B* (1982) 12 Fam Law 92 where the wife came from a wealthy family and

was a beneficiary under two substantial settlements – she was ordered to pay the husband a lump sum of £50,000 since the court considered it proper to treat the settlement as her assets – she could raise the lump sum by selling some of the assets or borrowing on the strength of them.

## Income of a new spouse on remarriage or of a new partner

After divorce a party may remarry or live with a new partner. The income of that new spouse or partner will be considered in so far as that income relieves the party of any bills or other financial obligations he or she would otherwise have to pay (see *Macey* v *Macey* (1981) 11 Fam Law 248 and *Slater* v *Slater* (1982) 3 FLR 364). To this extent a court can require information about a new spouse or partner's means. In *Wilkinson* v *Wilkinson* (1979) 10 Fam Law 49 the court required details of the means of the husband's new wife in order to get full details of his circumstances.

However no order will be made which effectively would be paid out of the new spouse or partner's income or capital. In *Brown* v *Brown* (1981) 11 Fam Law 247 the husband was unemployed. His new partner was working. As a result he received no state benefits and was entirely supported by her. No maintenance could be ordered against him since he had no means of his own. Similarly, in *Wynne* v *Wynne* [1981] 1 WLR 69; [1980] 3 All ER 659 the husband was unemployed. His new partner was wealthy and he lived with her in a luxurious apartment in Knightsbridge. Since he had no means of his own, no maintenance could be ordered against him.

## Property owned by a spouse before marriage

There is a widely held view that property owned by a spouse before the marriage should be treated differently from property acquired during the marriage. This view argues that in fairness, where such property still exists, the spouse to whom it was given should be allowed to keep it. The claim of the other spouse to it is weaker. In *White* v *White* (above) Lord Nicholls said that such property should be considered as part of 'all the circumstances of the case' and as a 'contribution to the welfare of the family' (under s25(2)(f)). The court should consider the nature and value of the property and the time and circumstances in which it was acquired. He was of the view that in the ordinary case such a factor could be expected to carry little weight, if any, where the claimant's financial needs could be met without recourse to such property.

## Property acquired after the divorce has been granted

Some spouses have argued that any property they have acquired after they have separated or been divorced should not been taken into account. This argument has not been accepted by the courts. In *Schuller* v *Schuller* [1990] 2 FLR 193, W and H divorced. W then went to work for an elderly friend. On the friend's death she inherited a flat. W argued that the flat was 'an after acquired asset' and had nothing to do with her marriage to H and should not be considered in settling financial relief between them. The Court of Appeal did not accept that argument and held that the flat was extremely relevant to deciding on financial provision.

## Section 25(2)(b)

These needs and obligations will include the everyday needs of the parties for food, clothing, accommodation, etc. The demands of bringing up the children will be of importance since their welfare is the first consideration.

The court will have regard to the need for a wife and children to be housed. See *Mesher* v *Mesher* [1980] 1 All ER 126 where the matrimonial home was held on a trust for sale in equal shares to the husband and wife, but the sale suspended for the wife and children to occupy the house until the youngest child became seventeen or finished full-time education. A similar order was made in *Allen* v *Allen* [1974] 1 WLR 1171; [1974] 3 All ER 385 taking into account the needs and obligations of a wife and children under s25(2)(b).

This will also apply to where the husband has the custody of the children. See *Browne* v *Pritchard* [1975] 1 WLR 1366; [1975] 3 All ER 721 where the court refused to order the sale of the matrimonial home in which the husband and the two children lived. The husband was unemployed. He could not buy the wife out. She was housed in a council house. The house was placed on a trust for sale with a one-third share to the wife and the sale postponed until the youngest child became eighteen and a half years of age.

The need for a house, to provide for contact visits, may also be considered. See *Calderbank* v *Calderbank* [1975] 3 WLR 586; [1975] 3 All ER 333 where the husband needed accommodation for the children when they came to stay with him for access visits.

In *M* v *B (Ancillary Proceedings: Lump Sum)* [1998] 1 FLR 53 it was confirmed that a lump sum could be ordered to allow a parent to have accommodation for contact. A similar decision was reached in *H* v *H (Financial Relief: Contact)* [1998] 1 FLR 971.

### The obligation of a second family

The fact that a husband has undertaken the legal responsibility of maintaining a new wife must be fully borne in mind and be given the same weight and degree as his responsibilities in any other respect (see *Barnes* v *Barnes* [1972] 1 WLR 1381; [1972] 3 All ER 872).

See also *Stockford* v *Stockford* (1982) 3 FLR 58 where the husband remarried and took on a second mortgage to buy a house for his second wife and their child. The second wife stopped working when the baby was due. The husband's only capital was tied up in the first home occupied by the first wife and the child of the first marriage. The court decided that the first wife could go out to work to earn more and because of the husband's new financial obligations the maintenance order for the first wife was reduced to allow the husband to maintain his second family.

See similarly *Furniss* v *Furniss* (1982) 3 FLR 46 where maintenance was reduced for the first wife to allow the husband to maintain his new wife and three children.

See *Delaney* v *Delaney* [1990] 2 FLR 457 where the husband and wife had three children. They divorced. The wife was in difficult financial circumstances. She applied for maintenance for herself and the children. The husband after a long period of unemployment got a job with a low wage. He lived with a woman whom he hoped to marry. They lived in a one-bedroomed flat which was unsuitable for when the children came for contact. He, therefore, acquired an interest in a three bedroomed house which significantly increased his outgoings to £179 a week from a joint income with his cohabitee of £212 a week. The judge held that the house exceeded the husband's needs and that he had incurred unnecessary and excessive obligations when his first obligation was to his children. He ordered the husband to pay £10 a week to each of the three children. The husband appealed.

HELD: When assessing the amount of financial provision the court should have first regard to the needs of the wife and the children for proper support. It should then consider the husband's ability to meet those needs in the light of the realities of the world. A former husband was entitled to balance his future aspirations for a new life against his responsibilities to his former family per Wood J:

> 'Whilst this court deprecates any notion that a former husband and ... father may slough off the tight skin of familial responsibilities and may slither into and lose himself in the greener grass on the other side nonetheless this court has proclaimed and will proclaim that it looks to the realities of the real world ... and that among the realities of life is that there is life after divorce. The respondent husband is entitled to order his life in such a way as will hold in reasonable balance the responsibilities to his existing family which he carried into his new life, as well as his proper aspirations for that new future.'

In this case the husband was entitled to have suitable accommodation for staying in contact with his children. He could not be said to be behaving extravagantly or unreasonably. Having regard to the husband's reasonable financial commitments and his girlfriend's due contribution there was insufficient properly to maintain the former wife and children. Social security benefits were available to the wife and children. The court would avoid making orders financially crippling to the husband. In the spirit of the clean break a nominal order would be made for each child (*Stockford* v *Stockford* applied).

These cases show the difficulties of paying for two families from one income.

### The 'reasonable requirements' approach
In the case of wealthy spouses the courts devised an approach whereby the wife would only receive such property as would meet her 'reasonable requirements' (see *O'Donnell* v *O'Donnell* [1975] 2 All ER 993, *Page* v *Page* (1981) 2 FLR 201, *Preston* v *Preston* [1981] 2 WLR 619; [1982] 1 All ER 41, *Thyssen-Bornemisza* v *Thyssen-Bornemisza* [1985] 2 WLR 715 and *Dart* v *Dart* [1996] 2 FLR 286). This approach resulted in a wife from a wealthy marriage receiving only a small proportion of the

matrimonial assets because this was all that was required to meet her reasonable needs (eg the wife in *Dart* v *Dart* received a lump sum of £9 million having sought £122 million). This approach was rejected by the House of Lords in *White* v *White* (above) which held that a claimant's needs could not be regarded as determining what she should receive. The court had to take into account the respective contribution of the spouses. A husband may have made a contribution to the welfare of the family through his business or employment and the wife through looking after the home and bringing up the children. Lord Nicholls asked: 'Why should the claimant wife be confined to the court's assessment of her reasonable requirements and the husband left with a much larger share?'; and 'In a case where the assets exceed the financial needs of both parties why should the surplus belong solely to the husband?' His answer was that the mere absence of financial need cannot, by itself, be a sufficient reason for such an approach. 'If it were, discrimination would be creeping in by the back door.' The court is required to look at all the circumstances and check any award against the yardstick of equality (as outlined above under *Section 25(1) – having regard to all the circumstances – the yardstick of equal division*).

### The next generation

If there are surplus resources available an extra award is permissible to allow a spouse to provide gifts and financial support and an inheritance for adult independent children and for grandchildren (see *Vicary* v *Vicary* [1992] 2 FLR 271 and *White* v *White* (above)). A parent's wish to be in a position to leave money to his or her children does not normally fall within s25(2)(b) unless the resources exceed the parties' financial needs. If there are such resources then the court can give such weight to such a wish as appropriate in all the circumstances of the case.

### Special needs

See *Smith* v *Smith* [1975] 2 All ER 19 where the wife had to care for a daughter with a serious kidney complaint. The wife could only work part time so that she could look after her. The wife had no job security because of her commitments to her daughter. She would not be able to house herself even if her daughter were able to leave home and the matrimonial home sold and the proceeds divided between the husband and wife. The court transfered the house to the wife absolutely.

## *Section 25(2)(c)*

An earlier provision required the court to seek to place the parties in the position in which they would have been had the marriage not broken down. This was considered unrealistic in relation to parties with limited or modest means where there is invariably a reduction in the standard of living. As a result the court has regard to the standard of living enjoyed by the family before the breakdown of the marriage. Where there is a reduction in the standard of living the courts will seek to distribute that reduction evenly (see *Scott* v *Scott* [1978] 1 WLR 723; [1978] 3 All ER 65).

In the case of wealthy spouses the court may be able to make orders which do not involve any significant reduction in the the parties' living standards. In *Calderbank* v *Calderbank* [1975] 3 WLR 586; [1975] 3 All ER 333 the wife was wealthy and the husband unemployed. They had enjoyed a rich lifestyle. The husband was given a capital award to enable him to purchase accommodation 'suitable to his station in life and suitable for the accommodation of the three children when they came to stay with him'. See also *Foley* v *Foley* [1981] 3 WLR 284; [1981] 2 All ER 857 and *B* v *B (Financial Provision)* [1990] 1 FLR 20. As can be seen from *White* v *White* (above) any orders should be checked against the yardstick of equality.

If spouses have chosen to live frugally while money is ploughed into a business this does not mean that the courts will make a frugal order. See *Preston* v *Preston* [1981] 3 WLR 619; [1982] 1 All ER 41 and *Vicary* v *Vicary* [1992] 2 FLR 271 in which orders were made to reflect the improved lifestyle of the spouses once the business had prospered.

## Section 25(2)(d)

The age of the parties can be an important factor. A young wife is more likely to be considered under the clean break provisions in s25A. An older wife may need financial security in her later years, especially if she has not worked and has few pension rights apart from a state pension. See the cases discussed in relation to ss5 and 10 MCA 1973 in relation to the financial protection of spouses in cases of divorce under s1(2)(d) and (e).

### The duration of a marriage

In earlier cases, even in the case of a very short marriage, financial provision could be ordered. See *Brett* v *Brett* [1969] 1 WLR 487; [1969] 1 All ER 1007 where after only five and a half months of marriage the wife was entitled to a large order to keep her in the wealthy lifestyle to which she had become accustomed. See also *Cumbers* v *Cumbers* [1974] 1 WLR 1331; [1975] 1 All ER 1 where after only eighteen months of marriage a wife was given a lump sum as compensation for the transfer of her third share in the house to the husband.

However, given s25A, short, childless marriages are likely to result in either no financial provision being ordered or being ordered for only a limited period.

See *Khan* v *Khan* [1980] 1 WLR 355; [1980] 1 All ER 499 where the marriage lasted nine months. Even though it was the husband who brought the marriage to an end, the maintenance order to the wife was limited to twelve months since the wife was young and able to go out to work. See the further discussion of s25A.

See *Attar* v *Attar (No 2)* [1985] FLR 653 where the husband was a wealthy Saudi Arabian who married an English air hostess. The marriage only lasted six months. The wife gave up her job as an air stewardess after the marriage. The court ordered a lump sum to allow the wife to readjust after the end of the marriage to leave her in a position as if the marriage had not taken place. She received the equivalent to two years of her wages which would enable her to get back into work and re-establish herself in society.

For an extreme case of a short marriage see *Krystmann* v *Krystmann* [1973] 1 WLR 927; [1973] 3 All ER 247 where the spouses only lived together for fourteen days before separating for the next twenty-six years. It was held that the wife had no entitlement to any financial provision from the husband.

### Cohabitation before marriage

Cohabitation before marriage is not normally considered as relevant under s25(2)(d). See *Campbell* v *Campbell* [1976] 3 WLR 572; [1977] 1 All ER 1 where there was an ill-considered affair between a seventeen-year-old youth and a woman aged thirty. They cohabited for three and a half years because the woman was already married. They then married. The marriage lasted two years.

HELD: The marriage was a short one. The cohabitation was irrelevant. The rights, duties and obligations of the parties only began on marriage. The court would not cheapen marriage by comparing it with cohabitation. The maintenance order would be reduced because of the shortness of the marriage.

See also *H* v *H* (1981) 2 FLR 392 where the parties cohabited 'on and off' for six years. They got married and the marriage lasted seven weeks.

HELD: The cohabitation lacked any permanence and should be ignored. Due to the shortness of the marriage the wife had suffered no financial loss and both she and the husband could go their separate ways and earn their living without any order being made except a lump sum of £3,500 to enable the wife to adjust to the change in her circumstances.

See *Foley* v *Foley* [1981] 3 WLR 284; [1981] 2 All ER 857 where the parties cohabited for seven years. They had three children in that period. They then got married. The marriage lasted five years.

HELD: Cohabitation was not the same as marriage and did not carry the same weight. However, cohabitation could be 'other circumstances' within the meaning of s25(2) to which the court could have regard. The weight to be attached to it depended on the circumstances.

In *Day* v *Day* [1988] 1 FLR 278 the wife had two children from a previous relationship. She formed a relationship with Mr Day which lasted over four years. They got married but the marriage last only six weeks because Mr Day prefered the bachelor life. *H* v *H* was distinguished since in that case both parties were capable of earning a living, there were no children and capital was available. In this case Mr Day had assumed responsibility for Mrs Day and for the children whom he knew were not his. He was ordered to pay maintenance to both her and the two children.

If parties are prevented from getting married and are, therefore, forced to cohabit then cohabitation can be a weighty factor. See *Kokosinski* v *Kokosinski* [1980] 3 WLR

55; [1980] 1 All ER 1106 where the parties cohabited for twenty-two years. They had a son and a matrimonial home was bought in that period. The wife changed her name to that of the husband by deed poll. They could not get married since the husband was already married and could not get divorced. They then did get married but a few months later the husband left. After six years of living apart the wife divorced the husband.

HELD: The wife had given the best years of her life to the husband during the time they lived together. She had helped him in his business and brought up his son. Those twenty-two years would be fully considered. The wife was given a large lump sum to enable her to buy a flat near where she worked.

In *S v S (Financial Provision)(Post-Divorce Cohabitation)* [1994] 2 FLR 228, H and W divorced in 1977 and a consent order dealing with financial matters was made. They then reconciled and lived together and did not separate until 1993. W successfully appealed against the consent order out of time. In recalculating her entitlement the court took into account the duration of the marriage (eight years). It also took into account the longer period they had lived together both before and after the marriage as part of 'all the circumstances of the case' since, during this time, W had helped run the family home, been a mother to the children, worked part of the time and been a loyal wife for H who was a rising and successful businessman. A lump sum of £285,000 was awarded to her.

### Section 25(2)(e)

See *Jones* v *Jones* [1975] 2 WLR 606; [1975] 2 All ER 12 where the wife was attacked with a knife by her husband. The tendon in her right hand was severed. She could not work again. She had no security for her later years. The matrimonial home was transferred to her absolutely.

See *B* v *B* (1982) 3 FLR 299 where the wife suffered from multiple sclerosis. Her future incapacity would result in substantial demands on her income and she was entitled to a higher award.

See *Seaton* v *Seaton* [1986] 2 FLR 398 where the husband had a severe heart attack after the divorce. As a result he could barely speak and his understanding was limited. His quality of life was greatly reduced. There was no prospect of recovery.

HELD: There was no need for court to require his wife to pay maintenance for his support. He lived with his parents and received a disability pension. Any payment from the wife could have little material effect in enhancing his limited enjoyment of life and there was no point in making an order.

In *Sakkas* v *Sakkas* [1987] Fam Law 414 the sole asset was the matrimonial home. The husband gave up work due to multiple sclerosis. His condition would deteriorate as the years went by whereby he would be confined to a wheelchair and would be in need of constant care. The wife and two children remained in the matrimonial home while the husband lived with his sister.

HELD: A *Mesher* order would be made allowing the wife to occupy the matrimonial home until the youngest child was twenty. The house would then be sold. The shares would not be determined until then since only then could a court assess the needs of the husband as well as providing the wife with a home.

In *Newton* v *Newton* [1990] 1 FLR 33 allowance had to be made for the wife's serious physical, emotional and psychological disabilities. This meant that she required resident companionship and help with transport. The court made provision for this.

## Section 25(2)(f)

It is this provision that usually gives rise to a non-working spouse's claim to a share in the matrimonial assets, particularly the matrimonial home. Lord Denning's views in *Wachtel* v *Wachtel* [1973] 2 WLR 366; [1973] 1 All ER 829 remain valid (though references to the 'wife' could now equally apply to a non-working husband):

> 'We may take it that Parliament recognised that the wife who looks after the home and family contributed as much to the family assets as the wife who goes out to work. The one contributes in kind, the other in money or money's worth. If the court considers that the home has been acquired and maintained by the joint efforts of both, then, when the marriage breaks down, it should be regarded as the joint property of both of them, no matter in whose name it stands. Just as a wife who makes substantial money contributions usually gets a share so should the wife who looks after the home and cares for the family for 20 years or more.'

The position was restated by Lord Nicholls in *White* v *White* (above):

> 'In seeking to achieve a fair outcome, there is no place for discrimination between husband and wife in their respective roles. Typically, a husband and wife share the activities of earning money, running their home and caring for their children. Traditionally, the husband earned the money and the wife looked after the children. This traditional division of labour is no longer the order of the day. Frequently both parents work. Sometimes it is the wife who is the money earner, and the husband runs the home and cares for the children during the day. But whatever the division of labour chosen by the husband and wife, or forced upon them by circumstances, fairness requires that this should not prejudice or advantage either party when considering s25(2)(f), relating to the parties' contributions. This is implicit in the very language of s25(2)(f). ...
>
> If in their different spheres, each contributed equally to the family, then in principle it matters not which of them earned the money and built up the assets. There should be no bias in favour of the money-earner and against the home-maker and the child-carer.'

The Court of Appeal emphasised the importance of the role of the homemaker in *Lambert* v *Lambert* [2003] 1 FLR 139 and awarded her half of the assets.

Illustrations of s25(2)(f) in action includes cases where the wife died before the ancillary relief orders were finalised. In such cases the wife's estate may still be awarded an order to recognise the wife's contribution to the welfare of the family (see *Smith* v *Smith* [1991] 2 All ER 306; [1991] 2 FLR 432 and *Barber* v *Barber* [1992] Fam Law 436). Contributions to the running of a family business which has produced the income for the family have also been recognised (see *O'Donnell* v *O'Donnell* [1975] 3 WLR 308; [1975] 2 All ER 993, *Gojkovic* v *Gojkovic* [1991] 3 WLR 621; [1990] 2 All ER 84, *Vicary* v *Vicary* [1992] 2 FLR 271, *Conran* v *Conran* [1997] 2 FLR 615 and *Dart* v *Dart* [1996] 2 FLR 286. Though these cases show increased orders for spouses who made such contributions they now have to be read in light of *White* v *White* (above) and the yardstick of equal division.

A lack of contribution can be a minus factor. In *West* v *West* [1977] 2 WLR 933; [1997] 2 All ER 705 the wife refused to leave her parents' house and set up home with her husband. Her lack of contribution to the family meant that she received a smaller order. In *E* v *E* [1990] 2 FLR 233 the wife was extravagant and neglected the three children. She had affairs (though the husband also had an affair). She abandoned the husband. Her behaviour was not considered as conduct under s25(2)(g) but as a negative contribution under s25(2)(f).

The contribution must be made during the marriage. Contributions during pre-marital cohabitation could be taken into account (see *Foley* v *Foley* and *Kokosinki* v *Kokosinski* (above)).

Future contributions which the parties are likely to make in the foreseeable future are also considered. This will be particularly relevant to the parent who is to look after the children after the divorce.

## Section 25(2)(g)

According to *Wachtel* v *Wachtel* (above) conduct would be relevant to the consideration of financial and property claims only if it was 'both obvious and gross'. The courts will wish to avoid going over allegations and counter allegations of matrimonial misconduct unless they are relevant to the financial claims.

NOTE Lord Denning's views in *Wachtel:*

'It has been suggested that there should be a "discount" or "reduction" in what the wife is to receive because of her supposed misconduct, guilt or blame (whatever word is used). We cannot accept this argument. In the vast majority of cases it is repugnant to the principles underlying the new legislation and in particular the 1969 Act. There will be many cases in which a wife (although once considered guilty or blameworthy) will have cared for the home and looked after the family for very many years. Is she to be deprived of the benefit otherwise to be accorded to her by section 5(1)(f) because she may share responsibility for the breakdown with her husband? There will be no doubt a residue of cases where the conduct of one of the parties is in the judge's words "both obvious and gross", so much so that to order one party to support another whose conduct falls into this category is repugnant to anyone's sense of justice. In such a case the court remains free to decline to afford financial support or to reduce the support which it would otherwise have ordered. But, short of cases falling into this category, the court should not reduce its order for financial provision merely because of what was formerly regarded as guilt or blame. To do so would be to impose a fine for supposed misbehaviour in the course of an unhappy married life. Counsel for the husband disputed this and claimed that it was justice that a wife should suffer for her supposed misbehaviour. We do not agree.

Criminal justice often requires the imposition of financial and indeed custodial penalties. But in the financial adjustments consequent on the dissolution of a marriage which has irretrievably broken down, the imposition of financial penalties ought seldom to find a place.'

In *Vasey* v *Vasey* [1985] FLR 596 Dunn LJ said that it is exceptional to take into account conduct because:

'… experience has shown that it is dangerous to make judgments about the cause of the breakdown of a marriage without full enquiry, since the conduct of the one spouse can only be measured against the conduct of the other and marriages seldom break down without fault on both sides.'

See *E* v *E* [1990] 2 FLR 233 as an illustration of the court's reluctance to take conduct into account (though behaviour during the marriage was considered under s25(2)(f) instead).

The Law Commission in its report on the financial consequences of divorce (Law Com No 112) also took the view that the courts could not be expected to apportion responsibility for the breakdown of the marriage, and it felt it would be quite wrong to require a court to hear the allegations and counter allegations made by the parties where they would have little effect on the outcome of the proceedings and where they would probably only hinder the process by which the parties come to terms with the breakdown of the marriage.

The Law Commission did recognise, however, that there would be exceptional cases where responsibility for the breakdown of the marriage can be identified, and should be when assessing financial orders. The Commission recognised the dangers of treating the phrase 'obvious and gross' as a statutory formula, fettering as it did the court's discretion in some cases. It felt that the court needs to examine sufficient of the matrimonial history to enable the judge to 'get the feel of the case', and thus be in a position to carry out its duty 'to take account of conduct in those cases where to do otherwise would offend a reasonable person's sense of justice'.

Section 25(2)(g), therefore, provides that conduct is to be considered as relevant only if it would be inequitable to disregard it.

### Where conduct is not relevant

After the spouses have separated they are free to lead their own lives. Therefore, cohabitation following separation is not normally conduct the court wishes to consider: see *Duxbury* v *Duxbury* [1987] 1 FLR 7, where both parties had had extra-marital affairs. The wife's conduct had not led to the breakdown of the marriage. The fact she was living with someone after they separated was not relevant. Section 25 was a financial exercise, not a moral one.

See also *Atkinson* v *Atkinson* [1987] 3 All ER 849 where a wife was living with another man after the parties had divorced. The husband asked that her conduct be taken into account in his application to reduce her maintenance order.

HELD: A punitive approach with regard to conduct was wrong. The variety of human folly is infinite. There may well be cases in which an ex-wife's conduct in the context of cohabitation, such as financial irresponsibility or sexual or other misconduct, may make it necessary and appropriate that a periodical payments order should be discharged or be a nominal order. The overall circumstances, particularly the financial consequences, may be such that it would be inappropriate for there to be a maintenance order (as in *Suter* v *Suter and Jones* [1987] 2 All ER 336, see below). But in general there is no statutory requirement that the court give decisive weight to such cohabitation. If the court were to do so it would impose an unjustified fetter on the freedom of an ex-wife to lead her own life as she chooses following a divorce.

In *Atkinson* v *Atkinson (No 2)* [1996] 1 FLR 51 (Court of Appeal), W was cohabiting. A maintenance order was made of £10,000 pa. H appealed on the basis that only a nominal order should have been made. His appeal was dismissed since on the facts the maintenance order was justified and not manifestly unjust.

### Where conduct is relevant

*Violence to a spouse.* See *Jones* v *Jones* [1975] 2 WLR 606; [1975] 2 All ER 12 where the husband attacked his wife with a knife causing her severe injuries which left her disabled in her right hand. She could not work. The husband's conduct had direct financial consequences. The matrimonial home was transfered to the wife absolutely to give her security (the husband was imprisoned for three years for the attack).

See *Armstrong* v *Armstrong* (1974) 118 SJ 579 where the wife fired a shotgun at her husband, and *Bateman* v *Bateman* [1979] 2 WLR 377 where the wife stabbed her husband on two separate occasions in the course of arguments. Such conduct was considered relevant.

In *Evans* v *Evans* [1989] 1 FLR 351 the husband regularly paid his wife her maintenance over many years. She was then convicted of inciting others to murder him. Her maintenance order was discharged.

In *H* v *H (Financial Provision)* [1994] 2 FLR 80, H and W were married and enjoyed a comfortable lifestyle. They jointly owned the matrimonial home. This lifestyle and the marriage was ended when H violently assaulted W. H was sent to prison for three and a half years. As a result of her injuries W became unemployed. She did receive £8,000 compensation from the Criminal Injuries Compensation Board. H was released from prison and W feared for her personal safety. He was unemployed. W worked part time and looked after the children.

HELD: As a result of H's conduct H's half-share in the matrimonial home would be transferred to W. This was the only way to give W and the children a stable home.

*Repugnant sexual behaviour.* In *Bailey* v *Tolliday* (1983) 4 FLR 542 the wife had an affair with her father-in-law. In *Dixon* v *Dixon* (1974) 6 Fam Law 58 the husband committed adultery with his daughter-in-law in the matrimonial home. In both cases the court considered such behaviour particularly repugnant and made orders as to financial provision accordingly.

**Financial misconduct.** See *Martin* v *Martin* [1976] 2 WLR 901; [1976] 3 All ER 625 where the husband left his wife and set up a series of unsuccessful business ventures with another woman, financed by mortgaging family assets. He dissipated over £33,000 of family assets. Meanwhile, the wife continued to run the farm and keep it viable.

HELD: All the assets the husband had dissipated should be taken into account. The wife was awarded the whole beneficial interest in the remaining assets, subject to paying off the mortgage the husband had incurred. She was also awarded a lump sum of £2,000 representing the husband's interest in his current venture.

In *Wells* v *Wells* [1992] 2 FLR 66; [1992] Fam Law 386 (decided in 1980) the husband had failed to comply with an order of maintenance pending suit. His conduct led to the wife incurring extra costs. As a result his entitlement to a half share in the former matrimonial home was reduced to a quarter share.

See *Suter* v *Suter and Jones* [1987] 2 All ER 336 where after the husband had left the matrimonial home, the wife invited her young lover to come and live with her and the children. The young man, who spent most nights with the wife, made no contribution towards the wife's new household, despite having the means to do so.

HELD: The wife's conduct in inviting the young man to live with her without requiring him to make any contribution to the running of the house was relevant and could not be disregarded. The husband's obligation to contribute to the wife's support was reduced to a nominal order.

In *Day* v *Day* [1988] 1 FLR 278 the husband encouraged the wife not to pay rent so that the money could be spent on other things. Rent arrears of £100 built up. The husband was ordered to pay a lump sum of £100.

In *B* v *B* [1988] 2 FLR 490 the wife's dishonesty in failing to disclose her income and disobeying the court's order to disclose her affairs was not only a contempt of court but conduct which it would be inequitable to disregard since it was primarily aimed at obstructing the husband's pursuit of remedies. The wife's lump sum was reduced.

The husband had a serious drink problem and personality disorder in *K* v *K* [1990] Fam Law 19; [1990] 2 FLR 225. He neglected the matrimonial home which had to be sold as a result. After being made redundant he did not work again and drifted around as a homeless person from one bed-sit to another. By contrast the wife had obtained well-paid employment and a flat of her own. The husband claimed 70 per cent of the proceeds of sale of the home so that he could buy a house plus maintenance of £5,000 a year for three years from the wife.

HELD: The test for conduct was whether a right thinking member of society would say that a spouse's conduct was such as to reduce or extinguish a spouse's entitlement. The husband's present situation had been largely self-inflicted whereas the wife had made great efforts to improve herself. The husband had caused the house to be sold. It would be unjust to order the wife to pay him maintenance. However, he did have an urgent need for accommodation, and so he was entitled to 60 per cent of the proceeds of sale.

*Abandoning the blameless spouse.* Where a spouse has unilaterally and unreasonably abandoned a spouse against whom there is no criticism courts have considered such conduct as relevant under s25(2)(g)

See *West* v *West* (above) where the wife refused to allow the marriage to work by refusing to live in the matrimonial home with the husband (though this was caused by a personality defect).

In *Cuzner* v *Underdown* [1974] 1 WLR 641; [1974] 2 All ER 357 the husband had paid for the matrimonial home. He put it in the joint names of himself and his wife. At this time she was having an affair with the co-respondent, and had the husband known of the affair he would not have transferred the house into joint names. The wife asked the court to require the house to be sold so that she could realise her half share and use it to set up home with the co-respondent.

HELD: The wife's application was an impudent one. She was trying to turn a blameless husband out of his own house. Given the way she had behaved her application was dismissed.

See *Robinson* v *Robinson* [1983] 2 WLR 146; [1983] 1 All ER 391 where the wife unilaterally and without excuse abandoned the husband. He appeared to be entirely blameless and in the circumstances the wife's conduct could not be disregarded. Her periodical payments were substantially reduced.

Similarly, in *Ibbetson* v *Ibbetson* [1984] FLR 545 the wife left her husband after five years of marriage. She could make no complaint against him to explain her conduct. The lump sum awarded to her was deleted.

*Pre-nuptial agreements.* In *M* v *M* [2002] Fam Law 177 H and W entered into a pre-nuptial agreement whereby if the marriage ended in divorce W would receive £275,000. After five years of marriage W filed for divorce. They had a child who lived with W. An order was made that W receive £875,000 from H's assets of £7.5 million. The first consideration was the child's welfare under s25(1). The pre-nuptial agreement was relevant as part of all the circumstances. It was also relevant under s25(2)(g). It was unjust to ignore the agreement but also to hold W strictly to it. It did not dictate W's settlement. Given the length of the marriage it was agreed that this not a case for equal division of the assets.

See also Chapter 14.

*Other cases.* *J(HD)* v *J(AM)* (*Financial Provision: Variation*) [1980] 1 WLR 124; [1980] 1 All ER 156. The wife suffered from chronic schizophrenia. She conducted a malicious campaign of persecution against her husband after his remarriage. She assaulted him and his new wife, sent letters and made telephone calls and made his and his new family's life a misery.

HELD: Such conduct could not be ignored even though it came after the divorce and after the wife's right to financial relief had been established. Some of the wife's behaviour was involuntary but some was intentional. If she carried on in this way she could forfeit her right to maintenance altogether.

In *Kyte* v *Kyte* [1987] 3 All ER 1041 the husband suffered from depression and was unpredictable and suicidal. The wife obtained an injunction excluding him from the matrimonial home and obtained a divorce on the grounds of his behaviour. The husband then discovered that his wife had been carrying on a secret affair with another man and the proceedings were in reality an attempt to get rid of him so that she could set up home with this other man. On one occasion when the husband had attempted suicide the wife had taken no steps to prevent the attempt. On a second occasion she had actively encouraged him and taunted him when he did not go through with it. The wife lied to the court about the extent of her relationship with the other man.

HELD: For the purpose of s25(2)(g) conduct included any relevant conduct during and after the marriage which might have contributed to its breakdown or which it would be otherwise inequitable to ignore, regardless of whether or not the other spouse's conduct was blameless. The wife's conduct not only in actively assisting or taking no steps to prevent the husband's suicide attempts, when she knew she would gain financially if he succeeded, but also in forming a deceitful relationship with another man was gross and obvious conduct which it would be inequitable to disregard even taking into account the husband's own conduct. The lump sum awarded to her was reduced from £14,000 to £5,000.

In *Whiston* v *Whiston* [1995] 3 WLR 405; [1998] 1 All ER 423; [1995] 2 FLR 268 W married H in 1973. In 1988 the parties separated. H then discovered that W was already married and was granted a decree of nullity because the marriage was void. W applied for ancillary relief. H argued that W should not be entitled to any financial relief because of her behaviour. The judge awarded her a lump sum of £25,000. On appeal this was reduced to £20,000. The husband further appealed.

HELD: Allowing the appeal and ordering that the wife receive no ancillary relief, the offence of bigamy strikes at the heart of marriage. Section 25(2)(g) allowed the court to consider matters of public policy. The court should be slow to allow a bigamist to assert a claim which arises out of her offending. The situation might be different if a party entered into a bigamous marriage genuinely and reasonably believing that he or she was free to do so. Such a person lacked the mental intention to be guilty of bigamy and may have an entitlement.

In *S-T (formerly J)* v *J* [1998] 1 All ER 431 J was born female but lived and was socially accepted as a male. He underwent sex-change surgery. He went through a marriage with S-T without advising her of his female gender and declared he was a bachelor and that there was no impediment to the marriage. When divorce proceedings were instituted, S-T discovered that J had been born female and petitioned for nullity under s11(c) MCA 1973. J applied for ancillary relief. The court dismissed his claim on the basis of his false declaration which amounted to a serious crime which struck at the heart of marriage. J appealed and it was held, dismissing the appeal, that the mere fact that the marriage had been contracted in circumstances which involved the commission of a serious crime (other than bigamy) could not debar a claim for ancillary relief (*Whiston* v *Whiston* distinguished). J's claim fell to be considered under s25 MCA 1973 which included consideration of his conduct. Section 25(1) allowed the court to take into account all the circumstances which included public policy considerations. In this case his conduct at the time of the marriage was such that that he was not entitled to any relief.

In *Rampal* v *Rampal (No 2)* [2001] 3 FCR 552 it was held that *Whiston* v *Whiston* was not authority for barring ancillary relief from every culpable bigamist whatever the circumstances. In the case the culpable bigamist, H, was entitled to ancillary relief. His 'second wife' had arranged the marriage, was aware of the bigamy and embraced the desired respectability for 22 years and only alleged bigamy when H applied for ancillary relief.

Note: The court should only take into account marital conduct – not misconduct during the litigation. Any litigation misconduct could be reflected in an order for costs (see *Tavoularos* v *Tavoularos* [1998] 2 FLR 418).

## 7.7 Considerations involving children

The Child Support Agency deals with almost all aspects of child maintenance. The courts retain jurisdiction to make child maintenance orders in the following areas:

1. child maintenance to a child of the family who is not the child of the payer (eg a step-child);
2. child maintenance to a child over 19 years of age (or between 16 and 19 years of age and not in full-time education);
3. in the case of a wealthy parents child maintenance above the maximum amount of child support which can be paid;
4. the payment of school fees;
5. child maintenance in relation to a child who is not habitually resident in England and Wales;
6. where the child is disabled and child maintenance is to meet expenses attributable to the child's disability (s8(3), (6)–(9) Child Support Act 1991).

There is jurisdiction for a court to make a child maintenance order if there is a pre-existing written agreement for payment of maintenance and the court order confirms that agreement (s8(5) Child Support Act 1991). A practice has been established whereby maintenance orders are made under s23(1)(a) MCA 1973 in favour of the spouse who cares for the children, for the benefit of the children, as a holding device until the Child Support Agency can carry out child support assessments. The spousal maintenance would then be reduced by the amount of the child support assessment. In *Dorney-Kingdom* v *Dorney-Kingdom* [2000] Fam Law

794 it was held by the Court of Appeal that such orders could be made and was allowed under s8(5) Child Support Act 1991. However, such orders should only be made where the parties consented to such an order.

The court can make lump sum and/or property orders for a child. The powers under ss23(1)(f), 24 and 24A MCA 1973 are not affected by the Child Support Act 1991.

Where the court does have jurisdiction to make a child maintenance order and/or a lump sum and/or a property adjustment order it must have particular regard to s25(3) MCA 1973, which provides:

'(a) the financial needs of the child;
(b) the income, earning capacity (if any), property and other financial resources of the child;
(c) any physical or mental disability of the child;
(d) the manner in which her was being and in which the parties to the marriage expected him to be educated or trained;
(e) the conisderations mentioned in relation to the parties to the marriage in paragraphs (a), (b), (c) and (e) of subsection (2) above.'

Examples of the court considering such matters include *O'Donnell* v *O'Donnell* [1975] 3 WLR 308; [1975] 2 All ER 993 and *Sibley* v *Sibley* (1979) 10 Fam Law 49 in which the husbands were ordered to pay for the private education of the children as had been jointly planned by the parties.

In relation any child of the family who is not a child of the payer the court must have regard to s25(4) MCA 1973, which provides:

'(a) as to whether that party assumed any responsibility for the child's maintenance, and, if so, to the extent to which, and the basis upon which, that party assumed such responsibility and to the length of time for which that party discharged such responsibility;
(b) to whether in assuming and discharging such responsibility that party did so knowing that the child was not his or her own;
(c) to the liability of any other person to maintain the child.'

In *Day* v *Day* [1988] 1 FLR 278 the husband and wife lived together for four years. The husband accepted responsibility for the wife's two children from a previous relationship. When the spouses got married the marriage only lasted six weeks. The children's natural father made no contribution to their maintenance. The court decided that the husband had fully understood his commitment and responsibility to the children and he was ordered to pay maintenance to each of them.

NOTE: Maintenance and/or lump sum orders to the children may be ordered even if the divorce petition is dismissed (though no property orders can be made) (s23(2) MCA 1973).

## 7.8 The clean break provisions

### General considerations

The courts have emphasised the following in considering whether or not to impose a clean break:

1. The court is not obliged to impose a clean break – it is obliged to consider whether a clean break is appropriate and fair in the circumstances of the case (see *Clutton* v *Clutton* [1991] 1 All ER 340).

2. The welfare of any children of the family does not rule out a clean break (see *Suter* v *Suter and Jones* (above)) but will often make a clean break inappropriate (see *Day* v *Day* (above) where a clean break was inappropriate in the case of a wife with dependant children aged 14 and 8).

3. Where a spouse's future is uncertain the courts have favoured a nominal maintenance order to provide a safety net (rather than impose a clean break). See *Suter* v *Suter and Jones* and *Scanlon* v *Scanlon* [1990] 1 FLR 193 where, in the latter case, a nominal maintenance order was made in favour of a wife whose health was uncertain. See also *SRJ* v *DWK (Financial Provision)* [1999] 2 FLR 176 in which the parties divorced after a long marriage. Both were in their fifties. The mother cared for the youngest child, aged ten. She only had a limited earning capacity. The husband had no assets apart from his pension entitlement since his business had failed. He had some earning capacity. A nominal maintenance order was made in the wife's favour to allow her to apply to increase the maintenance to a more reasonable level should the husband's income increase.

In practice clean break orders tend to be made where the parties are relatively young and/or financially independent and have no children (or no dependant children). See, for example, *Attar* v *Attar (No 2)* [1985] FLR 653 (decided before s25A was enacted but reflecting the principles behind the legislation) where a 27-year-old air hostess married a wealthy Saudi Arabian businessman. She gave up her work. The marriage failed after six months. The court considered that she was young and able to resume work. It gave her an adjustment period of two years to become self-sufficient and ordered the husband to pay a lump sum equivalent to two years of her pre-marital income to enable her to do this. In *Leadbeater* v *Leadbeater* [1985] FLR 789 the wife was aged 47 and had some earning capacity. The husband was ordered to pay her a lump sum to supplement that earning capacity which both reflected the enhanced lifestyle the spouses had enjoyed during the marriage and a clean break. In *Hobhouse* v *Hobhouse* [1999] Fam Law 212 the court made a clean break lump sum order to allow the wife of a four-year and childless marriage to return to Australia and resume her previous life and independence.

In other cases the courts show considerable caution before imposing a clean break. *Attar* can be contrasted with *C* v *C (Financial Relief: Short Marriage)* [1997]

2 FLR 26 in which the marriage lasted only nine-and-a-half months. They had a child who had special needs. The wife was not in good health, made worse by the husband's harassment of her after the end of the relationship. She was not able to return to the work she did before she married. The court ordered the husband to pay a lump sum and maintenance to the wife and maintenance for the child. The marriage had a profound and continuing impact of the wife's earning capacity, particularly in terms of her commitment to the child, making a clean break inappropriate.

A clean break has been considered appropriate in the case of an older couple. See *Schuller* v *Schuller* [1990] 2 FLR 193 where the parties divorced after a long marriage. The husband was retired and had a small pension, some modest savings and remained in the matrimonial home. The wife inherited a flat and was in reasonably well paid work. A clean break order was made whereby the husband paid the wife a lump sum which gave them an equality of assets. The court refused the wife's request that her interest in the home be preserved by a deferred charge on the house since this would leave the husband in an uncertain position given his age and future needs (eg paying for care in a nursing home).

## Section 25A(1)

Section 25A(1) encourages the court to consider the following kinds of order:

1. lump sum orders; and/or
2. outright transfers of the matrimonial home; and/or
3. pension–sharing orders

since such orders are final and provide for a clean break.

In the case of wealthy spouses one way of achieving a clean break is for one spouse to pay the other a lump sum sufficiently large to generate income, if invested, which will provide for the other spouse's needs. This has led to what is called the *Duxbury* calculation (after the case of *Duxbury* v *Duxbury* [1987] 1 FLR 7 in which the calculation of such a lump sum was discussed). A *Duxbury* lump sum can be calculated using a computer programme based on investment returns, life expectancy, rates of inflation, growth of capital and income tax rates. An example of a *Duxbury* calculation can be found in *F* v *F* [1996] 1 FLR 833 where the wife was 56 and the husband 57. The marriage lasted for 23 years. The husband had a net worth of £3.4 million. The wife had no assets apart from her joint interest in the matrimonial home. The court considered that the wife should receive £36,000 a year. Using the *Duxbury* calculation a lump sum order of £575,000 was ordered to produce such an income. There were additional orders which gave the wife a total of £1.1 million. See also *S* v *S* [1987] 2 All ER 312, *Boylan* v *Boylan* [1988] 1 FLR 282 and *Vicary* v *Vicary* [1992] 2 FLR 271. However, the *Duxbury* calculation led to what became called the *Duxbury* paradox, namely the older the wife, the smaller the *Duxbury* lump sum because the smaller her life expectancy. This could often be at odds with her increased contribution to the welfare of the family over the years of the marriage. See *B* v *B (Financial Provision)* [1990] 1 FLR 20 (where the court made a lump sum order of £570,000 when a *Duxbury* lump sum would only have been £300,000) and *Gojkovic* v *Gojkovic* [1991] 3 WLR 621; [1990] 2 All ER 84 (where a *Duxbury* lump sum would have been £532,000 but the court ordered a lump sum of £1 million to reflect her exceptional contribution to the marriage). The matter has been put beyond doubt by the House of Lords in *White* v *White* (above) where it was emphasised that the *Duxbury* calculation was merely a tool for the courts. The courts were entitled to order a lump sum in excess of any *Duxbury* calculation if this met the justice of the case, particularly taking into account a wife's contribution to the family and the yardstick of equality.

Section 25A(1) discourages the court to consider the following kinds of order:

1. maintenance payments to a spouse;
2. property settlements whereby the property is transferred to one spouse but on terms that it be sold at some future event and the proceeds of sale then divided between the spouses since the parties remain tied together 'financially'.

However, the courts will not hesitate to make such orders where in all the circumstances that is the fairest and most appropriate form of settlement.

For example, in *Clutton* v *Clutton* (above) the parties divorced after nearly 20 years of marriage. There was one child still at home with the wife. The husband remarried. The wife had a stable relationship with another man but did not intend to remarry or cohabit. The parties only asset was the matrimonial home worth £50,000 net of mortgage and in the sole name of the husband. The husband had a modest income and substantial debts. The wife had a small income. On the wife's application for ancillary relief a clean break order was not deemed appropriate. The husband was ordered to pay maintenance to the wife and to the child. The house was transferred to the wife but with a charge of £7,000 in the husband's favour. On appeal a clean break order was imposed, transferring the house to the wife absolutely and with the wife's maintenance order cancelled. The husband appealed to the Court of Appeal.

HELD: Although s25A(1) required the court to consider the appropriateness of a clean break that did not mean that the court had to strive for a clean break regardless of all other considerations. The home had been acquired by the joint efforts of both spouses and should be shared. The absolute transfer to the wife deprived the husband unfairly of his share. An order was made that the house be settled on the wife but to be sold when the wife died, remarried or cohabited with another man (a form of settlement known as a *Martin* order). It was stated by Lloyd LJ that such an order could only be said to offend against the clean break principle ‘the most extended sense of that term'.

## Section 25A(2)

This provision accepts that the court may not be able to impose a clean break straight away but may be able to allow an adjustment period during which maintenance is paid but after which the spouse can become self-sufficient.

The courts have shown caution in using this power. In *Morris* v *Morris* [1985] FLR 1176 the wife was aged 56 and could not adjust to the termination of payments from her husband without undue hardship. An order under s25A(2) could not be made. In *M* v *M* [1987] 2 FLR 1 the wife was aged 47. She had only worked part-time during the marriage. She could not easily find well paid work. She had lost the security of her wealthy husband's pension rights. The court had made an order that her maintenance terminate in five years' time. On appeal it was held that she would suffer hardship while her husband remained in a secure position. An order under s25A(2) was not appropriate. Similarly, in *Barrett* v *Barrett* [1988] 2 FLR 516 the wife was aged 44 and one of the three children was still dependent. The judge felt bound to impose a clean break and made an order terminating the wife's maintenance after four years. On appeal it was held that there no obligation to impose a clean break, only an obligation to consider whether one was appropriate. In this case the wife had no work experience, had limited job prospects and no pension entitlement. The husband had a good income with a pension scheme. It was inappropriate to end her maintenance while she was in such a weak financial position. If she got full time work the husband could always apply to reduce or terminate the maintenance under s31 MCA 1973. Similar views were expressed in *Whiting* v *Whiting* [1988] 1 WLR 565; [1988] 2 FLR 189, *Ashley* v *Blackman* [1988] 2 FLR 278 and *Fisher* v *Fisher* [1989] 1 FLR 423.

In *Suter* v *Suter and Jones* (above) the wife was aged 31, lived with a young man and had two children aged 14 and eight. The court felt that it was not possible to predict with any confidence when she would be able to adjust to financial independence. As the children grew up the wife would find it easier to increase her earning capacity but there were too many uncertainties. Her relationship with the young man was too uncertain and she had no intention of remarrying. A nominal maintenance order was made without any order under s25A(2).

A s25A(2) order was made in *CB* v *CB* [1988] Fam Law 471 which involved wealthy spouses, married for 20 years and with two sons aged 18 and 13. The wife was aged 44 and had an earning capacity. There had been protracted and bitter court proceedings. The wife had capital of £334,000. The court was of the view that any long term obligation on the husband to pay maintenance would result in future problems. The climate of opinion was in favour of clean breaks, particularly for young or young middle-aged wives with substantial capital. For them periodical payments for life was largely becoming obsolete. A limited term maintenance order was made whereby the husband paid maintenance of £10,000 a year to the wife for 1988–91, then £5,000 a year for 1991–93 and then her maintenance would cease. In addition the husband was ordered to pay her a lump sum. By that time the youngest child would be 18. A similar order was made in *Evans* v *Evans* [1990] 2 All ER 147 in similar circumstances, with the maintenance to the wife being limited to three years, by which time both the children would be at boarding school and the wife able to realise her earning capacity. A maintenance order limited to 18 months in *Hedges* v *Hedges* [1991] 1 FLR 196 was upheld on appeal. The wife was aged 37, there were no children and the limited term allowed her to adjust to her situation after the breakdown of a short, four-and-a-half-year marriage which had not caused a setback to her position in the employment market.

If the court makes a limited term maintenance order under s25A(2) it can also make an order preventing the payee from applying under s31 MCA 1973 for an extension of the order (see s28(1A) MCA 1973). The courts have again demonstrated reluctance to make such an order unless the future can be confidently foreseen. See *Waterman* v *Waterman* [1989] 1 FLR 380 in which the husband was ordered to pay maintenance to the wife, aged 38, for five years and a s28(1A) order made. She had responsibility for the child of the family, aged five. On appeal the s28(1A) order was set aside because, though the child would need less care, the circumstances did not justify preventing the wife from applying to extend the order should circumstances change.

For a further example of a case in which a s28(1A) order was made, see *L* v *L (Financial Provision: Appeal Procedure)* [1992] 2 FLR 145 in which a limited maintenance order was made in the context of acrimonious court proceedings and a s28(1A) order made. The wife was given 75 per cent of the immediately available capital. Her appeal against the order was dismissed.

NOTE: It is only possible for an application to be made to extend a limited term maintenance order during its term. Once the term has expired no application can be made. See *G* v *G (Periodical Payments: Jurisdiction to Vary)* [1997] 1 FLR 368 in which the wife applied to extend the term of her five-year limited maintenance order after it had expired. It was held that she could not do so. Again the court urged caution as to the use of s25A(2). Making limited term maintenance orders was a worthy purpose of a matrimonial law which strived to enhance self-respect and self-sufficiency after divorce. However, 'looking on the bright side' could not be at the expense of potential pitfalls in limited-term maintenance orders. Could anyone say with confidence and certainty that when a s25A(2) order was made the wife could achieve the goal of financial independence within a set period. In this case the wife clearly had not done so and was left in a weak financial position compared to her wealthy ex-husband. The application must be made before the expiry of the order. The fact that the court hearing is after the order has expired does not prevent the application from being heard. See *Richardson* v *Richardson* [1994] 1 WLR 186; [1994] 1 FLR 286 in which the parties made a consent order in 1988 that the husband pay the wife maintenance for a period up to 1 January 1991. Fourteen days before that date the wife applied for an extension of the period and for an increase in the amount of maintenance. In the absence of a s28(1A) order it was held that she was entitled to make the application. Her order was extended for five years, though with a s28(1A) order to prevent any further extensions (see *Richardson* v *Richardson (No 2)* [1994] 2 FLR 1051). See also *Jones* v *Jones* [2000] 2 FCR 201.

## *Section 25A(3)*

Section 25A(3) allows the court to dismiss an application for a maintenance order and direct that the applicant not be allowed to make any further application for a maintenance order in relation to that marriage. It encourages a once-and-for-all settlement. The case law on s25A(1) will assist courts in applying s25A(3).

For a more unusual application of s25A(3), see *Seaton* v *Seaton* [1986] 2 FLR 398 in which the husband drank heavily, committed an offence, lost his job and then had a severe heart attack which left him with limited speech and comprehension. He lived with his parents and received a disability pension. There were no children of the marriage. The wife was in full-time work. The court decided that there was little point in the wife paying him maintenance and an order was made under s25A(3) preventing him from making further application for maintenance payments.

## 7.9 Pension provision: ss24B–24D and 25B–25D MCA 1973

One of the most valuable assets a spouse may have is his or her pension provision. Regular pension contributions paid over a considerable period of time (for example, an employer's occupational pension scheme spread over the working life of the employee) may result in considerable amount of money being invested in pension provision by way of a lump sum and/or pension payments following the person's retirement. In addition, the person's spouse may have pension rights from the pension scheme should the person die. Where one spouse has worked throughout his or her working life and the other spouse has not there can be very unequal pension provision once retirement age is reached. On divorce any rights of the non-working spouse in the working spouse's pension entitlements may be lost. It is therefore important for the courts to consider the parties' pension provisions as a result of divorce.

Section 25B MCA 1973 imposes a duty on the court to consider the pension provision of the parties in settling financial provision. The court has a duty to have regard to any pension benefits under a pension scheme a party of the marriage has or is likely to have and any benefits which a party to the marriage is likely to lose the chance of acquiring because the marriage has been dissolved. If a party to the marriage has or is likely to have any benefit under a pension scheme the court must consider what order relating to that pension scheme should be made.

The court has three possible ways of dealing with pensions:

1. 'offsetting', ie lump sum or property orders in favour of the party with the least pension provision to compensate the party for the loss of pension provision and

to give the party some financial security on retirement (using powers under ss23, 24 and 24A MCA 1973);

2. a 'pension attachments' order (also called 'pension earmarking') whereby one spouse receives a share of the other spouse's pension rights earmarked for him or her and becomes payable when the other spouse retires (but which yields nothing if the spouse remarries or the other spouse dies before the pension becomes payable) (using powers under ss25B–25C MCA 1973);

3. an immediate order, called 'pension sharing', splitting the pension rights between the parties (using powers under ss24B–24D MCA 1973) (though this only applies to petitions filed on or after 1 December 2000).

## Lump sum and/or property orders – also referred to as 'offsetting'

See the cases on s5 MCA 1973 (Chapter 3, section 3.10) on defending a divorce and s10 MCA 1973 (Chapter 3, section 3.9) on delaying decree absolute which illustrate the court protecting the position of the weaker party in relation to pension rights. See also *T* v *T (Financial Relief: Pensions)* [1998] 1 FLR 1072 in which the court decided that maintenance and lump sum orders sufficiently compensated the wife for the loss of pension rights. It declined to make a pension attachments or earmarking order because the prospect of it benefiting the wife was too remote, the husband being aged 46. The court did order the payment of a lump sum from the husband's pension should he die still in work (see s25C below).

## Pension attachments or earmarking orders

Sections 25B–25D MCA 1973 give the court the power to direct trustees or managers of a spouse's pension scheme to make maintenance or lump sum payments (expressed in percentage terms) to his or her former spouse when the spouse retires. Such maintenance or lump sum payments cannot be paid until the pension scheme comes into effect (eg the spouse retires). The former spouse has to wait even if he or she retires first. There is also power to order the scheme member to exercise any right of nomination so as to give his or her former spouse all or part of any lump sum payable on death. See *Burrow* v *Burrow* [1999] Fam Law 83 in which an attachment or earmarking order was set aside because the husband was not likely to retire for 15 years or more and it was difficult to predict what future payments the wife needed. The future would be best dealt with by a variation of her maintenance order. An order earmarking capital was made reflecting the wife's contribution to the welfare of the family and the family assets.

## Pension sharing

Section 24B MCA 1973 allows the court to share a pension at the time of the divorce. For example, a wife may become a member of the husband's pension scheme in her own right or she might have a designated percentage of the husband's pension transferred into her own pension arrangements. There is no obligation to pension share or to share in equal amounts. A pension sharing order cannot be made at the same time as a pension attachments or earmarking order in relation to the same pension arrangement (s24B(5)). This power only applies to petitions for divorce filed on or after 1 December 2000.

Pension sharing orders can only be made in percentage terms (not in fixed cash amounts).

## Valuing pension rights

The starting point for the valuation of pension rights is the cash equivalent transfer value (CETV). Pensions come in different formats:

1. dependant on final salary;
2. accumulation of contributions;
3. eventual purchase of an annuity.

Professional advice is desirable in how to value these different forms of pension.

## Varying a post-nuptial settlement

Before the various reforms which gave the courts a wider range of powers to make orders concerning pensions the courts explored ways of using existing powers to achieve fairer provision. In the case of *Brooks* v *Brooks* [1995] 3 WLR 141; [1995] 3 All ER 257 the House of Lords allowed the courts to vary some pension arrangements under s24(1)(c) MCA 1973 as if they were 'post-nuptial settlements'. Now that the courts have much wider powers the decision in *Brooks* v *Brooks* has been nullified (see Welfare Reform and Pensions Act 1999, Sch 3, para 3).

## 7.10 Lump sum orders

Lump sum orders have a number of advantages. Since they are one-off payments they:

1. comply with the clean break provisions;
2. are easier to enforce than maintenance payments (and hence may be more suitable where a spouse is likely to default on maintenance payments, for example, in *Newton* v *Newton* [1990] 1 FLR 33 where a husband tried to conceal his wealth so a lump sum order was given to his wife as a once and for all settlement);
3. can provide compensation for the loss of a share in the matrimonial home or for pension rights;
4. can provide a spouse with an investment (eg to set up a business).

For example, in *Nicholas* v *Nicholas* [1984] FLR 285 a lump sum of £80,000 was given to a wife to enable her to set up in business running a guest house. In *Gojkovic* v *Gojkovic* [1991] 3 WLR 621 the wife received a large lump sum order to enable her to acquire and run a hotel business.

However, lump sum orders are only normally practicable if the spouse ordered to pay has the resources to do so. A lump sum order should not be made if the spouse would have to sell his or her business or home to raise the payment. In *Smith* v *Smith* (1983) 4 FLR 154 a lump sum order of £40,000 was quashed because it could only be raised by selling shares in the husband's private company – his only income-producing asset. This would jeopardise the company, which would benefit neither the husband nor the wife. A similar decision was reached in *P* v *P* [1989] 2 FLR 241. A lump sum order was quashed in *Kiely* v *Kiely* [1988] 1 FLR 248 because the husband could only raise the lump sum by selling the matrimonial home.

Normally a lump sum application should be disposed of once and for all. If there is a real possibility of capital from a specific source becoming available in the near future, then the court may adjourn the application so that a lump sum order can be made, particularly where this is the only way that justice could be done between the parties; for example, in *Roberts* v *Roberts* [1986] 2 FLR 152 it was decided that the longest period that the court should adjourn an application for capital provision where a party was likely to have financial resource in the foreseeable future was four or five years.

Lump sum orders can carry interest if they are not paid immediately or within the time scale allowed. They automatically carry interest in the High Court (see Judgments Act 1838), but in the county court only if an order is made under s23(6) MCA 1973.

## 7.11 Transfer of property orders

### What kind of property is covered?

The definition of property is wide so that courts may make orders with respect to different kinds of house or flat. The court may transfer protected tenancies or statutory tenancies within the meaning of the Rent Act 1977 and secure tenancies within the meaning of the Housing Act 1985 (see s53 and Schedule 7 Family Law Act 1996).

In the case of a local authority tenancy the local authority has the right to be heard, but its consent is not necessary to the court making an order: see *Lee* v *Lee* [1984] FLR 243 where the local authority opposed the transfer of a tenancy since it would disrupt its housing policy. The court balanced that hardship against that which would be caused to the wife if no transfer was ordered and ordered the transfer. In *Jones* v *Jones* [1997] 1 FLR 27, the Court of Appeal said that the court and a housing authority have different but interacting duties and functions, and the court must have regard to the manner in which the housing authority would perform its functions and whether that would have any consequences for the court's decision (for example, whether either party would be rendered homeless because of the local authority's housing policy). In that case the joint tenancy of a council flat was transferred to the husband (who was disabled) even though the local authority's housing policy would in effect leave the wife homeless for some time. However, evidence tended to show that wife had some means to find accommodation in the private sector, so the balance reverted in the husband's favour.

For a case involving a private tenancy see *Buckingham* v *Buckingham* (1979) 129 NLJ 52 where the landlord opposed the transfer of the tenancy but nevertheless it was transferred. See also *Hale* v *Hale* [1975] 1 WLR 931; [1975] 2 All ER 1090.

The court must consider the interests of a building society or bank which lent a mortgage and should obtain its consent, or at least give it an opportunity to be heard, before making a property order (*Practice Direction* [1971] 1 All ER 896).

Before ordering a sale of property under s24A the court must have regard to the interests of third parties (s24A(6)). See *Nicholas* v *Nicholas* [1984] FLR 285 where it was said that a court could not order a third party to sell property, namely property owned by a company where the husband was not the only shareholder.

The court should also consider the interests of third parties who live in the matrimonial home: see *Tebutt* v *Haynes* [1981] 2 All ER 239 where the husband's mother and aunt lived in the matrimonial home. They had the right to be heard if the wife was applying for an order which would in effect turn them out.

## When can orders be made?

Transfer of property orders can be ordered at any time after the divorce decree but not after the remarriage of either party.

## Outright transfers

It has become popular for a court to order an outright transfer of the matrimonial home to one party (often the wife) with compensation to the other spouse for his (or her) lost capital by way of not paying maintenance, or paying maintenance at a reduced rate, or a lump sum payment. This accords with the clean break. An important earlier case in this respect is *Hanlon* v *Hanlon* [1978] 1 WLR 592; [1978] 2 All ER 889. A house was bought on a mortgage by the husband, a police officer who, when the parties separated, went to live in police quarters, the wife remaining in the former matrimonial home with the four children of the marriage.

HELD: A deferred trust was not appropriate. The wife had conceded that she would be willing to forgo the periodical payment ordered to be made to her for the children. The house was, therefore, transferred to the wife absolutely on terms that the husband should be relieved from making periodical payments – a nominal order only was made for payment for the children.

An outright transfer is also appropriate where the court is of the opinion that a spouse is deceitful and is likely to fail to support the other spouse and any children on a long-term basis. This is what happened in *Bryant* v *Bryant* (1976) 6 Fam Law 108; (1976) 120 SJ 165 where the court transferred the husband's half interest to the wife because his past actions showed that he would not support her and the children and the only way of protecting them was by an outright transfer of the house to them.

## *The* Mesher *order*

Often there is a need to provide accommodation for one spouse and the children during their minority. The matrimonial home is likely to be the major family asset, but the equity in it may not be sufficient to allow for it to be sold and the proceeds used to buy alternative homes. It may also be unfair to order an outright transfer to the spouse with the children when there are no assets to compensate the other spouse for the loss of his interest in the home. A common form of order in these circumstances is to create a trust for sale, sale being suspended during the minority of the children: see *Mesher* v *Mesher* [1980] 1 All ER 126 where the matrimonial home was in joint names. The husband intended to remarry and had bought new accommodation. The wife also intended to remarry but wished to remain in the matrimonial home with the child of the family.

HELD: It would be wrong to transfer the property to the wife absolutely as that would deprive the husband of his interest in the home. It was right that the wife should have a home where she could live with the child. An order was made that the home be held on trust for sale, the sale suspended so long as the child was under 17 years of age, or until further order. The wife was to be equally responsible for the mortgage payments and was solely responsible for the outgoings on the property.

Such an order has come to be known as a *Mesher* order. The danger of it came to light in *Carson* v *Carson* [1983] 1 WLR 285; [1983] 1 All ER 478 where in 1975 the husband was ordered to settle the matrimonial home on trust for sale whereby the spouses held the proceeds of sale on equal shares, but the sale was postponed until each of the two children of the marriage became 18, or finished full time education, or the wife died or remarried, whichever was earlier. The wife got into financial difficulties. She asked the court to vary the order by ordering the complete transfer of the house to her in return for her forgoing periodical payments. It was confirmed that there was no power to vary the property settlement order. With only half of the proceeds of sale the wife found herself in great difficulty in rehousing herself. Similarly in *Dinch* v *Dinch* [1987] 1 WLR 252; [1987] 1 All ER 818 a *Mesher* order was made by consent which involved the husband in paying maintenance plus half of the mortgage. He stopped paying maintenance because he claimed voluntary redundancy. By that time the child had become 17 and the house fell to be sold under the terms of the *Mesher* order. The wife appealed, asking for a further postponement of the sale plus a lump sum order plus a further transfer of property order. If the house was sold she would be made homeless because she would have insufficient funds from the proceeds of sale, particularly in light of the non-payment of maintenance. The Court of Appeal made a new transfer of property order by transferring the house to her on trust for sale until she died, voluntarily moved or remarried. The husband appealed to the House of Lords.

HELD: The original order was a final and conclusive settlement which precluded any further claim in relation to the property. There was no power to vary the *Mesher* order under s31 MCA 1973 (following *Carson* v *Carson* and *Sandford* v *Sandford* [1986] 1 FLR 412) even though this left the wife in a very difficult position.

NOTE: The addition of the words 'or further order' to a *Mesher* order would allow the court to order an earlier sale should the need arise, although the nature of the order itself could not be varied (see *Thompson* v *Thompson* [1985] FLR 863). Such words would not allow a later sale.

*Mesher* orders are less popular with the clean break provisions which favour outright transfers. In *Dunford* v *Dunford* [1980] 1 All ER 122 a *Mesher* order was made which left the situation uncertain for the future. When the house was sold there might not be enough money for the wife and children to house themselves. It was held that a clean break remedy was appropriate, and the house was transferred to the wife. In *Harman* v *Glencross* [1986] 2 FLR 241 a *Mesher* order was criticised since it left the wife financially linked with the husband. The modern practice enshrined in s25A was to favour a clean break, ie an outright transfer (following *Minton* v *Minton* [1979] 1 All ER 79). In *Mortimer* v *Mortimer-Griffin* [1986] 2 FLR 315 a *Mesher* order was again inappropriate. The wife had shouldered the heavier burden since the breakdown of the marriage. A *Mesher* order was too open-ended, with too many problems and too harsh results. An outright transfer was ordered to the wife.

## The **Martin** *order*

A variation of the *Mesher* order is to settle the home on the remaining spouse on a trust for sale, with the house not to be sold until that spouse's remarriage or death or voluntary removal from the property or cohabitation with another person. This avoids the problem of the house having to be sold when the children are no longer minors and gives the remaining spouse greater security. This kind of order has been referred to as a *Martin* order after the case of *Martin (BH)* v *Martin (D)* [1977] 3 WLR 101; [1977] 3 All ER 762 which involved a marriage with no children. The husband had found his own accommodation. The wife needed a secure roof over her head. It was held that the property should be held jointly by the parties on trust for the wife's sole use during her lifetime or until her remarriage or voluntary removal from the property, whichever first occurred, provided that the wife henceforth paid the mortgage instalments. Only then could the house be sold and the proceeds divided equally.

In *Clutton* v *Clutton* [1991] 1 All ER 340 a *Martin* order was favoured (in preference to a *Mesher* order). It was said that a *Martin* order did not offend against the clean break provisions. The court took the opportunity to look at property orders:

1. An absolute transfer was not fair if both parties had jointly contributed to the matrimonial home and one spouse was unjustly deprived of his or her share.
2. A *Martin* order was a fairer order and did not offend against the clean break provisions.
3. A *Mesher* order was only appropriate where the proceeds of sale were amply sufficient to provide for both parties to buy alternative homes.

A variation of the *Martin* order is to oblige the remaining spouse to pay occupation rent to the other spouse under the terms of the *Martin* order. This may be appropriate if there is no outstanding mortgage or if the mortgage is paid off while the spouse is in occupation. He or she can compensate the other spouse for being in occupation by paying him or her occupation rent. This is what happened in *Harvey* v *Harvey* [1982] 2 WLR 283; [1982] 1 All ER 643 where a *Mesher* order was made. On the wife's appeal a *Martin* order was made instead, but after the mortgage had been repaid she should pay to the husband an occupation rent at a reasonable market rate to recognise her enjoyment of the property in which they had shares.

A similar order was made in *Brown* v *Brown* (1982) 3 FLR 161 where it was said that the *Harvey* form of order offered some way out of a difficult situation when the former matrimonial home was of modest value which, when sold, would not give either party sufficient capital to buy a house. Where the husband had secure accommodation and was not in immediate need of a capital sum, the best solution would be for the wife to pay an occupation rent when the youngest child attained 18 if the wife remained in occupation.

Like a *Mesher* order, a *Martin* order cannot be varied: see *Omielan* v *Omielan* [1996] 2 FLR 306 where a consent order was made in 1990 whereby the matrimonial home was settled on the wife to be sold if she died, remarried, cohabited with a man for more than six months or ceased to reside there on a permanent basis, whereupon the proceeds of sale would be 25 per cent to the wife and 75 per cent on trust for the children. In 1991 she gave birth to a child by a man who she conceded had been living with her for more than six months. In 1994 the husband applied for the sale of the house. In 1995 the wife applied for the 1990 order to be varied to postpone the sale until the youngest child attained 18 years or ceased full time education. The husband argued that the court had no jurisdiction to vary the property order. The court declared it had jurisdiction. The husband appealed.

HELD: Allowing the appeal and dismissing the wife's application, the property order was a final order and could not be varied under s31 MCA 1973. The court could not revisit such an order in the absence of something which vitiated the order (eg fraud, misrepresentation or material non-disclosure). The wife's cohabitation had ended her beneficial interest. The house had to be sold and the proceeds of sale divided.

## Property orders and the slump in the housing market

When there is a slump in the property market this affects the kind of property orders which can be made. An order for the sale of the matrimonial home may be impractical if the house cannot be sold or cannot be sold for a sufficient amount to rehouse the parties. Property transfer orders or settlements then have to be considered in order to retain the home for the children and/or one of the parties.

## Property orders and the Child Support Act 1991

The provisions of the Child Support Act 1991 are dealt with in section 7.17. In summary the parent (called the absent parent) who has left the children with the other parent (called the parent with care) may be required by the Child Support Agency to pay child support to the parent with care for the children's support. The child support is calculated using a rigid formula which obliges the absent parent to pay much higher amounts of child support than courts used to order in maintenance. In calculating whether the absent parent can afford to pay the child support any voluntary payments of the mortgage on the former matrimonial home made by the absent parent are ignored as outgoings. If the absent parent wishes to rehouse him or herself any mortgage payments for a new property are also ignored as outgoings until the mortgage is at least 12 months old. This may lead to the absent parent asking the court to immediately realise his or her interest in the former matrimonial home in order to have funds available to rehouse him or herself by ordering the sale of the house and the division of the proceeds of sale. Alternatively, the parent with care may have to raise a lump sum to compensate the absent parent for the loss of his or her interest. Another alternative might be a *Mesher* order preserving the absent parent's interest in the house until the children no longer need to live there. The trend of transferring the house absolutely to the parent with care in return for the absent parent not being ordered to pay any or reduced levels of maintenance may no longer be considered in the light of the Child Support Agency's independent right to assess and enforce child support regardless of any agreement reached in the divorce court. See *Crozier* v *Crozier* [1994] 2 WLR 444 in section 7.17.

## 7.12 The relevance of remarriage

Remarriage automatically terminates the periodical payments to the spouse who remarries (see s28(1) MCA 1973).

A spouse should disclose to the court if he or she is going to marry since this will affect what order the court makes.

In *Toleman* v *Toleman* [1985] FLR 62 the wife said she had no intention of remarrying. A consent order was made. She remarried within three months of the order. The husband successfully asked the court to set the order aside.

In *Livesey* v *Jenkins* [1985] 1 All ER 106 the wife failed to inform the court that she was going to remarry and the consent order, which did not take her remarriage into account, was set aside.

A remarried spouse is prevented from subsequently making an application for property orders (s28(3)) though applications made before the remarriage will not be affected and may continue to be determined after the remarriage.

Remarriage should, however, be disregarded in dividing capital assets unless a lump sum award represents the capitalisation of periodical payments. The wife is withdrawing her part of the capital from the former family partnership, and the amount she receives should not depend on what she proposes to do with it (see *Wachtel* v *Wachtel* above).

Cohabitation outside marriage may lead the court to conclude that the wife no longer needs the husband's support BUT such cohabitation is not to be equated with remarriage and there is no automatic ending of financial provision. Indeed, a wife may be worse off while living with another man and need the husband's periodical payments more than ever (see *Atkinson* v *Atkinson* [1987] 3 All ER 849). The relevance of the cohabitation will vary according to the circumstances.

## 7.13 Duration of maintenance orders

Unsecured periodical payments will not extend beyond the joint lives of the parties.

Secured periodical payments can continue after the payer's death and last until the payee's death.

On divorce or nullity, whether the periodical payments are secured or not, they will cease on the payee's remarriage.

On divorce or nullity, whether the periodical payments are secured or not, the court may direct that the payee shall not be entitled to apply under s31 for the extension of the term specified in the order (s28(1A) MCA 1981).

It is important that when any order limits the period of maintenance to a spouse and the parties intend that the limited period should not be extended the order contains a s28(1A) provision. Otherwise there is nothing to prevent a spouse applying to extend a limited period maintenance order even though the parties intended that no maintenance should be paid after the expiry of the period specified in the order. A husband discovered this to his cost in *Richardson* v *Richardson* [1994] 1 WLR 186; [1994] 1 FLR 286 when the parties agreed in 1988 to a consent order that he pay maintenance to his former wife for a limited period up to 1 January 1991. Fourteen days before that date the wife applied for an extension of that period and an increase in the amount of maintenance. In the absence of a s28(1A) order it was held that she was entitled to make the application. It is important for orders to be clearly drafted to include a s28(1A) provision where this is required. The maintenance order to her was subsequently extended for a further five years though with a s28(1A) order to prevent any further extensions (see *Richardson* v *Richardson (No 2)* [1994] 2 FLR 1051).

## Maintenance to spouses

Unless a limited term maintenance order is made, maintenance will be paid until:

1. the remarriage of the payee; or
2. the death of the payee in the case of secured maintenance; or
3. the death of the payer in the case of unsecured maintenance (s28 MCA 1973).

## Maintenance for children

Normally child maintenance orders are made until the child reaches the age of 17 (s29(2) MCA 1973) or finishes full-time education (s29(3)(a) MCA 1973). If there are special circumstances maintenance can be paid beyond these ages (eg where a child is disabled) (s29(3)(b) MCA 1973).

## 7.14 Variation of orders (s31 MCA 1973)

The court has the power to vary or discharge or suspend the following orders (including the power to revive suspended orders):

1. periodical payment orders;
2. instalments with respect to a lump sum order;
3. an order for the sale of property.

There is no power to vary a property adjustment order (unless the decree is one for judicial separation) or a lump sum order or the time within which to pay a lump sum (if instalments have not been ordered – though this could be overcome by an order, for example, to pay within twenty-eight days with liberty to apply for extension of time for payment). This is because property adjustment and lump sum orders are meant to be full and final settlements (see *Carson* v *Carson* [1983] 1 WLR 285; [1983] 1 All ER 478 and *Dinch* v *Dinch* [1987] 1 WLR 252; [1987] 1 All ER 818).

On an application to vary a child maintenance order, the court may make a lump sum order (eg to help with the child's education). Up to 1 November, 1998 the court could not vary a spousal maintenance order to a lump sum or property adjustment order. From 1 November, 1998 new powers were introduced which allow the court to discharge a spousal maintenance order and make a lump sum order or property adjustment order instead. As a result it will no longer be possible to guarantee a clean break if a spousal maintenance order is made (even a nominal order) because a variation could include fresh lump sum and property orders. The new powers will be useful to an ex-spouse who wishes to capitalise her maintenance (eg to pay off mortgage arrears by a lump sum payment). They could also apply if the paying ex-spouse becomes unexpectedly wealthy (eg by winning the lottery or profiting on a business deal) and the recipient ex-spouse wishes to convert her maintenance into a capital sum.

See for example *Cornick* v *Cornick (No 3)* [2001] 2 FLR 1240 in which H's wealth increased dramatically and then W and the children moved to Australia. W applied to vary and capitalise her maintenance payments. She received a lump sum of £800,000 (and the child maintenance payments were increased).

In exercising its powers under s31 the court must have regard to all the circumstances of the case, including any change in the matters to which the court was required to have regard when making the original order, first consideration being given to the welfare of a minor child.

Usually, applications to vary maintenance payments are made because:

1. a spouse's income has dropped or he has been made redundant or become unemployed whereby he can no longer afford the payments (a change in s25(2)(a) considerations);
2. his income has increased whereby the payments can be increased;
3. a spouse has acquired a second family to support so that he has new financial needs and obligations (a change in s25(2)(b) considerations) whereby his obligations to the first spouse should be reduced;
4. the spouse receiving the payments has increased needs (eg due to inflation or the children are older and more expensive to maintain) so that she requires more maintenance;
5. the spouse receiving the payments is living with another person (though has not remarried so s28 MCA 1973 does not apply) and is being supported by that person so that her payments should be reduced or discharged (but see *Atkinson* v *Atkinson* [1988] 2 FLR 353; [1987] 3 All ER 849).

The court shall consider whether in all the circumstances of the case it would be appropriate to vary the order so that payments to be made under it would be for a limited period, sufficient to enable the payee to adjust to the termination of those payments without undue hardship (s31(7)(a)).

Section 31(7)(a) reflects the clean break provisions in s25A. The courts have displayed similar caution in applying a clean break under s31(7) as under s25A (eg

*Morris* v *Morris* (1977) 7 Fam Law 244). A clean break was not applied under s31(7) in *Atkinson* v *Atkinson* (above) where the wife was living with another man, albeit of very limited means, and had no means of generating income herself. The husband applied to terminate her maintenance under s31(7) because she was living with another man. There was, however, no evidence to suggest that in the foreseeable future she would be able to adjust without undue hardship to the termination of periodical payments which the husband could well afford to pay. His application was rejected.

In *Whiting* v *Whiting* [1988] 1 WLR 565; [1988] 2 FLR 189 the spouses had been married for fourteen years and had three children. The wife gave up work to look after the children. They divorced. The husband was ordered to pay maintenance to the wife and children. When the children were older the wife obtained full-time employment as a teacher. Her maintenance was reduced to a nominal sum. The husband remarried. He was made redundant. He obtained another job but on a far lower salary. All his income was spent on his second family. After the children became independent he applied under s31(7) to terminate the wife's nominal maintenance order. His application was refused. He appealed.

HELD (Slade and Stocker LJJ): It was not appropriate to discharge the nominal maintenance order. Section 31(7) did not oblige a court, unless there were compelling reasons not to do so, to discharge a maintenance order. It obliged the court to consider whether a discharge was appropriate. It could not be assumed that the wife would be indefinitely financially independent from the husband. She had limited capital resources. She was vulnerable to ill health or redundancy. The nominal maintenance order was a 'last backstop' against such unforeseen contingencies. The judge at first instance could not be said to be plainly wrong. He had a wide discretion. The appeal was dismissed.

BUT Balcombe LJ dissented: To keep nominal maintenance orders alive just in case something happened (like winning the pools) was to negate entirely the clean break principle which had been introduced by Parliament for sound policy reasons.

In *Hepburn* v *Hepburn* [1989] 3 All ER 786 the spouses were married for ten years. They divorced. The wife was given a lump sum of one half the value of the matrimonial home and maintenance of £6,500 per year. She lived with another man, G, for eight years and was involved with G in business ventures in which she used substantial sums of her own money. The husband applied for the wife's maintenance to be discharged because she was living with G. The husband was then aged forty-nine and was wealthy. The wife was aged forty and was not well off. The court reduced her maintenance to a nominal sum but did not discharge it. The husband appealed. He argued that the wife had the capacity to support herself, that she had been financially irresponsible in her dealings with G and that she had been living with him for a long time. Now was the time for a clean break.

HELD: The nominal order was confirmed. The wife's cohabitation was not the same as remarriage (following *Atkinson*, above). A nominal order was appropriate since the wife's relationship with G might end. He had no financial obligations to her whereas the husband was a wealthy man and did have obligations to his ex-wife. It was wrong to pressure the wife into marrying G by discharging the order. The nominal order was not wrong in that it provided a last back stop for the wife (following *Suter* v *Suter and Jones* [1987] 2 All ER 336 and *Whiting* v *Whiting*, above).

In *Ashley* v *Blackman* [1988] 2 FLR 278 following a divorce the husband was ordered to pay maintenance to his wife. She was mentally ill. She lived on state benefits. The husband remarried. He had a very modest income as a painter/picture framer which was so low that he did not pay any income tax. He had to support his new wife. He applied under s31(7) to discharge his ex-wife's maintenance order.

HELD: Section 31(7) was intended to leave scope for those of limited means to be spared the burden of having to pay their former spouses a few pounds a week indefinitely. All the maintenance the husband could pay was swallowed up in the benefits the wife received. The clean break provisions were there to prevent the prospect of a divorced couple of acutely limited means remaining manacled together indefinitely by the necessity of returning at regular intervals to court for no other purpose than to thrash out at public expense the precise figure which one should pay to the other, not for the benefit of either, but solely for the relief of the tax paying section of the community to which neither of them had sufficient means to belong. A clean break was applied.

In *Fisher* v *Fisher* [1989] 1 FLR 423 following a divorce a husband was ordered to pay maintenance to his wife and to the child of the family. The wife then had a second child of whom the husband was not the real father. She could not obtain any maintenance for the second child since his father had disappeared. When the child of the family was fifteen the wife applied to increase both her order and his to keep pace with inflation. The husband cross-applied under s31(7) to discharge her order. His application was dismissed since the wife had a limited earning capacity given her responsibility towards the younger child even though that child was not the husband's responsibility. The husband appealed.

HELD: The appeal would be dismissed. Sections 25A and 31(7) were introduced to discharge 'meal tickets for life' in the case of short marriages, particularly where no children were involved. They required the court to consider whether it was appropriate to limit maintenance payments so that the supported spouse could achieve either partial or total financial independence. Both provisions were careful to qualify the requirement for adjustment by the words 'undue hardship'. Section 31(7) required the court to take into account all the circumstances. The court had a wide discretion. For the court to deny the wife's responsibility to the second child because he was not a child of the family would be to deny that wide discretion. Until that child was older it was premature to consider a limited term order under s31(7).

Was *Fisher* v *Fisher* fair to the husband? The child of the family was fifteen so, ignoring the second child, the wife could reasonably have been expected to go out to work and support herself. This decision led to newspaper headlines such as 'Divorce husband must pay for his ex-wife's affair' (*Daily Telegraph* 22 December 1988).

For an example of the court extending the term of a s25A(2) maintenance order see *Flavell* v *Flavell* [1997] 1 FLR 353 where after 18 years of marriage H and W divorced. The court ordered the sale of the matrimonial home with 60 per cent of the proceeds to W (aged 52 years) and 40 per cent to H. It also ordered maintenance to W of £450 a month for two years but no s28(1A) order was made prohibiting W from applying for the term to be extended. Two years later W applied to extend the term. The court removed the term of the order but reduced the payments to £250 a month. H appealed arguing that the court had no jurisdiction to vary unless W could show exceptional circumstances or at least a material change in position. It was held, dismissing the appeal, that there is nothing in the language of s31 MCA 1973 confining the exercise of the court's powers of variation to cases of exceptional circumstances or material change. The court will look at the matter afresh. In the present case the original order had deliberately left open the possibility of extending the maintenance if matters did not work out as anticipated at the original hearing. On the facts W had only been able to obtain part-time work with a small income and no pension provision. Her earning capacity was limited. In the circumstances the decision to extend the order was correct because the optimism of the original order had not been borne out. On the facts it was impossible to restrict payments for such further period as will be sufficient to enable W to adjust without undue hardship to the termination of maintenance (s31(7)(a)). It was not normally appropriate to provide for the termination of maintenance in the case of a woman in her mid-fifties. Limited term orders should not be made in hope rather than serious expectation.

Before 1 November, 1998 cases considered whether s31(7)(a) allowed courts to vary spousal maintenance to a clean break lump sum or property adjustment order. Section 31(5) precluded this. However the courts gave a broad interpretation to s31(5) and allowed a party to offer a lump sum payment in return for the termination of the other party's maintenance. See *S* v *S* [1987] 1 FLR 71; [1986] 3 All ER 566 where the court considered terminating a former wife's maintenance order on the basis of the former husband providing a once-and-for-all settlement to end his obligations to her. This approach received approval in *Boylan* v *Boylan* [1988] 1 FLR 282 where a former husband made a capital offer in return for ending his former wife's maintenance after four years. The capital offer proved inadequate so the maintenance order continued. There was an appeal in *S* v *S* when the above point was not in issue. The Court of Appeal appeared to favour a more strict interpretation of s31(5) but no ruling was made (see *S* v *S* [1987] 2 All ER 312). The broad construction of s31(5) was followed in *Peacock* v *Peacock* [1991] 1 FLR 324. The amendments to s31 from 1 November, 1998 now put the situation beyond doubt.

A spouse cannot apply for a new order as to financial provision as a way getting round s31. The leave of the court would be required. See *Pace* v *Doe* [1977] 1 All ER 176 where a wife's second marriage failed and she could not apply for a further order against her first husband to help her financial situation. Spouses who had financial provision ordered against them should be protected from unjust harassment or being put to expense to resist claims for financial provision made long after the divorce. Leave for such an application may be granted. See *Chatterjee* v *Chatterjee* [1976] 1 All ER 719 where the post-divorce situation had not settled and the wife was allowed to make a second application for a property adjustment order or a lump sum.

## The variation of consent orders

Consent orders can be varied like other court orders in terms of increasing or reducing periodical payments but the prohibitions against varying property adjustments orders and lump sum orders apply. This means that lawyers must be careful in advising their clients since the scheme created by a consent order may be final and the courts may have no power to vary it (see *Dinch* v *Dinch* [1987] 1 All ER 818). Parties should be aware of the consequences of the order since if something happens which upsets the basis of the order there may be nothing that can be done about changing the order to meet the new circumstances. A consent order may only be set aside if:

1. there is fresh evidence which could not have been known at the time the order was made; or
2. the consent order was based on wholly erroneous information upon which both the parties and the court relied; or
3. the consent order was obtained through the fraud of one party; or
4. there was not full and frank disclosure by one party *and* such disclosure would have led to a substantially different order; or
5. in exceptional circumstances when the fundamental basis on which the order was made has been destroyed.

The court will allow a consent order to be varied if the order has yet to be put into effect or was based on mistaken facts. See *Livesey* v *Jenkins* [1985] 1 All ER 106 where the wife failed to disclose that she was going to remarry, and *Thwaite* v *Thwaite* [1981] 2 All ER 789 where the husband was to transfer the matrimonial home to the wife when she returned to England from abroad with the children, so that they could be educated here. She did not return, therefore, the condition which had to be satisfied before the husband transferred the house was not satisfied, and the husband was allowed to ask the court to vary the order. In *Vicary* v *Vicary* [1992] 2 FLR 271; [1992] Fam Law 428 a wife agreed to a consent order on the basis of the husband having shares worth £347,000. After the consent order he sold his shares for £2.8 million. The consent order was set aside and the wife's award increased from £250,000 to £470,000.

The importance of consent orders being flexible was emphasised in *Potter* v *Potter* [1990] Fam Law 59 where a consent order was made whereby the wife was to pay to the husband £6,000 by 31 May 1988 whereupon the husband would transfer his interest in the matrimonial home to her. The wife could not raise the money by

31 May 1988 partly due to difficulties caused by the husband. The husband argued that the wife's failure freed him from any obligation to transfer his interest in the home. She had not complied with the consent order and the order could not be varied. The Court of Appeal held that the consent order had to be construed to give effect to its spirit and purpose. The house would be transferred at a later date when the wife had paid the lump sum. The addition of words such as 'or such other date as the court may order' to the order for payment of the lump sum would have introduced flexibility into the order and prevented the difficulty which had arisen.

See also *Thompson* v *Thompson* [1985] FLR 863 where the addition of the words 'or further order' in a *Mesher* order would enable a court to be flexible about the date of sale of a house held on trust and overcome difficulties which might arise (eg *Dinch* v *Dinch* above).

In *Harris* v *Manahan* [1997] 1 FLR 205 it was confirmed that formal agreements, properly and fairly arrived at with competent legal advice should not be displaced unless there were good and substantial grounds for concluding that an injustice would be done by holding the parties to the terms of the agreement. Bad legal advice could be a reason for not holding a party to the agreement. However a line had to be drawn and it was not right to add bad legal advice to the list of considerations which could justify setting aside consent orders. W's application to set aside the consent order was dismissed (even though as a result she lost the opportunity of a lump sum order, new accommodation and would be dependent on income support).

For a case where a consent order was set aside see *Middleton* v *Middleton* [1998] 2 FLR 821 in which the whole basis for the consent order was the sale of a house which also included a sub-post office business by H for over £50,000, each party receiving half the proceeds. Unknown to W, H moved the business elsewhere and allowed the house to fall into disrepair. When it was sold the net proceeds were only £652.19. The entire basis upon which the order was based had been deliberately frustrated by the unilateral actions of H which made the consent order a sham. The consent order was set aside and fresh provision made for W.

## Appealing against an order out of time

A party may seek to appeal against the order out of time rather than try to vary the order. Such leave will only be given in limited circumstances. See *Barder* v *Barder* [1987] 2 All ER 440; [1987] 2 FLR 480 (which had bizarre and tragic facts) where leave to appeal out of time would only be granted where:

1. new events invalidated the basis of the order and an appeal was likely to succeed; and
2. the new event occurred within a few months of the order; and
3. the application for leave is made reasonably promptly; and
4. if the appeal were granted it would not prejudice third parties who had acted in good faith and for valuable consideration on the basis of the order.

*Barder* v *Barder* was followed by *Hope-Smith* v *Hope-Smith* [1989] 2 FLR 56 where after a divorce a wife was awarded a lump sum of £32,000 to be paid by the husband within 28 days in full settlement of her claims. The house was valued at £116,000. The court applied a one-third guideline in calculating the lump sum which was to be used by the wife to buy a house for herself. Despite enforcement proceedings the husband deliberately delayed payment of the lump sum for three years. By then the house was worth £200,000. The wife sought to appeal out of time so that her lump sum could be increased to reflect the increase in the value of the house and the increased cost of housing herself.

HELD: Allowing the wife's appeal and applying the grounds in *Barder* the court considered that it would be unjust not to allow the matter to be re-opened. The wife's delay in enforcing the original order and in not appealing earlier were substantially due to the husband's wilful conduct and dilatory tactics. A new order was made whereby the wife was entitled to 40 per cent of the net proceeds of sale of the matrimonial home.

In *Smith* v *Smith* [1991] 2 All ER 306; [1991] 2 FLR 432 (CA) there were similarly tragic facts to *Barder* and a successful appeal against a court order out of time.

By contrast see *Edmonds* v *Edmonds* [1990] 2 FLR 202 where after a divorce the matrimonial home was transferred to W upon her paying a lump sum to H equal to one-fifth of the value of the house, The order was on the basis that W wanted to stay in the matrimonial home. The house was then valued £65,000. A year later W changed her mind and sold the house for £110,000. H was still entitled to his fifth share but he wished to appeal out of time because he argued that W's decision changed the basis of the order and that he should receive a greater share. He argued that the original value of the house had been wrong.

HELD: Applying *Barder* v *Barder*, the increase in value of the house was not a new event within the first condition laid down in *Barder*. It did not invalidate the order. It could have been foreseen by the parties. The same was true of W's change of mind. Leave to appeal was refused.

The courts have been reluctant to grant leave to appeal out of time. In *Penrose* v *Penrose* [1994] 2 FLR 621, H and W divorced. H's financial affairs were complicated. He was unreliable and failed to make proper disclosure of his financial affairs. He was thought to be worth £1 million. The judge ordered him to pay W a lump sum of £500,000 by instalments. A year later H applied for leave to appeal out of time because his income tax liability turned out to be much higher than that put to the court when the lump sum order was made and because of developments in legal proceedings in India which the court had not been fully aware of. Leave was refused. H appealed.

HELD: The appeal was dismissed on the basis that it is in the general public interest that a decision, once reached, is final and the grounds for upsetting it must be limited. H could not rely on events which could have been established by diligent enquiry at the original court. In any event, leave would have been refused because H had a remedy under s31 MCA 1973 to reduce or suspend the instalment payments of the lump sum order.

In *Worlock* v *Worlock* [1994] 2 FLR 689 a clean break order was made in 1984 following a divorce. The order was based on the value of H's interest in a building company owned by his mother. The company owned land which would dramatically increase in value once planning permission was granted. By 1988 H owned the company along with his brother and planning permission was granted. H's wealth dramatically increased. In 1990 W applied for leave to appeal out of time. Leave was refused and she appealed.

HELD: Her appeal was dismissed because at the time of the original court order all the relevant information about H's financial position and expectations was known to W. There had been no misrepresentation or failure to disclose H's assets. Applying *Barder* v *Barder* above, there had been no 'new event' whereby leave should be granted to appeal out of time.

In *Cornick* v *Cornick* [1994] 2 FLR 530, H and W divorced in 1992. W wanted a clean break. H and W's assets were worth £649,000 and included shares owned by H. The judge considered that there was insufficient capital to make a lump sum order large enough to meet W's reasonable requirements. He declined to make a clean break order. He ordered H to pay W a lump sum of £320,000 and maintenance of £20,000 a year. This order gave W over half of the available assets. Maintenance was also ordered for the children. By 1994 H's shares had increased in value dramatically and made him very wealthy. W's share under the court order shrank to 20 per cent of the combined assets. She applied for leave to appeal out of time.

HELD: Applying *Barder* v *Barder*, was the increase in the value of H's shares a 'new event'? The shares had been correctly valued in 1992. There had been no mistake or misrepresentation. A rise in the share value had been foreseeable though not the extent of the rise. In these circumstances there had not been a 'new event' and leave to appeal out of time would be refused. There had to be an additional factor more than a change in market price (such as the husband's behaviour which frustrated the original court order in *Hope-Smith* v *Hope-Smith* above).

NOTE: W then applied for a variation of the existing maintenance orders and succeeded in her application – her maintenance was increased from £20,000 pa to £35,000 pa and for each child from £4,200 pa to £8,500 pa (see *Cornick* v *Cornick (No 2)* [1995] 2 FLR 490).

A similar decision was reached in *B* v *B (Financial Provision: Leave to Appeal)* [1994] 1 FLR 219 where an order was made that the former matrimonial home be transferred to H by W with H paying a lump sum to W. By the time H was due to transfer the house, three years had elapsed and the value of the house had fallen from £340,000 to £250,000. H applied for leave to appeal out of time.

HELD: Leave to appeal was refused because the decline in value of the house was not a 'new event' as defined in *Barder* v *Barder*. The interval between the original order and the new event was too long to permit the case to be reopened.

NOTE: It is preferable when ordering payment of a lump sum which represents a share in the value of the matrimonial home to express the amount as a percentage of the value of the house rather than a fixed sum which may become out of date (as in *Hope-Smith*).

By contrast, in *Heard* v *Heard* [1995] 1 FLR 970, in 1992 a house was valued at £67,700 leaving an equity of £55,500. On this basis an order was made that house be sold with the wife receiving a lump sum of £16,000 and the husband the balance of the proceeds. The husband tried to raise the £16,000 by loan. He failed, so he put the house on the market for £80,000. Unfortunately the only offer he received was for £33,000. He applied for leave to appeal out of time. Leave was refused. He appealed.

HELD: Allowing the appeal, the discovery that the initial valuation was unsound or that the house could not be sold at the assumed price did amount to new events which satisfied the first condition in *Barder* v *Barder* (above). The basis of the order (that the husband be left with enough money to rehouse himself) had been invalidated. The husband's delay in seeking to reopen the matter was explicable and reasonable in the circumstances of the case.

One basis for appealing against an order out of time is a wife in whose favour an order has been made remarrying shortly after the making of the order. This occurred in *Wells* v *Wells* [1992] 2 FLR 66; [1992] Fam Law 386 (though decided in 1980) where an order was made transferring the former matrimonial home to the wife for her and the two children to live in. A few months later she remarried and went to live in her new husband's house with the children. The husband was granted leave to appeal out of time and a new order was made whereby the house was sold with the husband receiving a share of the proceeds.

By contrast in *Chaudhuri* v *Chaudhuri* [1992] 2 FLR 73; [1992] Fam Law 385 the home was transferred to the wife on the basis that it not be sold without her consent or until the younger child ceased full time education or until her death or remarriage or permanent cohabitation with another man (whichever occurred first) whereupon the house would be sold and the husband receive 25 per cent of the proceeds of sale and a lump sum of £27,000. The order was made so that the wife could provide a home for the children in a neighbourhood where she would have the support of friends. A little over a year later she remarried and moved to a new area. One of the children then went to live with the husband. The husband's application for leave to appeal out of time was refused because the possibility of the wife remarrying was included in the terms of the order. There had not been a sufficient change in the circumstances which underlay the original order, an appeal was not certain or very likely to succeed and the time which had elapsed since the making of the original order was on the borderline of being too great (applying *Barder* v *Barder*).

In *S* v *S* *(Financial Provision)(Post-Divorce Cohabitation)* [1994] 2 FLR 228, H and W divorced in 1977 and a consent order was made settling the financial provision. Shortly afterwards there was a reconciliation and they lived together until they finally separated in 1993. In late 1992 W applied for leave to appeal out of time against the original consent order made 15 years earlier. Leave was granted since the fundamental basis of the consent order had been that the parties would lead separate lives and this had been falsified by the reconciliation. There was a requirement that an application for leave be made promptly (following *Barder* v *Barder*). This had to be judged according to the circumstances of the case. In W's case she could be said to have acted with reasonable promptness.

It was held in *Crozier* v *Crozier* [1994] 1 FLR 126 that an obligation to pay child support under the Child Support Act 1991 did not constitute a new event sufficient to invalidate the basis of a consent order. This case is discussed in more detail in section 7.17 under **Consequences for existing orders**.

It was held in *S* v *S (Ancillary Relief: Consent Order)* [2002] Fam Law 422 that the decision in *White* v *White* was a supervening event within the meaning of *Barder* v *Barder* to allow a spouse to appeal against an order out of time. In the case W was awarded the matrimonial home and a lump sum of £800,000. The following month the House of Lords gave its judgement in *White* v *White* and W, six months later, applied to have her order set aside and reconsidered.

## Sue solicitors for negligence

Bad legal advice is not normally a ground for setting aside a consent order: see *Harris* v *Manahan* [1996] 4 All ER 454 where it was said that the policy of the law is to encourage a clean break, and public policy demanded that there should be some end to litigation. Given the lapse of time it would be unfair on the other party to set the consent order aside merely because of the bad legal advice given. Instead the injured party could sue his or her solicitors for negligence.

In *Dickinson* v *Jones Alexander & Co* [1990] Fam Law 137 the wife instructed solicitors who employed a junior member of staff to advise her on ancillary relief. He failed to appreciate that the husband had substantial means and failed to get proper disclosure of his wealth. A consent order was made whereby the husband paid a lump sum of £12,600 to the wife in full settlement of her claims and maintenance of £2,473 per year to the children. The husband stopped paying the children's maintenance. The wife was left dependent on social security. She sued the solicitors for negligence ten years after the consent order.

HELD (liability being admitted): The wife was entitled to damages for what she should have received, namely, one-third of the husband's gross income over the ten year period since the consent order. In addition, she was entitled to £5,000 in damages for the mental distress she had suffered as a result of the negligent conduct of the proceedings. In total she received £330,238 in damages.

In *Re Gorman* [1990] 2 FLR 284, H and W divorced but no property adjustment order was made. In particular the house was not transferred to W and the children. Three years later H became bankrupt. The trustee in bankruptcy took H's share in the house and successfully applied for the house to be sold. The court allowed W a limited postponement of the sale so that she could sue her original solicitors for not obtaining a property adjustment order and so protecting her position

## 7.15 Avoidance of transactions intended to defeat certain claims

Either party may apply to the court if he or she has brought proceedings under ss22–24, s27, s31 or s35 (see below) to set aside a disposition made by the other spouse, or to restrain the latter from making a disposition, provided that there is an intention to defeat a claim to financial relief for the spouse and children. For example, in *Hamlin* v *Hamlin* [1985] 2 All ER 1037 the husband was prevented from selling his house in Spain which was the only asset of the marriage.

If the disposition is within three years of the claim for provision *and* the disposition has defeated or will defeat the claim it is presumed that the other spouse intends to defeat the claim for financial relief (s37(5)).

But if the disposition is more than three years before the claim the spouse must prove that the other spouse had the intention to defeat the claim. This may be difficult to establish (see *K* v *K* (1982) The Times 16 February where the wife failed to establish such an intention).

The disposition cannot be set aside if it was made for valuable consideration (other than marriage) to a person who at the time of the disposition acted in good faith and without notice of any intention of the other spouse to defeat the spouse's claim for financial relief (s37(4)).

Notice means actual notice or constructive notice of the intention. See *Kemmis* v *Kemmis* [1988] 2 FLR 223 which considered the position of a bank who lent a mortgage to a husband who thereby wished to defeat the wife's claim for relief. If the bank knew of the wife's occupation and knew that she was making or about to make a claim for financial relief, it should have known that the wife would have objected to the disposition and it would have constructive notice that the husband intended to defeat her claim. The mortgage could then have been set aside under s37.

A spouse can safeguard her position by registering her application for financial relief as a pending land action which would then give a third party notice of her application (see *Whittingham* v *Whittingham* [1978] 2 WLR 936; [1978] 3 All ER 805) but there is no requirement for such registration if the third party would in any event be held to have constructive notice of her claim (see *Kemmis* v *Kemmis*).

See *Perez-Adamson* v *Perez-Rivas* [1987] 3 All ER 20 where the wife divorced the husband and made a claim for ancillary relief. The house was in the husband's sole name. She registered her claim as a pending action under s5 Land Charges Act 1972. The husband dishonestly tried to get his assets out of the jurisdiction of the court. He obtained a loan based on the security of the house. He then left the country. In agreeing to the loan the bank did not search the land charges register and was not aware of the wife's registration.

HELD: The bank had constructive notice of the wife's interest which took priority over the mortgage. Therefore, her claim for a property adjustment had priority over the bank's charge (*Whittingham* v *Whittingham* applied).

Section 37 could not apply since the bank gave valuable consideration and acted in good faith and without notice of any intention to defeat the wife's claim for financial relief (s37(4)). In such cases registration of a claim for ancillary relief as a pending action would seem to be a wise precaution.

In *Sherry* v *Sherry* [1991] 1 FLR 307 there were acrimonious divorce proceedings. The husband owned six properties. One property was unregistered land so the wife placed a class F land charge on it. The remaining properties were registered land and the wife registered 'inhibitions' in respect of them in accordance with injunctions she had obtained preventing the husband from disposing of them. After negotiations a consent order was made which apparently allowed the husband to dispose of all of the properties, though the wife disputed that this was what was intended. The husband then sold the properties to a friend who knew about the matrimonial difficulties. The friend's solicitor discovered the inhibitions registered with respect to some of the properties but was satisfied that the consent order discharged them. He did not discover the class F land charge. The husband received £105,000. He then disappeared with one of the children ('snatched' during a contact visit). The wife learnt of the sale of the properties. She applied to set aside the dispositions under s37. The judge found that the husband had made all the dispositions with the intention of defeating the claims of the wife and in order to 'snatch' the child. He found that the friend had given valuable consideration for the properties, though at an appreciable undervalue, but that since he knew of the matrimonial difficulties the friend was put on inquiry to see what the husband was trying to achieve. A simple search of the land registry was not sufficient. He should have inquired of the wife's solicitors. He found that the friend had constructive notice of the husband's intention with regard to two of the properties and so set aside these dispositions. The judge, however, found that the friend did not have constructive notice in relation to the remaining four properties because of what the consent order apparently said which released the friend from the duty of further investigation. The wife appealed against this part of the order.

HELD: The appeal would be allowed and all the dispositions set aside. In deciding whether the friend had constructive notice of the husband's intention the production by the husband of the consent order, though a factor to be taken into account, was not sufficient to discharge the friend's duty to make inquiries. The presence of the inhibitions had correctly raised doubts in the mind of the friend's solicitor. A simple inquiry of the wife's solicitor would have made the position clear. In light of the friend's knowledge of the acrimonious relations between husband and wife he had constructive notice of the husband's intentions throughout and all the dispositions were reviewable and could be set aside.

In *B* v *B* (*P Ltd Intervening*) (*No 2*) [1995] 1 FLR 374, H and W were living apart. They agreed that H should live in the former matrimonial home and that W should live elsewhere and that H should pay W £49,000. H persuaded W to wait for her money so that he could set up in business. There were divorce proceedings and W claimed financial provision from H. He continued to live in the former matrimonial home. H founded a company using a guarantee secured by way of a charge on the former matrimonial home. The business was a failure and the charge meant that there was no equity left in the former matrimonial home. H became unemployed and depended on social security. As a result he had no assets whereby any financial provision order could be made in W's favour. W applied to have the charge on the former matrimonial home set aside under s37 MCA 1973. The court found that H had intended to defeat W's claim for financial provision and that the mortgagee had constructive notice of this intention. It granted her application. The mortgagee appealed.

Held: Allowing the appeal, the charge was not a reviewable disposition under s37(4) unless the mortgagee had acted otherwise in good faith or had actual or constructive notice of H's intention to defeat W's claim for ancillary relief. All the mortgagee knew was that H was involved in matrimonial proceedings, that W had no legal interest in the former matrimonial home and that she lived in a different house. He had no actual knowledge of H's intentions. His only obligation was to inquire of the borrower (H) as to whether W had any interest or potential interest in the property. It was too much to expect him to check whether that information was true using other sources.

### The section envisages three situations

Where proceedings are brought for any of the forms of relief mentioned above, and an application is made in these proceedings. If the court is then satisfied that the other party has, with the intention of defeating that claim, made a disposition of any property and that if that disposition were set aside, financial relief, or different financial relief, would be granted to the applicant, it may make an order setting aside the disposition and give consequential directions.

Where the applicant has already obtained an order for financial relief and the disposition is intended to prevent the enforcement of that order or to deprive the other party of the means of complying with it. The court can take the same action as in the above.

Where no disposition has yet been made, but the applicant can satisfy the court that the other party is, with the intention of defeating the claim for financial relief, about to make any disposition, or transfer property out of the jurisdiction, or otherwise deal with it, the court can make such order as it thinks fit restraining the other party from so doing or otherwise for protecting the claim.

## 7.16 The Community Legal Service charge

Many parties to ancillary relief proceedings obtain state funding (which used to be called legal aid and is now called second stage community legal service funding) to pay for their legal representation. Such legal service funding is provided free to parties on low incomes or subject to a contribution for better off parties. However, there is a 'sting in the tale' in that the state can recover all or part of the monies it has paid via legal service funding from the assets awarded to the legally aided party. The recovery of legal aid costs used to be called the 'legal aid charge' but is now called the 'community legal service charge' or 'statutory charge' (following changes in the way in which funding for legal services was administered).

Section 10(7) of the Access to Justice Act 1999 provides that the amount spent on the legal service funding shall constitute a first charge on any property 'recovered or preserved' by the assisted party or in any compromise or settlement of any dispute. Such costs may be substantial and may destroy the benefit the successful party may gain from a court order.

In *Hanlon* v *Hanlon* [1978] 2 All ER 889 the wife was legally aided. After a protracted legal battle the court transferred to her the matrimonial home which had an equity of £10,000. Her legal aid costs were £8,025 and a charge to that amount was placed on the home she had recovered. In *Stewart* v *Law Society* [1987] 1 FLR 223 there was a charge of £4,600 placed on the wife's lump sum of £7,000 leaving her with very little. In *Mason* v *Mason* [1986] 2 FLR 212 nearly £23,000 in legal aid costs accumulated when the matrimonial home was worth only £53,000. Similar examples include *Dinch* v *Dinch* [1987] 1 All ER 818 and *Evan* v *Evans* [1990] 2 All ER 147. In the latter case the combined legal costs of £60,000 were out of all proportion to the available assets of £110,000. The Court of Appeal in *Evans* despaired of such a situation and reminded parties to agree evidence and keep it direct and relevant. The courts emphasise that legally aided parties should avoid protracted litigation and seek to reduce legal costs to avoid the consequences. There is a duty on legal advisers to inform litigants of the legal aid charge and its consequences and to keep them informed of the costs as they arise. Parker LJ in *Anthony* v *Anthony* [1986] 2 FLR 353 said:

> 'I cannot stress too strongly that it is incumbent on solicitors to explain and constantly reiterate to legally aided clients that legal aid does not mean that they conduct litigation free of charge forever. Often, particularly where relations between parties to a broken marriage are bitter, comparatively trivial issues are contested, the contesting of which issues can only result in a loss even if the contest is successful … Legal aid can in such circumstances, of course, be a disadvantage rather than a benefit, and the question which should always be to the forefront of everyone's mind is whether the contest of an issue is likely to produce or preserve more than the costs involved in success. If it is not so likely, contesting the issue is not only a useless exercise but a disadvantageous one.'

Solicitors are obliged to advise clients about the effects of the charge, provide them with two leaflets (*A Practical Guide to CLS Funding* and *Paying Back the Legal Services Commission: The Statutory Charge*) about it and sign a declaration that they have explained how the charge might affect their case and that this advice has been confirmed in a letter to the applicant for legal service funding. All applicants have to sign a declaration on the legal funding application form stating that they understand that they may be required to pay all or part of the costs of the proceedings at the end of the case, even if they are successful. A second warning about the effects of the charge is given to applicants when they receive their formal offer of legal funding. A solicitor's failure to make a client aware of the impact of the statutory charge may amount to professional negligence giving rise to a claim for damages.

There are income and capital limits whereby persons with an income above the limit and/or with capital above the limit are either ineligible for legal funding or liable to pay a contribution.

## Exemptions from the charge

Certain types of order are exempt or partially exempt from the charge:

1. periodical payments of maintenance are completely exempt (reg 44(1)(a) Community Legal Service (Financial) Regulations 2000);
2. the first £3,000 of any lump sum is exempt (reg 44(1)(d) and (2));
3. the first £3,000 of the value of any property made the subject of a court order under s24 MCA 1973 (reg 44(1)(d) and (2)).

NOTE: If the court orders the immediate sale of property under s24A MCA 1973 no part of the proceeds of sale is exempt.

The charge only applies to property 'recovered or preserved' and by implication only to property 'in issue' between the parties. It can be argued that if there has been no dispute over property and a consent order made that the charge will not apply. However, such a claim failed in *Curling* v *Law Society* [1985] 1 WLR 470; [1985] 1 All ER 705 where the charge was applied even though there was no dispute as to the wife's interest in the house. In *Parkes* v *Legal Aid Board* [1996] 4 All ER 272 B and P lived together and owned a house in joint names. When they separated B applied under s30 Law of Property Act 1925 to sell the property. After some negotiation, there was a consent order which allowed P and the child of the family to stay in the home until, inter alia, the child reached the age of 17. P applied for a declaration that the house had not been 'recovered or preserved' within the meaning of what is now s10(7) Access of Justice Act 1999 and that the only matter in dispute was the date on which the sale should be ordered. It was held that the long deferment of the sale conferred a benefit on P which had 'recovered or preserved' her interest in the property and the legal aid charge applied.

The charge applies even if a compromise or settlement is reached in order to avoid court proceedings (see s10(7) AJA 1999). In *Watkinson* v *Legal Aid Board* [1991] 2 All ER 953; [1991] 2 FLR 26 a wife obtained a maintenance order against her husband in divorce proceedings. There were then a series of variation proceedings increasing her maintenance. On each occasion she was legally aided but no legal aid charge arose because her maintenance was exempt from the charge. She applied for a further increase. She was legally aided by amending one of the earlier legal aid certificates to include the new application. The parties reached a settlement whereby the husband paid the wife £10,000 in a final settlement of her claim for maintenance. A legal aid charge of £1,900 was claimed on the lump sum. The wife argued that the lump sum represented a final payment of maintenance and was exempt from the charge. She also argued that the £10,000 was not a court order since (at that time) the court had no power to make such an order and the payment was an agreement between the parties upon which a consent order discharging her maintenance payments could be made. She argued that the money was not a compromise or settlement caught by what is now s10(7). It was held that the £10,000 attracted the charge since it was in effect a lump sum order. The charge included not only the legal aid costs of the new proceedings (£900) but also the costs originally incurred under the legal aid certificate (£1,000), notwithstanding that maintenance is normally exempt.

NOTE: Courts can backdate maintenance to the date of the application. This might result in a 'lump sum' of backdated maintenance becoming due to be paid. This would still be exempt and would not fall foul of the decision in *Watkinson*.

The charge applies to property acquired from the proceeds of any property recovered or preserved. See *Van Horn* v *Law Society* [1984] FLR 203 where the charge applied to a flat purchased by the wife using the proceeds of sale of the matrimonial home received in the course of complicated proceedings.

## Postponing the enforcement of the charge

### Postponing the enforcement of the charge over money (see reg 52 2000 Regulations)

Where a lump sum or proceeds of sale are recovered or preserved by a funded party under the MCA 1973 (or the Married Women's Property Act 1882 or the Inheritance (Provision for Family and Dependants) Act 1975), and the person wishes to purchase a home for him/herself and his/her dependants using the lump sum or proceeds of sale (or that is one of the terms of the agreement reached), and the person agrees in writing that any house he/she buys will be subject to the statutory charge and that simple interest will be charged while the charge is postponed, if the CLS agree, that the property purchased provides adequate security for the amount of the charge, then the charge can be postponed. The interest rate can be high so postponing the charge can be an expensive option.

### Postponing the enforcement of the charge over land (see reg 52 2000 Regulations)

Where the house has been recovered or preserved by a funded party and the person wishes to use the home for him/herself and his/her dependants, and the person agrees in writing that the house is subject to the statutory charge and that simple interest will be charged while the charge is postponed, if the CLS agree, that the property is adequate security for the amount of the charge, then the charge can be postponed. Again the interest rate can be high so postponing the charge can be an expensive option. The charged property can be sold and a new house purchased, subject to the agreement of the CLS, and the charge transferred to the new property, again provided the property can provide adequate security for the charge.

In *Scanlon* v *Scanlon* [1990] 1 FLR 193 the court indicated that while it could not direct the legal aid authorities to postpone the charge, it thought it extremely unlikely that the legal aid authorities would refuse to postpone enforcement and thereby frustrate a court order by leaving one or both parties with insufficient funds to rehouse themselves.

### The interest rate
The interest rate from 1 April 2002 is 1 per cent above the Bank of England official rate.

### The statutory charge and pension orders
The statutory charge does not apply to any pension sharing or pension attachment orders. It would attach to any lump sum order made to offset pension rights.

## Avoiding the charge

A court will not make artificial orders designed solely to avoid the effects of the charge (see *Manley* v *The Law Society* [1981] 1 All ER 401 which laid down the court's approach to such orders or schemes). In *Clark* v *Clark (No 1)* [1989] 1 FLR 174 the court rejected a scheme devised to protect a wife from the consequences of high costs incurred in enforcing maintenance arrears, holding that legal advisers had a duty to act on behalf of a legally aided client in the same manner as for a private client and should not endeavour to manipulate a situation to produce an artificial result at the expense of the legal aid fund (applying *Manley*).

In *Collins* v *Collins* [1987] 1 FLR 226 it was held to be wrong to make a higher lump sum order as a way of compensating a party for the additional burden of the legal aid charge. That case involved a deceitful husband whose actions forced the wife to adopt expensive legal remedies to discover the extent of his finances. However, the approach in *Collins* has not been followed in other cases. In *Wells* v *Wells* [1992] 2 FLR 66 (decided in 1980) the court allowed the wife a greater share in the matrimonial home to take account of the legal aid charge which was greater because of her efforts to force the husband to meet his obligations. If the charge destroys the whole basis of an order for the distribution of the matrimonial property between the parties then an appeal may be allowed and a new order made which better distributes the property (see *Simmons* v *Simmons* [1984] 1 All ER 83 and *Scanlon* v *Scanlon* [1990] 1 FLR 193).

The parties are entitled to ask the court to make orders in such a way that the most efficient use is made of their resources bearing in mind the legal aid charge, by:

1. making periodical payment orders (which are exempt);
2. making lump sum orders only to the extent of £3,000 (which is exempt);
3. not ordering the sale of the home (since all the proceeds attract the charge);
4. seeking to have the charge postponed (subject to warning the parties about the interest which may then accrue).

Such an approach can be found in *Anthony* v *Anthony* [1986] 2 FLR 353 where both parties were legally aided. The home was transferred ot the husband with a lump sum of £9,000 to the wife. She received a nominal maintenance order plus maintenance orders for the two youngest children who lived with her. The order rendered the wife homeless since her legal aid costs meant that she could only receive £2,500 (which was then the maximum exempt amount) of the lump sum. On appeal a new order was made transferring the house to the wife on a trust for sale for her to live in until she remarried, cohabited or either party applied for an earlier sale. The legal aid charge could be postponed while the wife needed the house. The maintenance to the children was increased since that was exempt from the charge. The court despaired of the costs incurred by the parties whereby nearly one-half of the assets could be swallowed by the charge. Solicitors were reminded that they should warn their clients that they could not conduct litigation free of charge.

### Costs

An obvious way to avoid the charge is to ask the court to award costs against the other party. However, costs do not necessarily follow the event in family cases particularly if a consent order is made (when each party may bear its own costs) or both parties are of inadequate means and any order for costs would reduce the financial provision which could be awarded. Costs ordered by the court may not cover the costs of the funding certificate. It was held in *Perry* v *Perry* [1986] 2 FLR 96 that it was wrong to award costs as a cloak for what was in effect a property adjustment order to compensate a party for the effects of the charge.

The new ancillary relief procedures are designed to reduce costs. As was said in *Piglowska* v *Piglowski* [1999] 2 FLR 763 there must be a proportionality between the amount at stake and the costs. It cannot be right to incur £128,000 in costs in relation to £127,400 of assets (as happened in that case).

## 7.17 Child Support Act 1991

The Child Support Act 1991 came into force on 5 April 1993. The jurisdiction of the courts to make maintenance orders for 'qualifying children' ended (s8(3) CSA 1991). A 'qualifying child' is a child whose parent(s) are absent from him or her and who is either under the age of 16 or under the age of 19 and receiving full time education. This means that from 5 April 1993 the courts ceased to be able to make maintenance orders for children except in a very limited number of cases:

1. Only natural or adopted children of parents are covered so courts will still be able to make maintenance orders for step-children who are children of the family.
2. Lump sum or property orders for children may still be made.
3. In the case of wealthy parents the courts may still be able to deal with child maintenance which exceeds the levels under the CSA 1991 and the courts will still be able to deal with ancillary matters like school fees.
4. Where the child is over 19 (or is between 16 and 19 but not in education).
5. Where one parent or the child is not habitually resident in the United Kingdom.
6. Where the child maintenance order is intended solely for educational purposes (eg school fees).
7. Where the child is disabled and the child maintenance is to meet expenses attributable to the child's disability.
8. Where there is a pre-existing written agreement between the parties concerning child maintenance (which can be converted into a court order: see section 7.7).

The child support officer in exercising any discretionary powers under the Child Support Act 1991 must have regard to the welfare of the child likely to be affected by the decision (s2). Since the amount of child support is fixed by formulas there is only limited scope for discretion.

### How it operates

### Making the application
The Agency provides special forms (called 'maintenance application forms') which the parent with the child(ren) must complete and return to the Agency if he or she wants an order against the absent parent (see Child Support Act 1991 (Maintenance Assessment Procedure) Regulations 1992).

In the case of a parent with children who is in receipt of benefit he or she is obliged to supply details of the absent parent and may be penalised if he or she fails to supply this information unless he or she can show that harm or undue distress would be caused to him or her or the children (see ss6 and 46 CSA 1991). In such a case the parent with children will be given written notice that his or her case will be referred to a child support officer in about eight weeks' time. The officer may reduce the amount of benefit received by 20 per cent for the first six months and 10 per cent for the following year (see Part IX CSA(MAP)R 1992). The parent does have a right of appeal to a Child Support Appeal Tribunal against such a benefit reduction (s46(7) CSA 1991) (for example, because the parent fears physical assault by the absent parent if his or her identity and whereabouts are revealed). New regulations from 7 October 1996 increase the reduced benefit direction to 40 per cent of the adult income support personal allowance for three years. This reduction is repeated at the end of each three years for parents who are still receiving benefit and are unwilling to co-operate. The measure is designed to penalise collusion between parents to defraud the taxpayer.

Guidelines have been issued to child support officers to assist them in deciding on reduced benefit directions. There is also power to review a reduced benefits direction once it has been imposed, particularly where the welfare of the child has been affected.

**Making the assessment** (see the Child Support Act 1991 (Maintenance Assessment and Special Cases) Regulations 1992)

Once an application has been made the Agency gives notice in writing to the absent parent and sends him or her a maintenance enquiry form which must be returned within 14 days. The absent parent is warned that maintenance is payable from the date the maintenance enquiry form is sent.

If the absent parent fails to return the maintenance enquiry form or fails to provide sufficient information for an assessment to be made then a child support officer (within the seven days following the expiry of the 14-day period for returning the form) may give 14 days' notice that he or she intends to make an interim assessment. The interim assessment is calculated by multiplying the maintenance requirement for the child(ren) (ie the income support rate for each child + the income support rate for the parent with care + one parent premium but less child benefit) by 1.5. Since this could produce a high figure there is an incentive to the absent parent to reveal his or her financial position quickly.

**The formula for calculating child support.**

There are four stages in calculating child support (see the Child Support (Maintenance Assessments and Special Cases) Regulations 1992):

*Calculating the Maintenance Requirement (MR).* This is the income support allowance for each qualifying child + the income support allowance for the caring parent (ie the rate for a claimant over 25) + income support family premium + income support lone parent premium (where the parent with care has no partner) but less the amount of child benefit received for each child. The income support allowance for the caring parent reduces, depending on the age of the youngest child. When the youngest child reaches 11 it goes down by 25 per cent and when the youngest child reaches 14 it goes down by a further 25 per cent and when the youngest child reaches 16 there is no allowance.

*Calculating the assessable income of the parent with care and the absent parent.* The net income of each parent is calculated. This is the take-home pay of each parent after tax and national insurance has been deducted. Only 50 per cent of contributions to a pension scheme are deducted. Any other source of income (eg from savings) is also taken into account. The income of any partner is *not* included. Child benefit is also *not* included. From each parent's net income is deducted 'exempt income'. 'Exempt income' is the income support allowance for a single claimant over 25 + 'reasonable' housing costs (up to a maximum amount of £80 a week or 50 per cent of income whichever greater) + other allowances if a parent is a lone parent or is disabled and/or has dependent children. If the absent parent has a new partner that partner is deemed to pay 25 per cent of the housing costs. There are also further deductions where there are step-children in the absent parent's household. Allowance is also made for high travel-to-work costs. Allowance is also made for property or capital transfers of at least £5,000 made by the absent parent before 5 April 1993.

*Calculating the deduction rate.* A deduction rate of 50 per cent is applied to the combined assessable income of both parents until the maintenance requirement is met. For example, a father is separated from the mother and the two children. The mother does not work. The maintenance requirement is £81.05. The father's assessable income is £140 a week. He would be required to pay 50 per cent of his assessable income ie £70 a week. He does not have enough income to meet the full maintenance requirement.

If the deduction rate is more than the maintenance requirement then there is provision for 'top up' payments of child support (called 'the additional element'). Where there is one child to support, 15 per cent of the balance is payable; if there are two children 20 per cent is payable and if there are three or more children 25 per cent is payable.

*Comparing the deduction rate with the absent parent's protected income.* The absent parent's income must not fall below a certain level, which is called 'protected income'. Protected income is the income support allowance for a single claimant over 25 (or the allowance for a couple if he has a partner) + housing costs (subject to a maximum amount) + other allowances (which apply if the absent parent is a lone parent or is disabled and/or has dependent children) + £30 a week + council tax + 15 per cent of any spare income after the allowances have been taken off. If the maintenance requirement reduces the absent parent's income below his protected income then the maintenance requirement has to be reduced so that he receives that protected income. For these purposes the income of any partner of the absent parent is added to the absent parent's income in making the above calculation.

A maintenance assessment cannot normally be reduced below a minimum amount of 5 per cent of the income support allowance for a single person over 25. This minimum amount does not apply to absent parents with dependent children or who are not fit for work. Absent parents on income support may have to pay the minimum amount, which may be taken directly from their income support.

There are provisions to require employers to provide information on the earnings of parents and for the charging of interest on any arrears in child support payments (see the Child Support Act 1991 (Information, Evidence and Disclosure) Regulations 1992 and the Child Support Act 1991 (Arrears, Interest and Adjustment of Maintenance Assessment) Regulations of 1992).

An absent parent may dispute that he or she is a parent of the child and that he or she is liable to pay child support. The Child Support Agency cannot then make a child support assessment and must apply to the family proceedings court for a declaration of parentage under s27 CSA 1991 (unless a court has already ruled on paternity eg in previous court proceedings whereupon the Agency can continue to make a child support assessment).

The caseload of the Child Support Agency was phased in from 1993 to 1997. Since April 1993 the CSA has dealt with new applications for child support. Then it took over existing maintenance orders where the parent receiving maintenance claimed income support or family credit over the period April 1993–March 1996. After that other maintenance orders were to be taken over at the request of the parent receiving maintenance on a phased alphabetical basis during 1996–97. Due to a backlog of work these provisions for taking over maintenance orders where the parent with care is not receiving benefit no longer apply (see ss4(1) and 7(10) Child Support Act 1995). Court maintenance orders made before 5 April 1993 in favour of parents with care who are not on benefit remain in force. Such a parent would have to apply to revoke the court order in order to ask the CSA to make a child support assessment. There were also plans for the CSA to take over the collection and enforcement of maintenance for spouses, but these plans have also been dropped due to the backlog of work.

## Where the absent parent has contact with the children

If a child spends two nights or more a week on average with the absent parent (or 104 nights a year) the amount of child support will be proportionately reduced. This may encourage some absent parents to have their children to stay with them which may result in more applications for contact being made to the court. Hopefully it will not result in absent parents trying to get their children to stay with them just so that the child support can be reduced which could cause conflict with the parent with care and not be in the child's best interests. One source of grievance since the Child Support Agency commenced calculating child support is that no account is taken of the cost to absent parents of contact visits, particularly if the children live some distance away. There is no provision to allow for such expenses. The absent parent would have to pay the child support first and then consider how he could afford to continue contact visits which might be expensive if his children lived some distance away.

## Consequences for existing orders

The consequences of the CSA 1991 for existing orders has been significant. Child support assessments are higher than existing child maintenance orders so absent parents have applied to have any maintenance orders they are paying to their spouse or former spouse revoked or reduced so that they can afford to pay the new amounts of child support. Existing clean break orders have not prevented the parent with care from applying for a maintenance assessment, which has altered the basis upon which the original order was made. This has become an issue where fathers have agreed to transfer their interest in the former matrimonial home to their former wife or continued to pay the mortgage in return for smaller maintenance payments. Such fathers have found that such settlements are not considered by the Child Support Agency when child support is calculated. Clean break orders may no longer be able to operate in the way anticipated given the element in child support for the parent with care – a kind of indirect maintenance for the spouse. In pre-1993, divorce settlements it was common to see the matrimonial home transferred to the wife with the children in return for the dismissal of her maintenance rights. Such a dismissal is ineffective in as much as the wife can apply to the Child Support Agency for a child support assessment which includes an element for herself.

In *Crozier* v *Crozier* [1994] 2 WLR 444; [1994] 2 All ER 362; [1994] 1 FLR 126, H and W were divorced in 1988. There was one child of the marriage. In 1989 a consent order was made whereby H would transfer to W his half share (worth £8,000) in the former matrimonial home. W's claim for maintenance was dismissed. A nominal maintenance was made for the child since the parties clearly intended that W should financially support the child and the transfer of H's interest in the home was partly for the child's benefit. The order was expressed as a full and final settlement of all property and financial claims between H and W save for child maintenance. W did not earn enough to support herself and the child and she claimed income support. In March 1993 the DSS obtained a maintenance order against H under the Social Security Administration Act 1992, whereby he paid the DSS £4 a week. When the Child Support Act 1991 came into force the Child Support Agency assessed H as being liable to pay £29 a week child support. By that time H was living with another woman and her child aged seven, and their own child aged two. He applied for leave to appeal out of time against the consent order arguing that the increased liability to support the child was a new event which undermined the basis of the consent order.

HELD: The demand for child support was not a reason to set aside a clean break consent order made in full and final settlement of a spouse's claim for herself and the children. While there could be a clean break between spouses there could not be a clean break with regard to children since the legal liability to maintain them continued for both parents. The state was empowered to seek the recovery of its expenditure on benefit for a child from a person who was liable to maintain the child and was not bound by any agreement made between the parents. The fact that the CSA 1991 had introduced a new administrative method which by-passed the courts did not constitute a new event which was sufficient to invalidate the consent order. Leave to appeal out of time was refused.

NOTE: Mrs Crozier came off income support before the hearing of the application so that Mr Crozier was never made subject to a formal assessment by the CSA – though he chose to continue his application and Mrs Crozier continued to defend it.

This may be perceived as a disincentive to clean break orders. *Mesher* orders may become popular again. The intention of the Child Support Act 1991 is to introduce a more consistent approach and more realistic levels of child support so defenders of child support do not accept that it discourages clean break orders. As a result child support should be taken into account by parties negotiating 'clean break' agreements since once a 'clean break' order is made it may not be possible to alter it in light of the absent parent being obliged to pay child support.

For an example of a case dealing with ancillary relief and child support see *Mawson* v *Mawson* [1994] 2 FLR 985 where H and W divorced. There was one child who lived with W. H was required to pay over £500 a month child support for the child. The district judge took this into account and ordered that the home be transferred to W, that H pay a lump sum to W of £2,000 and that W only have maintenance for three months so that she could adjust, without undue hardship, to a clean break from financial support from H after that date. W appealed since she wanted maintenance from H until either the death of either H or W or her remarriage. She also wanted a higher lump sum. She argued that the amount of child support might reduce and that she would be worse off. Her appeal was allowed. If the child support was reduced because H's income reduced, W would have no complaint against the order. However the child support might be reduced as a result of government changes and this had to be considered. The right balance was to make W's maintenance last for eight months and to give her the option of applying to extend that period, if circumstances justified it. The court would not therefore make an order under s28(1A) MCA 1973 which would prevent W from doing this.

From April 1995 the CSA will take account of property or capital transfers of at least £5,000 made before 5 April 1993 by the absent parent. An allowance for such a transfer is included in exempt income.

## Consequences for second families

Child support concentrates on the responsibility of an absent parent to contribute to his first family. If he remarries, or lives with another lady, and has a second family then only limited account is taken of this. Such second families can find themselves less well off as a result of the husband paying much larger amounts of child support (as opposed to court maintenance) for the children of his first family. This is a dramatic change from court based maintenance which made full allowance for a husband maintaining a second family, leaving the first family to make up any shortfall in income by claiming state benefits where this was appropriate.

## Departure directions

From 2 December 1996 absent parents can apply to the Child Support Agency for 'departure directions' (see ss28A–28H Child Support Act 1991 inserted by the Child

Support Act 1995). 'Departure directions' allow the CSA to take into account a wider range of expenses in calculating 'exempt income' than is allowed in the child support formula. This can lead to a reduction in the amount of child support payable.

There are three areas covered by 'departure directions':

*Special expenses.* These include travel to work expenses, expenses to visit children for contact visits, debts incurred before the absent parent became an absent parent. The first £15 is disallowed, and the child support officer has a discretion to allow such expenses as he or she considers reasonable to increase the amount of exempt income.

*Pre-1993 property or capital transfers.* Where a court order or other written agreement was in force before 5 April 1993 between the absent parent and the parent with care of children, and the amount of maintenance was reduced as a trade-off and was not properly reflected in the CSA assessment, the amount of exempt income can be increased to reflect this.

*Additional cases.* This includes 'inconsistent lifestyle' or unreasonably high housing costs of the absent parent or unreasonably diverting income, and allows the parent with care to ask the CSA to increase the amount of child support.

## Reform of child support through the Child Support, Pensions and Social Security Act 2000

Following continued criticism of the complexity, delay and inefficiency in the child support system the Government has agreed to move to a much simpler formula. The Child Support, Pensions and Social Security Act 2000 was enacted in July 2000. The new formula for calculating child support was supposed to come into force for new cases from April 2002. Unfortunately computer problems have delayed the implementation of the new reforms. In January 2003 the government announced that the new formula will apply to new cases from March 2003. Child support calculated under the existing formula will not be transferred to the new system until the government is satisfied that the computer system can cope.

The new formula is set out in s1 and Sch 1 CSPASSA 2000. There will be four rates:

1. a normal rate which obliges the non-resident parent (NRP) to pay 15 per cent of his net income for one qualifying child; 20 per cent for two qualifying children and 25 per cent for three or more qualifying children (with a 15 per cent reduction of net income if he has one dependant child from any new relationship, a 20 per cent reduction for two dependant children and a 25 per cent reduction for three or more dependant children);

2. a reduced rate where the NRP has a net income of between £100 and £200 a week;
3. a flat rate of £5 a week for NRPs on benefit or with a net income of less than £100 a week;
4. a nil rate for NRPs with a net income of less than £5 a week including students, child parents, long-stay hospital patients and prisoners.

There will be a reduction for the normal or reduced rate of child benefit if there is shared care between the NRP and the parent with care (PWC). If the NRP has overnight contact for between 52 and 103 nights a year there is a one-seventh reduction in the amount of child support paid. If the overnight contact is for between 104 and 155 nights a year the reduction is two-sevenths and for 156 to 174 nights three-sevenths. For shared care of 175 nights or more the reduction is one-half and £7 per child. There can be similar reductions for NRPs paying the flat rate.

Only the income of the NRP is considered. The income of the PWC is ignored. This will make the child support system administratively much easier to manage but may produce unfairness where the PWC has a substantial income. At present it is intended that net income will be gross income less tax, national insurance and all approved pension contributions. No other deductions such as travel or housing costs will be considered. There is a trade off for a simpler system at the expense of taking account of individual circumstances. There will be a cap on child support of £300 a week for one child or £200 a week for each of two children or £167 a week for each of three of more children. Courts will be allowed to make top-up maintenance orders for NRPs with high incomes.

The ability to vary the amount of child support calculated will be very much limited with much narrower grounds (compared to the existing scheme for departure directions). A NRP may argue that he has 'special expenses' which are child-related. This could include travel costs associated with contact visits or boarding-school fees and mortgage payments on the former matrimonial home where the NRP has no interest in it. Account can be taken of capital or property transfers to reflect pre-April 1993 clean break settlements. A PWC can also apply for increased payments where a NRP has capital assets which suggest that he could afford to pay more than his net income suggests.

# 8

# Property Rights and Financial Provision on Death

8.1 Introduction

8.2 Inheritance (Provision for Family and Dependants) Act 1975

8.3 The two-stage test under s2(1)

8.4 Matters which must be considered in applying both parts of the two-stage test (s3(1))

8.5 Who may apply for an order

8.6 How the two-stage test is applied to each kind of applicant

8.7 The orders the court can make

8.8 Clean break provision

## 8.1 Introduction

When a member of a family dies he or she may not have made provision for his or her relatives or dependants in his or her will or because he or she has died intestate. Such provision or lack of provision may require modification (see Inheritance (Provision for Family and Dependants) Act 1975, which replaced the Inheritance (Family Provision) Act 1938 and ss26–28 Matrimonial Causes Act 1965). In order to understand how the 1975 Act operates there must first be a discussion as to wills and as to intestacy.

NOTE: In *Moody* v *Stevenson* [1992] 2 WLR 640; [1992] 2 All ER 481; [1992] 1 FLR 494 it was stated that cases decided before the 1975 Act could not offer guidance since the law was radically changed by the 1975 Act.

### *Provision by will*

As long as the testator is of sound mind and has complied with the Wills Act 1837 the testator may dispose of his property in any way he sees fit (see *Re Coventry* [1979] 2 WLR 853; [1979] 3 All ER 815).

Generally, a will is revoked by the testator getting married (see s18 Wills Act 1837) and a new will has to be made. In the absence of any contrary intention in the will a gift to a spouse who is divorced from the testator will lapse and any appointment of the divorced spouse as an executor or trustee is ineffective (see s18A Wills Act 1837).

For example, in *Re Sinclair* [1985] 1 All ER 1066 the husband left his estate to his wife and if she predeceased him the estate would go to a charity. His wife was then divorced from him. The gift to her lapsed. She was still alive when the husband died so that the necessary condition for the estate to go to the charity was not satisfied.

HELD: The will was ineffective and the rules of intestacy applied.

Section 18A Wills Act 1837 is amended by s3 Law Reform (Succession) Act 1995 whereby the problem identified in *Re Sinclair* should no longer occur. If a will makes a similar provision to that in *Re Sinclair* and then there is a divorce then the gift to the spouse is revoked but can pass on as if the former spouse had died on the day on which the marriage was annulled or dissolved ie the charity would obtain the gift as the testator intended. The same applies to appointments of a spouse as an executor or trustee. This change only applies to persons dying on or after 1 January 1996.

## Intestacy

When someone dies without leaving a will or leaves a will which is invalid or ineffective the estate will be distributed according to the rules on intestacy (see Administration of Estates Act 1925). For the purposes of these rules children include children of unmarried parents (see s14 Family Law Reform Act 1969) but spouses do not include judicially separated spouses who cannot inherit on intestacy (see s18(2) MCA 1973).

An intestate's spouse cannot take a share on intestacy unless he or she survives the intestate by 28 days. Where the spouse does not so survive, the intestate's property will be dealt with as if there had been no spouse (see s1(1) Law Reform (Succession) Act 1995 – which only applies to deaths occurring on or after 1 January 1996).

Where the deceased was married and had children:

1. where the estate is worth £125,000 or less the spouse gets everything;
2. where the estate is worth more than £125,000 the spouse gets £125,000 and a life interest in half the remainder – the children get the rest.

Where the deceased was married but there were no children:

1. where the estate is worth £125,000 or less the spouse gets everything;
2. where one or both parents of the deceased are still living the spouse gets £200,000 plus half the balance and the rest goes to the surviving parent or is shared between the surviving parents;

3. where there are no surviving parents of the deceased but there are brothers and sisters of the deceased the spouse gets £200,000 and half the balance and the rest is shared between the brothers and sisters;
4. where there are no surviving parents or no brothers or sisters of the deceased then everything goes to the spouse.

The spouse will normally inherit all the personal possessions as well (eg motor car, china, linen, furniture, jewellery etc.) In practice, the spouse takes all or most of the estate under intestacy. This may produce an unfair result for surviving children. In *Sivyer* v *Sivyer* [1967] 1 WLR 1482; [1967] 3 All ER 429 the husband married his first wife. They had a daughter who was taken into local authority care. The first wife inherited a house in which she and her husband lived. She then died. The husband married again. The husband died intestate. Under the rules of intestacy the second wife inherited the whole estate and the daughter received nothing. This was particularly unfair in that the bulk of the estate was the house inherited by the daughter's mother (the deceased's first wife). The daughter made an application under the predecessor to I(PFD)A 1975 and was given a share of £2,500 from the estate which was worth £4,000.

Where the deceased was not married or has no surviving spouse:

1. if there are children the estate is shared equally between them;
2. if there are no children but one or both parents of the deceased are still alive the estate goes to the surviving parent or is shared equally between the surviving parents;
3. if there are no children and no surviving parents of the deceased but there are brothers and sisters then the estate is shared equally between them (brothers and sisters of the whole blood would inherit in preference to half brothers or sisters);
4. if none of the above applies but there are surviving grandparents then the estate is shared equally between them;
5. if none of the above applies but there are surviving uncles and aunts then the estate is shared equally between them;
6. if none of the above applies then the estate goes to the Crown.

If the estate goes to the Crown it does have a discretion to provide for people who depended on the deceased, but since I(PFD)A 1975 provides for this situation it is unlikely the Crown would be asked to exercise this discretion.

If children are under 18 then their share of the estate goes into statutory trusts until they reach the age of 18.

If any child of the deceased or any brother or sister of the deceased is already dead then the child's or brother's or sister's share passes to their children (ie the grandchildren or nephews/nieces of the deceased). The same applies to any predeceased aunts or uncles. Their issue would take the aunt or uncle's share.

Under these provisions an unmarried partner of the deceased would get nothing under intestacy.

The European Court of Human Rights considered intestacy in *Camp and Bourimi* v *Netherlands* [2000] 3 FCR 307 in which a mother was pregnant with a son, SB, when the father died intestate. The mother and father intended to marry. It was held by the Dutch courts that he could not inherit from his father's estate. It was held by the European Court that there had been a violation of art 14 in conjunction with art 8 of the European Convention on Human Rights. The right to inherit was not guaranteed by art 8 but art 8 encompassed inheritance. In this case there was a difference of treatment based on birth for which there was no objective or reasonable justification, and even allowing the state a margin of appreciation there had been a breach of the Convention. There had been no conscious decision by the father not to recognise SB and the exclusion of SB from inheriting from his father's estate was disproportionate. The legitimate heirs to the estate were aware of SB's existence. English and Welsh law, through the Inheritance (Provision for Family and Dependants) Act 1975, allows a child to make a claim from the estate of a parent, whether the child is legitimate or not. As a result a breach of the Convention is unlikely under English and Welsh law.

## 8.2 Inheritance (Provision for Family and Dependants) Act 1975

The Act provides a remedy for those who are left out of a will or as a result of intestacy but only in limited circumstances.

The Act applies when persons die after 31 March 1976 and are domiciled in England and Wales.

Applications may be made to the High Court or county court. The county court now has unlimited jurisdiction (see High Court and County Court Jurisdiction Order 1991 amending County Courts Act 1984).

No application can be made unless there has been a grant of probate or letters of administration concerning the deceased's estate. In *Re McBroom (deceased)* [1992] 2 FLR 49 an application under the 1975 Act was dismissed since this had not been done.

Since applications are expensive they should not be made in the case of small estates otherwise most of the estate will be used up in costs (see *Re Coventry* [1979] 2 WLR 853; [1979] 3 All ER 815; *Jelley* v *Iliffe* [1981] 2 WLR 801; [1981] 2 All ER 29; *Re Fullard* [1981] 3 WLR 743; [1981] 2 All ER 796).

There is a time limit on applications. Applications must be made within six months of administration of the estate unless the court gives leave for a late application (s4).

If there is a good reason for the delay the court may give leave. See *Re Salmon* [1986] 3 All ER 532 where the applicant had had long negotiations with the executors of the estate which delayed the application and leave was granted.

*Re Salmon* was followed in *Re C (deceased)(Leave to Apply for Provision)* [1995] 2 FLR 24. H and W had a child, C. W and C left H. Because of W's acrimonious relations with H, C ceased to have contact with him. H met another woman who had two children from a previous relationship. H and the woman married and a son was born. H died. He made no specific provision for C in his will. Two-and-a-half years later C (who was now aged eight) applied through W for leave to make a late application for provision from H's estate. Leave was refused. C appealed.

HELD: C had the burden of establishing the grounds for leave. While the court did not start with a general assumption that it should treat an applicant who was a minor child more favourably it did take into account that a refusal to give leave would cause the child hardship as a result of the fault of another person. While W's reason for delay was unsatisfactory it was C who was the claimant not W. C had no redress against W if leave were refused. The estate was sufficiently large to lessen any prejudice to the beneficiaries. The estate had also not been distributed so the beneficiaries would not be obliged to hand any capital back. C's prospects of success were good. Leave was therefore granted for her to make the application.

If there is no good reason for the delay leave may be refused. See *Re Dennis* [1981] 2 All ER 140 where the applicant was the son of the deceased who left an estate of £2.5 million. He used up his inheritance and got into debt with the taxman. He made a late application for greater provision from the will. There was an explanation for part of the delay but no good reason for the rest of the delay. His application also had little prospect of success. Leave was refused.

See also *Re Freeman* [1984] 3 All ER 906 where the will turned out to be invalid. The six months' time limit ran from when the will was found to be invalid, not the earlier time when the will had first been proved.

## 8.3 The two-stage test under s2(1)

In order to make an application two matters must be shown.

Has the deceased by will or intestacy failed to make reasonable financial provision for the applicant? This first matter is an objective test of fact and degree. It is based on the facts known at the time of the hearing and so circumstances which have occurred after the deceased's death can be considered since they might have frustrated the deceased's otherwise reasonable provisions (s3(5)).

If so, should the court in its discretion order financial provision for the applicant? How the test is applied depends on who is applying.

## 8.4 Matters which must be considered in applying both parts of the two-stage test (s3(1))

The court must consider the means of the applicant now and in the foreseeable future including his or her earning capacity and how that compares with his/her obligations and responsibilities.

The court must compare the applicant's circumstances with those of other applicants and with the beneficiaries under the estate.

The court must consider what obligations the deceased had towards the applicant and how such obligations compare with those to other applicants or beneficiaries (eg an obligation to a charity which benefits under a will may be less than that to an applicant who is a married spouse of the deceased) (*see Re Besterman* [1984] 2 All ER 656).

The size and nature of the estate must be considered. In particular, the court may ask who provided the assets making up the estate (see *Sivyer* v *Sivyer* (above) where the fact that the estate came from the applicant's mother (the first wife) as opposed to the second wife made the daughter's claim stronger).

Any physical or mental disability of the applicant must be considered and compared with those of other applicants or beneficiaries (see *Re Coventry* (above) where the court considered the merits of a claim made by a fit and healthy son as set against the claim of the beneficiary, his aged, frail and poor mother, and see *Re Debenham* [1986] Fam Law 101 where the applicant was the epileptic daughter of the deceased).

The court will then consider any other matter including the conduct (good or bad) which in the circumstances the court considers relevant (see *Re Coventry*, where the conduct of the son in forcing his mother to leave the family home counted against his claim, and *Jelley* v *Iliffe* (above) where the generosity of the applicant to the deceased strengthened his claim).

See *Re Snoek* (1983) 13 Fam Law 18 where the applicant was the wife of the deceased. He was terminally ill. During his illness she behaved very badly towards him. However, such behaviour did not justify his leaving her out of his will and did not cancel out her contributions over twenty years of marriage. She could make a claim under the 1975 Act.

Other considerations will also include statements made by the deceased (see *Kourkey* v *Lusher* (1983) 4 FLR 65 where the deceased repudiated his responsibility for maintaining his mistress so that she could not make a claim – see later).

## 8.5 Who may apply for an order

When a person dies domiciled in England and Wales and is survived by any of the following persons:

1.  the wife or husband of the deceased (s1(1)(a);
2.  a former wife or former husband of the deceased who has not remarried (s1(1)(b));
3.  an unmarried partner of the deceased but only if the deceased died on or after 1 January 1996 and during the whole of the period of two years ending immediately before the date when the deceased died the person was living in the

same household as the deceased and 'as the husband or wife' of the deceased (s1(1)(ba) and (1A) as added by s2 Law Reform (Succession) Act 1995);
4. a child of the deceased (s1(1)(c));
5. any person (not being a child of the deceased) who, in the case of any marriage to which the deceased was at any time a party, was treated by the deceased as a child of the family in relation to that marriage (s1(1)(d));
6. any person (not being included in the foregoing paragraphs of this subsection) who immediately before the death of the deceased was being maintained, either wholly or partly by the deceased (s1(1)(e));

that person may apply for an order under s2 of the 1975 Act.

## 8.6 How the two-stage test is applied to each kind of applicant

### Married spouses

A married spouse includes the spouse of a polygamous marriage (*Re Sehota (deceased)* [1978] 1 WLR 1506; [1978] 3 All ER 385 where the first wife applied since the second wife received everything under the deceased's will).

It includes void marriages where entered into in good faith and nullity proceedings have not been instituted and neither spouse has remarried during the deceased's lifetime (s25(4) I(PFD)A 1975). In *Ghandi* v *Patel* [2002] Fam Law 262 a void marriage not entered into in good faith fell foul of s25(4) and a claim by the 'wife' was dismissed.

It includes judicially separated spouses unless they have applied for financial provision under MCA 1973 and the court ordered that they be debarred from making application under the 1975 Act as part of the settlement of financial provision (see s15 1975 Act).

It includes divorced spouses where the decree was within twelve months of the death and no order has yet been made for financial provision. Otherwise divorced spouses must apply under s1(1)(b)(s14).

Applying the first part of the test: has the deceased by will or intestacy failed to make reasonable financial provision for the spouse?

Reasonable financial provision is defined in s1(2)(a) in the case of married spouses as such financial provision as would be reasonable in all the circumstances for a spouse to receive whether or not that provision is for his or her maintenance. Reasonable financial provision, therefore, has a wide meaning since it is not restricted to maintenance of the married spouse and can include more generous provision. Section 1(2)(a) does not apply to a judicially separated spouse where at the date of death the decree was still in force and the separation was continuing. Section 1(2)(b) would then apply (see below).

The court must consider the position of what the married spouse would be entitled to if there had been divorce proceedings (s3(2)). The court should then consider a similar amount in any provision it makes from the estate to that likely to be ordered under ss23 or 24 MCA 1973.

The age of the applicant and the duration of the marriage must be considered, as well as the contribution made by the applicant to the welfare of the family of the deceased, including any contributions made by looking after the home or caring for the family (s3(2)).

The courts will take account of the House of Lords decision in *White* v *White* [2000] 2 FLR 981. For example, in *Adams* v *Lewis* [2001] 2 WTLR 493 H and W had been married for 54 years. There were 12 children of the marriage, one of whom predeceased him. H died leaving an estate of £350,000 and left £10,000 to W plus his goods and personal effects. He left the balance to his children and the children of his deceased daughter. W was aged 86 and had assets of £6,000 and a state pension. While the children were not well off, none were in signficant need. W claimed greater provision. The court asked itself what W would have received had the marriage ended in divorce applying *White* v *White*. An order was made giving her roughly half the estate. In other cases the wife may be entitled to more than half of the estate. This happened in *Kusminow* v *Barclays Bank Trust Co Ltd* [1989] Fam Law 66, where the estate was valued at £100,000 with the wife having assets of £20,000. The deceased left all his estate to improverished relatives living in Russia. It was held that the wife was entitled to more than a half share of their joint assets because of her age (78) and her arthritis, namely £45,000 from the estate giving her £65,000 in total. The court will take account that a surviving spouse may need a capital reserve for future contingencies (eg to pay for private medical care). For example, in *Jessup* v *Jessup* [1992] 1 FLR 591 a surviving wife successfully claimed greater provision for this reason. In *Re Krubert (deceased)* [1996] 3 WLR 959 a conflict of emphasis was identified between *Moody* v *Stevenson* [1992] 2 WLR 640 (which stated that the starting point will be consideration of the presumed entitlement of the spouse under a notional divorce) and *Re Besterman* (above) (which stated that such a presumed entitlement was merely one of the factors, albeit an important one). It was said that the approach in *Re Besterman* was preferable since the divorce situation dealt with two spouses, while the 1975 Act was concerned with one surviving spouse. This may again mean that the surviving spouse could get a larger (or possibly smaller) share than a notional divorce settlement because of the wider picture.

Earlier decisions which gave the claimant wife a smaller share of the estate may have to be reconsidered in light of *White* v *White*. For example, in *Re Besterman* (above) the applicant wife was given a quarter of the estate. In *Re Bunning* [1984] 3 All ER 1 the wife was awarded a lump sum which allowed her to meet her 'reasonable requirements'. This approach was expressly rejected in *White*.

For an example of where a claim by a surviving spouse failed see *Re Clarke (deceased)* [1991] Fam Law 364 where a couple aged 71 and 78 married. The husband died leaving an estate of £179,501. He left his wife a life interest in the house and in his savings which would then pass to his children and grandchildren.

The wife had savings of £30,000. It was held that both in respect of divorce and inheritance what was required was that the wife should be housed, have an income to enable her to live reasonably comfortably and that she should have something to fall back on for future contingencies. The husband had made reasonable financial provision for the wife and her claim failed. See also *Parish v Sharman* [2001] 2 WTLR 593 in which H and W were married in 1967. They separated in 1985 and W petitioned for divorce but the decree was never made absolute and no application for ancillary relief was made. H then lived with S. In 1996 H died leaving his business to a friend and the rest of his property to S. W claimed reasonable financial provision from H's estate. The court dismissed her claim concluding that when H and W separated they had concluded their affairs conclusively and that W had allowed H to arrange his affairs on the basis that he was divorced from her. W's appeal was dismissed.

## Former spouses who have not remarried

Applying the first part of the test: has the deceased failed to make reasonable financial provision for the former spouse?

Reasonable financial provision is more narrowly defined in s1(2)(b) as such financial provision as would be reasonable for the applicant to receive for his or her maintenance. This may be a lot less than the wider definition applied in the case of married spouses under s1(2)(a).

There will be few cases where the test can be satisfied since such former spouses will have already been to the divorce court and already had the benefit of financial provision ordered by the court which, in the normal course of events, would have provided for their reasonable maintenance.

See *Re Fullard* [1981] 3 WLR 743; [1981] 2 All ER 796 where the deceased married the applicant, his first wife. They divorced. In the divorce settlement she was given the house and in return she paid him a lump sum to compensate him for the loss of his interest in the house. The deceased then remarried. He died leaving all his estate to his second wife. The applicant sought an order under the 1975 Act.

HELD: She had already had reasonable financial provision made for her in the divorce settlement. Her application was in effect an attempt to recoup the lump sum she had had to pay to the deceased for his share in the house. It was an unreasonable application and was dismissed.

*Re Fullard* was followed in *Barrass v Harding* [2000] Fam Law 878 in which H married W1. They had a son, S. After a marriage of 25 years H and W1 divorced in 1964. Ancillary relief was ordered by consent (though at a time when the law did not allow for extensive relief for W1). H then married W2. H had nothing further to do with W1, although he helped out S with respect to a car. W2 died in 1996 and H made a will leaving his property to W2's sister, B. Both W1 and S were in poor financial circumstances. W1 claimed financial provision from H's will. Financial provision was ordered. B appealed. The appeal was allowed since it was held that

H's failure to provide for W1 was not unreasonable on an objective basis. There were no special circumstances to justify an award (following *Re Fullard*). In this case H's freedom to dipose of his estate outweighed any sympathy for W1's parlous financial state.

But there may be circumstances where application can be made. See *Re Crawford* (1982) 4 FLR 273 where after the divorce settlement a large sum of money went into the deceased's estate from an insurance policy. The deceased failed to make any provision for the applicant from this money. Provision could be made for the applicant from this new source of money which had not been considered by the divorce court.

NOTE: The divorce court can order that a spouse be debarred from making application under the 1975 Act to provide a full and final settlement between the spouses. In such circumstances a divorced spouse would be prevented from making any application in any event (see s15 1975 Act).

If the court can hear the application it must consider in particular the age of the applicant and the duration of the marriage as well as the contributions made by the applicant to the welfare of the family, including any contributions made by looking after the home or caring for the children of the family (s3(2)).

In *Re Farrow (deceased)* [1987] 1 FLR 205 a wife divorced her husband. She was given a lump sum of £50,000 and maintenance of £5,500 a year. The husband made one maintenance payment and then stopped paying. The wife got into debt. The husband died and made no provision for the wife in his will. She applied for provision from his estate.

HELD: Having regard to the wife's age, the duration of the marriage, her contribution to the marriage and to s3 and the fact that the husband had not paid maintenance to her for seven years he should have provided for her in his will. The estate was ordered to pay £5,000 a year and a lump sum of £15,000 to the wife.

In *Cameron* v *Treasury Solicitor* [1996] 2 FLR 716, after 14 years of marriage H and W had divorced in 1971. There was a clean break order whereby W received £4,000. There was no order under s15 I(PFD)A 1975 preventing any applications under that Act. H died intestate, leaving an estate of £7,600 which passed to the Crown. W, who was financially in very straitened circumstances, claimed financial provision. The court ordered that the whole estate be paid to her. The Treasury Solicitor appealed.

HELD: Allowing the appeal, the question was whether it was reasonable or not in all the circumstances of the case for H not to have made financial provision for W. Section 3(1) I(PFD)A 1975 provided guidance to the court. It was particularly relevant to consider whether H had any obligations or responsibilities towards W (s3(1)(d)). Although there had been a continuing friendship between H and W this did not suffice to constitute any new or continuing obligation on H. Special circumstances would have to be shown to justify an award (see *Re Fullard* [1981] 2 All ER 796). In this case there were none.

## Unmarried partners

This class of claimant was only introduced where the deceased died on or after 1 January 1996 and during the whole of the period of two years ending immediately before the death of the deceased the claimant was living in the same household as the deceased and as the husband or wife of the deceased (s1(1A) 1975 Act). In addition to the general considerations in s3, the court must consider the age of the applicant and the length of time he/she lived as husband or wife in the same household as the deceased. The court must also consider the contribution made by the applicant to the welfare of the family of the deceased including any contributions made by looking after the home or caring for the family (s3(2A) 1975 Act).

In *Re Watson (deceased)* [1999] 1 FLR 878 A and W had a relationship for 30 years. They did not marry and lived apart caring for their respective elderly parents. After those parents died, A (in her mid forties) left the house she owned to live with W. She contributed half of the outgoings and cooked, cleaned and washed for W. They slept in separate bedrooms and did not have sexual relations (though they had previously had sexual relations earlier in their relationship). After ten years W died intestate and with no relations. His estate passed to the Crown as bona vacantia. A claimed provision under s1(1A) of the 1975 Act. It was held that A met the criteria in s1(1A) and the lack of provision for her was not reasonable and that provision should be made for her.

## Children of the deceased

Children include legitimate and illegitimate children (s25(1)), children adopted by the deceased and children conceived while the deceased was alive but who were born after he had died (s25(1)). There is no restriction on age (see *Re Debenham* [1986] Fam Law 101). Many claimants are 'adult' children of the deceased. There is no restriction if the child is married. Children of the deceased who are then adopted by another person cease to be children of the deceased and cannot claim (see *Re Collins* [1990] 2 All ER 47).

Applying the first part of the test: has the deceased failed to make reasonable financial provision for the child? Reasonable financial provision is given the restricted meaning in s1(2)(b), so is such financial provision as would be reasonable for the child to receive for his or her maintenance. Maintenance does not include the payment of debts (eg debts to the tax authorities – *Re Dennis* [1981] 2 All ER 140). Maintenance involves living expenses such as housing, food, clothing and entertainment. It does not mean a basic or subsistence level but in a manner suitable to the claimant's circumstances (see *Re Coventry* [1979] 2 WLR 853; [1979] 3 All ER 815) or to live decently and comfortably according to the claimant's station in life (see *Re Leach* [1985] 2 All ER 754 and *Re Christie* [1979] 2 WLR 105; [1979] 1 All ER 546).

Applying the second part of the test: should the court in its discretion order financial provision for the child? There appear to be two schools of thought. The older cases obliged the claimant to establish a moral claim to be provided for and would not grant provision merely because the claimant was the child of the deceased, particularly if the child is young, healthy and able to go out to work. Examples of such cases include:

1. *Re Dennis* (above) where the claim by the son failed because he established no moral claim and the court was of the view that he was a 'rolling stone', a spendthrift who was well able to earn his living if he got down to it.
2. *Re Coventry* (above) where the claim by the son also failed because he established no moral claim. He had lived with his father free of charge and though he had looked after him this was an arrangement of mutual convenience and there was little love lost between them. His claim would have reduced his needy mother's share of the estate.
3. *Williams* v *Johns* [1988] 2 FLR 475 which involved an adopter daughter claiming from her adoptive mother's estate. The daughter had had a stormy life but was supported by her mother who got nothing in return. In the end the mother repudiated her and expressly left her out of her will. She left her estate to her natural son who had been dutiful and helpful to his mother. He disliked his adoptive sister because of her treatment of his mother. He opposed her claim since he had been made redundant and was anxious to keep his family (though he had sufficient earning capacity to meet his obligations). The daughter was unemployed and in poor financial circumstances. The daughter's claim failed because she failed to establish some sort of obligation to be maintained beyond the mere fact of an adoptive relationship. She was capable of maintaining herself and had been independent for many years. It was not unreasonable that the mother had made no provision for her in her will (*Re Coventry* and *Re Dennis* followed).
4. *Re Jennings* [1994] 3 WLR 67; [1994] 3 All ER 27; [1994] 1 FLR 536 in which the son, who was a successful businessman who lived comfortably but not excessively, claimed provision from his father's estate of £300,000 left to three charities. He had lived separately from his father since the age of two. In the absence of any moral obligation, taken with the son's financial circumstances, his claim failed.

Claims succeeded where a moral claim was established. For example see:

1. *Sivyer* v *Sivyer* [1967] 1 WLR 1482: [1967] 3 All ER 429 where the daughter argued that her step-mother had unfairly inherited property which originally came from the daughter's real mother
2. *Re Christie* [1979] 2 WLR 105; [1979] 1 All ER 546 where the son was able to show that his mother had intended to treat her two children equally, but had made a will which mistakenly left him worse off than his sister, and thereby establish a moral claim whereby his application was successful
3. *Re Debenham* [1986] Fam Law 101 where the daughter relied on a promise made

by her mother to provide for her in her will. When the mother died leaving an estate of £172,000 she only left £200 to her daughter and the rest to animal charities. The daughter was disabled and had a husband who had been made redundant. In light of the promise it was held that the mother had failed to make reasonable financial provision for her. The court awarded her £3,000 and periodical payments of £4,500 for her lifetime.

4. *Re Collins* (above) where the mother had made an invalid will and her property passed under intestacy to her violent husband from whom she was separated. Her two children had been taken into care. Her illegitimate daughter (who was unemployed) was awarded £5,000 from her estate. Her legitimate son's claim failed because he had been adopted.

5. *Re Goodchild* [1996] 1 WLR 694; [1996] 1 All ER 670; [1996] 1 FLR 4 in which a son's claim succeeded because of an understanding that his mother's estate would pass to her husband and then to their son when in fact the husband passed the property to his second wife. The son was on a limited income. It was held that the husband (or the claimant's father) was wrong to pass the property to his second wife, particularly in relation to property owned by his first wife (the claimant's mother).

6. *Re Abram (deceased)* [1997] 1 WLR 1216; [1996] 2 FLR 644 in which the son had worked for his mother's business for many years at a low wage in the expectation that the business would be his. He and his mother then fell out and she altered her will, disinheriting him. They were then reconciled but the mother did not change her will, though she said she would do so. There was overwhelming evidence of a moral obligation whereby her failure to provide for her son was unreasonable. Financial provision was ordered.

More recent cases suggest that adult children do not need to establish a moral obligation or special circumstances. For example, see:

1. *Re Hancock (deceased)* [1998] 2 FLR 346 in which H was married to W and had seven children. He died in 1985 leaving a plot of land (then valued at £100,000) to four of his sons and one of his three daughters, D1, involved in the family business. He left the residue to W. His will expressed the wish that W should make provision in her will for the two remaining daughters, D2 and D3, not involved in the business. In 1986 D2, aged 58 years, applied for financial provision under the 1975 Act. By that time the family business had sold the land for £663,000. W died and left £1,000 to D2. D2 was in straightened financial circumstances. She was awarded £3,000 a year from the estate. The four brothers and sister, D1, appealed arguing that D2 had failed to establish some moral obligation on H towards D2 (following *Re Coventry* and *Re Jennings*). The appeal was dismissed. It was held that an adult child did not necessarily have to show that the deceased owed to the child a moral obligation or that there were other special circumstances. However, a claim made by an adult child with an established earning capacity may well fail in the absence of such factors.

2. *Re Pearce (deceased)* [1998] 2 FLR 705 in which P had a son, S, aged 29 years. P lived with a woman for some three-and-a-half years. When he died he left his estate worth £285,000 to her and nothing to S. S applied for financial provision. The judge held that P was under a moral obligation to S arising from substantial work S had put into P's farm coupled with promises that S would inherit the farm. He awarded S £85,000. The legatee appealed. The appeal was dismissed. Following *Re Hancock* (above) there was no prerequisite that a moral obligation or special circumstances had to be shown to justify an award. The existence of a moral obligation was relevant under s3(1)(d). The court considered S's needs under s3(1)(a) and those of the legatee under s3(1)(c) in determining that reasonable financial provision had not been made for S (*Re Jennings* (above) distinguished). Though awards (save for surviving spouses) are restricted to what is required for maintenance, the capital award in this case could be justified as meeting income needs of a recurrent nature).

3. *Espinosa v Bourke* [1999] 1 FLR 747 in which D agreed to care for her elderly father, F. D gave up her part-time job and F sold his home, discharged the mortgage on D's home and paid for home improvements and family outgoings. F disapproved of D's lifestyle, which included a number of marriages, the last of which was to an unemployed Spanish fisherman. In the last year of his life, D spent most of her time in Spain, leaving F, aged 87, in the care of D's son and a cleaner. F left his estate to D's son and nothing to D. D claimed provision based in part on a promise F made to his wife before she died that he would leave his shares to D. The court dismissed her claim since F had no continuing obligation to D in light of the financial contributions he had made and the lack of commitment by D to F in the last year of his life. D appealed. It was held, allowing the appeal, that a 'moral obligation' was not an essential requirement for an adult child's claim to succeed. The court had wrongly focused too much on the requirement to show a moral obligation and had failed to consider the needs and resources of D. She had little earning capacity and was in financial need. The court had failed to give proper weight to F's promise to his wife. D was awarded £60,000. Although the question of a moral obligation was not a threshold requirement, it was the case that an applicant of working age with a job (or job capacity) would have to identify some very weighty factor to establish a failure to make reasonable financial provision.

## Persons treated by the deceased as children of the family

A child of the family is any child who is not the real child of the deceased but has been treated by the deceased as his or her child nevertheless. Under the 1975 Act the term 'child of the family' is given a wide definition. It includes an adult child of the family who may not have been brought up as a young child by the deceased but who became a child of the deceased's family later.

See *Re Leach* [1985] 2 All ER 754, where the applicant had been brought up in her parents' house. Her mother died when the daughter was aged thirty-two and lived away from home. Her father married again. He died leaving his property to his second wife. The second wife never maintained the daughter. The daughter never lived in the second wife's household. However, the daughter visited the second wife (her stepmother) and they had a close relationship which was more like a mother-daughter relationship than a stepmother-stepchild relationship. The second wife died intestate and her estate went to her brothers and sisters who had had little contact with her. The daughter was then aged fifty-five.

HELD: The daughter could make a claim as a child of the deceased's family even though she had never lived in the deceased's household or been maintained by her.

See *Re Callaghan (deceased)* [1985] FLR 116; [1984] 3 All ER 790. After a son was born his father was killed in an accident. His mother then met another man. He treated the son as his own son. However, he and the mother did not get married until the son was twenty-three. The mother purchased the house where she and her second husband lived. The son then married. His children treated the second husband as their grandfather. His mother then died intestate so that all her estate went to her second husband. He then became ill. The son and wife took care of him during four months of illness. He nominated the son as his next of kin. He then died intestate. All the estate went to his sisters in Ireland who had had little contact with their brother. The son made a claim from the estate on the basis that he was a child of his step-father's family.

HELD: The son was a child of the family. His stepfather had treated the son as his child before he married the son's mother. The son had a moral claim on his stepfather's estate because of the care he and his wife had given to the deceased during his distressing illness. That obligation was stronger than any claim the sisters of the deceased had.

Applying the first part of the test: has the deceased failed to make reasonable financial provision for the child of the family?

Reasonable financial provision has the restricted meaning in s1(2)(b) and so is restricted to such financial provision as would be reasonable for the applicant to receive for his or her maintenance.

See *Re Leach* above, where the applicant was a spinster aged fifty-five who needed financial independence since it was unlikely she would marry. When she retired she would suffer a serious drop in her income. The fact that she received nothing from the deceased meant that she had not received reasonable financial provision under s1(2)(b).

Applying the second part of the test: should the court in its discretion order financial provision for the child of the family?

In *Re Leach* most of the deceased's estate in fact came from the applicant's father. The deceased had encouraged the applicant to buy a house in the expectation that she would receive something on the deceased's death. The applicant had established a moral claim whereby the court would make an order in her favour. She received a lump sum of £14,000 to enable her to buy a house.

In *Re Callaghan* most of the estate came from a house purchased by the applicant's mother. Given that fact and the care he and his wife had provided to the deceased during his illness a moral claim on the deceased's estate had been established. The applicant was awarded a lump sum of £15,000 to enable him to buy a house for his family.

The court is directed to have particular regard to the following in applying the test:

1. the manner in which the applicant was being or in which he might expect to be educated or trained;
2. did the deceased assume any responsibility for the applicant's maintenance and, if so, to what extent, on what basis and for how long;
3. whether the deceased did so knowing the applicant was not his own child;
4. the liability of other persons to maintain the applicant.

## Persons being maintained either wholly or partly by the deceased

Being maintained by the deceased is defined in s1(3) as being otherwise than for valuable consideration (and so excluding paid housekeepers, servants, companions etc); and the deceased made a substantial contribution in money or money's worth towards the reasonable needs of that person.

This definition excludes a couple living together who pool their resources and equally provide for each other.

In *Re Beaumont* [1979] 3 WLR 818; [1980] 1 All ER 266 Mr Martin lived with Mrs Beaumont. She provided the accommodation for which he paid rent. She paid the outgoings of the household but he contributed towards the shopping bills. She did the cooking and washing. He did the household and gardening jobs. He bought the car and paid for its running expenses. She paid for it to be insured. The court took the view that each provided equally to each other's maintenance. Mrs Beaumont died. Mr Martin applied for provision from her estate.

HELD: There was no undertaking or assuming of responsibility by Mrs Beaumont for Mr Martin's maintenance. He did not fall within the definition in s1(3). His application was dismissed.

However, a number of cases can be contrasted with *Re Beaumont* where claims did succeed.

See *Jelley* v *Iliffe* [1981] 2 WLR 801; [1981] 2 All ER 29 where two pensioners lived together and pooled their resources. The deceased provided the applicant with rent free accommodation and cooked and washed for him. The applicant did the gardening and household jobs and provided companionship for the deceased.

HELD: There was a substantial contribution made by the deceased towards the reasonable needs of the applicant, namely, the provision of free accommodation. The applicant could make a claim for financial provision.

See *Re Wilkinson* [1978] 1 All ER 221; [1977] 3 WLR 514 where two elderly sisters lived together. The deceased was a childless widow who had worsening arthritis. She provided rent free board and lodging to her sister, the applicant, and paid all the household bills. The applicant helped her sister to dress and did light chores. She provided companionship. A home help did all the heavy work.

HELD: The applicant was being maintained under s1(3) because of the provision of free board and lodging. The services she rendered to the deceased were not for valuable consideration and did not exclude her application. The onus was upon her to satisfy the court that she was within the statute and this she had done.

See *Harrington* v *Gill* (1983) 4 FLR 265 where a couple lived together. The deceased provided the applicant with a free accommodation and paid all the outgoings. The applicant did all the housework. When the deceased died he left all his money to his comfortably off daughter.

HELD: The applicant was being maintained within the meaning of s1(3). She was given a lump sum of £10,000 to provide for her maintenance and the deceased's house was settled on her for her lifetime.

See *Bishop* v *Plumley* [1991] 1 All ER 236 where Mrs Bishop and Mr Plumley were married to other people. They lived with each other for ten years in rented accommodation pooling their state benefits and Mr Plumley's modest earnings. A relative of Mr Plumley died leaving him a sum of money which he used to buy a house in which he and Mrs Bishop lived. She cared for Mr Plumley as he progressively became more ill with angina. During a short period when they were separated Mr Plumley made a will leaving his estate to his children. They then lived together until Mr Plumley died. Mrs Bishop had no assets of her own. She claimed provision from his estate. Her claim was dismissed since she was held not to have been maintained by the deceased (since their resources were pooled) and the benefit to her of rent-free accommodation was balanced with the valuable consideration of her care for him. She appealed.

HELD: Allowing the appeal, the test whether an applicant was being maintained by the deceased wholly or partly before his death was whether the applicant had received a substantial contribution in money or money's worth towards the applicant's needs from the deceased otherwise than for valuable consideration. The court had to make a common sense comparison of the benefits which flowed between the couple. If the flow of benefits was broadly equal between them, that would show that the applicant had given valuable consideration for the benefits conferred by the deceased. If there was an obvious imbalance in the flow of benefits because those conferred by the deceased outweighed those conferred by the applicant, that would show that the deceased had made a substantial contribution towards the applicant's needs within s1(3). Where the deceased had provided a secure home for his partner and she had provided him with connubial services, that would show that the deceased had made such a substantial contribution for the purposes of s1(3). Mrs Bishop's care and attention of Mr Plumley was not valuable consideration for him providing her with a secure rent-free home but was part of their relationship (*Jelley* v *Illiffe*, above, applied).

In *Graham* v *Murphy* [1997] 1 FLR 6 G and M lived together for 17 years. M earned £50,000 annually from a family business while G was an HGV driver and manager earning £8,500 a year. They first lived in rented accommodation then in a house bought by M. They enjoyed a high standard of living mostly financed by M. M became ill and G cared for her. M died in 1994 intestate leaving a net estate of £240,000. Under the rules of intestacy M's parents inherited the estate. They had no need for the additional capital. G claimed provision from the estate. It was held that M had maintained G for nine years of their relationship. He had obtained free accommodation and received substantial subsidies in relation to their standard of living. He qualified as a 'dependant' under s1(1)(e) of the 1975 Act. G established that the rules of intestacy meant that reasonable provision had not been made for him. The absence of any other dependency or strong moral claim, the length of G and M's relationship and his care for M in her last illness were influential factors. A lump sum of £35,000 (to buy a house) and the transfer of a motor vehicle to G was ordered.

In *Rees* v *Newbery* [1998] 1 FLR 1041 R, with a modest income, lived in flat owned by the deceased, D, for ten years at substantially below the market rent. D given instructions for a new will under which this arrangement would continue for the rest of R's life but died before the will could be completed. D left an estate worth £700,000. D had no family and the money was left to charities. R applied for financial provision. It was held that the provision of accommodation at less then market rent constituted maintenance under the 1975 Act and on the facts D had assumed responsibility for R's maintenance. R was entitled to apply for provision. Objectively D had failed to make reasonable financial provision taking into account D's wishes (*Jelley* v *Iliffe*). It was in the interests of the charities that the flat be sold with vacant possession. R was awarded a lump sum of £64,000 which capitalised the loss of the value of accommodation.

Persons being maintained wholly or partly by the deceased may include mistresses; see *Malone* v *Harrison* [1979] 1 WLR 1353 where the deceased had a wife. He was separated from her. He lived with a woman whom he treated as his wife. However, he also had a mistress whom he took on holidays. He also paid her living expenses. He promised to marry her if he was free to do so. He told her that he would not provide for her in his will but he did point out that she might be able to claim under the 1975 Act. He died leaving his estate of £480,500 to his separated wife and to the woman he lived with.

HELD: The deceased had assumed full responsibility for his mistress's maintenance for twelve years. He had intended that she should be provided for after his death. She was entitled to financial provision which had to be balanced with his obligation to provide for the woman he had lived with. The mistress received a lump sum of £19,000 to give her a steady income. She was already working but could only earn a low wage.

But if the deceased clearly abandoned his responsibility for the applicant then a claim will fail. See *Kourkey* v *Lusher* (1983) 4 FLR 65 where the deceased maintained a mistress. He went on holiday with his wife. On his return he declared clearly that he regarded his responsibility for maintaining the mistress to be at an end. He died nine days later.

HELD: The mistress could not make a claim. The responsibility for her maintenance had finished before the deceased had died, and so she did not qualify under s1(2)(e) or (3).

See *Layton* v *Martin* [1986] 2 FLR 277 where a woman became a man's mistress for four years. He paid her a monthly 'salary' as his 'secretary' plus housekeeping. He made a will leaving her £15,000. The relationship then ended. He cut the woman out of his will. Two years later he died leaving an estate of £365,000. The woman claimed provision from his estate.

HELD: She had no claim under the 1975 Act since she had ceased to live with the deceased.

NOTE: She made claims against his estate based on the promise of financial security the man had given to her. She argued that there was a constructive trust or a proprietary estoppel or an enforceable contract based on that promise whereby she was entitled to provision from the estate. The court rejected all her claims since the man's promise was too vague to be enforceable and the woman had simply lived with him without making any relevant contribution to the acquisition or preservation of any assets, and so there could be no trust. This illustrates how difficult it can be for a mistress to make any claim if she falls outside the scope of the 1975 Act.

There is no need for the deceased to have declared responsibility for the applicant. Section 1(2)(e) and (3) are based on the deceased's actions, not on his or her intentions. The question is whether the applicant has been placed in a position of dependency.

The court will look at the arrangements made generally before the death of the deceased. It may ignore fluctuations in the deceased's final weeks where during such an emotional time changes may occur which may be contrary to what the deceased may have done for many years. In *Kourkey* v *Lusher* (above) the deceased's change of mind was considered to be fully considered and not a 'fluctuation'.

Applying the first part of the test: has the deceased failed to provide reasonable financial provision for the dependent person?

Reasonable financial provision is again given the restricted meaning in s1(2)(b).

The court must in particular have regard to the extent to which, the basis on which, and for how long, the deceased assumed responsibility for the applicant's maintenance (s3(4)).

The cases already reviewed show how the first part of the test as well as the second part of the test work in practice.

In *Bouette* v *Rose* [2000] 1 FLR 363 it was held that the mother could be a dependant of her child and on the child's death was entitled to claim maintenance from the child's estate. The case involved a child awarded a large sum of compensation. The payments by the Court of Protection had to be used to meet the financial and material needs of the child's mother who was providing day-to-day care so that the mother could look after the daughter's physical and emotional needs. Since that Court could be taken to have appreciated that their payments were going to meet the mother's needs as well as those of the daughter, the mother was a dependant on the child.

## 8.7 The orders the court can make

Section 2 Inheritance (Provision for Family and Dependants) Act 1975 provides:

'(1) Subject to the provisions of this Act, where an application is made for an order under this section, the court may, if it is satisfied that the disposition of the deceased's estate effected by his will or the law relating to intestacy, or the combination of his will and that law, is not such as to make reasonable financial provision for the applicant, make any one or more of the following orders –

(a) an order for the making to the applicant out of the net estate of the deceased of such periodical payments and for such terms as may be specified in the order;

(b) an order for the payment to the applicant out of that estate of a lump sum of such amount as may be so specified [the most common form of order eg *Re Leach* and *Re Callaghan* where a lump sum was provided so that applicant could buy a house];

(c) an order for the transfer to the applicant of such property comprised in that estate as may be so specified;

(d) an order for the settlement for the benefit of the applicant of such property comprised in that estate as may be so specified [eg *Harrington* v *Gill* where the house was settled on the applicant for her life];

(e) an order for the acquisition out of property comprised in that estate of such property as may be so specified and for the transfer of the property so acquired to the applicant or for the settlement thereof for his benefit;

(f) an order varying any ante-nuptial or post-nuptial settlement (including such a settlement made by will) made on the parties to a marriage to which the deceased was one of the parties, the variation being for the benefit of the surviving party to that marriage, or any child of that marriage, or any person who was treated by the deceased as a child of the family in relation to that marriage.'

The court in considering what order to make must have regard to the matters in s3(1).

The court has power to make interim provision if the applicant is in need of immediate financial assistance (s5) and also to vary, discharge or suspend orders for periodical payments (s6) and to order the payment of lump sums by instalments (s7). The court has no power to vary lump sum or property orders, and so when making such orders the court must allow for future contingencies.

Section 16 authorises the court on an application under s2 of this Act to vary or discharge secured periodical payments orders made under MCA 1973. (NOTE: where there is no application under s2, then former spouses will have to rely on s31 MCA 1973 to vary or discharge the order and also if s15 (above) applies.)

Section 17 also authorises the court, on an application under s2 of this Act, to revoke or vary a maintenance agreement expressed to continue after death, so that a separate application under s36 MCA 1973 will not be necessary in such circumstances. (Although, as before, where there is no s2 application, s36 will have to be relied upon to vary the maintenance agreement and also where s15 above applies.)

Conversely, s18 provides that a court hearing an application for variation after death under s31(6) or s36(1) MCA 1973 may exercise any of the wider powers available under the 1975 Act (eg powers under ss10 and 11 1975 Act to review dispositions or contracts made by the deceased during his lifetime).

## 8.8 Clean break provision

On the grant of a decree of divorce, nullity or judicial separation or at any time thereafter, the court, if it considers it just to do so, may on the application of either party to the marriage, may order that the other party to the marriage shall not on the death of the applicant be entitled to apply for an order under s2 (s15(1)).

The court can, therefore, dismiss the claim a party may have had on the estate of the other spouse, with or without the consent of that party, as part of a clean break order.

An order under s15 should not be made automatically. In order to consider whether such an order is 'just' the court should be given some indication of what an estate is likely to consist of and some details of the persons whom the applicant considers to have a prior claim on his estate in the event of his death (ie there must be evidence to support a s15 order) (see *Whiting* v *Whiting* [1988] 1 WLR 565).

# 9

# Financial Relief During the Marriage

9.1 Introduction

9.2 High Court and county court

9.3 Orders

9.4 Child support

## 9.1 Introduction

Spouses may wish to apply for financial relief when they have separated but have not divorced so that they remain married. If a wife has suddenly been abandoned by her husband she will want maintenance quickly to provide for her and the children until she decides whether to seek long term relief through divorce. She will have the following options open to her:

1. to petition for divorce and apply for maintenance pending suit under s22 MCA 1973;
2. apply for maintenance to the High Court or county court under s27 MCA 1973 (dealt with below);
3. apply for maintenance to the magistrates' court under s2 or s6 Domestic Proceedings and Magistrates' Courts Act 1978 (see Chapter 11);
4. apply to the High Court or county court or magistrates' court for maintenance for the children (not for herself) under s15 and Sched 1 Children Act 1989 (see Chapter 11);
5. apply for child support through the Child Support Agency.

Normally the quickest, cheapest and most convenient remedy is to apply to the magistrates' court. As far as maintenance for the children is concerned application must be made to the Child Support Agency for child support since the courts are unlikely to have any jurisdiction to deal with child maintenance.

195

## 9.2 High Court and county court

Section 27(1) Matrimonial Causes Act 1973 (as amended by s63 Domestic Proceedings and Magistrates' Courts Act 1978) provides:

'(1) Either party to a marriage may apply to the court for an order under this section on the ground that the other party to the marriage (in this section referred to as the respondent) –
(a) has failed to provide reasonable maintenance for the applicant; or
(b) has failed to provide, or to make a proper contribution towards, reasonable maintenance for any child of the family.'

## 9.3 Orders

The orders which may be made are periodical payments, secured periodical payments and lump sum orders. Lump sums are subject to s27(7):

'(7) Without prejudice to the generality of subsection (6)(c) or (f) above, an order under this section for the payment of a lump sum –
(a) may be made for the purpose of enabling any liabilities or expenses reasonably incurred in maintaining the applicant or any child of the family to whom the application relates before the making of the application to be met;
(b) may provide for the payment of that sum by instalments of such amounts as may be specified in the order and may require the payment of the instalments to be secured to the satisfaction of the court.'

The court will have regard to the matters mentioned in s25 when deciding upon an order subject to the same amendment regarding conduct made in regard to magistrates' courts. Where an application is also made in respect of a minor child of the family, first consideration shall be given to the welfare of the child.

### Scope of orders

Orders are subject to same rules as to duration as in divorce and judicial separation, etc (see ss28 and 29 MCA 1973).

It can be ordered for the wife and the children even though there has only been neglect to maintain one or the other.

It can be granted after judicial separation.

Maintenance pending suit cannot be awarded. However, the court can make an interim order before liability for maintenance is established if there is a need for immediate financial assistance. When a full order is made the payments can be backdated to cover the period from when the application was made to when the order is made by the court.

If an order is made, the court may deal with the residence of and contact with the children.

## 9.4  Child support

Following the coming into force of the Child Support Act 1991 most applications for the financial support of children must be made to the Child Support Agency, *not* the court.

# 10

# Occupation of the Family Home and Property Rights

10.1 Introduction

10.2 Applications under s17 Married Women's Property Act 1882

10.3 How an interest in land may be acquired

10.4 Contractual licence

10.5 Proprietary estoppel

10.6 Equitable accounting

10.7 When the court values the interest under a trust

10.8 Proposals for reform to the law of property rights between unmarried couples

10.9 Trusts of Land and Appointment of Trustees Act 1996

10.10 Allowances for housekeeping and maintenance

10.11 Bank accounts

10.12 Engagements

10.13 The protection of beneficial interests against third parties

10.14 Matrimonial home rights

10.15 Occupation of the matrimonial home when one spouse is bankrupt

10.16 Excluding the violent partner from the family home

## 10.1 Introduction

Courts have a very wide discretion to make orders concerning the matrimonial home in divorce proceedings under s24 MCA 1973 having regard to s25 MCA 1973. However, disputes over the matrimonial home do not only arise in divorce, nullity and judicial separation proceedings. Parties may ask the court to resolve such disputes in other ways. In particular, unmarried couples cannot use MCA 1973.

The main remedies available to resolve disputes are:

1. an order under s17 Married Women's Property Act 1882;
2. a declaration of property interest under the inherent jurisdiction of the court;
3. enforcing a trust for sale under the Trusts of Land and Appointment of Trustees Act 1996;
4. establishing rights of occupation under the Family Law Act 1996; and
5. excluding a violent spouse or partner under the Family Law Act 1996 and under the inherent powers of the court.

## 10.2 Applications under s17 Married Women's Property Act 1882

Parties who may apply under s17 MWPA 1882:

1. husband or wife;
2. former parties to the marriage if application is made within three years of decree absolute of divorce or nullity (eg where a wife has failed to make an application under s24 MCA 1973, and has remarried and so cannot make a new application under s24, she may apply under s17 MWPA 1882 as long as it is within three years of decree absolute); and
3. formerly engaged couples if an application is made within three years of the termination of the engagement.

Applications under s17 MWPA 1882 are not as frequent as those under s24 MCA 1973. However, s17 may still be important in the case of a spouse who fails to apply under s24 (as above) or who does not wish to commence divorce proceedings, or in the case of one or both spouses going bankrupt (where a decision as to who owns property may be important), or where questions of taxation arise in relation to ownership of property, or where one spouse dies and a dispute as to title to property arises.

### What the court has to consider under s17

Section 17 is widely framed. The court may consider any question 'as to the title to or possession of property' and may make 'such order with respect to the property in dispute as it thinks fit'.

The court may consider the property even if it has been sold since it may order payment from one spouse to the other or the sale of such property as represents the proceeds of the original property (s7 Matrimonial Causes (Property and Maintenance) Act 1958).

For many years the courts used s17 to do what they thought fit with matrimonial property having regard to the wife's often inferior position in having no legal interest in the home. The court took into account such general considerations as the wife's contribution to the family as a wife and mother as well as any financial contributions she had made to the home and thereby gave her a share in the matrimonial home. However, in two House of Lords decisions it was held that such general considerations were irrelevant and should not be considered. The courts had to decide applications on the legal and equitable principles of property law in order to decide who owned the property and the shares of each party.

In *Pettitt* v *Pettitt* [1970] AC 777; [1969] 2 WLR 966; [1969] 2 All ER 385 Lord Morris of Borth-y-Gest stated:

> 'In my view, all the indications are that s17 was purely a procedural section ... the procedure was devised as a means of resolving a dispute or question as to title rather than as a means of giving some title not previously existing.'

In *Gissing* v *Gissing* [1971] AC 886; [1970] 3 WLR 255; [1970] 2 All ER 780 Lord Diplock stated:

> '... the legal principles applicable to the claim are those of the English law of trusts and, in particular, in the kind of dispute between spouses that comes before the courts, the law relating to the creation and operation of "resulting, implied or constructive" trusts'.

The court must, therefore, apply principles of property law in resolving such a dispute. The question is 'whose is this?' according to the principles of property law, not 'to whom shall this be given?' according to what the court thinks is fair and just. The approach is totally different from that used under the MCA 1973 where the court is given a wide discretion to do what it feels is just and reasonable.

In order to understand how the courts will decide on disputes under s17 it is necessary to understand some basic principles of property law. Some of the cases relate to unmarried couples. They cannot make application under s17 but may, nevertheless, ask the court to declare their interests. The same principles apply to such an application as to one under s17.

## 10.3 How an interest in land may be acquired

### The conveyance

All conveyances of land or any interest in land must be by way of deed (see s52 Law of Property Act 1925).

A husband and wife may acquire an interest in land by conveying the land into their respective names by deed. Their interest in the land is recorded in the deeds to the land.

The conveyance (or lease) may not only declare in whom the legal title is to vest but also in whom the beneficial title is to vest. Any such declaration will be conclusive evidence as to ownership unless the conveyance can be set aside on the grounds of fraud or mistake.

For example, in *Goodman* v *Gallant* [1986] 1 All ER 311 the husband and wife purchased the matrimonial home. It was conveyed into the husband's name but it was not in doubt that the wife had a half share. The husband left the wife who remained in the house. She lived there with Mr Goodman. She and Mr Goodman agreed that the husband should sell them the house. He did so and a clause of the conveyance to the wife and Mr Goodman expressly stated that they held the property on trust as joint tenants (ie each entitled to half shares). The wife claimed a larger share.

HELD: The conveyance contained an express declaration of trust which declared the beneficial interests in the property. Until the conveyance was set aside or rectified those were the interests. There was no room for the wife trying to claim a larger share under the doctrine of resulting, implied or constructive trusts.

In *Turton* v *Turton* [1987] 2 All ER 641 a conveyance which conveyed a house into the names of an unmarried couple living together, contained an express declaration of trust that the couple held the property as beneficial joint tenants. The woman had made no contribution to the purchase of the property. The couple then separated and the woman asked the court to declare her interest in the house.

HELD: Where there was an express declaration regarding an unmarried couple's beneficial interest in a property that declaration was conclusive and excluded any discretionary jurisdiction to value the interests in any other way.

An unsigned deed or covenance may be used to decide interests. See *Re Gorman* [1990] 2 FLR 284 where a house was transferred to H and W in equal shares. The declaration of interests was unsigned. The court held that it pointed unequivocally to the house being held in equal shares even though W had contributed the largest share through a gift from her father and payment of the morgage after H had left.

In *Huntingford* v *Hobbs* [1993] 1 FLR 736 an unmarried couple bought a property and had it transferred into their joint names. The transfer contained a declaration that 'the survivor of them can give a valid receipt for capital money arising on the disposition of the land'. Of the purchase price £38,860 had been provided by the respondent from the sale of her previous house with the balance paid by a mortgage of £25,000 which the appellant agreed to pay. The appellant then left and married another woman. The house was then worth £95,000 with the mortgage liability still £25,000. The judge ordered that the house should be sold and the proceeds divided on the basis of the actual monetary contributions of the parties which left the appellant with only a £3,500 share of the proceeds. He appealed on the basis that the transfer of property contained a declaration of beneficial interests which entitled him to a half share.

HELD: Following *Goodman* v *Gallant* a declaration of trust in the transfer would conclusively define the parties' respective beneficial interests. The crucial question was whether the transfer contained the declaration the appellant alleged. In *Re Gorman* a declaration in the transfer that the parties were entitled 'for their own benefit' had been held to unequivocally point to a joint tenancy. However in *Harwood* v *Harwood* [1991] 2 FLR 274 a declaration in terms identical to the present case was held not to be a declaration of beneficial interests but one for the benefit of third parties. The court followed *Harwood* and determined that there was no declaration of beneficial interests in the transfer. In the absence of such a declaration the parties' respective beneficial interests fell to be determined by resulting trust principles and therefore by their respective contributions to the purchase price. In this case the most likely inference from the conduct of the parties was that they had a common intention on the date of purchase that the respondent provide a cash sum and the appellant provide the balance by way of mortgage. On that basis the respondent was entitled to a 39 per cent share in the proceeds of sale and the respondent 61 per cent.

NOTE: One of the judges, Dillon LJ, expressed the view that *Harwood* was distinguishable since there was no third party who could have benefited from the interpretation applied to the declaration and that *Re Gorman* could have been followed. One of the judges delivering the majority judgment, Steyn LJ, considered that it was impossible to infer precisely the common intention of the parties and that he had hoped a more equitable result could have been reached. His view demonstrates the continued difficulties presented by this kind of case.

## By resulting, implied or constructive trust

Though one spouse may have the legal right to the house the other spouse may have an equitable interest in it (eg the house is in the name of one spouse but the other spouse contributed his or her own money to purchase it). Such an equitable interest must be evidenced by a document in writing (see s53(1)(b) Law of Property Act 1925). As from 27 September 1989 such an interest can only be created by a contract in writing incorporating all the terms which the parties have expressly agreed to and such a contract must be signed by or on behalf of each party (see s2(1) and (3) Law of Property (Miscellaneous Provisions) Act 1989).

In everyday life spouses (or unmarried couples) often fail to comply with the strict requirements of ss52 and 53(1)(b) Law of Property Act 1925 and s2 Law of Property (Miscellaneous Provisions) Act 1989. They do not regulate their interests in a property in legal documents as the law requires. As a result s53(2) Law of Property Act 1925 and s2(5) Law of Property (Miscellaneous Provisions) Act 1989 allow a spouse or other person, who cannot establish his or her interest in the home in the conveyance, or by a written and signed contract, to ask the court nevertheless to declare his or her interest under a resulting, implied or constructive trust.

See *Gissing* v *Gissing*:

'A resulting, implied or constructive trust ... is created by a transaction between the trustee and the cestui que trust in connection with the acquisition by the trustee of a legal estate in land, whenever the trustee has so conducted himself that it would be inequitable to allow him to deny the cestui que trust a beneficial interest in the land acquired. And he will be held so to have conducted himself if by his words or conduct he has induced the cestui que trust to act to his own detriment in the reasonable belief that by so acting he was acquiring a beneficial interest in the land.'

Lord Diplock went on to state:

> 'This is why it has been repeatedly said in the context of disputes between spouses as to their respective beneficial interests in the matrimonial home, that if at the time of the acquisition and transfer of the legal estate into the name of one of them an express agreement has been made between them as to the way in which the beneficial interest shall be held, the court shall give effect to it – notwithstanding the absence of any written declaration of trust. Strictly speaking this states the principle too widely, for if the agreement did not provide for anything to be done by the spouse in whom the legal estate was not be vested, it would be a merely voluntary declaration of trust and unenforceable for want of writing. But in the express oral agreements contemplated by these dicta it has been assumed 'sub silento' that they provide for the spouse in whom the legal estate in the matrimonial home is not vested to do something to facilitate its acquisition, by contributing to the purchase price or to the deposit or the mortgage instalments when it is purchased upon mortgage or to make some other material sacrifice by way of contribution to or economy in the general family expenditure. What the court gives effect to is the trust resulting or implied from the common intention expression in the oral agreement.'

More recently Lord Templeman in *Winkworth* v *Edward Baron Development Co Ltd* [1987] 1 All ER 114 restated the position:

> 'Equity is not a computer. Equity operates a conscience but is not influenced by sentimentality. When a man (it usually is a man) purchases property and his companion (married or unmarried, female or male) contributes to the purchase price, or contributes to the payment of a mortgage, equity treats the legal owner as a trustee for the property for himself and his companion in the proportions in which they contribute to the purchase price because it would be unconscionable for the legal owner to continue to assert absolute ownership unless there is some express agreement between the parties, or unless the circumstances in which the contributions were made established a gift or loan or some relationship incompatible with the creation of a trust.'

The court will, therefore, prevent the spouse with the legal interest from standing on his strict legal rights when it is clear that the other spouse has a beneficial or equitable interest.

It is not easy to distinguish between a resulting, implied or constructive trust since the courts have blurred the distinction between them in the cases. However, one can identify particular instances in which resulting and constructive trusts arise.

## Establishing a resulting or constructive trust

A resulting or constructive trust requires:

1. clear evidence of a *common intention* between the parties that at the time of the purchase of the property (or exceptionally some time after the purchase) though one party has the legal title to the property *both* parties clearly intended that the other party have a beneficial interest in the property; and
2. the other party has acted to his or her detriment based on that common intention.

The difficulty in many cases is how the applicant establishes the *common intention*. In more recent cases a stricter approach has been applied as to what evidence there has to be before the court will declare a beneficial interest under a resulting or constructive trust. There now appear to be only two ways to satisfy a court that the requirements have been met:

1. by the party without a legal interest showing that he or she has made a direct financial contribution towards the purchase of the property (where there is an obvious inference that there must have been a common intention between the parties that the contributing party should acquire a beneficial interest in the property in accordance with the amount of the financial contribution) – this gives rise to a presumption of a resulting trust; or

2. clear evidence of conversations between the parties showing that they both formed a common intention that the party without legal title has a beneficial interest in the property (preferably with the shares in the property quantified) and the party without legal title acting to his or her detriment based on that common intention – this gives rise to a *constructive trust* where the court will construct a trust giving effect to that common intention and preventing the party with legal title denying the common intention and insisting on his or her strict legal title. The party without legal title must act to his or her detriment based on the common intention since equity will not perfect an imperfect gift ie will not enforce an unwritten common intention unless the applicant has acted upon it.

The judgment of Lord Bridge of Harwich in *Lloyds Bank* v *Rosset* [1990] 2 WLR 867 illustrates this approach:

'The first and fundamental question which must always be resolved is whether, independently of any inference to be drawn from the conduct of the parties in the course of sharing the house as their home and managing their joint affairs, there has at any time prior to acquisition, or exceptionally at some later date been any agreement, arrangement or understanding reached between them that the property is to be shared beneficially. The finding of an agreement or arrangement to share in this sense can only, I think, be based on evidence of express discussions between the partners, however imperfectly remembered and however imprecise their terms may have been. Once a finding to this effect is made it will only be necessary for the partner asserting a claim to a beneficial interest against the partner entitled to the legal estate to show that he or she acted to his or her detriment or significantly altered his or her position in reliance on that agreement in order to give rise to a constructive trust or proprietary estoppel.

In sharp contrast with this situation is the very different one where there is no evidence to support a finding of an agreement or arrangement to share, however reasonable it might have been for the parties to reach such an agreement if they had applied their minds to the question, and where the court may rely entirely on the conduct of the parties both as the basis from which to infer a common intention to share the property beneficially and as the conduct relied on to give rise to a constructive trust. In this situation direct contributions to the purchase price by the partner who is not the legal owner, whether initially or by payment of mortgage instalments, will readily justify the inference necessary to the creation of a constructive trust. But, as I read the authorities, it is at least extremely doubtful whether anything less will do.'

It seems from this judgment that courts either will refuse to infer or will find it very difficult to infer any common intention which could be reasonably assumed from the way the parties have behaved towards each other if there is no evidence of direct conversations or financial contributions. No matter how long or close their relationship, no matter what has been done together in relation to 'their home' no property rights may arise unless the parties clearly talked about the party without legal title having an interest in the property or that party made a direct financial contribution to its purchase.

The approach in *Rosset* was followed in *Hammond* v *Mitchell* [1991] 1 WLR 1127 where Waite J described the difficulties facing a woman in relation to her claim that she had a beneficial interest in property owned by a man with whom she lived but did not marry:

'... in general, their financial rights have to be worked according to their strict entitlement in equity, a process which is anything but forward looking and involves, on the contrary, a painfully detailed retrospect.

The template for that analysis has recently been restated by the House of Lords and the Court of Appeal in *Lloyds Bank* v *Rosset* [1991] AC 107, [1990] 2 FLR 155 and *Grant* v *Edwards* [1986] Ch 638, [1987] 1 FLR 87. The court first has to ask itself whether there have, at any time prior to acquisition of the disputed property, or exceptionally at some later date, been discussions between the parties leading to any agreement, arrangement or understanding reached between them that the property is to be shared beneficially. Any further investigation carried out by the court will vary in depth, according to whether the answer to that initial enquiry is "yes" or "no". If there have been discussions of that kind and the answer is therefore "yes", the court then proceeds to examine the subsequent course of dealings between the parties for evidence of conduct detrimental to the party without legal title referable to a reliance upon the arrangement in question. If there have not been discussions and the answer to that initial inquiry is therefore "no", the investigation of subsequent events has to take the form of an inferential analysis, involving a scrutiny of all events potentially capable of throwing evidential light on the question, whether in the absence of express discussion, a presumed intention can be spelt out of the parties' past course of dealing. This operation was vividly described by Dixon J in Canada as "the judicial quest for the fugitive or phantom common intention" (*Pettkus* v *Barker* (1980) 117 DLR (3rd) 257) and by Nourse LJ in England as a "climb up the familiar grounds which slopes down from the twin peaks of *Pettitt* v *Pettitt* and *Gissing* v *Gissing*". The process is detailed, time consuming and laborious.'

A further illustration can be found in *Springette* v *Defoe* [1992] 2 FLR 437; [1992] Fam Law 489 where S and D lived together as man and wife in a council flat and then a council house of which S was the tenant. They then bought the council house for £14,445 which represented a discount of 41 per cent on its estimated market value because S had been a tenant of the council for 11 years. S and D obtained a mortgage for £12,000 which they were both liable to pay. By agreement they each contributed one half of the mortgage payments. D contributed £180 and

D paid the balance of the purchase price. The property was transferred into their joint names but the transfer did not declare their beneficial interests. The relationship broke down three years later. S claimed a 75 per cent share in the property. At first instance it was held that S and D were entitled to a half share each because there was evidence from both parties that each of them had in his or her mind an uncommunicated belief or intention that they were to share the property equally, although neither had said anything expressly along these lines. S appealed.

HELD: The case for equal beneficial shares rested on an uncommunicated belief. The fact that after the purchase the mortgage was paid in equal shares was not evidence that they had a common intention that the property should belong to them in equal beneficial shares but merely that they had agreed that each should pay half of the mortgage instalments. In the absence of any express declaration of beneficial interests the parties held the property on resulting trust in the proportions in which they had contributed directly or indirectly to the purchase price, unless there was sufficient specific evidence of their common intention that they should be entitled to other proportions (following *Walker* v *Hall* [1984] FLR 126). Common intention must be founded on evidence such as would support a finding that there was an implied or constructive trust. The court did not 'sit, as under a palm tree, to exercise a general discretion to do what the man in the street, on a general overview of the case, might regard as fair'. A common intention must mean a shared communication – it was not sufficient for the parties happening to think on the same lines without one knowing what the other was thinking. In the present case it was clear that there had never been any discussion between the parties about what their respective beneficial interests were to be. There was a presumption of resulting trust based on actual contributions which had not been displaced. The appeal was allowed and the court declared that the parties were beneficially entitled in the proportions of 75 per cent to S (taking into account the discount she had brought to the purchase price) and 25 per cent to D.

Earlier cases in which a common intention was based not on express conversations or direct financial contributions but on behaviour from which a common intention could be indirectly inferred (an approach apparently rejected in *Rosset* and *Springette* v *Defoe*) appear no longer to represent the correct approach. However, such cases have not been overruled so there remains some uncertainty whether a claimant could establish a common intention by such indirect means.

*Evans* v *Hayward* [1995] 2 FLR 511 (which also concerned a dispute over a council house bought by the plaintiff at a considerable discount) reached a similar conclusion to *Springette* v *Defoe*. In that case the beneficial interests were determined on the basis of the parties respective direct financial contributions to the purchase of the property (ie mortgage payments) and the plaintiff's contribution by way of discount as a result of her long-standing occupation of the property.

However a different approach was taken in *Midland Bank* v *Cooke* [1995] 4 All ER 562; [1995] 2 FLR 915 where H and W married in 1971. W's parents paid for the wedding and the reception. H's parents gave them a wedding gift of £1,100. They bought a house in H's sole name with the £1,100 plus £1,000 from H and the balance of £6,450 by mortgage. Neither party discussed how the property should be beneficially owned. Both parties worked during the marriage. H paid the mortgage and W paid the other household outgoings, though it was not clear whether this arrangement was the only way in which H could afford to make the mortgage payments. W did a considerable amount of work to maintain and improve the house. In 1978 a bank advanced a considerable sum secured on the house to fund H's company. In 1979 (following the decision in *Williams & Glyn's Bank* v *Boland* [1979] 2 WLR 550) W signed a form postponing any interest she might have in the house to the bank's security interest. In 1984 W brought proceedings under the Married Women's Property Act 1964 and by consent it was declared that the house belonged to the spouses jointly. Later the bank brought possession proceedings in order to recover £52,491 due to it. It was ruled that the 1979 waiver by the wife had been obtained by undue influence. The court then declared that W was only entitled to a 6.47 per cent share in the property since her only financial contribution had been via her half share of the wedding present from H's parents. W appealed arguing that she should have a greater share. The bank cross-appealed arguing that W had no beneficial interest.

HELD: W's parents had paid for the wedding and reception. H's parents had made a contribution to the cost of the intended matrimonial home. The correct inference was that H's parents had intended a gift to both parties. W had therefore contributed half of the £1,100 towards the purchase price and held an equivalent share in the home by way of resulting trust.

Furthermore, once W had established a beneficial interest, the court was entitled to draw inferences as to the parties probable common understanding about the ownership of the property. The court was required to look at all the dealings between the parties which related to the ownership and occupation of the house. The court was not confined to the limited range of direct contributions. In this case the parties had behaved in a way that showed that they intended to share everything equally. The reasonable inference was that W was entitled to 50 per cent beneficial interest. The fact that the parties had not made any agreement about the ownership of the property is not conclusive. *Springette* v *Defoe* could be distinguished because that was of a part pooling of resources by a middle-aged couple already established in life whose house purchasing arrangements were clearly regarded as having the formality of a business relationship.

Per Waite LJ:

'The general principle to be derived from *Gissing* v *Gissing* and *Grant* v *Edwards* can in my judgement be summarised in this way. When the court is proceeding in cases like the present where the partner without legal title has successfully asserted an equitable interest through direct contribution, to determine (in the absence of express evidence of intention) what proportions the parties must be assumed to have intended for their beneficial ownership, the duty of the judge is to undertake a survey of the whole course of dealing between the parties relevant to their ownership and occupation of the property and their sharing of burdens and advantages. That scrutiny will not confine itself to the limited range of acts of direct contribution of the sort that are needed to found a beneficial interest in the first place. It will take into consideration all conduct which throws light on the question what shares were intended. Only if that search proves inconclusive does the court fall back on the maxiim "equality is equity".'

In *Drake* v *Whipp* [1996] 1 FLR 826, Mrs D and Mr W had cohabited since 1985. In 1988 they decided to buy a barn. The house was conveyed into W's sole name. D paid 40 per cent and W 60 per cent of the purchase price of £61,000. Substantial improvements of £130,000 were made to the barn to make it into a luxury house. D paid 10 per cent of the costs of the improvements and did about 30 per cent of the manual work in terms of hours. W provided the rest of the money and the manual work. In 1989 D and W moved into the house. D's name was added to W's bank account and their respective earnings paid into this one account. D paid for the food and household running expenses while W paid for the household accounts and the running of his car. In 1993 D left. She sought a declaration that the house was held in trust for D and W in equal shares. The court found the circumstances led to a resulting trust in D's favour and that her share was limited to her actual monetary contribution. It assessed D's share as 19.4 per cent. D appealed.

HELD: Allowing the appeal, the evidence pointed to the creation of a constructive trust rather than a resulting trust. The evidence supported a finding that the parties had a common intention. Where a constructive trust existed the court adopted a broad brush approach to quantifying the beneficial interests under that trust. The court was not restricted solely to the parties' direct contributions but included the entire course of conduct of the parties together. This included the parties' intention to buy the house as a home, and the fact that they had a joint bank account and had contributed unequally to the work on the house. W held the house on trust in the shares two thirds to himself and one third to D.

Following *Midland Bank* v *Cooke* and *Drake* v *Whipp*, it now appears that once a beneficial interest has been established, unless the parties have a clear common intention as to what shares they respectively have, the court will adopt a broad brush approach and quantify those shares in a way that appears reasonable in all the circumstances. Hence a 5 per cent contribution to the purchase price can lead to a 50 per cent share (as in *Midland Bank* v *Cooke* and a 19 per cent contribution can lead to a 33 per cent share (as in *Drake* v *Whipp*).

NOTE: Whether the broader interpretation in *Midland Bank* v *Cooke* and *Drake* v *Whipp* will be applied, as opposed to the more literal application of *Lloyds Bank* v *Rosset* and *Springette* v *Defoe*, remains to be seen.

### Cases where there were direct financial contributions leading to a presumption of resulting trust

In *Re Rogers' Question* [1948] 1 All ER 328 the house was in the husband's name but it was purchased using £100 paid by the wife for the deposit and the balance of £900 paid by the husband by way of mortgage. The wife did not work and made no other financial contributions. The court held that it was reasonable to infer that each party intended to contribute to the house in the proportions they provided so the husband had a nine-tenths share and the wife a one-tenth share.

In *Cowcher* v *Cowcher* [1972] 1 WLR 425; [1972] 1 All ER 943 the wife contributed a third share to the purchase of the house which was in the husband's name. She claimed a half share but it was held that her beneficial interest was in the same proportion to her financial contribution. There was insufficient evidence of a common intention at the time of the purchase of the house that they were to be treated as having equal shares.

In *Walker* v *Hall*, above, W and H lived together in a house owned by H. They paid the mortgage from their pooled earnings. They then moved and bought a new house. Each provided £195 from their savings to the purchase price of £3,580. A further £1,000 was provided by a bank loan for which both were equally liable. The balance came from the proceeds of sale of H's house. Their relationship then ended and W left. W claimed a beneficial share. It was held that W and H were beneficially entitled as between themselves in the proportion in which they had provided the purchase money. It was not open to the court, in the absence of a specific intention to the contrary, to hold that the house belonged to W and H in equal shares notwithstanding their unequal contributions simply because it was bought to be their family home and they intended that their relationship last for life. It was not open to the court to 'top up' W's share beyond what it would be on the basis of her financial contribution on the broad notion that it would be fair because the house had been purchased as a family home. The judge's proportions of a one quarter share to W and three-quarters to H were in principle correct subject only to adjustment for the appropriate proportion of the bank loan repayments made by H after W had left.

In *Sekhon* v *Alissa* [1989] 2 FLR 94, D bought a house for £36,500 which was conveyed into her sole name. Her mother (M) contributed £22,500 to the purchase price. The house was large and in poor condition. Over £21,000 was spent improving it. M contributed £5,000 to the cost of the improvements. The house was then valued at £120,000. D argued that M's contribution was a gift and that she was the sole beneficial owner though she accepted an obligation to repay M if she wanted her money back. M argued that the purchase was a joint venture and that she and D should hold the house in shares equivalent to the proportion of their financial contributions. It was held that the law presumed a resulting trust in M's favour. That presumption had to be rebutted by evidence that M intended a personal loan without acquiring any interest in the property. In the absence of sufficient evidence in rebuttal M had a beneficial interest in the house with her share corresponding to the value of her contribution.

See also *Huntingford* v *Hobbs* discussed above.

Mention should be made at this stage of the *presumption of advancement*. This only applies to a married or engaged couple. If a wife buys a property using her own money but conveys it into her husband's name then ordinary resulting trust principles would apply and the husband would hold the property on trust for her. If the husband uses his money to buy the property and conveys it into his wife's name the converse may not apply since there is an established legal presumption that he must have intended this is an outright gift to his wife. This is called the presumption of advancement and derives from the days when it was unusual for women to have property or any earning power. It is doubtful whether the presumption would be applied today in light of the changed economic position of women. Indeed it was questioned in *Pettit* whether the presumption was valid at all. However the presumption was applied in *Tinker* v *Tinker* [1970] 2 WLR 331; [1970] 1 All ER 540.

### Cases where direct financial contributions did not lead to a presumption of resulting trust

Not all financial contributions will lead to a presumption of resulting trusts. Such contributions may only have been loans or gifts or payment of rent and so the presumption will not apply.

See *Savage* v *Dunningham* [1973] 3 WLR 471; [1973] 3 All ER 429 where D purchased a long lease in a flat he shared with S and Y. S and Y contributed to the rent and provided some of the furniture. The only agreement had been one that each would share in the payment of rent and the outgoings of the flat. S and Y argued that they held an interest in the flat under a resulting trust. It was held that S and Y's contributions were not to any purchase money. They simply paid rent. Their flat sharing was an entirely informal arrangement. They was no common intention to acquire property rights. The law of trusts played no part in such a situation of flat sharing.

In *Re Sharpe* [1980] 1 WLR 219; [1980] 1 All ER 198 an aunt loaned £12,000 to her nephew so that he could buy a house worth £17,000. He was then made bankrupt. The aunt claimed that she was entitled to a beneficial interest in the house under a resulting trust. It was held that a loan could not give rise to a resulting trust since there was no common intention that a property interest be acquired, merely an agreement that the loan be repaid. On the facts of this particular case the aunt's interests were however held to be protected under a constructive trust.

*Re Sharpe* can be contrasted with *Risch* v *McFee* [1991] 1 FLR 105 where a woman lent money to a man to enable him to buy out his wife's interest in the former matrimonial home. She then lived with the man in the house. He did not pay her any interest or repayments under the loan. She then made further payments to help pay the mortgage. It was held that in those circumstances the loan became part of the money which established her beneficial interest in the property and increased her share.

## Cases where there was evidence of conversations which established a common intention – the constructive trust

In *Eves* v *Eves* [1975] 1 WLR 1338; [1975] 3 All ER 768 a woman met a married man. They lived together in the man's house and she had two children by him. The house was sold and a new house bought using the proceeds of sale and a mortgage which the man paid. The woman made no direct financial contribution to the purchase. The house was put into the man's name. The man told the woman that it would be their house and that the only reason it was not transferred into their joint names was because she was under age (ie under 21). The house was very dirty and dilapidated. The woman, acting in reliance on the common intention expressed between the parties, did considerable decoration work inside the house and labouring work outside including some heavy demolition work. It was held that the man's promise to her which she accepted and relied on enabled the court to impose a constructive trust in which the woman was entitled to a quarter share in the property.

In *Re Densham* [1975] 1 WLR 1519; [1975] 3 All ER 726 there was clear evidence of a common intention since the husband had stated in letters to his solicitor that the purchase of the house was meant to be a joint one. The house was subsequently conveyed into the husband's sole name by mistake but the wife's interests were protected by the court under a trust.

In *Grant* v *Edwards* [1986] 3 WLR 114; [1986] 2 All ER 426, G went to live with E. G had E's child and E purchased a house for himself, G and their child to live in. It was conveyed into E and his brother's name. G made no direct financial contribution to the purchase. E told G that he would have conveyed the house into their joint names but it might prejudice G's divorce proceedings against G's husband. E and G had a second child. In reliance on E's words G made very substantial contributions to the housekeeping after she had gone out to work and paid some of the mortgage payments since E's income was too small to manage to pay both for the mortgage and the housekeeping. There was a fire at the house. Insurance money was used to pay for the repairs and the balance put into E and G's joint account. It was held that there was a common intention that G have a beneficial interest in the home because of what E had said. G had acted to her detriment based on that common intention. She was held to be entitled to a half share in the house.

In *Stokes* v *Anderson* [1991] 1 FLR 391; [1991] Fam Law 310, S and A lived together but were not married. S had been married and he and his ex-wife owned the former matrimonial home in equal shares. He bought his ex-wife's share for £45,000. He said that he would put A's name on the deeds. Relying on his promise A gave him £5,000 and then £7,000 towards the £45,000. They planned to get married but S cancelled the plans. A lived in the house. She decorated it and worked in the garden spending £2,500 of her own money. The relationship then broke down. S applied for possession saying that the payments made by A had been loans and gave rise to no interest in the house. A claimed a beneficial interest. It was held that there was evidence of a common intention that she should have a beneficial interest. She had paid the money on the understanding that they would marry and that the house would be their home. Her payments constituted conduct acting on that common intention. The extent of her beneficial interest had never been discussed by the parties. Its quantification depended upon the parties' common intention, not necessarily ascertained at the time the interest was acquired, but seen in light of all payments made and acts done by A. She was entitled to a quarter share subject to the mortgage.

In *Hammond* v *Mitchell* [1992] 2 All ER 109; [1991] 1 WLR 1127, H and M lived together for 11 years and had two children. They never married. H bought a bungalow using the proceeds of sale of his flat and a mortgage. It was transferred into his sole name. He told M that this was for tax reasons though he said M would have a half share as soon as they were married. M relied on H's promise. She used earnings from her work to help run the household. She agreed to allow any right she had in the bungalow to be used as security for H's speculative business ventures which, had they failed, would have meant the loss of the bungalow. She and H were described as beneficial owners of the bungalow to the bank which offered the loan for the business ventures. She fully supported the business ventures which succeeded and brought great wealth. It was held that there had been express discussions about the bungalow which amounted to a common intention or understanding that it was to be shared beneficially and that M had acted to her detriment based on that common intention. She had a one half beneficial interest. Her claim in relation to another property failed because there had never been any discussions concerning its ownership.

In *Savill* v *Goodall* [1993] 1 FLR 753; [1993] Fam Law 289, S moved in to live with G in 1977. They lived in a council house of which G was the tenant. They had a difficult relationship. In order to strengthen their relationship and to take advantage of the right to buy provisions in relation to the council house, they both signed a notice in 1984 claiming a joint right to buy the council house. Using G's years of tenancy (and those of her former husband who had the tenancy before her) they bought the house with a 42 per cent discount using a mortgage to pay for the balance. The conveyance did not declare their beneficial interests. It was agreed that S pay the mortgage which he did. In 1986 S left. G then paid the mortgage. S claimed a half share in the house. The judge found that S and G had contributed equal amounts of money to the purchase and on the basis of that conduct they had a common intention that they owned the house in equal beneficial shares. G appealed arguing that she was entitled to a 42 per cent share before the remainder was distributed.

HELD: Allowing the appeal in part, the judge had been wrong to look at the parties' contributions. Following *Lloyds Bank* v *Rosset* [1990] 2 WLR 867 the first question was whether, independently of any inference to be drawn from the conduct of the parties in the course of their sharing the house, there was at any time prior to the acquisition of the house (or exceptionally at some later date) any agreement, arrangement or understanding between the parties that the property should be shared beneficially. In this case S and G had reached an agreement before they purchased the house that it be owned jointly by claiming the right to buy jointly. The extent of their beneficial interests was governed by that agreement independently of any inference to be drawn from their conduct. They were each entitled to a half share after adjustments had been made for the payments made with respect to the mortgage.

See also *Le Foe* v *Le Foe and Woolwich plc* [2001] 2 FLR 970 in which indirect contributions to the mortgage payments (made by the wife paying household expenses while the husband paid off the mortgage and by her using an inheritance to pay off a previous mortgage) gave rise to a beneficial interest under a resulting trust. W got 50 per cent share. It seems that *Lloyds Bank* v *Rosset* was not given a strict interpretation. Provided the indirect contribution clearly relates to the house purchase it can give rise to a beneficial interest.

## Cases where the applicant failed to satisfy the court that there was any beneficial interest

### Where there was insufficient evidence of a common intention

In *Burns* v *Burns* [1984] 2 WLR 582; [1984] 1 All ER 244 the parties lived together as man and wife for 19 years but never married. The woman changed her surname to that of the man. The man purchased a house in his sole name in which the parties lived. The woman made no contributions to the purchase. There were two children of the relationship. The woman looked after the house and brought up the children. The man paid all the household expenses. The woman did not go out to work until the children were older. When she did earn she did contribute to the household expenses by paying rates, household bills and buying such goods as a washing machine. Since the man was relatively well off her contributions were not essential to enable him to pay the household expenses and the mortgage. He never asked her to contribute to the house. He never suggested that the house was jointly owned.

HELD: The woman had no beneficial interest in the property. The court had no power to make such property adjustments as the court thought fair and reasonable. The woman's interest had to be ascertained by the application of the law of trusts. In this case there was no express agreement that the plaintiff had an interest in the house. She had made no contributions to the purchase price. There was no evidence of a common intention at the time of purchase or subsequently. She had made no substantial contributions to the family finances so as to enable the man to pay the mortgage. It was not enough for her to show that she had looked after the house and raised the children.

In *Thomas* v *Fuller-Brown* [1988] 1 FLR 237, T and FB lived together as an unmarried couple. T owned the house in which they lived. FB had made no financial contribution to its purchase. FB obtained an improvement grant on T's behalf. He did substantial work using the improvement grant to finance his labour and buy materials. The house increased in value. The relationship ended. T left as a result of FB's behaviour. She applied to have FB excluded so that she could return to the house. FB defended the action by saying that the work he had done gave him a beneficial interest in the house.

HELD: FB had no beneficial interest in the house. The fact that he had spent money or labour on T's property did not of itself entitle him to an interest. There could be no interest unless there was an express agreement or common intention giving rise to a trust or a promise giving rise to a question of estoppel. In this case there had been no agreement or common intention. FB was a mere licensee who had done work in the house in return for board and lodging. A man who does work by improvement to his cohabitee's property without a clear understanding as to the financial basis on which the work is done does so at his own risk.

In *Windeler* v *Whitehall* [1990] 2 FLR 505 D owned his own house from which he ran his business. P went to live with him and became his mistress. D wanted P to marry him but she refused. P looked after D's house and entertained for him. D sold the house and moved into a larger one. P made no contribution to its purchase. She did not work and was supported by D. She supervised some minor building work done on the house. D made a will in P's favour. Their relationship then ended. P claimed an interest in the house and business.

HELD: A man had no legal obligation to support his mistress. The courts had no jurisdiction to disturb existing property rights which existed at the end of a relationship no matter how long that relationship had lasted or how deserving the claimant. In this case there was no direct evidence of any common intention that P should have any interest in the house or business. Such an intention could not be inferred from the parties' conduct. P had made no direct or indirect financial contributions to the property. The mere fact that P lived with D and did the ordinary domestic tasks was no indication that either party intended to alter existing property rights (following *Burns* v *Burns* above). D's will was a recognition of some moral obligation to P should D die suddenly. There was no evidence of proprietary estoppel. Even if P had been encouraged to believe that she would inherit the property on D's death that was only if she continued to live with D until he died. That contingency was ended when the relationship ended.

In *Lloyds Bank* v *Rosset* (above) a husband and wife decided to buy a semi-derelict farmhouse in order to renovate it and live in it as a family home. Over £80,000 was needed to both buy and renovate the house. The husband had a wealthy family in Switzerland. They offered him the money on the condition that the house be in his sole name. Before the house was bought the vendors allowed the spouses to start work on it. They engaged builders to do the substantial work. Since the husband spent a lot of time abroad in his work the wife had to supervise the builders and do a lot of decoration work herself. Three days before the completion of the sale, unbeknown to the wife, the husband arranged a loan for £15,000 from

Lloyds Bank to help meet the renovation costs since he had spent some of the £80,000 on other things. The house was used as security for the loan. The house was sold and transferred into the husband's name. A year or so later there were matrimonial difficulties and the husband left. Repayments of the loan had not been made to the bank so it applied for possession. The wife resisted the application by claiming a beneficial interest in the house which would be protected as an 'overriding interest'. The judge at first instance and the Court of Appeal held that she did have a beneficial interest. On appeal to the House of Lords.

HELD: There was no concluded agreement, arrangement or any common intention formed before contracts were exchanged for the purchase of the property that the wife have any beneficial interest in the house. The husband, under pressure from his family, always intended that the house would be in his sole name. The intention held by the spouses that the house was to be renovated and that it be shared as a family home did not throw any light on the spouses' intention with respect to the beneficial ownership of the property. The wife's considerable work in planning and supervising the builders and doing some work herself could not possibly justify any inference that there was a common intention that she should have a beneficial interest. She only acted in the way any wife would in hurrying the work along while her husband was abroad. The monetary value of any work she did was so trifling compared to the cost of the house as to be almost de minimis. The finding that the husband held the house as constructive trustee for himself and his wife could not be supported. The judge would not have fallen into error if he had kept clearly in mind the distinction between the effect of evidence on one hand which was capable of establishing an express agreement or an express representation that the wife was to have an interest in the property and evidence on the other hand of conduct alone as a basis for an inference of the necessary common intention.

## Where there was evidence of a common intention but there was no acting to detriment based on that common intention

In *Midland Bank* v *Dobson* [1986] 1 FLR 171 there was some evidence of a common intention between the husband and wife that the wife should have a beneficial interest in the home which was in the husband's name. There was an agreement 'to share everything'. However the wife did nothing to her detriment acting in reliance on that common intention. She made no financial contribution to the purchase of the house. She only earned an income late on in the marriage. She used her income to pay for some household items in the same way as any ordinary spouse. She also did some decoration in the same way as an ordinary spouse. Her behaviour was consistent with the husband having absolute beneficial ownership. Her claim to a beneficial interest failed.

*House improvements.* There is a special provision for married people contained in s37 Matrimonial Proceedings and Property Act 1970:

'37. It is hereby declared that where a husband or wife contributes in money or money's worth to the improvement of real or personal property in which or in the proceeds of sale of which either or both of them has to have a beneficial interest, the husband or wife so contributing, shall, if the contribution is of a substantial nature and subject to any agreement between them to the contrary express or implied, be treated as having then acquired by virtue of his or her contribution a share or an enlarged share, as the case may be, in that beneficial interest of such an extent as may have been then agreed or, in default of such agreement, as may seem in all the circumstances just to any court before which the question of the existence or extent of the beneficial interest of the husband or wife arises (whether in proceedings between them or in any other proceedings).'

This provision does *not* apply to unmarried couples.

The contribution in money or money's worth must be substantial. In *Re Nicholson (deceased)* [1974] 1 WLR 476; [1974] 2 All ER 386 the wife paid for the installation of central heating which increased the value of the property and gave her a 21/41st share as opposed to a half share.

The contribution must refer directly to the improvement of the house. In *Harnett* v *Harnett* [1973] 3 WLR 1; [1973] 2 All ER 593 the wife drove a builder's van, dealt with the contractors and did some office work but neither paid for nor did any of the building work herself. It was held that her contributions did not directly give rise to the building work which improved the house and that she acquired no interest.

Simple decoration work and the normal DIY work any ordinary householder might do will not suffice since such work will neither satisfy s37 MPPA 1970 nor amount to any kind of evidence to support a claim for a resulting or constructive trust. Examples where such claims failed include *Pettitt* v *Pettitt* (where there was some decoration, a wardrobe was built, a lawn was laid and a garden wall constructed), *Gissing* v *Gissing* (where there was some decoration and some gardening) and *Button* v *Button* [1968] 1 WLR 457; [1968] 1 All ER 1064 (where there was normal DIY work such as installing a gas fire).

In the case of unmarried couples where more substantial work is done the situation is less clear. Following *Rosset* it would appear that house improvements are only likely to give rise to a beneficial interest under a constructive trust if there is clear evidence of a common intention (as was the case in *Eves* v *Eves*).

A less clear example can be found in *Ungurian* v *Lesnoff* [1990] 2 FLR 299 where L gave up her promising career in Poland as well as her flat there in order to come to England to live with U. U bought a house in his name for L, her two sons and his son to live in. There was an understanding that U would provide a home for L. L and her two sons carried out substantial improvements to the house though U paid for the materials. The relationship ended and U asked L to leave. It was held that direct evidence of an agreement between U and L that L should have a beneficial interest in the house or have it absolutely was unsatisfactory. However the intention of the parties, based on why the house was bought and the parties' subsequent conduct (in particular the building work) meant that U held the house on constructive trust for L to live for her life.

NOTE: The decision in this case had a dramatic impact in that the terms of the trust meant that L became a tenant for life under the Settled Land Act 1925. This obliged U to vest the house in L's favour so that she could sell it and use the proceeds to buy another house or invest the proceeds (applying *Binions* v *Evans* [1972] 2 All ER 70; *Bannister* v *Bannister* [1948] 2 All ER 133) even though this had not been the intention of the parties.

Whether this case would be decided in the same way in light of *Rosset* is not clear.

In *Cooke* v *Head* [1972] 1 WLR 518; [1972] 2 All ER 38 a plot of land was purchased by H. He paid the deposit and the mortgage. His cohabitee, C, did substantial building work including demolishing a building, removing hard core and working a cement mixer. Both saved and the savings were used to pay the mortgage. It was held that where two people by their joint efforts acquired property for their joint benefit the legal owner held the property on trust for both of them. In this case C was entitled to a third share. Again this case may have to be regarded with caution in the light of *Rosset*.

*Helping in the business.* There have been some cases where one partner has helped in the other partner's business and this has given rise to a claim of a constructive trust. See *Re Cummins (deceased)* [1971] 3 WLR 580; [1971] 3 All ER 782; *Nixon* v *Nixon* [1969] 1 WLR 1676; [1969] 3 All ER 1133; and *Meutzel* v *Meutzel* [1970] 1 WLR 188; [1970] 1 All ER 443. Unless there is evidence of a common intention it is doubtful that a claim could be based on contributions to a business in light of *Rosset* and remarks made in *Hammond* v *Mitchell* where a claim that help in business activities gave rise to a beneficial interest were rejected.

*Quantification of interests under a trust.* The circumstances in which a resulting or constructive trust can arise have been described. However, once the court finds that there is the evidence to support either kind of trust how does the court quantify the interests under the trust? If the court finds that a resulting trust arises from direct financial contributions to the purchase price then the shares will be in proportion to those contributions. However, in the case of a constructive trust the position may be less clear. The quantification of the shares will depend on the common intention found by the court. Since the common intention can be vague the court may not be able to quantify the shares on the basis of an express agreement. The court will then look at all the circumstances to determine the amount of the shares. For example in *Grant* v *Edwards* [1986] 3 WLR 114 the court noted the substantial contributions made by the claimant and the fact that both parties behaved in a way consistent with joint ownership (eg by putting the fire insurance money into a joint account). The court held that the claimant had a half share.

A useful illustration of the complexities involved is provided by *Passee* v *Passee* [1988] 1 FLR 263 where the plaintiff bought a house which was conveyed into his name. The defendant (his aunt) contributed £500 and her daughter contributed

£250 to the purchase. The aunt and her daughter paid the plaintiff a weekly amount to cover the mortgage. Other members of the family lived in the house. They also paid money but this was treated as rent. The daughter then died and the aunt left then shortly returned. The plaintiff spent over £8,000 improving the property. The court was asked to determine whether the aunt and the daughter's estate had beneficial interest in the property and, if so, to quantify their shares.

HELD: The house had been bought with a common intention that the plaintiff hold the house on trust for himself, his aunt and her daughter. The common intention was not that they have equal shares and their shares were not limited to the precise contributions they had made. The court had to decide what was fair having regard to their total contributions. The payment of mortgage was relevant and could not be discounted simply because the payments had gone off the interest rather than the capital. The payment of rent by the other members of the family was not relevant and did not diminish the payments made by the aunt and her daughter. On the facts and giving full credit for the plaintiff's capital improvements the aunt held a 30 per cent share and the daughter's estate held a 10 per cent share – these shares to be realised when the house was sold.

In earlier cases the courts had adopted the maxim 'equality is equity' and decided an equal division of shares was fair in all circumstances. That approach was rejected in *Gissing* v *Gissing* where courts were reminded that they must quantify the shares on the basis of the common intention and subsequent behaviour consistent with that common intention. Examples of this approach can be seen in *Eves* v *Eves* (where the claimant was entitled to a quarter share) and *Stokes* v *Anderson* (where the claimant only contributed at the most £14,500 to a house worth £100,000 but was held to be entitled to a 25 per cent share). In *Midland Bank* v *Cooke* it was held that the quantification of shares was not limited to direct contributions. The court could look at all the dealings between the parties which related to the ownership and occupation of the house. This approach was followed in *Drake* v *Whipp* [1996] 1 FLR 826.

## 10.4 Contractual licence

The courts may have to consider property rights in a less substantial relationship. The courts have recognised property rights where couples cohabit without getting married but have been reluctant to recognise such rights where a couple have a relationship without living together on a settled or permanent basis. The position of the mistress with whom a man may have a 'visiting' relationship is, therefore, less secure than with wives or cohabitees. Where no resulting, implied or constructive trust can be said to exist a person, such as a mistress, may nevertheless have a right of occupation protected by a contractual licence, namely, a contract giving her a licence to remain in occupation which, if breached, may give rise to a claim for damages for breach of contract. It is, therefore, not a property right, in that no interest is given in the property, but it may still be a valuable protection. See

*Ashburn Anstalt* v *Arnold* [1985] 2 All ER 147 where it was confirmed that a contractual licence is not an interest in land binding on a purchaser even with notice.

In order for a contractual licence to exist there must be an intention to create a legally binding relationship; and the claimant must show that she has provided consideration for the contract.

The cases are not consistent and it is not easy to predict when a contractual licence will be found and when not.

In *Tanner* v *Tanner* [1975] 1 WLR 1346; [1975] 3 All ER 776 a married man had a visiting relationship with a woman. She was the tenant of a rent-controlled flat. She had twins. The man bought a house for her and the children. She put no money or work into the house. The man then broke off the relationship and ordered the woman and the children to leave the house.

HELD: The woman had furnished consideration by giving up the security of her flat. She had a contractual licence entitling her to stay until the children had finished their education or until circumstances changed. She was entitled to damages if that licence was breached.

In *Hardwick* v *Johnson* [1978] 1 WLR 683; [1978] 2 All ER 935 the husband's mother allowed the husband and his wife to live in a house bought by the mother. At first they paid rent to her but after a while they ceased. The mother did not insist on payment since she knew the couple were short of money. The marriage broke down. The wife and child of the marriage remained in the house. The mother applied for possession of the house. The wife offered to continue paying rent to the mother.

HELD: The wife's occupation of the house was protected by a contractual licence whereby if she resumed payment of rent her licence to occupy could not be revoked.

In *Chandler* v *Kerley* [1978] 2 All ER 942 the husband and wife sold their former matrimonial home to the plaintiff on the understanding that the wife (who was to divorce her husband) and the children of the marriage would remain in the home and live with the plaintiff. The relationship between the plaintiff and the wife broke down soon afterwards.

HELD: The wife's occupation was protected by a contractual licence (though it was not clear what consideration the wife had supplied), but since the plaintiff could not have intended to assume the burden of housing the wife and another man's children indefinitely the licence could be terminated on her being given twelve months' notice which would enable her to find alternative accommodation.

But contrast *Horrocks* v *Foray* [1976] 1 WLR 230; [1976] 1 All ER 737 where a woman became a man's mistress at the age of fifteen. He bought her a house. She had his child. The relationship lasted seventeen years with the woman being maintained very generously. The man died suddenly in a road accident. His wife then learned of the relationship and sought possession of the house bought for the mistress and the child. The woman argued that she had a contractual licence because she had given consideration by leaving her previous home and not applying for a maintenance order for the child.

HELD: On the facts there was no contractual licence. The man had died suddenly without expressing any intention as to what he intended if the relationship ended. The mistress had been maintained in a manner beyond what one would reasonably expect a man to provide by way of contract. The subject of contractual licence was far from the parties' mind.

See also *Coombes* v *Smith* [1987] 1 FLR 352; [1986] 1 WLR 808 where a man provided a house for his mistress and their child while he continued to live with his wife and family. The woman had left her husband to live with him. She asked the man to put the house in their joint names but he assured her that she had no need to worry because he would always provide a roof over her head. The relationship ended. She claimed the right to remain in the house by virtue of proprietary estoppel (see below) and contractual licence. She claimed that she had left her husband, had given birth and cared for the man's child, had spent money and labour on decorating the house and had refrained from furthering her career. She claimed that this constituted acting to her detriment or consideration for the purposes of contractual licence.

HELD: She had provided no consideration. She had left an unhappy marriage. She had given up a job but that was because she was expecting a baby. There was no evidence to support an enforceable contract that the man provide her with a roof over her head for the rest of her life.

## 10.5 Proprietary estoppel

Where one person has acted to his or her detriment in reliance on a belief, which was known of and encouraged by another person, that he or she either has or is going to be given a right in or over the other person's property, the other person cannot insist on his or her strict legal rights if to do so would be inconsistent with the person's belief – the other person will be 'estopped' from relying on his or strict legal rights (see *Re Basham* [1986] 1 WLR 1498).

This is similar to a constructive trust but there is no need to establish a common intention, only that the claimant has been misled in the manner described above.

In *Jones* v *Jones* [1977] 2 All ER 232 the father bought a house for his son. He told the son it was a gift so that the son and his family could live near him. The son paid one-quarter of the purchase price but the father assured him that the house was a gift. The son gave up his job and his own house to come and live in the new house. He paid no rent to the father. He did pay the rates. The father died. His widow claimed the house or, failing that, she demanded rent from the son.

HELD: The widow was estopped from dispossessing the son. She could not demand rent. She and the son owned the house equally. She could not have the house sold since the purpose of the promise was to provide the son and his family with a home. The father's conduct had led the son to reasonably believe that the house belonged to him for life, therefore, causing him to give up his house and work, to contribute £1,000 to the purchase price and carry out work on the house.

In *Pascoe* v *Turner* [1979] 2 All ER 945, P met T, who was a widow. T moved into P's house as a housekeeper but the relationship became that of man and wife. T helped P with his business. She refused his offer of marriage. P bought a house and T moved into it. She continued to help him in his business. P started a relationship with another woman. He told T that she had nothing to worry about and that the house and contents were hers. With P's knowledge and encouragement T spent one quarter of her modest capital on repairs and improvements to the house. P tried to reclaim the house.

HELD: P was required to honour his promise. A life time licence was not sufficient to give protection to T. P was required to convey the house to T.

In *Greasley* v *Cooke* [1980] 1 WLR 1306; [1980] 3 All ER 710 a maid stayed with a family from the age of sixteen years for over thirty years. She was not paid. She became part of the family. When she was young she lived with the son of the family. She was assured she could live in the family home for all her life. The family then required her to leave.

HELD: She had been given a promise that she could live in the house. As a result she had received no wages. The family was estopped from denying her occupation. She could remain in the house until she died.

In *Maharaj* v *Chand* [1986] 3 All ER 107 a man and woman lived together. The man told the woman that when he bought a house he would provide her with a permanent home for her and the children. The woman gave up her flat. She supported his application to the housing authority to acquire the land. She used her earnings to pay for the household expenses. She looked after the man and the children.

HELD: The woman had to be allowed to live in the house until the children no longer needed a home. The man was estopped from denying his promise to her.

NOTE: In *Maharaj* v *Chand* the woman did not claim a beneficial interest binding on third parties but one binding on the man with whom she lived. The proprietary estoppel was based on his promise not to assert his right to terminate her occupation. He was estopped from denying that promise since she had acted to her detriment in reliance upon it. This can be compared with *Pascoe* v *Turner* where the property right claimed did bind third parties. The proprietary estoppel was based on one party leading the other to believe that he or she would become entitled to a beneficial interest in the property. Effect is given to that claim by, if necessary, obliging one party to convey the house to the other.

But contrast *Coombes* v *Smith* where a woman left her husband to live with the defendant. He made no promises to her nor encouraged her in any way concerning the house. She had no mistaken belief that she had the right to remain in the defendant's house indefinitely. She had not acted to her detriment since she had left an unhappy marriage and had given up her job to live with the defendant because she was expecting a baby.

HELD: She had no property rights. There was no contractual licence. There was no estoppel (*Pascoe* v *Turner* distinguished).

In *Matharu* v *Matharu* [1994] 2 FLR 597, F bought a house for his son, H, and his wife, W, to live in. H and W lived in the house from 1971. H made extensive improvements to it. In 1988 the marriage broke down. In 1990 W obtained an order excluding H from the house. In 1992 F applied for possession of the house. His application was dismissed on the basis that W had a right of occupation by virtue of proprietary estoppel. F appealed.

HELD: Dismissing the appeal, W had to show:

1. she had made a mistake as to her legal rights;
2. she had expended money or done some act on the faith of her mistaken belief;
3. the possessor of the legal title, F, must have known of his legal right, which was inconsistent with W's mistaken belief;
4. that F knew of W's mistaken belief but encouraged W directly or indirectly (by not asserting his legal title) to expend money or otherwise act on the faith of her mistaken belief.

In this case W had satisfied these requirements. However, this did not give her a beneficial interest but gave her a licence to occupy the house for life or as long as she wished.

In *Wayling* v *Jones* [1995] 2 FLR 1030, W and J lived together in a homosexual relationship from 1971 to 1975 and from 1976 to 1987 when J died. J ran several catering businesses. W worked in those businesses and acted as a companion and chauffeur to J. He received little payment. J made a will leaving a hotel to W. J then bought another hotel; he said he would change his will but did not do so. J said that this hotel was for W to run and then inherit. When J died all W received was a car and furniture of negligible value. W claimed a share of J's estate on the basis of proprietary estoppel. His claim was dismissed on the basis that he would have stayed with J even if the promises had not been made to him so he had not suffered detriment in relying on J's promises. He appealed.

HELD: Allowing the appeal, there was a sufficient link between the promises relied on and the conduct which constituted the detriment. W's conduct in helping run J's various enterprises for little more than pocket money was conduct from which his reliance on J's clear promises could be inferred. Once this had been established the burden of proof passed to the defendants to prove that W did not rely on the promises. The defendants failed to discharge that burden. W was awarded over £72,000 plus interest.

This case seems to follow the broad approach in *Re Basham* and not the narrower approach in *Coombes* v *Smith*.

In *Gillett* v *Holt* [2000] 2 FLR 266 G had been brefriended by H as a child and had worked for H on his farm and eventually as his business partner for 40 years. G claimed that H had assured him that he would leave his estate. H made a will leaving his estate to another person. The court held that a proprietary estoppel was made not out because H had no made no irrevocable promise to G and that, even if he had, G had failed to show that he had suffered any detriment. On appeal it was held that even where a promise or assurance is in terms linked to the making of a will, the circumstances may make it clear that the assurance is more than a mere statement of a present and revocable intention and is tantamount to a promise. H's assurrances were repeated over a long period, usually before family witnesses and in some cases were unambiguous. They were intended to be relied upon and were relied upon. Too much emphasis had been placed on whether H's promise was irrevocable. It was G's detrimental reliance which made it irrevocable. There had to be a sufficient link between the promises relied upon and the conduct which constituted the detriment. Detriment is not a narrow or technical concept. It need not consist of spending money or another quantifiable financial detriment, so long as it is substantial. The test of detriment is whether it would be unjust or inequitable to allow the assurance to be disregarded. In this case G had an exceptionally strong claim on H's conscience. G and his wife devoted the best years of their lives to working for H. They relied on H's assurance because they trusted him and they deprived themselves of the opportunity to better themselves in other ways. It would be startling if the law did not give a remedy. A clean break order would be made whereby the freehold of the farmhouse would be granted to G together with a sum of £100,000 to compensate him for the exclusion from the rest of the farming business.

A claim failed in *Taylor* v *Dickens* [1998] 1 FLR 806 in which a promise made by a woman to remember the claimant in her will in return for unpaid work in the garden was held not to establish a promissory estoppel. In this case the court allowed for the fact that the woman was able to change her mind.

## 10.6 Equitable accounting

After one party has left the other party may remain in the home. The party in the home may continue to pay the mortgage and make improvements to the property and may ask the court to take these payments into account. The other party may argue that the party in the property has enjoyed the occupation of it while he/she has had to find alternative accommodation and that this should be taken into account. The courts can make adjustments to take into account the value of such payments or improvements or enjoyment of occupation in order to more fairly distribute the shares in the property. This process is called equitable accounting.

### Mortgage instalments

A party who voluntarily leaves the home will usually have to give credit for the capital element in the mortgage instalments paid by the party in the home since these payments increase the value of the equity. The court reflects this by crediting one half of those repayments to the party in occupation who paid the capital mortgage instalments. See *Cracknell* v *Cracknell* [1971] 3 WLR 490; [1971] 3 All ER 552 where the wife left and the husband remained in occupation paying £864 of mortgage instalments. He was given credit for £432 of those payments. In *Leake* v *Bruzzi* [1974] 1 WLR 1528; [1074] 2 All ER 1196 the wife left and the husband was given credit for half of the mortgage instalments he paid after she left in so far as they represented payments from capital.

Where the mortgage payments only relate to interest (since they do not reduce the equity) they may not be credited at all. In certain circumstances they can be treated as occupation rent (see below). In *Suttill* v *Graham* [1977] 1 WLR 819; [1977] 3 All ER 1117 the husband and wife were beneficially entitled in equal shares in the home. W left, leaving H in the home. He paid the mortgage instalments. He was credited with half of the amount of mortgage instalments so far as they related to capital but not so far as they represented interest. More recently in *Turton* v *Turton* [1987] 2 All ER 641 an unmarried couple had equal shares in the home. The woman left. The man continued to pay the mortgage. Up to the time the house was sold for £35,000 he had paid £5,000 representing payments of capital. He was given credit for those repayments leaving £30,000 to be divided between the parties. In *Re Pavlou (A Bankrupt)* [1993] 3 All ER 955, H and W bought a house in 1973 which they owned jointly. In 1983 H left. W remained in occupation paying the mortgage and paying for improvements to the house. She petitioned for divorce in 1986. In 1987 H was made bankrupt and his half interest in the house vested in the trustee in bankruptcy. The trustee applied for a declaration of interests and for the house to be sold. W argued that she should be reimbursed for her expenditure on the property.

HELD: W was entitled to credit for one half of the increase in equity resulting from the capital element of the mortgage payments from the date from when H left the home.

## Occupation rent

If the parties are co-owners each is entitled to possession. If one leaves voluntarily he or she is not entitled to expect the other party to pay occupation rent simply because the occupying party is enjoying occupation while the absent party has to find alternative occupation.

However, if one party is forced to leave then the court can treat the occupying party as being liable to pay occupation rent to the party who was forced to leave. This reasoning was applied in *Dennis* v *MacDonald* [1982] 2 WLR 275; [1982] 1 All ER 590 where the woman had to leave because of the man's violence. She was entitled to compensation equivalent to one half of a fair rent under the Rent Act 1970. In such situations, if the occupying party has been paying the mortgage any payments which only represent payments of interest (which are not normally taken into account) can be treated as payments of occupation rent, since this represents a simple form of equitable accounting in order to avoid costs in obtaining valuations (see *Leake* v *Bruzzi* above).

The situation was reviewed in *Re Pavlou (A Bankrupt)* (above) where it was held that occupation rent applied not only where one party had been forced to leave but where it was necessary to do equity between the parties. Where the property was a matrimonial home, and where the marriage had broken down, the party who had left could be regarded as having been excluded so that occupation rent was payable by the party in occupation. If the party left voluntarily and was free to return it would not be just to expect the party in occupation to pay occupation rent. The position when H left to when W petitioned for divorce was not clear and rent would not be charged. However, from 1986 when W had petitioned for divorce (which signalled her refusal to take H back) she was liable to pay occupation rent. She was entitled to reimbursement for the interest element in the mortgage payments, but if the trustee in bankruptcy would not agree to set this off against the occupation rent the necessary accounts and inquiries would have to be ordered.

### Improvements after one party has left

In *Bernard* v *Josephs* (1983) 4 FLR 178; [1982] 2 WLR 1052; [1982] 3 All ER 162 the proceeds of sale were divided between the parties only after the plaintiff had paid £2,650 to the defendant to compensate him for the sum he had spent on decorating the house and so increased the sale price.

A more recent example of equitable accounting can be found in *Re Gorman* [1990] 2 FLR 284 where H and W held the matrimonial home in equal shares. H left. W paid off the mortgage arrears which had accrued, improved the property and paid the mortgage instalments after he had left. W's half share was credited with one-half of the mortgage instalments she had paid plus half of the sum she had spent on improvements. However, her share was then debited with one-half of the occupation rent due to H for his loss of his right to occupy the home.

In *Re Pavlou (A Bankrupt)* (above) W was entitled to one half of the increase in value of the home resulting from her improvements or one half of her actual expenditure, whichever the lesser.

## 10.7 When the court values the interest under a trust

There had been some doubt, if a wife or mistress had a beneficial interest under a resulting or constructive trust, when the court should value her interest. Should it be valued at the time when the parties separated or when the house is sold? There may be a considerable gap between those dates during which the value of the house may have dramatically increased. The point has hopefully been conclusively determined in *Turton* v *Turton* (above). The date is the date of the sale of the house and not earlier (following *Walker* v *Hall* [1984] FLR 126).

Beneficial interests existing under such a trust are property interests which are absolute and indefeasible and continue until the property is sold and then attach to the proceeds of sale. Beneficial interests under a trust cannot be defeated or diminished by the exercise of the court's discretion that the interest should be determined or valued at another date (eg the date when the parties separated).

The importance of this can be illustrated by the facts in *Turton* v *Turton*. An unmarried couple each had a half share in a house. They separated in 1975. The house was then valued at £10,500. The court did not order the sale of the house until 1987 when the house was valued at £35,000. The court had to give credit of £5,000 to the man for his payment of the mortgage after the woman had left. If the woman's share was valued at the date of separation she was only entitled to £2,750 (ie half of £10,500 after £5,000 deducted). If it was valued at the date the house was sold she was entitled to £15,000 (ie half of £35,000 after £5,000 deducted). The court held that the latter date was the correct date for the valuation of her interest.

## 10.8 Proposals for reform to the law of property rights between unmarried couples

The Civil Partnerships Bill was launched in January 2002 as a private member's Bill. It aims to provide sweeping reforms of the law relating to the property rights of unmarried couples (including same sex couples). There would be a presumption of equal ownership or the registration of a property agreement. If the partnership comes to an end a cessation order could be made and there would then be wide powers to distribute property.

The Relationships (Civil Registration) Bill was also introduced as a private member's Bill (in October 2001). The Bill would allow partners to register their relationship and thereafter have the same rights and responsibilities as married couples in terms of inheritance, housing succession, incapacity, pensions, social security and domestic violence. The partners would be able to lodge any pre-registration agreement about property rights on dissolution. Financial relief could be granted in the same terms as for married persons.

Two discussion papers were published in July 2002. First, the Law Commission published its discussion paper *Sharing Homes*. The Law Commission attempted to devise a scheme which could provide greater certainty and consistency in evaluating beneficial interests in a shared home. The scheme would encompass direct financial contributions to the purchase of the home and indirect financial contributions such as one party paying for household expenditure to allow the other to pay the mortgage. It considered the difficulties in evaluating non-financial contributions (eg looking after the home and children) and came to the view that a fair scheme was unattainable. It concluded that the existing case-law approach to resulting, implied and constructive trusts offered flexibility, though a more generous attitude to non-financial contributions was recommended. It commended *Midlands Bank* v *Cooke* [1995] 2 FLR 915 in allowing the courts, once a resulting or constructive trust had been established, to take into account all the circumstances in quantifying the beneficial entitlements under the trust. It was considered that codification of the common law would make the law too rigid. It looked at the law in other jurisdictions such as Australia, New Zealand and Canada and found no clear solutions there.

The second discussion paper was published by the Law Reform Board of the Law Society and was called *Cohabitation: The Case for Clear Law*. The paper recommended that the law should permit the registration of same-sex relationsips. It also recommended that unmarried couples (including same sex couples) who have been in a relationship for a continuous period of two years or have a child should have specific rights, including the right to apply to the court for capital provision. It did not recommend a general right to maintenance, confining court orders to lump sum and/or property orders. The case for a clean break can be seen as even stronger where parties have not entered into the commitment of marriage. It did recommend a limited right to maintenance (eg for no more than four years) to allow a partner to retrain for work and to reflect any economic disadvantage caused by the separation which could not be compensated by capital orders. This approach is similar to that advocated by the Scottish Law Commission and to systems adopted in Australia. It recommended that there be a standard definition of cohabitation.

## 10.9 Trusts of Land and Appointment of Trustees Act 1996

The Trusts of Land and Appointment of Trustees Act (TOLATA) 1996 came into force on 1 January, 1997 and replaced, inter alia, s30 Law of Property Act 1925 and the Settled Land Act 1925.

Prior to the TOLATA 1996 coming into force a husband and wife could only purchase a house jointly under the terms of a trust for sale which deemed the beneficial interest to be in the proceeds of sale rather than in the land itself. The spouses held the land as trustees on trust to sell it (although with a power to delay sale). Land could be owned successively under a trust for sale. However, unless a trust for sale was expressly created a strict settlement would be applied. This was a complicated and difficult kind of settlement which could be costly to operate.

The TOLATA 1996 replaces trusts for sale and strict settlements with a new single system of co-ownership known as 'trusts for land'. Trusts for sale are abolished and existing trusts for sale became trusts for land as from 1 January 1997. No new strict settlements can be created (with very limited exceptions). Under a trust for land, title is vested in the trustees who are given power both to sell and to retain the land rather than being placed under a duty to sell. The doctrine of conversion is abolished so that a joint beneficial interest in land is treated as an interest in land rather then in the proceeds of sale. This reflects the fact that most co-ownership is for the purpose of providing a home rather than an investment. Conveyancing has been made simpler as a result.

Under s14 TOLATA 1996 it is possible for the court to order the sale of the property. This is discussed in more detail in 10.15 Occupation of the matrimonial home when one spouse is bankrupt.

## 10.10 Allowances for housekeeping and maintenance

### Section 1 Married Women's Property Act 1964

'If any question arises as to the right of a husband or wife to money derived from any allowance made by the husband for the expenses of the matrimonial home or for similar purposes, or to any property acquired out of such money, the money or property shall, in the absence of any agreement between them to the contrary, be treated as belonging to the husband and the wife in equal shares.'

NOTE:

1. The Act only applies if the allowance is provided by the husband (not vice versa).
2. What are 'expenses of the matrimonial home or similar purposes'? Does it cover mortgage repayments?

*Tymosczuk* v *Tymosczuk* (1964) 108 SJ 656 – mortgage repayments are not within the Act.

*Re Johns' Assignment Trusts* [1970] 1 WLR 955; [1970] 2 All ER 210.

HELD: Obiter, there is no reason why mortgage repayments should not be subject to the Act.

## 10.11 Bank accounts

Ownership of money in a joint bank account and property bought therewith depends on the intention of the parties and, in particular, whether there was established a 'common purse'.

The leading case is that of *Jones* v *Maynard* [1951] 1 All ER 802 where there was a joint bank account. Into this were paid the husband's earnings and various incomes of the wife. The husband paid more into the account than the wife. There was no evidence of specific intention but the spouses regarded the fund as joint savings to be invested from time to time. The husband withdrew the money and purchased various investments in his own name. The wife also withdrew money though in lesser amounts. The parties divorced. The husband closed the account.

HELD: It was a joint account and they were entitled to it equally. As to investments, they must be regarded as a continuation of the joint account. Therefore, the husband held it on trust for the wife. The wife was entitled to half the account and half of the investments purchased with money from the account.

Vaisey J said:

'In my judgment, when there is a joint account between husband and wife, a common pool into which they put all their resources, it is not consistent with that conception that the account should thereafter be picked apart, and divided up proportionately to the respective contributions of husband and wife, the husband being credited with the whole of his earnings and the wife with the whole of her dividends. I do not believe that, when once the joint pool has been formed, it ought to be, and can be, dissected in any such manner. In my view, a husband's earnings and salary, when the spouses have a common purse and pool their resources, are earnings made on behalf of both; and the idea that years afterwards the contents of the pool be dissected by taking an elaborate account as to how much was paid in by the husband and the wife is quite inconsistent with the original fundamental idea of a joint purse or common pool.

In my view the money which goes into the pool becomes joint property.

The husband, if he wants a suit of clothes, draws a cheque to pay for it.

The wife, if she wants any housekeeping money, draws a cheque, there is no disagreement about it.'

*Jones* v *Maynard* was distinguished in the case of *Re Bishop (deceased)* [1965] 2 WLR 188; [1965] 1 All ER 249. The husband and wife had both withdrawn from a joint bank account and purchased shares which had been registered in their separate names. The husband died. The wife claimed that the shares bought by the husband in his name with money drawn from the joint account were hers.

HELD (by Stamp J): The spouse in whose name the shares had been purchased was entitled to the whole beneficial interest in them.

'Where a husband and wife open a joint account at a bank on terms that cheques may be drawn on the account by either of them, then ... each spouse can draw upon it not only for the benefit of both spouses but for his or her own benefit. Each spouse, in drawing money out of the account, is to be treated as doing so with the authority of the other ... if one of the spouses purchases a chattel for his own benefit or an investment in his or her own name, that chattel or investment belongs to the person in whose name it is purchased or invested.'

NOTE: W was entitled to the money in joint account.

## Presumption of advancement

If one spouse uses his money to buy property but that property is conveyed into the other spouse's name or into their joint names who owns the property? One way to answer the question is to apply the equitable presumption of advancement whereby if the husband provides the purchase money but the property is conveyed into his wife's name then it is presumed that she acquires the sole beneficial interest in it. If the husband provides the purchase money but the property is conveyed into joint names the presumption gives the wife a joint beneficial interest. For example a husband paid his salary into a joint account in *Re Figgis (deceased)* [1968] 2 WLR 1173; [1968] 1 All ER 999. It was presumed that the money belonged to the husband and wife jointly. The presumption has not been applied where the wife transfers property to the husband. In *Heseltine* v *Heseltine* [1971] 1 WLR 342; [1971] 1 All ER 952 the wife paid her money into a joint account with her husband. It was held that the presumption of advancement did not apply. The joint account was for the convenience of family administration. The assets bought by her using the account belonged to her.

The presumption was designed to give wives greater protection when their financial position was very weak compared with their husbands. As the position of wives has strengthened the presumption has ceased to be as important. In *Pettitt* v *Pettitt* [1969] 2 WLR 966; [1969] 2 All ER 385 it was doubted whether the presumption continued to be relevant. The courts prefer to construe the deeds and contracts relating to property or the intention of the parties. The presumption is a judicial instrument of last resort if all other attempts to discover beneficial interests have failed.

It is also possible to apply the presumption to other family members. In *McGrath* v *Wallis* [1995] 2 FLR 114 a father and son bought a house. About 70 per cent of the purchase price came from the sale of the father's previous house. The house was conveyed into the son's sole name because the father had not been able to obtain a mortgage (because he was aged 63 and unemployed). A declaration of trust was prepared whereby the son held the house in shares of 80 per cent to the father and 20 per cent to himself but this declaration was never executed. The father then died intestate. His daughter claimed a share of his property under the rules of intestacy. The son argued that he held the property outright by virtue of the presumption of advancement. The judge held that the presumption had not been rebutted and that the son owned the property. The daughter appealed.

HELD: Allowing the appeal, following *Pettitt* v *Pettitt* (above) the presumption of advancement was a judicial instrument of last resort – to be used only after the court had exhausted other ways of discovering property rights. It could be rebutted by comparitively slight evidence. In this case the presumption was rebutted. The only reason the house was conveyed into the son's name was because the father could not obtain a mortgage. There was no reason why the father wanted to give up his interest in the house in favour of his son. The father had a 70 per cent share in the house (ie the amount he had contributed to the purchase price) and the daughter was entitled to her share under the rules of intestacy.

## 10.12 Engagements

*Disputes over property between engaged couples*

### Agreement to marry

Even if an agreement to marry is unenforceable at common law an applicant may use s17 MWPA 1882 to resolve property disputes. In *Shaw* v *Fitzgerald* [1992] 1 FLR 357 the parties lived together in a property. The applicant was already married. The parties agreed to marry. The relationship broke down. The applicant claimed a beneficial interest in the property (because he had bought out the respondent's divorced husband's share in the property) and the return of a ring he had given to the respondent. The respondent claimed that there had been no agreement to marry but if there had been it would have been unenforceable since the applicant was already married. She argued that the court had no jurisdiction under s17 MWPA 1882 despite the Law Reform (Miscellaneous Provisions) Act 1970 extending the procedure to cover engaged persons. The judge agreed with the respondent and dismissed the application. The applicant appealed.

HELD: Allowing the appeal, s1 LR(MP)A 1970 referred to agreements to marry and not just to agreements which would have been enforceable at common law. The applicant could use s17 MWPA 1882 to resolve the dispute as to the property and the ring.

### Engagement ring

This is presumed to be an absolute gift to the partner who receives it (see s3(2) Law Reform (Miscellaneous Provisions) Act 1970).

This presumption may be rebutted by proof that it was a gift given with a condition that it be returned should the engagement be broken off (eg the ring is a family heirloom to be retained in one particular family).

### Engagement presents from third parties

Such presents are presumed to be conditional on getting married and so should be returned if the engagement is broken off.

### Gifts between the parties (other than the engagement ring)

This is a question of fact. The gifts may be classed as absolute gifts (eg birthday or Christmas presents) or as conditional gifts which are meant to be returned if the engagement is ended (eg furniture bought for the intended matrimonial home which may be conditional on getting married).

The donor is not prevented from recovering the property by reason of he or she being the one who terminated the engagement (see s3(1) 1970 Act).

### Disputes over property

The same rules apply to engaged couples as to husband and wife concerning beneficial interests in property acquired during the engagement (see s2(1) 1970 Act). So the law of resulting, implied and constructive trusts will apply as does s37 Matrimonial Proceedings and Property Act 1970 in relation to improvements to property. Engaged couples may apply for a declaration under s17 MWPA 1882 provided that proceedings are instituted within three years of the termination of the engagement (see s2(2) 1970 Act).

There must be a firm engagement – an unconditional agreement to marry. The above provisions do not apply to unofficial or informal engagements. It does not matter that the engagement is unenforceable when made (eg because one party is still married). Provided there is a firm agreement to marry; jurisdiction is given by the 1970 Act to deal with an application under s17 MWPA 1882 (see *Shaw* v *Fitzgerald* above).

The presumption of advancement can apply. If a man buys property with his own money and puts it into his fiancée's own name it is presumed to be a gift to her (see *Moate* v *Moate* [1948] 2 All ER 486, which involved a fiancée claiming that a house transferred into her name by her fiancé was hers pursuant to s17 MWPA 1882).

However, the position of an engaged couple is not the same as that of a married couple. The court cannot make orders in similar terms to s24 MCA 1973 with respect to engaged couples (see *Mossop* v *Mossop* [1988] 2 All ER 202, where a fiancée's application that her fiancé transfer to her part of his interest in a house which they had both lived was dismissed since there was no cause of action).

### Wedding presents

To whom such presents belong is a question of the intention of the donor.

See *Samson* v *Samson* [1960] 1 All ER 653, where wedding gifts did not necessarily belong to both parties, and *Kilner* v *Kilner* [1939] 3 All ER 957, where £1,000 was given to a newly married couple by the wife's father and paid into their joint account. The money was to be divided equally between them.

In *Midland Bank* v *Cooke* [1995] 4 All ER 562 W's parents paid for the wedding and H's parents made a wedding gift of £1,100 in order to help with the purchase of the matrimonial home. The only sensible inference was that H's parents intended that the wedding gift was to H and W jointly.

## 10.13 The protection of beneficial interests against third parties

A brief introduction to conveyancing is helpful to the understanding of how a beneficial interest may be protected against third parties. If a husband is the legal owner of property he may wish to mortgage the house with a third party (usually a bank or building society) in order to raise money. He may not wish his wife (who has a beneficial interest in the house) to know of the mortgage. He mortgages the house without informing her. He then defaults in payment of the mortgage. The third party will wish to take possession of the house and sell it in order to recover the money loaned to the husband on the security of the house. Can the wife protect her right of occupation on the strength of her beneficial interest?

One has to look at how title to land is conveyed. There are two systems of conveyancing – one for registered land; another for unregistered land. In the case of registered land the third party wishing to acquire title over the land must examine the registered title. There are certain matters which will affect title:

1. the third party will be bound by interests entered as Notices or Cautions on the register at the Land Registry (under the Land Registration Act 1925) – otherwise the third party will take title free of any other interests not entered on the register;
2. certain minor interests not entered on the register will be overreached and so will not bind the third party;
3. BUT certain interests called 'overriding interests' (see ss3(xvi) and 70(1) LRA 1925) will bind the third party even though they are not on the register and the third party has no knowledge of them. The reason for this is that public policy allows such interests to override even at the expense of the register thereby not recording all the interests which will bind the purchaser.

In the case of unregistered land the third party wishing to acquire title over the land must examine the title deeds. There are certain matters which will affect title:

1. the third party will be bound by interests entered as land charges at the Land Charges Registry (under the Land Charges Act 1972);
2. certain equitable interests not entered as land charges will be overreached and so will not bind the third party;
3. BUT the third party will be bound by certain interests which are neither registerable nor overreachable but which can only be discovered by inquiries being made by the third party – the third party will be bound by them since he will either have actual notice of them (namely, he discovered the interest as a result of his inquiries) or constructive notice of them (he failed to discover them but it is deemed that he should have discovered them had he made reasonable inquiries) (see s199(1) Law of Property Act 1925).

The question that needed to be answered was whether under these methods of conveyancing a wife's beneficial interest was protected against the third party purchaser.

At first the answer was no. In *National Provincial Bank Limited* v *Ainsworth* [1965] 3 WLR 1; [1965] 2 All ER 472 the House of Lords held that the rights of a deserted wife were purely personal rights enforceable against her husband and that these rights could not as a matter of law affect third parties. (This decision led to the enactment of the Matrimonial Homes Act 1967.) There was no 'deserted wife's equity' and the bank was entitled to possession.

Later the answer was yes. See *Williams & Glyn's Bank Limited* v *Boland and Another; Williams & Glyn's Bank Limited* v *Brown and Another* [1981] AC 487; [1980] 2 All ER 408. These were conjoined appeals to the House of Lords by Williams & Glyn's Bank Limited from decisions of the Court of Appeal, which had allowed appeals by Mr and Mrs Boland and by Mrs Brown against possession orders made in favour of the bank. The question raised by the appeals was whether a husband or a wife (in each case a wife) who had a beneficial interest in the matrimonial home by virtue of having contributed to its purchase price, but whose spouse was the legal and registered owner, had an 'overriding interest' binding on a mortgagee who claimed possession under a mortgage granted to that spouse alone. In each case the husband was registered in the Land Registry as the proprietor of the matrimonial home and the husband had mortgaged the home to the bank without the knowledge of the wife who was living in the house.

HELD: The appeals would be dismissed. The wives were entitled to resist claims for possession brought by the bank when the husbands did not pay the charges because the wives were 'in actual occupation' within s70(1)(g) of the Land Registration Act 1925, and so held 'overriding interests' to which the bank's charges were subject. The wives were further protected because by reason of their contributions to the purchase of the houses they were equitable tenants in common of the houses.

The property in both cases was registered under the Land Registration Act 1925. It was unclear whether the decision would affect unregistered titles where the purchaser's position would depend on notice, although in their speeches the Lords suggested that a purchaser might be deemed to have constructive notice of a wife's interests if he made no enquiry about them.

The question was answered in *Kingsnorth Finance Ltd* v *Tizard* [1986] 1 WLR 783; [1986] 2 All ER 54 which dealt with unregistered land. The matrimonial home was bought by the husband and wife and conveyed into the husband's name. The marriage broke down. The wife slept away from the house but returned virtually every day once the husband had left for work so that she could feed and look after the children. She also slept at the house when the husband was away which was frequently. The husband arranged a loan of £66,000 with the finance company using the house as security without the wife's knowledge. He told the company that his wife had left him and that he was single. He arranged for the company's agent to inspect the property when he knew the wife would not be there. The money was loaned to him. He then disappeared off to the USA with it. The company sought possession of the house.

HELD: The wife was in actual occupation of the property. Physical presence could amount to actual occupation without being exclusive, continuous or uninterrupted. It was not negatived by repeated absence. Her rights should have been revealed by a proper inspection or search. The company knew that the husband was married and that there were children. The company, therefore, had constructive notice of the wife's rights and took subject to those rights under s119(1) Law of Property Act 1925.

It was pointed out in *Lloyds Bank* v *Carrick* [1996] 2 FLR 600; [1996] 4 All ER 630 that in the case of unregistered land the intending purchaser only has constructive notice of matters that would have come to light had he/she made a reasonable inspection/enquiry in the circumstances. If he/she acts in a prudent fashion and does not find the wife in occupation or evidence that would give notice of occupation he/she is protected from the wife's interest.

See *Lloyds Bank* v *Rosset* [1988] 3 All ER 915 where a husband and wife decided to buy a semi-derelict farmhouse. The husband was Swiss and his Swiss family provided him with the money to buy the house and renovate it through a trust stipulating that the house had to be put into the husband's name. Before the house was bought the vendors allowed the husband and wife to start work on the house. They engaged builders who were supervised by the wife since the husband spent a lot of his time away at work. The house was uninhabitable and so the wife and children lived elsewhere. The only person who did occupy the house was one of the builders who slept 'rough' in the house. When the house was sold the husband arranged a loan for £15,000 with Lloyds Bank without the wife's knowledge. The house was used as security. The Bank did not inspect the property and relied on the husband's misleading statements and so was unaware of the wife's possible interest in it. The sale was completed as well as the loan. The house was on registered land and it took two months for the transaction to be registered at the Land Registry. In between the completion of the sale and the registration of the Bank's charge sufficient work was done to enable the wife to actually occupy the house. The marriage failed. The husband left. He did not repay the loan. The Bank sought possession. The wife resisted the claim by claiming an overriding interest under s70(1)(g) LRA 1925.

HELD (by the Court of Appeal): Three questions had to be answered:

## *What was the relevant date when deciding if an overriding interest bound by a third party?*

For there to be an overriding interest the wife had to show that she had a beneficial interest in the house; and that she was in actual occupation *before* the charge to the Bank took effect. If her beneficial interest was created *after* the charge took effect or she was in actual occupation *after* that date her claim failed.

When did the Bank's charge take effect? Was it when the purchase was completed or was it when title was formally registered two months later? The court was unanimous in deciding that the relevant date was the completion of the purchase. Though any purchase of registered land only took formal effect when title was registered at the Land Registry (s20(1) LRA 1925) any interest binding on the purchaser had to exist at the time of completion. This was because the purchaser made his inquiries before completion. Any overriding interest had to exist before that date so that the Bank could reasonably discover it. It would be unfair and unworkable to say that any binding interest could be created after completion and after all reasonable inquiries had been made by the purchaser.

## Did the wife have a beneficial interest before completion?

The court held that she did have a beneficial interest, but this part of the decision was overruled by the House of Lords (see section 10.3).

## Was the wife in actual occupation before completion?

The court was divided. Nicholls and Purchas LJJ said that she was. What constituted actual occupation depended on the nature and state of the property. A person could be in actual occupation through another (eg a caretaker) or in the wife's case through workmen. In the wife's case there was a physical presence throughout the period before completion which given the state of the property was a physical presence one would expect of an occupier. If the Bank had inspected the property they would have found the wife there. They should then have inquired of her possible interest and at least got her written consent, knowing that the house was to be a matrimonial home. Common sense indicated that they should be bound by her interest.

BUT Mustill LJ disagreed. The presence of builders in itself could not amount to occupation. They were simply tradesmen going about their business. The wife did not have sufficient continuity of presence through herself and the builders to amount to 'actual occupation'. She and the builders were getting the house ready for actual occupation. Her presence did not disclose anything about the possibility of interests adverse to the husband's legal title. Since she was not in actual occupation she had no overriding interest.

The court also considered the justice of the case. The Bank should have inspected the property. It should not have relied on the word of a deceitful husband. It could pursue the husband for its money. It could recover the loan and accrued interest when the house was eventually sold. Equity did not mean that the Bank would lose its money. It deprived the Bank of immediate possession thereby making the wife and children homeless.

The wife had an overriding interest which defeated the Bank's claim for possession (Mustill LJ dissenting).

The House of Lords allowed the Bank's appeal in *Lloyds Bank* v *Rosset* [1990] 1 All ER 1111, holding that the wife did not have a beneficial interest in the property.

The decision of the Court of Appeal that the relevant date had been the completion of the purchase was upheld and further confirmed by the House of Lords in *Abbey National Building Society* v *Cann* [1990] 1 All ER 1085 where G lived with his parents, Mr and Mrs C, in a house he owned. Mrs C claimed a beneficial interest in that house, partly on the basis that G had assured her that she would always have a roof over her head. In 1984 G sold that house and used the proceeds of sale to buy another house. He secured a £25,000 mortgage from a building society to fund the difference in the purchase price. He stated that the house was for his sole occupation. In fact, he did not live in it and it was occupied by Mr and Mrs C. He defaulted in paying the mortgage. The building society claimed possession. Mrs C claimed an overriding interest under s70(1)(g) LRA 1925 on the basis that her beneficial interest in the first house had transferred to the second house and that she was in actual occupation of the second house. Following *Lloyds Bank* v *Rosset* the relevant date for considering actual occupation was the date of the completion of the purchase when the mortgage took effect. On that day Mrs C was on holiday in the Netherlands but Mr C and G on her behalf unloaded her furniture and effects into the new house and organised the laying of her carpets. Such acts amounted to no more than preparatory steps leading to actual occupation and could not be actual occupation. Therefore, she had no overriding interest.

In any event Mrs C must have known that G had to raise a mortgage to buy the house and so she had impliedly authorised it. Her rights were against G, not the building society. The purchase of the house and the charge took effect at the same time since the acquisition of legal title depended on the provision of funds through the mortgage. A purchaser had no prior claim over that of a bank or building society. As a result Mrs C could not have any prior claim, through G, over the building society. Her rights were in the proceeds of sale.

## Where there will be no overriding interest

### Where a wife has no beneficial interest
In order to have an overriding interest a wife must have a beneficial interest as well as be in actual occupation. If a wife has no beneficial interest she cannot have an overriding interest (as was the case in *Midland Bank* v *Dobson* and *Lloyds Bank* v *Rosset*).

### Where the wife agreed to the loan
If a mortgage or loan is granted with the full knowledge of a wife or cohabitee there is no overriding interest. If the mortgage is a joint project then a wife or cohabitee can hardly claim the right to indefinitely stay in the property without paying the mortgage she agreed to. Her beneficial interest takes effect under a trust which allows the holder of the legal title to raise the mortgage and the mortgage takes priority over her beneficial interest in the property (see *Bristol and West Building Society* v *Henning* and *Winkworth* v *Edward Baron Development Co Ltd*).

See *Equity and Law Home Loans Ltd* v *Prestidge* [1992] 1 WLR 147 where P and B lived together. They decided to buy a house. B paid £10,000 and the balance was raised by a mortgage of £30,000 with the Britannia Building Society in the name of P, with B's knowledge and agreement. A year later P remortgaged the property to Equity and Law for nearly £43,000, without B's knowledge. P redeemed the mortgage with Britannia and pocketed the balance. P then left without paying the new mortgage. Equity and Law applied for possession. B resisted the claim.

HELD: B had a beneficial interest in the house (following *Grant* v *Edwards*). Had the mortgage remained with Britannia B would have had no answer to an order for sale since she agreed to it. Her consent must in common sense apply to the new mortgage in replacement of the old provided it did not make her position worse. If it was just to enforce the first mortgage it must be just to enforce the second by virtue of an imputed consent which applied to the creation of both. Possession was granted to Equity and Law (applying *Bristol and West Building Society* v *Henning*).

NOTE: The possession order only allowed Equity and Law to enforce the mortgage to the extent of £30,000 plus accrued interest leaving B in no worse position.

### Where there are two trustees under the trust

*Williams & Glyn's Bank* v *Boland* was not followed in *City of London Building Society* v *Flegg* [1987] 3 All ER 435 where the parents of the wife provided over half of the purchase price and were equitable tenants in common in the home which was in the legal names of the husband and wife. The wife and husband lived beyond their means. They took out a second mortgage with the building society. They defaulted on the mortgage. The building society applied for possession. The parents argued that they had an overriding interest in that they were in actual occupation and had an equitable interest under a resulting trust. Their argument failed since the building society had dealt with *two* trustees. The building society did not need to inquire if there are beneficial interests behind them. The parents' interest was in the proceeds of sale. If there was more than one trustee in a resulting trust there was no overriding interest. There had to be a balance between the public interest in securing that land held on trust was freely marketable and the protection of beneficial interests under a trust.

## Undue influence, duress or misrepresentation

Following the decision in *Williams & Glyn's Bank* v *Boland* it became the standard practice of banks and other lending institutions to ensure that, if they lent money to a person and used a house to secure the loan, any other person living in the property (usually the person's spouse) signed a form that he or she agreed to the house being used as a security for the loan. The banks hoped to avoid the consequences of *Williams & Glyn's Bank* v *Boland* in this way, since it could demonstrate that the other person had clearly agreed to the loan and to the house being used as a security for that loan.

However, even where a spouse had signed such a document it was still possible for that spouse to defeat a claim for possession if that document had only been signed by him/her or a result of 'duress' or 'undue influence' or 'misrepresentation'. This is because the courts recognise that a spouse or partner is likely to have an emotional involvement with the debtor (normally the husband) which makes him/her vulnerable.

In *Barclays Bank* v *O'Brien* [1993] 3 WLR 786; [1993] 4 All ER 417 H and W owned the matrimonial home jointly. H had an interest in a company. In order to raise capital for the company H obtained a loan from the bank using the home as security. H misrepresented the situation to W by saying that she was signing a mortgage on the house which would last for three weeks. When W went to sign the legal charge the effect of the documents was not explained to her, nor was she advised to seek independent legal advice. She signed the documents without reading them. H then defaulted on the loan and the bank applied for possession of the house.

HELD: When a wife stood surety for her husband's debts having been induced by undue influence, misrepresentation or similar wrong, she had a right to have the transaction set aside if the third party (in this case the bank) had actual or constructive knowledge of the wrong. The bank had a duty to take reasonable steps to satisfy itself that the wife entered into the obligation freely and in knowledge of the true facts. A bank would be put on enquiry if the transaction was not to the financial advantage of the wife and because of the substantial risk that a husband might act wrongly (eg to further his business interests or safeguard his debts)

A bank must warn such a spouse or partner, in the absence of the debtor, as to the amount of the potential liability and the risks involved and advise her to seek independent legal advice before signing the document. Otherwise the bank will be fixed with actual or constructive notice of the duress, misrepresentation or undue influence. In this case the bank had failed to take any steps to verify the situation and therefore had constructive knowledge of H's wrongful misrepresentation. W was entitled to have the charge set aside.

In *Royal Bank of Scotland* v *Etridge (No 2)* [2001] 3 FCR 481 it was confirmed that a bank is put on inquiry when a wife offers to stand surety for her husband's debts. On its face such a transaction is not to the financial advantage of the wife and there is a substantial risk that the husband has acted wrongly whereby the wife could set aside the transaction. There is no need for the wife to prove financial disadvantage or any wrongdoing by the husband. The wife does not have to show to the bank that she is cohabiting or that she placed implicit trust and confidence in the husband in relation to financial affairs. The bank is put on inquiry even if the wife is a director or secretary of the company for whose benefit the loan is sought. There is no need for the wife to show 'manifest disadvantage'. This term (used in earlier cases) has caused difficulty and misunderstanding and should be discarded. In future banks should be put on enquiry in every case where the relationship between the surety and the debtor is non-commercial. The types of relationship which give scope for misuse cannot be listed exhaustively. The greater the disadvantage to the vulnerable person, the more cogent the explanation for the transaction must be (applying *Allcard* v *Skinner* (1887) 36 Ch D 145). The court can then infer, in the absence of a satisfactory explanation, that the transaction could only have been obtained by undue influence.

A bank is not put on inquiry in the case of a joint loan for the husband and wife unless the bank is made aware that the loan is being made for the husband's purposes as opposed to their joint purposes. This was the decision in *CIBC Mortgages* v *Pitt* [1993] 3 WLR 802; [1993] 4 All ER 433 in which W agreed to a joint mortgage on the matrimonial home under undue influence. H and W stated that it was to be used to pay off an existing mortgage and to buy a holiday home. The money was paid into their joint account but was then used by H to speculate on the stock market. H defaulted on the mortgage and the lender sought possession of the home. It was held that even if W could prove actual undue influence she still had to show that the lender had actual or constructive notice of the undue influence. In this case there was nothing to indicate that this was anything other than a normal loan for H and W's benefit. See also *Brittania Building Society* v *Pugh* [1997] 2 FLR 7.

What must the bank do to avoid constructive notice of undue influence, duress or misrepresentation? The House of Lords in *Royal Bank of Scotland* v *Etridge (No 2)* set out the options. The clearest course is for the wife to attend a private meeting with the bank at which she is told the extent of her liability as a surety, warned of the risk she is running and urged to take independent legal advice. In exceptional cases the bank has to insist that the wife is separately advised. There is no obligation to arrange a private meeting. A suitable alternative is for the bank to rely on an independent legal adviser bringing to the wife's attention in a meaningful way the practical implications of the loan so that she enters into the transaction with open eyes. The bank should provide the solicitor with the financial information for the solicitor to properly advise the wife. The bank can rely upon confirmation from a solicitor acting for the wife that the solicitor has advised her appropriately. In the ordinary case deficiencies in the advice are a matter between the wife and the solicitor and the bank is entitled to proceed in the belief that the solicitor has advised the wife properly. Independent legal advice should be given at a face-to-face meeting in the absence of the husband. The solicitor could act for the husband or the bank provided the solicitor was satisfied that there was no conflict of interest. In *Credit Lyonnais Bank Nederland* v *Burch NV* [1997] 1 FLR 11; [1997] 1 All ER 144 the bank sent a standard form to the respondent which she signed and returned. This was held not to be sufficient to avoid the bank being fixed with constructive notice of undue influence (in this case the respondent's employer). It was necessary that the respondent receive advice either from the bank or from an independent legal adviser. An independent solicitor was bound to have told her on no account to enter a transaction so manifestly disadvantageous to her.

In *TSB* v *Camfield* [1995] 1 WLR 430; [1995] 1 All ER 951 W agreed to stand surety on H's misrepresentation that her liability would be limited to £15,000. She would not have agreed to the charge if a higher figure had been contemplated. The bank's legal executive failed to correct her misapprehension. When the bank sought to enforce the charge W claimed the charge should be set aside following *Barclays*

*Bank* v *O'Brien*. The bank accepted that W was entitled to have the charge set aside but only on the terms that she had accepted a valid security for £15,000. It was held that the charge should be set aside in full. The bank had constructive notice of H's misrepresentation. W's right to have the charge set aside was an 'all or nothing process'. If she had known of the true circumstances she would not have agreed to the charge at all.

## 10.14 Matrimonial home rights

Occupation under the Family Law Act 1996:

### *Where one spouse is entitled to occupy a dwelling-house and the other is not*

Where one spouse is entitled to occupy a dwelling-house by virtue of a beneficial estate or interest or contract or any enactment giving that spouse the right to remain in occupation and the other spouse is not so entitled then the spouse not so entitled has the following rights:

1. if in occupation, a right not to be evicted or excluded from the dwelling-house or any part of it by the other spouse except with the leave of the court given by an order under s33.
2. if not in occupation, a right with the leave of the court so given to enter into and occupy the dwelling-house (see section 30(2) FLA 1996).

A spouse who has an equitable interest in a dwelling-house or in its proceeds of sale but has no legal interest in the dwelling-house is treated for these purposes as not being entitled to occupy the dwelling-house by virtue of that interest (see s30(9) FLA 1996).

Payments of rent, mortgage or other outgoings affecting the dwelling-house can be made by the spouse with a right to occupy under s30(2) must be accepted as if the payments were made by the spouse who is entitled to occupy the house (though payment of the mortgage by the spouse with the right to occupy under s30(2) would not affect any claim by the that spouse against the other spouse to an interest in the home by virtue of that payment) (see s30(3) and (5) FLA 1996).

Section 30 does not apply to a dwelling-house which has at no time been and which was at no time intended by the spouses to be a matrimonial home of theirs (see s30(7) FLA 1996).

The rights of occupation under s30 continue only so long as the marriage subsists (except where s33(5) otherwise provides) and only so long as the other spouse is entitled to occupy the dwelling-house (except where those rights are a charge on an estate or interest in the dwelling-house) (see s30(8) FLA 1996).

## *Right of occupation as a charge on the estate or interest in the dwelling-house*

If one spouse is entitled to occupy a dwelling-house by virtue of a beneficial estate or interest the other spouse's matrimonial home rights are a charge on the estate or interest (see s31(1) and (2) FLA 1996). This takes the form of a Class F land charge in the case of registered land. Such a charge has the same priority as if it were an equitable interest created at whichever is the latest of the following dates:

1. the date on which the spouse entitled to occupy by virtue of a beneficial estate or interest acquired the estate or interest;
2. the date of the marriage;
3. 1 January 1968 (when the MHA 1967 came into force) (see s31(3) FLA 1996).

When a spouse's matrimonial home rights are a charge on an interest of the other spouse under a trust (provided that there are no persons, apart from the spouses living or unborn who are or could become beneficiaries under the trust, ignoring any potential exercise of a general power of appointment by the spouse(s)) the rights are a charge on the estate or interest of the trustees for the other spouse (see s31(4), (5) and (7) FLA 1996). Such a charge has the same priority as if it were an equitable interest created (under powers overriding the trusts) on the date when it arises (see s31(6) FLA 1996).

The matrimonial home rights are brought to an end by:

1. the death of the other spouse; or
2. the termination (otherwise than by death) of the marriage

unless the court directs otherwise by an order under s33(5) (see s31(8) FLA 1996).

Matrimonial home rights are not binding on third parties unless they are registered. In the case of registered land the right of occupation under FLA 1996 can be registered by notice under the Land Registration Act 1925, though such matrimonial home rights are not an overriding interest within the meaning of LRA 1925 even though the spouse is in actual occupation of the dwelling-house (see s31(10) FLA 1996). In the case of unregistered land the charge must be registered as a Class F land charge under the Land Charges Act 1972.

It is important to get the correct form of registration. If the wrong form of registration is adopted it will not bind a purchaser; see *Miles* v *Bull (No 2)* [1969] 3 All ER 1585 where the wife lost the protection which she would have obtained against a purchase from her husband because her solicitor had registered a Class F land charge instead of a Notice under the Land Registration Act 1925. The title to the land was registered.

A right may be registered even if the wife is not in actual occupation of the house: see *Watts* v *Waller* [1972] 3 WLR 365; [1972] 3 All ER 257. A spouse who is out of occupation has a conditional right of occupation which, although it cannot be enforced without leave of the court, is capable of registration.

Registering rights of occupation will only bind if transactions are completed after the registration (eg a mortgage taken out before rights are registered will not be affected) (see *Hastings & Thanet Building Society* v *Goddard* [1970] 1 WLR 1544; [1970] 3 All ER 954 where the wife registered her rights only after the mortgage and also used the wrong form of registration – a Class F land charge in the case of registered land instead of a Notice, so she was not protected).

The registration of rights can also be abused. See *Wroth* v *Tyler* [1973] 2 WLR 405; [1973] 1 All ER 897 where the wife registered her rights and thereby prevented the husband from selling the house and so making him liable in damages to a prospective purchaser.

The court may cancel the registration if there has been misuse. See *Barnett* v *Hassett* [1982] 1 All ER 80; [1981] 1 WLR 1385 where the spouses each had their own house. The husband sold his house in anticipation of the wife selling her house and they both moving into a new house. While he was selling his house he moved into the wife's house. The marriage did not work. The husband left. He stopped the sale of his house (losing a large amount of money in the process). The husband registered a Class F land charge on the wife's house, not because he want to live in her house, but as a bargaining tool in ancillary relief proceedings.

HELD: The husband had rights of a spouse not in occupation under s1(1)(b) MHA 1983 (the predecessor of FLA 1996). However, he did not want to occupy the house. He only wanted a share in the proceeds of sale. The MHA 1983 was not concerned with that. The Act was concerned with rights of occupation. The registration of the husband's right of occupation was cancelled.

## 10.15 Occupation of the matrimonial home when one spouse is bankrupt

If a spouse is declared bankrupt or cannot otherwise pay his/her debts the other spouse's occupation of the matrimonial home may not be protected either under the FLA 1996 or by virtue of his/her beneficial interests (eg under a resulting trust). The courts have to balance the interests of the creditors (including the principle that a person should pay his/her debts) against those of the debtor/bankrupt's family. The courts have tended to favour the interests of the creditors.

### Applying for an order to sell the property

The Trusts of Land and Appointment of Trustees Act (TOLATA) 1996 came into force on 1 January, 1997. Section 14 of the 1996 Act replaced s30 Law of Property Act 1925 and allows an application to be made for the sale of property. Section 15 sets out the criteria to be applied in deciding whether to order a sale.

Where one spouse is bankrupt a sale is likely to be ordered even though the other spouse objects. See *Bank of Baroda* v *Dhillon* [1998] 1 FLR 524 where, although W was ignorant of H's action in charging the house, the bank would have no other way to get its money in the foreseeable future, the children were adult children and would not suffer hardship and W would be left with enough money to re-accommodate herself. W had an overriding interest under s70(1)(g) LRA 1925 and the bank's legal charge took subject to that interest. However this did not prevent a sale in which half the proceeds went to the bank and half (representing W's equitable interest) to W.

See also *Bank of Ireland Home Mortgages Ltd* v *Bell* [2001] 2 FLR 809 in which H and W lived in a house owned by H but mortgaged to BIHM. H fell into arrears and subsequently left the property. BIHM applied for the house to be sold pursuant to ss14 and 15 TOLATA 1996. W was in poor health and occupied the house with her son. It was held that s15 TOLATA 1996, by requiring the court to have regard to particular matters, had given scope for some change in the court's previous practice that a creditor's interest should prevail except in exceptional circumstances. Nevertheless, the creditor's need for recompense remained a powerful consideration. The debt in this case of £300,000 was increasing daily and eventually the bank would be entitled to all the proceeds of sale. The home was no longer a matrimonial home. The child was not far short of 18 years of age and was therefore a slight consideration. W's health was only a ground for postponing the sale, not refusing it. W was only entitled to at most a 10 per cent beneficial interest. It was ordered that the property be sold.

## Where the spouse is bankrupt

Where a spouse has no legal or equitable interest in the property but has matrimonial home rights under the FLA 1996, the Insolvency Act 1986 makes those rights binding on the trustee in bankruptcy. If the trustee wishes to obtain possession and terminate the spouse's right of occupation he must apply under FLA 1996 and terminate the spouse's right of occupation (see s336(2) IA 1986).

The trustee in bankruptcy may apply for an order for the sale of the property under the TOLATA 1996. Section 335A Insolvency Act 1986 (inserted by the TOLATA 1996) requires the court having jurisdiction in the bankruptcy to make such order as it thinks just and reasonable having regard to:

1. the interests of the bankrupt's creditors (that is ordinary as well as secured creditors);
2. in the case of the home or former home of the bankrupt or bankrupt's spouse or former spouse, the conduct of the spouse or former spouse and the needs of any children;
3. all the circumstances of the case other than the needs of the bankrupt.

If the application is made under TOLATA 1996 after one year from the vesting of the property in the trustee in bankruptcy, the interests of the creditors are to prevail in the absence of exceptional circumstances.

In the case of *Dhillon* (above) the bank could have brought bankruptcy proceedings. H's interests would then have vested in the trustee in bankruptcy who could then apply for an order under s14 of the 1996 Act. The application would be governed by s335A Insolvency Act 1986. Re-accommodating the family or interrupting the children's schooling are not regarded as exceptional circumstances to avoid a sale once the one-year period laid down in s335A has elapsed. In *TSB Bank* v *Marshall* [1998] 2 FLR 769 a bank sought an order for possession in relation to a family home when the mortgage payments fell into arrears. The bank had an equitable charge over the house and applied for an order under the 1996 Act. H and W argued that the house was still intended as a home for two of the children still living there, notwithstanding that the children were now adults. It was held that the principles under s30 Law of Property Act 1925 applied to s14 of the 1996 Act. The purpose of s14 is to allow the court to do what is equitable, fair and just in all the circumstances, including (but not confined to) those set out in s15(1). The interests of the bank will prevail except where there are exceptional circumstances. Here there were no exceptional circumstances.

In *The Mortgage Corporation* v *Silkin and Shaire* [2000] Fam Law 402 a more generous approach appeared to be advocated. In the case H and W jointly owned the matrimonial home. They had one child, S. W began a relationship with F and H moved out of the home. In divorce proceedings the house was transferred into the joint names of W and F and a lump sum of £15,000 paid to H. W and F raised the £15,000 by a mortgage on the house. W, F and S lived in the house. W had modest earnings from a part time job. F paid the mortgage and household expenses. F died in 1992. It then came to light that he had forged W's signature on several documents, including a mortgage to TMC which he had used to pay off earlier mortgages and debts. TMC brought proceedings for possession of the house in which W and S were living. It was held that W was not bound by the TMC mortgage since she had clearly not agreed to it. W was beneficially entitled to a 75 per cent interest in the house. She had originally had a joint interest in the house with H. In the absence of any express agreement between W and F her equitable interest had to be determined from contemporary and subsequent conduct. Looking at the available evidence it should be inferred that H's 50 per cent share was to be distributed between W and F equally. The TMC mortgage was only valid against F's 25 per cent share. The question of whether the house should be sold was governed by the Trusts of Land and Appointment of Trustees Act (TOLATA) 1996 (which had replaced s30 Law of Property Act 1925). Under the old law there was no distinction between cases in which a trustee in bankruptcy or a mortgagee asked for the sale. The normal rule was that, save in exceptional circumstances, the wishes of the person wanting the sale would prevail over the interests of the children and families in occupation (see *Re Citro* and *Lloyds Bank* v *Byrne*). However, the law had been changed by s15 TOLATA 1996 which set out the specific factors to be taken into account in exercising the court's discretion and indicated in s15(4) that a different approach applied in bankruptcy cases. The balance had tipped more in favour of families and against banks and other charges. As a result of s15 the court had greater flexibility. The old authorities under s30 had to be treated with caution and in many cases would be unlikely to be of great assistance. In this case an order of sale was refused if the parties could agree to TMC's equity being converted to a loan on which W would pay interest at the TMC's normal market rate.

As can be seen from the above the interests of the creditors generally prevail. However, see *Judd* v *Brown* [1998] 2 FLR 360 (High Court) for an example of exceptional circumstances which justified the refusal of the sale of a matrimonial home jointly owned by a bankrupt. The wife was suffering from cancer and her recovery was directly affected by the prospect of having to leave her home. Postponement of the sale during her treatment was also likely to impose stress on her. No sale would be ordered (even after the 12 months' period in s335A Insolvency Act 1986 had elapsed). There was an appeal in *Judd* v *Brown*, reported at [1999] 1 FLR 1191, but the issue of the wife's occupation of the home was not in issue.

A postponement of a year was granted to the bankrupt's wife in *Re Raval (A Bankrupt)* [1998] Fam Law 590 since she suffered from mental illness and she needed a delay to enable her to adjust to a move while maintaining her mental stability. By contrast, a sale was ordered in *Trustees of the Estate of Eric Bowe (A Bankrupt)* v *Bowe* [1998] 2 FLR 439 even though the proceeds of sale were insufficient to satisfy all the debts owed to creditors.

Cases decided before the TOLATA 1996 reflect a similar approach:

1. *Re Bailey* [1977] 2 All ER 26: an immediate sale was ordered.
2. *Re Lowrie* [1981] 3 All ER 353: the sale of the home was ordered within three months despite the hardship that would be caused to the wife and children.
3. *Re Citro* [1990] 3 All ER 952; [1991] 1 FLR 71: orders postponing the sale of the houses of two families until the youngest children reached the age of sixteen were set aside on appeal and short period of suspension substituted.
4. *Re Gorman* [1990] 2 FLR 284: only a six months' postponement in sale was allowed.
5. *Barclays Bank* v *Hendricks* [1996] 1 FLR 258: the dislocation of the wife and children to new accommodation did not constitute exceptional circumstances to delay a sale in which the bank sought to recover 20 per cent of the money owed by the husband secured on a charge on the matrimonial home.

By contrast delays in the sale were allowed in:

1. *Re Holliday* [1980] 3 All ER 385: the sale was postponed for five years until the youngest child reached the age of seventeen years.
2. *Austin-Fell* v *Austin-Fell* [1990] 2 All ER 455; [1989] 2 FLR 497: the court allowed a postponement of the charging order on the matrimonial home for ten years by which time the youngest child would be eighteen years of age.
3. In *Claughton* v *Charalambous* [1999] 1 FLR 740 where a sale was postponed

because of exceptional circumstances under s335A IA 1986 because the wife, aged 60, had poor health, could only walk with great difficulty and had a reduced life expectancy. The home was fitted with a chair lift.

4. In *Re Bremner (A Bankrupt)* [1999] 1 FLR 912 in which the sale was postponed until three months after the death of the bankrupt (aged 79 and not expected to live more than six months) who was being cared for by his 74-year-old wife. The interests of common humanity outweighed any difficulties caused by the delay in the sale of the home.

It is possible for a spouse to apply to annul the bankruptcy if the other spouse has declared himself bankrupt purely as a device to frustrate the spouse's claim for financial provision (see s282(1) Insolvency Act 1986). For example in *F* v *F (Divorce: Insolvency: Annulment of Bankruptcy Order)* [1994] 1 FLR 359 the wife successfully applied to annul the husband's bankruptcy order because the bankruptcy petition showed an inaccurate picture of his financial position, was a device against the wife and an abuse of the process of bankruptcy.

An obligation arising under a financial provision order made in family proceedings is not provable in bankruptcy. As a result the trustee in bankruptcy has no duty to investigate and account for the money or property which is the basis of the financial provision order. See *Woodley* v *Woodley (No 2)* [1993] 2 FLR 477 where the wife unsuccessfully tried to enforce payment of a £60,000 lump sum after her husband had been made bankrupt. In *Re Bradley-Hole (A Bankrupt)* [1995] 1 WLR 1097; [1995] 4 All ER 865 a wife was able to claim some arrears of maintenance and other debts which had accrued after the husband had been made bankrupt (though this case may be confined to its facts since the husband was made bankrupt and then entered into a voluntary arrangement before being made a bankrupt a second time).

## Cohabitees

Unmarried partners have no rights under the Insolvency Act 1986 and cannot resist an application by the trustee in bankruptcy for possession unless he/she has an interest in the property. Application then has to be made for a sale under s14 TOLATA 1996. As specified above the interests of the creditors will prevail after one year.

## Transactions which could defeat the claims of creditors

Transactions at undervalue which are meant to defeat the claims of creditors may be set aside so that the position is restored to what it would have been if the transaction had not been entered into. The court must be satisfied that the debtor's purpose was to put assets beyond the reach of a person making a claim against him or who will at some time make a claim against him or, alternatively, a transaction that might prejudice the interests of such a person (see s423 Insolvency Act 1986).

For example, in *Lloyds Bank* v *Marcan* [1973] 1 WLR 1381; [1973] 3 All ER 754 the husband leased his horticultural business to his wife thereby depriving his bank of the ability to sell it to realise the asset when he was made bankrupt. The husband had done that knowing that the bank wanted possession. The lease was set aside.

Transactions at undervalue within a specified time of a bankruptcy may also be set aside without the need to show any intention to defeat the claims of creditors (see s339 of the 1986 Act). This applies to transactions within five years ending with the day of the presentation of the bankruptcy petition. If the transaction is more than two years from that time the creditor must show that the husband could not pay all his debts at the time of the transaction, or became insolvent in consequence of entering into the transaction (s341). Therefore, if a husband has transferred his interest in a property to his wife, then such a transaction may not survive against the trustee in bankruptcy because of ss423 and 339. For an example of a case where a wife acquired a beneficial interest which did survive against a trustee in bankruptcy see *Re Densham* [1975] 3 All ER 726 (where a wife's beneficial interest of a one-ninth share in a house survived the trustee in bankruptcy's application to have it set aside so that she retained that share of the proceeds of sale).

NOTE: A wife cannot register her rights of occupation or acquire rights of occupation once the bankruptcy petition has been presented (s336).

In *Re Flint (A Bankrupt)* [1993] 1 FLR 763, H and W divorced in March 1990. In May 1990 a bankruptcy petition was presented against H. On 18 July 1990 a transfer of property order was made whereby the jointly owned house was transferred to W. On 24 July 1990 H was adjudicated bankrupt. The property transfer was declared void under s284 Insolvency Act 1986 and the house held on trust for the trustee in bankruptcy and W in equal shares.

Please also note that s39 MCA 1973 specifically states that the fact that a transfer is made in compliance with a court order does not prevent it from coming within the scope of s339 IA 1986.

In *Re Kumar (A Bankrupt)* [1993] Fam Law 470, H and W were joint tenants of the matrimonial home worth £140,000 with a mortgage of £30,000. In June 1990 H transferred his interest in the house to W. In January 1991 W obtained a decree nisi of divorce and in April 1991 a clean break order was made dismissing W's claim for financial provision in light of H's transfer to his interest in the home. In July 1991 a bankruptcy order was made against H. The trustee in bankruptcy applied under s339 Insolvency Act 1986 to set aside the transfer.

HELD: Granting the trustee's application, the June 1990 transfer was at an undervalue. W provided no consideration other than taking on the whole of the mortgage which was considerably less than the value of H's interest. No divorce court would have required H to transfer what was all his capital to W (who had a superior earning capacity), depriving him of having the means to rehouse himself.

## 10.16 Excluding the violent partner from the family home

### Introduction

In 1992 the Law Commission published a report entitled *Family Law, Domestic Violence and Occupation of the Family Home* (Law Com No 207). It criticised the existing law on domestic violence as being inconsistent and spread over a range of statutes, with different levels of courts having different powers and applying different considerations. Some victims of domestic violence only had limited remedies or no remedy at all. The Law Commission recommended a uniform code which would offer a consistent set of remedies for a wider range of people in all courts having jurisdiction in family proceedings. There was then widespread consultation which resulted in the Family Homes and Domestic Violence Bill. This Bill met with considerable Parliamentary opposition and was dropped. Eventually the proposals were incorporated in Part IV of the Family Law Act 1996 which was passed in July 1996 and came into force in October 1997.

### What Part IV of the Family Law Act 1996 replaces

The Domestic Violence and Matrimonial Proceedings Act 1976 and Matrimonial Homes Act 1983 are repealed, as are ss16–18 DPMCA 1978. These provisions were replaced by a single code which is set out in Part IV of FLA 1996.

### Occupation and non-molestation orders

#### To which court should application be made?

Application can be made to the High Court, county court or magistrates' court (see s57 FLA 1996). There is a provision allowing magistrates' courts to transfer more difficult cases to the county court. Magistrates' courts will not be allowed to deal with any application involving disputes concerning a party's entitlement to occupy a property by virtue of a beneficial interest estate or interest or contract unless it is unnecessary to determine the question in order to deal with the application or make the order (see s59(1) FLA 1996). This is because magistrates' courts do not have the expertise to deal with such applications. The magistrates can decline to deal with applications which may be more conveniently dealt with in another court (eg a county court) (see s59(2) FLA 1996).

#### Definition of terms

'Cohabitants' are a man and woman who, although not married to each other, are living together as husband and wife (see s62(1)(a) FLA 1996).

'Former cohabitants' is to be read accordingly but does not include cohabitants who have subsequently married each other (see s62(1)(b) FLA 1996).

'Relevant child' means any child who is living with or might reasonably be expected to live with either party to the proceedings and any child in relation to whom an order under the Children Act 1989 or Adoption Act 1976 is in question in relation to the proceedings and any other child whose interests the court considers relevant (see s62(2) FLA 1996).

A 'child' means a person under the age of 18 years (see s63(1) FLA 1996).

The phrase 'significant harm' carries a similar meaning to that in the Children Act 1989. 'Harm' means in relation to a person aged 18 years or more ill-treatment or the impairment of health. In relation to a child it means ill-treatment or the impairment of health or development. 'Development' means physical, intellectual, emotional, social or behavioural development. 'Heath' includes physical or mental health. 'Ill-treatment' includes forms of ill-treatment which are not physical and, in relation to a child, includes sexual abuse (see s63(1) FLA 1996). Where the question of whether harm suffered by a child is significant turns on the child's health or development, his or her health shall be compared with that which could reasonably be expected of a similar child (see s63(3) FLA 1996).

'Dwelling-house' includes any building or part of a building which is occupied as a dwelling and any caravan, house-boat or structure occupied as a dwelling and any yard, garden, garage or outhouse belonging to it and occupied with it (see s63(1) FLA 1996). It can include, for instance, the whole of a hotel owned by a husband and wife (and not just their living quarters) if there is only one entrance and one kitchen (see *Kinzler* v *Kinzler* (1985) 15 Fam Law 26).

A person is 'associated' with another person if –

1. they are or have been married to each other;
2. they are cohabitants or former cohabitants;
3. they live or have lived in the same household otherwise than merely by reason of one of them being the other's employee, tenant, lodger or boarder;
4. they are relatives;
5. they are engaged (whether or not that engagement has been terminated);
6. they are parents of a child or have parental responsibility for the child (or are a natural parent of a child and the adoptive parents or a child who has been or is the process of being adopted);
7. they are parties to the same family proceedings (other than proceedings under Part IV FLA 1996) (see s62(3), (4) and (5) FLA 1996).

'Relative' is defined by reference to a list which includes fathers, mothers, step-parents, siblings, stepsiblings, grandparents and grandchildren (including such relatives by virtue of that person's spouse or former spouse or cohabiting partner), brothers, sisters, uncles, aunts, nephews and nieces (see s63(1) FLA 1996).

## *Application for occupation orders*

There are five kinds of application for occupation orders:

1. application by a person with occupation rights or with matrimonial home rights against an 'associated' person (pursuant to s33 FLA 1996);
2. application by a former spouse with no existing right to occupy against the other former spouse who has a right to occupy (pursuant to s35 FLA 1996);
3. application by a cohabitant/former cohabitant with no right to occupy against a cohabitant/former cohabitant with a right to occupy (pursuant to s36 FLA 1996);
4. application by a spouse with no right to occupy against a spouse who also has no right to occupy (pursuant to s37 FLA 1996); and
5. application by a cohabitant/former cohabitant with no right to occupy against the cohabitant/former cohabitant who also has no right to occupy (pursuant to s38 FLA 1996).

It may be important to make the right kind of application since different provisions apply depending on the kind of application to be made. Applicants may have to clarify their rights of occupation in order to determine which kind of application should be made. However, if an applicant makes an application under one section but the court considers that it should have been made under another section, then the court can make the order under the correct section (see s39(3) FLA 1996).

### Application for an occupation order by a person with occupation rights or with matrimonial home rights (the s33 occupation order)

*Who may apply for a s33 occupation order?* If a person is entitled to occupy a dwelling-house by virtue of a beneficial estate or interest or contract, or by virtue of any enactment giving him or her the right to remain in occupation, or has matrimonial home rights in relation to a dwelling-house (eg under s30(2) FLA 1996), *and* the dwelling-house is or at any time has been the home of the person entitled and of another person with whom he or she is associated, and was at any time intended by the person entitled and any such other person to be their home, then the person entitled may apply for an occupation order against that other person ('the respondent') (see s33(1) FLA 1996).

For these purposes, if an agreement to marry is terminated no application can be made under s33 FLA 1996 by reference to that agreement after the end of three years beginning with the date on which it is terminated (see s33(2) FLA 1996).

### *What is a s33 occupation order?*

A s33 occupation order is an order which:

1. enforces the applicant's entitlement to remain in occupation as against the respondent; or
2. requires the respondent to permit the applicant to enter and remain in the dwelling-house or part of the dwelling-house; or

3. regulates the occupation of the dwelling-house by either or both parties; or
4. prohibits, suspends or restricts the exercise by the respondent of his or her rights to occupy the dwelling-house by virtue of his or her beneficial estate or interest or contract or enactment giving him or her the right to remain in occupation; or
5. if the respondent has matrimonial rights in relation to the dwelling-house and the applicant is the other spouse, restrict or terminate those rights; or
6. requires the respondent to leave the dwelling-house or part of the dwelling-house; or
7. excludes the respondent from a defined area in which the dwelling-house is situated.

(See s33(3) FLA 1996.)

A s33 occupation order may also declare that the applicant is entitled to occupy a dwelling-house or has matrimonial home rights (see s33(4) FLA 1996).

If the applicant has matrimonial home rights and the respondent is the other spouse, an occupation order made during the marriage may provide that those rights are not brought to an end by the death of the other spouse or the termination (otherwise than by death) of the marriage (see s33(5) FLA 1996). The court may exercise such powers in any case where it considers that in all the circumstances it is just and reasonable to do so (see s33(8) FLA 1996). Otherwise a s33 occupation order ceases to have effect on the death of either party and in any event may not be made after the death of either of the parties (see s33(9) FLA 1996).

A s33 occupation order may be made for a specified period or until the occurrence of a specified event or until further order (see s33(10) FLA 1996). Under the previous law the period of an exclusion order was normally limited to three months (see *Practice Direction (Injunction: Domestic Violence)* [1978] 1 WLR 1123). In exeptional cases where the respondent's behaviour has been particularly serious and persistent, the order may be unlimited (see *Galan v Galan* [1985] FLR 905 and *Spencer v Camacho* (1983) 4 FLR 662).

### What the court must consider before making a s33 occupation order
The court must have regard to all the circumstances including:

1. the housing needs and housing resources of each of the parties and of any relevant child; and
2. the financial resources of each of the parties; and
3. the likely effect of any order, or of any decision by the court not to exercise its powers, on the health, safety or well-being of the parties and of any relevant child; and
4. the conduct of the parties in relation to each other and otherwise.

(See s33(6) FLA 1996.)

The court must balance the risk of significant harm – if it appears to the court that the applicant or any relevant child is likely to suffer significant harm attributable to conduct of the respondent if an occupation order is not made the court shall make the occupation order unless it appears to the court that:

1. the respondent or any relevant child is likely to suffer significant harm if the order is made; and
2. the harm likely to be suffered by the respondent or child in that event is as great as, or greater than, the harm attributable to conduct of the respondent which is likely to be suffered by the applicant or child if the order is not made (see s33(7) FLA 1996).

In *Chalmers* v *Johns* [1999] Fam Law 26 a wife applied for a s33 occupation order on the basis of occasional acts of minor violence by the husband. It was held that s33(7) only came into play if the applicant or child was likely to suffer significant harm if the order was not made. Given the slight nature of this particular domestic violence, s33(7) did not apply. An occupation order was draconian in nature and on the facts of this case was not appropriate. A non-molestation order was the correct remedy.

In *B* v *B (Occupation: Order)* [1999] 1 FLR 715 H was violent to W. W moved out of the matrimonial home (a council house) with their two-year-old daughter into bed and breakfast accommodation. H remained in the house with a six-year-old son from a previous relationship. W obtained a s33 occupation order against H obliging him and his son to leave the house. The court also transferred the council house tenancy to her (pursuant to Sch 7 FLA 1996) and made a non-molestation order in W's favour (pursuant to s42 FLA 1996). H appealed. It was held, allowing the appeal, that the court had mistakenly analysed H's housing needs and resources in that it was thought that the local authority had a duty to rehouse him. He would not be rehoused because he was treated as making himself intentionally homeless due to his violence. By contrast the local authority had a duty to rehouse W and the daughter. The court was entitled to find under s33(7) FLA 1996 that W and the younger child were likely to suffer significant harm attributable to H's conduct if an occupation order were not made. However, weighing the respective likelihoods of harm so far as the two children were concerned the balance came clearly down in favour of H's child, if an occupation order were made. If he were to move he would also have to change schools and being taken away from his father was not a solution.

In *Banks* v *Banks* [1999] 1 FLR 726 H, aged 75, lived with W, aged 79. They were joint tenants of the matrimonial home. W suffered from manic depression and dementia but could be cared for at home with assistance. She was verbally and physically aggressive which caused H strain. H was physically and emotionally frail. H petitioned for divorce and applied for an occupation order and a non-molestation order. If W's behaviour deteriorated she would be hospitalised. It was held, dismissing the application, that W's behaviour did not significantly threaten H's health, even allowing for his age and uncertain health. If an occupation order was made W would be caused significantly greater harm than the harm H would suffer if the order was not made. Occupation was a temporary issue given the divorce proceedings. It was also wrong to make a non-molestation order since W's behaviour was a symptom of her condition over which she had no control. An order would serve no practical purpose even if she were capable of understanding it.

In *G v G (Occupation Order: Contact)* [2000] Fam Law 466 H and W divorced. There were proceedings relating to ancillary relief and the residence of the two children of the family. W also applied for an occupation order under s33 FLA 1996. H had not used violence against W. The atmosphere in the house was tense. The judge dismissed the application for the s33 occupation order. He considered s33(7) but found that H's conduct was unintentional and that any harm W suffered was unattributable to it. W appealed. It was held, dismissing the appeal, that the making of a s33 occupation order was a draconian act and was an exceptional order to make. The court first had to consider s33(7). The judge was wrong to consider that H's conduct had to be intentional. The court was concerned with the effect of the conduct rather than whether it was intentional. In the circumstances s33(7) did not apply since there was no significant harm. The court then had to move to s33(6) and the four factors set out therein. In the case there was an absence of violence, the conduct complained of amounted to friction arising from the divorce process, H was often away on business and the ancillary relief and residence hearings were a matter of weeks away. To exclude H and part him from the children was undesirable.

## Application by former spouse with no existing right to occupy (a s35 occupation order)

### What is a s35 occupation order?
If one former spouse is entitled to occupy a dwelling-house by virtue of a beneficial estate or interest or contract or has a right of occupation by virtue of any enactment; and the other former spouse is not so entitled; and the dwelling-house was at any time their matrimonial home or was at any time intended by them to be their matrimonial home, then the former spouse not so entitled may apply to the court for an occupation order against the other former spouse (see s35(1) and (2) FLA 1996).

For these purposes a former spouse who has an equitable interest in the dwelling-house or in the proceeds of sale but who has no legal interest is treated as not being entitled to occupy the dwelling-house (see s35(11) FLA 1996).

### Meaning of a s35 occupation order
For these purposes a s35 occupation order *must* contain the following provisions:

1. where the applicant is in occupation:

   a) an order giving the applicant the right not to be evicted or excluded from the dwelling-house or any part of it by the respondent for the period specified in the order; and

   b) prohibiting the respondent from evicting or excluding the applicant during that period.

2.  where the applicant is not in occupation –

    a)  an order giving the applicant the right to enter into and occupy the dwelling-house for such period specified in the order; and
    b)  requiring the respondent to permit the exercise of that right.

(See s35(4) FLA 1996.)

A s35 order *may* also –

1.  regulate the occupation of the dwelling-house by either or both of the parties;
2.  prohibit, suspend or restrict the exercise by the respondent of his or her right to occupy the dwelling-house;
3.  require the respondent to leave the dwelling-house or part of the dwelling-house; or
4.  exclude the respondent from a defined area in which the dwelling-house is situated.

(See s35(5) FLA 1996.)

### What the court must consider

In deciding whether to make an occupation order under s35(3) or (4) and, if so, in what manner, the court shall have regard to all the circumstances. In particular the court must consider:

1.  the housing needs and housing resources of each of the parties and of any relevant child;
2.  the financial resources of each of the parties;
3.  the likely effect of any order, or of any decision by the court not to exercise its powers to make an occupation order, on the health, safety or well-being of the parties and of any relevant child;
4.  the conduct of the parties in relation to each other and otherwise;
5.  the length of time that elapsed since the parties ceased to live together;
6.  the length of time that has elapsed since the marriage was dissolved or annulled; and
7.  the existence of any pending proceedings between the parties:

    a)  for an order under s23A or 24 MCA 1973;
    b)  for an order under para 1(2)(d) or (e) Sch 1 CA 1989; or
    c)  relating to the legal or beneficial ownership of the dwelling-house.

(See s35(6) FLA 1996.)

In deciding whether to make a s35(5) provision (eg excluding the respondent) and, if so, in what manner, the court shall have regard to all the circumstances including the matters mentioned in s35(6)(a) to (e) FLA 1996.

The court must add a s35(5) provision if it appears that the applicant or any relevant child is likely to suffer significant harm attributable to the conduct of the respondent if such an order is not made, unless it appears to the court that –

1. the respondent or any relevant child is likely to suffer significant harm if a s35(5) order is made; and
2. the harm likely to be suffered by the respondent or child in that event is as great or greater than the harm attributable to conduct of the respondent which is likely to be suffered by the applicant or child if the s35(5) provision was not made.

(See s35(8) FLA 1996.)

An order may not be made under s35 after the death of either of the former spouses and ceases to have effect on the death of either of them (s35(9) FLA 1996).

An order under s35 must be limited so as to have effect for a specified period not exceeding six months. It may be extended on one or more occasions for a further specified period not exceeding six months (s35(10) FLA 1996).

As long as a s35 order remains in force s30(3)-(6) applies in relation to the applicant as if he or she were the spouse entitled to occupy the dwelling-house by virtue of s30 and as if the respondent were the other spouse (s35(11) FLA 1996).

For an example of a court making an occupation order under s35 FLA 1996, see *S v F (Occupation Order)* [2000] 2 FCR 365 which involved M and F who had divorced. They had two teenage children, I and S, who lived with their mother, M, in the former matrimonial home in London. F lived abroad. M, without consulting F, decided to move the children from London to Somerset. I, who was in the middle of his A levels, refused to move. F, who supported I, and moved back to England, applied for an occupation order to permit him to go back into the London home and look after I. F was unable to establish a beneficial interest in the home so could not apply under s33 FLA 1996. He applied for an order under s35 FLA 1996. Applying the s35(6) criteria the court considered F to be in the most difficult financial position in terms of finding accommodation for himself and I. He had no income. M was able to find accommodation in Somerset, supported by her new husband who had an income. M had caused the crisis with I. The parties had been separated for five years but continued to be involved with the children. An occupation order was granted for six months permitting F to return to the London home.

### Where the applicant is an unmarried cohabitant or former cohabitant with no existing right to occupy (a s36 occupation order)

*What is a s36 occupation order?*

Where one cohabitant or former cohabitant is entitled to occupy a dwelling-house by virtue of a beneficial estate or interest or contract or by virtue of any enactment giving him or her the right to remain in occupation; and the other cohabitant or former cohabitant is not so entitled; and that dwelling-house is the home in which they live together as husband and wife or a home in which they at any time so lived together or intended so to live together then the cohabitant or former cohabitant not so entitled may apply for an occupation order against the other cohabitant or former cohabitant ('the respondent') (s36(1) and (2) FLA 1996).

### What a s36 occupation order means

If the applicant is in occupation a s36 order *must* contain provisions:

1. giving the applicant the right not to be evicted or excluded from the dwelling-house or any part of it by the respondent for the period specified in the order; and
2. prohibiting the respondent from evicting or excluding the applicant during that period.

(See s36(3) FLA 1996.)

If the applicant is not in occupation a s36 order must contain provisions:

1. giving the applicant the right to enter into and occupy the dwelling-house for the period specified in the order; and
2. requiring the respondent to permit the exercise of that right.

(See s36(4) FLA 1996.)

A s36 order *may* also:

1. regulate the occupation of the dwelling-house by either or both of the parties;
2. prohibit, suspend or restrict the exercise by the respondent of his/her right to occupy the dwelling-house;
3. require the respondent to leave the dwelling-house or part of the dwelling-house; or
4. exclude the respondent from a defined area in which the dwelling-house is included.

(See s36(5) FLA 1996.)

For these purposes a person who has an equitable interest in the dwelling-house or in the proceeds of sale but no legal interest is to be treated as not being entitled to occupy the dwelling-house (see s36(11) FLA 1996).

### What the court must consider

In deciding whether to make a s36(3) or (4) order and, if so, in what manner the court shall have regard to all the circumstances including:

1. the housing needs and resources of each of the parties and of any relevant child;
2. the financial resources of each of the parties;
3. the likely effect of any order, or of any decision by the court not to exercise its powers under s36(3) or (4) on the health, safety or well-being of the parties and of any relevant child;
4. the conduct of the parties in relation to each other and otherwise;
5. the nature of the parties' relationship;

6. the length of time during which they lived together as husband and wife;
7. whether there are or have been any children who are children of both parties or for whom both parties have or have had parental responsibility;
8. the length of time that has elapsed since the parties ceased to live together; and
9. the existence of any pending proceedings between the parties:

a) for an order under para 1(2)(d) or (e) Sched 1 CA 1989; or
b) relating to the legal or beneficial ownership of the dwelling-house.

(See s36(6) FLA 1996.)

In deciding whether to exercise its powers to include any s36(5) provision (eg an order excluding the respondent) and, if so, in what manner the court must have regard to all the circumstances including the matters mentioned in s36(6)(a) to (d) (see s36(7)(a) FLA 1996).

The court must also ask the questions:

1. whether the applicant or any relevant child is likely to suffer significant harm attributable to conduct if the s36(5) provision is not included; and
2. whether the harm likely to be suffered by the respondent or child if the provision is included is as great or greater than the harm attributable to conduct of the respondent which is likely to be suffered by the applicant or child if the provision is not included.

(See s36(7)(b) and (8) FLA 1996.)

If the balance of harm test shows that the harm to the applicant or relevant child is greater if the order is not made than the harm to the respondent or relevant child if it is made then the court is not obliged to make an occupation order (unlike with a s33 occupation order).

In considering the nature of the parties' relationship the court must have regard to the fact that they have not given each other the commitment involved in marriage (see s41 FLA 1996).

### Duration of the order

A s36 order must be limited so as to have effect for a specified period not exceeding six months but may be extended on one occasion for a further specified period not exceeding six months (see s36(10) FLA 1996).

A s36 order may not be made after the death of either of the parties and ceases to have effect on the death of either of them (see s36(9) FLA 1996).

So long as the order remains in force s30(3)–(6) apply in relation to the applicant as if he or she were a spouse entitled to occupy the dwelling-house by virtue of s30 and as if the respondent were the other spouse (see s36(13) FLA 1996).

For an example of a court making a s36 occupation order see *Gay* v *Sheeran* [1999] 3 All ER 795; [1999] 2 FLR 519 in which S and P held a council tenancy of the flat in which they lived. P left and G moved into the flat and cohabited with S. S then moved out but the tenancy was not terminated. Eighteen months later the council discovered that S and P no longer lived in the flat and sought possession. G applied for a transfer of the tenancy but was refused. G then applied for an occupation order under s36 protecting her from eviction from S's flat. This had the legal effect of enabling the transfer to be granted. The occupation order was made but the council appealed on the basis that the order was a device to gain the transfer. It was held, dismissing the appeal, that the court was entitled to make the s36 occupation order because on the facts there was a real possibility that S might return. The order served a practical purpose. It was a short term holding order (limited to six months in length). It was not intended to determine property rights.

## Where neither spouse is entitled to occupy (a s37 occupation order)

### *What is a s37 occupation order?*

Where a spouse or former spouse and the other spouse or former spouse occupy a dwelling-house which is or was the matrimonial home but neither of them is entitled to remain in occupation then either may apply to the court for an occupation order (see s37(1) and (2) FLA 1996). Both parties must be in occupation for s37 to apply.

### *What a s37 occupation order means*

A s37 occupation order means an order:

1. requiring the respondent to permit the applicant to enter and remain in the dwelling-house or part of the dwelling-house;
2. regulating the occupation of the dwelling-house by either or both of the spouses;
3. requiring the respondent to leave the dwelling-house or part of it; or
4. excluding the respondent from a defined area in which the dwelling-house is included.

(See s37(3) FLA 1996.)

### *What the court must consider*

In deciding whether to exercise its powers and, if so, in what manner the court shall have regard to all the circumstances including:

1. the housing needs and housing resources of each of the parties and of any relevant child;
2. the financial resources of each of the parties;
3. the likely effect of any order, or of any decision by the court not to exercise its powers under s37(3), on the health, safety or well-being of the parties and of any relevant child; and
4. the conduct of the parties in relation to each other and otherwise.

(See ss37(4) and 33(6) FLA 1996.)

If it appears to the court that the applicant or any relevant child is likely to suffer significant harm attributable to conduct of the respondent if a s37(3) order is not made, the court shall make the order unless it appears to it that:

1. the respondent or any relevant child is likely to suffer significant harm if the order is made; and
2. the harm likely to be suffered by the respondent or any relevant child in that event is as great as, or greater than, the harm attributable to conduct of the respondent which is likely to be suffered by the applicant or child if the order is not made (see ss37(4) and 33(7) FLA 1996).

### Period of the order
A s37(3) order must be limited to have effect for a specified period not exceeding six months but may be extended on one or more occasions for a further specified period not exceeding six months (see s37(5) FLA 1996). The maximum period of the order is one year.

## Application for a s38 occupation order – where neither cohabitant nor former cohabitant is entitled to occupy
### Who may apply for a s38 occupation order?
If one cohabitant or former cohabitant and the other cohabitant or former cohabitant occupy a dwelling-house which is the home in which they live or lived together as husband and wife but neither of them is entitled to remain in occupation then either of them may apply to the court for an order against the other (see s38(1) and (2) FLA 1996).

### What a s38 occupation order means
A s38 occupation order means an order:

1. requiring the respondent to permit the applicant to enter and remain in the dwelling-house or part of the dwelling-house;
2. regulating the occupation of the dwelling-house by either or both of the parties;
3. requiring the respondent to leave the dwelling-house or part of the dwelling-house; or
4. excluding the respondent from a defined area in which the dwelling-house is included (see s38(3) FLA 1996).

### What the court must consider
In deciding whether to exercise its powers to make a s38(3) order and, if so, in what manner the court must have regard to all the circumstances including:

1. the housing needs and housing resources of each of the parties and of any relevant child;
2. the financial resources of each of the parties;
3. the likely effect of any order, or of any decision by the court not to make a s38(3) order, on the health, safety or well-being of the parties and of any relevant child;

4. the conduct of the parties in relation to each other and otherwise (see s38(4) FLA 1996).

The court must also ask itself whether the applicant or any relevant child is likely to suffer significant harm attributable to the conduct of the respondent if the s38(3) order is not made and whether the harm likely to be suffered by the respondent or child if the s38(3) order is made is as great or greater than the harm attributable to conduct of the respondent which is likely to be suffered by the applicant or child if the provision is not included (see s38(5) FLA 1996).

Again there is no duty on the court to make an occupation order where the balance of harm is greatest in relation to the applicant or a relevant child.

### Period of a s38(3) order

A s38(3) order shall be limited so as to have effect for a specified period not exceeding six months but may be extended on one occasion for a further specified period not exceeding six months (see s38(6) FLA 1996). The order is limited to a maximum period of one year.

### General provisions concerning occupation orders

An occupation order under s33, s35, s36, s37 or s38 may be made in other family proceedings or without any other family proceedings being instituted (see s39(2) FLA 1996).

If an application is made for an occupation order under one of those sections and the court considers that it has no power to make the order under the section concerned but that it has power to make an order under one of the other sections the court may make an order under that other section (see s39(3) FLA 1996).

The fact that a person has applied for an occupation order or that an occupation order has been made does not affect the right of any person to claim a legal or equitable interest in any property in any subsequent proceedings (see s39(4) FLA 1996).

The court may on, or at any time after, making an occupation order under ss33, 35 or 36:

1. impose on either party obligations to repair and maintain the dwelling-house and to pay rent or mortgage or other outgoings affecting the dwelling-house;
2. order the party occupying the dwelling-house to make periodical payments to the other party for accommodation he/she has had to find where that other party has a legal right to occupy the dwelling-house (but for the occupation order);
3. grant either party possession or use of furniture or other contents of the dwelling-house;
4. order either party to take reasonable care of any furniture or other contents of the dwelling-house;
5. order either party to take reasonable steps to keep the dwelling-house and any furniture or other contents secure (see s40(1) FLA 1996).

In deciding whether and, if so, how to exercise its powers under s40(1) the court must have regard to all the circumstances of the case including the financial needs and resources of the parties and the financial obligations which they have or are likely to have in the foreseeable future including financial obligations to each other and to any relevant child (see s40(2) FLA 1996).

A s40(1) order ceases to have effect when the occupation order to which it relates ceases to have effect (see s40(3) FLA 1996).

In *Nwogbe* v *Nwogbe* [2000] 2 FLR 744 a husband excluded from the local authority accommodation occupied by him and his wife was ordered to pay the rent pursuant to s40 FLA 1996. He failed to pay. The Court of Appeal held that there was no power to enforce such an order (eg by way of imprisonment for contempt) and that there was a serious statutory lacuna.

## Case law

Part IV of the Family Law Act 1996 provides a new framework for occupation orders. As a result existing case law (which interpreted the provisions in the Matrimonial Homes Act 1983, the Domestic Violence and Matrimonial Proceedings Act 1976 and the Domestic Proceedings and Magistrates' Courts Act 1978) can only offer a guide to some aspects of the new provisions.

### Housing needs and housing resources

The question the court is likely to ask is how easy is it for each of the parties to find alternative accommodation? The court may well require information on how easy it is for either of the parties to rehouse themselves (for example, through the council as in *Thurley* v *Smith* [1985] Fam Law 31). The court may well favour the mother if she has the children since she will find it more difficult to arrange alternative accommodation than a father on his own (see *Lee* v *Lee* [1984] FLR 243). The housing needs of any relevant child are *not* paramount and do not override those of the respondent.

### The parties' conduct

The court is also likely to ask itself how reasonable the applicant's wish to exclude the respondent is. This may depend on the extent of the conduct by the respondent as well as the behaviour of the applicant. If there is no conduct justifying an order the application is likely to be refused.

Where the 'balance of harm' test applies and the applicant or any relevant child is likely to suffer greater significant harm attributable to the respondent's conduct (if the order is not made) than any significant harm which the respondent or relevant child would suffer (if the order is made) then the occupation order either must be made or is likely to be made (depending on the kind of occupation order applied for). 'Significant harm' includes not only significant physical injury but also mental harm. Examples of existing case law include:

1. *Phillips* v *Phillips* [1973] 1 WLR 615; [1973] 2 All ER 423 where the parties were divorced but continued to live together in a council flat – this caused a strain to the wife and son whereby they would become 'psychiatric invalids' – an exclusion order was made to protect the mental health of the wife and child.
2. *Walker* v *Walker* [1978] 1 WLR 533; [1978] 3 All ER 141 where an exclusion order was granted since the wife suffered from a depressive illness as a result of living with the husband.
3. *Scott* v *Scott* [1992] 1 FLR 529 where a husband continually molested the wife despite undertakings and court orders; he was never violent, but the exclusion order was upheld because of his conduct.
4. *Brown* v *Brown* [1994] 1 FLR 223 where the jealous, argumentative and unyielding nature of the husband resulted in behaviour which was sufficiently serious to the wife and the daughter – his conduct, short of violence or the threat of violence, was of sufficient severity to make it just and reasonable to justify an exclusion order.

In other cases where the conduct of the respondent is not causing significant harm to the applicant or child then the court has a discretion and may refuse to exclude the respondent. Examples of existing case law include:

1. *Myers* v *Myers* [1982] 1 WLR 247; [1982] 1 All ER 776 where there was only one physical assault by the husband on the wife which was not serious, plus verbal abuse; the violence was not likely to be repeated, and the ouster order was refused.
2. *Summers* v *Summers* [1986] 1 FLR 343 where a married couple had repeated loud quarrels but there was no violence; both parties were equally to blame. The judge considered that it was not in the children's best interests to witness their parents' quarrels and excluded the husband for two months to give the parties a 'breathing space'. The husband's appeal was allowed since an ouster order was not justified in these circumstances.
3. *Wiseman* v *Simpson* [1988] 1 All ER 245 where the parties lived with a young child in a council flat. There was no violence, but the flat was small and relations between the parties were strained. An exclusion order was quashed on appeal because the applicant woman had not demonstrated that it was just and reasonable to make such an order.
4. *Gibson* v *Austin* [1992] 2 FLR 437 where an unmarried couple lived in rented accommodation with four children. The couple's relationship then deteriorated and the mother threatened the father with a knife on two occasions (though this was not considered to be serious). The father's application for an order excluding the mother was refused, and this decision was confirmed on appeal.

It is important to note that the welfare of any child in the home is *not* paramount. It is not corrrect to grant an exclusion order simply because this would be for the benefit of the child's welfare (see *Richards* v *Richards* [1983] 3 WLR 173;

[1983] 2 All ER 807 and *Summers* v *Summers, Wiseman* v *Simpson* and *Gibson* v *Austin* above). However, the likely effect of any exclusion order (or a decision not to make an exclusion order) on the health, safety or well-being of any relevant child must be considered in applications for occupation orders. The 'balance of harm' test (which includes likely significant harm to any relevant child attributable to the respondent's conduct) may well be decisive. Where the 'balance of harm' test is not decisive the needs of any child are likely to be important and will considerably strengthen the case of the parent with whom the child resides. The needs of the children were particularly important in *Anderson* v *Anderson* [1984] FLR 566 and *Lee* v *Lee* (above).

## Third parties

An interesting example of an existing case which might well have been decided differently under FLA 1996 is *Kaur* v *Gill* [1988] 2 All ER 288; [1988] 2 FLR 328 where a husband owned a family home and the wife had no legal right in the house. As a result she had matrimonial home rights. The marriage failed and the wife left as a result of the husband's conduct. The husband sold the house to S who was a blind man. Before the sale the wife registered her right of occupation by a notice under LRA 1925 so that S had notice of those rights. She then applied for an order declaring her right to occupy the house and to prohibit S from occupying it. She also asked that S or the husband be ordered to pay the outgoings on the property while she occupied the house. Her application was refused, taking into account S's interests. On appeal it was decided that S's interests were validly considered, and the wife's appeal was dismissed. Under FLA 1996 the wife could have applied for a s33 occupation order. The court would have considered s33(6) FLA 1996 which includes the financial resources of the parties and their housing needs. The wife and a young child were living in cramped accommodation. The 'balance of harm' test would also apply. In these circumstances the decision would probably have been in the wife's favour.

## Non-molestation orders

### Meaning of non-molestation order

A non-molestation order means an order prohibiting the respondent from molesting another person who is associated with the respondent and/or prohibiting the respondent from molesting a relevant child (see s42(1) FLA 1996).

The order may refer to molestation in general or to particular acts of molestation or both (see s42(6) FLA 1996).

Molestation includes violence, but also has a wider meaning, including pestering or harassing: see *Vaughan* v *Vaughan* [1973] 1 WLR 1159; [1973] 3 All ER 449 where the husband was described as a 'perfect nuisance' as a result of his unwelcome visits to his separated wife, and *Horner* v *Horner* (1983) 4 FLR 50; [1982] 2 WLR 914; [1982] 2 All ER 495 where the husband made annoying telephone calls in which he made disparaging remarks to his separated wife. If violence is relied upon it need not be voluntary (see *Wooton* v *Wooton* [1984] FLR 871: violence during epileptic fits). In *Johnson* v *Walton* [1990] 1 FLR 350 'molestation' was defined as including behaviour with an intent to cause distress or harm. This included the sending of embarrassing revelations and photographs to a newspaper with the intent to cause distress and to cause the newspapers to molest her (applying *Horner* v *Horner*).

The first reported case after the FLA 1996 came into force was *C* v *C (Application for Non-Molestation Order)* [1998] 1 FLR 554; [1998] 2 WLR 599 which concerned a couple who were divorced. W then published articles in two national newspapers about H's relationship with W and three other former wives which spoke about H in unflattering terms. H applied for a non-molestation order under s42 Family Law Act 1996 to prevent W from causing the publication of any accounts of events during the marriage. It was held that although there was no legal definition of 'molestation' under s42 FLA 1996 the word implied some deliberate conduct which was aimed at a high degree of harassment of the other party so as to justify the intervention of the court. Molestation does not include enforcing an invasion of privacy per se. There has to be some conduct which clearly harasses and affects the applicant to such a degree that the intervention of the court is called for. The material complained came nowhere near molestation as envisaged by s42. The conduct complained of was not 'molestation' as such but damage to his reputation.

### Who can apply for a non-molestation order?

Application can be made by a person who is associated with another person. The definition of a person 'associated' with another person has already been given.

In *G* v *G (Non-molestation Order: Jurisdiction)* [2000] 2 FLR 532 G lived with F. G stated that she did not strictly speaking live with F but that they spent four or five nights together. F said that they had discussed marriage and he had sold his house and put the proceeds in a joint account from which he spent money on G's house since it was 'soon to be our marital home'. The justices found that G and F were not 'associated' within the meaning of s42(1)(a) FLA 1996 since they had never lived in the same household under s62(3)(c). They found that they had separate households, were not cohabitants under s62(3)(a), did not have children and the relationship was not stable. They found insufficient evidence of an agreement to marry under s62(3)(e). They refused to grant a non-molestation order. G appealed and admitted she had only stated that she did not live with the man in order to preserve her state benefits.

It was held, allowing the appeal, that G was not permitted to say to a court that she was living with a man whilst maintaining to the DSS that she was not. The evidence was sufficient to support G and F being cohabitants. Three of the signposts set out in *Crake* v *Supplementary Benefits Commission* [1982] 1 All ER 498 were present: sexual relations, living in the same household and a joint bank account. Where domestic violence is concerned the 1996 Act should be given a purposive construction. Jurisdiction should not be declined unless the facts are plainly incapable for being within the statute. The justices should have considered s62(3)(b) before (c).

## When can a non-molestation order be made?

The court may make a non-molestation order if an application for a non-molestation order has been made (whether or not in other family proceedings) by a person associated with the respondent or on the court's own motion if it is hearing family proceedings to which the respondent is a party and the court considers such an order should be made for the benefit of any other party to the proceedings or any relevant child (even though no such application has been made) (see s42(2) FLA 1996).

Where an agreement to marry is terminated no application can be made for a non-molestation order by reference to that agreement after the end of the period of three years beginning with the date on which it is terminated (see s42(4) FLA 1996).

## What the court must consider

In deciding whether to make a non-molestation order and, if so, in what manner the court must have regard to all the circumstances including the need to secure the health, safety and well-being of the applicant (or, where the court is making the order of its own motion, the person for whose benefit the order would be made) and of any relevant child (see s42(5) FLA 1996).

## How long can a non-molestation order last?

A non-molestation order may be made for a specified period or until further order (see s42(7) FLA 1996). However if the order is made in other family proceedings it ceases to have effect if those proceedings are withdrawn or dismissed (see s42(8) FLA 1996).

See *Re BJ (Power of Arrrest)* [2000] 2 FLR 443 where M and F had a volatile relationship. They had one child, C. They separated with C remaining with M. F applied for parental responsibility and contact. C was unwilling to see his father. After protacted litigation the court made a parental responsibility order but also made a non-molestation order of unlimited duration with a power of arrest attached for a period of two years. The order was to prevent F from pestering M and C. F appealed. It was held, dismissing the appeal and overruling a decision of the High Court in *M* v *W* [2000] 1 FLR 107, a non-molestation order could last for an indefinite period and there was no obligation for the courts to find exceptional or unusual features before making such an order. There was no reason to limit the period of a non-molestation order because a power of arrest was limited in duration. Section 47(2) FLA 1996 did allow for a power of arrest to be for a shorter period than the order to which it attached.

## Application by a child for an occupation order or a non-molestation order

A child aged 16 years or more can apply for an occupation order or a non-molestation order in his or her own right. A child under the age of 16 years may not apply for such an order except with the leave of the court. The court may only grant leave if it is satisfied that the child has sufficient understanding to make the proposed application (see s43 FLA 1996).

## Engagements – evidence required

A court cannot make a s33 occupation order or a non-molestation order with respect to an engaged person unless there is produced to the court evidence in writing of the existence of the engagement. The requirement for written evidence does not apply if the court is satisfied that the engagement was evidenced by the gift of an engagement ring by one party or if an engagement ceremony took place in the presence of one or more other persons assembled for the purpose of witnessing the ceremony (see s44 FLA 1996).

## Ex parte orders

An occupation or non-molestation order can be made ex parte where the court considers that it is just and convenient to do so (see s45(1) FLA 1996). The court must have regard to all the circumstances including:

1. any risk of significant harm to the applicant or a relevant child attributable to conduct of the respondent if the order is not made immediately;
2. whether it is likely that the applicant will be deterred or prevented from pursuing the application if an order is not made immediately; and
3. whether there is reason to believe that the respondent is aware of the proceedings but is deliberately evading service and the applicant or a relevant child will be seriously prejudiced by the delay involved in effecting service (or substituted service) of the proceedings (see s45(2) FLA 1996).

If the court makes an ex parte order it must give the respondent an opportunity to make representations relating to the order as soon as just and convenient at a full hearing (that is, a hearing notice of which has been given to all the parties) (see s45(3) FLA 1996). The length of an order made at a full hearing is treated as starting from the date of the ex parte order and any extension may be made as if the ex parte order and the order made at the full hearing are one order (see s45(4) FLA 1996).

## Undertakings

Instead of making an occupation or non-molestation order the court may accept an undertaking from any party to the proceedings. Such an undertaking is enforceable as a court order (see s46(1) and (4) FLA 1996). A power of arrest cannot be attached to an undertaking and an undertaking cannot be accepted where a power of arrest would be attached to an order (see s46(2) and (3) FLA 1996). Courts will therefore have to decide whether an undertaking can adequately protect the applicant given that it cannot be enforced using a power of arrest.

### Attaching a power of arrest

If a court makes an occupation order or non-molestation order and it appears to the court that the respondent has used or threatened violence against the applicant or relevant child it *must* attach a power of arrest to the order unless satisfied that in all the circumstances of the case the applicant or child will be adequately protected without such a power of arrest (see s46(2) FLA 1996).

In *Chechi* v *Bashier* [1999] 2 FLR 489 the Court of Appeal held that the court had a discretion not to make a non-molestation order in circumstances in which there was a mandatory application of a power of arrest. In the case the Court was of the view that a power of arrest would give too much power to the defendants, namely the power to oblige the police to respond to a request to arrest the appellant without any investigation into the truth of the allegations. The case was more suitable for undertakings or an injunction in civil proceedings.

A power of arrest cannot be attached to an ex parte order unless it appears to the court that the respondent has used or threatened violence against the applicant or a relevant child and that there is a risk of significant harm to the applicant or child attributable to the conduct of the respondent if the power of arrest is not attached immediately (see s46(3) FLA 1996). If the court does attach a power of arrest to an ex parte order it may provide that the power of arrest is to have effect for a shorter period than the occupation or non-molestation order (see s46(4) FLA 1996). Any such period may be extended by the court on one or more occasions on an application to vary or discharge the occupation or non-molestation order (see s46(5) FLA 1996).

Where a power of arrest is attached a constable may arrest without warrant a person whom he has reasonable cause for suspecting to be in breach of the occupation or non-molestation order (see s46(6) FLA 1996). The person must be produced before a court within 24 hours of his or her arrest (excluding Christmas Day, Good Friday or any Sunday) where he or she may be dealt with or remanded to appear before a later court (see s46(7) FLA 1996). The power to remand includes a remand for medical examination and report (whether on bail or in custody) (see s48 FLA 1996).

Where no power of arrest is attached to an order the applicant may apply to the court for the issue of a warrant for the respondent's arrest if the applicant considers that the respondent has failed to comply with the order. The application must be substantiated on oath and the court must be satisfied that there are reasonable grounds for believing that the respondent has failed to comply with the order (see s46(8) and (9) FLA 1996).

In *Re H (Respondent under 18: Power of Arrest)* [2001] 1 FLR 641 it was confirmed that a power of arrest could be attached to an occupation order and non-molestation order even though the respondent was under 18. The respondent could be arrested even though there was a serious gap in the law whereby such a respondent could not be committed into custody for contempt.

## Enforcement of an occupation or non-molestation order

The High Court, county court and (to a lesser extent) magistrates' court have power to commit a respondent to prison for disobeying an occupation or non-molestation order. This committal power may be suspended for such period or on such terms and conditions as the court may specify.

## Variation and discharge of an order

Either party may apply to vary or discharge an occupation or non-molestation order (or a power of arrest attached to the order) (see s49(1) and (4) FLA 1996). Where the court has made a non-molestation order on its own motion it may vary or discharge the order on its own motion (see s49(2) FLA 1996).

A s33 occupation order may be varied or discharged on the application of a person who derives title under the respondent spouse or under the trustees for that spouse (see s49(3) FLA 1996).

## Appeals

An appeal shall lie to the High Court against the making of an occupation or non-molestation order (or the refusal to make an order) by a magistrates' court (see s61(1) FLA 1996). Appeals against decisions of the county court and High Court lie to the Court of Appeal.

## *The inherent powers of the court*

Note the use of the inherent jurisdiction of the court to grant injunctions under, inter alia, s37 Supreme Court Act 1981. This jurisdiction will be exercised only if the injunction sought is incidental to other proceedings, and there is sufficient link between the relief sought by way of the injunction and those other proceedings, and the injunction is in support of a recognised legal or equitable right (see *Ainsbury* v *Millington* [1986] 1 All ER 73; [1986] 1 FLR 331).

Application may be made by married or unmarried persons, and the application must be made incidental to other proceedings such as residence or divorce proceedings. In the case of an emergency, the court may hear an application even though other proceedings have not been commenced, if an undertaking is made to file the appropriate petition or make the appropriate application (see *Re W (A Minor)* [1981] 3 All ER 401). The court will only grant an ouster order if it is required in relation to the main proceedings (eg it is necessary to protect the children in residence proceedings – see *Ainsbury* v *Millington* where one of the reasons why the ouster order was refused was that the court was not convinced it was necessary to protect the child in the course of such proceedings). The court is unlikely to grant an ouster order if it only meant to give one spouse an advantage in an application to settle the matrimonial home (see *O'Malley* v *O'Malley* [1982] 1 WLR 244; [1982] 2 All ER 112) since that may be viewed as abusing the court's powers in an attempt to gain possession of the property.

Perhaps the most difficult hurdle in relation to the inherent power of the court to exclude a spouse or partner is that the court will only act in support of a recognised legal or equitable right. If the applicant has no right, or no greater right than the person the court is being asked to exclude from the home, the application may fail (as happened in *Ainsbury* v *Millington*, where the woman was a joint tenant of a council flat and the court refused her application partly on the basis that this was not a sufficient right to warrant the court ordering her unmarried partner out of the home). *Ainsbury* v *Millington* was followed in *Pearson* v *Franklin* [1994] 1 WLR 186.

One example of a recent consideration of the powers under s37 SCA 1981 and s38 County Courts Act 1984 is *C* v *K (Inherent Powers: Exclusion Order)* [1996] 2 FLR 506 where a grandmother, C, looked after her grandson. C lived with a man, K. They were joint tenants of a council house. K violently assaulted C and was abusive to the grandson. C obtained a residence order for her grandson and an injunction to exclude K. It fell to be determined whether there was jurisdiction to grant the injunction.

HELD: An injunction under s37 SCA 1981 or s38 CCA 1984 could be granted in support of legal and equitable rights which included rights under a residence order. Where neither MHA 1983 nor DVMPA 1976 applied, a non-residential parent could be restrained from interfering with the residential parent's exercise of parental responsibility. These powers extended to the grant of injunctions against third parties. Thus a third party could be restrained from interfering with the exercise of parental responsibility by a person with a residence order. This included a power to exclude the third party from property in which he had a beneficial interest. However, such powers should be exercised with extreme caution. By analogy with s100(4) CA 1989 the jurisdiction was likely to be exercised only when the court was satisfied that if an injunction was not granted the child was likely to suffer significant harm. On the facts of the case an exclusion order was not made (but various orders to limit K's behaviour were made).

NOTE: The fact that C and K were joint tenants did not appear to have been dealt with. In *Ainsbury* v *Millington* (above) an injunction was refused where there was a joint tenancy and the applicant had no superior right of occupation.

An injunction granted under s37 SCA 1981 (or s38 County Courts Act 1984) can exclude the respondent from a specified area (for example, he or she is excluded from coming or remaining within 250 yards of the plaintiff's home address). In *Burris* v *Azadini* [1996] 1 FLR 266 it was confirmed that there is power at common law to grant an injunction restraining a defendant from entering a designated area if such is necessary for the protection of the plaintiff. The general power of county courts to grant an injunction is the same as that of the High Court, and s37(1) of the Supreme Court Act 1981 is cast in the widest terms. An injunction may be granted at common law to restrain conduct which is not in itself tortious or otherwise unlawful, if it is necessary to protect the legitimate interests of a plaintiff who has invoked the court's jurisdiction. Exclusion zone orders should not, however, be made without good reason, reconciling the interests of the defendant to liberty and the plaintiff to protection. This included an exclusion zone order.

Another example of a case involving the court using its inherent jurisdiction to exclude a former spouse is found in *P* v *P (Interim Exclusion Order)* [1997] 1 FLR 69 in which a divorced wife successfully applied to exclude her former husband from the former matrimonial home. The Matrimonial Homes Act 1983 was not available to her since the parties were divorced. The Domestic Violence and Matrimonial Proceedings Act 1976 was not available since the parties were living apart. The former wife had an interest in the home. She feared her former husband would return and use violence against her. The court granted in interim exclusion order to protect her property rights. The Family Law Act 1996 now provides a specific remedy for this situation.

## Procedural considerations

Only the High Court and the county court have such an inherent power (not the magistrates' courts).

There may be an ex parte application but only in exceptional circumstances and if there is a real, immediate danger of serious injury or incurable damage.

There may be an application with a minimum two days' notice.

## No power to exclude a parent from the family home under the Children Act 1989

There is no power to exclude a parent from the family home under the Children Act 1989. In *Pearson* v *Franklin* above, F and M were unmarried and were joint tenants of a house. They had two children, twins born in January 1992. As a result of arguments the relationship broke down and in September 1992 M left with the children and went to live at her parents' house. F remained in the house. There was no allegation that F had been violent to M or the children. In March 1993 M applied for a specific issues order under s8 Children Act (CA) 1989 to allow her and the children to live in the house and to exclude F. F applied for a contact order. The judge held that he had no power to make the order sought by M and dismissed her application. He made a contact order in F's favour. M appealed against the refusal to make the specific issues order.

HELD: The appeal was dismissed because, although a specific issues order under s8 Children Act 1989 could be used to determine where a child should live, it was not appropriate to make an order under s8 where a right of occupation was involved since such an order would have the effect of an ouster order and it had not been Parliament's intention that ouster orders should be made under the guise of specific issues orders. M was not entitled to an ouster order under the inherent jurisdiction of the court because as joint tenants neither party had a right to occupy the property to the exclusion of the other (*Ainsbury* v *Millington* [1986] 1 All ER 73 followed).

M was not without remedy since she could apply for a property transfer order under s15 and Schedule 1 of the Children Act 1989 (as happened in *K v K (Minors: Property Transfer)* [1992] 2 All ER 727).

In *D v D (Ouster Order)* [1996] 2 FCR 496, H and W married in 1980. They had three young children. H left in 1995, leaving W and the children in the matrimonial home. H worked abroad but returned to live in the matrimonial home for three days each week. The atmosphere was tense, so W left to stay with friends. W sought a prohibited steps order to prevent H from staying overnight, and this order was granted. H appealed.

HELD: Allowing the appeal, there was no jurisdiction to make an ouster order under CA 1989. Such an order could only be made by applying s1(3) MHA 1983. The judge had failed to take into account the conduct of the parties and the fact that an ouster order was draconian and not to be made lightly. There was no conduct by H which amounted to him making life intolerable for W and the children whereby an ouster order was just and reasonable. The ouster order was quashed.

In *Nottinghamshire CC v P* [1993] 2 FLR 134 the Court of Appeal ruled that a s8 order could not be used to exclude a parent from his or her home for the protection of a child as a result of an application by a local authority.

## Application for a personal protection injunction based in tort

In *Khorasandijian v Bush* [1993] 2 FLR 68 it was decided that the High Court or county court had jurisdiction to grant an injunction to any person who requires personal protection from molestation or harassment which amounts to a recognised form of tort. However the House of Lords in *Hunter and Others v Canary Wharf Ltd* [1997] 2 FLR 342; [1997] 2 WLR 684 ruled that *Khorasandijian v Bush* was wrongly decided and should be overruled. It now appears that only a person with a proprietary right in land can sustain an action in nuisance and only to protect an interest in land and not to protect any right to personal privacy.

## The criminal law

Often the first point of contact for a family member subject to domestic violence is the police. If the police are satisfied that a criminal offence has been committed then the perpetrator can be arrested and either released on bail with conditions (eg to stay away from the alleged victim) or brought before the magistrates' court for a remand in custody. The powers of remand and sentence (including binding a defendant in a sum of money to keep the peace) can be used to prevent domestic violence.

The Protection from Harassment Act 1997 (which largely came into force in June 1997) provides additional remedies. It creates two criminal offences:

1. criminal harassment (s2) (namely the pursuit of a course of conduct which

amounts to harassment and which the accused knows or ought to have known amounts to harassment of the victim); and

2. aggravated fear of violence (s4) (namely the pursuit of a course of conduct which causes the victim to fear that violence will be used against him/her and which the accused knows or ought to know would cause the victim to so fear).

In addition to a prison sentence and/or fine the court can make restraining orders to prevent further harassment (s5). Breach of a restraining order can be punished with imprisonment. A statutory tort of harassment is created (s3 which came into force in September 1998) which allows criminal courts to punish the breach of civil orders since the breach of a civil injunction under s3 is a criminal offence. An actual or apprehended breach of s1 (the prohibition against harassment of another) may be the subject of a civil claim for damages. A plaintiff can apply ex parte for the arrest of the defendant for breach of a civil order which is punishable either as a civil contempt or as a criminal offence. There are special defences including that the accused was acting reasonably in all the circumstances. The Act may considerably assist victims of domestic violence since with the co-operation of the police, the criminal courts can deal with incidents without the need to seek occupation and non-molestation orders in the civil courts.

Following the House of Lords decision in *R* v *Ireland* [1997] 3 WLR 534; [1998] 1 FLR 105 an accused who made repeated phone calls followed by silence can be prosecuted for assault occasioning actual bodily harm. In this respect the criminal law now has greater scope in dealing with domestic violence.

## Other remedies

A local authority has the power to issue an injunction for anti-social behaviour (including threats of violence) under s152(3) Housing Act 1996 (eg see *Manchester City Council* v *Worthington* [2000] Fam Law 238).

# 11

# Magistrates' Courts

## 11.1 Introduction

The Domestic Proceedings and Magistrates' Courts Act 1978 repealed the Matrimonial Proceedings (Magistrates' Courts) Act 1960 and, by inference, the case law that grew up around that statute. Before the 1978 Act came into force the magistrates' courts still operated on the basis of the matrimonial offence. These offences were based on the pre-1969 divorce grounds: adultery, cruelty and desertion. In addition, there were specific offences such as violence and giving the spouse VD. Wilful failure to maintain was also a ground for an order. The grounds

274

such as adultery were subject to bars such as condonation. A 'guilty' wife, who had, for example, herself committed adultery, could not obtain an order.

The 1978 Act followed the recommendations of the Law Commission Report No 77 and assimilated the law of matrimonial proceedings in magistrates' courts to that of the higher courts.

The Act came fully into force on 1 February 1981.

## 11.2 Jurisdiction

Section 30 provides that magistrates shall have jurisdiction to hear an application under Part I if at the date of making the application either the applicant or the respondent ordinarily reside in the commission area of the court.

Jurisdiction exists notwithstanding that the respondent resides in Scotland or Northern Ireland, if the applicant resides in England and Wales and the parties last ordinarily resided there as man and wife.

Jurisdiction also exists where the applicant resides in Scotland or Northern Ireland and the respondent resides in England and Wales.

Domicile is irrelevant.

## 11.3 Applicants

Applicants for an order for maintenance under ss2, 6 or 7 of the Act must be a party to a marriage.

Applications are usually made when parties first separate. An order can be obtained quickly and cheaply in the magistrates' court to provide financial provision until the parties decide whether to divorce and obtain a final and comprehensive settlement in the county court. It is easier to obtain a magistrates' courts order than maintenance pending suit in the county court.

Normally, if proceedings have begun in the county court at the same time as proceedings in the magistrates' court, then the magistrates should not proceed, so that two courts are not considering the same matters at the same time (see *Kayne* v *Kayne* [1965] 1 All ER 620), BUT if there is a need for a quick resolution concerning residence and/or maintenance which the magistrates can provide, then the magistrates may decide those issues if the county court proceedings are likely to be delayed (see *Lanitis* v *Lanitis* [1970] 1 All ER 466; *Jones* v *Jones* [1974] 3 All ER 702).

## 11.4 Grounds for applications under s2

There are four grounds available to husbands and wives when making application for an order under s2. The grounds are specified in s1:

1. the other party to the marriage has failed to provide reasonable maintenance for the applicant (s1(a));
2. has failed to provide or make proper contribution towards reasonable maintenance for any child of the family (s1(b));
3. has behaved in such a way that the applicant cannot reasonably be expected to live with the respondent (s1(c));
4. has deserted the applicant (s1(d)).

There is no requirement in the 1978 Act that failure to maintain should be wilful.

The ground of behaviour in the magistrates' courts will be dealt with in the same way as it is in the divorce courts (ie using the hybrid test of viewing the parties subjectively) and then asking, taking into account each party's personality, characteristics, etc, whether the parties can reasonably be expected to live together (see *Bergin* v *Bergin* [1983] 1 WLR 279; [1983] 1 All ER 905; (1983) 4 FLR 344).

The ground of desertion is the same as in divorce except there is no need to show a continuous period of two years.

There may be a six months time limit whereby the ground of application must have arisen within six months of the making of the application (see s127 Magistrates' Courts Act 1980).

The Law Commission in its report *The Ground for Divorce* (1990 Law Comm No 192) recommended the abolition of the grounds of behaviour and desertion in s1 DPMCA 1978 in order to avoid bitterness and conflict which could hinder prospects of saving the marriage. These recommendations have been included in the Family Law Act 1996. The grounds for making a maintenance order under s2 DPMCA 1978 are amended so as to delete the grounds of behaviour and desertion (see s18(1) FLA 1996 deleting s1(c) and (d) DPMCA 1978). This part of the Family Law Act 1996 is not yet in force.

## 11.5 Orders by a magistrates' court

Section 2 DPMCA 1978:

'(1) Where on an application for an order under this section the applicant satisfies the court of any ground mentioned in section 1 of this Act, the court may, subject to the provisions of this Part of the Act, make any one or more of the following orders, that is to say –
(a) An order that the respondent shall make to the applicant such periodical payments and for such terms, as may be specified in the order;

(b) An order that the respondent shall pay to the applicant such lump sum as may be specified;

(c) An order that the respondent shall make to the applicant for the benefit of a child of the family to whom the application relates, or to such a child, such periodical payments, and for such term, as may be specified;

(d) An order that the respondent shall pay to the applicant for the benefit of a child of the family to whom the application relates, or to such a child, such lump sum as may be so specified.

(2) Without prejudice to the generality of subsections (1)(b) or (d) above, an order under this section for the payment of a lump sum may be made for the purpose of enabling any liability or expenses reasonably incurred in maintaining the applicant, or any child of the family to whom the application relates, before the making of the order, to be met.

(3) The amount of any lump sum required to be paid by an order under this section shall not exceed £1,000 or such larger amount as the Secretary of State may from time to time by order fix for the purposes of this subsection.'

## 11.6 Relief available

Periodical payments (which need not be only on a weekly basis).

Lump sum provision subject to a ceiling of £1,000.

NOTE: On an application for variation of an order the court may not only vary instalments but may award another lump sum in addition to that awarded originally. The award can be made to cover expenses which accrued before the date of the order.

There is no power to award secured periodical payments – all periodical payments ordered by the magistrates' court are unsecured. There is no power to make a property adjustment order. As has been seen, lump sums are limited to £1,000.

The powers to order financial relief are, therefore, not nearly as extensive as in the county court. In such circumstances spouses may consider using the alternative procedure under s27 MCA 1973, since this allows secured periodical payments and unlimited lump sum orders to be made. However, such an application is not as cheap, or as quick, as an application before the magistrates' court.

In determining the financial provision for spouses, statutory guidelines are laid down in s3 of the Act and are closely similar to those in s25 of the 1973 Act.

## 11.7 Section 3(1) Domestic Proceedings and Magistrates' Courts Act 1978

(As substituted by s9 Matrimonial and Family Proceedings Act 1984.)

'(1) Where an application is made for an order under section 2 of this Act, it shall be the duty of the court in deciding whether to exercise its powers under that section and, if so, in what manner, to have regard to all the circumstances of the case, first consideration being given to the welfare while a minor of any child of the family who has not attained the age of eighteen.

(2) As regards the exercise of its powers under subsections (1)(a) or (b) of section 2 the court shall in particular have regard to the following matters –

(a) the income earning capacity, property and other financial resources which each of the parties to the marriage has or is likely to have in the foreseeable future, including in the case of earning capacity any increase in that capacity which it would in the opinion of the court be reasonable to expect a party to the marriage to take steps to acquire;

(b) the financial needs, obligations and responsibilities which each of the parties to the marriage has or is likely to have in the foreseeable future;

(c) the standard of living enjoyed by the parties to the marriage before the occurrence of the conduct which is alleged as the ground of the application;

(d) the age of each party to the marriage and the duration of the marriage;

(e) any physical or mental disability of either of the parties to the marriage;

(f) the contributions made by each of the parties to the welfare of the family, including any contribution made by looking after the home or caring for the family;

(g) the conduct of each of the parties, if that conduct is such that it would in the opinion of the court be inequitable to disregard it.'

These provisions are virtually the same as under s25 MCA 1973, though the clean break provisions do not apply to magistrates' courts, the authorities on s25 will equally apply to magistrates' courts (see *Macey* v *Macey* (1982) 3 FLR 7; *Vasey* v *Vasey* [1985] FLR 596; *Blower* v *Blower* [1986] Fam Law 56).

The one-third principle may be applied by the magistrates' court BUT is inappropriate in the many cases involving low income families which come before the magistrates' courts (eg *Cann* v *Cann* [1977] 3 All ER 957).

## 11.8  Orders in respect of children

The age limits which apply under s29 of the 1973 Act will also be applicable in the magistrates' court, that is, up to eighteen years (s5(1)) (and not sixteen as previously), and beyond (not terminating at twenty-one as previously) if the child is undergoing further training or education, or where the child's welfare requires that there should be an extension (s5(2)).

The guidelines for maintenance claims in respect of children are laid down in s3(3) and are closely similar to the provisions in the 1973 Act, that is, the financial needs of the child, income and earning capacity, if any, property and other financial resources of the child; any physical or mental disability of the child, the standard of living enjoyed by the family before the occurrence of the conduct which is the ground of the application; the manner in which the child was being and in which the parties intended him to be educated or trained; and the matters referred to in s3(2)(a) and (b) in relation to the parties to the marriage.

Payment may be made to the child direct, and the child may later apply for variation should this be necessary.

In an application for maintenance of a child of the family who is not a child of the respondent, the court will have regard to the same factors as are contained in s25(3) of the 1973 Act, namely:

1. whether the respondent has assumed any responsibility for the child's maintenance;
2. the basis upon which and the extent to which he had done so;
3. whether in assuming and discharging such responsibilities the respondent did so knowing that the child was not his own;
4. the liability of any other person to maintain the child (s3(4)).

The jurisdiction to order child maintenance has virtually ceased since the Child Support Agency now deals with nearly all periodical payments for children.

## 11.9 Reconciliation provisions (s26)

The court may at any stage adjourn an application if there is a reasonable possibility of a reconciliation.

If such an adjournment is made, the court may seek the assistance of a probation officer to effect a reconciliation.

If the parties live together for a continuous period exceeding six months then the maintenance order ceases to be enforceable (though this does not apply to maintenance orders for the children) (s25).

## 11.10 Agreed orders (s6)

Under s6 of the 1978 Act, the magistrates' court has power to make orders for financial provision (periodical payments and lump sum) which have been agreed between the parties. There is no need for the applicant to prove any grounds. A party who applies for an order under s2 may change the proceedings to s6 if agreement is reached in court.

The court will make an agreed order where there is nothing to suggest that so to do would be contrary to the interest of justice and the court is satisfied that proper provision is being made for the child.

There is no upper limit on lump sum provisions so long as the other party agrees.

No order will be made unless there is evidence to hand of the means of the parties and the consent of the other party. The other party must be either present or represented in court to indicate consent or must send in a signed and witnessed document showing his consent (see s6(9) and r17 Family Proceedings Courts (Matrimonial Proceedings) Rules 1991).

## 11.11 Orders where parties living apart by agreement (s7)

Under s7 of the 1978 Act, where the spouses have been separated for a continuous period exceeding three months, neither party being in desertion, and one spouse has been making periodical payments for the benefit of the other party or a child of the family, that other party may apply to the magistrates for an order, specifying in the application the aggregate amount received during the three months immediately preceding the application. On hearing the application, the court may order the respondent to make such periodical payments to the applicant or for the benefit of a child of the family. The amount of the order must not exceed the aggregate amount stated in the application.

If, as a result of the above limitation, the magistrates feel that reasonable maintenance cannot be awarded, they may refuse to make an order on this ground and treat the application as one for financial provision under s1 and make a suitable order under s2.

## 11.12 Interim orders (s19)

The magistrates have power to make one interim maintenance order of no more than three months' duration.

In certain circumstances, the court may order the interim order to continue for a further period not exceeding three months.

## 11.13 Variation and revocation (s20)

Either party to the marriage may subsequently apply to vary or revoke an order for financial provision.

The powers of the court are as follows:

1. When the court has made an order under s2, it has power to vary, revoke, suspend or revive that order and also make a lump sum order (not exceeding £1,000).
2. Where the court has made an order under s6, it has power to vary, etc, that order, and also to make a lump sum order (which may exceed £1,000 if the respondent agrees) to the other party of the marriage or to a child of the family or to the other party for the benefit of the child.
3. Where the court has made an order under s7, it has power to vary, etc, that order, but not to make a lump sum order.

Once a child has reached the age of sixteen, then he may apply for variation on his own account.

If an order in favour of a child ceases when the child reaches either sixteen or eighteen, the application to vary must be made before the child reaches twenty-one.

In exercising its power to vary, the court, so far as it is just to do so, will give effect to any agreement reached between the parties to the application.

If no agreement, or the court decides not to give effect to it, the court will have regard to all the circumstances of the case, including any change in any of the matters to which the court was required to have regard when making the original order.

## 11.14 Arrangements for the children

Whenever an application is made for an order under s2, s6 or s7 the court must be informed if there are children of the family under eighteen. If there are such children the court cannot decide on the maintenance application until it has decided whether to exercise any of its powers under the Children Act 1989 with respect to the child(ren): see s8 DPMCA 1978 as amended by para 36, Sch 13 CA 1989). The magistrates' court will be able to make residence orders, contact orders, prohibited steps orders and specific issue orders (see Chapter 15 for an explanation of these terms).

Third parties (eg grandparents) have the ability to intervene in the proceedings and apply for orders under s8 CA 1989.

The power to make care orders and supervision orders has been repealed. The court can ask the local authority to investigate whether a child is in need (see s37 CA 1989) and will be able to make family assistance orders (see s16 CA 1989 – explained in Chapter 15).

The welfare of the child is paramount (see s1(1) CA 1989). In deciding whether to make a s8 order the court must have regard to a checklist of considerations (see s1(3), (4) CA 1989 detailed in Chapter 15). The court must have regard to the principle that delay in resolving a dispute over the upbringing of a child is likely to prejudice the child's welfare (see s1(2) CA 1989). The court must also consider that making a s8 order would be better for the child than making no order at all (see s1(5) CA 1989). This may mean that few orders will need to be made pursuant to s8 DPMCA 1978 (as amended) since in many cases the parents will have settled what should happen to their child(ren) and any court order is unlikely to make things better for the child.

## 11.15 Applications specifically for children

Application may be made to the High Court, county court or magistrates' court by a parent or guardian of a child or by a person in whose favour there is a residence order with respect to the child requiring:

1. either or both parents to pay maintenance to the child or to the applicant for the benefit of the child (which in the case of the High Court or county court can be secured maintenance);
2. either or both parents to pay a lump sum to the child or to the applicant for the benefit of the child (subject to a £1,000 limit in the magistrates' court);
3. either or both parents to transfer property to the child or to the applicant for the benefit of the child (this power is not available in the magistrates' court) (see s15 and para 1, Sch 1 CA 1989).

Where no maintenance order is in force and a child's parents are separated a child aged eighteen years or more receiving education or training (or where special circumstances justify it) may apply for orders of maintenance and lump sum from one or both of his or her parents (see para 2, Sch 1 CA 1989).

An unmarried parent as well as a married parent can make use of these provisions to provide for his or her child.

'Parent' includes a party to the marriage who has treated a child as a child of his or her family (though this does not apply to para 2). Such 'parents' can both apply for and be ordered to make financial provision for such children of the family.

'Parent' does not include a cohabitee who is not a father or mother of the child concerned. See *Re J (A Minor: Property Transfer)* (1992) The Times 12 November where a mother and her child lived with a man (who was not the child's father) for ten years. She applied under s15 and Sch 1 CA 1989 for an order transferring the joint tenancy of the house into her sole name. Her application was dismissed since the cohabitee could not be a parent under s15 and because he had not married the mother he could not be a step-parent who had treated the child as a child of the family.

The court in deciding whether to use its powers above must have regard to all the circumstances and in particular to:

1. the income, earning capacity, property and other financial resources of the child's parents, the applicant (and the person with a residence order for the child, if that is appropriate) as they are now and are likely to be in the foreseeable future;
2. the financial needs, obligations and responsibilities such persons have or are likely to have in the foreseeable future;
3. the financial needs of the child;
4. the income, earning capacity (if any), property and other financial resources of the child;
5. any physical or mental disability of the child;
6. the manner in which the child was being, or was expected to be, educated or trained (see para 4(1) Sch 1 CA 1989).

The court must also be satisfied that to make an order for financial provision would be better than making no order at all (s1(5)).

If a person is not the mother or father of the child the court must have regard, when considering whether to make an order and, if so, in what manner, to:

1. whether that person had assumed responsibility for the maintenance of the child, for how long, why and to what extent;
2. whether he or she did so knowing that the child was not his or her child;
3. the liability of any other person to maintain the child (see para 4(2), Sch 1 CA 1989).

When a court makes a residence order it may make an order for financial provision of its own motion (see para 1(6) Sch 1 CA 1989).

If application is made under Sch 1 CA 1989 the court may also of its own motion make s8 orders relating to the child (see s10(1)(b) CA 1989).

For an example of a case where a county court considered an application under s11B Guardianship of Minors Act 1971 (the predecessor to Sch 1 CA 1989) for a property order see *K* v *K (Minors: Property Transfer)* [1992] 1 WLR 530 where a court transferred a joint tenancy held by an unmarried couple to the mother for the benefit of the children.

In *Philips* v *Pearce* [1996] 2 FLR 230 applications for lump sum/property orders under Sch 1 CA 1989 were refused because the reason for the application was to make up for a lack of child support payments of £90 a week. Lump sum/property orders could only be made to meet the child's needs in respect of a particular item of expenditure, for example to furnish the child's home, or to assist with the child's education or medical costs or with costs associated with the birth. No provision could be made for the child's regular support. The case involved a father who lived in a house worth £2.6 million and owned cars worth £190,000 but was assessed as being liable to pay no child support because he had no income.

See also *J* v *C (Child: Financial Provision)* [1999] 1 FLR 152 in which a father, who won £1.4 million on the National Lottery, was ordered to settle £92,000 on his three year old son. This was a case in which the CSA had failed to make a suitable child support assessment because the father had no regular income.

## 11.16 Child Support Act 1991

The Child Support Act 1991 has already been discussed. The power of magistrates' courts to order child maintenance under DPMCA 1978 and of the High Court, county court and magistrates' court to order child maintenance under the CA 1989 has virtually ceased. Applications for lump-sum orders and/or property orders may still be made since these are not dealt with by the Child Support Agency. Applications in relation to step-children may also be made since the CSA does not deal with the financial support of step-children.

# 12

# State Benefits

12.1  The benefits available to families

12.2  Duties to maintain

12.3  The diversion procedure

12.4  Relationship between state benefits and maintenance orders

## 12.1  The benefits available to families

An understanding of the benefits which may be claimed by families will assist in those cases where the spouse ordered to pay maintenance cannot pay a sufficient sum to his separated or divorced spouse and the children, and they have to rely on state benefits for all or part of their income.

### Child benefit (ss141–147 Social Security Contributions and Benefits Act 1992)

Any parent responsible for a child under sixteen who lives with the parent can claim child benefit. A claim can also be made for a child aged between sixteen and nineteen who is in full-time education up to and including A-level or equivalent standard. Child benefit may also continue for some weeks for a school leaver aged under eighteen who is registered for work or a YTS course at a careers office or job centre.

Child benefit ceases when a child starts work full time or starts a YTS course or starts higher education. It will also normally stop when a child marries or is otherwise able to claim income support.

Child benefit is a set sum payable for each child whatever the parent's income. It is £15.75 for the eldest or eldest qualifying child and £10.55 for each subsequent child (April 2002 rates). Child benefit is tax free.

The parent who has the child living with him or her claims the child benefit. If the other parent contributes to the child's upkeep at a rate equal to or more than the child benefit, he or she may claim it instead.

## Working Families Tax Credit and Children's Tax Credit

See Chapter 16, section 16.2 for help given to working families on low incomes.

**Other help**

There is an automatic entitlement to free NHS prescriptions, dental treatment and sight tests and help with the cost of glasses.

## Income support (ss124–127 SSCBA 1992)

This benefit is designed to help parents out of work or who work less than 16 hours a week and whose income is below a certain level. If one parent works 16 hours or more a week then no claim can be made for income support.

A claimant must be 16 or more though claims cannot usually be made by or for any person aged 16 or 17 (since they are supposed to be on a government training scheme for which they are paid a training allowance). There are exceptions for lone parents who are under 18 who can claim income support or for young people who are forced to live away from home (eg because of physical or sexual abuse) or who have previously been in the care of the local authority.

A parent may claim income support which covers him or herself, his or her partner and any child living with them who is under 16 or who is 16, 17 or 18 and doing a full time course leading to a qualification not above A level or equivalent standard.

A claim cannot be made if there are savings or capital of £8,000 or more. If there are savings between £3,000 and £8,000 this will reduce the amount of income support.

The first £5 of each parent's earnings or the first £20 of a single parent's income do not affect the amount of income support (as from April 2001). Any income above these amounts will reduce the amount of income support received. All maintenance or child support payments are counted as income and will reduce the amount of income support received pound for pound.

Income support is made up of the following allowances:

1. a personal allowance – the April 2002 rates are £53.95 a week for a single claimant over 25, £37.00 a week for a child under 16;
2. premiums – lone parent premium is £15.90 a week and family premium is £14.75 a week (April 2002 rates);
3. plus housing costs payments to cover certain accommodation payments not met by housing benefit (eg mortgage interest payments – though since October 1995 new claimants for income support receive no interest payments for the first two months and only half for the next four months. Income support will not cover any mortgage interest for 39 weeks for new mortgages entered into after 1 October 1995 which includes new mortgages swapped for old mortgages to take

advantage of lower interest rates. Income support will also not pay any interest on mortgages of over £100,000).

The amount a person gets is worked out by adding up the weekly personal allowances and any premiums the person qualifies for plus any payments for mortgage interest and certain other housing costs which are not covered by housing benefit. From this is taken away any income from part time work or maintenance (subject to the exempted amounts detailed above).

### Other help
There is entitlement to the same help as with family credit.

### Income support and mortgage payments
If a non-earning spouse is left on his/her own in the matrimonial home with the children, and the earning spouse has left the home and is no longer paying the mortgage, the non-earning spouse can claim income support. Under normal circumstances, where a mortgage was taken out on or after 2 October 1995 no payment of mortgage interest would be made for the first 39 weeks of the claim. Thereafter, 100 per cent of the mortgage interest is payable. However, there is an exception which relates to a person who claims income support after being abandoned by his/her partner and where that person's family includes a child. The word 'abandoned' is important. If the spouse leaves by agreement then the more generous provisions for paying mortgage interest payments will not apply. Where the exception does apply, for the first eight weeks no claim can be made with respect to the mortgage. For the next 18 weeks half the mortgage interest will be paid. After 26 weeks the full mortgage interest will be paid. During the eight-week period when no payments are made the spouse in the home may be able to obtain an occupation order with an order under s40 FLA 1996 requiring the other spouse to pay the mortgage. Such an order would have no effect on the spouse's income support entitlement.

### Housing benefit (see s130 SSCBA 1992)

Housing benefit is paid by local councils to people on low incomes who are paying rent. It does not cover mortgage interest payments or fuel costs (which might be covered by income support) or water charges. It does not pay for the cost of meals which may be included in the rent (eg only the bed part of bed and breakfast rent may be covered). It does not pay for lighting or cooking.

If the claimant, or the claimant and his or her partner together, have more than £16,000 in savings and investments he or she cannot claim, the amount of housing benefit is reduced to take into account savings between £3,000 and £16,000.

If a claimant is entitled to income support and has to pay rent or rates, then the claimant qualifies automatically for maximum housing benefit. If the claimant does not receive income support, he or she may still qualify for maximum housing benefit if the money coming in is less than the amount required to meet his or her needs. If the money coming in is more than the needs, the housing benefit is reduced in proportion to the difference.

The maximum housing benefit covers all rent. If there are other people living with the claimant who do not depend on the claimant to support them, then less help may be given with rent.

Housing benefit is claimed from the local authority.

### Council Tax benefit

Council tax is based on an estimated property value of a person's home, with one bill per dwelling. Council tax benefit is available for owner occupiers and tenants on low incomes. The maximum benefit will cover 100 per cent of the council tax bill. The benefit is based on income and savings. Savings of over £16,000 make the claimant ineligible. Savings between £3,000 and £16,000 reduce the amount of benefit.

### The Social Fund (see ss138–140 SSCBA 1992)

These are grants or loans for dealing with exceptional expenses.

#### Funeral costs

If arrangements have to be made for a funeral by a person in receipt of income support, working families tax credit or housing benefit, then the person may be able to claim a Funeral Payment from the Social Fund. Any money which the person or their partner have over £500, or which is available from the estate of the person who died, or from insurance policies or charities, will be taken into account. Funeral payments are repayable from the deceased person's estate so can be reclaimed by the Social Fund. Application must be made within three months of the date of the funeral.

#### Sure Start Maternity Payments

Sure Start Maternity Payments are available from the Social Fund to help buy things for a new baby if the mother or her spouse/partner is receiving income support, income based jobseeker's allowance or working families tax credit. The claim must be made either during pregnancy or within three months of the child's birth. There is a grant of £500 for each qualifying child.

#### Cold weather payments

A family with a child under five, in receipt of income support, may be able to get a cold weather payment during a period of cold weather (when the average temperature for seven days in a row is, or is forecast to be, 0°C or below).

## Community Care Grants

If a person is receiving income support, then he or she may claim a Community Care Grant to help elderly or handicapped people to lead independent lives in the community. Grants may be awarded to people leaving institutional or residential care, or to help people remain in the community. Any savings over £500 are taken into account.

Grants may also be paid to help cope with difficult family problems (eg after the break-up of a marriage).

Grants do not have to be repaid but are discretionary and come out of a limited budget, and so there is no guarantee that a person will actually receive a grant.

## Budgeting Loans

If a person is in receipt of income support then he or she may be able to claim a Budgeting Loan. These are interest-free loans to help people spread the payment for exceptional expenses over a longer period. Such payments could cover such items as essential household equipment, furniture, repairs, maintenance or removal expenses. The amount is decided by the Social Fund Officer and will be according to the person's needs. The award cannot be greater than the person can afford to repay. If the person or his or her partner or spouse have savings over £500 then this is taken into account.

A Budgeting Loan has to be repaid. The rate of repayment and the period over which the person pays back the loan is calculated on the basis of the person's income and circumstances.

## Crisis Loans

Crisis Loans are to help people who cannot meet their immediate short-term expenses in an emergency or following a disaster, provided that the award of a loan is the only means by which serious risk to the health or safety of the person, or a member of the family, may be prevented. A Crisis Loan could cover expenses for up to fourteen days or such items as essential household equipment or travel costs.

The amount is decided by the Social Fund Officer but an award cannot be made for a greater amount than the person can afford to repay. A Crisis Loan has to be repaid. The rate of repayment and the period over which the person pays it back is again worked out based on the person's income and circumstances. The loans are made at the discretion of the Social Fund Officer and come out of a limited local fund. A person cannot owe the fund more than £1,000.

## One parent benefit

One parent benefit used to be paid for the first child in one parent families. The benefit was phased out in April 1998.

## Widowed parents (see ss36–38 SSCBA 1992)

When a spouse dies the surviving spouse may be able to claim a bereavement payment of £2,000. This will usually be claimed by the surviving spouse under 60 and the deceased spouse should have paid national insurance contributions.

If the surviving parent has at least one dependent child then he or she may claim Widowed Parent's Allowance if the surviving parent claims child benefit or is a widow pregnant by her late husband. To get the full rate the deceased spouse must have paid national insurance contributions for virtually all his/her working life. If he/she paid less then the surviving parent will get less. The allowance ends on remarriage. If the surviving parent lives with a person of the opposite sex the allowance is lost while the relationship lasts. It is not possible to claim Widowed Parent's Allowance at the same time as the bereavement allowance.

The Widowed Parent's Allowance is £75.50 a week plus extra payments for each child (April 2002 rates). The allowance stops on retirement when it is replaced by retirement pension. There is also a benefit called Bereavement Allowance which could be claimed by someone not otherwise entitled to Widowed Parent's Allowance.

## 12.2 Duties to maintain

Section 78(6) Social Security Administration Act 1992 provides that:

'(a) a man shall be liable to maintain his wife and any children of whom he is the father;
(b) a woman shall be liable to maintain her husband and any children of whom she is the mother.'

(NB this means that unmarried fathers and mothers have a duty to maintain their children though not their respective unmarried partners.)

If a person is receiving income support for him or herself or for him or herself and his or her children and another person is liable to maintain them, then the DSS can either:

1. encourage the claimant to apply for a maintenance order against that liable person (eg encourage an unmarried mother to apply for a maintenance order for her children against her separated partner under Sched 1 CA 1989); or
2. take proceedings itself against the liable person through their local magistrates' court to oblige that person to pay an equivalent sum to the income support paid for the children (so that the DSS recovers all or part of the money it has paid out in income support – see s106 SSAA 1992). The court must have regard to 'all the circumstances and, in particular, to the income of the liable person'.

As a last resort the DSS can take criminal proceedings since it is an offence for any person to persistently refuse or neglect to maintain any person he or she is liable to maintain and in consequence of his or her refusal or neglect income support is paid in respect to such a person. The offence is punishable by a fine of up to £1,000 and/or imprisonment of up to three months (see s105 SSAA 1992).

The Child Support Agency now largely deals with obliging absent parents to pay child support where state benefits are being paid to the parent caring for the children.

## 12.3 The diversion procedure

A wife may be in receipt of both maintenance and benefits. Her entitlement to benefit will be reduced by how much maintenance she is supposed to receive. If the husband does not pay the maintenance or is irregular in his payments the wife will receive a fluctuating and reduced income. In order to avoid this, such a wife may make an arrangement with the DSS (the 'diversion procedure') whereby any maintenance payments made by the husband to the magistrates' court will be sent by the court direct to the DSS. The DSS will then pay the wife her full amount of benefit ignoring the maintenance order as far as she is concerned. The DSS will then receive the maintenance in order to recoup the benefit paid to the wife, which she would not otherwise receive when she was entitled to the maintenance direct herself. The wife will get her full entitlement to benefit whether the maintenance is paid or not. The DSS will normally seek enforcement of the maintenance order on the wife's behalf.

The wife then receives a regular income from benefit and does not have to worry about the maintenance which is either never paid or paid sporadically.

If the wife's order is for a larger amount than her allowance, the DSS may not adopt this procedure if it might involve it in the work of repaying the wife. It will only do so if it seems likely that the husband will not pay at all or only irregularly.

The diversion procedure only applies to maintenance orders made in, or registered in, the magistrates' courts.

## 12.4 Relationship between state benefits and maintenance orders

The courts' attitude has changed in recent times so that the availability of state benefits has become more important in matrimonial proceedings. The courts have applied have considered the following:

### *A husband cannot throw the burden of maintaining his wife and children which he ought to bear on to the state*

If a husband can afford to pay maintenance he cannot argue that no order should be made simply because his wife and children will receive income support and that any maintenance order he pays will either be deducted from their income support or paid direct to the DSS, so that it will make no difference to them. See *Peacock* v *Peacock* [1984] 1 All ER 1069 where a husband was ordered to pay £5 weekly to his wife and £5 weekly to each of his two children even though these sums were totally swallowed up by the state benefit the wife received (following *Barnes* v *Barnes* below).

See *Day* v *Day* [1988] 1 FLR 278 where the husband also argued that he should not have to pay maintenance to his wife and her children because 'she will be in a better financial position on benefits' and that any maintenance he paid would be diverted to the DSS. His argument was rejected and the maintenance order was confirmed.

The principle in *Barnes* v *Barnes* was described in *Ashley* v *Blackman* below, by Waite J as:

'... a salutary principle, protecting public funds from feckless or devious husbands who seek to escape their proper responsibilites by throwing the burden of their wife's maintenance upon social security. It is also a rigorous one, because by its very nature it is hard to squeeze the resources of a husband with small means until the shoe really pinches'.

## Where there is not enough money to go around state benefits should be considered as a resource (eg under s25(2)(a) MCA 1973)

A court should not make a maintenance order which the husband cannot afford to pay and which will bring him below subsistence level. He should be left to have enough money to live on or maintain his new family. The DSS will then be left to make up the deficit by providing the appropriate benefits for the wife and children. The availability of state benefits enables the court to deal with a larger purse than otherwise be available (see *Barnes* v *Barnes* above).

The same consideration was applied in *Reiterbund* v *Reiterbund* [1975] 2 WLR 375; [1975] 1 All ER 280 in relation to s5 MCA 1973 and the question of grave financial hardship and the right of the wife to supplementary benefits in the event of her husband dying before she was sixty. Supplementary benefit was most relevant.

In *Claxton* v *Claxton* [1982] 3 FLR 415 and *Chase* v *Chase* (1983) 13 Fam Law 21 it was emphasised that there was no point in bringing a husband below subsistence level.

This approach was adopted in *Stockford* v *Stockford* [1982] 3 FLR 58 and applied in *Delaney* v *Delaney* [1990] 2 FLR 457 where a wife had failed to apply for state benefits for herself and the three children. The court considered her entitlement and only made nominal maintenance orders for the children against the husband since proper maintenance orders would have financially crippled him.

The court will also consider the 'passport benefits' a spouse may be entitled to as a result of claiming income support or family credit. If a maintenance order is made a spouse may lose not only the entitlement to income support or family credit but also entitlement to 'passport benefits' such as council tax benefit, free dental care and free prescriptions. These are also resources which may persuade a court not to make a maintenance order if it would leave the recipient spouse worse off (see *C* v *C (Financial Provision)* [1995] 2 FLR 171).

## Using the 'liable relative' formula to assess maintenance

In *Smethurst* v *Smethurst* [1977] 3 WLR 472; [1977] 3 All ER 1110 Sir George Baker said that the court should have regard to the 'guideline calculation' used by the Supplementary Benefit Commission in assessing maintenance. That calculation involved adding the rent to the supplementary benefit rates for the husband and his second family to a quarter of earned income to reach a figure which is what is deemed as necessary for his household. Any extra amount could then be paid by way of maintenance.

However, in *Shallow* v *Shallow* [1978] 2 WLR 583; [1978] 2 All ER 483 the Court of Appeal rejected the use of the 'liable relative' formula applied by Sir George Baker in *Smethurst* v *Smethurst*. The formula is merely a starting point for discussion – 'a ranging shot which suggested a figure which could then be considered in detail in the light of all the circumstances of the particular case.' In the case rigidly applying the formula produced an unreasonable result whereby the wife was left far worse off than the husband.

In *Stockford* v *Stockford* (above) it was said that the statutory provisions, such as s25 MCA 1973 and s3 DPMCA 1978, must be applied without superimposed judicial glosses (such as the liable relative formula or one-third rule).

## Should a husband claiming state benefits be ordered to pay maintenance?

If a husband is unemployed and claiming benefit the court cannot assume that he has an earning capacity and should be working and thereby order him to pay maintenance. If he is claiming benefit the state accepts that he is genuinely out of work and unable to find work (see *Williams* v *Williams* [1974] 3 WLR 379; [1974] 3 All ER 377 and *Girvan* v *Girvan* (1983) 13 Fam Law 213).

If a husband is unemployed the court may nevertheless order him to pay maintenance. A husband cannot assume that if he is receiving state benefit he is always at subsistence level and that he cannot be ordered to pay maintenance since this will take him below that subsistence level. The court will make an order it considers fair and reasonable. See *Freeman* v *Swatridge* [1984] FLR 762 where an unemployed husband was ordered to pay 50p a week to each of his two children. His appeal was dismissed. There was no rule of law that a court could not order maintenance in such circumstances.

However, in many cases the most appropriate order will be a nominal order (eg £1 a year of 5p a week) while the husband remains unemployed. See *Berry* v *Berry* [1986] 3 WLR 257; [1986] 2 All ER 948 where a husband was claiming supplementary benefit. He was ordered to pay £5 weekly maintenance which was then reduced to £2 weekly. He appealed.

HELD: Where the husband was dependent on state benefits the proper conclusion, in the absence of special circumstances, was that there was no margin between the husband's level of subsistence and the amount of benefit he received to justify the making of a substantial order for maintenance against him. The order was reduced to a nominal sum.

## The relevance of state benefits to the clean break provisions

In *Ashley* v *Blackman* (above) a husband was ordered to pay maintenance to his mentally ill wife. He had a small income which was wholly used up keeping his second family. His former wife was dependant on state benefits. The husband applied under s31(7) MCA 1973 to discharge the maintenance order.

HELD: The principle in *Barnes* v *Barnes* (above) was required to stop devious and feckless husbands who sought to throw the burden of his wife's maintenance on to the state. Section 31(7) was intended to leave scope for those of limited means to be spared the burden of having to pay former spouses a few pounds a week indefinitely. A clean break was applied to prevent the prospect of a divorced couple of acutely limited means remaining manacled together indefinitely by the necessity of returning at regular intervals to court for no other purpose than to thrash out at public expense the precise figure which one should pay to the other, not for the benefit of either, but solely for the relief of the tax paying section of the community to which neither of them had sufficient means to belong.

A clean break was also imposed in *C* v *C (Financial Provision)*, above, where a husband's income and resources were entirely consumed by the care he required following a bad accident. The wife was dependent on state benefit. A clean break order was made with no maintenance provision for her and with an order prohibiting her from making a claim under the Inheritance (Provision for Family and Dependants) Act 1975.

## The Child Support Act 1991

From 5 April 1993 the relationship between state benefits and maintenance orders changed dramatically since the Child Support Act 1991 came into force. Its provisions are outlined in Chapter 7. Parents with the care of children who are in receipt of income support, family credit or disability working allowance and who have maintenance orders in their favour for their children will be contacted by the Child Support Agency who will 'take over' the child maintenance. The Agency will assess the child support payable and the court maintenance order will cease to have effect.

Any parent with the care of the children who first claims income support or disability working allowance after 5 April 1993 is asked to apply for child support maintenance at the same time.

By March 1996 virtually all children whose families receive income support or disability working allowance were the subject of child support assessments collected and enforced by the Child Support Agency. The courts have no role to play except a limited role in helping the Agency to enforce payment.

As with existing maintenance orders if a parent with care is receiving income support the amount of child support received will lead to a £ for £ reduction in income support so that the parent with care and the children will be no better off unless the amount of child support is more than the income support received.

Parents with care claiming Disability Working Allowance, housing benefit or Council Tax Benefit will have the first £15 of their child support ignored in the calculation of these benefits.

Though parents with care should be better off as a result of child support, some parents on income support may be worse off. This is because the higher amounts of child support paid by absent parents may take the parent with care above income support levels but not sufficiently to compensate for the loss of the fringe benefits which go with income support, namely housing benefit, council tax benefit, free prescriptions, free dental care and free school meals.

# 13

# Consortium

13.1 Nature of consortium

13.2 Incidents of consortium

13.3 Termination of the right to consortium

## 13.1 Nature of consortium

'Consortium' means living together as husband and wife with all the incidents that flow from that relationship (ie mutual duty to cohabit).

The old concept of marriage was the *doctrine of unity* whereby when the wife married her husband they became one person – the husband. The legal existence of the woman was suspended.

The doctrine of unity was never fully applied but was only finally disapproved of in *Midland Bank Trust Co Ltd* v *Green (No 3)* [1981] 3 All ER 744 where a husband and wife were sued for conspiracy and it was argued that they could not be liable on the basis that they were one person in law and could not conspire together. It was held that the doctrine of unity had no place in modern law. It was a medieval fiction. The husband and wife had to be treated as separate and equal.

In *R* v *Leggatt* (1852) 18 QB 781 the Court of Queen's Bench held that they would not force a wife to return to her husband against her will by enabling him to obtain custody of her by habeas corpus.

Later, in *R* v *Jackson* [1891] 1 QB 671; [1891-4] All ER 61, the wife's personal liberty was enhanced further. The wife had gone to live with relations whilst the husband was absent in New Zealand. After his return, she refused to live with him again, and failed to comply with a decree of restitution of conjugal rights. Consequently, he arranged with two men that they should seize her as she came out of church, and she was then put into a carriage and taken to her husband's residence, where she was allowed complete freedom of the house, but was not permitted to leave the building. She then applied for a writ of habeas corpus.

HELD (by the Court of Appeal): It was no defence that the husband was merely confining her in order to enforce his right to her consortium.

From the date of that decision 'the shackles of servitude fell from the limbs of married women as they were free to come and go at their own will' (see McCardle J in *Place* v *Searle* [1932] 2 KB 497).

Scrutton LJ in the same case commented:

'It seems to be clear that at the present day, a husband has a right to the consortium of his wife, and the wife to the consortium of her husband.'

The action of obtaining a decree for the restoration of conjugal rights was abolished in s20 Matrimonial Proceedings and Property Act 1970.

Actions for harbouring, enticing and stealing a spouse away were abolished by ss4 and 5 Law Reform (Miscellaneous Provisions) Act 1970 (recognising a wife's freedom to leave her husband).

If a husband steals, carries away or secretes his wife against her will he is guilty of kidnapping (see *R* v *Reid* [1972] 3 WLR 395; [1972] 3 All ER 1350). A husband cannot enforce his right to consortium.

These rights must now be regarded as reciprocal.

## 13.2 Incidents of consortium

In *Best* v *Samuel Fox & Co* [1952] 2 All ER 394 Lord Reid stated that consortium consisted of a 'bundle of rights some hardly capable of precise definition which stem from the common home and common life'.

### Examples

**Wife's right to her husband's name**
This survives divorce and the husband's death. No injunction is possible to prevent the use thereof unless used for purposes of defrauding the former husband, or if some other right is being invaded.

**Mutual right to choose the matrimonial home**
Neither has an absolute right and both must act reasonably. In a large number of cases, the earning spouse will be entitled to the last word for the simple reason that he or she will be the breadwinner and must be able to live near his or her place of work (per Denning LJ in *Dunn* v *Dunn* [1948] 2 All ER 822 and *King* v *King* [1941] 2 All ER 103).

In *Dunn* v *Dunn* the wife was very shy due to profound deafness. She wanted to stay at the first matrimonial home. The husband wished to move to where he worked. He was unreasonable in refusing to live where the wife wanted to live and thus the husband was in desertion.

In *King* v *King* the wife ran three businesses from her matrimonial home, namely, a small dairy, the growing of fruit and flowers for the market and a guesthouse. Her future was bound up in the house and she would be destitute without the house. The husband initially accepted that he and the wife should treat her house as the matrimonial home. He then refused to move from his family home. The husband was held to be unreasonable in refusing to live at the wife's house. He was in desertion.

The wife's dislike of the husband's offer of accommodation was unreasonable and she was in desertion in *Mansey* v *Mansey* [1940] 2 All ER 424. In *Munro* v *Munro* [1950] 1 All ER 832 the husband's insistence that the wife live with his mother was unreasonable.

## Mutual right to normal sexual intercourse

This continues after the marriage has been consummated provided that it is reasonably exercised. But one spouse is not bound to submit to the demands of the other if they are inordinate, perverted, or otherwise unreasonable, or if likely to lead to a breakdown in health.

A husband is not entitled to insist upon using contraceptives or practising coitus interruptus against the wife's will if it is unreasonable to deprive her of the opportunity of bearing children.

If the spouse does so insist, the other will be entitled to withdraw from cohabitation without being in desertion. This may also amount to behaviour for purposes of divorce or judicial separation proceedings (see *Hutchinson* v *Hutchinson* [1963] 1 WLR 280; [1963] 1 All ER 1, but contrast *Weatherley* v *Weatherley* [1947] 1 All ER 563).

Until recently criminal courts accepted Sir Matthew Hale's proposition in 1736 that a husband could not be guilty as a principal of rape of his own wife. This was assumed to be the law in *R* v *Miller* [1954] 2 WLR 138; [1954] 2 All ER 529 (even when a divorce petition had been filed – since the petition could be disputed the implied consent to intercourse remained – unless there was an agreement to live apart). However, this rule has gradually been whittled away until it no longer applies.

In *R* v *Clarke* [1949] 2 All ER 448 Byrne J held that a husband could be guilty of rape if the wife had obtained a judicial separation or separation order in the magistrates' court, because this relieves her of the duty of cohabiting, and thus of having sexual intercourse with him. The principle was extended in *R* v *O'Brien* [1974] 3 All ER 663 to the case where a decree nisi of divorce had been obtained, for the marriage is de facto dead and, consequently, the wife's consent must be regarded as revoked.

In *R* v *Leak* [1975] 2 All ER 1059 the husband was convicted of aiding and abetting a third party to rape his wife.

In *R* v *Roberts* [1986] Crim LR 188 the marriage between the husband and the wife had broken down. A non-molestation order and ouster order had been granted to the wife for two months against the husband. There was also a separation agreement. The ouster and non-molestation order expired. The husband forcibly had intercourse with the wife. He argued that, since the injunction against him had expired and the separation agreement made no reference to non-molestation, his wife's implied consent to intercourse remained. He was convicted of rape. His appeal was dismissed. The question was whether the parties had, by agreement between themselves or through a court or by a court order, made it clear that the implied consent to sexual intercourse no longer existed. Clearly, on the facts there was no longer any implied consent – it had been terminated. It had not been revived simply because the injunction had expired.

A husband can indecently assault his wife. See *R* v *Kowalski* [1988] 1 FLR 447 where a marriage was failing and the husband and wife were beginning to live separate lives. They continued to share a home and bed. While the wife was in the lavatory the husband burst in carrying a knife and placed it against her throat and forced her to commit fellatio (sexual stimulation by her mouth) after which he had normal intercourse with her. Though it was settled law that a man could not be guilty of rape on his wife, that depended on an implied consent to sexual intercourse which arose from the married state and continued until that consent was put aside by a decree nisi of divorce, a separation order or, in certain circumstances, by a separation agreement. Such implied consent did not apply to other sexual acts. The wife had in the past consented to fellatio but had shown that she found it indecent, repellent and abhorrent. Her consent to fellatio, once given and even long practised, could not run backwards and attach to the marriage vows. Consent to fellatio had to be a particular consent if it were not to be an assault. Circumstances of indecency depended on all the facts of a particular case. Since it was clear that the wife had not given positive consent, the husband was guilty of indecent assault. He was sentenced to two years' imprisonment concurrent on two counts of indecent assault and assault.

The House of Lords has now ruled on the position in *R* v *R* (*Rape: Marital Exemption*) [1992] 1 FLR 217; [1991] 3 WLR 767; [1991] 4 All ER 481 stating that the rule that a husband cannot be criminally liable for raping his wife was no longer part of the law. A husband and wife are equal partners in marriage. It is unacceptable that by marriage a wife submits herself irrevocably to sexual intercourse in all circumstances. Lord Keith of Kinkel referred to Sir Matthew Hale's proposition in the following terms:

> 'It may be taken that the proposition was generally regarded as an accurate statement of the common law of England. The common law is, however, capable of evolving in the light of changing social, economic and cultural developments. Hale's proposition reflected the state of affairs in these respects at the time it was enunciated. Since then the status of women, and particularly of married women, has changed out of all recognition in various ways which are very familiar and upon which it is unnecessary to go into detail. Apart from property matters and the availability of matrimonial remedies, one of the most important changes is that marriage is in modern times regarded as a partnership of equals, and no longer one in which the wife must be the subservient chattel of the husband.

Hale's proposition involves that by marriage a wife gives her irrevocable consent to sexual intercourse with her husband under all circumstances and irrespective of her state of health or how she happens to be feeling at the time. In modern times any reasonable person must regard that conception as quite unacceptable.'

In the case a husband was sentenced to three years' imprisonment for attempting to rape his wife who had left him and gone to live with her parents.

R appealed to the European Court of Human Rights against the decision in *R* v *R*. In *CR* v *United Kingdom* [1996] 1 FLR 434 the European Court unanimously held that the decision did not violate art 7 of the Convention for the Protection of Human Rights and Fundamental Freedoms (no one can be held guilty of a criminal offence which was not a criminal offence at the time it was committed). The European Court recognised that United Kingdom courts can develop case law provided that any change was 'reasonably foreseeable'. The situation has now been confirmed by statute (see s142 Criminal Justice and Public Order Act 1994).

## Mutual right to protection
Each spouse is entitled to use such force as is reasonably necessary to protect the other from attack or other physical harm.

## Either party's right to maintenance
See Chapters 7, 9, 11 and 12.

## Duty to respect marital confidences
See *Argyll* v *Argyll* [1965] 2 WLR 790; [1965] 1 All ER 611 where two years after divorce, the defendant wrote a series of newspaper articles some of which contained information relating to the plaintiff's 'private life, personal affairs and private conduct, communicated to the defendant in confidence during the subsistence of the marriage'.

HELD: Equity's general jurisdiction to restrain breach of confidence was sufficiently wide to enable the court to grant an injunction to prevent the defendant from divulging these secrets and the newspaper from publishing them.

Ungoed-Thomas J said:

'There could hardly be anything more intimate or confidential than is involved in that relationship of husband and wife, or than in the mutual trust and confidences which are shared between husband and wife. The confidential nature of the relationship is of its very essence and so obviously and necessarily implicit in it that there is no need for it to be expressed.'

## Evidence in legal proceedings
*The competence of spouses to give evidence.* A spouse may give evidence for any party in civil proceedings (see s1 Evidence Amendment Act 1853).

A spouse may give evidence for the prosecution, the accused or co-accused in criminal proceedings (unless the husband and wife are jointly charged, when neither is competent for the prosecution as long as they are liable to be convicted, see s80 Police and Criminal Evidence Act 1984).

*The compellability of spouses to give evidence.* Spouses are compellable in all civil proceedings.

Spouses are compellable for the accused in all criminal cases unless the spouses are jointly charged. They are only compellable for the prosecution in certain cases – where an offence of assault is alleged against a spouse or child, or a sexual offence is alleged against a child (see s80 Police and Criminal Evidence Act 1984).

*Privilege.* A spouse cannot claim privilege against questions asking about communications between himself or herself and his or her spouse in civil proceedings (see s16(3) Civil Evidence Act 1968) and in criminal proceedings (see s80 Police and Criminal Evidence Act 1984).

Communications between spouses are not necessarily treated as being confidential and may be intercepted. See *Rumping* v *DPP* [1962] 3 All ER 256 where the police intercepted a letter written by the accused to his wife virtually confessing his guilt to the charge of murder. The letter was held to be admissible and the accused was convicted.

## The effect of marriage on contracts
*The capacity of a spouse to enter into a contract.* A wife may enter into her own contracts with third parties and be sued in her own name in the same way as a husband (see s1 Law Reform (Married Women and Tortfeasors) Act 1835).

*Contracts between spouses.* Spouses may contract with each other but any contract which purports to regularise their domestic affairs is likely to be unenforceable since the courts do not wish to regulate domestic life and it is presumed that spouses do not intend to enter into legal regulations with each other. See *Balfour* v *Balfour* [1919] 2 KB 271 where an agreement by a husband to pay a wife £30 a month housekeeping while he was abroad if the wife did not look to him for any other maintenance was held to be unenforceable; *Spellman* v *Spellman* [1961] 2 All ER 498 where an agreement between spouses about the ownership of a car was held to be unenforceable; and *Gould* v *Gould* [1969] 3 All ER 728.

BUT an agreement when spouses are not living together amicably may be legally enforceable (see *Re Windle* [1975] 3 All ER 987). Where they have separated the presumption that they do not intend to be legally bound may not apply (see *Merritt* v *Merritt* [1970] 2 All ER 760).

*One spouse entering into a contract as agent for the other.* Problems can arise if one spouse has no money in his or her own name (eg a wife with no income) and uses the other spouse's money to buy goods. If a married woman lives with her husband there is a presumption that she has his authority to pledge his credit to buy goods and services which are *necessary* for running the household (eg food, clothing and other household items). This was called the *agency of necessity* and enabled a wife to contract with a third party on her husband's behalf. The third party was able to sue the husband if payment was not made (see *Debenham* v *Mellon* (1880) 6 App Cas 24).

However, if the wife cannot be said to be the husband's agent it is she who will be liable in contract (see *Miss Gray Ltd* v *Cathcart* (1922) 38 TLR 562 and *Callot* v *Nash* (1923) 39 TLR 292).

Articles of luxury cannot be 'necessaries' unless the couple have a lifestyle which shows that such luxuries are 'necessaries' to them and not extravagant.

If a husband has already forbidden the third party to give his wife credit or forbidden his wife to pledge his credit (even if the third party may be unaware of that) then the presumption in the agency of necessities may be rebutted. The above may apply if a husband gives his wife a fixed allowance which may imply that his wife is prohibited from spending anything over that fixed allowance.

NOTE: If the husband has allowed the wife to pledge his credit to a particular third party for goods or services in the past he cannot simply forbid his wife to pledge his credit without telling the third party, otherwise he might be estopped from denying his wife's authority to buy goods on his credit since that would not be fair to that particular tradesman having regard to the husband's past behaviour.

## 13.3 Termination of right to consortium

The right to consortium is terminated by:

1. Judicial separation or magistrates' court order.
2. An order excluding one spouse from the matrimonial home will have the practical effect of ending consortium.
3. Separation agreement – although once the agreement comes to an end, the right will revive.
4. Decree nisi of divorce or nullity.
5. One party providing just cause for leaving. A court may prevent one spouse from interfering with another after they have separated. See *Nanda* v *Nanda* [1968] 2 WLR 404; [1967] 3 All ER 401 where the husband was entitled to an injunction to prevent his wife from entering the flat where, after deserting his wife, he had set up home with another woman and their two children, since the wife was trespassing on the husband's property, his flat never having been the matrimonial home.
6. One party losing the intention of living with the other partner (see *Santos* v *Santos* [1972] 2 WLR 889; [1972] 2 All ER 246).

# 14

# Separation and Maintenance Agreements

14.1 Introduction

14.2 The relationship between separation agreements and the courts

## 14.1 Introduction

### What is normally included in a separation or maintenance agreement

Separation or maintenance agreements may be in the form of an agreement or by way of a deed. To be legally enforceable the agreement must constitute a contract between the parties. Unless the agreement is by deed then a party seeking to enforce the agreement would have to show that he or she furnished consideration. Such consideration could be the agreement to separate or the resolution of competing claims over property. The agreement would normally be enforced by the law of contract though there are special provisions for altering agreements in some circumstances (see below).

An agreement between spouses who remain living together would normally be regarded as a domestic arrangement with no intention to create legal relations. For the purposes of this chapter it is assumed that the parties are no longer living together and have either agreed to separate and/or agreed to settle their financial affairs in place of a court order or in anticipation of a court order confirming what they have agreed.

A separation/maintenance agreement could include the following:

1. in the case of a separation agreement, an agreement for the spouses to live apart and separate (which would prevent either party from being in desertion);
2. agreements about with whom the children will live and the contact arrangements for the other parent (though such an agreement could not have the effect of surrendering or transferring parental responsibility – s2(9) CA 1989);
3. an agreement about who is to live in the former matrimonial home and/or whether and when it should be sold and how the proceeds of sale should be divided;

4. agreements that one spouse pay the other spouse maintenance (including over what period and in what amount);
5. the payment of capital sums and/or the dividing up of other assets;
6. the payment of maintenance or other financial provision for any children of the marriage.

Separation agreements *cannot* include the following terms:

1. an agreement to separate in the future or to provide for future separation (see *Wilson* v *Wilson* (1848) 1 HLC 538; *Re Meyrick's Settlement* [1921] 1 Ch 311 and *Re Johnson's Will Trusts* [1967] 2 WLR 152; [1967] 1 All ER 553) – this would be considered to be contrary to public policy as tending to harm the status of marriage);

Note: An agreement for immediate separation or after separation has taken place is quite lawful;

2. an agreement preventing application being subsequently made to the court for financial provision (see s34(1)(a) MCA 1973 – such a term would not invalidate the rest of the agreement – s34(1)(b) MCA 1973);
3. an agreement preventing application being subsequently made to the Child Support Agency for child support.

## 14.2 The relationship between separation agreements and the courts

### Cannot oust the jurisdiction of the court

Any provision in a separation agreement which supposedly ousts the jurisdiction of the courts to make a maintenance order will be void (eg an agreement preventing either party from applying to the courts in the future would have no effect; see s34(1)(a) MCA 1973).

An agreement about paying maintenance for or to a child could not prevent application being subsequently made to the Child Support Agency. However the existence of a written agreement about child maintenance does provide an exception to the general rule that courts can no longer make maintenance orders for the children. If there is a written agreement as to child maintenance a court would have jurisdiction to convert that agreement into a court order for child maintenance (see Child Maintenance (Written Agreements) Order 1993 and s8(5) Child Support Act 1991).

### Can form basis of subsequent court order

If the spouses, each having received appropriate advice and with full knowledge of the other spouse's financial circumstances, have freely reached a separation agreement then the courts are likely to uphold that agreement in subsequent court proceedings and confirm the financial arrangements made in that agreement in the court order unless there is some clear and compelling reason otherwise.

In *Edgar* v *Edgar* [1980] 1 WLR 1410; [1980] 3 All ER 887 the wife entered into an agreement whereby she accepted property worth £100,000 from her husband. She agreed not to apply to the court for any further financial provision. She entered into this agreement even though she was given advice that she would be better off applying to the court for financial provision. Three years later she petitioned for divorce and applied for ancillary relief. Initially she was awarded a lump sum of £750,000. On appeal the court overturned that decision and confirmed the £100,000 transfer set out in the agreement.

A similar approach was adopted in *N* v *N (Consent Order: Variation)* [1993] Fam Law 676 where the parties divorced in 1987. The wife agreed in a consent order that her maintenance should cease after five years, though no order was made under s28(1A) MCA 1973 preventing her from applying to extend that period. However, she agreed in writing in a letter not to apply for an extension. In 1991 she changed her career and applied to extend the term of her maintenance for a further period of three years. Her application was refused because she had freely entered into an agreement with which the court would not interfere. Her appeal was dismissed. Though the signed letter could not oust the court's jursidiction it was highly relevant and amounted to conduct which it was inequitable to ignore. The court would uphold an agreement freely entered into by properly advised parties, subject to the court having a duty to give first consideration to the welfare of any child of the family (pursuant to s25(1) and s31(7) MCA 1973). In this case the financial difficulties of the wife could not harm the child, though the child's home might be at risk. The child's maintenance would be increased but the wife's maintenance would not be extended (*Edgar* v *Edgar* followed).

See also *G* v *G (Financial Provision: Separation Agreement)* [2000] Fam Law 472 in which a separation agreement between the parties was considered when the parties divorced and the court was asked to make ancillary relief orders. The agreement was part of all the circumstances (under s25(1) MCA 1973) and was also conduct which it was inequitable to ignore (under s25(2)(g) MCA 1973 and following *Edgar* v *Edgar*). In the case the parties had attached importance to the agreement and acted upon it and the ancillary relief reflected the separation agreement.

See also *X* v *X (Y and Z Intervening)* [2002] 1 FLR 508 in which a couple reached agreement on a clean break settlement. W then sought to resile from the agreement. It was ordered that the agreement become the court order since it had been a formal agreement properly and fairly arrived at with competent legal advice and there were no grounds for concluding that it would cause any injustice by holding the parties to it (applying *Edgar* v *Edgar* [1980] 1 WLR 1410). In the case H had performed his part of the agreement. The court would not permit parties to depart from an agreement properly and fairly reached between themselves without good and substantial grounds for concluding that an injustice would arise from holding the parties to it.

By contrast, in *Smith* v *Smith* [2000] 3 FCR 374 a separation agreement, in which the wife accepted £16,000 in final settlement of her claims on H, did not prevent a later application by her for ancillary relief following divorce, in which she was awarded a lump sum of £60,000. The separation agreement did not carry great weight since it had not been negotiated with the benefit of legal advice and W had only agreed to it under pressure. The court then looked at a fair settlement in the case of a young wife and a short, childless marriage. It imposed a clean break order with the £60,000 lump sum order.

Maintenance agreements are most commonly used as the basis for consent orders.

In *Beach* v *Beach* [1995] 2 FLR 160 the husband and wife made a separation agreement under which a farm (which was loss-making) was to be sold and the wife paid £450,000 as a final settlement of any claim under MCA 1973. The wife was persuaded not to insist on the immediate sale of the farm. The farm business deteriorated, the husband was made bankrupt and evicted from the farm by his creditors. He then went to live with his parents and lived on income support. The wife received £415,000 from the trustee in bankruptcy under the terms of the settlement. Following divorce the husband asked for a lump sum order of £270,000 against his wife so he could pay off some of his creditors and set up a new business.

HELD: The financial disparity between the parties was now so great that applying s25 MCA 1973 the husband should receive £60,000 so he could obtain accommodation, while leaving the wife with the financial contribution she had made over the years of the marriage. The principle in *Edgar* v *Edgar* did not bar the husband's application because of the change of circumstances after the separation agreement. However the husband's conduct in dissipating the family assets was so inequitable it could not be disregarded and reduced the amount of the lump sum he claimed.

## Variation of maintenance agreements

Application can be made to the court to vary a maintenance agreement provided it is in writing – an oral agreement could not be varied by the court (see s34(2) MCA 1973). For the these purposes the agreement must be:

1. an agreement containing financial arrangements, whether made during the continuance or after the dissolution or annulment of the marriage; or
2. a separation agreement in writing between the parties while they are still married containing such arrangements.

'Financial arrangements' is given a wide meaning (see s34(2) MCA 1973).

Either party may apply to either a county court or to a magistrates' court (subject to jurisdictional requirements) during the lifetime of both parties provided:

1. that there has been a change in the circumstances in the light of which the financial arrangements contained in the agreement were made or omitted to be made (including any change foreseen by the parties) whereby the agreement should be altered or amended to include financial arrangements; or
2. that the agreement does not contain proper financial provision for any children of the family (see s35 MCA 1973).

The court can vary, revoke or insert such financial arrangements as appear to the court to be just in all the circumstances. A magistrates' court is restricted to dealing with maintenance (and not property transfers or settlements).

The court will consider from an objective point of view what circumstances reasonable people would have taken into account when making the agreement in considering any change in circumstances. It will then consider whether the agreement has become unjust; see *Gorman* v *Gorman* [1964] 1 WLR 1440; [1964] 3 All ER 739), where *Gorman* v *Gorman* there was a separation agreement whereby the husband maintained the children and paid the rates and repair costs on the house in which the wife and children lived. The wife undertook to maintain herself and not to apply to a court for maintenance. The husband's income then quadrupled, while his wife became ill and could no longer work. She was then in receipt of state benefit and some voluntary payments from the husband. She applied to vary the agreement by inserting a provision that he pay maintenance to her. The court ruled that the provision forbidding her from applying for maintenance was void but refused to alter the agreement since the wife had been reasonably provided for.

In *D* v *D* (1974) 118 SJ 715 the wife, on independent advice, agreed with her husband to transfer her interest in the matrimonial home for £1,500. The value of the property then increased to £13,250. She applied to vary the agreement. By that time the husband had remarried and had spent money improving the house. In these circumstances the agreement had not become unjust and the wife's application was refused.

In *Simister* v *Simister (No 2)* [1987] 1 FLR 194 a maintenance agreement provided that a husband on a modest salary should pay one-third of that salary to his wife. His salary then unexpectedly and dramatically increased. He applied to vary the agreement on the grounds that he now paid too much to his wife for her needs. The court agreed that the wife received in excess of her needs and varied the amount to be paid under the agreement.

There are also provisions to vary an agreement after the death of one of the parties (see s36 MCA 1973).

Similarly, there are provisions to alter maintenance agreements relating to children in paras 10 and 11, Sch 1 CA 1989.

# 15

# Parent and Child

## 15.1 The interests of parents and the interests of the child

### The rights and duties of the parent

Historically the law gave parents (particularly the father of a legitimate child) the right to determine all matters relating to their child.

Gradually statutes introduced the principle that the welfare of the child was more important than parental rights (eg s2 Custody of Infants Act 1873 provided that agreements in separation deeds could not be enforced if they were not of benefit to the child; s5 Guardianship of Infants Act 1886 provided that the court had to have regard to the welfare of the infant as well as the conduct and wishes of the parents in making orders as to custody and access).

## The welfare of the child is the paramount consideration

### Children Act 1989
Section 1:

> '(1) When a court determines any question with respect to –
> (a) the upbringing of a child; or
> (b) the administration of a child's property or the application of any income arising from it,
> the child's welfare shall be the court's paramount consideration.'

The paramountcy of the child's welfare applies to most proceedings concerning children, in particular:

1. care proceedings;
2. proceedings to settle the arrangements where a child should live following his or her parents' separation and how the child should have contact with the other parent.

However, the paramountcy principle does not apply to all proceedings. For example:

1. in adoption proceedings the child's welfare is the first consideration and not paramount to the interests of the natural parents (see s6 Adoption Act 1976; *Re D (An Infant) (Adoption: Parent's Consent)* [1977] 2 WLR 79);
2. in applications for financial relief the child's welfare is the first consideration and does not override other considerations (see s25(1) MCA 1973; *Suter* v *Suter and Jones* [1987] 2 All ER 336);
3. in applications for occupation orders (excluding a violent parent from the home) the interests of the child are only one of a number of factors (see ss33–38 Family Law Act 1996).

Where the interests of the child are paramount the meaning of the term has been interpreted in *J* v *C* [1969] 2 WLR 540; [1969] 1 All ER 788. In that case the child's parents were Spanish nationals resident in Spain. They sent their son to live in England. Up to the age of ten he lived for all except 18 months of his life with foster parents in England. He had been brought up as an English boy, spoke little Spanish and hardly knew his parents. The courts ordered that he live with his foster parents and not with his parents on the ground that they 'would be unable to cope with the problems of adjustment or with consequential maladjustment' if the boy were to go and live in Spain with them.

Lord MacDermott:

> '... when all the relevant facts, relationships, claims and wishes of parents, risks, choices and other circumstances are taken into account and weighted the course to be followed will be that which is most in the interests of the child's welfare as that term has now to be understood. That is the first consideration because it is of the first importance and the paramount consideration because it rules upon or determines the course to be followed.'

All other considerations are relevant only insofar as they cast light on what is in the best interests of the child.

## The right to family life: art 8 of the European Convention for the Protection of Human Rights and Fundamental Freedoms (the European Convention on Human Rights)

There has been some debate about whether s1 Children Act 1989 is compatible with the European Convention on Human Rights which is applied to English and Welsh law by the Human Rights Act 1998 from 2 October 2000. In particular art 8 states:

'(1) Everyone has the right to respect for his private and family life, his home and his correspondence.
(2) There shall be no interference by a public authority with the exercise of this right except such as is in accordance with the law and is necessary in a democratic society in the interests of national security, public safety or the economic well-being of the country, for the prevention of disorder or crime, for the protection of health or morals, or the for the protection of the rights and freedoms of others.'

Where there is a conflict between the rights of the child and the rights of the parent which should prevail? In English and Welsh law the rights of the child are likely to be paramount. Under European law the answer is less clear cut. However, in practice the European Court of Human Rights attaches particular importance to the best interests of the child. Taking into account the cases quoted below (in particular *Scott* v *United Kingdom*) it appears that English and Welsh law is likely to be compatible with the Convention

An example of the balancing between the rights of the parents and the child can be found in the *K and T* v *Finland* [2001] 2 FLR 707 in which K had two children, P and M, by two different fathers, F1 and F2. K had mental health problems and on occasion she was voluntarily admitted to a mental hospital. In 1991 she formed a relationship with another man, T. In 1992 the custody of P was transferred to F1, her father. M was voluntarily accommodated in a children's home and F2 played no part in his life. In 1993 K gave birth to her third child, J. The child was immediately removed from K after birth and placed into care. M was placed in compulsory care. K showed signs of mental illness and all unsupervised contact between K and T and the two children, J and M, was prohibited. K had some contact with both children. T established a relationship with J. He was told that he could not take over J's care while he continued his relationship with K. Care orders with respect to J and M were confirmed. In 1994 J and M were placed with foster parents 120 km from the home of K and T. Contact was restricted to one supervised visit per month.

In 1995 K gave birth to her fourth child, N. K was then committed to compulsory psychiatric care and T cared for the baby. Eventually K was allowed home and, with support, she and T cared for N. All appeals by K with regard to the care orders for and restrictions on contact with J and M were dismissed. K and T complained to the European Court arguing breaches of arts 8 and 13.

It was held that the state was given a wide margin of appreciation in relation to a decision to take a child into care, due to the importance of protecting children. Consideration of the best interests of the child was of crucial importance in every case. Stricter scrutiny was called for in respect of restricting parental rights of contact with the children otherwise family relations between parents and children could be effectively ended.

In respect of emergency care orders it would not always be possible to involve parents in the decision-making process. However, the state had to make a careful assessment of the impact of the proposed measures on parents and children and that any possible alternatives to removing the children had been weighed. In the case of J, it had been reasonable not to give K advance warning of the emergency care order since this could have had dangerous consequences. However, the reasons were not sufficiently compelling to justify the extremely harsh measure of taking a new-born baby into public care at the momemt of birth. Other possible protective measures could have been considered. The removal of the child from her care was disproportionate and not necessary in a democractic society. There had been a violation of art 8 in relation to J. In relation to M, K and T had recognised that K could not care for M. He had already been separated from his family as a result of his voluntary placement. There had been no violation of art 8 in relation to him.

In relation to the care orders, the state had a primary task to safeguard the children. The state had been entitled to place the children into public care given K's serious mental illness and the family's social problems. However, a care order should be a temporary measure with the ultimate aim of reuniting parent and child, subject to the best interests of the child. In this case no serious or sustained effort had been made to see if K and T could bond with the children. The state should have re-examined the situation from time to time so see if there had been any improvement in the family situation. Rare or non-existent contact between natural parents and children could progressively diminish and eventually destroy the possibility of re-unification. The state had breached art 8 by its failure to take sufficient steps to reunify the family.

There had been no breach of art 13 since rights of appeal had been available to, and had been exercised by, K and T.

By contrast in *L* v *Finland* [2000] 2 FLR 118 L was married to W. They had two children, A and B. W became mentally ill after the birth of B and went into hospital on a number of occasions. Social services helped the family. In 1992 the marriage was in difficulties and the children were placed in interim care, principally on the basis of suspected sexual abuse of A. The sexual abuse was not proved but the local authority decided to keep the children in care because of L and W's inability to care for them and the damage done to their development. The children were placed with foster parents and the parents' contact with them restricted. Contact by the paternal grandparents was prohibited. Appeals against the orders of the local authority were dismissed. L was deprived of the right to an oral hearing in relation to his appeal. L and W then divorced. After further reviews of the case A said that she had been sexually abused by L and her paternal grandfather. Both she and B were nervous about contact with L. Contact with L was limited to four times a year. W and the maternal grandmother supported A and B staying in foster care. L and the paternal grandfather complained that their rights under arts 6, 8 and 13 had been violated.

It was held, dismissing the complaints under arts 8 and 13 but upholding the complaint under art 6, the decision of the authorities that care in the foster home had better prospects of success than the continuation of support for the family was reasonable. There was nothing to suggest that the decision-making process failed to involve L to a sufficient degree to protect their interests. The authorities acted within the margin of appreciation afforded to them in such matters.

A fair balance had to be struck between the interests of the child in remaining in public care and those of the parent in being reunited with his child. In carrying out this balancing exercise the court will attach particular importance to the best interests of the child which, depending on the circumstances, may override those of the parent. In particular, a parent cannot be entitled under art 8 to have such measures taken as would harm the child's health and development. In this case the parents had separated and no longer constituted a family. The rights and interests of W must also be taken into account. The authorities in the exercise of its discretion could decide that the maintenance of the care order was in the best interests of the children.

While the alleged sexual abuse had never been confirmed by a judicial finding, the children's interests made it justifiable for the authorities to reduce the father's right to access. The refusal of all contact, even in the case of a child–grandparent relationship, was very drastic: the court accepted that in these circumstances the authorities could reasonably consider it necessary in a democratic society.

The right to a public hearing under art 6(1) entails an entitlement to an oral hearing unless there are exceptional cirumstances that justify dispensing with such a hearing. In view of the lack of any previous oral hearing prior to L's appeal to an administrative court, and bearing in mind what was at stake for the applicants, there were no exceptional circumstances justifying the lack of an oral hearing before the court. There had been a violation of art 6.

In *Scott* v *United Kingdom* [2000] 1 FLR 958 S had a severe alcohol problem. In 1991 she gave birth to a child, C. In 1992 C was placed with foster parents after C's father placed her into the care of the local authority and S started attending a unit for assessment and family therapy. The local authority planned to rehabilitate C with S. There was a difference in expert opinion as to how S could control her drinking and care for the child. In June 1993 S relapsed. In July 1993 S entered a clinic for alcohlics at the local authority's expense. The local authority reconsidered its plans for C. Relations between S and the local authority broke down. At a meeting in September 1993, to which S was invited but did not attend, it decided to plan for C's adoption. In October 1993 S left the clinic and relapsed into drinking again on learning of the local authority's plans. In 1994 care proceedings were started and a care order eventually made. In October 1994 the court dispensed with S's consent in relation to freeing C for adoption. It dismissed her application to discharge the care order. In November 1994 C was moved to her adoptive parents and in July, 1996 she was adopted by them. S complained under art 8 that she had not been properly consulted as to the decision in October 1994 to free C for adoption and that the court had not properly supervised the local authority pursuant to art 13.

It was held that the application was inadmissible. There was no violation of art 8 because the interference with S's right to family life was necessary in a democratic society and porportionate to the aim of protecting the rights of the child (art 8(2)). Authorities enjoyed a wide margin of appreciation in assessing the necessity of taking a child into care. Stricter scrutiny was required for any further limitations where they might curtail family relations between parents and a young child. It had not been established that the authorities had acted in a way which did not allow S to put her case across. The decision-making process was not unfair. S had been given a proper opportunity to make her views known. She had been legally aided and represented in the 1994 court proceedings. She had been invited to, and taken part in, meetings organised by the local authority concerning C's future. The September 1993 meeting was an internal administrative meeting designed to formulate the local authority's strategy. The decision was not irrevocable and S had ample opportunity to challenge it thereafter. Even allowing a narrow margin of appreciation the domestic court could not be criticised on the merits of the case for protracted proceedings nor for finally reaching the conclusion that C be freed for adoption. There was no indication that the authorities contributed to S's failure to overcome her drinking problem. In the absence of any violation of art 8, there was no violation of art 13.

## 15.2 The legal position of parents with respect to their children

### Married parents of children

*Parental responsibility.* Parents have *parental responsibility* for their children (see s2(1) CA 1989). 'Parental responsibility' means 'all the rights, duties, powers, responsibilities and authority which by law a parent of a child had in relation to the child and his property' (see s3(1) CA 1989).

That parental responsibility stays with the parent even if some other person subsequently acquires parental responsibility for the child (see s2(6) CA 1989) though he or she cannot act in any way which would be incompatible with any order made with respect to the child under the Children Act 1989 (see s2(8) CA 1989). Adoption will end parental responsibility.

*Mothers and fathers have equal parental responsibility.* Each parent shall have parental responsibility for the child (see s2(1) CA 1989).

NOTE: The rule of law that a father is the natural guardian of his legitimate child is abolished (see s2(4) CA 1989).

Parental responsibility may be shared between parents and in some cases with third parties (see s2(5) CA 1989).

*Parental responsibility cannot be transferred or lost.* A person who has parental responsibility for a child may not surrender or transfer any part of that responsibility to another but may arrange for some or all of it to be met by one or more persons acting on his or her behalf (see s2(9) CA 1989). The person with whom any such arrangement is made may himself or herself be a person who already has parental responsibility for the child concerned (eg the other parent) (see s2(10) CA 1989).

BUT the making of any such arrangement cannot affect any liability of the person making it which may arise from any failure to meet any part of his or her parental responsibility for the child (see s2(11) CA 1989).

NOTE: As has already been seen a person who has parental responsibility for a child shall not cease to have parental responsibility solely because some other person subsequently acquires parental responsibility for the child (s2(6)) (eg on a divorce if a residence order is made in favour of the mother and stepfather, the stepfather will acquire parental responsibility under the residence order, but the natural father will continue to have parental responsibility and share it with the mother and stepfather, each being able to act independently from the others, though not in a way inconsistent with court orders).

*A person with parental responsibility can act independently.* Where more than one person has parental responsibility for a child each of them may act alone and without the other (or others) in meeting that responsibility (s2(7)) (excluding matters requiring parental consent, eg adoption). Such action cannot be in any way which would be incompatible with any order made with respect to the child under the Children Act 1989 (see s2(8) CA 1989).

### Unmarried parents of children

Where a child's mother and father were not married to each other at the time of the child's birth the mother shall have parental responsibility for the child (see s2(2)(a) CA 1989).

The father cannot have parental responsibility unless he applies to have such responsibility under s4(1)(a) CA 1989 or under a 'parental responsibility agreement' with the mother (see s4(1)(b) CA 1989) or he is appointed a guardian (see s5 CA 1989) or he obtains a residence order (see s12(1) CA 1989).

The reason that unmarried fathers do not have the same legal status as married fathers is that the position of the unmarried father can range from an isolated act of intercourse with the mother (after which the man has nothing to do with the mother or child) to a father living with the mother and playing a full part in the child's life. An unmarried father with commitment to a child can take steps to acquire parental responsibility by agreement or by court order.

The court will follow the principles established under s4 Family Law Reform Act 1987 which s4 CA 1989 replaced. In *Re H (Minors) (Local Authority: Parental Rights) (No 3)* [1991] 2 All ER 185; [1991] Fam Law 151 and *Re C (Minors)* [1992] 2 All ER 86 three criteria were laid down for considering whether an unmarried father should be given parental responsibility for his child.

1. the degree of commitment he had shown towards his child;
2. the degree of attachment between him and his child;
3. the reason why he wanted parental responsibility for his child.

The fact that he may not be able to exercise his parental responsibility in practice (eg because the mother refused to allow him to have anything to do with the child) was not necessarily fatal to an application that he be granted parental responsibility.

This reasoning was applied in *Re H (Minors) (Parental Responsibility)* [1993] 1 FLR 484 where an unmarried couple, M and F, had a child, C, now aged two. M left taking C with her. She developed a relationship with another man, H, whom she married. She refused to allow F to have contact with C because H refused to allow it. H and M wished to apply to adopt C. F applied for a contact order. By agreement he was given contact fortnightly but H later said that the contact was endangering his marriage to M. H and M and C went to live in Scotland and contact ceased. F applied for contact again and for a parental responsibility order. The judge refused both applications. F appealed.

HELD: Allowing the appeal, though the judge's decision about contact was not plainly wrong it was clear that a parental responsibility order should have been made under s4 CA 1989 since this would protect F's position should there be an adoption application or should any misfortune befall M and H. In considering such an application the child's welfare was paramount. The court would consider the extent of the father's commitment to the child, his current relationship with the child and the reasons for his application (following *Re H* and *Re C*, both considered above). The fact that the father could not enforce such an order because of the mother and her new relationship did not prevent such an order from being made.

This approach was applied in *Re A (Minors) (Parental Responsibility)* [1993] Fam Law 464 where F had lived with M for three months, had been present at the child's birth and his name appeared on the birth certificate. M and F's relationship deteriorated. F then did not see the child for a year. He applied for contact and parental responsibility both of which M opposed.

HELD: Refusing the order for contact but granting the order for parental responsibility, F had shown considerable commitment to the child.

*Re A* was followed in *Re C and V (Minors) (Parental Responsibility Order)* [1998] 1 FLR 392 where it was again emphasised that parental responsibility and contact are different concepts. It is therefore possible to refuse an order for contact to an unmarried father but grant him a parental responsibility order. The granting of parental responsibility was not concerned with day to day decisions about the child's life or the decision as to where the child should live. It conferred the status held by a married father. A child should grow up with a favourable and positive image of an absent parent. It was important that wherever possible the law should confer on the concerned father the stamp of approval where he had shown himself willing and anxious to pick up the responsibility of fatherhood. The court should not deny or avoid it. An appeal by an unmarried father against an order dismissing his application for contact failed but his appeal against the refusal to make a parental responsibility order was allowed.

In *Re G (A Minor) (Parental Responsibility Order)* [1994] 1 FLR 504 the father and mother, who were not married, had a six-year-old child. The parents separated. The child remained with the mother but was taken into the care of the local authority while the mother underwent a detoxification programme to deal with her abuse of alcohol. The father had contact with the child at the discretion of the local authority. Social workers found the father awkward, difficult and unresponsive to them. He applied for parental responsibility. His application was refused. He appealed.

HELD: The appeal was allowed as the welfare of the child was paramount (see s1(1) Children Act 1989). It was assumed that an order would be in the child's interests if the father satisfied the criteria set out in *Re H* (above), namely: he had shown a sufficient degree of commitment between himself and the child; that there was a sufficient degree of attachment between him and the child; and that his reasons for applying for parental responsibility were not improper or wrong. The criteria in *Re H* were not exhaustive but indicated the factors to be considered. Once these criteria had been satisfied the court ought to grant the father parental responsibility even though the father was difficult, unresponsive and awkward. In this case the father had shown a lack of insight into the child's needs. He had been awkward and difficult with social workers. However, this was not a reason in itself to refuse parental responsibility. He had a good relationship with the child who was clearly attached to him. It was obviously in the child's interests that the father be given the legal status of parental responsibility.

In *Re P (A Minor) (Parental Responsibility Order)* [1994] 1 FLR 578 the child, P, was born to unmarried parents, M and F. F and M had a relationship for four years but lived with their respective parents. They then lived together for two months but separated in 1989, P staying with her mother, M. F successfully applied for contact and it was ordered that P reside with M. In 1992, M gained employment and allowed P to stay with F for four or five days a week. Relations between M and F became strained. In 1993 F applied for residence, contact and parental responsibility. The court dismissed his applications for residence and parental responsibility but made a contact order with the consent of both M and F which included staying contact for P with F. F's application for parental responsibility was dismissed because the court was concerned about the acrimony between M and F and that F would interfere in the day-to-day decisions affecting P's welfare.

HELD: The appeal was allowed as F had shown great love and concern for the child. He had played a major role in the child's life. An order that he have parental responsibility did not allow him to override the mother. Section 2(8) of the Children Act 1989 prevented him from acting in a way incompatible with another order such as the residence order. The fact that parents cannot co-operate is not a ground for refusing the order. If there was a dispute about any major decision affecting the child either party could apply for a specific issues order. If parental responsibility was misused either party could apply to the court for a prohibited steps order. Parental responsibility did not allow the father to interfere in the day-to-day management of the child's life when the child lives elsewhere.

*Re P* was followed in *Re S (Parental Responsibility)* [1995] 2 FLR 648 where the parents of a seven-year-old girl had intended to marry, had bought a flat in joint names and jointly registered the girl with the father's surname. The relationship broke down, but the father continued to pay maintenance plus the nursery fees for the child. In 1990 he was convicted of possessing obscene literature. The mother became reluctant to allow contact because she feared he might abuse the child. The father applied for defined contact and parental responsibility. No order was made for contact following s1(5) CA 1989. The court refused to make a parental responsibility order. The father appealed against the second decision.

HELD: Allowing the appeal, the father had satisfied the criteria for being granted parental responsibility. What was in issue was not the rights he might obtain but the conferring of status on a committed father. A child should grow up with self-esteem and have a favourable positive image of the absent parent. Wherever possible the law should confer the stamp of approval on a committed father to avoid the child growing up with some belief that the father is disqualified from fulfilling his parental role.

The grant of parental responsibility did not entitle the father to interfere in matters within the day-to-day management of the child's life. Any abuse of parental responsibility could be dealt with by applying to the court for a s8 order. Parental responsibility is about duties and responsibilities as well as rights and powers. A father who has shown real commitment to the child and to whom there is a positive attachment ought to assume the weight of those duties and cement that commitment and responsibility by sharing the responsibilities for the child with the mother.

A court should not use its power to make a parental responsibility order as a weapon to force a father to make maintenance. In *In Re H (Minors) (Parental Responsibility Order: Maintenance)* [1996] 1 FLR 867 the father had demonstrated a genuine interest in the children's welfare and education and was attached to them and had maintained contact with him. The fact that he had failed to provide maintenance for their upkeep was not a good reason for refusing to make a parental responsibility order until he had made such payments.

It is possible to terminate a parental responsibility order or agreement if a father acts in a way which is obviously harmful to the child (eg by seriously assaulting the child) (see *Re P (Terminating Parental Responsibility)* [1995] 1 FLR 1048).

An application for parental responsibility was refused in *Re P (Minors: Parental Responsibility Order)* [1997] 2 FLR 722 in which M and F were not married. They had two children, B born in 1989 and G in 1993. During the relationship F served a number of prison sentences for robbery offences. For his last offence he received a sentence of 15 years in 1994. His earliest date of release was 1998 or 1999. During 1995 relations between M and F became strained and contact between her and the children and F (via prison visits) reduced. She wished to move abroad and make a fresh start. In November, 1995 she decided to change the children's surname, both of whom had been registered at birth with F's surname. In 1996 F applied for contact and parental responsibility and for a specific issues order for the children's surnames to revert back to his surname. A contact order was made by agreement. The application for parental responsibility was dismissed and no specific issues order made. H appealed. It was held, dismissing his appeal, that the level of attachment between F and the children was minimal because of F's prison sentences. The court had applied the correct principles in dismissing the applications for parental responsibility. The change of name had taken place some time ago, the children were known by their new names at school and their medical records had presumably been changed. Though the children would have contact with F and their paternal grandparents it was unlikely that F would be able to play any physical role in their upbringing and the advantages of being known by the name of the only person who had their effective care was in their best interests. The conduct which led to his imprisonment was also relevant particularly since it was damaging for the children.

In *Re H (A Minor) (Parental Responsibility)* [1998] 1 FLR 855 a father who enjoyed supervised contact failed in his application for parental responsibility because on one occasion he had deliberately physically abused his son, had not been truthful about what had happened and had not shown the capacity to be necessarily responsible for the grant of a parental responsibility order. He had physically abused another child in the past. He had not been truthful about what had happened and had made no attempt to come to terms with what he had done. The judge considered him unfit to have contact unsupervised and made an order for supervised contact. An appeal against the decision refusing him parental responsibility was dismissed. The three factors of the degree of commitment towards the child, the degree of attachment already existing between the child and his father and the reasons of the father in applying for the order were starting points but were not the only relevant factors. The judge had been fully justified in deciding that a man who behaved in this manner towards his son was not fit to have parental responsibility for him, particularly because he had made no attempt to come to terms with what he had done.

In *Re P (Parental Responsibility)* [1998] 2 FLR 96 an unmarried father had shown commitment to the child but his motivation in seeking parental responsibility was improper and wrong (he had obscene photographs of young children and posed a risk of sexual abuse to the child) so the court used its discretion to refuse parental responsibility.

A father with severe, permanent brain injury was refused parental responsibility since he had a badly impaired memory, very poor reasoning ability and a propensity for violent and unpredictable behaviour and could not exercise parental responsibility (see *M* v *M (Parental Responsibility)* [1999] 2 FLR 737).

See also *Re M (Contact: Parental Responsibility)* [2001] 2 FLR 342 in which an unmarried father had shown commitment to his daughter and was attached to her. However, relations between the father and the mother and her husband were very strained. Despite the father displaying the three factors of commitment, attachment and motivation, parental responsibility was refused because of the predicted misuse of parental responsibility by the father and the stress to the mother which would undermine her ability to care for the child (who was severely disabled).

## Government proposals on parental responsibility

Section 111 of the Adoption and Children Act 2002 (when in force) will amend s4 CA 1989 to give an unmarried father parental responsibility if he is registered as the child's father on the birth certificate. The mother would have to consent to him being registered. The change will not apply to fathers who are registered on the child's birth certificate before s111 comes into force. It will only apply to fathers who are registered after s111 has come into force.

Section 112 of the Adoption and Children Act 2002 (when in force) will create a s4A Children Act 1989 allowing a step-parent to acquire parental responsibility for a child of his or her spouse either by agreement with the spouse or by order of the court. This would provide an alternative to adoption since it would give the step-parent parental responsibility.

## European Convention on Human Rights and parental responsibility

It has been argued that English and Welsh law discriminates against unmarried fathers by treating them differently to married fathers in terms of parental responsibility. In particular, it has been argued that the law infringes art 14 of the European Convention on Human Rights which prohibits any discrimination in the enjoyment of Convention rights and freedoms (eg the right to family life under art 8). This argument was determined in *B* v *United Kingdom* [2000] 1 FLR 1 in which J was born to unmarried parents, F and M (who was an Italian national), in 1994. F and M separated soon afterwards, J remaining with his mother. F, the father, had regular contact. In February 1997 F applied for a parental responsibility order, a contact order, a prohibited steps order to prevent M from taking J to Italy and a specific issues order regarding J's surname. In March 1997 M took C to Italy. A few days later F sought ex parte orders for J's return. The High Court held that J's removal was not unlawful since F did not have parental responsibility. It declined to make any order since J had always lived with M and it was inappropriate to order M and J's return. F's appeal failed. F then appealed to the European Court of Human Rights, arguing that his rights as an unmarried father had been wrongfully breached under art 8 (right to family life) and art 14 (no discrimination in applying rights) of the European Convention on Human Rights. It was held that the application was inadmissible. For the purpose of art 14 a difference in treatment is discriminatory if it has no objective or reasonable justification, ie does not pursue a legitimate aim or if there is no reasonable relationship or proportionality between the aims employed and the aim sought to be realised. The relationship between unmarried fathers and their children varies from ignorance and indifference to a close stable relationship indistinguishable from the conventional family-based unit. There exists an objective and reasonable justification for the difference in treatment between married and unmarried fathers with regard to the automatic acquisition of parental rights (*McMichael* v *United Kingdom* (1995) 20 EHRR 205 followed).

### Third parties

Any person in whose favour a residence order is made will have parental responsibility for the child while the residence order is in force (see s12(2) CA 1989).

Any person without parental responsibility but who is caring for the child will be able to do what is reasonable in all the circumstances to safeguard or promote the child's welfare (see s3(5) CA 1989).

## What is parental responsibility?

'Parental responsibility' is only given a general definition in s3(1) CA 1989. In general terms it means the responsibility and right to make choices over important issues regarding the child such as:

1. choosing where the child should live;
2. deciding where a child should be educated (including the right to see school reports);
3. choosing which religion (if any) the child will be brought up in;
4. deciding on what medical treatment the child should receive;
5. deciding on where the child should travel (including the right to apply for a passport for the child).

However, family life is too complicated for there to be an exhaustive list of what parents (or other people with parental responsibility) can and should do. However, certain aspects of parental responsibility have received particular attention in both statute and caselaw.

### The responsibility to care for and control the child

This general responsibility ends when:

1. a child reaches the age of majority, namely, eighteen years (see s1 Family Law Reform Act 1969); or
2. when a child marries (which may be once the child becomes sixteen); or

3. when a child enters the armed forces; or
4. when an adoption order is made.

The responsibility to control the child dwindles as the child gets older and becomes mature enough to make his or her own decisions. That responsibility may end up as nothing more than a responsibility to give advice to the child (see *Hewer* v *Bryant* [1969] 3 WLR 425; [1969] 3 All ER 578 quoted with approval by the House of Lords in *Gillick* v *West Norfolk and Wisbech Area Health Authority* [1985] 3 All ER 402).

The responsibility to control the child includes moderately and reasonably punishing the child. However, unreasonable physical punishment can give rise to criminal proceedings (eg *R* v *Smith* [1985] Crim LR 42) and/or to a breach of the child's rights. See *A* v *United Kingdom (Human Rights: Punishment of Child)* [1998] 2 FLR 959 in which a child, A, aged nine, was beaten on more than one occasion by his stepfather, S, with a garden cane which was applied with considerable force. S was charged with assault occasioning actual bodily harm but raised the defence of reasonable chastisement. He was found not guilty. A subsequently complained to the European Commission of Human Rights that the state had failed to protect him from ill-treatment by S in violation of art 3 of the Convention for the Protection of Human Rights and Fundamental Freedoms. The Commission expressed the opinion that there had been a violation of art 3 and referred the case to the European Court of Human Rights. It was held that art 3 required contracting states to ensure that individuals were not subject to inhuman or degrading treatment or punishment. Children and other vulnerable individuals were entitled to state protection by way of effective deterrence against serious breaches of personal integrity. Under English law on a charge of assault on a child the prosecution had to prove beyond reasonable doubt that the assault went beyond reasonable chastisement. In A's case the beating by S reached the necessary level of severity to be prohibited by art 3 yet S was acquitted. Accordingly the law had not provided A with adequate protection against ill-treatment contrary to art 3. The UK government had accepted that the law failed to provide adequate protection and required amendment. A was awarded compensation of £10,000 plus costs.

The decision cannot be said to prohibit the use of physical punishment against children. In *Costello-Roberts* v *United Kingdom* (1995) 19 EHRR 112 three slaps with a slipper on the child's clothed buttocks were not regarded as sufficiently serious as to amount to a violation of art 3. One has to balance the nature and degree of force used and the age and situation of the child.

In *R* v *H (Assault of Child: Reasonable Chastisement)* [2001] 3 FCR 144 it was held that a father charged with assaulting his son with a leather belt across his back several times could plead reasonable chastisement. The jury had to decide whether the chastisement was reasonable and moderate. For punishment to be degrading and in breach of art 3 of the European Convention on Human Rights (ECHR) it had to attain a particular level of severity, the degree of severity being judged on the facts of each case. Not every case of corporal punishment breached art 3.

In *R (On the application of Williamson)* v *Secretary of State for Education and Employment* [2003] 1 FLR 1 the claimants were head teachers and parents at certain Christian schools who wished to maintain the right of teachers to administer reasonable chastisement in independent Christian schools. They argued that the restriction on using corporal punishment in s548 Education Act 1996 infringed their human rights. It was held that while a religious belief in the correctness of corporal punishment could attract the protection of art 9 ECHR, the restriction did not interfere with the manifestation of religious belief since the parents (rather than the teachers) could administer reasonable chastisement.

In January 2000 the government issued a consultation document on the physical punishment of children called *Protecting Children, Supporting Parents*. It ruled out the possibility of making unlawful all smacking and forms of physical rebuke. It said that some mild physical rebuke was considered acceptable by most loving parents. However, it discussed *A* v *United Kingdom* (above) in which the level of physical punishment inflicted on a child was such that it breached art 3 of the European Convention on Human Rights. The step-parent was not punished for the injuries he inflicted on the child because he was acquitted by a jury of assault occasioning actual bodily harm on the basis of 'reasonable chastisement'. UK law was held to be in breach of the Convention for not protecting the child given that art 3 had been breached. The consultation document asked for views on defining what 'reasonable chastisement' should mean so that the term was in accordance with the European Convention. Another option was to exclude the defence of reasonable chastisement once actual bodily harm had been inflicted on a child. The document also considers whether there should be limits on who can inflict physical punishment on children (eg restricted to parents).

The Scottish Executive proposed in 2001 a total ban on blows to the head, shaking and the use of implements, and a ban on the physical punishment of children up to the age of two years. Parents would retain the right to reasonably chastise their children within these limits. The government may include proposals on reasonable chastisement in the Criminal Justice Bill before the 2002–3 Parliament.

Article 19 of the UN Convention on the Rights of the Child 1989 obliges member states to protect the child from all forms of physical violence.

## Parental consent is required for the marriage of a child aged sixteen to under eighteen

A child who wishes to marry between the ages of sixteen and eighteen needs the consent of his or her parent to marry (see s3 Marriage Act 1949) but this is subject to the child's right to apply to a court for the court to give consent which replaces the consent which the parent refuses to give. If no consent has been given to the marriage the marriage will not be void in any event.

## The child's surname

Children usually take the same surname as their parents. Problems can arise if the parents separate and perhaps divorce. The mother may have the child living with her. She may then live with another man and remarry. The mother may then wish to take the surname of her new husband. The mother and stepfather may want the child to be known by their new surname. This may strengthen the new relationship, avoid embarrassment for the child and be convenient. The child's natural father may oppose the loss of an important link with his child, namely the use of his surname. The legal position in dealing with such a dispute is as follows:

*Where a residence order is in force.* No person may take steps to cause the child named in the residence order to be known by a new surname without the written consent of every person with parental responsibility or with the leave of the court (s13(1) CA 1989).

See *Re B (Change of Surname)* [1996] 1 FLR 6 in which W and H divorced. The three teenage children lived with her, had no contact with H and wished to have nothing to do with him. W remarried and applied for a specific issues order under s8 CA 1989 for the three children to be known by her new surname. The children supported the application. H opposed the application on the basis that it would sever any relationship between him and the children. The court refused W's application. She appealed but her appeal was dismissed. It was held that her application was not one under s8 CA 1989 but an application under s13 CA 1989 for leave for the children to be known by the new surname. The welfare of the children was paramount but the court did not have to apply the welfare checklist in s1(3). Residence or contact orders would not normally be made if they ran flatly contrary to the wishes of normal adolescent children. This did not apply to a formal change of surname. In the present climate of divorce, remarriage and cohabitation there was no opprobrium for a child to have a different surname from other adults in the same household. It would damage the link between the children and their natural father. The grant of leave would have served to give the court's approval to a process not in the children's best interests.

Another example can be found in *Re C (Minors) (Change of Surname)* [1998] 1 FLR 549 in which M and F were the unmarried parents of children aged eight and seven. The children originally used M's maiden name. From 1992 the children lived with F under a residence order and from 1993 he caused them to use his surname, not realising that such a change was prohibited except with M's consent or leave of the court. M had since remarried and no longer used her maiden name. However she wished the children to retain it for official purposes in order to preserve links with her. The court granted leave to cause the children to be known by F's name (though with M's surname as a middle name). M appealed. It was held, dismissing the appeal, although it was of fundamental importance for children to have an enduring relationship with both parents, notwithstanding their separation, where the mother no longer carried her maiden name, it would not appear to be in the interests of the children, who were living with their father and had informally adopted his name, to carry her maiden name. Although *Re B (Change of Surname)*

[1996] 1 FLR 791 recognised the importance to such links, nothing in that judgement should be taken as indicating that it was desirable in principle that children should have different names for different purposes. Although the stamp of parenthood reflected by a surname should not lightly be erased, M herself no longer used the name so it was hard to see how its retention by the children for any purpose could significantly assist to preserve a link with her.

*Where there is no residence order in force and both natural parents have parental responsibility.* The parent wishing to change the child's surname can only do so with the consent of the other natural parent or by a court order (eg a specific issues order pursuant to s8 CA 1989). See *Practice Direction (Child: Change of Surname)* [1995] 1 WLR 365; [1995] 1 All ER 832; [1995] 1 FLR 458).

For example, see *Re PC (Change of Surname)* [1997] 2 FLR 730 in which F and M were married and had three children aged 12, 10 and 6. F and M separated in 1993 and divorced in 1994. The children lived with M. Contact with F ceased in 1995. In May 1996 M remarried. She had known her second husband (H2) since 1993 and the children knew him well. The children began to use H2's surname in 1996. Their names were then changed by deed poll in October 1996. The children signed the deed poll. The headmaster of the children's school sought advice when asked by M to amend the school records. The advice was that their names could not be changed without F's consent. The family doctor recorded the change of surname. M applied for a specific issues order that the school recognise the change of name. She argued that s2(7) Children Act 1989 allowed her to change the names unilaterally and that F's consent was not required. It was held that a parent with parental responsibility could not unilaterally change a child's surname if the other parent also had parental responsibility. Although s2(7) CA 1989 enabled one person with parental responsibility to act alone this did not extend to change the child's surname without the agreement of the other parent with parental responsibility (*Y v Y (Child Surname)* [1973] Fam 147 applied). Where a residence order was in force, s13 CA 1989 applied which prevented a change of name without the consent of every person with parental responsibility or leave of the court. Where a residence order was not in force the situation was the same. If only one parent had parental responsibility then that parent could change a child's name without the consent of the other parent.

In this particular case the court criticised the children being asked to sign the deed polls stating that this should not have happened.

Another example can be found in *Re C (A Minor) (Change of Surname)* [1998] 2 FLR 656 in which M and F were unmarried. In 1992 they had a child, C who was registered in F's name. In 1994 the relationship ended and shortly after M changed C's surname by deed poll. In 1995 F applied for parental responsibility and contact. After prolonged litigation it was agreed that he have parental responsibility and staying contact. In 1997 F applied under s8 CA 1989 for a specific issues order that C be known by F's surname. His application was refused. F appealed. It was held, dismissing the appeal, that disputed issues about a child's name should be referred to the court. A change of name was a profound matter and not simply a formal factor. A child's name was important and changes should be made gradually. Preserving and strengthening the link between the child and the absent parent through the maintenance of the child's surname was as important when good contact was being enjoyed as when there is not sufficient contact. The welfare checklist applied (as it also applied for an application under s13 Children Act 1989). A change of name must be justified as being in the child's best interests. Was this the case in 1994? M's justification for the change of name was insufficient. However the court did not consider, on the facts of this case, it was in the child's interests to change his/her name back to that of F. The child's name had been changed for three years. There was a heavy responsibility on those who seek to change a child's name. Good and cogent reasons should be shown to allow such a change. Changes of name should be dealt with by the court and not by deed poll. Another example of a court disapproving of a change of name but confirming the change because it had been in place for some years can be found in *Y* v *Y (Child: Surname)* [1973] 3 WLR 80; [1973] 2 All ER 574 in which a mother unilaterally changed the surname of her daughters but the court was not called upon to rule upon the matter until four years had elapsed.

See also *Re T (Change of Surname)* [1998] 2 FLR 620 in which M was married to H. They had two children who had H's surname. She had a third child by another man who also carried H's surname. M then cohabited with T and gave birth to twins who were registered with T's surname. T was granted parental responsibility. The relationship ended. M changed the surnames of the twins by deed poll to H's surname. Seven months after the change of name T applied for contact and for a specific issues order that his children use his surname. The judge held that in the absence of a residence order there was nothing to prevent M changing the twin's surname without T's consent. T appealed. It was held, allowing the appeal, the decision was wrong. Either the consent of the other parent or the leave of the court was required before a child's name could be changed, certainly when both parents had parental responsibility. The fact that the children had become known by the new surname by a wrongful act was not a justification for refusing T's application. The convenience of medical and school records showing the same surname for all the children in the same family was slight compared with T's application.

In *A* v *Y (Child's Surname)* [1999] 2 FLR 5 the parents were married. When the child was born the mother registered the child's surname in her maiden name since the marriage was in difficulties. The parents divorced. The father did not realise that he could take action about the child's surname until the child was aged two-and-a-half. He then applied for a specific issues order under s8 CA 1989. His application was dismissed. The child was then four years old and was known by her mother's name at nursery school. The father's delay had allowed a status quo to become established and a change would cause confusion and embarassment for the child.

See also *Re S (Change of Name: Cultural Factors)* [2001] 2 FLR 1005 which dealt with difficult issues involving a child being called by a Sikh or Muslim surname.

*Where there is no residence order in force and only the mother has parental responsibility (ie the natural father is an unmarried father who has not acquired parental responsibility either by agreement or by court order).* The mother can act unilaterally in changing the child's surname though the father can seek to prevent this by applying for a prohibited steps or specific issues order (pursuant to s8 CA 1989).

For example see *Dawson* v *Wearmouth* [1999] 2 WLR 960; [1998] 2 All ER 353; [1999] 1 FLR 1167 in which M was married to H and had two children. They then separated, the children living with M. M then had a relationship with F and a child, A was born. One month later M and F separated. M wished A to be known by her surname which was H's surname. F applied for a specific issues order so that A would have his surname. He stressed the importance of his link with A being marked by her using his surname. The order was made. M appealed. It was held, allowing the appeal, since this was not a case in which s13 Children Act 1989 applied (since there was no residence order in force) then the matter had to be dealt with by a s8 order. Changing a child's name was a profound matter whatever the age of the child. The court had to apply the welfare checklist. M's choice of surname was logical and could not be criticised. These circumstances coupled with the important factor that M's married surname was the child's duly registered name were very powerful factors in M's favour which could only be displaced by strong countervailing circumstances. No specific issues order was made. There was an appeal to the House of Lords which dismissed the appeal. Section 1 CA 1989 applied so any change in the child's surname had to lead to an improvement in the child's welfare. In particular s1(5) applied so it was for the party seeking the change to establish that such a change was better for the child than to refuse it. Lord Mackay expressed the view that any dispute about a child's surname should be referred to the court whether or not a residence order was in force, whoever has or has not parental responsibility. A disputed change should not be made unilaterally.

If the court is called upon to resolve a dispute about a child's surname it will treat the child's welfare as its paramount consideration and, if considering a specific issues or prohibited steps order, apply the welfare checklist (see s1(3), (4) CA 1989). Courts treat a child's surname as a serious matter, particularly in relation to the link it may provide with a natural father. Other examples of cases in which leave was refused because of it would sever the link with the natural father include:

1. *W* v *A (Child: Surname)* [1981] 1 All ER 100 even though the children were emigrating to Australia with their mother and step-father and were aged 12 and 13 years and wanted the change.
2. *Re F (Child: Surname)* [1994] Fam Law 12 in which, after a divorce, the mother

wished her and the children to be known by her maiden name – it was held that there was no justification for the change of the children's name.

3. *Re W; Re A; Re B (Change of Name)* [1999] 2 FLR 390 which concerned three appeals involving disputes between parents about their child's surname. In *Re W* the parents had a child who was given the mother's surname. The parents later married and had a second child who was given the father's surname. The court refused the father's application for the first child to be known by the father's surname. In *Re A* the parents had a child who was given the father's surname. The parents then married but the father was sentenced to a long term of imprisonment. The mother divorced him. The court allowed her to change the child's surname to her maiden name so that he was not identified with his father. In *Re B* the children were registered with their father's surname. He was convicted of indecent assault on two older children. The court allowed the mother to change the children's surname to her own. It was held that where the parents remain unmarried the degree of the father's commitment to the child, the quality of any contact and the existence or absence of parental responsibility were all relevant factors. Where the parents got married the legitimation of the child was but one factor. If the child had been registered in the father's surname there had to be strong reasons to change that surname.

4. *Re R (A Child)* [2001] 2 FLR 1358 in which the child lived with his mother but was registered with his father's surname. The mother then changed the child's surname to that of her partner by deed poll. The Court of Appeal held that the use of the partner's surname had an insecure foundation. The better solution would be to combine the father's and mother's surnames. This reflected Spanish custom (Spain being where the mother and child intended to move).

See *Re H (Child's Name: First Name)* [2002] Fam Law 340 which considered a dispute between separated married parents concerning their baby's first name. It was held that first names were less concrete than surnames. Children commonly had more than one first name. The courts could not prevent the parent caring for the child (in this case the mother) from using the first name of her choice at home and with outside bodies, provided she recognised that fact that the child had a fixed series of names on his/her birth certificate.

## Medical treatment of the child
Generally speaking:

1. a parent with parental responsibility for a child under 16 must consent to medical treatment of his or her child before such treatment can be lawfully given;

2. a child aged 16 or over may consent to medical treatment without parental consent (s8 Family Law Reform Act 1969);

3. in some cases the court will allow a child under 16 to give a valid consent to medical treatment;

4. the court retains the right to override the wishes of the parent and/or the child (even if 16 years or older) and allow lawful medical treatment to be given in the best interests of the child against the wishes of the parent and/or child;

5. a person who does not have parental responsibility for a child but who has care of the child may do what is reasonable in all the circumstances of the case for the purposes of safeguarding or promoting the child's welfare (s3(5) Children Act 1989 – eg allowing a teacher or child minder to respond to an emergency without parental consent).

*A child under 16 years giving valid consent to medical treatment without the agreement of his/her parents.* The leading case is *Gillick* v *West Norfolk and Wisbech Area Health Authority* [1985] 3 All ER 402 in which the House of Lords decided that a doctor could lawfully give contraceptive advice to a girl under 16 years of age without her parents' consent. Lord Fraser accepted that parental rights to control a child existed for the benefit of the child and not the parents and that, in most cases, parents relaxed their control over their children gradually as the child developed. The degree of parental control varied according to the child's understanding and intelligence. In the overwhelming majority of cases the best judges of a child's welfare were the parents and normally important medical treatment would be carried out only with parental consent. However, there could be circumstances in which a doctor was a better judge than the parents of medical advice and treatment in the interests of the child's welfare. There was no provision which compelled him to hold that a girl under the age of 16 lacked the legal capacity to give a valid consent to such medical treatment, provided she had sufficient understanding and intelligence to know what was involved. Lord Scarman agreed, holding that, unless or until Parliament intervened, the courts should establish flexible principles to do justice in the particular circumstances of each case.

The *Gillick* case has led to the concept of the *Gillick* competent child, ie the child with sufficient understanding and intelligence to give a valid consent to medical treatment.

*Gillick* competence has to have a lasting basis. In *Re R (A Minor) (Wardship: Medical Treatment)* [1992] 1 FLR 190; [1991] 4 All ER 177 a 15-year-old girl had a history of disturbed behaviour. She suffered from a psychotic state in which she was sometimes rational and sometimes not. When rational she refused medical treatment. She was made a ward of court. It was held that for a child to a have *Gillick* capacity there had to be a full understanding on a lasting basis as to the consequences of the treatment and its withdrawal. The girl did not have a lasting capacity and so the court could authorise medication.

In *Re L (Medical Treatment: Gillick Competence)* [1998] 2 FLR 810 a 14-year-old girl received serious burns. She was a Jehovah's Witness and did not want a blood transfusion which was needed to save her from a painful death. The dreadful consequences of her refusal were not explained to her because it was considered too distressing for her. She was held not to be *Gillick* competent for the proposed treatment. She had led a sheltered life in the context of her family and religious community. She had only a limited understanding of her grave situation. The proposed treatment was vital to her survival and was authorised. The case illustrates that *Gillick* competence relates to the particular child and the particular treatment. A child may be *Gillick* competent in relation to minor treatment but not in relation to major treatment. In any event the court can override a *Gillick* competent child when the court is of the view that the treatment is vital to the child's welfare.

***Overriding the wishes of* Gillick *competent child.*** The extent of a 16-year-old's right to determine her own medical treatment was discussed in *Re W (A Minor) (Medical Treatment)* [1992] 3 WLR 758; [1992] 4 All ER 627. Here a 16-year-old girl (W) was in local authority care. W suffered from severe anorexia nervosa and was admitted to a specialist residential unit. The local authority wished to remove her to a hospital but W wished to stay where she was and cure herself. The local authority asked the court to direct that W be moved to the hospital and be given medical treatment without her consent. The court granted the application. W appealed. Her condition then deteriorated to the extent that she had to be removed to the hospital as an emergency measure. It was held, dismissing the appeal, that the court could override her wishes in her best interests even where she had sufficient understanding and intelligence to make an informed decision about refusing medical treatment where such refusal would lead to death or serious injury. The court approached its decision by strongly favouring the child's wishes. Section 8 FLRA 1969 enabled a child of 16 years or older to consent to medical treatment which would otherwise trespass on the child's person but s8 did give such a child the absolute right to refuse medical treatment.

***Overriding the wishes of a non-*Gillick *competent child.*** If a child is held not to be *Gillick* competent then the court will have little hesitation in overriding his/her wishes in the child's best interests (see *Re S (A Minor) (Consent to Medical Treatment)* (below)).

*Gillick* competence can be applied to an older child. In *A Metropolitan Borough Council v BB* [1997] 1 FLR 767 a 17-year-old crack-cocaine addict refused to consent to medical treatment. She was treated as not being *Gillick* competent and treatment was authorised.

***Overriding the wishes of the parent and/or the child***
WHEN THE CHILD DOES NOT CONSENT BUT THE PARENT DOES. In *Re R (A Minor) (Wardship: Medical Treatment)* (above) Lord Donaldson held that where a *Gillick* competent child had the capacity to consent to medical treatment that capacity was concurrent with that of the parent. Only failure to consent or refusal of consent by both parent and child could then create a veto. The consent of either parent or the child enabled treatment to be lawfully undertaken. In the absence of such consent the court could override the wishes of the parent and the child in the best interests

of the child. This approach was followed in *Re K, W and H (Minors) (Medical Treatment)* [1993] 1 FLR 855 which involved two 15-year-olds and a 14-year-old in separate appeals relating to their refusal to consent to medical treatment in a special unit. In each case the child's parents consented to the treatment. It was held that while a *Gillick* competent child could consent to medical treatment, if he or she declined to do so then consent could still be given by someone else with parental rights and responsibilities. Only a refusal by all those having power of veto could create a veto. See also *Re M (Medical Treatment: Consent)* [1999] Fam Law 753 in which the court authorised an urgent transplant operation against the wishes of a 15-year-old *Gillick* competent child.

WHEN THE CHILD IS NOT *GILLICK* COMPETENT AND THE PARENT REFUSES CONSENT. This situation will apply when the child is too young and/or immature to be *Gillick* competent. For example, in *Re B (A Minor) (Wardship: Medical Treatment)* [1981] 1 WLR 1421 the parents decided not to allow medical treatment which would have prolonged the life of their Down's syndrome baby. The court held that it was in the best interests of the child that it should live and ordered the treatment to be given. By contrast in *Re T (A Minor) (Wardship: Medical Treatment)* [1997] 1 FLR 502; [1997] 1 WLR 242 a baby was born with a life-threatening liver defect. He had an unsuccessful operation which caused him pain and distress. The parents, who were healthcare professionals, refused to allow T to have any further operations, in particular a liver transplant. It was held that while there was a strong presumption in favour of prolonging the child's life that was not the sole objective. In that case the best interests of the child required that his further treatment be left in the hands of his parents. In *Re P (A Minor)* [1986] 1 FLR 272 the High Court authorised an abortion for a child in the care of the local authority against the wishes of her parents.

The well publicised case of Mary and Jodie, the conjoined Siamese twins, illustrated the dilemmas for the courts called upon to authorise their separation when the parents had refused to give consent. The High Court authorised the operation. The parents appealed. In *Re A (Conjoined Twins: Medical Treatment)* [2001] 1 FLR 1 the Court of Appeal on 22 September 2000 dismissed their appeal. It found that the twins were separate persons. It balanced the paramount welfare of each child. The prospect of full life for Jodie was counterbalanced by an acceleration of the certain death of Mary. The court chose the lesser of the inevitable loss – the loss of Mary over the loss of both Jodie and Mary. It also considered the consequences in terms of the criminal law – namely that necessity justified the killing of Mary. Distinguishing *R v Dudley and Stephens* (1884) 14 QBD 273, three conditions were laid down to satisfy the defence of necessity. First, the act was needed to avoid inevitable and irreparable evil. Second, no more should be done than was reasonably necessary to achieve the purpose to be achieved. Third, the evil inflicted must not be disproportionate to the evil avoided. All three conditions were satisfied in this case. Ward LJ also decided that the doctors would be acting in legitimate self-defence of Jodie. Nothing in the Human Rights Act 1998 called for a different answer.

In some cases the parents refuse to consent to treatment and the courts agree with that refusal even though this means that the child will die. This will apply if the court is of the view that this is in the child's best interests. In *Re C (A Baby)* [1996] 2 FLR 43 a baby was born eight weeks prematurely. She developed meningitis which led to serious brain damage. She needed artificial ventilation and tube feeding. She was blind and deaf and suffered pain and distress. There was no prospect of improvement in her condition. The doctors and parents agreed that it was in the child's best interests that artificial ventilation be stopped. She was made a ward of court and the court granted approval for the cessation of ventilation. A similar decision was reached in *Re C (A Minor) (Medical Treatment)* [1998] 1 FLR 384.

In other cases the parent wants treatment which is opposed by the medical authorities or a local authority. For example, in *Re D (A Minor) (Wardship: Sterilisation)* [1976] 2 WLR 279; [1976] 1 All ER 326 the mother of a girl wanted the child to be sterilised. An educational psychologist made the child a ward of court to prevent such treatment and the court held that such treatment was not in the child's best interest. By contrast in *Re B (A Minor) (Sterilisation)* [1987] 2 All ER 206 the House of Lords allowed the sterilisation of a mentally handicapped 17-year-old girl, this being the only effective form of contraception and in her best interests. The court emphasised that such an operation should only be undertaken with the consent of the wardship court. A similar decision was reached in *Re M (Wardship: Sterilisation)* [1988] 2 FLR 479 which again involved a mentally handicapped 17-year-old girl. She had a mental age of five or six and there was a real danger she would find a pregnancy traumatic. There was a 50 per cent chance that she would give birth to a mentally retarded child and might have to undergo an abortion. She would be sterilised in her own interests and not for eugenic reasons. In *Re J (Specific Issues Order: Child's Religious Upbringing and Circumcision)* [2000] Fam Law 246 the court refused to allow a child to be circumcised at the request of his Muslim father but opposed by his non-Muslim mother, with whom he lived. Circumcision was irreversible and had considerable consequences. Where parents disagreed one could not act without the consent of the other because it was an exceptional course (despite s2(7) CA 1989). The court's consent was required.

WHEN THE CHILD IS *GILLICK* COMPETENT AND REFUSES CONSENT AND THE PARENTS REFUSE CONSENT. In *Re E (A Minor)(Wardship: Medical Treatment)* [1993] 1 FLR 179 the court was asked to allow a hospital to treat a 15-year-old who was suffering from leukaemia and required blood transfusions. He and his parents refused to agree to such treatment because of their religious beliefs as Jehovah's Witnesses. The court dispensed with the consent of both the 15-year-old and his parents and authorised the treatment. The child's veto was not considered binding. Great weight was given to his religious beliefs and his decision, taken with that of his parents. However, his welfare was paramount. If the blood transfusions were not given he would die. Similar decisions were reached in *Devon County Council* v *S* [1993] Fam Law 40 and *Re S (A Minor) (Consent to Medical Treatment)* [1994] 2 FLR 1065. In *Re S* the child was held not to be *Gillick* competent and her wishes could be more readily overridden.

***Dealing with a contested issue as to medical treatment.*** Where there is a dispute about the medical treatment of a child which is an emergency the recommended procedure is to use the inherent jurisdiction of the High Court through s100 CA 1989 (as opposed to using applying for a specific issues order under s8 CA 1989 or an emergency protection order under s44 CA 1989 or an interim care order under s32 CA 1989). See *Re O (A Minor) (Medical Treatment)* [1993] 2 FLR 151 which concerned a child who needed a blood transfusion which was opposed by the child's parents who were Jehovah's Witnesses. The local authority applied for a care order. This was inappropriate since the parents were caring, committed and capable apart from this one issue. The most appropriate remedy was through the inherent jurisdiction of the High Court. A contrasting opinion was voiced in *Re R (A Minor) (Blood Transfusion)* [1993] Fam Law 577 which dealt with similar circumstances and recommended that application be made to the High Court for a specific issues order under s8 CA 1989.

Many of the reported cases involve the wardship jurisdiction being invoked.

## The child leaving the United Kingdom

Where a residence order is in force with respect to a child, no person may remove the child from the United Kingdom without either the written consent of every person with parental responsibility for the child or the leave of the court (see s13(1) CA 1989). This does not prevent the child from being taken abroad for a period of less than one month by the person in whose favour the residence order is made (see s13(2) CA 1989) (eg to take the child on a foreign holiday).

When the court is asked to consider whether to grant leave it will:

1.  treat the welfare of the child as paramount (this includes the importance of maintaining the link with the parent with whom the child does not live which may be severed if the child goes abroad to live);
2.  normally place great importance on any realistic and well thought out plans of the parent with the child to go abroad and give leave rather than frustrate the plans for the family's future (eg to live abroad);
3.  apply the welfare checklist in s1(3) CA 1989 (see *H* v *H (Residence Order: Leave to Remove from Jurisdiction)* [1995] 1 FLR 529).

Leading cases include *Re H (Application to Remove from Jurisdiction)* [1998] 1 FLR 848 in which both parents shared the care of their five-year-old daughter before she went to school, whereupon she lived with her mother. The mother married an American and wanted to settle in the USA though she could have continued with her job as an air hostess in the UK. The judge gave leave for the child to be taken to the USA. The father appealed. It was held, dismissing the appeal, the law was as laid down in *Poel* v *Poel* [1970] 1 WLR 1469 and subsequent cases had not altered it. The question was 'is the proposed move a reasonable one from the point of view of the adults involved ie properly thought out and planned?' If the answer is 'yes' then leave should only be refused if it is clearly shown beyond any doubt that the interests of the children and the interests of the residential parent are incompatible. The court should not in principle interfere with the reasonable decision of the residential parent. Otherwise the resulting bitterness or disappointment of the applicant may directly or indirectly harm the children.

In *Payne* v *Payne* [2001] Fam Law 346 the above principles were confirmed. The court needs to be satisfied that there is a genuine motivation for the move and not an intention to bring contact between the child and the other parent to an end. The European Convention on Human Rights did not necessitate any fundamental revision of the principles applied by the courts since *Poel* v *Poel*. This was also the view of the court in *Re A (Permission to Remove Child from Jurisdiction: Human Rights)* [2000] 2 FLR 225 which considered the respective rights of each parent to a family life under art 8. Leave was granted to take the children to the USA.

Other examples of cases include:

1. *MH* v *GP (Child: Emigration)* [1995] 2 FLR 106 in which the the relationship with the absent parent was such that the detriment to the child outweighed the presumption in favour of the mother's application.
2. *Re T (Removal from Jurisdiction)* [1996] 2 FLR 352 in which the mother's plans to remove the child to France were ill thought out and plainly incompatible with the child's welfare.
3. *M* v *M (Minors) (Jurisdiction)* [1993] Fam Law 396 in which the mother's application for leave to remove the children to Israel was refused since the views of the children, who were articulate and intelligent and opposed to the move, carried considerable weight. The move to Israel would disrupt their contact with their father and would mean a substantial change in their education and the main language they used.

The court may seek assurances that contact will be maintained with the parent remaining in England. In *Re S (Removal from Jurisdiction)* [1999] 1 FLR 850 the mother was required to lodge a security of £135,000 to ensure that an English contact order was authenticated in Chile (where the children went to live). In other cases the parent removing the child has been obliged to obtain a 'mirror' order in the foreign country giving contact rights to the absent parent (see *Re K (Removal from Jurisdiction)* [1999] Fam Law 754).

## The responsibility to financially maintain the child

A married parent has a responsibility to financially maintain his or her child. That responsibility can be enforced by:

1. an application under ss23, 24 and 24A Matrimonial Causes Act 1973 (in divorce, nullity and judicial separation proceedings) or under s27 MCA 1973 (for failing to maintain the child);
2. an application under the Domestic Proceedings and Magistrates' Courts Act 1978 (see Chapter 11);
3. an application under Sched 1 CA 1989 (see Chapter 11);
4. an application under s106 Social Security Administration Act 1992 whereby the Department of Social Security may apply to a magistrates' court to recover the cost of income support paid for a child from a parent who is liable to maintain the child.

In the case of an unmarried parent a responsibility to financially maintain a child can be enforced under Sched 1 CA 1989 and under the Social Security Administration Act 1992.

From 5 April 1993 s1 Child Support Act 1991 imposed a duty on each parent to financially maintain his or her child. That duty can be enforced in the case of an absent parent by the making of a maintenance assessment which obliges the parent to pay child support maintenance and which largely replaces the above provisions.

**The responsibility to protect the child from physical harm**
Breach of this responsibility may result in criminal liability (eg manslaughter where the prosecution must show a deliberate or reckless act or failure). See *R* v *Lowe* [1973] 1 All ER 805 where an unintelligent father failed to foresee the consequences of not calling a doctor when his nine week old child fell ill. The child died ten days later of dehydration and gross emaciation. He was acquitted of manslaughter.

*Cruelty to children* where it is an offence for a person (aged sixteen or more) who has custody, charge or care of any child to wilfully assault, ill-treat, neglect, abandon or expose the child in a manner likely to cause him or her unnecessary suffering or injury (see s1 Children and Young Persons Act 1933).

A genuine lack of appreciation through stupidity, ignorance or inadequacy may be a defence. The offence is not based on an objective test of what a reasonable parent would have done. See *R* v *Sheppard* [1981] AC 394; [1980] 3 All ER 899 where a young couple of low intelligence had a sixteen-month-old baby. The baby fell ill. The parents thought it was a minor upset and did not call a doctor. The child died from hypothermia and malnutrition. The prosecution had to prove deliberate or reckless neglect. The couple were acquitted.

**The responsibility to protect the child from moral harm**
Breach of this responsibility may also result in criminal liability. The Sexual Offences Act 1956 sets out offences of incest (ss10, 11); indecent assault (ss14, 15); permitting a girl under thirteen or sixteen to use premises for intercourse (ss25, 26); causing or encouraging prostitution of, intercourse with, or indecent assault on a girl under sixteen (s28) etc ...

## The responsibility to see that a child receives education

It is the duty of the parent of every child of compulsory school age to cause that child to receive efficient full-time education suitable to his or her age, ability, aptitude and any special educational need he or she may have either by regular attendance at school or otherwise (see s7 Education Act 1996).

This duty can be enforced by a local education authority requring parents to comply with their duty through a 'school attendance order' and by prosecuting parents for the offence of failing to send their child to school (see ss443 and 444 Education Act 1996).

Failure to attend may be a ground for the making of an education supervision order (see s36 CA 1989) or, if the child is suffering 'significant harm' as a result, for care proceedings (see s31 CA 1989).

For an example of the court deciding on a dispute between parents as to how a child should be educated see *Re P (A Minor) (Education)* [1992] 1 FLR 316 where the parents of a child were divorced. There was a dispute about whether the father should pay the school fees for the child to attend a public school which was a boarding school and for which he had obtained a music bursary. The judge decided that the child should attend this school. The father appealed.

HELD: The views of the child had not been obtained. He was keen to attend another school which was a local day public school. This would enable him to have more time with his father. The court found that his views had been independently formed and that he was mature and sensible. On that basis full recognition should have been given to the child's views and it was ordered that the child attend the school he wanted to attend.

## 15.3 When a family breaks down what should happen to the children?

When a family breaks down and the parents separate, then a court may be asked to make orders as to what should happen to the children.

### Section 8 orders

The court can make 'a section 8 order', namely:

### A residence order

This is an order settling the arrangements to be made as to the person with whom a child is to live.

*Shared residence orders.* Normally a residence order specifies that the child should live with one person. However, the courts can also make shared residence orders whereby a child spends part of his or her time living with one parent and the rest of the time living with the other parent. See *A* v *A (Minors) (Shared Residence)* [1994]

1 FLR 669 in which the Court of Appeal made a shared residence order which confirmed that the children lived with their mother most of the time but lived with their father on alternate weekends and half of school holidays. Earlier cases (such as *Riley* v *Riley* [1986] 2 FLR 429) which disapproved of such shared orders had been decided before the Children Act 1989 and were no longer good law. Section 11(4) CA 1989 specifically provides for shared residence orders. The Court of Appeal was more cautious in *Re H (A Minor) (Shared Residence)* [1994] 1 FLR 717, saying that shared residence orders should only be rarely made and would depend on exceptional circumstances. Subsequent cases have not followed *Re H*. In *Re D (Children) (Shared Residence Orders)* [2001] 1 FLR 495 the Court of Appeal said that there was no need to show exceptional circumstances or a positive benefit before such an order could be made. It was sufficient that a shared residence order was in the child's best interests. That case involved three children who lived with their mother but who had substantial contact with their father. The parents repeatedly returned to court to settle disputes about education and passports and precise schedules which the court concluded were caused by the mother having sole residence. Shared residence recognised the reality of the situation. In *Re A (Children) (Shared Residence)* [2001] EWCA Civ 1795 the Court of Appeal again said that shared residence orders were not necessarily exceptional. However, a shared residence order was not appropriate where a child lived with one parent and had limited contact with the other parent, simply as device to give the parents equal status. A residence order settled where the child should live. In the appeals orders were made that the girls live with their mother and have contact with their father and the boy live with his father and have contact with his mother.

*Attaching conditions to residence orders.* It is possible to attach conditions to a s8 order, including a residence order, but the scope for such conditions is limited. See *Re E (Residence Order: Imposition of Conditions)* [1997] 2 FLR 635 in which a residence order was made in favour of the mother but with a condition that she and the children live in London (rather than move to Blackpool where the mother wanted to live). The father was unreliable with contact and it was feared that if the children moved to Blackpool contact might cease. The mother appealed and the appeal was allowed. It was held that while s11(7) CA 1989 allowed the imposition of conditions to a residence order the court could not put unwarranted restrictions on where a suitable residential parent wished to live. It would be exceptional for the court to keep that kind of control over the residential parent. The father's unreliability over contact did not justify such a condition. That would penalise the mother for his inadequacy. In *Re S (A Child) (Residence Order: Condition) (No 2)* [2003] 1 FCR 138 it was held that the general principle is that a suitable parent entrusted with the primary care of a child by way of a residence order should be able to choose where she lived and with whom (following *Payne* v *Payne* [2001] 1 FLR 1052). However, it was also held that a condition that the residential parent not move to Cornwall without the leave of the court was validly imposed because of the truly exceptional circumstances of the case (namely emotional harm to a particularly vulnerable and handicapped child). This did not mean that the court had to find fault with the residential parent. It meant that the paramountcy of the child's welfare exceptionally required the imposition of restrictions on the residential parent which would otherwise be unacceptable. A condition not to remove the children to Northern Ireland was upheld in *Re H (Children) (Residence Order: Condition)* [2001] 2 FLR 1277 because the case was 'highly exceptional' given the drastic consequences for the children if moved too far away from the non-residential parent.

## A contact order

This is an order requiring the person with whom a child lives, or is to live, to allow the child to visit or stay with the person named in the contact order, or for that person and the child otherwise to have contact with each other.

*Types of contact.* Contact can include:

1. visiting contact (eg the child visiting or being visited by the non-residential parent);
2. staying contact (eg the child staying overnight with the non-residential parent);
3. indirect contact (eg contact by letter, birthday and Christmas cards and by telephone).

Examples of indirect contact include:

1. *Re M (A Minor) (Contact: Conditions)* [1994] 1 FLR 272 in which a court ordered contact by letter between a child and his father who was serving a prison sentence.
2. *A v L (Contact)* [1998] Fam Law 137 in which M and F had a short-lived and violent relationship. They had a son born in 1994. By that time M was living with P and the child took P to be his father. F was sentenced to a long period of imprisonment. M was opposed to any contact between the child and F. The court held that the child should know that he had two fathers. An order for indirect contact would enable the nettle to be grasped now rather than later. F should send letters and presents via M's solicitor.
3. *Re O (Contact: Imposition of Conditions)* [1995] 2 FLR 124 where the court made an order that the mother send the father photographs of the child every three months, copies of all nursery or playgroup reports, information about any serious illnesses and to accept delivery of cards and present for the child through the post and to read and show the child any communication and to give him any presents. It was held that a child should grow up knowing of the love and interest of the absent parent with whom, in due course, contact could be established. The mother had no right to veto contact and the court could compel her to send information to the father.

Contact can also be supervised, for example through a contact centre. See *Re M (Contact: Supervision)* [1998] 1 FLR 721 where a parent with significant shortcomings (drug and alcohol abuse, a lack of a permanent home and occasional inability to control his temper) could have contact through a contact centre since the child could benefit from such contact even within the confines of the contact centre.

*The right of the child to contact with the non-residential parent.* Contact is considered to be the right of the child and not the right of either parent (see *M v M* [1973] 2 All ER 81). If the child's welfare demands that the child remain in contact with the non-residential parent (eg because that parent had an important relationship with the child before the family broke up) then contact should be ordered. If contact will be detrimental to the child it should not be ordered (see *Re KD (A Minor) (Ward: Termination of Access)* [1988] AC 806; [1988] 2 FLR 139).

Under the European Convention on Human Rights the mutual enjoyment by parent and child of each other's company, even if the relationship between the parents has broken down, is a fundamental element of family life and protected by art 8(1). That right could be interfered with if the interference was necessary in a democratic society under art 8(2). Consideration of the child's best interests is of crucial importance. A fair balance has to be struck between the interests of a parent and the interests of a child, with particular importance being attached to the child's interests. As a result a decision to limit a father's rights of contact in order to protect his daughter's psychological health did not breach art 8 in *Hoppe v Germany* [2003] 1 FCR 176.

*A presumption in favour of contact?* The courts have stated that no court should deprive a child of contact to either parent unless it was wholly satisfied that it was in the interests of the child that contact should cease. That is a conclusion at which courts may be extremely slow to arrive. See *Re H (Minors) (Access)* [1992] 1 FLR 148 in which it was said that when parents separated and one had care of the child, contact with the other often resulted in some upset to the child. These upsets were usually minor and superficial and were heavily outweighed by the long term advantages to the child of keeping in touch with the parents concerned. Save in exceptional cases, to deprive a parent of contact was to deprive a child of an important contribution to the child's emotional and material growing up in the long-term (following *M v M* (above)). In *Re M (Contact: Welfare Test)* [1995] 1 FLR 274 it was stated that the court should use the welfare checklist in s1(3) CA 1989. The court should ask whether the fundamental emotional need of every child to have an enduring relationship with both parents (see s1(3)(b)) was outweighed by the harm, in the light of the child's wishes and feelings (see s1(3)(a)), the child would be at risk of suffering (s1(3)(e)) if a contact order was made. This was in line with *Re H* above. In the case the mother's application for contact was refused because children, aged nine and seven, did not want to see their mother and were emotionally secure in their new family.

In *Sahin* v *Germany* [2002] 3 FCR 321 the European Court of Human Rights looked at contact between a child and his father. F lived in an unmarried relationship with M. They had a child, C, born in June 1988. F and M separated. F had contact with C until November 1990 when M stopped contact. The court found that contact with F was not in C's interests but did not hear evidence from C. F appealed. The appeal court took evidence from an expert who examined C and advised that C (then aged five) should not be asked directly about F because of the risk that C might think her views were decisive. The appeal was dismissed. A further appeal was dismissed. F appealed to the European Court of Human Rights on the ground that the refusal to allow him contact breached art 8 (the right to family life). It was held that the decision to deny F contact with C breached art 8(1). The interference was in accordance with law and had a legitimate aim, namely the protection of the child in accordance with art 8(2). However, in order for the denial of contact to be necessary in a democratic society (also in accordance with art 8(2)) there had to be a fair balance between the rights of the child and those of the parent, with particular importance being attached to the interests of the child, which could override those of the parent. In striking that balance the state was afforded a margin of appreciation. In failing to hear evidence from the child the court had failed to have complete information on C's relationship with F. This was an indispensable prerequisite for finding out C's true wishes. The expert's comments about C were too vague. The state had exceeded its margin of appreciation and there had been a violation of art 8. The decision appears to encourage courts to either have a child attend to give evidence (currently frowned on by UK courts) or for the children and family reporter to ask the child directly about his/her relationship with his/her father. English courts will have to be careful that the child's views have been sought in reaching conclusions about the child's relationship with his/her father and whether contact should be ordered. The Court of Appeal in *Re T (A Child: Contact)* [2003] 1 FCR 303 recognised that *Sahin* v *Germany* raised policy issues which the government and judiciary needed to consider.

### When contact was not ordered

WHERE THERE IS NO BOND WITH THE CHILD. See *Re SM (A Minor) (Natural Father: Access)* [1991] 2 FLR 333 in which contact was refused where there was no postive benefit to the child from contact with his father. There was no bond between them. The only bond was between the child and the mother and stepfather. If the father were to have regular contact there was likely to be confusion created in the child's mind and risk destabilising the family unit. Contact should cease. In *Re F (A Minor) (Access)* [1992] Fam Law 484 a similar conclusion was reached. Any theoretical benefit to the child of having contact between the child and his father was outweighed by evidence of potential harm. See also *Re D (A Minor) (Contact: Mother's Hostility)* [1993] Fam Law 465).

WHEN OLDER CHILDREN DO NOT WANT TO SEE THE APPLICANT PARENT. See *Re M* (above) in which children aged nine and seven did not want to see their mother. In *Re S (Contact: Children's Views)* [2002] 1 FLR 1156 the wishes and feelings of a 16-year-old daughter and a 14-year-old son (both of whom did not wish to have contact with their father) were respected and no orders as to contact were made. The court had to respect the wishes and feelings of the children, even to the extent of allowing them, as occasionally they do, to make mistakes.

WHERE THE EFFECT ON THE PRIMARY CARER WOULD BE TOO ADVERSE. See *Re H (Contact Order) (No 2)* [2001] Fam Law 795 where a mother would suffer a nervous breakdown if direct contact between the father and his children were ordered. The need for the children to have a competent and confident primary carer, able to meet their needs and bring them up properly, outweighed their need for direct contact with their father. This case may be confined to its unusual facts. The father suffered from a brain disorder which resulted in violent mood swings.

*Contact in cases involving domestic violence.* Courts have been concerned at the consequences for children and parents (usually mothers) arising from contact with violent parents (usually fathers). Courts have paid attention to research which shows the possible harmful consequences of contact in such cases. For an example of such research see 'Domestic Violence Research' [2000] Fam Law 156 which indicated:

1. the risks to the safety and welfare of the women and children were not adequately assessed by the courts when contact orders were granted to violent men;
2. poor provision was made for the safety of the abused parent and children (the abusive parent discovered the new address of the abused parent in many cases);
3. two-thirds of parents were further abused as a result of contact and three-quarters of children physically abused by their fathers were abused again during contact visits;
4. three-quarters of abused parents opposed the making of contact orders because of fear of harm to their children;
5. one-third of abused parents were threatened with imprisonment for opposing contact;
6. Eight-three per cent of children's wishes and feelings were not taken into account by the court.

The Lord Chancellor commissioned *A Report to the Lord Chancellor on the Question of Parental Contact in Cases where There is Domestic Violence* (April 2000). It did not consider that there was any need to amend the Children Act 1989 to provide a presumption against contact where domestic violence was established (as is the case in New Zealand). Its recommendations were accepted in *Re L, V, M and H (Contact: Domestic Violence)* [2000] 2 FLR 334 which involved four conjoined appeals against orders refusing contact in cases with a background of domestic violence. It was held that where domestic violence is alleged the court should first adjudicate on the allegations and find them proved or not proved. If found proved there was no presumption of no contact but the violence was a factor in the balancing exercise of the court's discretion. The court had to consider the past and present conduct of both parties, the effect on the children and on the residential parent and the motivation of the parent seeking contact. The ability of the parent to recognise their past conduct, to be aware of the need to change and to make genuine efforts to do so would be likely to be an important consideration. All the appeals by fathers, whose applications for contact had been refused, were dismissed. Courts were warned of the dangers of making interim contact orders pending a proper investigation (see also *Re M (Interim Contact: Domestic Violence)* [2000] 2 FLR 377).

*Enforcing contact.* Contact can be a very difficult matter. When parents separate there can be much bitterness. The residential parent with the child living with them may want nothing further to do with the non-residential parent. The residential parent may remarry and want the new partner to be the child's new father or mother. Any contact order may be disobeyed. The court has limited sanctions in such cases. It can fine or imprison or reconsider with whom the child should reside. However, in reality such options may be unrealistic or counter-productive (see *I v D (Access Order: Enforcement)* [1988] 2 FLR 286; *Re L (Minors) (Access Order: Enforcement)* [1989] 2 FLR 359; and *Re S (Minors: Access Appeal)* [1990] 2 FLR 166).

The European Court of Human Rights examined the difficulties of enforcing contact in *Glaser v United Kingdom* [2000] 3 FCR 193. That case involved a married couple, G and W, with three children. G and W separated with the children living with W. W then stopped G having contact with the children after she alleged that G had sexually abused them. The court made contact orders but only two contact visits took place. W and the children then disappeared and were eventually traced. The court then made fresh contact orders but only if the children agreed to it. No further contact took place. G then complained to the European Court of Human Rights alleging that his right to family life under art 8 of the European Convention on Human Rights had been infringed by the failure of the UK courts to enforce the contact orders and the delays in dealing with his case. The European Court held that the state had a positive obligation to secure respect for family life, including reuniting the parent with his child. Whilst the state had to do their utmost to facilitate co-operation over contact, any obligation to apply coercion had to be limited to take account the rights of the other parent and children. Coercive measures could damage the children. There was no absolute obligation on the state to enforce the right to contact. In this case the state would have been irresponsible to impose stringent coercive measures on W without proper and careful investigation of the requirements of the children's welfare. G's appeal was dismissed. By contrast in *Hokkanen v Finland* [1996] 1 FLR 289 the state was criticised for failing to take all reasonable steps to enforce contact orders in favour of a father whose children were cared for by grandparents. The state was found to have failed to enforce the contact orders sufficiently vigorously when faced with the obstinate refusal of the grandparents to comply with the orders.

For a more recent example of the difficulties in enforcing contact, see *Re K (Contact: Committal Order)* [2003] Fam Law 11 in which a mother was imprisoned for refusing to comply with contact orders and residence of the children transferred to the father. On appeal the imprisonment and residence orders were set aside and supervised contact ordered. The Court of Appeal looked at the balancing exercise within art 8 of the European Convention on Human Rights (the right to family life). The court must ask whether the removal of a mother from young children was proportionate. In this case it was not.

In 2002 the Children Act Sub-Committee of the Lord Chancellor's Advisory Board on Family Law published *Making Contact Work: A Report to the Lord Chancellor on the Facilitation of Arrangements for Contact between Children and Their Non-residential Parents and the Enforcement of Court Orders for Contact* (Lord Chancellor's Department, 2002). The report looked at the effects of contact and children. It commissioned a report from two clinical psychologists. While contact was deemed to be generally beneficial to children, more research was needed. The report also recommended a broadening of the court's powers to enforce contact. It recommended a first step which would be facilitative and non–punitive. This could include parenting programmes. The second step would involve penal sanctions, such as being placed on probation or community punishment.

## A prohibited steps order

This is an order that no step which could be taken by a parent in meeting his or her parental responsibility for a child, and which is of a kind specified in the order, shall be taken by any person without the consent of the court.

A prohibited steps order cannot order that parents have no contact with each other since an order can only relate to what a parent can or cannot do in meeting his or her parental responsibility for his or her child. See *Croydon LBC* v *A* [1992] 3 WLR 267; [1992] 2 FLR 341.

It is possible to make a prohibited steps order against someone who is neither a parent nor a party to the proceedings. See *Re H (Prohibited Steps Order)* [1995] 1 WLR 667; [1995] 4 All ER 110; [1995] 1 FLR 638 where an order was made preventing a third party (who had abused the children) from having contact or seeking to have contact with the children.

## A specific issues order

This is an order giving directions for the purpose of determining a specific question which has arisen, or which may arise, in connection with any aspect of parental responsibility for a child (see s8(1), (2) Children Act 1989).

These orders are intended to be neutral and less adversarial. The aim is to remove some of the conflict which existed in contests for 'legal rights' over children. 'Parental responsibility' will continue regardless of with whom the child is living under a residence order thereby both parents will retain parental responsibility to their child after a separation or divorce (see s2(6) CA 1989). A residence order gives any person who is not a parent parental responsibility (eg a step-parent) while the residence order remains in force (see s12(2) CA 1989).

A court cannot make a specific issue or prohibited steps order with a view to achieving a result which could be achieved by making a residence or contact order (see s9(5) CA 1989). This provision was emphasised in *Nottinghamshire County Council* v *P* [1993] 3 All ER 815 where a local authority sought to use a prohibited steps order to achieve what could have been achieved by residence and contact orders. The case concerned two girls aged 16 and 13 whom, it was alleged, had been sexually abused by their father. The local authority did not wish to seek care orders. They asked for a prohibited steps order forbidding the father from residing with the girls and forbidding him from having contact with them unless it was supervised. Applying s9(5) the Court refused to make a prohibited steps order.

## Who can apply for a s8 order?

The parents of a child (whether married or unmarried) may apply for any s8 order (see s10(4) CA 1989). The status of an unmarried father with no parental responsibility was considered in *Re C (Minors) (Parent: Residence Order)* [1993] 3 All ER 313 where it was confirmed that such a father could apply for any s8 order as of right and did not need the leave of the court (though in that case the child had been freed for adoption which deprived the unmarried father of the status of 'parent' and meant that he had to apply for leave to apply for a s8 order).

Any person in whose favour a residence order is in force may apply for any s8 order (see s10(4) CA 1989).

A party to the marriage to whom the child is a child of the family may apply for a residence order or a contact order (see s10(5)(a) CA 1989) (ie a step-parent).

Other third parties can apply for certain s8 orders (see later).

## Child of the family

A child of the family, in relation to the parties to a marriage, means a child of both of those parties and any other child who has been treated by both of those parties as a child of their family (excluding children fostered out to foster parents by local authorities or voluntary organisations) (see s105(1) CA 1989).

Treatment as a child of the family is tested objectively. It involves behaviour towards a child, who must, therefore, be living, and an unborn child will not fall within the category.

See *W(RJ)* v *W(SJ)* [1972] 2 WLR 371; [1971] 3 All ER 303 where the wife committed adultery. It was not clear whether the children born to her were her husband's. Despite the uncertainty he treated them as his children and so he was liable to maintain them as 'children of the family'.

In *A* v *A* *(Family: Unborn Child)* [1974] 2 WLR 106; [1974] 1 All ER 755 the husband had married the wife knowing her to be pregnant and believing himself to be the father. Six days after the marriage the wife left him. When the child was born it was obviously not the child of the husband but the daughter of a Pakistani with whom the mother had also had intercourse before the marriage. The husband had only treated the child as his before she was born – that was insufficient to make the child a child of his family.

This case has been followed in *W* v *W* *(Child of the Family)* [1984] FLR 796 and in *Re Leach* [1985] 2 All ER 754.

It is immaterial whether the husband realises the child is his own or not if he in fact treats the child as his own (see *W* v *W* [1972] 2 WLR 371; [1971] 3 All ER 303).

The fact that the child's natural parent is paying maintenance is not decisive, so that the child may still be a child of the step-parent's family (see *Carron* v *Carron* [1984] FLR 805).

It has been decided that a child is not a child of the family if he or she was born after the family had broken up and there is no longer a family for the child to be a child of, even though the husband made occasional visits after he had left and sent cards to the child signed 'Dad'.

See *M* v *M* [1981] 2 FLR 39 where a husband and wife separated. The wife became pregnant by another man. She did not want the rest of her family to know that the husband was not the father. She persuaded him to allow her family to believe he was the father. He made occasional visits and sent cards to the child. When they divorced on the ground of five years living apart the child was held not be a child of the family since the husband had never lived with the child so that there was no family for the child to be a 'child of the family'.

In *Re A* *(A Minor)* *(Child of the Family)* [1998] 1 FLR 347 A was born in 1990 when her mother was aged 17 years. From the age of one A lived with her maternal grandparents whom she called 'Mum' and 'Dad'. The grandparents took all the major decisions about A's health and schooling and bore the cost of her upbringing with some small assistance from A's paternal grandparents. In 1994 the grandfather left the grandmother and in 1995 the grandmother petitioned for divorce. An issue arose as to whether A was a child of the grandparents' family as defined in s52 Matrimonial Causes Act 1973. The court held she was. The grandfather appealed. It was held, dismissing the appeal, grandparents could treat their grandchild as a child of the family within the meaning of s52 MCA 1973 where the child's parent(s) had irrevocably abdicated leaving the grandparents to assume primary responsibility for the child for the foreseeable future. If the grandparents were simply providing emergency or secondary cover then the child was unlikely to be a child of their family.

## *What the court must consider before making a s8 order?*

### The welfare of the child is paramount (s1(1) CA 1989)

This has already been discussed in section 15.1.

### Delay is harmful to the child (see s1(2) CA 1989)

In any proceedings in which any question with respect to the upbringing of a child arises, the court must have regard to the general principle that any delay in determining the question is likely to prejudice the welfare of the child (s1(2)).

In order to minimise delay the court can draw up a timetable with a view to determining the question without delay; and give such directions as it considers appropriate for the purpose of ensuring, so far as is reasonably practicable, that that timetable is adhered to (see s11(1) CA 1989).

### The no order principle (see s1(5) CA 1989)

The court cannot make a s8 order unless it considers that doing so would be better for the child than making no order at all (s1(5)). The court should not interfere unless it will improve things for the child by making an order.

Section 1(5) CA 1989 was discussed in *B* v *B (Grandparent: Residence Order)* [1992] 2 FLR 327; [1992] Fam Law 490 where a grandmother applied for a residence order with respect to her 11-year-old granddaughter. The child had lived with the grandmother for most of her life and the child's mother agreed to the order. Magistrates refused to make an order since they were not satisfied that making an order would be better than no order at all. The grandmother appealed.

HELD: If the parties to an application for a residence order were the parents of the child and they agreed on where their child should live then, in the absence of an issue upon which it was necessary for the court to decide, the court would usually decline to make the order even though it was a consent application. However in this case the child was living with her grandmother who did not have the status of having parental responsibility for the child. The grandmother had found that this lack of status meant that she had no authority in relation to the child's education (eg giving consent for the child to go on a school trip), no power to consent to medical treatment in an emergency and the mother could remove the child from the grandmother's care without warning. A residence order would give the grandmother parental responsibility automatically and give the child stability. Therefore a residence order would make things better for the child than making no order at all and the appeal would be allowed.

In *K* v *H (Maintenance)* [1993] Fam Law 464 F made voluntary payments of £20 a week to M for the support of their child. Both wanted the agreement made into a court order so application was made under s15 and Schedule 1 CA 1989. The justices applied the no order principle and made no order. On appeal.

HELD: Allowing the appeal, the no order principle did not apply to applications for financial relief under CA 1989. The considerations for such an application were laid down in Schedule 1 CA 1989. Even if the no order principal had applied a court order would have provided greater security than a voluntary written agreement between the parents, so an order should have been made.

## The checklist (see s1(3), (4) CA 1989)

If the court is considering whether to make a s8 order and the making of the order is opposed by any party to the proceedings the court must have regard in particular to:

*The ascertainable wishes and feelings of the child concerned (considered in light of the child's age and understanding).* The importance of the child's wishes and feelings will depend on the age and understanding of the child. If the child is sixteen years old or more the court is unlikely to make an order contrary to the child's wishes, particularly following *Gillick* and *Hewer* v *Bryant*. And see *Stewart* v *Stewart* [1973] 3 Fam Law 107 where a girl aged fifteen-and-a-half wished to be with her mother. Custody was granted to the mother.

Under sixteen years of age the court will take the child's views into account but may treat them with caution.

In *M* v *M* (1977) 7 Fam Law 17 the wishes of a six-year-old girl to stay with her father were treated with caution. Similarly, in *B(M)* v *B(R)* [1968] 1 WLR 1182 the wishes of a girl aged seven-and-a-half to stay with her father carried scarcely any weight.

However, in *Marsh* v *Marsh* (1978) 8 Fam Law 103 the custody of two children aged eight and five was given to the father despite the children's wish that they live with their mother. When the children were twelve and nine the mother sought custody. Again the children expressed the desire to live with the mother. There was nothing against the father's care. The court granted custody to the mother since it was of the opinion that the children were old enough to decide – their wishes were not paramount but were important in deciding what was in their best interests.

In *M* v *M* *(A Minor: Custody Appeal)* [1987] 1 WLR 404 there were two children, a girl aged twelve and a boy aged nine. When the parents separated the children lived with the mother for a short time. The girl then went to live with the father. The mother sought custody of both children. The girl was strongly opposed to returning to the mother and wished to stay with the father. Her views were given great weight by the Court of Appeal who gave custody of the girl to the father, as she wanted, and custody of her younger brother to the mother.

But the views of a child may be ignored if the child has been 'coached' by one of the parents. In *Re P (Minors) (Wardship: Care and Control)* [1992] 2 FCR 681 the views of two boys aged 13 and 11 that they wished to live with their father were disregarded. The 11-year-old was found to be immature, had been brought up by his mother, continued to need her and was close to his eight-year-old sister who lived with the mother. The father had campaigned to transfer the affections of the boys and this had resulted in the elder boy's difficult behaviour. It was desirable to keep the children together. The welfare of the children diverged from the wishes of the children and the decision that all three children live with their mother was plainly right.

The wishes and feelings of a 13-year-old girl to live with her father were not followed in *Re M (Family Proceedings: Affidavits)* [1995] 2 FLR 100. His application for a residence order was dismissed and the daughter remained living with her mother. The welfare officer considered both parents suitable to care for the girl but that the girl had not fully thought through what it would be like to live with her father permanently. The judge therefore gave less weight to her views. An appeal against his decision was dismissed.

In *M v M (Minors) (Jurisdiction)* [1993] Fam Law 396 the views of the children aged 11 and ten were important. They lived with their mother. Both wished to stay in England and retain contact with their father who was separated from their mother. The court made an order in the mother's favour allowing her to remove the children to Israel and lose contact with their father. The welfare report recommended that it was in the children's best interests that they remain in England. The father appealed.

HELD: Allowing the appeal, the court had only paid lip service to the views of the children. Orders should be made respecting their wishes and feelings allowing them to remain in England and retain contact with their father.

As a matter of court procedure a contested s8 application will be referred to conciliation where a welfare officer will speak privately to the parties and try to reach agreement. It has been directed that any child of nine years or over should be brought to such a conciliation appointment. If there are younger brothers or sisters then they may also attend. This recognises the importance of allowing the child to make his or her wishes and feelings known (see *Practice Direction (Family Division: Conciliation)* [1992] 1 WLR 147).

Since the welfare checklist applies to care proceedings (see later) the wishes and feelings of a child subject to care proceedings must be considered. However, such children may be vulnerable and disturbed so that their views may not be decisive. For example in *Re C (A Minor) (Care: Child's Wishes)* [1993] 1 FLR 832; [1993] Fam Law 400 a father was left caring for two children aged 12 and 13. He was a bitter, lonely and pathetic person who allowed his children to become out of control. His 13-year-old daughter associated with bad company, became involved in crime, failed to develop emotionally and was a victim of a serious sexual offence. She felt responsible and protective towards her father and strongly wished to return to him. The court made a care order since she was too young to carry the burden of deciding her own future.

***The child's physical, emotional and educational needs.*** The courts have considered various aspects of the child's needs:

MOTHERS CARING FOR YOUNG CHILDREN. The courts used to give great weight to the consideration that young children should be brought up by their mother, given the natural bond between young children and their mother. This consideration is not as decisive as it used to be but may still be an important factor.

See *Greer* v *Greer* (1974) 4 Fam Law 187 where the father and the mother separated. Their children, two girls aged eight and five, remained with the father who took care of them for two years. Prior to leaving the house the mother had been inefficient and lazy about running the household and was more interested in her career. She then applied for custody. She was in full-time employment. She had kept in close and regular contact with the children. There was no criticism of the father's care of the children. The judge at first instance awarded custody to the father. On appeal custody was awarded to the mother since the natural rhythm of childhood in their earlier days was with their mother.

See *Ives* v *Ives* [1973] 3 Fam Law 16 where after the parties separated the father cared for the two daughters for four years. The mother then applied for custody. The welfare report supported the father's claim. Both parents could provide a stable home. There was no criticism of the father's care. The court decided in favour of the mother and declared that, other things being equal, small children should be in the care of their mother.

See *Re K (Minors) (Children: Care and Control)* [1977] 2 WLR 33 discussed later.

See *Re W (A Minor: Custody)* (1983) 4 FLR 492; (1983) 13 Fam Law 47 where after the parties separated the father cared for his daughter aged two years in a wholly satisfactory way for virtually all the two years of her life. The mother maintained close contact with her daughter. Both could offer a good home. The court decided in favour of the mother: 'If all factors balanced then probably it is right for a child of tender years to be brought up by his or her natural mother.'

It was not correct to make a generalisation about the view of courts on the matter of a young child being with its mother. The Court of Appeal preferred to say that as a matter of general experience the individual circumstances of each case varied so much that any generalisations had to be qualified in the light of a sensitive grasp of the realities of all the relationships between the child and the adults concerned. Further, the capacity of the adults to form a loving relationship with the child was of the utmost importance. If all such factors were nicely balanced then probably it was right that a young child be brought up by the mother.

The same decision was reached in *Allington* v *Allington* [1985] 15 Fam Law 157 where the court reversed a decision that a father keep custody despite doubts concerning the mother and how permanent her new relationship was.

See also *C* v *C (Minors: Custody)* [1988] 2 FLR 291 where Heilbron J said that:

> 'All things being equal it is a good thing for a young child to be brought up by his mother, though that is not to say that fathers cannot also look after children of that age and even younger; they can and they do.'

The custody of the four-year-old son was given to the mother.

Contrast *B* v *B (Custody of Child)* [1985] Fam Law 29. The mother left the father with their eleven-month-old child in his care. He was given custody of the child by a magistrates' court. Nearly two years later the mother applied for custody, since she was then in a position to provide full-time care in a stable home. There was no criticism of the way the father had cared for the child. The child was strongly attached to him. A sudden transfer of custody might harm her. Since the father was unemployed he could provide full-time care for her. Custody was granted to the father.

However, the court was not happy that the father was unemployed. It noted that he had not become deliberately unemployed in order to care for the child – he had been made redundant. The court would have frowned if he had deliberately given up work to care for the child, though it stopped short of saying that a father had a moral duty to find work.

In *Re H (A Minor: Custody)* [1990] 1 FLR 51 the Court of Appeal said that it was well recognised that in dealing with the upbringing of children of tender years, given the normal commitment of the father to support the family, the mother was usually the right person to bring up her children. However, in that case a mother's claim for custody was dismissed in favour of an aunt and uncle – see below in relation to preserving the status quo in a child's life.

In *Re W (A Minor) (Custody)* [1990] Fam Law 261 the court started with the assumption that as between an eighteen-year-old mother and a forty-seven-year-old father, a child aged eight months was prima facie better with the mother, though of course that was an assumption that could be displaced.

In *Re S (A Minor) (Custody)* [1991] 2 FLR 388; [1991] Fam Law 302 the parents of a little girl, now aged two years, separated when the mother walked out (after allegedly being assaulted by the father) leaving the child with the father. The mother failed to contact her daughter for some time and the father looked after the child with the help of his family. The mother renewed contact with her daughter and applied for custody. Two welfare officers' reports recommended that the mother be given custody. The magistrates awarded custody to the father with access to the mother. However, the mother kept the child after an access visit. She appealed and the judge reversed the custody order in the mother's favour. The father appealed.

HELD: Allowing the appeal – the child's welfare was the first and paramount consideration. There was no presumption that one parent should be preferred to another parent for the purpose of looking after a child at a particular age. It was likely that a young child, particularly a little girl, would be expected to be with her mother but that was subject to the overriding factor that the child's welfare was the paramount consideration. It was natural for young children to be with mothers, but where there was a dispute, it was a consideration rather than a presumption. The case was remitted back to a fresh bench of magistrates to reconsider custody.

In *Re A (A Minor) (Custody)* [1991] 2 FLR 394 married parents had six children aged 20, 18, 16, 12, ten and six years. The mother developed an interest in the occult and had an affair with a married man. The parents separated. The mother left with the 12-year-old daughter. She could not take the youngest two children since she could not practically care for them. The father cared for the ten-year-old boy and the six-year-old girl (the older children being treated as independent). Due to bitterness between the parents the mother had problems having access to the children in the father's care. The mother claimed custody of the three youngest children. The judge awarded her custody of the 12-year-old daughter (already living with her) and the six-year-old daughter leaving the ten-year-old boy in the father's custody. The father appealed against the order relating to the six-year-old daughter.

HELD: Allowing the appeal, it was natural for young children to be with their mothers, but in a dispute it was a consideration, not a presumption. Where very young children remained throughout with the mother the unbroken relationship of mother and child would be difficult to displace, unless the mother was unsuitable to care for the child. Where mother and child had been separated, as here, and the mother now sought the child's return, other considerations apply. There was no presumption which required the mother, as mother, to be considered as the primary caretaker in preference to the father. The welfare of the child was paramount and each parent had to be assessed carefully before one could be chosen as the custodial parent. It was in the six-year-old daughter's interests that she did not move, so custody should go to the father with generous access to the mother. This view was supported by the House of Lords in relation to an appeal from a Scottish court (see *Brixey* v *Lynas* [1996] 2 FLR 499).

In the case of very young babies it has been held that, other things being equal, they should live with their mother (see *Re W (A Minor) (Residence Order)* [1992] 2 FLR 333; [1992] Fam Law 493 where the residence of a four-week-old baby was transferred from the father to the mother). There was a rebuttable presumption that a baby's best interests were served by its mother although the situation might be different with older children.

In *Re A (Children: 1959 UN Declaration)* [1998] Fam Law 72 it was again confirmed that there is no principle that mothers should care for young children. It was a consideration. In the case the relevance of the 1959 Declaration to family law (in particular Principle 6 that a child of tender years should not, save in exceptional circumstances, be separated from his/her mother) was doubted.

FATHERS CARING FOR OLDER BOYS. It has been said that older boys (eg aged eight years or more) should be cared for by their fathers, but this consideration has not been nearly as strongly expressed as the consideration in favour of mothers and young children (see *W* v *W and C* [1968] 1 WLR 1310; [1968] 3 All ER 408; *Re C(A) (An Infant), C* v *C(A)* [1970] 1 WLR 288; [1970] 1 All ER 309 where it was said that there was no principle to that effect).

PROVIDING THE BEST LIVING CONDITIONS. A child's welfare is not measured by material advantage or physical comfort alone. However, other things being equal, a parent who can offer the child good accommodation must have the edge over the one who cannot (see *Re F (An Infant)* [1969] 3 WLR 162; [1969] 2 All ER 766). But see *D* v *M (A Minor: Custody Appeal)* where the mother was unemployed and cared for the child in basic but adequate conditions. The father was materially much better off and could provide better housing and facilities. However, the court considered that the mother was the best person to bring up the child and the father's material advantages did not outweigh that. It was also said in *Stephenson* v *Stephenson* [1985] FLR 1140 that material disadvantage usually carried little weight.

In *B* v *T (Custody)* [1989] 2 FLR 31 a magistrates' court was criticised for looking too much at material matters, namely, the father being able to provide a semi-detached home with a garden as opposed to the mother's ninth floor flat with a play area five minutes' walk away and ignoring the advantages of a young child remaining with her mother.

KEEPING BROTHERS AND SISTERS TOGETHER. It is generally desirable to keep brothers and sisters together and not to split the family up more than is necessary. This will not usually be decisive, particularly if staying access to both parents will mean that the children will meet frequently during the holidays (see *Re P (Infants)* [1967] 1 WLR 818; [1967] 2 All ER 229).

See *Clarke-Hunt* v *Newcombe* (1983) 4 FLR 482 where there were two brothers. It was in the best interests of the younger brother that he should stay with his mother. The court, therefore, decided that, since the two brothers should not be separated, the elder brother should live with the mother as well, even though this was against his wishes and he might have been better off with his father.

In *Adams* v *Adams* [1984] FLR 768 the mother sought custody of her daughter but not her son. She failed to get custody of either child since the court considered it preferable that the two children should be kept together.

In *C* v *C (Minors: Custody)*, above there was a four-year-old son and a seven-year-old daughter. The son had a strong bond with his father but also a close relationship with his sister. The daughter was in the mother's custody. The son's custody was disputed. Custody was granted to the mother because the court considered that brothers and sisters should be brought up together unless there were strong reasons to suggest the need for different arrangements. Children would be of mutual support following their parents' separation. This could not be remedied by generous and frequent access. Both children should live in the same household, namely, that of the mother. The father was given generous access.

However, this consideration was not applied in *B* v *T (Custody)*, above, where the parents had two children, a boy aged three and a girl of fifteen months. They separated. The mother left with the baby girl. Both parents applied to a magistrates' court for custody of both children. Custody of both children was given to the father. On appeal to the High Court custody of both children was granted to the mother. On further appeal to the Court of Appeal.

HELD: The magistrates had been wrong to order custody of both children to the father. The High Court had also been wrong to order custody of both children to the mother based on insufficient evidence since the boy would lose his close bond with his father. No consideration had been given to the practicability and desirability of making an order giving custody of one child to one parent and the other child to the other parent. The case would be remitted back to the magistrates' court for the whole matter to be explored in depth.

In *B v B (Residence Order: Restricting Applications)* [1997] 1 FLR 139 (Court of Appeal) the mother (M) and father (F) married in 1975. They had three children, all boys, R aged 17 years, A aged 14 years and J aged 10 years. In 1993 the parents separated. M remained in the matrimonial home while F went to live with his grandfather. The children moved between the two houses. In 1994 an application was made for residence orders. R was living with F and A and J lived with M. In view of R's age no order was made with respect to him. A residence order was made that A and J live with M. In 1995 A went to live with F. In October, 1995 R went to live with M. F applied for residence orders with respect to the A and J. The court ordered A live with F and J live with M. F appealed. It was held, dismissing the appeal relating to the residence orders, that it was normally in the children's interests that they should live together. However, A had voted with his feet and the court pays great attention to the views of a 14-year-old. J had always lived and was settled with his mother. A change of residence would be damaging for him. There would be extensive contact between A and J since the parents lived near each other. The decision that they live with different parents could not be faulted.

NOTE: an order preventing F from making further applications with respect to J was set aside. Such a restriction was a drastic order to be made and should only be made in clear and exceptional circumstances.

THE EDUCATION OF THE CHILD. The court will wish to keep a child at the school where he or she is settled. The parent with the better attitude towards education may be favoured. In *May v May* [1985] Fam Law 106 the father laid emphasis on academic achievement, while the mother and her cohabitee had a somewhat free and easy attitude to education. As a result the father got care and control of the children.

THE CHILD'S RELIGION. Nowadays, the question of religious upbringing will probably have little bearing on the issue of care and control. But if the child has already had religious instruction, the continuation of his religion may be of vital importance if a break in it would produce emotional disturbance. It may be relevant to consider whether adherence to a religious sect (eg Jehovah's Witnesses or Scientology) would lead to the child's isolation or other psychological damage. See *Re B and G (Minors) (Custody)* (1985) 15 Fam Law 127 where both parents were loving and able to offer good homes to the children, but the Court of Appeal refused the father's appeal against the custody order in favour of the mother because of the grave risks involved for the children in his adherence to Scientology. Scientology was described as 'immoral' and 'obnoxious' and the father and the step-mother were deprived of custody even though they had had the child for five years.

See *Hewison v Hewison* (1977) 7 Fam Law 207 where the father belonged to a religious denomination called the Exclusive Brethren whose practices would deprive the child of normal social contact and limit the opportunities for the child's education. The mother got custody.

A number of cases have dealt with parents who are Jehovah's Witnesses. See *Re C (Minors) (Wardship: Jurisdiction)* [1978] 2 All ER 230; [1977] 3 WLR 561 where the court considered the harm that might be caused to a child by the refusal of parents who are Jehovah's Witnesses to allow blood transfusions and in taking children on house-to-house visiting. Such factors do not mean that such a parent cannot be awarded custody but will weigh against him or her. In *Jane v Jane* (1983) 13 Fam Law 209 the court was concerned with the blood transfusion problem and as a result made an unusual order – a split custody order, by giving actual custody to the mother who was a Jehovah's Witness, but legal custody to the father who was not and could, therefore, consent to a blood transfusion if the child needed one.

Custodial parents may have to give undertakings to continue a child's religion. See *Re E (An Infant)* [1964] 1 WLR 51; [1963] 3 All ER 874 where a Jewish couple were required to bring a child up as a Roman Catholic. See *J v C* [1969] 2 WLR 540 where the Protestant couple were required to bring the child up as a Roman Catholic.

In *Re P (Section 91(14) Guidelines) (Residence and Religious Heritage)* [1999] 2 FLR 573 it was emphasised that the right of parents to expect a child to have a particular religious upbringing is subservient to the welfare of the child. In that case the child was living with a non-practising Roman Catholic family. The child's parents were Orthodox Jews and wanted the child to be returned to them so that she could be brought up as an Orthodox Jew. Their application was dismissed. The child was very young and had limited understanding of her religious background. While s1(3)(d) CA 1989 required the court to have regard to the child's religious and cultural upbringing, the overwhelming factor was the need to preserve the child's present family in which she was thriving.

RACIAL AND CULTURAL BACKGROUND. If the parents propose to live in different countries, the court must take into account the possible psychological damage that might be done to the child by removing him from his native country to another, where his native tongue is not spoken, where he will be divorced from the social customs and contacts to which he is used, and where his education may be adversely affected (see *Re L* [1974] 1 All ER 913).

*The likely effect on the child of any change in his or her circumstances.* Courts have looked at two aspects of this consideration:

PRESERVING THE STATUS QUO IN A CHILD'S LIFE. The courts recognise that stability is important in the life of a child. If a child has been in the care of one parent for a long time the court may be very slow to change care and control and disrupt the child's life with all the upset that might cause. This consideration has grown more important in recent years.

See *J v C* (above) where the child had spent all but eighteen months of his life with his English foster parents. Though his Spanish parents were unimpeachable the importance of preserving the 'English' status quo of the child's life outweighed their claim for custody.

See *S(BD)* v *S(DJ)* *(Children: Care and Control)* [1977] 2 WLR 44; [1977] 1 All ER 656 where the mother had had the care of a son and daughter aged eight and six respectively for one year. The father then remarried and applied for custody. The court decided in favour of the mother to preserve the status quo of the children's lives and avoid the risks of moving them to a strange home in a strange area.

See *D* v *M* *(A Minor: Custody Appeal)* [1982] 3 WLR 891; [1982] 3 All ER 897 where the mother had had care of an illegitimate child all his life, namely, one and a half years. The father only applied for custody after he had married. The court decided in favour of the mother given the considerable upset of transferring the child away from the home he was settled in.

In *Stephenson* v *Stephenson*, above, the mother left her seven-month-old daughter when she left the matrimonial home. The child was cared for by the father and his cohabitee for two and a half years during which the mother only had access six times. The father and cohabitee had a happy and stable relationship and provided the child with a loving and constant relationship. The judge granted custody to the mother since he considered that a young girl should be with her natural mother. She lived with a man who had a criminal record and who, it was alleged, had used violence against the mother. The Court of Appeal allowed the father's appeal. He provided a stable, loving and happy home. The importance of the mother being the natural mother was reduced by her earlier abandonment of and inconsistency to her daughter.

Preserving the status quo was also important in *B* v *B* *(Custody of Child)*. In *B* v *T* *(Custody)*, above, the court pointed to the fact that the child of fifteen months had spent all her life with her mother in giving custody to her despite the fact that the father could provide better living accommodation.

In *Re H* *(A Minor)* *(Custody)* [1990] 1 FLR 51 the parents separated and the mother returned to India (her native land) with their son. Both parents decided that the child should be educated in England and so he came back to live in this country. He lived with his uncle and aunt. The father failed to tell the mother how the son was progressing and so she returned to England to see him. The father refused her access. She then divorced the father and applied for custody. The uncle and aunt also applied for custody. The court heard that the mother was warm and loving and had much love to offer her son. She wished to take him back to India. However, he had settled with his aunt and uncle. He had lived with them for two and a half years. He had developed from being a shy, difficult and backward boy into a normal eight-year-old schoolboy. The court gave custody to the aunt and uncle with generous access to the mother. The mother appealed. Her appeal was dismissed because the court had taken into account the relevant considerations (including the claim of an unimpeachable mother) and could not be said to be plainly wrong.

But a change will be ordered where appropriate. See *Re DW* *(A Minor)*

*(Custody)* (1984) 14 Fam Law 17 where a ten-year-old boy was transferred from the care of his step-mother, against his wishes, after she had cared for him for five-and-a-half years (though such a decision might well not be reached today). See also *Allington* v *Allington* and *Re W (A Minor: Custody)* (1983) where custody was transferred away from the father to the mother who had kept in close touch with the children so that the transfer would not necessarily be so upsetting.

In *Re G (Minors)* (1992) The Times 9 October an order was made transferring the residence of the children from the mother to the father even though the children had lived with the mother for three years. The transfer in residence was based on the mother's admission that she had been taking drugs in the presence of the children. The case concerned an interim residence order being made in the father's favour – the outcome of the final hearing was not reported.

In *Re B (Residence Order: Status Quo)* [1998] 1 FLR 368 H and W had a child, B. H cared for B from the age of two years. When B was three the marriage was dissolved and a residence order was made in H's favour. There were difficulties with contact. W applied for residence when B was aged eight and a residence order was made in her favour, partly on the grounds that contact might work better that way. H appealed. The appeal was allowed. The overwhelming importance for securing the child's future was plainly the status quo. The difficulty in contact had to be endured and tackled.

PROVIDING CONTINUITY OF CARE. The courts prefer a child to be looked after continuously by one adult, without there being any break in the provision of care, rather than a child being looked after in a fragmented way by a succession of adults (eg a parent who goes out to work using child minders and relatives to look after the child while he or she was away at work).

See *Re K (Minors) (Children: Care and Control)* [1977] 2 WLR 33 where the mother could provide continuous care whereas the father, who was a busy clergyman, could only arrange for the children to be cared for by a succession of 'worthy persons'. The mother was given custody.

See *S(BD)* v *S(DJ)* above, where the mother was not working and could provide full-time care for the child, whereas the father was working, as was his new wife who would have been overstretched if she also had to have care of the children. The mother again was awarded custody.

See *D* v *M (A Minor: Custody Appeal)* above where the mother of the child (who was illegitimate) was unemployed and could care for the child full-time. The father had married. His plan was that the child should be cared for by him, his wife, a relative (for two days) and a child minder (for the remaining periods). The court favoured the mother in that she could provide continuous care.

In *S* v *S (Minors) (Care and Control)* [1990] 2 FLR 341 W offered full-time care of the children. H worked long hours as a builder and offered that the children be cared for by him and the children's grandmother. The court preferred W's offer of day-to-day care but postponed its decision until W's claims with respect to the home had been resolved.

In some cases the parents have arranged that the children spend part of the week with one parent and the rest of the week with the other. This can be confirmed by the court making a shared residence order provided this is in the child's best interests (see *A* v *A (Minors) (Shared Residence)* [1994] 1 FLR 669 and *Re A (A Minor) (Shared Residence Order)* [1994] Fam Law 431). The court will balance a need for a child to have a settled home with the benefits of sharing his/her time between both parents.

*The child's age, sex, background and any characteristics of the child which the court considers relevant.* Some of the factors discussed above equally apply under this consideration.

*Any harm which the child has suffered or is at risk of suffering.* This consideration is more relevant to care proceedings. One aspect which has received attention is the parent's new partner. In *Scott* v *Scott* [1986] Fam Law 301 the mother's cohabitee had a criminal record and had committed acts of indecency against the child. That fact more than offset any advantages the mother had in taking care of the child.

The mother's cohabitee was also important in *Stephenson* v *Stephenson*, above, since he had a criminal record and had allegedly been violent to her. Her claim for custody failed.

*How capable each of the child's parents, and any other person in relation to whom the court considers the question to be relevant, is of meeting the child's needs.* The court has considered aspects of this consideration:

THE RELEVANCE OF THE PARENT'S CONDUCT. The behaviour of a parent is only relevant in the way that it affects the child's welfare. The behaviour between parents may be considered to be irrelevant. See *Re K* [1988] 1 All ER 214 where there was a 'moral' parent, namely, the father who was a clergyman who tried to effect a reconciliation with the mother who had left him, and an 'immoral' parent, namely, the mother who had left the husband and was living in adultery. The court considered the respective behaviour of the parents as not being relevant – the welfare of the children meant that they should live with the mother and so she got custody. In *S(BD)* v *S(DJ)*, above, the phrase 'unimpeachable parent' was criticised. The mother had had three affairs whereas the father was 'unimpeachable'. She was given custody.

Otherwise misconduct may be relevant as throwing light on probable behaviour of the parents in the future and might tip the scales where each parent has an equal claim (see *Re F* [1988] 2 FLR 116).

See *Re H (A Minor: Custody Appeal)* [1991] Fam Law 422 where it was held that a father's allegations of adultery and persistent lying against the mother were unlikely to have any relevance in deciding who should have custody of their fourteen-year-old son. When marriages break down spouses can behave in a reprehensible way towards each other but this did not of itself necessarily disentitle either spouse from being a good or adequate caretaker of a child. The mother had cared for her son for the previous three years whereas the father had failed to take any interest in him. Custody was given to the mother.

ATTITUDES TO CONTACT. Attitudes to contact between the child and the other parent can reveal whether a parent is genuinely concerned with the welfare of the child by allowing the other parent contact to the child, or whether a parent is more interested in hurting the other parent by refusing contact, even though it is in the child's interest to keep contact with the other parent. See *D v M (A Minor: Custody Appeal)* above, where the father was reluctant to allow the mother to have contact if he were given custody. The court considered that a serious matter which weighed against his claim for custody.

See *Re S (Minors: Access Appeal)* [1990] 2 FLR 166 where H and W had two children C and B (both boys). C went to live with H while B remained with W. W refused to allow H access to B and thereby deprived B of access to his brother. The Court of Appeal said that where a custodial parent resolutely refused to obey an access order (as there was in this case) there was usually no effective sanction to enforce the order (eg imprisonment). However, the court could look at custody afresh and decide whether B's welfare required that he be given the opportunity to know his brother and his father even if this meant depriving W of custody.

PARENTS WITH HOMOSEXUAL RELATIONSHIPS. In *Re C* [1991] 1 FLR 223 it was held that a parent (in this case a mother) with a homosexual/lesbian relationship was not necessarily unfit to have care and control of his or her child. However, such a relationship was important in deciding which of the alternative homes offered by the parents is most likely to advance the child's welfare. The upbringing most likely to be in the child's best interests is the one which comes closest to the ideal norm by the standards of society (ie that a child should be brought up in a home by a father and mother).

In this case H and W separated in 1984 when the child (C) was one. W had care and control. H had access. In 1988 H remarried. In 1989 W, who was employed as a prison officer, formed a lesbian relationship with a prisoner released after serving a sentence for violence. C had a strong bond with W. The judge at first instance decided that W's lesbian relationship played no significant part in deciding where C should live. C was going to have to cope with the relationship whether C stayed with W on visiting access or permanently. H appealed.

HELD: The judge's conclusion on the effect on C of the lesbian relationship was plainly wrong. Despite the vast change in attitudes towards marriage, sexual morality and homosexual relationships the ideal environment for the upbringing of a child was the home of a loving, caring and sensible mother. When the marriage was at an end that ideal could not be sustained. The court then had to decide between two possible alternatives with the preference for the one which came closest to that ideal. A lesbian relationship was an unusual background in which to bring up a child. It was undesirable that a young child should understand the nature of the mother's relationship. What would be the effect on C's school friends on learning of the relationship? W's partner's previous conviction was also relevant. The appeal was allowed and the case listed for rehearing.

NOTE: After the rehearing care and control was given to H (*Re C* [1990] Fam Law 413).

The opposite conclusion was reached in the case of *B v B (Minors) (Custody, Care and Control)* [1991] 1 FLR 402; [1991] Fam Law 174 where the parents had three children aged ten, nine and two. The mother left to live in a lesbian relationship. There was a divorce. The father formed a new relationship with a woman whom he hoped to marry. The parents agreed to have joint custody of all three children and that the oldest two should live with their father. Care and control of their two-year-old son was disputed.

HELD: In determining whether a child should be brought up in a lesbian household two factors had to be considered: the effect on the sexual identity of the child and the effect of stigmatization. Neither factor weighed heavily against the mother since the father would play a role in the boy's life whoever had care and control and the mother was not a militant lesbian parading her relationship in public. The boy had closely bonded with the mother. There was a wide difference in ages between him and the older children so the desirability of keeping siblings together was not overriding. The mother was a caring and loving mother with a good understanding of the psychological needs of children. Care and control of the youngest child was granted to her.

NOTE: In this case the court was assisted by a report from an eminent consultant psychiatrist to the effect that the dangers to a child of living in a lesbian household tended to be overestimated and that the little boy would be better off with the mother. Against this was the welfare report which expressed concern about the mother's lesbianism and recommended that the child live with the father and the siblings be brought up together. Also, if the child was to live with the father, a child minder would have had to be employed whereas the mother was available to provide continuous care.

*The range of powers available to the court under the Children Act 1989.* This completes the checklist of considerations under s1(3), (4) CA 1989.

A number of other considerations should also be mentioned:

## Guidance from other decisions

The circumstances of each case and the personalities of the parties and the children are infinitely variable. The course followed in one case may of little assistance in guiding one to the course to be adopted in another (see *Re K (Minors) (Children: Care and Control)*, above, and *Pountney* v *Morris* [1984] FLR 381).

## Long-term and short-term welfare

Generally, the court is concerned to do what is best for the child's long-term welfare unless this is ruled out by short-term disadvantages. See *Thompson* v *Thompson* [1987] Fam Law 89 where the husband and the wife separated. The husband retained custody of their daughter. Both applied for custody. The husband proposed to care for the daughter with the assistance of his mother. The daughter was happy where she was. The court considered that the husband's plans were unrealistic. However, the wife wanted the daughter to come and live in her new family, and it was uncertain whether she would settle in her new family. The court granted custody to the husband. The best approach was what was in the daughter's short-term welfare, given that it was not clear if either party could provide for her long-term welfare. The situation could be reviewed in three years' time.

For illustrations of the courts favouring a long-term approach see *B* v *T (Custody)* [1989] 2 FLR 31 where magistrates were criticised for looking at what was best for young children in the short term. They granted custody of young children to an unemployed father after considering the mother's accommodation problems. They ignored the long-term, such as the possibility of the father obtaining work and not being able to care for the children and the possibility of the mother finding a better place to live. Custody was given to the mother. See also *Re M (A Minor: Custody Appeal)* [1990] 1 FLR 291 where a child was born to a seventeen-year-old father and sixteen-year-old mother. They decided to place the child for adoption and the child went to live with local authority foster parents. The father then changed his mind and applied for custody of the child stating that his parents could help him bring up the child. His application was dismissed since in the long-term the father's immaturity and the stresses and strains of any new relationship he might develop might conflict with his duties to the child. The child's long-term future lay with two loving adoptive parents.

## The CAFCASS report

The court will often ask the Children and Family Advisory and Support Service (CAFCASS) to prepare a report to help the court make its decision. The report will be prepared by an officer called the children and family reporter. Courts often give great weight to the recommendations in the CAFCASS report. The court is not bound by such recommendations but should give reasons for not following them (see *Stephenson* v *Stephenson* [1985] FLR 1140). In *W* v *W (A Minor: Custody Appeal)* [1988] 2 FLR 505 it was said that if a court failed to give its reasons for not following the report's recommendations there would be grounds for an appeal. More recently in *Re W (Residence)* [1999] 2 FLR 390 the importance of giving adequate reasons for not agreeing with such recommendations was emphasised.

## When outside help is needed

Courts cannot make care or supervision orders in matrimonial (called 'private law') proceedings. The court can invite the local authority to investigate a child's circumstances if the child is in need (see s37 CA 1989) or make a family assistance order (see s16 CA 1989). A family assistance order will require either a social worker or a probation officer to be made available to 'advise, assist and (where appropriate) befriend any person named in the order' (ie parents or any person with whom the child is living or any person in whose favour a contact order has been made or the child). Such an order will be aimed at providing short-term help for a family (eg in their problems associated with a separation or divorce). Such an order can only be made in exceptional circumstances and only with the consent of the named person. An order will only last up to six months though a second order could be made.

## 15.4 Checking the arrangements for children after divorce

In any proceedings for divorce, nullity or judicial separation, if there are any children of the family under 16 (or older children the court has directed should be considered), the court must consider whether (in the light of the arrangements which have been, or are proposed to be made, for the children's upbringing and welfare) it should exercise any of its powers under the Children Act 1989 with respect to any of them (see s41(1) MCA 1973 as amended by para 31, Sch 12 CA 1989). Section 41(1) provides:

> 'If it appears to the court that –
> (a) the circumstances of the case require it, or are likely to require it to exercise any of its powers under the Children Act 1989; and
> (b) it cannot exercise its powers without further considering the case; and
> (c) there are exceptional circumstances which make it desirable in the interests of the child that the court should give a direction.
> it may direct that the decree of divorce or nullity cannot be made absolute or the decree of judicial separation granted until the court orders otherwise.'

Considering the arrangements for the children will usually be a paperwork exercise. Normally only children under 16 will be considered. The children of the family have to be named in the divorce petition. The petitioner must prepare a statement about the present and proposed arrangements for the children. The petitioner should try and agree its contents with the respondent in advance of petitioning for divorce and get his/her counter signature on the statement. If the respondent refuses to countersign then the petitioner files his/her statement and the respondent can file a statement of his/her own (ie when returning the acknowledgement of service). The statement is eight pages long and requires detailed information about the children of the family. At the end of the form the petitioner is asked whether he/she would agree to attend conciliation with the respondent if the arrangements are not agreed. Most family hearing centres have a conciliation appointment scheme where parties attend in order to see if a settlement is possible in a relatively informal, relaxed manner with a court welfare officer (see *Practice Direction (Family Division: Conciliation)* [1992] 1 WLR 147). The aim of the statement is to make both parents look at the change in the lives of their children and to provide the court with a written picture of what has happened to them.

The statement (and, where applicable, counter statement) are reviewed by a district judge. He/she decides whether the court needs to exercise its powers under s8 CA 1989. If satisfied that no direction is needed then no court attendance is required and a certificate of satisfaction is issued and a date set for decree nisi. If the district judge is not satisfied then he/she can direct that a welfare report be prepared and further evidence filed and require both parties to attend a hearing. A date is set for decree nisi but decree absolute is postponed until the situation concerning the children is resolved to the satisfaction of the court.

## 15.5 Third parties wanting to care for the children

### *Third parties applying for s8 orders*

Residence or contact orders (but *not* specific issue or prohibited steps orders) may be applied for by:

1. a step-parent (ie a party to the marriage in relation to whom the child was a child of the family);
2. a person with whom the child has lived for the last three years out of the last five (this period need not have been continuous but must not have ended more than three months before the application);
3. any person who:

   a) where the child is subject to a residence order, has the consent of each of those in whose favour the order was made;
   b) where the child is in care, has the consent of the local authority in whose care the child is; or
   c) in any other case, has the consent of those who have parental responsibility for the child (see s10(5) CA 1975).

Other people may apply for any kind of s8 order if:

1. the court considers that the order should be made even though no application has been made (see s10(1)(b)); or
2. the person has obtained the leave of the court to make the application (see s10(1)(a)(ii) CA 1989).

In considering whether to grant leave the court must have particular regard to:

1. the nature of the proposed application for the s8 order;

2. the applicant's connection with the child;
3. any risk there might be of the proposed application disrupting the child's life to such an extent that the child would be harmed by it; and
4. where the child is being looked after by a local authority – the authority's plans for the child's future; and the wishes and feelings of the child's parents: see s10(9) CA 1989.

The leave requirement is to filter out cases of unwarranted interference by third parties. The final requirement relates to foster parents seeking leave and obliges the court to take the parents' interests and those of the local authority into account.

The requirements for granting leave were considered in *Re A and Others (Minors) (Residence Order)* [1992] 3 WLR 422; [1992] 3 All ER 872; [1992] 2 FLR 154; [1992] Fam Law 439 where a foster parent had had highly disturbed children living with her for two years. Good progress was made but the placement broke down when the relationship between the foster parent and the local authority broke down. The children were removed. The foster mother applied for leave to apply for residence orders for the children. The court granted leave holding that the children's welfare was paramount in considering whether to grant leave or not. On appeal it was held that the children's welfare was not paramount in considering whether to grant leave. It was only paramount if leave was granted and the application considered on its merits. In considering whether to grant leave the court must have regard to the criteria laid down in s10(9) CA 1989 which included the wishes and feelings of the children's mother, the future plans of the local authority and the risk that the proposed applications would disrupt the children's lives to the extent that they would be harmed. In this case the court had not applied the correct criteria and the appeal would be allowed. Leave for the foster mother to make an application for the residence order was refused particularly in light of the views of the children who were old enough to know their minds and did not wish to return to live with the foster mother.

The court also held that in considering whether or not to grant leave a court did not have to assume it should not interfere with the plans of the local authority save in the most exceptional circumstances since that principle had been superseded by CA 1989. However a court should assume that a local authority's plans were in accordance with its duty under s22(3) CA 1989 to safeguard and promote the welfare of the child and that any departure from those plans might well disrupt the child's life to such an extent that the child would be harmed by it.

In the case of a person who has been a local authority foster parent of a child within the last six months, that person cannot apply for leave un~~~~ he or she has the consent of the local authority (unless he or she is a relative ~~~~~~~ or the child has lived with him or her for three out of the past five ~~~~~~ 1989).

Third parties can either make direct applications for resid~~~~ or may intervene in existing proceedings (eg adoption procee~~~~

domestic violence proceedings, maintenance proceedings under DPMCA 1978 and divorce proceedings under MCA 1973) subject to the leave of the court.

In *G* v *Kirklees MBC* [1993] 1 FLR 805; [1993] Fam Law 278 an aunt sought leave to become a party in care proceedings (pursuant to r7(2) Family Proceedings Courts (Children Act 1989) Rules 1991) so that she could seek an order for residence or contact to the child. The local authority wished to obtain a care order with a view to placing the child for adoption so opposed the application. The child's mother's views were inconsistent but she strongly opposed any member of her family having contact with the child so she too opposed the application made by the aunt. The justices refused her application holding that the welfare of the child was paramount. The aunt appealed.

HELD: That the justices had applied the wrong test. In considering whether to grant leave the welfare of the child was not paramount (applying *Re A and Others* (above)). The purpose of seeking leave was for the aunt to seek a s8 order. The matters set out in s10(9) CA 1989 assisted in considering the application for leave since the aunt would have had to apply for leave under s10 to apply for a s8 order were it not for the care proceedings. The applicant also had to show that her application was likely to succeed if she was joined as a party. Since the aunt had no reasonable prospect of obtaining a s8 order there was no purpose in joining her as a party.

Applications for prohibited steps orders and specific issues orders by third parties will need the leave of the court (see s10(1), (2) CA 1989).

NOTE: Such orders cannot be made if a child is in the care of a local authority (see s9(1) CA 1989).

In *G* v *F (Shared Residence: Parental Responsibility)* [1998] 2 FLR 799 G and F formed a lesbian relationship in 1991. They wanted a child of the relationship. F had a child by artificial insemination from an anonymous donor and a child was born in September 1994. The relationship broke up in 1997 and G applied for leave to apply for contact and a shared residence order in respect of the child. F opposed the application for leave arguing that G did not satisfy s10(9) CA 1989. It was held that G had an arguable case for a shared residence order in order to acquire parental responsibility for the child. She had played an important role in the child's life and upbringing. G had deep affection and concern for the child. The background of the lesbian relationship was no basis for discriminating against G. Her application for leave was granted.

## Children applying for orders

A child may apply for leave to apply for a s8 order. The court must be satisfied that the child has sufficient understanding to make the proposed application (see s10(8) CA 1989). There have been a number of cases where children have obtained leave and then obtained their own orders. Some cases were reported in the media under headlines such as 'Girl, 11, first in England to "divorce" parents' (see *Independent* 12

November 1992). In that case an 11-year-old girl obtained the leave of the court to make an application for a residence order. Her application was successful and an order made that she reside with her grandparents as opposed to her mother and step-father.

In another case a 14-year-old girl sought a residence order whereby she could live with the parents of her 18-year-old boyfriend as opposed to her parents. She was made a ward of court (see *Re AD (A Minor) (Child's Wishes)* [1993] Fam Law 405). In *Re SC (A Minor) (Leave to Seek Residence Order)* [1993] Fam Law 618 a 14-year-old girl had been in care for eight years. She lived in a children's home after foster placements had broken down. She wished to live with a family friend and sought leave to apply for a residence order. Her mother opposed the application for leave.

HELD: The girl had sufficient understanding under s10(8) CA 1989 to make the application. It did not follow that the court was bound to grant her leave. There was no statutory guidance equivalent to s10(9) to show how the court should consider whether to grant leave. The court should have regard to the likelihood of success of the application. Following *Re A and Others* (above) the welfare of the child was not paramount in considering whether leave should be granted.

In *Re C (Residence: Child's Application for Leave)* [1995] 1 FLR 927 a 14-year-old girl applied for leave to apply for an order under CA 1989. Her parents had been separated and there was a long history of proceedings. She felt that she had not been able to convey her wishes to the court in those proceedings. She lacked confidence that her true views would be adequately represented by the court welfare officer in the proceedings currently before the court (which were for variation of existing residence and contact orders).

HELD: If the court was satisfied that the child had sufficient understanding to make the application then it had a discretion whether or not to grant leave. The child's welfare was important but not paramount. The court had to be cautious since this area of law is developing. The court had to balance two considerations. Firstly a child is a human being with individual wishes and feelings which should command serious attention. Secondly a child may be vulnerable and impressionable. He or she may lack maturity and be unable to weigh the long term against the short term. He or she may lack insight and imagination in judging how he or she or others may react in certain situations. If a child was given party status in proceedings between warring parents then the child would be present when the parents gave evidence and were cross-examined. He or she may hear things which it would be better for the child not to hear. The child could be cross-examined. In the present case the child was of sufficient understanding, her application had some prospect of success and the issue to be decided was of great importance. Leave was granted.

In another case an 11-year-old was successful in obtaining a residence order that she live with a couple who had fostered her as a baby rather than with her mother.

NOTE: It is wrong to say that a child can 'divorce' his or her parents. A child may obtain a residence order but his or her parents still retain parental responsibility which they hold along with the person named in the residence order (though the parents cannot act against the residence order eg by demanding that the child return to live with them).

Any application by a child for leave to apply for his/her own s8 order should be heard by the High Court because of the difficult issues raised (*Practice Direction* [1993] 1 All ER 820).

In *Re S (A Minor) (Adopted Child: Contact)* [1999] 3 WLR 504; [1999] 1 All ER 648 Y a nine-year-old child (adopted into one family) applied for leave to apply for contact with S, her seven-year-old half-brother (adopted into a separate family). Leave was refused because of the risk that Y's application would disrupt S's life to the extent that he would be harmed by it.

## 15.6 Guardianship

### Appointing a guardian – by the parents

A parent who has parental responsibility for his or her child may appoint another individual to be the child's guardian in the event of that parent's death (see s5(3) CA 1989). Such an appointment must be made by a written and dated document signed by the parent making the appointment or signed at the direction of the parent in the presence of two witnesses who each attest the signature (see s5(5) CA 1989). An appointment may be made by will or deed as before.

The appointment of such a guardian only takes effect if:

1. on the death of the parent making the appointment there is no other parent with parental responsibility for the child; or
2. immediately before the death of the parent making the appointment a residence order in that parent's favour was in force with respect to the child (see s5(7) CA 1989).

Otherwise if no residence order has been made in the deceased parent's favour the surviving parent (if he or she has parental responsibility) retains responsibility for the child and the guardian's appointment only takes effect once that parent has also died (see s5(8) CA 1989).

Once the appointment does take effect the guardian has parental responsibility for the child (see s5(6) CA 1989).

More than one guardian may be appointed.

The guardian may appoint a replacement guardian following the same formalities.

A guardian cannot be appointed save in accordance with s5 Children Act 1989. The High Court's inherent jurisdiction can no longer be exercised (subject to rules of court) (see s5(11) and (13) CA 1989).

An appointment of a guardian is revoked if the person appointed is the spouse of the person who made the appointment and either the marriage is dissolved or annulled either by a court in England and Wales or via a foreign divorce or annulment recognised in England and Wales (unless a contrary intention appears by the appointment) (s6(3A) Children Act 1989 as added by s4 Law Reform (Succession) Act 1995). This provision only applies to an appointment made by a person dying on or after 1 January 1996 (regardless of the date of the appointment and the date of the dissolution or annulment). This amendment to the law seeks to avoid a situation which can arise with second marriages. For example a mother has children from a previous unmarried relationship. She marries. She appoints her second husband as guardian of his step-children. She then divorces him. Unless she changed her will he would remain the children's guardian if she died which may not be her wish. The new provision revokes the appointment automatically on divorce.

### Appointing a guardian – by the court
An individual may apply to the court to be a child's guardian if:

1. the child has no parent with parental responsibility for the child; or
2. a residence order has been made with respect to the child in favour of a parent (or guardian) of the child who has died while the order was in force (see s5(1) CA 1989).

The court may also appoint a guardian in the above circumstances if the court considers that the order should be made even though no application has been made for it (see s5(2) CA 1989).

### Revocation and disclaimer of an appointment
A later appointment of a guardian by a parent (or by a guardian) revokes the earlier appointment unless it is clear the purpose of the later appointment is to appoint an additional guardian (see s6(1) CA 1989).

An appointment by a parent can be revoked by a written, dated and signed document (in the same way as appointing a guardian) or by destroying the appointment document (other than one made in a will or codicil) (see s6(2) and (3) CA 1989).

If the appointment is made it shall be revoked if the will or codicil is revoked (see s6(4) CA 1989).

A person may disclaim his or her appointment as a guardian by a written and signed document made within a reasonable time of the guardian's first knowing that the appointment has taken effect (see s6(5) CA 1989).

Any appointment of a guardian under s5 may be brought to an end at any time by order of the court:

1. on the application of any person who has parental responsibility for the child;
2. on the application of the child concerned, with leave of the court; or
3. in any family proceedings, if the court considers that it should be brought to an end even though no application has been made (see s6(7) CA 1989).

**General considerations**

Application is made to the High Court, county court or magistrates' court (see s92(7) CA 1989).

The child's welfare is paramount (see s1(1) CA 1989).

The court must be satisfied that making an order will be better than making no order at all (see s1(5) CA 1989).

The court must assume that any delay in determining any question of guardianship is likely to prejudice the child's welfare (see s1(2) CA 1989).

The Guardianship of Minors Act 1971 and Guardianship Act 1973 are repealed and the concept of guardianship as a complex mixture of common law, equity and statute becomes a single concept under the Children Act 1989.

A guardian has parental responsibility for the child and may give consent to the child's adoption (see s5(6) CA 1989 and s16 Adoption Act 1976).

## 15.7 Wardship

Wardship is largely a creature of the common law. It originated in medieval times. A ward of court is a child whose guardian is the High Court. Wardship can be more flexible than other forms of proceedings and provides an immediate remedy (which may be particularly useful in emergencies such as children being 'kidnapped' and taken abroad by one parent against the wishes of the other). However, wardship does have drawbacks. Hearings before the High Court can be subject to long delay. Hearings are expensive since barristers appear in the High Court (as opposed to solicitors in magistrates' court or in some county court hearings).

### When a local authority may use wardship

A local authority *cannot* use wardship as an alternative to care proceedings (see s100(2) CA 1989).

Where a child's case is before the High Court it cannot make a care order or supervision order itself but may direct a local authority to investigate the child's circumstances (s7 Family Law Reform Act 1969 is repealed by s100(1) CA 1989 – see also s37 CA 1989).

No application for the exercise of the wardship jurisdiction with respect to children may be made by a local authority unless the authority obtains the leave of the court (see s100(3) CA 1989).

The court may only grant leave if it is satisfied that:

1. the result which the local authority wish to achieve could not be achieved in any other way open to the local authority (eg under CA 1989); and
2. there is reasonable cause to believe that if the court's inherent jurisdiction is not exercised with respect to the child, the child is likely to suffer significant harm (see s100(4), (5) CA 1989).

This limits the powers of the local authority so that in most cases it must use Parts IV and V of the Children Act 1989 which balances the interests of family autonomy and child protection.

These provisions were discussed in *Devon County Council* v *S* [1995] 1 All ER 243 where M had nine children. Y was married to the eldest child. Y, who had convictions for sexual offences, was considered to be a serious risk, particularly to the youngest three children. M did not consider Y to be a risk and allowed him to visit her and the children. The local authority did not want to take care proceedings since it considered that this would do more harm than good. It considered that M's care of the children was otherwise good and it did not wish to invade her parental responsibility for the children and risk destabilising their care. The local authority applied for leave to make the children wards of court. The court refused leave on the ground that the local authority could protect the children by taking care proceedings.

HELD: Allowing the appeal and granting leave, s100 CA 1989 should not be construed restrictively. There were valid reasons why care proceedings were not appropriate. Equally an application for a supervision order was not appropriate since such an order would require M to be supervised, rather than Y. Since there was reasonable cause to believe that if the court's powers were not exercised the children would suffer significant harm, the local authority was allowed to bring wardship proceedings.

Where the local authority wishes to supplement its powers or gain the authority of the High Court to confirm its decisions, it may apply for leave.

In *Re B (A Minor) (Wardship: Sterilisation)* [1987] 2 FLR 314 the local authority asked the High Court to sanction the sterilisation of a mentally handicapped child.

See *Practice Note (Sterilisation)* [1990] Fam Law 375 where it was said that the sterilisation of a minor (or a mentally incompetent adult) will in virtually all cases require the prior sanction of a High Court Judge. In the case of a child this would be through wardship in the Family Division. The court must be satisfied that those proposing sterilisation are seeking it in good faith for the best interests of the child rather than for their own convenience or that of the public. The proceedings will normally involve a thorough adverserial investigation of all possible viewpoints and possible alternatives to sterilisation. The court will normally require evidence clearly establishing:

1. the child cannot give valid consent;
2. the condition which it is sought to avoid will in fact occur (ie there is a real danger of pregnancy as opposed to a mere chance);
3. the child will experience substantial trauma or psychological damage if the pregnancy occurs which would be greater than that resulting from the sterilisation *and* the child is incapable of caring for a baby even with reasonable assistance;
4. there is no practicable, less intrusive alternative means of avoiding the problem other than immediate sterilisation.

For a case involving abortion see *Re B (Wardship: Abortion)* [1991] 2 FLR 426 where a twelve-year-old girl became pregnant. She was of normal intelligence and understanding for her age. She asked for an abortion. She was in the care of her maternal grandparents with her unmarried mother keeping in close touch. The local authority made her a ward of court. The child was represented by the Official Solicitor. The mother opposed the abortion. The risks of continuing the pregnancy included premature labour, a difficult birth and possible physical and mental injury. The abortion was sanctioned.

In *Re D* [1987] 3 WLR 1400; [1987] 3 All ER 717 a local authority started care proceedings because of the educational problems of a severely handicapped child. The parents replied by making the child a ward of court. The local authority allowed the wardship to continue and asked the High Court to provide guidance in balancing the wishes of the parents and the special needs of the child.

In *Re C (A Minor) (No 1)* [1989] 2 All ER 752 a local authority used wardship to ask the High Court to deal with the difficult and sensitive case of an extremely handicapped child who was born terminally ill. The Court directed that she should received treatment to relieve her of pain, suffering or distress but that she should otherwise be allowed to end her life peacefully and with dignity.

In *Re Baby J* [1990] 3 All ER 930 a child was born with severe handicap. He suffered from a life threatening condition. He was made a ward of court. The Court asked whether he could be allowed to die or whether he should be kept alive. The first and paramount consideration was the welfare of the child. Since treatment would cause increased suffering and would produce no benefits the court would be justified in refusing to consent to medical treatment. There was a strong presumption in favour of action which would prolong life but that presumption was not irrebuttable. See also *Re B* [1990] 3 All ER 927 where the court reached the opposite conclusion in relation to a less severely handicapped child.

In *Re J (A Minor)(Wardship: Medical Treatment)* [1992] 3 WLR 507; [1992] 4 All ER 614 a 16-month-old child was profoundly mentally and physically handicapped. His life expectancy was short. He required 24-hour attention. The local authority shared parental responsibility for J. The question arose as to, if J suffered a life threatening event (particularly in relation to J's difficulties in breathing), whether he should be treated. The doctors considered that to use measures to prolong his life (in particular artificial ventilation) would be cruel. The local authority and J's mother sought an order requiring the doctors to continue to provide all available treatment to him to prolong his life. An order was made in those terms. The health authority, J (through the Official Solicitor) and the local authority (who had changed its mind) appealed against the order.

HELD: Allowing the appeal, the court would not use its inherent jurisdiction over minors to order a doctor to treat a minor in a manner contrary to the doctor's clinical judgment. The doctor's duty was to treat the patient in accordance with his/her best clinical judgment. The doctors should be left free to treat J as they saw fit subject to those with parental responsibility for J consenting to him being treated by those doctors. There could not be an obligation on doctors to treat a patient in a particular way.

See *Re LH* [1986] 2 FLR 306 where a local authority had to deal with a schizophrenic father and a depressive mother seeking access to a child in its care, and wardship was used to resolve a very difficult situation.

In *Re L (A Minor) (Wardship: Freedom of Publication)* [1988] 1 All ER 418; [1988] 1 FLR 255 a local authority used the wardship jurisdiction to restrict media reports about a child who had lost her parents and grandmother in a ferry disaster. In particular, the local authority wished to protect the child's privacy at the funeral and asked the High Court to make orders accordingly which the authority had no power to do itself.

## When other people can use wardship

People cannot use wardship to challenge the decisions of local authorities.

In *A* v *Liverpool City Council* [1981] 2 WLR 948; [1981] 2 All ER 385 a mother sought to challenge a local authority's decision to refuse her access to her child who had been made the subject of a care order by making the child a ward of court. The House of Lords dismissed the wardship stating that the court had no power to review the decisions of a local authority which had been given the statutory power and duty to take such decisions as it saw fit as to the welfare of a child in its care.

This was followed in *Re W (A Minor) (Wardship: Jurisdiction)* [1985] 2 WLR 892; [1985] 2 All ER 308 (also called the *Hertfordshire* case) where the relatives of a child who had been the subject of care proceedings tried to use wardship in order to become involved in what was to happen to the child since they had no right to appear in the care proceedings. They argued that their only remedy was wardship. Following *A* v *Liverpool City Council* the House of Lords again said it had no power to review a local authority acting within its statutory powers and dismissed the wardship.

In *Re M and H (Minors) (Parental Rights Resolution: Access Orders)* [1988] 2 FLR 431 the House of Lords again confirmed its earlier decisions and declined to allow a putative father to seek a challenge to the decision of a local authority to refuse him access to a child in its care under a parental rights resolution.

Once care proceedings have started an individual cannot use wardship to challenge the proceedings since this would interfere with the procedure laid down by Parliament. See *NSPCC* v *H and H* [1989] 2 FLR 131 where a stepfather tried to use wardship because the rules of care proceedings did not allow him to be a party at that time. See also *Re E (Minors) (Wardship: Care Proceedings)* (1983) 4 FLR 668; *W* v *Shropshire County Council* [1986] 1 FLR 359 and *W* v *Nottinghamshire County Council* [1986] 1 FLR 565 which stated that wardship could not be used to forestall a local authority contemplating care proceedings.

Individuals may ask the High Court to authorise important decisions concerning a child through wardship or to prevent harm from coming to the child. See *Re D (A Minor) (Wardship: Sterilisation)* [1976] 2 WLR 279; [1976] 1 All ER 326 where an educational psychologist made a child a ward of court to prevent the child's mother from sterilising her child and *Re B (A Minor) (Wardship: Medical Treatment)* [1981] 1 WLR 1421 where wardship was used to allow a handicapped child to receive medical treatment which his parents refused to consent to since they wished to allow the child to die. More recent examples include *Re Baby J* and *Re B*, both considered above.

## Procedural considerations

A child can only be made a ward of court by order (see s41 Supreme Court Act 1981).

An unborn child cannot be made a ward of court. In *Re F* [1988] 2 All ER 193; [1988] 2 FLR 307 the court was told of a mentally unbalanced drug addict mother who disappeared while pregnant. There was concern for the welfare of the unborn child. The court refused to ward the unborn child since a foetus had no right of action in English civil law and had no existence independent of the mother. The court refused to impose controls over the mother for the benefit of an unborn child.

Immediately a summons for an order from the Family Division of the High Court is issued the child becomes a ward. An appointment to confirm the wardship must be within twenty-one days (see s41(2) SCA 1981) or the wardship will cease. At this stage any frivolous applications may be dismissed (eg *Re Dunhill* (1967) 111 SJ 113 where a night club owner attempted to ward one of his striptease artists as a publicity stunt and his application was dismissed as an abuse of process).

The applicant must state his or her relationship to the child (*Practice Direction* [1967] 1 WLR 623). Application is usually made by a parent or a local authority but may be made by any person (eg the educational psychologist in *Re D (A Minor) (Wardship: Sterilisation)* above).

The wardship will continue until the child becomes eighteen or until the court ends the wardship (see s41(3) SCA 1981). The rights of the child's parents are superseded and no step can taken without the consent of the High Court.

## Principle on which the court will act

The welfare of the child is the paramount consideration when dealing with the child's custody and upbringing though it may not be in relation to other aspects (eg allowing the press to report a particular case as in *Re L* [1988] 1 All ER 418 or allowing a child to give evidence in a criminal case as in *Re K* [1988] 1 All ER 214) where other considerations may have equal weight.

The balance between the interests of the child and that of the freedom of the press was considered in *Re M and N (Wards) (Publication of Information)* [1990] 1 All ER 205. The child's welfare was not the first and paramount consideration. The media should generally have the maximum freedom to publish, the child the maximum protection. A court should not automatically grant an injunction prohibiting publication. If an injunction was needed it should be no wider than necessary to protect the child (eg simply to prevent the child's identity from being revealed).

See also *Re C (A Minor) (No 2)* [1989] 2 All ER 783 where the Court of Appeal considered the freedom of the press to publish details of a difficult and sensitive case involving a terminally ill, severely handicapped child who was a ward of court.

The court must assume that any delay in determining a question with respect to the upbringing of a child is likely to prejudice the child's welfare (s1(2) CA 1989).

The High Court in wardship may make s8 orders as with the county court and the magistrates' court in family proceedings (ie residence orders, contact orders, prohibited steps orders and specific issues orders).

## 15.8 Adoption

### Introduction

The concept of adoption was introduced in 1926. It is now governed by the Adoption Act 1976 which came into force in 1988 (and replaced previous provisions in the Children Act 1975 and the Adoption Act 1958). An adoption order ends the legal relationship between a child and his or her natural parents and creates a new and exclusive relationship between the child and the adopters. Applications for adoption have fallen dramatically in recent years. In 2001 there were 4,452 adoptions (nearly half of them being applications by a natural parent and a step-parent) compared with 22,500 in 1974.

### What an adoption order means

An adoption order gives parental responsibility for a child to the adopters (see s12(1) AA 1976 as amended by Sch 10 CA 1989).

It extinguishes the parental responsibility which any person has for the child immediately before the making of the order and extinguishes any order made under the Children Act 1989 (see s12(3) AA 1976 as amended) though it does not affect parental responsibility so far as it relates to any period before the adoption order was made (see s12(2) AA 1976 as amended).

It extinguishes any maintenance order or agreement with respect to the child in the same way as outlined above.

An adoption order is final and effects a permanent change in the status of the child and the parties. If an adoption order has been properly made and acted upon and has not been appealed it cannot be later set aside. See *Re B (Adoption: Jurisdiction to Set Aside)* [1995] 3 WLR 40; [1995] 2 FLR 1 where a baby was born to an English woman and an Arab father. He was adopted and mistakenly brought up by a Jewish couple. As an adult he learned of his true background and wished to travel and work in the Middle East. He applied to have the adoption order set aside on the basis of the fundamental mistake about his background. His application was dismissed.

Adoption does not deprive the child who has been adopted of a interest in possession already vested in the child (despite the fact that on adoption the child is treated as the child of the adopters and of no other person). As a result a great-grandson was able to inherit under his great-grandmother's will (she died in 1990) even though he was subsequently freed for adoption (see s42(4) AA 1976 and *Staffordshire County Council* v *B* [1998] Fam Law 8.

## Adoption orders with conditions

An adoption order may contain such terms and conditions as the court thinks fit (see s12(6) AA 1976).

The power to impose terms and conditions when making an adoption order has been considered by the House of Lords in *Re C (A Minor) (Adoption: Conditions)* [1988] 1 All ER 705:

1. Adoption vested all parental rights and duties in the adoptive parents and extinguished the rights of natural parents. Therefore, in normal circumstances a court would not order that a third party be given access to the adopted child since it is desirable that there should be a complete break on adoption.
2. There would have to be exceptional circumstances for a court to impose a condition of access without the agreement of the adoptive parents.

But the need for a complete break on adoption with a child's past relationship was not an inflexible rule. It may be undesirable that there should be contact between a child and his or her parents since an adoption order was meant to cut them out of the child's life. That did not mean that the same reasoning necessarily applied to other natural relatives.

On the facts of the case it was held that it was right for an access order to be made as a condition in an adoption order allowing the elder brother to see his thirteen-year-old sister who had been adopted. They were closely attached. It was in the interests of the welfare of the girl to be adopted but at the same time it was in her interests to maintain contact with her brother.

Adoptions have come to be classified as 'closed adoptions' or 'open adoptions'. A 'closed adoption' means that there is no contact between the child and his or her natural family after the adoption order is made. An 'open adoption' is an adoption where the child's natural family continue to have contact with the child even though the parental responsibility for the child now vests entirely with the adopters. In practice an 'open adoption' is only practical if the adoptive parents agree to it (as recommended in *Re C* (above). The adopters did not agree with contact between the child and her grandmother in *Re GR (Adoption: Access)* [1985] FLR 643. The court refused to attach a condition to the adoption order providing for such contact. Such a conditon would detract from the rights and duties of the adoptive parents by limiting or depriving them of the right to stop contact if they thought it was disturbing or unsettling the child. Such a condition might provide a fertile source of future litigation between the adoptive parents and the grandmother. She could only see the child if the adoptive parents allowed it.

A similar view was taken in *Re T (Adoption: Contact)* [1995] 2 FLR 251 where a mother agreed to an adoption but wanted to continue to have contact with her daughter. The adopters agreed to contact but only once a year. The mother wanted more frequent contact. The adoption order was made together with a contact order that there be annual contact between the child and her. The adopters, local authority and guardian appealed against the condition. The adopters argued that the no order principle should apply since the contact order obliged them to do what they had already agreed to. The local authority and guardian argued that the adopters should have control over contact and that the child should not be obliged to do what she may not want to do.

HELD: Allowing the appeal, the mother had to trust the adopters. The adopters had the welfare of the child as their primary consideration in deciding on contact between the child and her mother. If there was a contact order and contact ceased to be suitable the onus would be on the adopters to go back to court to vary or suspend the order. This was an unjust burden on the adoptive family. There was benefit in there being no order as to contact since the adopters needed the flexibility to change with the circumstances and not feel constrained by the order. If the adopters stopped contact unreasonably then the mother could apply for leave to apply for contact.

See also *Re G (Children: Contact)* [2002] 3 FCR 377 which said that current research was in favour of some contact in adoption. One of the possible benefits is that of children simply knowing who their natural parents were. To quote Ward LJ, contact removes 'the sense of the ogre, as they reach adolescence and begin to search for their own identity, with the double crisis not only of adolescence but also of coming to grips with the fact that they are adopted'. The appeal was concerned with children in the process of being adopted having minimal contact with their mother and father (minimal contact being once or twice a year).

In some cases the adoptive parents will indicate that they will allow contact between the child and his or her natural family, but the court sees no need to impose a condition in the adoption order to this effect. If the adoptive parents do not then abide by the agreement for contact, a member of the child's natural family could apply for leave to apply for a contact under s10 CA 1989. This is what happened in *Re T (Minors) (Adopted Children: Contact)* [1996] 1 All ER 215; [1995] 3 WLR 793; [1995] 2 FLR 792 where there was an agreement that the child's half sister have contact with the child after the adoption was made. The court held that it was of the highest importance that adoption proceedings be conducted in a spirit of co-operation between the adopters and the natural family whenever possible. Leave was granted for the half sister to apply for a contact order.

An earlier case, *Re C (A Minor) (Adopted Child: Contact)* [1993] 3 All ER 259, advocated a more restrictive approach.In the case a child, A, was taken into care in 1988. His mother last saw him in July 1989. In 1990, following a contested hearing in which the mother's consent was dispensed with, an adoption order was made without any condition as to contact. In 1993 the mother applied for leave to apply for a contact order and a specific issue order with regard to A. She argued that recent research had shown the importance of the biological family and that adopted children should be able to re-establish contact with their roots. Her application was dismissed. The court held that in the absence of a condition for contact in the adoption order there could be no reopening of the issue of contact unless there was a fundamental change of circumstances. Adoption orders were intended to be permanent and final. This approach was not followed in *Re T (Adoption: Contact)* or in *Re T (Minors) (Adopted Children: Contact)* and it appears that there is now a more flexible approach.

It is rare for any other kind of condition to be attached to an adoption order. In *Re S (A Minor) (Blood Transfusion: Adoption Order: Condition)* [1995] 2 All ER 122; [1994] 2 FLR 416 an adoption order was made in favour of a couple who were Jehovah's Witnesses. The child had lived with them for two years and adoption was clearly in her interest. The court was concerned that the couple (because of their religious beliefs) would refuse to consent to the child being given a blood tranfusion should she require one. The couple said they would not consent but that they would not impede a doctor who lawfully carried out a blood transfusion. The court attached a condition requiring the couple not to refuse to give their consent to blood transfusions without applying to the court which could give or refuse consent. The adopting couple appealed.

HELD: Allowing the appeal, in this case the choice between adoption and no adoption was clear. It was not right to remove the child merely because of a small risk that she might one day require a blood transfusion which might give rise to legal difficulties. The welfare of the child was the first consideration. There were established procedures for the medical authorities to deal with this situation. There was no need for the condition. The imposition of conditions in adoption orders should be rare.

## Who can be adopted

A child can be adopted if he or she is under the age of eighteen (see s72 AA 1976). An adoption order cannot be made if a child is or has been married (see s12(5) AA 1976).

An adoption order may be made notwithstanding that the child is already an adopted child (see s12(7) AA 1976).

## Who may apply for an adoption order

### Application by a married couple

A married couple may apply for an adoption order. Each partner should be at least twenty-one years of age but if the husband or the wife is the father or mother of the child and is at least eighteen years of age and his or her spouse is at least twenty-one years of age, then application can be made (see s14(1) AA 1976 and s14(1), (1A), (1B) AA 1976 as amended by Sch 10 CA 1989).

## Application by a single person

A single person may apply for an adoption order if he or she is at least twenty-one years of age.

The applicant must either be unmarried or, if he or she is married, the court must be satisfied that:

1. his or her spouse cannot be found; or
2. the spouses have separated and are living apart and the separation is likely to be permanent; or
3. the spouse is incapable of making an application for an adoption order by reason of physical or mental ill-health (see s15(1) AA 1976).

If the person is the mother or father of the child, the court cannot make an adoption order unless it is satisfied that:

1. the other parent is dead or cannot be found; or
2. there is some other reason justifying the exclusion of the other natural parent (which must be recorded by the court) (see s15(3) AA 1976).

It can be seen from the above provisions that an unmarried couple could not apply for adoption. However it is possible for one partner to apply for adoption. If an adoption order is made a joint residence order could also be made whereby the other partner acquired parental responsibility for the child. This happened in *Re AB (Adoption: Joint Residence)* [1996] 1 FLR 27. Unmarried foster parents had lived together for more than twenty years. They had two daughters. They had fostered a 5-year-old boy for two years. The foster father applied to adopt the boy. An adoption order was made. The foster father also applied with his partner for a joint residence order. The court granted the joint residence order holding that such an order did not circumvent the provisions of s14 AA 1976 which prohibited the granting of a joint adoption order to an unmarried couple. There was nothing inconsistent in the making of both orders. While the residence order gave the foster mother parental responsibility it did not give her the full rights she would have had under an adoption order.

In *Re B (A Child) (Sole Adoption by Unmarried Father)* [2002] 1 FLR 196 the House of Lords confirmed that an unmarried father could apply to adopt his daughter without the involvement of the child's mother. In the case F (the father) and M (the mother) were the parents of B. M showed no interest in B and, without seeing her, put her up for adoption. B was fostered with a view to adoption. F was not aware that M had been pregnant and had given birth to B. Social services contacted F and told him of what had happened. F and M then jointly registered the birth and made a parental responsibilty agreement giving F parental responsibility. F applied to adopt B. M consented to his application. The Official Solicitor representing B opposed the application on the ground that ending M's relationship with B could not be said to safeguard and promote B's welfare and there was no basis under s15(3)(b) Adoption Act 1976 (namely 'other reasons justifying the exclusion of the other natural parent) to grant the adoption. M only wanted indirect contact once a year and wanted nothing further to do with B. The judge regarded the circumstances of the case as exceptional because M had rejected B from birth and on account of M's failure to play any part in B's upbringing and that s15(3)(b) was satisfied. The court made the adoption order. The guardian appealed to the Court of Appeal which allowed the appeal. It interpreted s15(3)(b) as dealing with something comparable to death, disappearance or anonymous sperm donation in order to exclude a natural parent. It considered such an interpretation compatible with art 8 of the European Convention on Human Rights. F appealed to the House of Lords. Allowing the appeal, the House of Lords held that there was sufficient 'other reason justifying the exclusion of the other natural parent' under s15(3)(b) Adoption Act 1976 for an adoption order to made in favour of the natural father alone. The Court of Appeal had been wrong to adoption a restrictive interpretation. On its face the permanent exclusion of the child's mother from the life of the child was a drastic step. The court had to be satisfied that the course was in the best interests of the child. Consent of the excluded parent was not itself a sufficient reason, but it was a factor to be taken into account. Its weight would depend on the circumstances. There was no discordance between s15(3)(b) and art 8 of the European Convention of Human Rights. The balancing exercise required by art 8 did not differ in substance from that undertaken by a court in deciding whether adoption would be in the best interests of the child. The court's conclusion that adoption was in the child's best interests, even though it would exclude the mother from the child's life, identified the pressing social need for adoption and represented the court's considered view on proportionality. The judge could not be said to have misdirected herself.

A single person cohabiting in a homosexual relationship can apply for adoption. There was no public policy consideration preventing such an application. The court would have regard to all the circumstances with the first and overriding consideration being the welfare and best interests of the child. The child, W, had been taken into care and then placed two years ago with a single woman living in a lesbian relationship with a view to adoption. W was well-settled and thriving. An order was made freeing W to be adopted by the single woman. See *Re W (A Minor) (Adoption: Homosexual Adopter)* [1997] 2 FLR 406.

## *The child must live with the applicant(s) before the making of the application*

If the applicant or one of the applicants is a parent, step-parent or relative of the child (or the child was placed with the applicants by an adoption agency or by the

High Court) the child must be at least nineteen weeks old and must have had his or her home with the applicants or one of them for at least the thirteen weeks preceding the making of the order (see s13(1) AA 1976).

If the applicant or one of the applicants is not so related to the child the child must be at least twelve months old and must have had his or her home with the applicants or one of them for at least the twelve months preceding the making of the order (see s13(2) AA 1976).

The court places great reliance on the report prepared for it by the adoption agency or the local authority in order to assess the adoption application. The court must be satisfied that either the adoption agency (if it placed the child for adoption) or the local authority within whose area the home is (in other cases) have had sufficient opportunities to see the child with the applicant, or, in the case of an application by a married couple, both applicants together in the home environment (see s13(3) AA 1976).

Adoption proceedings are 'family proceedings' (see s8(4) CA 1989) and so the court considering the adoption application may make a s8 order with respect to the child if an application has been made by a person entitled to apply for a s8 order or by a person who has obtained the leave of the court to make such an application or the court considers that such an order should be made even though no application has been made (see s10(1) CA 1989). As a result the court could make, for example, residence and/or contact orders instead of an adoption order. Third parties (eg grandparents) could apply for leave to intervene in the proceedings. The court has a greater flexibility in finding an alternative to adoption if that is appropriate.

## The duty to promote the welfare of the child

In reaching any decision relating to the adoption of a child a court shall have regard to all the circumstances, first consideration being given to the need to safeguard and promote the welfare of the child throughout his childhood; and shall so far as is practicable ascertain the wishes and feelings of the child regarding the decision and give due consideration to them, having regard to his age and understanding (s6).

NOTE: This is not the same test as that applied in s1(1) Children Act 1989. It is logical that a different test applies to adoption proceedings (which extinguish parental responsibility) from that which applies to proceedings under the Children Act 1989 (which regulate parental responsibility). The words 'first consideration' allow the court to consider matters other than the child's welfare. This includes the rights of the natural parent(s), public policy and the social consequences of an adoption for the child. In an adoption case involving the child moving from one country to another there are also questions of immigration status and family life abroad (see *Re B (A Minor) (Adoption Application)* [1995] 2 FCR 749).

In *Re W (A Minor) (Adoption)* [1984] FLR 402 the child was born illegitimate. The natural father paid maintenance for the child and obtained a magistrates' court order granting him access to the child. The mother married and applied with her husband to adopt the child. The father objected, claiming that the child would benefit from a continued relationship with him. An adoption order was made, the judge taking the view that the child's interests were paramount and that he was not concerned whether it was fair and just to the mother or the natural father. The father appealed.

HELD: Allowing the appeal, the judge had materially misdirected himself in holding that the child's interests were paramount. There was a distinction, albeit a fine one, between the test to be applied in adoption proceedings and that set out in what is now s1 CA 1989. 'All the circumstances of the case' included the interests or claims of all the parties, namely, the child, the natural parents and the adopting parents.

See also *Re D (An Infant) (Adoption: Parent's Consent)* [1977] 2 WLR 79; [1977] 1 All ER 145 where it was said that in adoption proceedings the welfare of the child is not the paramount consideration as with custody, but is the first consideration. While the child's welfare remains the single most important factor it does not necessarily outweigh all other circumstances.

In *Re A (A Minor) (Adoption: Parental Consent)* [1987] 1 WLR 153 the Court of Appeal commented that on the facts of the case the result could properly be said to be the same whatever form of words was used, in that the importance of giving a child the right degree of security was so great as to be overwhelming when deciding between adoption and any other type of order. The distinction between s6 Adoption Act 1976 and what is now s1 CA 1989 did not trouble the court in that case.

The court must have regard to the general principle that any delay in determining the question of adoption is likely to prejudice the child's welfare (see s1(2) CA 1989).

## The need for parental consent

An adoption order cannot be made unless:

1. the child has been freed for adoption (see below); or
2. in the case of each parent or guardian of the child the court is satisfied that:

   a) the parent or guardian freely and with full understanding of what is involved agrees unconditionally to the making of an adoption order (whether or not the parent or guardian knows the identity of the applicants which can be kept secret if the applicants wish); or

   b) the agreement of the parent or guardian to the making of the adoption order should be dispensed with on a ground specified in s16(2) (see s16(1) AA 1976).

Agreement cannot be given by the mother until at least six weeks after the child's birth (see s16(4) AA 1976 – to avoid any immediate post-natal depression that might influence a mother's wishes following the birth).

A parent for these purposes does not include an unmarried father of a child unless he has parental responsibility for his child through a residence order or pursuant to s4 Children Act 1989 (see s72(1) Adoption Act 1976). This was confirmed in *Re L (A Minor) (Adoption: Procedure)* [1991] 1 FLR 171. Such a father need not even be named in the adoption application or be made aware that his child is the subject of an adoption application. The court could not require the social worker preparing the adoption report to interview him. That was a matter for the social worker's discretion. *Re L* was followed by *Re C (Adoption: Parties)* [1995] 2 FLR 483 which again confirmed that an unmarried father was not a 'parent' for the purposes of the Adoption Act 1976 and that there was no requirement to join him as a party.

However, in more recent cases courts have recognised that an unmarried father has a right to family life under art 8 and the right to a fair hearing under art 6 of the European Convention on Human Rights. In *Re H (A Child) (Adoption: Disclosure)*; *Re G (A Child) (Adoption: Disclosure)* [2001] 1 FLR 646 it was held that an unmarried father without parental responsibility should be informed of adoption proceedings and be heard unless there were good reasons not to do so. Each case depended on its own facts. In most cases a mother's wish for confidentiality ought not to deprive the father of his right to be informed and consulted about the future of his child. In *Re H* the father had a family life with the mother and their eldest child and had shown commitment to him. After they separated the mother concealed the birth of their second child, H, and placed H for adoption. It was held that the father was entitled to respect for his family life with H. To place H for adoption without notifying him would also breach art 6. He should be consulted as to the adoption. By contrast in *Re G* the parents had never cohabited and their relationship did not have sufficient constancy to be a de facto family. Their relationship therefore did not constitute family life as protected by art 8 and the father need not be identified or be notified as to the adoption. In *Re R (Adoption: Father's Involvement)* [2001] 1 FLR 302 the unmarried parents, F and M, cohabited periodically. When R was born the relationship between them had broken down and F did not know of R's birth. R was placed with foster parents. F and M then got back together and R returned to live with them. However, the relationship only lasted a few days and R was returned to foster parents. F offered to look after R but this came to nothing. F was then sentenced to three years' imprisonment for assaulting M. An application was made to adopt R. It was held that F should be joined as a party. F had had sufficient involvement with R. If he was allowed to be heard in the adoption proceedings he would not be able to challenge any adoption order, which could be disastrous for the child. In *Re M (Adoption: Rights of Natural Father)* [2001] 1 FLR 745 it was held that an unmarried father need not be notified of adoption proceedings since the parents had never had a meaningful relationship at any time relevant to the child's birth. In addition, the father had been violent to the mother and there was a strong case for saying that any interference with the father's right to a family life with the child was justified in order to protect the mother and child. Under art 6 the father did not have an unqualified right to be notified of the child's existence or that he be notified and consulted about the adoption. The decision not to involve the father was necessary, just and proportionate.

In some cases the rights of the unmarried father may persuade the court that an adoption order is not appropriate. In *Re B (Adoption Order)* [2001] 2 FLR 26 an adoption order in favour of a foster carer was set aside in favour of a residence order to the foster carer and a contact order to the father. He had maintained frequent contact with his child and had an excellent relationship with him. The adoption order was not a necessary and proportionate interference with his right to maintain a family life with his son.

## Grounds for dispensing with parental consent (s16(2))

### Has persistently failed without reasonable cause to discharge his parental responsibility for the child (s16(2)(c))

Parental duties include the obligation to maintain the child and to show affection, care and interest in the child. See *Re P (Infants)* [1962] 1 WLR 1296; [1962] 3 All ER 789 where the mother of two illegitimate children left them with a local authority and took no further interest in them. Her consent to adoption was dispensed with on this ground. See *Re B(S)* [1967] 3 WLR 1438; [1967] 3 All ER 629 where the child was born to a Spanish father and English mother. The mother left the father in Spain and returned to England when pregnant with the child. She placed the child for adoption. The father refused to give his consent. First he doubted the paternity of the child. This was established by blood tests. He then wrote bitter and hostile letters to the mother. He showed no interest in the child. He never visited her. He said he was entitled to the child and wanted the child but did nothing to discharge any obligations to her. He sent no maintenance or letters or presents for the child. He had 'washed his hands of her'. His consent was dispensed with on this ground.

But contrast *Re D (Minors) (Adoption by Parent)* [1973] 3 WLR 595; [1973] 3 All ER 1001. The father of two children left the mother for another woman. He refused to maintain the mother and the two children who lived on social security. He did send Christmas and Easter presents and some clothes. Over a period of two and a half years he saw the children on eight or ten occasions in the course of spasmodic access visits. The mother remarried and moved away. The father had to trace her. When he did so she refused him access and with her new husband applied to adopt the two children. The father refused to give his consent. The mother applied for his consent to be dispensed with on the basis of persistent failure to discharge parental duties.

HELD: Whether a parent had persistently failed to discharge his obligations was a matter of fact and degree. It had to be shown that the failure was not only culpable to a high degree but also that the failure was so grave and so complete that the child would derive no advantage from maintaining contact with the natural parent. Persistent failure meant 'permanent' failure. The case fell far short of that. There had been a temporary withdrawal or drifting apart on the breakdown of the marriage, but the father had searched for the children. He had never abrogated his duties by washing his hands of them. The adoption was refused.

## Has abandoned or neglected the child (s16(2)(d))

In *Watson* v *Nickolaisen* [1955] 2 WLR 1187; [1955] 2 All ER 427 a mother left her child in the hands of people in whom she had confidence since they wished to adopt the child. She initially gave her consent to adoption but then changed her mind and withdrew it.

HELD: Her consent could not be dispensed with on the basis of her having 'abandoned' the child. She had not left the child to her fate but in the hands of a couple who would care for her. A parent only abandoned a child if the child was abandoned in such a way that a criminal offence would be committed (eg wilful neglect or abandonment in a manner likely to cause suffering under s1 Children and Young Persons Act 1933).

## Has persistently ill-treated the child or has seriously ill-treated the child (and because of that ill-treatment or for other reasons the rehabilitation of the child within the household of the parent is unlikely) (s16(2)(e) and (f), (5))

See *Re A (A Minor) (Adoption: Dispensing with Agreement)* [1981] 2 FLR 173 where severe and repeated assaults over a period of three weeks sufficed under this ground.

Therefore, a single act of violence to a child would not necessarily mean that the offending spouse's consent could be dispensed with. There would have to be no likelihood of rehabilitation as a result of the violence or some other reason (eg the parent being sent to prison).

## Is withholding agreement unreasonably (s16(2)(b))

The leading case on withholding agreement unreasonably is *Re W (An Infant)* [1971] 2 WLR 1011; [1971] 2 All ER 49 where the mother gave birth to an illegitimate son who was taken into care and had been with foster parents since shortly after his birth. His mother had not seen him at all for seventeen months so that she was a total stranger to the child. The mother initially gave her consent to adoption but then withdrew it and wanted to take care of the child herself. She had a precarious and unstable lifestyle. She was a warm-hearted but unstable and inconsistent young woman. Her refusal to consent to the adoption was motivated by her feelings of guilt and regret and some sentimentality but not by the best interests of the child. If the child was returned to her there were serious doubts whether she could cope with the child. By contrast the child had settled well with the foster parents. Was the mother refusing to give her consent unreasonably?

HELD: Whether a parent was withholding agreement unreasonably:

1. was judged at the date of the hearing;

2. was an objective test, namely, would a reasonable parent withhold agreement? That was a question of fact and degree depending on all the circumstances;

3. the welfare of the child is not paramount – it is not the sole consideration – the parent has legitimate rights which would be extinguished by an adoption order and so had the right to veto the adoption – adoption could not be granted simply because the welfare of the child suggested it;

4. in judging reasonableness one must take into account the welfare of the child. A reasonable parent gives great weight to what is better for the child. A reasonable parent does not ignore or disregard any risk or ill likely to be avoided by adoption or some appreciable benefit (such as material and financial prospects, the child's education and his or her happiness and stability) likely to accrue if the child is adopted;

5. in order to establish unreasonableness there is no need to show culpability on the part of the parent. There is no need to show callousness or self-indulgent indifference. There is no need to show a failure or probable failure in parental duty. The test is reasonableness in the context of the totality of the circumstances.

A parent's anguish in considering whether to give consent is understandable but the court must nevertheless see what a reasonable parent in his or her place would do in all the circumstances of the case.

On the facts of the case the mother was withholding her agreement unreasonably. Her consent was dispensed with and the adoption granted.

In *Re C (An Infant)* [1964] 3 All ER 483 an illegitimate child was allowed to go into care by the parents. She was then placed with a view to adoption. The mother vacillated on whether she would agree to adoption. She gave her consent and then withdrew it. She accepted that she could not care for the baby herself but she wished to find a foster mother for the child. At the hearing medical evidence was given that the child would suffer adverse effects if separated from the applicants, who were fond of the child and had established good relations with her.

HELD: The question is not what would be in the interests of the child but what would be the reasonable attitude of the mother when confronted with all the circumstances, in particular, the medical evidence and the uncertainty of the child's future with her natural mother. Her consent was being unreasonably withheld. Adoption granted.

In *O'Connor* v *A and B* [1971] 1 WLR 1227; [1971] 2 All ER 1230 a married man had an affair with the mother. A son was born. The man returned to his wife. The mother delivered the child to the father saying that he was his responsibility. The father sent him into the care of the local authority. He was placed with a couple for adoption. He settled with the adopters and was happy and well integrated into their family. The mother consented to the adoption. The father then divorced his wife and married the mother. The mother withdrew her consent, as did the father, on the basis that they were married and could provide an adequate home for the child.

HELD: Strong reasons have to be shown for dispensing with consent where the parents are married, wish to have the child and have suitable accommodation for the child. On balance there was a greater risk of the child's future with the parents than with the adopters. In the circumstances, in particular, in view of the doubts about the stability of the parents' character and union, their consent had been unreasonably withheld. Regard also had to be given to be lapse of time and the disruptive effect of removing a child who was three years old and had been in the care of his adopters for two and a half years. Adoption granted.

In *Re PA (An Infant)* [1971] 1 WLR 1530; [1971] 3 All ER 522 the mother was unmarried and gave birth to a baby. She handed the baby over to a young couple for adoption. She gave her consent, but largely under pressure from a relative. She then withdrew her consent. She became engaged to be married and was able to take care of the child. The prospective adopters provided excellent care for the child.

HELD: If the welfare of the child was the only consideration it might be right for the child to remain where she was. However, that was not the law. The natural parent was entitled to withhold her consent so long as she was not unreasonable in so doing. The mother never really wanted the child to be adopted. She withheld agreement reasonably in the hope and expectation that she would be able to provide a secure home for the child. The upset of moving the child (who was just one year old) would be temporary and she would then benefit from the love and care of her natural mother. She was not unreasonably withholding her agreement. Adoption refused.

In *Re D (An Infant) (Adoption: Parent's Consent)* [1977] 2 WLR 79; [1977] 1 All ER 145 the father was a practising homosexual. His wife had divorced him and remarried. She and her new husband wanted to adopt the son of the first marriage. The father opposed the adoption.

HELD: If the father was to continue to have access the boy was bound to come into contact with other homosexuals. The father had nothing to offer for the son in the future. He was unreasonably withholding his agreement, since a reasonable father in the circumstances would want to protect the child from such a situation and give him a secure and stable future.

The court is not required, pursuant to s6 Adoption Act 1976, to give first consideration to the welfare of the child in determining whether consent is unreasonably withheld. However, since a reasonable parent would take the child's welfare into account it is one of the considerations to which the court should have regard.

In *Re P (An Infant) (Adoption: Parental Consent)* [1977] 1 All ER 182; [1976] 3 WLR 924 a sixteen-year-old girl gave birth to an illegitimate son. He was placed in care at her request and then placed for adoption. The mother consented but then changed her mind. The baby was nine months old and did not know its mother.

HELD: The court had to balance a young, single and inexperienced girl living with her family on social security with an uncertain future with a secure and warm relationship established with the proposed adopters. The mother's change of mind was not relevant to the question. If it were possible for this young mother to look at the problem without emotion and to be that impossible person, the reasonable mother, the court entertained no doubt that her decision would, but for the fact of the love which the mother bears her child, be in favour of adoption. Her agreement was unreasonably withheld and the adoption granted.

In *Re F (A Minor) (Adoption: Parental Consent)* [1982] 1 WLR 102; [1982] 1 All ER 321 a son was seriously neglected by his mother and then gravely assaulted by the mother and the man she was living with. The mother received a sentence of borstal training. The son was taken into care and placed with foster parents. He was severely disturbed but greatly improved under the skilled care of the foster parents. They became the only stable factor in his life. He was disturbed by his mother's visits. The visits stopped and he did not see her for two years. When he was three the foster parents applied for adoption. The mother accepted that the child should be brought up by the foster parents but wished to keep contact with her son since she hoped that one day he would be returned to her.

HELD: In applying the objective test of whether in all the circumstances a reasonable parent would have refused her agreement to adoption the court was required to have regard to the practical consequences to the child of making or refusing to make an adoption order.

It was clearly established that it would not be in the child's best interests to have contact with the mother, and that adoption would give him a settled and secured home with no threat of interference from the mother. No reasonable parent could have concluded that contact with the child would be beneficial to him given that there were no chances of a successful reintroduction to, or continuance of contact with, the child.

In *Re H(B) (An Infant) and W(N) (An Infant)* (1983) 4 FLR 614 the court stated that within the parameters set by the House of Lords, the court had moved towards a greater emphasis upon the welfare of the child as one of the factors to be considered when dealing with s16(2)(b) Adoption Act 1976 but that short of amending legislation or further consideration by House of Lords there must be a limit to that shift. There was room for reasonable withholding of consent by the natural parent even though those responsible for the child's welfare, who were normally professionals, held an acceptable view that the child's welfare demanded adoption. The court must, therefore, look to the attitude of the natural parent as one of the potential factors. Further, where the natural parent presented himself or herself at the time of the hearing as someone capable of caring for the child, that was another relevant factor, together with other circumstances including the ultimate welfare of the child. Where there was an inherent defect in the parent which was likely to persist, that was also important, but where the unsuitability could only be related to past history, unless the past history was likely to influence the future position, then it should carry little weight in the mind of the hypothetical reasonable natural parent. The chances of a successful reintroduction to, or continuation of contact with, the natural parent was a critical factor.

In both cases the adoption was refused since there were chances of a successful reintroduction. There had been access between the child and the parents in one case, and access was sought in the other. The parent's refusal to give consent came within the band of reasonableness since though the children, aged ten and eleven, were well integrated into foster families and wished to be adopted, they were aware of their natural families and wished to keep in contact with them.

In *Re M (A Minor) (Custodianship: Jurisdiction)* [1987] 2 All ER 88 a daughter was born to a handicapped 17-year-old girl, married to a much older man. The child was seriously assaulted and taken into care. It was not clear who had inflicted the injuries. The parents denied so doing. She was placed with foster parents. There was access between the child and the parents but that ceased. Nearly two years went by without any contact. The foster parents applied for adoption.

HELD: The proper test of whether the parents had reasonably withheld their agreement was whether on all the evidence, but having regard to the fact that there was room for two reasonable attitudes which were mutually conflicting, a hypothetical reasonable parent would have withheld agreement in the circumstances. The chances of reintroduction to the natural parent were minimal. There were foster parents whose fitness to care for the child was not in question. The mother was physically handicapped. The father had had some problems with drink. It was most unlikely that the child had any recollection of them. Any attempt at access would be damaging and disruptive to the child. Their agreement would be dispensed with.

In *Re E (A Minor) (Adoption)* [1989] 1 FLR 126 the mother had a sad history of physical and sexual abuse when young. Her first two children were adopted. Her third child, Mark, was taken into care but allowed to live with his mother and the care order was discharged. She had a fourth child, Glyn. Glyn suffered physical injuries and was taken into care. The mother and Mark visited Glyn at his foster home and Mark formed a close relationship with Glyn. The local authority wished to arrange for Glyn's adoption. The mother opposed the application. The local authority sought to have her consent dispensed with on the ground that she was withholding consent unreasonably since there was no prospect that Glyn could ever be rehabilitated with his mother.

HELD: The court had to ask itself two questions:

1. Was adoption in the child's best interests having regard to all the circumstances, first consideration being given to the need to safeguard and promote the welfare of the child throughout his childhood (as provided for in s6 AA 1976)? If the answer to the question was 'yes', then the court had to ask the second question.
2. Was the natural parent withholding her agreement unreasonably? The child was *not* the first consideration in answering that question. Section 6 AA 1976 did *not* apply.

In this case the answer to the first question was 'yes'. However, in answering the second question the court could not substitute its own view for that of the mother. What would the hypothetical reasonable parent with knowledge of all the relevant circumstances do? She would consider the sibling's interests, namely, the close relationship between Glyn and Mark. She would not assume that it was a foregone conclusion that she would never resume the care of Glyn. The mother's refusal was, therefore, within the bounds of possible reasonable decisions. It might have been wrong or mistaken but it was unreasonable. Her consent was not dispensed with and adoption could not be granted.

In *Re L (A Minor)* [1990] 1 FLR 305 parents gave birth to a daughter, D. The father was sent to prison. D received injuries and a care order was granted to the local authority on the basis that she was not receiving proper care and attention. She was placed with foster parents with a view to adoption. Access to the mother was terminated. The foster parents applied to adopt D who was then five and half and had not seen her natural mother for over two years. The mother did not consent to the adoption. Her consent was dispensed with on the ground that is was unreasonably withheld. The mother appealed.

HELD: The appeal was dismissed. There was no principle that access should be retained with the natural parent. The question was whether the mother's agreement was being unreasonably withheld. A court should not substitute its own decision for that of the parent. The question was whether a parental veto came within a band of reasonable possible decisions, not whether it was right or mistaken. Not every reasonable exercise of judgment was right. Not every mistaken exercise of judgment was unreasonable (*Re W (An Infant)*, above, applied). In this case the mother's decision did not come within the reasonable band of decisions and the adoption was rightly granted.

In *Re B (A Minor) (Adoption: Parental Agreement)* [1990] 2 FLR 383 two children, N and S, were taken into care because their mother, M, neglected them. N settled well. S did not and was eventually returned to M. N's foster parents applied to adopt him. M's right of access to N was terminated but the foster parents encouraged N to keep in touch with M and his sister, S. M refused to give consent to the adoption. The court was asked to dispense with her consent because she was withholding consent unreasonably. The court applied the two–stage test. First, adoption was found to be in N's best interests. He would be given security. He was eleven years old and wanted adoption. Secondly, the court found that continued contact between N, M and S was important. It also found that M had a sense of grievance against the local authority over its past approach to her access to N and S while in care. It found that M's refusal to give consent did not fall outside the bank of reasonable decisions in those circumstances. M's consent could not be dispensed with and so the adoption was refused. The foster parents appealed.

HELD: Allowing the appeal, there was a strong case in favour of the adoption. Applying *Re W* (above) a reasonable parent would recognise the great benefit to N of adoption. The reasonable parent would desire that contact between her, S and N should continue but would observe that adoption would not have endangered that contact given the attitude of the foster parents. N wanted adoption. If adoption was refused he might resent M. M's sense of grievance against the local authority was irrelevant to the issue. A reasonable parent would have agreed to adoption since she would have recognised that the benefit to N from adoption was decisive.

The case of *Re D (A Minor) (Adoption: Freeing Order)* [1991] 1 FLR 48 is useful in that it applies all the main authorities. A young mother had a baby. The father left before the birth. The mother cohabited with another man. The child, K, failed to thrive and received minor injuries. A care order was made. The mother had a second child, D. She left her cohabitee. K was returned to the mother and D on a trial basis but there were more injuries and K failed to thrive. K was removed and places with prospective adopters. The mother established a new relationship and planned to marry. She had access to K although it was sporadic. The local authority applied to free K for adoption. The mother refused to give her consent. The judge refused to dispense with her consent holding that the tests 'is adoption in the best interests of the child?' and 'is the mother unreasonable in withholding consent?' were really the same. The local authority appealed.

HELD: Following *Re E* (above) the test under s6 (is adoption in the child's best interest?) and that under s16(2) (was the mother unreasonably withholding consent?) were not the same and had to be considered separately. In the case given the lack of a bond between the mother and K rehabilitation was not feasible. The long-term future of the child lay with adoption. This satisfied the first test under s6. In relation to the second test (applying *Re W* and *O'Connor* v *A and B* (both considered above)) this involved considering how a parent in the mother's situation but (hypothetically) endowed with a mind and temperament capable of making responsible decisions would approach a complex question involving a judgment as to the present and the future and the probably impact upon K. Looking at the hypothetical reasonable parent in the circumstances of this mother the factors in her favour are that she is the mother and K lived with her for two main periods totalling eighteen months; she was now settled with a potential husband and with S who was being cared for satisfactorily; and she wishes to reunite the family. She has access which is having no ill effects on K. The contrary factors are: rehabilitation has failed in the past because of physical injuries and a failure to bond; K has not lived with the mother for two years; there is no evidence of any close or warm or effective relationship between them; there is no evidence of any relationship between K and S; and there is no prospect of rehabilitation at any time in the future. In conclusion, the mother's aspirations to have K back and reunite the family are unrealistic. Continued access to K is not likely to be beneficial to K in any real sense and would be entirely superficial and would upset K with her present family as she got older. A reasonable parent in the position of the mother would recognise the overwhelming force of the negative points and the unreasonableness of withholding consent. Her consent would be dispensed with and K freed for adoption.

NOTE: There is one other ground for dispensing with consent – that the parent cannot be found or is incapable of giving agreement (s16(2)(a)).

## Prohibition on private placements and payments for adoption

Section 11(1):

> 'A person other than an adoption agency shall not make arrangements for the adoption of a child, or place a child for adoption, unless –
> (a) the proposed adopter is a relative of the child, or
> (b) he is acting in pursuance of an order of the High Court.'

Contravention of s11(1) is an offence punishable with up to three months' imprisonment and/or a fine not exceeding £5,000 (s11(3)).

Section 57(1):

> 'Subject to the provision of this section, it shall not be lawful to make or give to any person any payment or reward for or in consideration of –
> (a) the adoption by that person of a child;
> (b) the grant by that person of any agreement or consent required in connection with the adoption of a child;
> (c) the transfer by that person of the actual custody of a child with a view to the adoption of the child; or
> (d) the making by that person of any arrangements for the adoption of a child.'

Again, contravention constitutes an offence punishable with up to three months' imprisonment and/or a fine not exceeding £5,000 (s57(2)).

The above does not apply to payments with respect to the reasonable expenses of an adoption agency or to any payment or reward authorised by the court to which application for an adoption order in respect of a child is made (s57(3)).

See *Re Adoption Application (Surrogacy)* [1987] 2 All ER 826 where a husband and wife were a childless couple unable to have a child of their own. X was a happily married woman with two children. X enjoyed pregnancy. She advertised in a magazine to help childless couples. The husband and wife answered the advertisement and it was agreed that X would bear the husband's child. X was in full-time employment. It was agreed that the husband and wife should pay her £10,000 to represent her loss of earnings, expenses in connection with the pregnancy and for emotional and physical factors. X was paid £5,000, but refused the balance as she had made money on a book she had written about her experiences. The child thrived with the husband and wife. When the child was two years old they applied for adoption. The question for the court was whether the payment had contravened s57(1)?

HELD: The financial arrangements did not contravene the section. There was no element of profit or financial reward. X had been sincere and not motivated by profit. She had turned down a couple who had offered her a much larger sum since she had wanted a couple with whom she could establish a rapport. The arrangement was really one of trust – there had been no written contract.

Alternatively, the court had a discretion under s57(3) to authorise payments and this could be done retrospectively. The adoption order would be granted.

NOTE: There is also a prohibition on advertisements in relation to adoption (s58).

In other cases breaches of ss11 and 57 have not prevented an adoption order from being made. The legal position with regard to a breach of s11 or s57 was considered in *Re Adoption Application (Non Patrial: Breaches of Procedure)* [1993] 1 FLR 947; [1993] Fam Law 275 (which concerned an adoption application for a baby from El Salvador) where it was held that a court could not authorise a breach of s11 which had already taken place. The court could retrospectively authorise a breach of s57. However, a breach of s11 did not prevent the court making an adoption order. The court must take the breach into account and consider whether public policy required that the adoption be refused. The welfare of the child remained the first consideration (s6).

In *Re ZHH (Adoption Application)* [1993] 1 FLR 83 (decided in 1987) an unmarried mother gave birth to a daughter in 1984. She was not able to look after her but wanted to do the best for her child. She gave the child to a divorced woman, A, who could not have children but wanted a child. The placement contravened s11 AA 1976. A applied to adopt the child.

HELD: Granting the application, the child was extremely well cared for and the adoption was entirely in the child's interests. The prohibition in s11 did not prevent the High Court from making an adoption order in this case.

In more deliberate cases the application will fail. See *Re C (A Minor) (Adoption Application)* [1993] 1 FLR 87 where H and W adopted a child in 1986 who was placed with them by a relative (so not contravening s11). In 1989 they arranged to adopt another child. They arranged with a pregnant woman, M, who did not want to keep her child that H would pass himself off as the child's father and that when the child was born it would live with H and W. H and W paid the woman various sums before the child was born and £2,000 after the child was born. The child was falsely registered as the child of the woman and H. In 1990 H and W applied to adopt the child. M began to regret giving up the baby and informed the local authority of the true circumstances. The child was then aged 20 months. At the last minute H and W withdrew their adoption application but the court still ruled on its merits and the breaches of ss11 and 57.

HELD: The placement contravened s11 AA 1976. If the court considered the adoption application it should exercise its discretion with great caution and only give authorisation when the placement and the adoption was in the child's best interests. The payments contravened s57. The court could not authorise what was in effect the sale of the baby for adoption. The application would have failed on this ground alone. The child should be rehabilitated with her mother.

By contrast in *Re AW (Adoption Application)* [1993] 1 FLR 62 Mr and Mrs B had adopted a child earlier. They knew that because of their age (they were 62 and 60), their health, strains in their marriage and Mr B's alcoholism that they would not be considered as suitable applicants for adoption. They set out to arrange an adoption which contravened both s11 and s57. They arranged with a pregnant woman, who did not wish to keep her baby, to travel to Germany where she would have the child. They paid her £1,000 in expenses. The child was born in 1987. The child was brought back to England and lived with Mr and Mrs B. They delayed any application for adoption until 1990.They then delayed and hindered the enquiries made by the local authority so that the child remained with them for so long that no one was likely to remove the child because of the danger to her welfare. By the time the High Court considered the adoption the child was aged four. The mother gave her consent. The child's father was not married to the mother and played no part in the proceedings.

HELD: Granting the adoption, Mr and Mrs B had breached s11 AA 1976 since all the arrangements had been made in England and the physical handover of the child had been in England. The payment of £1,000 breached s57(1) AA 1976 whether or not there was a commercial or profit motive. However, the breaches of ss11 and 57 did not prevent the adoption. The court had to balance public policy against the welfare of the child. The child's welfare was the first consideration. The behaviour of Mr and Mrs B, their health, the status of their marriage and the deliberate breaches of ss11 and 57 fully justified the court in refusing to sanction the breaches and refusing the adoption. However, in this case the child's welfare demanded the making of an order so that she could stay with the only family she knew. She was settled, received love and a good standard of care. An interim adoption order was made for a probationary period of two years.

In *Re MW (Adoption: Surrogacy)* [1995] 2 FLR 759 a married coupled entered into a surrogacy arrangement with a woman whereby she would be fertilised with the husband's sperm, give birth to a child, hand the child to the couple who would then apply to adopt the child. The couple made payments to the mother. A child was born and handed over to the couple who then applied for adoption. Relations between the woman and the couple deteriorated and the woman, the child's natural mother, opposed the adoption and began a media campaign to draw attention to her plight. This involved publishing photographs of the child and causing the couple great distress.

HELD: The adoption application breached both the prohibition on private placements (since the applicants were not both 'relatives' of the child – the wife having no biological link with the child) and the prohibition of payments for adoption. However the court had a discretion to make the order and retrospectively authorise the payments (*Re ZHH* and *Re C* (both considered above) followed). The child had been settled happily with the applicants for over two years. The mother's consent would be dispensed with and an adoption order made.

From 30 April 2001 s14 Adoption (Interagency Aspects) Act 1999 inserted s56A into the Adoption Act 1976 making it an offence for any person habitually resident in the UK (other than a relative of the child) to bring a foreign child into the UK for the purposes of adoption unless requirements set down by the Secretary of State have been satisfied. The regulations require an adoption agency to oversee the arrangements. The provision is designed to strengthen the safeguards against foreign children being inappropriately brought into the UK for adoption.

## Procedure

If the adoption is unopposed the court will appoint a reporting officer (an independent social worker) who will ensure that any parental consent is properly and freely given by investigating the circumstances and witnessing the consent of the parent on a special form.

If the adoption is contested the court will appoint a children's guardian (again an independent social worker) who will investigate the case on the child's behalf and prepare a report from the child's point of view. A guardian may also be appointed if there are any other circumstances justifying it.

When application is made for an adoption order, notice must be given to the local authority (unless they have placed the child for adoption) so that they have at least three months in which to investigate the application and prepare a written report for the court. The child becomes a 'protected child' (s32). It is the duty of the local authority to secure the well-being of the protected child as well as to prepare the required report (s33).

## Freeing for adoption

A local authority adoption agency may wish to plan in advance for adoption. It may apply for an order 'freeing the child for adoption' which vests parental responsibility for the child in the adoption agency. Any parent or guardian cannot then veto the adoption. The agency is free to plan the adoption without the fear that the parents or guardians might change their minds or in any way oppose the adoption. Long-term plans can be made for the child and for proposed adopters without the pressure of a contested adoption hearing in the future.

A freeing for adoption order can only be made on application by an adoption agency and only if the court is satisfied that (as with adoption applications) each parent or guardian freely and with understanding gives consent to the freeing for adoption or his or her consent is dispensed with on a ground specified in s16(2) (see s18(1) AA 1976).

In the case of an unmarried father the court must also be satisfied that if he does not have parental responsibility for the child he has no intention of applying for an order under s4(1) CA 1989 or a residence order under s10 CA 1989 or that if he did make such an application it would be likely to be refused.

There are provisions for keeping a parent or guardian informed as to whether the child has been adopted, and allowing them to apply to revoke the freeing order if twelve months elapses and the child has not been adopted or not placed for adoption.

The House of Lords has ruled on what steps a court can take to protect a child should a freeing for adoption order be revoked. See *Re G (A Minor) (Adoption: Freeing Order)* [1997] 2 WLR 747; [1997] 2 FLR 202 where a child, G, had been taken into care while a baby because of his mother's inability to care for him. He was freed for adoption in 1993, the mother's consent being dispensed with. The child's adoption placement broke down and he was placed in a residential special school. The mother was informed that he had not been adopted and she applied for the freeing order to be revoked. At the hearing it was clear that G may never be adopted but that his mother could not care for him. The dilemma for the court was that if the freeing order was revoked parental responsibility was restored to the mother and removed from the local authority. The court refused to revoke the order. The mother appealed. Her appeal was dismissed. She appealed to the House of Lords which allowed her appeal. The freeing order would be revoked but only once a care order had been applied for and made under s31 CA 1989. The court has jurisdiction to make a conditional revocation order so that the child can be protected whether by making the revocation conditional on some other order or under the court's inherent jurisdiction.

For a further illustration of the problems which can result from an order freeing a child for adoption see *Re J (Freeing for Adoption)* [2000] 2 FLR 58 in which a child, J, who was the subject of a care order, was freed for adoption. His mother's consent was dispensed with on the basis that she was withholding her consent unreasonably. The freeing order had the effect of revoking the care order and severing J's relationship with his natural family. No prospective adopters could be found. J was placed with long-term foster parents. The local authority wanted the freeing order revoked since adoption was no longer planned. The only person who could apply to revoke the freeing order was the mother and only after 12 months had elapsed since the freeing order. The mother was unlikely to make any such application. In addition, if the freeing order was revoked then the mother would be the only person with parental responsibility for J since the care order would not be revived. The High Court exercised its inherent jurisdiction to revoke the freeing order and make a fresh care order. It was held that the inherent jurisdiction existed outside the statutory scheme in the Adoption Act 1976 and could be used to supplement those powers in the interests of protecting the child. A care order could only be made provided the criteria in s31 CA 1989 were satisfied. This case follows the approach of the House of Lords in *Re G (A Minor) (Adoption: Freeing Order)* (above) which identified the gap in the law concerning freeing orders. A similar result was reached in *Oldham MBC v D* [2000] 2 FLR 382.

## Adoption and Children Act 2002

The law on adoption will be radically changed when the Adoption and Children Act 2002 (enacted in November 2002) comes into force, probably in 2004. The Act came into being after a long period of consultation. In 1993 the government published a White Paper called *Adoption: The Future* (Cm 2288). In 1996 a Bill was published which then lapsed. In 2000 the Prime Minister announced a major review of adoption and a fresh White Paper *Adoption Procedure: A New Approach* (Cm 5017) was published in the same year with the aim of reducing delay and inefficiency in adoption proceedings. It also aimed to increase the number of adoptions.

The Act will make the welfare of the child paramount in all decisions relating to adoption (as opposed to it being a first consideration) (s1(2) ACA 2002). A welfare checklist similar to that in s1(3) Children Act 1989) will be applied by the courts in deciding whether to make an adoption order (s1(4) ACA 2002). The checklist will include extra considerations, eg the relationship between the child and any relatives and how such relatives contribute to the child's welfare and the relatives' wishes and feelings. The delay principle in s1(2) CA 1989 is also introduced into adoption proceedings (s1(3) ACA 2002). With a view to this the court must draw up a timetable to ensure that the application is dealt with without delay (see s109 ACA 2002).

An application for adoption can be made by an unmarried couple (see s50 ACA 2002) as well as a married couple or single person (like the existing law).

The grounds for dispensing with parental consent will be reduced to three where:

1.  the parent or guardian cannot be found; or
2.  the parent or guardian is incapable of giving consent; or
3.  the welfare of the child requires that consent be dispensed with (see s52 ACA 2002).

Freeing for adoption which be replaced by placement orders (ss18–25 ACA 2002).

There will be an obligation on local authorities to provide post-adoption support. A national adoptions register will be created to allow for a speedier matching of children with prospective adopters (in contrast to the up to two years it can take at present). The child's welfare will be paramount so an adoption could not be denied because the child and the parents do not share the same racial or cultural background. There will be an independent review mechanism for prospective adopters who feel that they have been turned down unfairly.

There will be a new special guardianship order which will be a halfway house between adoption and no order, giving the applicant parental responsibility but not severing links with the child's natural family. A wider group of people will be able to apply for guardianship than can apply for adoption (see new ss14A–14G CA 1989 inserted by the ACA 2002).

## 15.9  Care proceedings

**Who can hear the application for a care order?**
Care proceedings are heard by the Family Proceedings Court comprised of magistrates from the *family panel* (see s92 CA 1989).

Care proceedings must be started in the local magistrates' court (called the Family Proceedings Court for these purposes) (r3(1) Children (Allocation of Proceedings) Order 1991 – though care proceedings can be commenced in a suitable High Court or county court which asked for a case to be investigated under s37 CA 1989). The magistrates' court can transfer the case to another magistrates' court if this is in the interests of the child because it is likely to significantly accelerate the determination of the proceedings or to consolidate with other family proceedings or for some other reason and the other court consents to the transfer (r6 C(A of P)R 1991). A magistrates' court can transfer the application to the county court where it is in the interests of the child to do so because of the complicated nature of the evidence, the number of the parties or some novel or difficult point of law or because of some question of general public interest or to consolidate with other family proceedings of the transfer would significantly accelerate the determination of the proceedings (and there is no alternative) (r7 C(A of P)R 1991). Only certain types of county court can hear care proceedings. These are called care centres and are staffed by judges experienced in family proceedings (r18 C(A of P)R 1991). The county court can transfer the case to the High Court if that would be the most appropriate venue in the interests of the child (r12 C(A of P)R 1991). Either the family proceedings court, a single justice or the justices' clerk can direct a transfer. It is anticipated that long and complex cases involving controversial issues such as sexual abuse can be heard by the higher courts if that will mean a more convenient and speedier hearing.

### Who will apply for care proceedings?

Only a local authority or an authorised person can apply for a care order (s31(1)). At the moment only the NSPCC is authorised. Application may be made with a minimum of three days' notice. The respondents to the application are each parent of the child but only if the parent has parental responsibility (ie an unmarried father is not a respondent) and any other person who has parental responsibility for the child (eg through a residence order). The following people have to be notified of the application (though they are not respondents unless they apply to the court): any parent without parental responsibility (eg an unmarried father) and any person who is caring for the child at the time proceedings are commenced (Sch 2 FPC (CA 1989) R 1991).

An unmarried father can apply to be made a party to the proceedings if he can show that he has been involved in the child's life and can contribute to the decision-making process. Ordinarily he ought to be given the opportunity to be heard unless there are good reasons for him not to. See *Re B (Care Proceedings: Notification of Father without Parental Responsibility)* [1999] 2 FLR 408 and *Re P (Care Proceedings: Father's Application to be Joined as a Party)* [2001] 2 FCR 279. In *Re P* the father applied to be joined as a party at the last minute. His application was rightly refused because it would have delayed the final hearing. The denial of his rights under art 8 had the legitimate and proportionate aim of avoiding undue delay.

## The duty to take care proceedings

In *Z v United Kingdom* [2000] 2 FCR 245 the European Court of Human Rights held that the protection of children required not only the protection provided by the criminal law but also a positive obligation on authorities to take preventative measures to protect a child who was at risk from another individual. To do otherwise would amount to a breach of art 3 (which prohibits inhuman or degrading treatment). Although a local authority could be justified in taking steps to maintain a family unit by providing support, where such steps failed to show a significant and timely improvement then there was a positive obligation to consider care proceedings. While it was accepted that local authorities face difficult and delicate decisions and that it was impossible to prevent all instances of abuse and neglect, local authorites had to demonstrate that they had taken adequate measures to protect against inhuman and degrading treatment. In this particular case the local authority failed to take effective measures. The ruling by the House of Lords that victims of abuse could not sue a negligent local authority was held to violate access to the courts pursuant to art 6.

See also *D, P and JC v United Kingdom* [2003] 1 FLR 50 which followed *Z v United Kingdom* [2001] 2 FLR 612 in holding that local authorities who had failed to protect children from sexual abuse should not be immune from being sued for negligence. There was a positive obligation under art 3 of the European Convention on Human Rights to protect children from harm. In the particular circumstances there was no breach of art 3 since there was insufficient information available to the local authority to know about the sexual abuse. However, there was a breach of art 13 (the right to a remedy) because one of the children had sued the local authority but had the claim struck out because of the House of Lords' decision in *X v Bedfordshire County Council* [1995] AC 633. Article 13 required the state to provide a thorough and effective investigation of complaints of sexual abuse and for an individual to establish the liability of the state for acts or omissions involving the breach of Convention rights. A similar decision was reached in *TP and KM v United Kingdom* [2001] Fam Law 590.

## What will be the ground of the application?

There is a single ground referred to as the *threshold criteria* (s31(2)):

> 'A court can only make a care order or supervision order if it is satisfied –
> (a) that the child is suffering *significant harm* or is likely to suffer *significant harm*; and
> (b) the harm, or likelihood of harm, is attributable to –
> (i) the care given to the child being not what is would be reasonable to expect a parent to give to his or her child (or the care likely to be given to the child falls below that standard); or
> (ii) the child being beyond parental control.'

The criteria combine the finding of fact of *significant harm* or future risk of *significant harm* with an objective test that such *significant harm* or future risk of such harm arises from the failure of the parents to provide objectively reasonable care for their child now or in the future or the child being beyond their control.

The *threshold criteria* can involve future harm, namely, harm which has not yet occurred but which is likely to happen.

Harm in the words *significant harm* is given a wide meaning. Harm includes ill-treatment or impairment of health or development. Ill-treatment includes sexual and emotional abuse. Development includes physical, intellectual, emotional, social and behavioural development. Health includes physical or mental health (see s31(9) following *F* v *Suffolk CC* [1981] 2 FLR 208). The court can judge a child's health and development against what would reasonably be expected of a similar child (s31(10)). Significant harm has been held to mean any harm which the court should take into account in considering a child's future (see *Humberside County Council* v *B* [1993] 1 FLR 257).

Section 31(10) was considered in *Re O (A Minor) (Care Order: Education: Procedure)* [1992] 1 WLR 912; [1992] 4 All ER 905; [1992] 2 FLR 7; [1992] Fam Law 487 which concerned a child said to be suffering from significant harm because she was not attending school. A 'similar child' in s31(10) meant a child of equivalent intellectual and social development who has gone to school and not merely an average child who may or may not have gone to school.

The phrase 'is suffering significant harm' in s31 Children Act 1989 was considered in *Re M (A Minor) (Care Order: Threshold Conditions)* [1994] 3 All ER 298; [1994] 3 WLR 558 where the child's father brutally murdered the mother in front of their four-month-old child, G, and his two half-brothers and his half-sister. The children were taken into police protection. The mother's maternal cousin, W, obtained a residence order for the older siblings but did not feel able to cope with such a young child as G. He was placed with short-term foster parents. The local authority applied for a care order. W then decided that she could cope with G and, with the support of the local authority, applied for a residence order. The father was sentenced to life imprisonment. He and the guardian ad litem supported the making of a care order with a view to G being adopted outside the natural family. The judge found that the phrase 'is suffering significant harm' in s31(2) Children Act 1989 referred to the time immediately before protective measures had been taken. She found that the threshold criteria in s31(2) had been satisfied. She made a care order and dismissed the application for a residence order. W appealed and the Court of Appeal held that the phrase 'is suffering significant harm' referred to the time when the court was deciding if it could make a care order. In this case the court could not make a care order since the child had ceased to suffer significant harm at the date of the hearing. It could not be shown that the child was likely to suffer such harm in the future (which was the second limb to s31(2)(a)) since the father was in prison and W was able to provide the child with a home with his siblings. The care order was quashed and G was placed with W, where he settled well. G's father appealed to the House of Lords.

HELD: The phrase in s31(2) 'is suffering significant harm' meant that where a child had suffered significant harm but arrangements were then made to protect the child (eg via an emergency protection order and/or interim care orders) and those arrangements had continuously been in place up to the date when the court was deciding whether s31(2) had been satisfied then the relevant date is the date when the local authority initiated its protective procedures. If, after the local authority had initiated protective procedures, the need for them ended so that the child was no longer subject to them (eg by being returned to the parents), then the court could not look back to the situation when the protective arrangements started. In G's case, the threshold criteria had been satisfied and the care order would be restored. Since G was doing well living with W the local authority would continue that arrangement and monitor the situation.

The case of *Re H and R (Child Sexual Abuse: Standard of Proof)* [1996] 2 WLR 8; [1996] 1 FLR 80 has considered the meaning of the phrase 'is likely to suffer significant harm' in s31(2) CA 1989. M had four daughters. D1 and D2 were children of M's marriage to H. She left H and commenced living with R by whom she had two more daughters, D3 and D4. In 1993 when D1 was 15 years old she made a statement that she had been sexually abused by R since she was seven or eight years old. She was accommodated with foster parents and R was charged with rape. In 1994 the local authority applied for care orders with respect to D2, D3 and D4. Interim care orders were made followed by interim supervision orders. R was acquitted of rape but the local authority continued with the applications for care orders on the basis of alleged sexual abuse by R on D1. It asked the court to find on the balance of probabilities that R had sexually abused D1 or, at least, there was substantial risk that he had done so and that as a result the threshold conditions were satisfied with respect to D2, D3 and D4. The court dismissed the applications holding that though it was more than a little suspicious that R had abused D1 it was not sure to the requisite high standard of proof that D1's allegations were true. The local authority appealed to the Court of Appeal which dismissed its appeal. The local authority appealed to the House of Lords.

HELD: Dismissing the appeal (Lord Browne-Wilkinson and Lord Lloyd of Berwick dissenting), s31(2) marked the boundary line between the interests of the parents in caring for their own children and the interests of the child in which there could be circumstances where there might be a need for the child's care to be entrusted to other. In s31(2)(a) 'likely' means a real possibility, a possibility which cannot be ignored having regard to the nature and gravity of the feared harm in the particular case. It did not mean 'more likely than not'. The burden is on the local authority. The standard of proof is on the balance of probabilities, namely what is more likely than not. The first limb of s31(2)(a) predicated an existing state of affairs to be decided on facts admitted or proved on the balance of probabilities. The same approach applied to the second limb of s31(2)(a). However, the more serious the allegation the less likely it is that the event occurred and hence the stronger the evidence needed before the allegation can be established on the balance of probabilities. The court must decide on disputed facts. Having found the facts, the court must reach a decision on how highly it evaluates the risk of significant harm befalling the child. In this case the local authority based its application on D1's allegation that she had been subject to repeated sexual abuse. To decide that D2, D3 and D4 were at risk because there was a possibility that D1 had been abused was not sufficient to satisfy s31(2)(a). Parents were not to be at risk of having their children taken away on the basis only of suspicions.

NOTE: Both Lord Browne-Wilkinson and Lord Lloyd agreed that the evidence had to show that there was a real possibility that D1 had been abused. They concluded that the evidence did suggest such a real possibility and therefore would have allowed the appeal.

In *Re C and B (Care Order: Future Harm)* [2001] 1 FLR 611 the parents had four children. Their first two children, A and A1, were made the subject of care orders because of significant harm caused to A and the likelihood of harm to A1. The parents were capable of caring for children in the short term but not in the long term. When their third and fourth children (B and C) were born care orders were made on the basis of likelihood of future harm. On appeal, the care orders were quashed because B and C were not at risk of immediate harm. Though there was a real possibility of future harm the response must be a proportionate response to the nature and gravity of the feared harm. The local authority should have supported the family and eventually reunited it unless the risks were so high that the welfare of the children required alternative care. Article 8 of the European Convention on Human Rights emphasises that the intervention has to be proportionate to the legitimate aim.

The House of Lords again considered the threshold criteria in *Lancashire County Council* v *B* [2000] 1 FLR 583 17 in which child A, a girl aged 7 months, suffered non-accidental injuries as a result of violent shaking. It was not clear who had caused the injuries, the child's mother, father or child minder. Care proceedings were taken with regard to child A and with regard to child B, the child of the child minder. The court dismissed the applications for care orders because it could not be satisfied who had caused the injuries and construed that the threshold criteria could not be made out. The local authority and guardian appealed. The Court of Appeal allowed the appeal in relation to child A. The Court construed s31(2)(b)(i) CA 1989 (the care being given to the child or likely to be given to him if the order were not made, not being what it would be reasonable to expect a parent to give to him) as not implying any duty to find a parent responsible for the significant harm. 'Attributable' meant a causal connection of some kind but did not necessarily import any degree of individual responsibility or culpability. The Court found that where the parenting and care of a child was shared amongst a range of people, and the child suffers serious harm through lack of care, the child must not be left at risk simply because it is not possible for the court to be sure which part of the care network and which identifiable individuals have failed. It considered that this would be inconsistent with the purposive construction of the Children Act 1989. A care order could be considered in relation to the girl. The Court dismissed the appeal in relation to child B. The basis of the decision was that child B was likely to suffer significant harm in light of the significant harm suffered by child A. There were no allegations or evidence of any injury. There was no proof of injury to child B. Risk of future harm could only be established on the basis of proven facts, not just suspicion. It had not been proved to the requisite standard that the child minder had been the perpetrator of injuries to child A. The parents of child A appealed to the House of Lords. As part of their appeal they argued that the continued proceedings infringed their right to a private and family life under art 8 of the European Convention.

HELD: Dismissing the appeal, the threshold conditions could be satisfied where there was no more than a possibility that parents, rather than one of the other carers, were responsible for inflicting the injuries on the child.

Per Lords Nicholls, Slynn, Nolan and Hoffmann – under s31(2)(b)(i) the court had to be satisfied that the harm suffered by the child was attributable to 'the care given to the child'. This normally referred to the care given by the parents or other primary carer. However, different considerations from the norm apply in a case of shared caring where the care given by one or other of the carers is proved to have been deficient and the child has suffered harm but the court is unable to identify which of the carers provided the deficient care. In such a case the phrase 'the care given to the child' is apt to embrace the care given by any of the carers. The attributable conditions may be satisfied where there was no more than a possibility that the parents were responsible for inflicting the injuries. This interpretation was necessary to permit the court to intervene to protect a child at risk where the individual responsible could not be identified.

Per Lord Clyde – s31(2)(b)(i) simply defined the standard of care and did not point to the necessity of identifying the individual who caused the harm. No restriction limiting its scope to care given by particular kinds of people could be read into it.

There was no breach of art 8(1). The steps taken by the local authority had been those reasonably necessary to pursue the legitimate aim of protecting the child from further injury within the exception set out in art 8(2).

It by no means followed that because the threshold conditions were satisfied that the court would make a care order. That question fell to be determined by a detailed assessment of the child's welfare in all the circumstances. The court's discretion would have to take account of the fact that the parents had not been shown to be responsible for the child's injuries.

A similar conclusion was reached in *Re B (Minors) (Care Proceedings: Practice)* [1999] 1 WLR 239 in which an eight-month-old baby was subject to serious non-accidental injury. It was not clear which parent had caused the injury. It was held that the injuries were inflicted whilst the child was living in their care and this satisfied s31(2) CA 1989. It was also found that there was a likelihood of the child's twin brother suffering significant harm because of the risk that he would suffer significant harm if left in the care of either or both of his parents. The parent had either injured the child or failed to protect the child from harm.

There is a two-stage test in care proceedings:

1. is s31(2) satisfied? – this is a matter of factual proof;
2. whether or not to make an order and, if an order is to be made, what kind of order(s) should be made – this is a matter of judicial discretion bearing in mind the welfare checklist and the no order principle (see below).

This was the approach recommended in *Humberside County Council* v *B*, above.

### How should the court reach its decision?
*The welfare of the child.* The welfare of the child is the paramount consideration (s1(1)). This will mean that the child's welfare will override all other considerations (see *J* v *C* [1969] 1 All ER 788) and determines what order should be made.

*The no order principle.* The court cannot make an order unless it considers that doing so would be better for the child than making no order at all (s1(5)). The court must be satisfied that its intervention will improve things for the child. This is an entirely new consideration in care proceedings.

*Particular considerations – the checklist.* In particular, the court must have regard to:

1. the ascertainable wishes and feelings of the child (considered in the light of his or her age and understanding);
2. the child's physical, emotional and educational needs;
3. the likely effect on the child of any change in his or her circumstances;
4. the child's age, sex, background and any characteristics of his or hers which the court considers relevant;
5. any harm which the child has suffered or is at risk of suffering;
6. how capable each of the child's parents, and any other person in relation to whom the court considers the question to be relevant, is of meeting the child's needs;
7. the range of powers available to the court (s1(3), (4)).

This list of considerations is referred to as the welfare checklist and is the same as that used to consider applications for residence or contact orders.

It was emphasised in *Humberside County Council* v *B* (above) that a court must consider *all* the orders available to it (as directed by s1(3)(g)) and not just the options of making a care order or a supervision order.

### How should the court control care proceedings?
*Reducing delay.* The court must assume that any delay in deciding upon the care proceedings is likely to prejudice the child's welfare (s1(2)).

In order to reduce delay the court has a duty to draw up a timetable when care proceedings have started detailing when the parties should have finished their investigations and when a full hearing should take place. The court will be able to give directions to ensure that parties adhere to that timetable (s32(1)).

Regulations provide more detail as to how courts can control and reduce delay. This includes the power to arrange for medical examinations to take place by the experts from all the parties or for the disclosure of such reports.

*Twin-track planning.* In some cases the future of the child lies in being taken into care and then being adopted in a new family, cutting off all links with the natural parents. If this is the case the local authority is encouraged to reduce delay by dealing with adoption, or freeing for adoption, proceedings at the same time as the care proceedings. For an example of twin-track planning see *B Metropolitan Council v H (Goodman Project: Concurrent Planning)* [2000] Fam Law 237 in which care proceedings and freeing for adoption proceedings proceeded alongside each other (following *Re D and K (Care Plan: Twin Track Planning)* [1999] 2 FLR 872). The idea is to limit the number of court proceedings and placement moves for children in the care system. A special pilot project for concurrent planning, the Goodman Project, is testing this approach.

*Disclosure of evidence.* It is provided that each party must disclose the evidence they wish to call in advance of the hearing. Each witness must sign a written statement of the substance of their oral evidence and file and serve the statements on the court and other parties. If a party fails to disclose its evidence it may not be allowed to call the evidence at the hearing (see r17 Family Proceedings Courts (Children Act 1989) Rules 1991). This allows each party to know what the other party's case is in advance so that a more informed hearing can take place. The court is expected to have read the evidence before the hearing so that it is aware in advance of the issues involved (r21 FPC(CA 1989)R 1991).

The issue of disclosure in care proceedings was dealt with by the European Court of Human Rights in *L v United Kingdom* [2000] 2 FLR 322 in which L was a heroin addict. Her child ingested methadone. L said this was accidental. The local authority took care proceedings because it considered L had deliberately administered the drug. In the care proceeings L was granted leave to disclose court papers to an expert to prepare a report, subject to the condition of disclosure to all the parties. The expert found no evidence that the child had been habitually provided with methadone but doubted the mother's account. The police applied successfully for the disclosure of the report. L appealed unsuccessfully to the Court of Appeal and the House of Lords. She further appealed to the European Court arguing violation of arts 6 and 8 of the Convention. It was held, declaring the application to be inadmissible, that the obligation to disclose the report did not deprive L of a fair trial looking at the proceedings as a whole. Legal representation enabled her to counter adverse aspects of the report. She had not been deprived of the opportunity to present her case nor disadvantaged in relation to the other parties. There was no breach of the right to self-incrimination since no criminal proceedings were brought. The disclosure did not amount coercion of an accused to give evidence against herself.

Any interference with L's family and private life was justified under art 8(2) in order to protect the child. A parent must be able to participate in the decision-making process concerning her child, but here the disclosure was in the child's best interests and did not deprive the mother of the opportunity to protect her own interests.

The appeal confirms the House of Lords majority decision in *Re L (Police Investigation: Privilege)* [1996] 1 FLR 731 in which it was held that litigation privilege does not attach to expert reports in care proceedings obtained pursuant to a court direction. Such privilege does not arise in such non-adverserial proceedings.

### Interim care orders and interim supervision orders

Where in any proceedings on an application for a care order or supervision order the proceedings are adjourned the court may make an interim care order or interim supervision order with respect to the child (s38(1)).

The court must be satisfied that there are reasonable grounds for believing that the circumstances with respect to the child satisfy the threshold criteria (see s31(2) and s38(2)).

*Duration of interim care and supervision orders.* An interim order lasts as long as the period specified in it. That period is limited to:

1. a single period of eight weeks;
2. if the care or supervision proceedings are finished in less than eight weeks the date the application is finally decided;
3. two or more orders may be made after the first order but only for up to four weeks at a time (though there can be longer interim orders if the court makes a short interim order at first) (s38(4), (5)).

The court in determining how long an interim order should last must consider whether any party who was, or might have been, opposed to the making of the interim order, was in a position to argue his or her case against the making of the order in full (s38(10)).

*Interim assessment.* Where the court makes an interim care or supervision order the court may give such directions (if any) as it considers appropriate with regard to the medical or psychiatric examination or other assessment of the child (BUT if the child is of sufficient understanding to make an informed decision the child may refuse to submit to the examination or assessment) (s38(6)).

Such a direction may be to the effect that there is to be:

1. no such examination or assessment; or
2. no such examination or assessment unless the court otherwise directs (s38(7)).

An assessment direction may be:

1. given when the interim order is made or at any time while it is in force; and
2. varied at any time on the application of any person (who falls within classes of persons prescribed by rules of court yet to be enacted) (s38(8)).

An alternative to an interim supervision order coupled with an assessment direction would be a child assessment order. However, a child assessment order has less compulsion about it than an interim supervision order and so the court will have to choose which form of order is appropriate in each case.

In *Re B (Interim Care Orders: Directions)* [2002] Fam Law 252 it was confirmed that the court had wide powers to order assessments under s38(6), including directing a residential placement for a mother and baby against the wishes of the local authority (following *Re C (Interim Care Order: Residential Assessment)* [1997] 1 FLR 1).

### Exclusion order

The Family Law Act 1996 gives the courts the power to make an exclusion order at the same time as making an interim care order (or an emergency protection order). For example if a child is being abused by his father or step-father and an interim care order is made the court can make an order excluding the father or step-father (thereby avoiding the local authority having to remove the child). The court must be satisfied that there is reasonable cause to believe that if a person is excluded from a dwelling house in which the child lives then the child will cease to suffer or cease to be likely to suffer significant harm and another person living in the dwelling house (whether a parent or not) is able and willing to care for the child and that person consents to the exclusion requirement.

*Interim residence or contact order.* The court may at any time during the course of the proceedings make an interim residence or contact order though it is not in a position to dispose finally of the proceedings (s11(3)). Such an interim residence or contact order may only take effect for a specific period (s11(7)(c)).

If the court makes an interim residence order it *must* at the same time make an interim supervision order with respect to the child *unless* it is satisfied that the child's welfare will be satisfactorily safeguarded without such an order being made (s38(3)).

### The care plan

The local authority must file with the court and the parties a care plan describing what plans it has made for the child assuming that a care order is made. The details in the care plan can be the most controversial part of the care proceedings. A parent may accept that the grounds for making a care order have been made out but hope that the local authority will return the child home, albeit subject to a care order allowing the local authority to impose protective measures. What can the parent do if he/she disagrees with the care plan? What can the court do if it finds that the grounds for making a care order have been made out but disagrees with the care plan? In *Re S, Re W (Children: Care Plan)* [2002] 2 WLR 720 the House of Lords considered two cases. In *Re S* three children were made the subject of care orders with care plans that the eldest child live with foster parents and the younger two children be rehabilitated with their mother. There were concerns that the care plans would not be acted upon by the local authority and that this would constitute a major breach of the rights of the mother. The concerns were justified when the local authority failed to implement the care plan due to budgetary problems. In *Re W* two children were made the subject of care orders with care plans that they live with their maternal grandparents (who lived in the USA but who were prepared to come to England) and have contact with their parents. There were uncertainties, including when the grandparents might move to England. Despite the uncertainties the court made care orders. The Court of Appeal purported to make two major adjustments and innovations in the construction and application of the Children Act 1989. First, courts were to be given a wider discretion to make interim care orders when there were gaps in the care plan or where the passage of a relatively brief period would see some event happening vital to the deciding the future. In *Re W* the care orders were set aside and interim care orders made. Second, courts would be able to identify 'starred' milestones in the care plan when important stages in the plan should be completed. If a starred milestone was not achieved the local authority would be obliged to reactivate the interdisciplinary process which helped create the care plan and inform the children's guardian. Either the guardian or the local authority would be able to apply to the court for directions which could grant relief pursuant to ss7 and 8 Human Rights Act 1998. On appeal, the House of Lords held that the introduction of a starred system could not be justified as a legitimate exercise in interpreting the 1989 Act in accordance with s3 Human Rights Act 1998. The Court of Appeal had gone well beyond the boundary of interpretation allowed by s3. The starred system constituted an amendment to the 1989 Act, not an intepretation. Courts were not empowered to intervene in the way local authorities discharged their parental responsibilities under final care orders. Parliament had entrusted to local authorities, not the courts, the responsibility for looking after children under care orders. The starring system departed from that principle. Sections 7 and 8 Human Rights Act 1998 did not provide a legal basis for the introduction of the new system.

The failure of the state to provide an effective remedy for a violation of art 8 of the European Convention on Human Rights did not make the Children Act 1989 incompatible with the Convention. The making of the care order involved a process which was compatible with arts 6 and 8. Any infringement of rights after a care order had been made flow from the local authority's failure to comply with its obligations under the 1989 Act. A parent could bring proceedings against a local authority under s7 Human Rights Act 1998. Alternatively, there are administrative and complaint procedures available to such a parent. There is also the ability to apply to discharge a care order under the 1989 Act.

An interim care order was to enable the court to safeguard the child until the court was in a position to decide whether or not to make a care order. It was a temporary 'holding' measure. An interim care order could not be used to supervise the local authority. Before making a care order the court should have before it a sufficiently firm and particularised care plan so that there was a reasonably clear picture of the foreseeable future of the child. The court had to balance the need to be satisfied about the appropriateness of the care plan and the avoidance of over-zealous investigation into matters which were properly within the administrative discretion of the local authority.

The government was asked to give urgent attention to the serious practical and legal problems identified by the Court of Appeal. One of the most urgent questions is whether some degree of court supervision of local authorities' discharge of parental responsibilities would bring about an overall improvement in the quality of child care provided by local authorities. An example of a local authority failing to implement an effective care plan can be found in *Re F* [2002] Fam Law 8 in which the local authority's failure to implement its care plan led to the children being further harmed.

Courts can affect the implementation of a care plan through applications for contact (s34) and applications to discharge care orders (s39). For example, in *Re B (Minors) (Termination of Contact: Paramount Consideration)* [1993] Fam Law 301 the Court of Appeal held that while the plans of the local authority must command the greatest respect and consideration from the court, Parliament had given to the courts, not the local authority, the duty to decide on contact between child and parent. By allowing rehabilitative contact under s34 the court set the care plan (which was for the child to be permanently placed with another family) in a new direction. See section 15.11.

If a supervision order is made the role of the children's guardian continues until the supervision order ends (s12(5)(b) Criminal Justice and Court Services Act 2000). This could allow the guardian to monitor how the local authority operates the supervision order.

The government has introduced an amendments to the Children Act 1989 via the Adoption and Children Act 2002 which requires the court to consider the care plan (called a s31A plan), and obliges the local authority to file the plan and keep it under review. These changes are not yet in force.

### What orders can be made?
If the threshold criteria are satisfied and having considered the 'check list' (in s1(3)) the court has a much wider range of orders available to it. Some of these orders can only be made if the threshold criteria has been satisfied. Some may be made even if that criteria has not been met.

*No order at all.* If the court decides that no order will make things better for the child it may choose to make no order at all (applying s1(5)).

*Care order.* The threshold criteria must be satisfied before a care order can be made (s31(1)(a)). A care order gives parental responsibility of the child to the local authority. The parents retain their parental responsibility for their child (s2(5), (6)) and theoretically hold their responsibility jointly with the local authority. The local authority must consult the parents about its plans for the child (s22(4)) and must give the parents' views due consideration (s22(4)). However, the local authority has the power to limit what a parent may do to meet his or her parental responsibility for the child (s33(3)). The local authority may only so limit the parent's actions if it is necessary to do so in order to safeguard and promote the child's welfare (s33(4)). In turn the local authority cannot prevent a parent from doing what is reasonable in all the circumstances of the case for the purpose of safeguarding or promoting the child's welfare (s33(5)). A care order will not, therefore, give a local authority all parental rights and duties. This is also reflected in the provisions for parents having contact with their children in care dealt with later.

The limits on the powers of a local authority were illustrated in *Re X (Parental Responsibility Agreement: Children in Care)* [2000] Fam Law 244 in which care orders were made with respect to child A (aged five) and child B (aged two). The local authority's care plan was to place them for adoption. A and B's parents were M and F. F was an unmarried father who had no parental responsibility. He was serving a prison sentence. The court refused to make a parental responsibility order. F appealed. M agreed that F should have parental responsibility even though the children were unlikely to return to her care. The local authority opposed F having parental responsibility. The court had to consider whether it could prevent F and M reaching a parental responsibility agreement. It was held, making no order on F's appeal, the local authority could not prevent M from entering a parental responsibility agreement with F. They were at liberty to enter into such an agreement. To create the agreement both parents must act in unison, each signing the agreement. The agreement was a self-contained process which did not depend on the exercise of parental responsibility. F was not exercising parental responsibility when he signed. He would acquire parental responsibility if he married M. The local authority could not prevent that process so why should it be able to prevent the signing of a parental responsibility agreement? If F gained parental responsibility he could not act incompatibly with the care order (ss2(8) and 33(3)(b) CA 1989) and the local authority could determine the extent to which the parents could meet their parental responsibility. It gave him status whereby, for example, he could refuse to consent to an adoption order. Given the Human Rights Act 1998 the law must be very clear before it permitted invasion of parental autonomy by public authorities.

In *Re S (Change of Surname)* [1999] 1 FLR 672 S and T were two girls aged 15 and 16 who were made the subject of care orders following allegations by T that she had been sexually abused by her father. Both girls applied to change their surname to that of their deceased mother. Under s33(7) CA 1989 the written consent of every person with parental responsibility is required for a change of surname. The father refused his consent. Application was made to the court who granted the application for T but not for S. The court took account of the fact that the father was acquitted of allegations of sexual abuse in the criminal court. S appealed and it was held, allowing her appeal, that the acquittal in the criminal court did not necessarily strengthen the father's case. It was unlikely to result in a reconciliation and might increase the antipathy of both girls towards their father. The court had failed to identify S as *Gillick* competent and accord her wishes and feelings proper consideration.

*Supervision order.* The threshold criteria must be satisfied before a supervision order can be made (s31(1)(b)). The supervisor will have a duty to advise, assist and befriend the supervised child (s35(1)). A supervision order will only last for one year (Sch 3 para 6(1)) though it may be extended subject to an overall maximum of three years (Sch 3, para 6(3)). A care order vests parental responsibility in the local authority. It has effective sanctions available to it and it has clear duties. It is fundamentally different from a supervision order, which cannot be seen as a watered-down version of a care order (see *Re S(J) (A Minor) (Care or Supervision Order)* [1993] 2 FLR 919; *Re V (Care or Supervision Order)* [1996] 1 FLR 776).

In *Re O (Supervision Order)* [2001] 1 FLR 923 it was emphasised that art 8 of the European Convention on Human Rights obliged the court to provide a proportionate response to the legitimate aim fo protecting family life. On the facts of the case a care order would have been a disproportionate response to the risk to the child (which was at the lower end of the spectrum). A supervision order was the proportionate response. A similar decision was reached in *Re C (Care Order or Supervision Order)* [2001] Fam Law 580.

*Family assistance order.* The threshold criteria need not be satisfied for this order to be made. The court must be satisfied that the circumstances of the case are *exceptional* and that every person named in the order, other than the child, has *consented* to it (s16(3)).

A family assistance order is an order requiring a social worker (or probation officer) to advise, assist and (where appropriate) befriend any person named in the order, namely:

1. any parent (or guardian of the child);
2. any person with whom the child is living;
3. any person in whose favour a contact order is in force with respect to the child;
4. the child.

The order may direct that any person named in the order should take specified steps to enable the social worker (or probation officer) to be kept informed of that person's address and to be allowed to visit the person (s16(4)).

A family assistance order can only last for up to six months (s16(5)).

*Residence order.* A residence order is an order settling the arrangements to be made as to the person with whom the child is to live (s8(1)). The threshold criteria need not be satisfied before a residence order is made.

A local authority cannot apply for a residence order (as a short cut to obtaining a care order) and a court cannot make a residence order in favour of a local authority (as an alternative to a care order) (s9(2)). This provision was considered in *Nottinghamshire County Council* v *P* [1993] 3 All ER 815; [1993] 2 FLR 134 where two girls aged 16 and 13 had allegedly been sexually abused by their father. The local authority did not wish to apply for care orders. Section 9(2) prohibited it from applying for a residence or contact order. It therefore applied for a prohibited steps order forbidding the father from living with the girls and forbidding him from having contact with them unless supervised. This request contravened s9(5) CA 1989 which prevents a court from making a prohibited steps order which would achieve the same result by the making of a residence or contact order.

A court may make a residence order if it considers that such an order should be made even though no application for such an order has been made (s10(1)(b)).

A court made a residence order in favour of foster parents in *Gloucestershire County Council* v *P (A Minor)* [1999] 3 WLR 685; [1999] 2 FLR 61 despite the restriction imposed in s9. Such an order would, however, be most exceptional and be made on cogent reasons based on the clear needs of the child.

Parents or other parties or persons involved in the care proceedings can apply for residence orders or for leave to make application for a residence order rather than leave the matter to the discretion of the court:

1. a parent (or guardian) can apply as of right (s10(4)(a)) (eg where one parent has abused a child, the other 'innocent' parent may wish to apply for a residence order);
2. any party to a marriage (whether or not subsisting) in relation to whom the child is a child of the family can apply as of right (s10(5)(a));
3. any person with whom the child has lived for a period of at least three years can apply as of right (s10(5)(b));
4. any person who applies with the consent of each of the persons in whose favour a residence order has been made or with the consent of each person who has parental responsibility for the child can apply as of right (s10(5)(c)).

Most of the above categories will be more relevant to family proceedings following divorce or parental separation rather than care proceedings. Perhaps of more direct relevance will be the right of parents to apply for residence orders and of third parties (eg foster parents or grandparents or other relatives) to apply for leave to apply for residence orders.

A foster parent who is, or was, at any time within the preceding six months, a local authority foster parent may apply for leave to apply for a residence order if:

1. he or she has the consent of the local authority; or

2. he or she is a relative of the child; or
3. the child has lived with him or her for at least three years preceding the application (s9(3)).

Any other person may apply for leave to apply for a residence order if he or she does not qualify as of right (s10(1)(a)(ii) and (2)(b)).

The court in deciding whether or not to grant leave must have particular regard to:

1. the nature of the proposed application for a residence order;
2. the applicant's connection with the child;
3. any risk there might be of that proposed application disrupting the child's life to such an extent that he or she would be harmed by it; and
4. where the child is being looked after by a local authority:

   a) the authority's plans for the child's future; and
   b) the wishes and feelings of the child's parents (s10(9)).

The child may apply for leave to apply for a residence order to settle with whom he or she wishes to live. As well as the above considerations the court must be satisfied that the child has sufficient understanding to apply for a residence order before leave can be given (s10(8)).

***Where s8 orders should not be used in the place of care proceedings.*** A local authority should not apply for s8 orders as an alternative to care proceedings where it believes that children are suffering significant harm. See *Nottinghamshire County Council* v *P* (above) where a father had persistently abused the eldest of his three daughters. The mother was under the father's control and did not protect her children. The two younger daughters were at serious risk of abuse. Instead of applying for care orders the local authority applied for a prohibited steps order that the father should not reside in the same household as his daughters, and that any contact with them should be supervised by social workers. If the father was forced to leave the home there was a real risk that the daughters would run away to see him. The judge refused to make the prohibited steps order. The local authority appealed. The judge did make a residence order (on the father's application) that the children live with their mother which included a condition that the father leave the home, against which the mother, father and the children's guardian ad litem appealed.

HELD: Dismissing the father's appeal and allowing the mother's, father's and guardian's appeal, the local authority's application for a prohibited steps order was made with a view to achieve what could be achieved by a residence or contact order. A local authority was not able to apply for a residence or contact order (s9(2) CA 1989). There was no power in this case to make a prohibited steps order which was a back door way of applying for residence or contact orders. As a matter of public policy the route chosen by the local authority was wholly inappropriate. Part IV CA 1989, covering care proceedings, gave the authority wide powers and discretion. An authority could choose to place children with their parents even when a care order had been made. A prohibited steps order did not give the local authority any authority as to how to deal with the children. The local authority had a statutory duty which it had failed in not seeking care orders. The court could not force the authority to take proceedings and if the authority refused to act then the court was powerless to make an appropriate order. The residence order with its conditions was artificial and inappropriate and could not stand.

*Contact order* (see also section **15.11 Contact with children in care**)
CONTACT ORDERS AFTER A CARE ORDER IS MADE. Before a care order can be made the court must:

1. consider the arrangements which the authority has made, or proposes to make, for affording the child's parents (or guardian); and any person in whose favour a residence order was in force immediately before the making of the care order contact with the child; and
2. invite the parties to the proceedings to comment on those arrangements (s34(11)).

The local authority must allow the child reasonable contact with such persons while the child is in care (s34(1)) unless the local authority (or the child) applies for an order authorising the authority to refuse to allow contact between the child and such a person (who must be named in the order) (s34(4)). When making a care order the court may make a contact order or an order authorising the local authority to refuse to allow such contact, if it considers that such an order should be made, even if no application is made for such an order (s34(5)).

A contact order may be made either at the same time as a care order or later (s34(10)) and may be subject to such conditions as the court considers appropriate (s34(7)).

If a contact order is made there is provision for the local authority to refuse to allow contact in an emergency (s34(6)).

Once a care order has been made a contact order may only be made with respect to a parent. Any other person must apply for leave to apply for a contact order before one can be made (s34(3)). If a parent's application for a contact order or another person's application for leave to so apply is refused then no further application can be made for the next six months and the leave of the court is required for a further application to proceed (s91(17)).

CONTACT ORDERS IF NO CARE ORDER IS MADE. If no care order is made the court has a wider discretion to make contact orders. Similar provisions to those which apply to applying for residence orders or for leave to apply for residence orders apply in relation to contact orders (s10(1), (2), (4), (5) and (8)).

**Appeal**
An appeal lies to the High Court (s94(1)).

A parent or child may appeal against the making of a care order or supervision order (s94(1)(a)).

A local authority or child may appeal against a magistrates' court's refusal to make a care order or supervision order (s94(1)(b)).

If a court dismisses an application for a care order in a case where the child is the subject of an interim care order the court may make a 'temporary' care order pending the appeal subject to such directions and for such specified period as the court determines (s40(1), (4)). There is also provision for a 'temporary' supervision order (s40(2)). Such 'temporary' orders are themselves subject to appeal.

There is no appeal against a magistrates' court declining jurisdiction because it considers that the case can more conveniently be dealt with by another court (s94(2)).

Magistrates must give a judgment containing the reasons for their decision which must be recorded in writing (r21 FPC (CA 1989) R 1991). This contrast with the previous situation where magistrates simply made their decision without giving any reasons.

## Non-school attendance

If a child of compulsory school age and is not being *properly educated* a local education authority may apply to a family proceedings court for an *education supervision order* (s36(1) and (3)). Care proceedings will only apply on this basis if the child is suffering *significant harm* or likely to do so as a result of not being properly educated.

A child is treated as being properly educated only if he or she is receiving efficient full-time education suitable to his or her age, ability and aptitude and any special educational needs he or she may have (s36(4)).

A child is assumed not to being educated if he or she:

1. is the subject of a school attendance order (under s437 Education Act 1996) which is not being complied with; or
2. is a registered pupil at a school which he or she is not attending regularly (within the meaning of s444 Education Act 1996);

A child already in care cannot be made the subject of an education supervision order (s36(6)).

The local education authority must consult the authority social services committee before making application for an education supervision order (s26(8), (9)).

An order places a duty on the supervision to advise, assist and befriend and give directions to the supervised child and his or her parents in such a way as will, in the supervisor's opinion, secure that the child is properly educated (Sch 3 Part III para 12(1)(a)). Before giving directions the supervisor must, so far as is reasonably practicable, ascertain the wishes and feelings of the child and his or her parents, including, in particular, the parents' wishes as to the place at which their child should be educated (Sch 3 Part III para 12(2)). In setting the terms of the directions the supervisor must give due consideration to those views (para 12(3)).

An education supervision order can only last one year (para 15(1)). It may, however, be extended by application for up to three years. Application cannot be made earlier than three months before its expiry (para 15(2), (3) and (5)). The order may be extended more than once but must end if the child ceases to be of compulsory school age or is made the subject of a care order (para 15(4), (6)).

For an example of a case where non-school attendance was the basis for granting a care order see *Re O (A Minor) (Care Order: Education: Procedure)* [1992] 1 WLR 912; [1992] 4 All ER 905; [1992] 2 FLR 7; [1992] Fam Law 487 where a fifteen-year-old girl had been truanting from school for three years. Since the education welfare officer had already made numerous attempts to advise, assist and befriend the girl and her parents which had failed the local authority considered that applying for an education supervision order was pointless and applied for a care order. The magistrates found that the child had suffered significant harm to her social and intellectual development and made a care order. The child appealed against the care order. The care order was confirmed because the child had suffered significant harm as a result of not going to school and that harm must be due to the child either being beyond the control of her parents or her not receiving the care it was reasonable to expect. The court considered that the child was not coping and would not cope in the future with society and its boundaries and rules or with the ups and downs of adult relationships. She would not learn to take responsibility for her own actions and show commitment towards preparing herself for adult life.

### Representing the child and appointment of a children's guardian
*Appointing a children's guardian.* The court, on an application for a care order or a supervision order, *must* appoint a guardian ad litem for the child *unless* satisfied that it is not necessary to do so in order to safeguard the child's interests (s41(1), (6)(a)).

A children's guardian is an independent social worker who is not connected with the local authority bringing the care proceedings. He or she investigates the proceedings from the child's point of view. The guardian will be under a duty to safeguard the interests of the child in the manner prescribed by such rules (s41(2)).

The guardian will appoint a solicitor for the child (s41(4)(a)). The court may appoint a solicitor for the child if:

1. no guardian has been appointed for the child; and
2. the child has sufficient understanding to instruct a solicitor and wishes to do so; and
3. it appears to the court that it would be in the child's best interests for the child to be represented by a solicitor (s41(4)).

A solicitor must represent the child in accordance with rules of court (s41(5)).
A guardian will have a right of access to local authority records (s42).

*Guardian's report.* The court may take account of:

1. any statement contained in the guardian's report;
2. any evidence given in respect of matters referred to in the report in so far as the statement or evidence is, in the opinion of the court, relevant to the question which the court is considering *regardless* of any act or rule of law which would otherwise prevent the court from taking account of the statement or evidence (eg the hearsay rule) (s41(11)).

## Before care proceedings are stated – investigating the child's circumstances and/or protecting the child in emergencies

### Child assessment orders

WHAT IS A CHILD ASSESSMENT ORDER? A child assessment order is an order requiring the child's parents or other persons caring for a child to produce the child (eg to a hospital) or allow the child to be visited at home (eg by a doctor) so that the child's health or development or the way in which the child has been treated can be assessed. This enables the local authority to decide whether the child is suffering, or is likely to suffer, from *significant harm* before deciding whether to commence care proceedings (s43(1)(b), (2) and (6)).

WHO MAY APPLY FOR A CHILD ASSESSMENT ORDER? The local authority or an authorised person (ie the NSPCC) may apply for a child assessment order (s43(1)).

WHAT NOTICE MUST BE GIVEN OF THE APPLICATION? The applicant must take such steps as are reasonably practicable to ensure that notice of the application is given to:

1. the child's parents; and
2. any person who is not a parent of the child but who has parental responsibility for him; and
3. any other person caring for the child; and
4. any person in whose favour a contact order is in force with respect to the child; and
5. the child;

before the hearing (s43(11)).

WHAT ARE THE GROUNDS FOR SUCH AN APPLICATION? The applicant must satisfy the court that:

1. the applicant has reasonable cause to suspect that the child is suffering, or is likely to suffer, *significant harm*; and
2. the assessment of the state of the child's health or development, of the way in which the child has been treated, is required to enable the applicant to determine whether or not the child is suffering, or is likely to suffer, *significant harm*; and

3. it is unlikely that such an assessment will be made, or be satisfactory, in the absence of a child assessment order (s43(1)).

The child's welfare is paramount (s1(1)). The court must be satisfied that to make the order would be better than making no order (s1(5)). This emphasises that a child assessment order should only be made, for instance, where parents are unreasonably refusing to allow their child to be assessed and where such an assessment is likely to improve things for the child.

WHAT SHOULD BE SPECIFIED IN THE ORDER.

1. What kind of assessment is to be carried out;
2. the date on which the assessment is to be begun (s43(5)(a));
3. how long the assessment is to last (with a maximum period of seven days) (s43(5)(b));
4. the person to whom the child should be produced (s43(6)(a));
5. what directions are necessary to enable the assessment to be carried out (eg to allow a home visit by a person on a certain date or for the child to be kept at a hospital for a specified period) (s43(6)(b));
6. if the child is to be kept away from home during the assessment (eg at a hospital) such directions as the court thinks fit with regard to the contact that the child must be allowed to have with other persons (eg parents) while away from home (s43(10)).

HOW LONG CAN A CHILD ASSESSMENT ORDER LAST? The order can only take effect for a maximum of seven days commencing from a date specified in the order (s43(5)).

The order can only be effective in keeping a child away from home in accordance with the directions in the order; and only for as long as it is necessary for the purposes of the assessment (s43(9)).

WHAT IF A CHILD ASSESSMENT ORDER IS NOT COMPLIED WITH? There appears to be no direct power to enforce a child assessment order should, for instance, a parent refuse to allow a child to be assessed. However, such a refusal could result in application being made to remove the child compulsorily under an emergency protection order (eg s44(1)(c)).

If a child is of sufficient understanding to make an informed decision he or she can refuse to be medically or psychiatrically examined or assessed in any other way (s43(8)).

WHAT IF THE COURT CONSIDERS THAT THE CHILD IS IN IMMEDIATE DANGER? The court, on an application for a child assessment order, may be satisfied that the circumstances are far more serious. It may be satisfied that the child *is* suffering, or *is* likely to suffer, *significant harm* so that the grounds for removing the child under an emergency protection order are made out. The court *cannot* then make a child assessment order and must proceed to decide whether an emergency protection order should be made (s43(4)). The court is allowed to treat the child assessment order application as an application for an emergency protection order (s43(3)).

### Emergency powers of the police to protect children

TAKING A CHILD INTO POLICE PROTECTION. Where a police constable has reasonable cause to believe that a child would otherwise be likely to suffer significant harm the constable may remove the child to suitable accommodation; or take reasonable steps to prevent the child being removed from any hospital or other place in which the child is then being accommodated (s46(1)).

This is called taking the child into *police protection* (s46(2)).

INFORMING PEOPLE OF WHAT HAS HAPPENED. As soon as is reasonably practicable after taking the child into police protection the constable must:

1. inform the local authority in whose area the child was found of the steps that have been taken and are proposed to be taken with respect to the child and the reasons for taking them; and

2. give details to the local authority within whose area the child is ordinarily residence of the place at which the child is being accommodated (assuming this is a different local authority to that indicated above); and

3. inform the child (if he or she appears capable of understanding) of what is being done and why and what is going to happen and, so far as is reasonably practicable, sound out the child's wishes and feelings; and

4. cause a police officer (called the *designated officer* and appointed to deal with children's cases) to inquire into the case; and

5. if the child is not already there, move the child to local authority accommodation (or to any suitable place registered as a 'refuge' for children (under s51)); and

6. take such steps as are reasonably practicable to inform the child's parents; and every person who is not a parent of his but who has parental responsibility for the child; and any other person with whom the child was living immediately before the child was taken into police protection of what has happened to the child, why and what further steps may be taken (s46(3), (4)).

INVESTIGATING THE CASE. The *designated police officer* (appointed to deal with children's cases) inquiring into the case must within the seventy-two hours complete his or her inquiries and as soon as the inquiries are completed *must* release the child from police protection *unless* he or she considers that there is still reasonable cause for believing that the child would be likely to suffer significant harm if released (s46(5)).

Neither the designated officer nor the officer who took the first action are given parental responsibility for the child as a result of the child being in police protection (s46(9)(a)). The designated officer has a duty to do what is reasonable in all the circumstances of the case for the purpose of safeguarding or promoting the child's welfare. He or she must have particular regard to the length of the period during which the child will be kept in police protection (ie keep the period as short or as long as is needed to safeguard or promote the child's welfare) (s46(9)(b)).

At the same time the local authority, on being informed that a child who lives, or is found, in its area is in police protection must make (or cause to be made) such enquiries as it considers necessary to enable it to decide whether it should take any action to safeguard or promote the child's welfare (s47(1)(a)(ii)). In particular, the enquiries must be directed towards establishing whether any application (eg for an emergency protection order) should be made (s47(3)(a)) and whether the authority should ask the designated officer to apply for an emergency protection order on its behalf (ss46(7) and 47(3)(a)). Unless it has sufficient information already the authority must take such steps as are reasonably practicable to see the child or ensure that the child is seen by a person authorised to act on its behalf (s47(4)). If the child is ordinarily resident in the area of another authority it must consult that other authority who may undertake the necessary enquiries in place of the first authority (s47(12)).

CONTACT WITH THE CHILD. The designated officer (or if the child is in local authority accommodation, the local authority) *must* allow the child to have such contact (if any), which in the opinion of the officer (or local authority) is both reasonable and in the child's best interests, with:

1. the child's parents; and
2. any person who is not a parent of the child but who has parental responsibility for the child; and
3. any person with whom the child was living immediately before the child was taken into police protection; and
4. any person in whose favour a contact order is in force with respect to the child; and
5. any person acting on behalf of any of those persons (s46(1) and (11)).

FURTHER SAFEGUARDING THE CHILD. If the designated officer does consider that there is still reasonable cause for believing that the child would be likely to suffer significant harm the officer may apply for an emergency protection order (s46(7)) whether or not the local authority know of or agree to such an application being made (s46(8)).

*Emergency protection orders*
WHAT IS AN EMERGENCY PROTECTION ORDER? An emergency protection order:

1. operates as a direction to any person who is in a position to do so to produce the child to the applicant when requested to do so by the applicant (s44(4)(a)); or
2. authorises the applicant to remove the child at any time to accommodation

provided by or on behalf of the applicant and authorises the child being kept there (s44(4)(b)(i)); or

3. prevents the child being removed from any hospital or other place in which the child was being accommodated immediately before the making of the order (s44(4)(b)(ii)); and gives the applicant parental responsibility for the child (s44(4)(c)) but only to the extent of taking such action in meeting that parental responsibility as is reasonably required to safeguard or promote the welfare of the child (having regard in particular to the welfare of the child) (s44(5)(b)).

The authority to remove the child (under s44(4)(b)(i)) can only be exercised to the extent needed to safeguard the welfare of the child (s44(5)(a)). Therefore, if it appears to the applicant that it is safe for the child to be returned the child must be returned (s44(10)(a)). Similarly, the authority to prevent the child's removal (under s44(4)(b)(ii)) can only be exercised to the extent needed to safeguard the welfare of the child (s44(5)(a)). Therefore, if it appears to the applicant safe to allow the child to be removed from the hospital or other place the child must be allowed to be removed (s44(10)(b)).

The order must, wherever reasonably practicable, name the child. Where it does not the order must describe the child as clearly as possible (s44(14)).

Who may apply for am emergency protection order? There are three categories or persons who may apply for an emergency protection order:

1. any person (whether a local authority social worker, or NSPCC officer or any other person, eg a school teacher or police officer); or
2. a local authority; or
3. an authorised person (ie the NSPCC) (s44(1)).

What notice must be given of the application? Application can be made with one day's notice. In an emergency the application may be made ex parte (ie without notice). The applicant must firstly obtain the leave of the justice's clerk of the local magistrates' court (r4(4) Family Proceedings Courts (Children Act 1989) Rules 1991). If an order is made ex parte then it must be served on the respondents (particularly the parents) within forty-eight hours of the making of the order (r21(8) FPC (CA 1989) R 1991) otherwise it appears that it cannot be enforced. This then allows the parents to challenge the emergency protection order (eg by applying for it to be discharged which can be done after seventy-two hours have elapsed since it was made).

In *P, C and S* v *United Kingdom* [2002] 2 FLR 631 the European Court of Human Rights found that an application for an ex parte emergency protection order did not breach art 8 since the parents in the case were aware that this might happen and there were relevant and striking reasons for making such an application. However, the way in which the emergency protection order was implemented (namely a new born baby being removed from the parents) was not in this case supported by sufficient and relevant reasons. The removal could not be regarded as necessary in a democratic society for the purpose of safeguarding the baby. As a result the right to family life under art 8 ECHR had been breached. The local authority should have looked at alternatives for removal – for example, the child remaining with the parents under supervision. The message for local authorities and courts is that while emergency applications can be made to protect children, the way emergency measures are taken must be proportionate to the risk the particular child faces.

To whom may the application be made?. An application will normally be made to a single magistrate on the family proceedings panel (r2(5) FPC (CA 1989) R 1991). In most cases this will be ex parte after the justices' clerk has given leave. The relevant application forms have to be completed together with sufficient copies for each respondent. As with the order these must be served on the respondents within forty-eight hours of the making of the order (r4(4) FPC (CA 1989) R 1991).

What are the grounds for such an application? There are three grounds:

1. *The general ground.* Where *any person* makes application (whether a local authority social worker, NSPCC officer or any other person) the court may make an emergency protection order only if it is satisfied that there is *reasonable cause to believe the child is likely to suffer significant harm* if the child is not removed to accommodation provided by or on behalf of the applicant (eg to foster parents); or the child does not remain in the place in which he or she is then being accommodated (eg in a hospital) (s44(1)(a)).
2. *Local authority enquiries are being frustrated.* If the local authority has *reasonable cause to suspect that a child in its area is suffering, or is likely to suffer, significant harm* it has a duty to make such enquiries as it considers necessary to enable it to decide whether any action should be taken to safeguard or promote the child's welfare (s47(1)(b)).

    If those enquiries are being frustrated by access to the child being unreasonably refused to a local authority social worker (or other person authorised by the local authority in connection with their enquiries) and the local authority has reasonable cause to believe that access to the child is required as a matter of urgency the court may make an emergency protection order (s44(1)(b) and (2)(b)(ii)).

    NOTE: A social worker (or other person) seeking access to a child for such enquiries must carry official identification which must be produced, if requested to do so (eg by a parent) (s44(3)).
3. *NSPCC enquiries are being frustrated.* As with the previous ground if the NSPCC has reasonable cause to suspect that a child is suffering, or is likely to suffer, *significant harm*, it may make enquiries with respect to the child's welfare.

    If those enquiries are being frustrated by access to the child being unreasonably refused to an NSPCC officer and the NSPCC has reasonable cause to believe that access to the child is required as a matter of urgency a court may make an emergency protection order (s44(1)(c) and (2)(b)(ii)).

NOTE: An NSPCC officer seeking access to a child for such enquiries must, as with a social worker, carry official identification, which must be produced if requested (s44(3)).

WHAT EVIDENCE CAN BE PUT TO A JUSTICE OR TO A COURT? A justice or court considering an application for an emergency protection order can consider any report or evidence which in the opinion of the justice or of the court is relevant to the application regardless of rules of evidence which might otherwise make that report or evidence inadmissible (eg the hearsay rule) (s45(7)).

WHAT MAY BE SPECIFIED IN AN EMERGENCY PROTECTION ORDER? The court may give certain directions when the emergency protection order is made or at any time while the order is in force (s44(9)(a)). There are two types of direction:

1. *Assessing the child.* The court may give such directions as it considers appropriate for the medical or psychiatric examination or other assessment of the child (s44(6)(b)).

   NOTE: As with child assessment orders the child, if he or she is of sufficient understanding to make an informed decision, may refuse to submit to the examination or assessment (s44(7)).

   A direction may be that there should *not* be any such examination or assessment or that there be no such examination or assessment unless the court directs otherwise (s44(8)).

   The court may direct that the applicant for the emergency protection order, if he or she chooses, be accompanied by a doctor, registered nurse or registered health visitor, in exercising powers under the emergency protection order (s44(12)).

2. *Contact with the child.* The applicant should allow the child reasonable contact with the child's parents; and any person who is not a parent of the child but who has parental responsibility for the child; and any person with whom the child was living immediately before the making of the emergency protection order; and any person acting on behalf of any of those persons (s44(13)).

   This presumption in favour of contact is subject to the directions of the court. The court may give directions as it considers appropriate with respect to the contact which is, or is not, to be allowed between the child and any named person (s44(6)(a)). The court may impose conditions on a contact direction (s44(8)).

Either of these forms of direction may be varied subject to rules of court (s44(9)(b)).

There are further directions which may be included where the whereabouts of the child are not known.

1. *Discovering the child's whereabouts.* Where it appears to a court making an emergency protection order that adequate information as to the child's whereabouts is not available to the applicant for the order; but is available to another person the court may include in the emergency protection order a provision requiring that other person to disclose, if asked to do so by the applicant, any information that he or she may have as to the child's whereabouts (s48(1)).

   No person can be excused from complying with such a requirement on the ground that complying might incriminate him or her (or his or her spouse) of an offence (BUT a statement or admission made in complying shall not be admissible in evidence against either the person or his or her spouse in proceedings for any offence (other than perjury)) (s48(2)).

2. *Entering premises to search for the child.* An emergency protection order may authorise the applicant to enter premises specified in the order and search for the child with respect to whom the order is made (s48(3)).

   Any person who intentionally obstructs any person exercising the powers of entry and search is guilty of a summary offence punishable with a maximum level 3 fine (currently £1,000) (s48(7), (8)).

3. *Searching for other children.* Where the court is satisfied that there is reasonable cause to believe that there may be another child on those premises with respect to whom an emergency protection order ought to be made the court may make an order authorising the applicant to search for that other child on those premises (s48(4)). Wherever it is reasonably practicable such an order should name such a child and where it does not name the child it must describe him or her as clearly as possible (s48(13)).

   The same provisions about the offence of intentionally obstructing the exercise of powers of search and entry apply (s48(7), (8)).

   If such another child is found on the premises and the applicant is satisfied that the grounds for making an emergency protection order exist with respect to the other child the order to search for him or her shall have effect as if it were an emergency protection order for that other child (s48(5)).

   The applicant must notify the court whether such another child is found (s48(6)).

4. *Issuing a warrant to enforce an emergency protection order.* If it appears to a court, on application by any person, that a person attempting to exercise powers under an emergency protection order has been prevented from doing so by being refused entry to the premises concerned or access to the child concerned; or that any such person is likely to be so prevented from exercising such powers the court may issue a warrant authorising any constable to assist the person exercising the powers under the emergency protection order to exercise those powers. The constable may use reasonable force if necessary (s48(9)).

   The warrant must be addressed to a constable. Wherever it is reasonably practicable the warrant must name the child and where it does not it must describe the child as clearly as possible (s48(3)). The warrant must be executed by a constable who must be accompanied by the person applying for the warrant, if that person so desires, unless the court has directed otherwise (s48(10)).

The court may direct that the constable concerned may, in executing the warrant, be accompanied by a doctor, registered nurse or registered health visitor, if the constable so chooses (s48(11)).

RETURNING THE CHILD. An emergency protection order ceases to be binding if the applicant considers it safe to return the child or to allow the child to be removed (eg from hospital) since the applicant must then return the child or allow the child to be removed (s44(10)).

The child must be returned to the care of the person from whose care he or she was removed. If that is not reasonably practicable the child must alternatively be returned to a parent of the child; or any person who is not a parent of the child but who has parental responsibility for the child; or such other person as the applicant (with the court's agreement) considers appropriate (s44(11)).

If, however, there appears to be a change in circumstances during the remainder of the period of the emergency protection order which makes it necessary the applicant may again remove the child (or prevent the child's removal) (s44(2)).

ENFORCING AN EMERGENCY PROTECTION ORDER. If a person intentionally obstructs any person exercising powers under an emergency protection order to remove a child or prevent the removal of a child he or she is guilty of a summary offence punishable by a maximum level 3 fine (presently £1,000) (s44(15), (16)). See also the power to issue a warrant (s48(9)).

FOR HOW LONG CAN AN EMERGENCY PROTECTION ORDER LAST?' An emergency protection order can last for a period of up to eight days (s45(1)). If the order is for eight days and the eighth day is a public holiday (which means a Sunday, bank holiday, Christmas Day or Good Friday) the justice or court making the order can specify that the order ends at noon on the day after (or if that day is also a public holiday) on the day after that (s45(2)).

CAN AN EMERGENCY PROTECTION ORDER BE EXTENDED? A local authority (or NSPCC) who obtains an emergency protection order can apply, before the order expires, to extend the order (s45(4)). The order may be extended for up to seven days but only if the court has reasonable cause to believe that the child is likely to suffer significant harm if the order is not extended (s45(5)). The order can only be extended once (s45(6)).

APPLYING TO DISCHARGE AN EMERGENCY PROTECTION ORDER. Application may be made to the court by the child; or a parent of the child; or any person who is not a parent of the child but who has parental responsibility for the child; or any person with whom the child was living immediately before the making of the emergency protection order for an emergency protection order to be discharged (s45(8)). Presumably the basis of such an application would be that there were no grounds for the making of the order.

If such a person was given notice of the application for the emergency protection order and was present at the hearing of the application he or she cannot apply to discharge the order (s45(11)(a)).

Such an application can only be heard by the court after 72 hours have elapsed since the making of the emergency protection order.

No application to discharge can be made once an emergency protection order has been extended (s44(11)(b)).

The Family Law Act 1996 allows the court to make an 'exclusion order' against a named individual, or a non-molestation order.

## 15.10 Children accommodated by the local authority

Every local authority must provide accommodation for any child in need within their area who appears to them to require accommodation as a result of:

1. there being no person who has parental responsibility for the child;
2. the child being lost or having been abandoned; or
3. the person who has been caring for the child being prevented (whether or not permanently, and for whatever reason) from providing the child with suitable accomodation or care (see s20(1) CA 1989).

A local authority may not accommodate a child if any person who has parental responsibility for the child and is willing and able to provide or arrange for accommodation for the child objects (see s20(7) CA 1989).

Any person who has parental responsibility for a child may at any time remove the child from accommodation provided by or on behalf of the local authority under s20 (see s20(8) CA 1989).

There is no need for notice, written or otherwise. If the local authority wishes to prevent the child's removal it will have to apply for compulsory powers using the emergency protection order and care proceedings.

The powers of a local authority when a child is accommodated under s20 CA 1989 are limited. It cannot act in direct contradiction of the parents' wishes since it is the parents who hold parental responsibility. The local authority is restricted to exercising mundane day-to-day powers of management. This was illustrated in *R* v *Tameside Metropolitan Borough Council, ex parte J* [2000] Fam Law 90 in which a severely disabled 13-year-old girl had been accommodated by the local authority since the age of nine. She lived in a residential home. The local authority wished to place her with foster parents. Her parents disagreed. The local authority nevertheless proceeded to introduce her to prospective foster carers. The parents successfully obtained judicial review, holding that the local authority had no power to move the child against the expressed wishes of the parents.

## 15.11 Contact with children in care

Where a child is being looked after by a local authority, the authority shall, unless it is not reasonably practicable or consistent with the child's welfare, endeavour to promote contact between the child and:

1. the child's parents;
2. any person who is not a parent of the child but who has parental responsibility for the child; and
3. any relative, friend or other person connected with the child (see para 15, Sch 2 CA 1989).

To support this duty the local authority must take reasonable steps to inform the child's parents and any other person who had parental responsibility for the child of the child's address (see para 15, Sch 2 CA 1989) unless the child is under a care order and it would prejudice the child's welfare to give it (see para 15, Sch 2 CA 1989). The local authority may also make payments to assist visits between the child and a parent or other person connected with the child, if the visits would otherwise cause undue financial hardship and the circumstances warrant payment (see para 16, Sch 2 CA 1989).

Where a child is in care the local authority must allow reasonable contact with the child's parents, any guardian of the child and where there was a residence order in force immediately before the care order was made the person in whose favour the order was made (see s34(1) CA 1989).

The court on application may make appropriate orders with respect to such contact (see s34(2), (3) CA 1989).

If the local authority wish to refuse contact between the child and a parent it must apply to the court for an order refusing contact (see s34(4) CA 1989) unless the court made an order refusing contact when the care order was made (see s34(5) CA 1989).

The local authority can refuse contact in an emergency for a maximum of seven days (see s34(6) CA 1989).

The effect of s34 was considered in *Re B (Minors) (Termination of Contact: Paramount Consideration)* [1993] 3 All ER 542 where two girls born in 1988 and 1990 were made the subject of care orders in 1991 because of the unstable lifestyle of their mother, M, and her lack of care for them. They were placed with foster parents while plans were made for their adoption. M kept in touch with them only erratically. M then had a third child in 1992 who was also subject to care proceedings. After considerable support from social services M was able to set up home with her third child and look after him well. She started to see the girls regularly and had frequent unsupervised contact with them in her new home. The girls enjoyed the visits with their mother and baby brother. The local authority applied for an order under s34(4) CA 1989 authorising them to refuse contact between the girls and M so that the girls could be placed with prospective adoptive parents. M hoped that they would be eventually returned to her and opposed the application. The judge made the order taking the view that he had no power to interfere with the plans put forward by the local authority for the adoption of the two girls. The children's guardian ad litem, supported by M, appealed.

HELD: Allowing the appeal, following *A* v *Liverpool City Council* (above) the court had no general power to review the plans of the authority. However, the *Liverpool* principle did not apply to the intervention of the court in response to an application properly made under CA 1989 (in this case under s34 CA 1989). In considering the application under s34 the child's welfare was paramount. The plans of the local authority based on its appreciation of the best interests of the child must command the greatest respect and consideration by the court, but Parliament had given to the court, not the local authority, the duty to decide on contact between the child and those named in s34(1). The court may require the local authority to justify its long term plans to the extent that those plans exclude contact between parent and child. If the court were unable to intervene it would make a nonsense of the welfare of the child being paramount and would subordinate that welfare to the administrative decision of the local authority in a situation where the court has the duty to determine the issue. M's potential to care for all her children should be investigated and the contact between her and the girls should continue.

This approach was followed in *Re E (A Minor)* [1993] Fam Law 671.

In *KA* v *Finland* [2003] 1 FCR 201 the European Court of Human Rights said that the taking of a child into public care should normally be regarded as a temporary measure, with the ultimate aim of reuniting the child with the natural parent. There was a positive duty not to restrict parental contact where circumstances might improve to allow for the family to be reunited. In the case there had been a violation of art 8 because the parental contact had been unnecessarily restricted. There had been a failure to take sufficient steps towards possible reunification of the father and his children, despite improvements in his circumstances.

Difficulties may arise where a teenage mother has a child and both the mother and child are made the subject of a care order and the local authority wish to terminate contact between mother and child. This was the case in *Birmingham City Council* v *H (No 3)* [1994] 1 All ER 12 where care orders were made with respect to a 16-year-old girl and her son. The mother had behavioural problems. Her son was placed with foster parents. This distressed the mother who attempted to injure herself. The local authority applied under s34(4) CA 1989 to terminate contact because it wished to place the boy for adoption since he was likely to be harmed by his mother if returned to her. The judge held that the son's welfare was paramount and took priority over that of the mother and granted the order. On appeal the

Court of Appeal held that since both mother and son were in care the welfare of both was to be regarded as paramount and the welfare of one could not take priority over the other. It concluded that it was premature to terminate contact having regard to the benefit this would provide to the mother, and that it would not be detrimental to the son provided contact was monitored. The son, through his guardian ad litem, appealed to the House of Lords.

HELD: Allowing the appeal, s34 was concerned with categories of persons who could have contact with a child in care. In this case the child in care was the son and the mother was in one of the categories of persons whose position the court could consider in relation to contact. The issue of contact concerned the upbringing of the son and it was his welfare which was paramount under s1 CA 1989. The mother's upbringing was not in question so her welfare was not paramount. There was therefore no balancing exercise to be carried out between the son's and mother's welfare since the son's welfare was the paramount consideration. It was therefore appropriate to authorise the local authority to refuse the mother contact with her son.

See also *Re W (Section 34(2) Orders)* [2000] Fam Law 235 in which W, X and Y were made the subject of care orders and an order was made under s34(2) prohibiting contact between the children and their parents. The mother, M, then applied for contact and the local authority proposed that contact be at its discretion and an interim order was made to that effect. At the adjourned hearing the guardian sought an order under s34 CA 1989 prohibiting the local authority from exercising its discretion to permit staying contact. The court refused and made an order for contact at the local authority's discretion. The guardian appealed. It was held, dismissing the appeal, the court had no jurisdiction under s34 to prohibit a local authority into whose care a child had been placed from permitting parental contact with the child. The legislation was never meant to prevent contact which the local authority considered to be in the child's interests. This would be undue and unnecessary judicial invasion of a difficult and sensitive area. Such an order would be unenforceable since reg 3 Contact with Children Regulations 1991 allowed the local authority, with parental agreement, to depart from a contact order.

See also *Re F (Care Proceedings: Contact)* [2000] Fam Law 708 in which a family proceedings court made care orders with respect to three children. The court made an order under s34(4) CA 1989 authorising the local authority to terminate contact with the mother, M. M appealed against the s34(4) order, arguing that the justices failed to give due weight to arts 6 and 8 of the European Convention on Human Rights. She argued that the s34(4) order allowed the local authority to make an administrative decision to terminate contact. It was held, dismissing the appeal, there was little merit to the arguments under the Convention which added little substance to the appeal. The s34(4) order was a judicial order, not an administrative one. The court retained the power to vary or revoke the order if the care plan was changed or the basis for the original order changed.

## 15.12 Status of a child

### The presumption of legitimacy

If a child is conceived by or born to a mother who is married at the time of the conception or birth it is presumed at common law that the child is the legitimate child of the mother and her husband. This presumption applies even if the marriage is dissolved after the child has been conceived but before the child is born (see *Knowles* v *Knowles* [1962] 2 WLR 742; [1962] 1 All ER 659). The presumption also applies if the husband dies after the child has been conceived but before the child is born.

However in *Re H and A (Paternity: Blood Tests)* [2002] 1 FLR 1145 it was held that the paternity of a child was to be established by science and not by legal presumption or inference. In the nineteenth century, when science had nothing to offer and illegitimacy was a social stigma, the presumption of the legitimacy of children born during marriage was a necessary tool. However, with the advances of science and with more children born out of marriage, paternity was to be established by science (ie DNA testing). Establishing scientific fact allowed for planned management. This could be contrasted with the risk of perpetuating uncertainty that bred rumour and gossip with the risks to the children in the future. Unpalatable truth could be easier to live with than uncertainty. On the facts of this case the court had been wrong to dismiss the application for DNA tests brought by the wife's lover, and to rely on the presumption of legitimacy because of fears that the truth of the parentage of twins would be disastrous to the family unit, the husband believing he was their father.

Earlier cases, such as *B* v *B and E* [1969] 3 All ER 1106, *Re F (A Minor) (Blood Tests: Parental Rights)* [1993] 3 All ER 596 and *O* v *L (Blood Tests)* [1995] 2 FLR 930, in which husbands were held to have reasonably relied on the presumption of legitimacy and reasonably declined to provide blood tests, are unlikely to be followed today.

### Rebutting the presumption of legitimacy

This presumption may be rebutted on the balance of probabilities (see s26 Family Law Reform Act 1969). However, the courts have considered the status of a child to be a grave matter and the burden of proof is more than a narrow balance of probabilities (see *W* v *K (Proof of Paternity)* [1988] 1 FLR 86; *Serio* v *Serio* (1983) 4 FLR 756).

### The sterility of the husband
If the husband is sterile this can be used to rebut the presumption of legitimacy (see *W* v *K* (above)).

## The absence of the husband during the time of conception

If the husband was away during the time when the child must have been conceived this can be used to rebut the presumption of legitimacy: see *Preston-Jones* v *Preston-Jones* [1951] 1 All ER 124. The court will apply present-day standards of medical science in deciding the possible dates of conception, taking into account the nature of the pregnancy and when the child was born.

## DNA testing

In any civil proceedings in which the paternity of a child falls to be determined, the court may, on the application of any party to the proceedings, direct that scientific tests be carried out (s20 Family Law Reform Act 1969).

Scientific tests will take the form of DNA tests using mouth swabs taken from the child, the mother and the putative father. The courts accept DNA tests as virtually conclusive in determining parentage, hence the decision in *Re H and A* (above).

A scientific test is directed pursuant to s20(1) Family Law Reform Act 1969. There is no power to order a person to provide a sample. A person has to consent to a sample being taken (see s21 FLRA 1969). The person with the care and control of the child has to consent to a sample being taken from the child. However, if that person refuses to allow a sample to be taken from the child, the court can nevertheless order that a sample be taken from the child. If an adult fails to take any step required of him/her for a scientific test (eg by refusing to supply a sample) then the court may draw such inferences, if any, from that failure as appear proper in the circumstances (see s23(1) FLRA 1969). Since DNA testing is assumed to produce a positive certainty in its results a refusal may be taken to prove the result the refusing party fears. For example, in *Re A (A Minor) (Paternity: Refusal of Blood Test)* [1994] 2 FLR 463 a man, alleged to be one of three possible fathers to a child, refused to undergo DNA tests. It was held that he must be the child's father. Any man unsure of paternity could put his doubts to rest by submitting to a DNA test. The inference that a man who refuses to submit to such a test is the child's father is virtually inescapable. Such a man would have to advance clear and cogent reasons as to why he refused to be tested. For an example of courts ordering a sample to be taken from a child even though her mother refused, see *Re T (Paternity: Ordering Blood Tests)* [2001] Fam Law 738. It was held that DNA tests should be ordered since certainty of parentage was in the child's best interests.

The courts consider that the truth of a child's parentage should be established even if one or both parents disagree. Generally it is considerered not to be in a child's long term interests for the matter of parentage to remain unresolved and capable of being asserted when the child is older and when greater distress could be caused. Adults need to found their future relationship with a child on facts, rather than on what they would wish the situation to be (see *Re G (A Minor) (Blood Tests)* [1994] 1 FLR 495). Similarly, in *Re H (A Minor) (Blood Tests: Parental Rights)* [1996] 3 WLR 506; [1996] 4 All ER 28 it was held that the child had a right to know the truth unless his or her welfare clearly justified it being covered up. The sooner the child knew the truth the better. He or she should grow up knowing that he might have two fathers, his psychologicial father and his biological father rather than have a time bomb ticking away. See also *Re G (Parentage: Blood Samples)* [1997] 1 FLR 360.

There have been cases in which scientific tests have not been ordered. See *B v B and E* [1969] 3 All ER 1106 and *O v L (Blood Tests)* [1995] 2 FLR 930. See also *Re F (A Minor) (Blood Tests: Parental Rights)* [1993] 3 All ER 596 where the mother had intercourse with her husband and another man, A, at the time the child, F, had been conceived. The mother's relationship with A ended as soon as she discovered she was pregnant. F had been brought up by the mother and her husband. A had no contact with F. A applied for DNA tests to establish F's parentage. The court refused to order scientific tests. F's welfare was paramount. While this normally meant that the truth of her parentage be established, the chances of A successfully obtaining a parental responsibility or contact order were remote. It would be unfair to F to disturb the presumption that the parents bringing her up were anything other than her legitimate parents. The court would not disturb the stability of the family unit upon which F's emotional welfare depended (following *S v S; W v Official Solicitor* [1970] 3 WLR 366; [1970] 3 All ER 107). In *K v M (Paternity: Contact)* [1996] 1 FLR 312 scientific tests were not ordered because the child was securely based in a two-parent family and it was in the interests of the child to disturb the settled family upon which the welfare of the child depended.

As can be seen from the above cases the court has to balance the risks to the child of disturbing his or her security against the certainty of the child knowing who his or her parents really are. The court must take into account the prospects of success of the man claiming to be the father in obtaining a parental responsibility or contact order. The more recent authorities have tended towards ordering scientific tests to get to the truth. In the case of *Re T (Paternity: Ordering Blood Tests)* (above) reference was made to the European Convention on Human Rights. In balancing the various rights to family life of the child and adult parties under art 8 the child's right to know his true roots and identity carried the most weight. Any interference with the adult parties' rights to a private and family life was proportionate to the legitimate aim of providing such knowledge to the child. The UN Convention on the Rights of the Child 1989 also supports a child knowing his identity.

## Declaration of parentage

A free-standing application for a declaration of parentage can now be made (see s55A Family Law Act 1986 as introduced by the Criminal Justice and Court Services Act 2000).

## *Legitimation*

### Section 2 Legitimacy Act 1976

A child is legitimated by the subsequent marriage of his parents if his father was domiciled in England at the date of marriage and even if, at the time of his birth, one or both parents were married to someone else.

Legitimacy dates from the marriage; or 1 January 1927, if later; or 29 October 1959, if later, and if either parent was married to someone else at the date of his birth.

### Section 3 Legitimacy Act 1976

Where the parents of an illegitimate person marry, or have married, one another, and the father of the illegitimate person was, or is, at the time of the marriage, domiciled in a country other than England and Wales, by the law of which the illegitimate person became legitimated by virtue of such subsequent marriage, that person, if living, shall be recognised in England and Wales as having been so legitimate from the date of the marriage, notwithstanding that his father was not, at the time of the birth of that person, domiciled in a country in which legitimation by subsequent marriage was permitted by law.

### Section 1 Legitimacy Act 1976

'(1) The child of a void marriage, whenever born, shall, subject to subsection (2) below and Schedule 1 to this Act, be treated as the legitimate child of his parents if at the time of the insemination resulting in the child's birth, or at the time of the act of intercourse resulting in the birth (or at the time of the celebration of the marriage if later) both or either of the parties reasonably believed that the marriage was valid.

(2) This section only applies where the father of the child was domiciled in England and Wales at the time of the birth, or, if he died before the birth, was so domiciled immediately before his death.'

In relation to a child born after 4 April 1988 it is presumed that one of the parties had such a reasonable belief that the marriage was valid, unless the contrary is shown (see s28 Family Law Reform Act 1987 introducing a new s1(4) Legitimacy Act 1976). This will make it easier for such children to claim to be legitimate since they are in effect presumed to be legitimate. It is also made clear that a spouse's mistake as to the law in believing that the marriage was valid can be a reasonable belief (see s28 FLRA 1987 introducing a new s1(3) LA 1976). There had been doubt expressed on this point which is now resolved.

Section 1(1) LA 1976 cannot legitimate a child if he or she was born *before* his or her parents entered into the void marriage. See *Re Spence* [1990] 2 All ER 827 where A married L. L then left A and lived with S. Two children were born, J and P, who were illegitimate. L then married S. The marriage was void because of L's earlier marriage but S reasonably believed that the marriage was valid. J died intestate. P claimed the estate under the rules of intestacy. However, the claim could only succeed if he was J's legitimate brother and thereby entitled under intestacy. If he and J were illegitimate he was not entitled. The court held that L's subsequent marriage to S *after* J and P had been born could not legitimate them under s1(1) LA 1976.

NOTE: This decision does not apply where a person died intestate on or after 4 April 1988 since, as a result of s18 FLRA 1987, the general principle in s1 FLRA 1987 applies whereby the children of unmarried parents are treated in the same way as children of married parents in cases of intestacy.

## Voidable marriages

So far as voidable marriages are concerned, such children thereof are legitimate by virtue of s16 Matrimonial Causes Act 1973 (see Chapter 2).

## Effects of legitimation

1. Section 8 Legitimacy Act 1976

   'A legitimated person shall have the same rights, and shall be under the same obligation in respect of the maintenance and support of himself or of any other person as if he had been born legitimate ... and any claim for damages, compensation, allowances etc that could be made by or in respect of a legitimate child shall apply in the case of a legitimated person.'

2. He and his spouse may take property:

   a) under a deed executed after legitimation;
   b) on a death occurring after legitimation;
   c) on a death occurring after 31 December 1969;
   d) under an entail created after legitimation;
   e) under a deed made on or after 1 January 1970.

3. Further, the provision that legitimation must precede the date on which the disposition comes into operation has been removed by the Children Act 1975 if the instrument was made on or after 1 January 1976; or in the case of a disposition made by will, the testator died on or after that date.

4. A legitimate person cannot, however, succeed to a title created before legitimation or to property settled with it; or claim under a special power of appointment created before, but exercised after, legitimation.

## Declaration of legitimacy and legitimation

Section 56 Family Law Act 1986 has extended the existing law under s45 Matrimonial Causes Act 1973 for declarations as to legitimacy and legitimation, in that s56 allows for declarations to cover legitimations recognised at common law (the provision came into force on 4 April 1988).

Jurisdiction exists only if:

1. the applicant is domiciled in England or Wales at the date of the application; or
2. has been habitually resident in England and Wales for a period of one year ending with that date (s56(3)).

Under s56(1) any person may apply to the court for a declaration that he is the legitimate child of his parents.

Under s56(2) any person may apply to the court for one of the following declarations:

1. that he has become a legitimated person; or
2. that he has not become a legitimated person.

A 'legitimated person' means a person legitimated or recognised as legitimate under s2 or s3 Legitimacy Act 1976, or under s1 or s8 Legitimacy Act 1976, or by a legitimation (whether or not by virtue of the subsequent marriage of his parents) recognised by the law of England and Wales and effected under the law of another country.

The application will be made to the High Court or a county court.

## Status of children of unmarried parents

The Family Law Reform Act 1987 improved the status of children born to unmarried parents.

### General principle

In statutes passed after 4 April 1988 references to any relationship between two persons shall, unless the contrary intention appears, be construed without regard to whether or not the father or mother of either of them, or the father and mother of any person through whom the relationship is deduced, have or had not been married to each other at any time (see s1 FLRA 1987).

### Rights of intestate succession

In relation to rights under intestacy arising when a person dies on or after 4 April 1988, children born to unmarried parents will have the same rights as children born to married parents (see s18 FLRA 1987).

## The position of unmarried fathers

An unmarried father may obtain parental responsibility for his child by:

1. applying to the court for an order that he should have parental responsibility for the child (see s4(1)(a) CA 1989); or
2. the father and mother making a 'parental responsibility agreement' which

provides for the father to have parental responsibility for the child (see s4(1)(b) CA 1989. Regulations will set out the form and content of such an agreement); or
3. applying for a residence order with respect to the child (see s10 CA 1989).

## Children born by artificial insemination

The common law presumption that a child is the legitimate child of married parents does not apply if the husband is not the biological father. Invariably the child will in any event be treated as a child of the family or the parents may choose to adopt the child (as in *Re Adoption Application (Surrogacy)* [1987] 2 All ER 826).

A child born after 4 April 1988 in England and Wales as a result of artificial insemination of a woman who was at the time of the insemination married, and who was artificially inseminated with the semen of some man other than her husband, is treated in law as the child of the parties to the marriage and shall not be treated as the child of any other person, unless it is proved to the satisfaction of the court that the husband did not consent to the insemination (see s27 FLRA 1987).

NOTE: In *Re P (Minors) (Surrogacy)* [1988] 1 FLR 140 – an artificially inseminated mother refused to hand over twins she had given birth to on behalf of a husband and wife. The twins were made wards of court. The court held that the care and control of the children should go to the mother since that was in their best interests – their welfare being the first and paramount consideration. She was their natural mother and had had them for five months so that they were bonded to her.

The legal status of children born by artificial methods is regulated by the Human Fertilisation and Embryology Act 1990, the relevant provisions of which finally came into force on 1 November 1994. Section 27 FLRA 1987 has been replaced, but will still apply to women who received treatment before 1 August 1991.

Children may be born as a result of certain methods:

1. *Artificial insemination* (AID) (where male sperm is artificially inseminated into a woman's womb).
2. *In vitro fertilisation* (IVF) (where the woman's egg is fertilised by male sperm outside the womb and then inserted into it).
3. *Gametes intra-fallopean transfer* (GIFT) (where the woman's egg and the male sperm are placed into a woman's womb to fertilise there).

The child's parents could then be:

1. The woman in whose body the baby develops and who gives birth (her husband could be treated as the father).
2. The woman who donated the egg.
3. The man who donated the sperm.

All three could be unrelated people, eg a woman donates an egg, it is fertilised using the sperm of an unrelated man (an 'anonymous donor') and the baby develops in a 'surrogate' mother. Who are the child's parents? ... the genetic parents who donated egg/sperm (and their spouses) or the woman who gives birth (and her spouse)?

Where the genetic mother and the birth mother are the same and the genetic father is the woman's husband/partner then the mother and husband/partner are the legal parents. This covers situations where parents cannot conceive naturally and use either AIH or IVF with their own eggs/sperm and the woman bears the resulting child.

BUT where the child is conceived using frozen sperm or a frozen embryo after the death of the man who supplied the sperm the child is legally fatherless. This could happen, for example, where a husband had cancer. He donates sperm which is then stored frozen. He undergoes radiation treatment for his cancer which could render him infertile. If he then dies from the cancer his wife could use her husband's frozen sperm to have a child but the husband would not be the child's father. The law seeks to discourage children being born to a widow and having a dead father (see s28(6)). There is a rule that a child cannot have two fathers (s28(4)).

Where a child is born to a married woman using sperm donated by a man who is not her husband (eg by AID) the child is treated as the child of the married parents unless it is proved to the satisfaction of the court that the husband did not consent to the insemination (s28(2) HFEA 1990). The presumption that a child born in wedlock is the legitimate child of the married parents appears to apply so the husband might have to dispute paternity (eg using DNA tests) in the same way as a child born after natural conception (s28(5) HFEA 1990). The genetic father (ie the donor of the sperm, who might be anonymous) would not be the legal father in these circumstances. An anonymous donor who gives his consent to the use of his sperm for licensed artificial insemination cannot be the father (s28(6)). Section 28(2) was applied in *Re CH (Contact)* [1996] 1 FLR 569. H married W1, and they had a daughter. H then had a vasectomony, after which he divorced W1 and married W2. H tried unsuccessfully to reverse the vasectomony, and he and W2 then received fertility treatment whereby W2 was artificially inseminated with the sperm of an anonymous donor for which H gave his written consent. A child was born in April 1993. H was present at the birth and was registered as the child's father. H and W2 separated in March 1994 and W2 started a new relationship. W2 tried to deny contact between H and the child on the basis that he was not the child's biological father.

HELD: By virtue of s28(2) HFEA 1990, H was treated in law as the child's father. The child had only been born with H's consent and his participation in the treatment. It was accepted that H loved the child and had a right to contact. W2 could not prevent contact unless there were compelling reasons which made contact unwise or undesirable. There were no such reasons, and contact was ordered.

By contrast, in *Re Q (Parental Order)* [1996] 1 FLR 369 a married couple, H and W, entered into a surrogacy arrangement whereby an unmarried woman agreed to have placed in her an embryo created from W's egg and the sperm from an anonymous donor. The treatment was provided through a licensed clinic, and payments totalling £8,280 were made to the surrogate mother. A child was born, and H and W sought a parental order under s30 HFEA 1990 (see below).

HELD: The child had no natural father since the surrogate mother was unmarried and the sperm donor was anonymous (see s28(6)(a)), therefore no consent was required under s30(5) before a parental order could be made. Payments to the surrogate mother could be authorised under s30(7) retrospectively *(Re Adoption Application (Adoption: Payment)* [1987] 2 FLR 291). H could not be regarded as the child's father under s28(3) since no treatment had been provided for him. His status as father was confirmed by the s30 parental order.

Where a child is born to an unmarried woman using sperm donated by a stranger if she received treatment at a licensed clinic together with her unmarried partner then he is treated as the child's father even though he is not the genetic father (s28(3) HFEA 1990). As with any unmarried father he would not have parental responsibility under the Children Act 1989 though he could acquire such responsibility by agreement with the mother or by court order.

Section 28(3) was considered in *Re D (Parental Responsibility: IVF Baby)* [2001] 1 FLR 972 in which a child was born to M after her egg was fertilised with the sperm of an anonymous donor. At the time she agreed to the treatment she said she had a stable relationship with B. She and B had initial fertility treatment. By the time of the second treatment the relationship between M and B was no longer stable and M had a relationship with another man. M misled the authorities in order for the treatment to continue. The parties asked the court to apply s28(3) and treat B as the child's father. M opposed B having any relationship with the child. B applied for contact and parental responsibility. An order for indirect contact was made. Without the agreement the child's father could theoretically have been the anonymous donor or M's new partner.

Where there is a surrogacy arrangement involving a woman bearing a child on behalf of genetic parents who have donated eggs or sperm or both (eg because the genetic mother has no womb) the surrogate mother who gives birth to the child is the legal mother (not the genetic parents) (s27 HFEA 1990). The surrogate mother has parental responsibility for the child which she cannot transfer or surrender (s2(9) Children Act 1989). Any agreement between the surrogate mother and the genetic parents to hand the child over to the genetic parents is unenforceable (s1A Surrogacy Arrangements Act 1985) and no payments can be made for a surrogacy arrangement unless it is authorised by the court (eg to cover surrogacy expenses).

BUT the child can be treated in law as the child of married genetic parents even though the child has been born to a surrogate mother if the genetic parents apply to the court within six months of the child's birth (or in the case of a child born before the coming into force of s30 within six months of s30 coming into force). The genetic parents must each be at least eighteen years old and the child be living with them. The court must be satisfied that the surrogate mother (and her husband in some cases) have freely and with full understanding of what is involved, agreed unconditionally to the making of the order. The agreement of the surrogate mother is ineffective until the child is at least six weeks old. No payment can have been made for the surrogacy arrangements unless authorised by the court. Proceedings under s30 HFEA 1990 are family proceedings under the Children Act 1989 and so the child's welfare is the first consideration. If s30 does not apply an alternative is for the genetic parents to bring adoption proceedings assuming that the child has lived with them for the minimum period required by the Adoption Act 1976.

See *Re W (Minors) (Surrogacy)* [1991] 1 FLR 385 where the genetic mother had no womb but could produce eggs. Eggs were taken from her and fertilised in vitro by sperm from her husband. Two embryos were implanted in a surrogate mother who gave birth to twins. The twins went to live with the genetic parents. The local authority made the children wards of court and applied for declarations as to who the children's legal parents were.

HELD: The welfare of the children was paramount. They were happy in their home. The application was adjourned to allow the genetic parents to apply under s30 HFEA 1990 within twenty-eight days of it coming into force for an order that they be declared the twins' legal parents.

See *Re C (Application by Mr and Mrs X under s30 HFEA 1990)* [2002] Fam Law 351 in which H was married to W. W could not conceive a child. With the assistance of an organisation called COTS they entered into a surrogacy agreement with M which included a payment of £12,000 covering potential loss of earnings and expenses. M was unemployed. H and W did not wish for her to work during any pregnancy. M conceived a child using H's sperm and a child was born. Application was made to justices for an order under s30 HFEA 1990 giving parental responsibility for the child to H and W. The justices refused to make the order because of the payment of £12,000. On appeal the payment was authorised and the s30 order made. The payment was held not to be disproportionate and entered into in good faith. It was manifestly in the interests of the child that the order be made.

If the natural parent does not agree to the s30 application then it cannot succeed. For an illustration of such circumstances see *Re MW (Adoption: Surrogacy)* [1995] 2 FLR 759 where a married couple who entered into a surrogacy arrangement whereby a woman was fertilised with the husband's sperm applied to adopt the resulting child. The applicants could not have applied for a s30 order since the birth mother refused to give her consent. In the adoption application her consent was dispensed with and the adoption order made.

NB: Section 30 came into force on 1 November 1994.

The above does not apply to unmarried genetic parents where the surrogate mother remains the legal mother.

NB: A male donor may give written consent for the use of his sperm so that he is not treated as the legal father of any child born using it (s28(6)(a) HFEA 1990). Otherwise he may be treated as the legal father even though he donated the sperm 'anonymously'. The HFEA 1990 creates the Human Fertilisation and Embryology Authority which regulates clinics providing assisted conception services. Such clinics must provide the authority with the names and other details of donors of eggs or sperm otherwise they cannot be used. Essentially a donor can remain anonymous in that his or her name and address should not be revealed, eg to a child enquiring about his or her genetic parent(s) (though some limited information on the characteristics of the donor may be provided).

A woman cannot be treated unless account has been taken of the welfare of any child who may be born as a result of the treatment (including the need of a child for a father) and of any other child who may be affected by the birth (s13(5) HFEA 1990). The woman being treated and any man treated with her must be given an opportunity to receive proper counselling about the implications of the treatment (s13(6) HFEA 1990). A donor must also be given an opportunity for counselling (para 3, Sch 3 HFEA 1990).

In *Rose* v *Secretary of State and HFEA* [2002] 2 FLR 962 it was held that art 8 of the European Convention on Human Rights gave the right to a child born by artificial information to have information about the donor. The child had the right to establish details of his or her identity and this included the right to information about a biological parent. Whether the HFEA 1990 in its restrictions on providing information about anonymous donors was incompatible with the Convention was left as an open question.

In *Leeds Teaching Hospital NHS Trust* v *Mr and Mrs A* (2003) The Times 28 February the court had to determine the parentage of twins born to Mrs A. Mr and Mrs A underwent IVF treatmnet but Mrs A's eggs were accidentally fertilised with Mr B's sperm. Under common law Mr B was declared to be the father. Section 28 HFEA 1990 did not assist. Mr A had not consented to the embryo being mistakenly placed in Mrs A so s28(2) did not apply. Section 28(3) did not apply since Mr and Mrs A could not be considered as having treatment together in these circumstances. Mr and Mrs A then determined to apply to adopt the twins so that they could gain exclusive parental responsibility for them.

# 16

# Taxation on Separation and Divorce

16.1  Introduction

16.2  Income tax

16.3  Maintenance payments

16.4  Inheritance tax

16.5  Capital gains tax

## 16.1  Introduction

It was stated by the Court of Appeal in *S* v *S* [1977] Fam 127 that the legal advisers to the parties in a divorce should always be aware of the tax implications of any proposed financial settlement and be able to inform the court of the tax effects of any order it may propose to make. In many cases a careful utilisation of the provisions of taxation statutes and Inland Revenue extra-statutory concessions can result in financial benefits to both parties (see also *Lewis* v *Lewis* [1977] 1 WLR 409; [1977] 3 All ER 992; *Preston* v *Preston* [1982] 1 All ER 41; [1981] 3 WLR 619).

The tax which is most frequently considered in dealing with financial arrangements on divorce is income tax, but considerations of capital gains tax (CGT) and inheritance tax (IHT) could arise.

## 16.2  Income tax

### *Spouses living together*

Spouses are taxed separately. Each spouse is taxed on his or her own income. Each spouse claims his or her own personal allowance to offset against his or her own income. Each spouse is responsible for paying his or her own income tax and can keep his or her private affairs private from his or her own spouse if they so choose.

There used to be a married couple's allowance but this allowance ceased in 2000 (save for spouses over the age of 65).

The personal allowance for 2002–2003 is £4,615.

## Rates and bands of income tax for 2002–2003

| | | |
|---|---|---|
| Lower rate | 10 per cent | £1,880 a year or less |
| Basic rate | 22 per cent | £1,881 to £28,400 a year |
| Higher rate | 40 per cent | over £28,400 a year |

## Working Families Tax Credit

The Working Families Tax Credit (WFTC) is an allowance paid to low-paid workers with children. It is administered by the Inland Revenue and is available to all couples (married or unmarried) or single parents with one or more children under 16 (or under 19 if still in full time education) living with them. One or both of the parents must work 16 hours a week or more. From April 2002 it comprises:

1. a basic tax credit of £60 a week;
2. an extra tax credit of £11.65 a week if one partner works at least 30 hours a week;
3. a tax credit for each child of £26.45 from birth, £27.20 from the September after their 16th birthday until the day before they are 19;
4. a childcare tax credit of up to 70 per cent of eligible child care costs to a maximum of £135 a week for one child, £200 a week for two or more children;
5. extra credits for disabled children.

The WFTC is reduced by 55p for each £1 of net income above £94.50 a week. There are reductions if there are savings above £3,000, and the person is not eligible if there are savings over £8,000. Payments of child maintenance or child support are disregarded as income.

To illustrate how the WFTC works take a lone parent who works 27 hours a week and earns £200 a week net. She has a child aged seven and pays £60 a week childcare. She will receive:

1. a basic tax credit of £60;
2. a tax credit for her child of £26.45;
3. a childcare tax credit of £42 (ie 70 per cent of £60)

Total tax credit = £128.45.
    Less 55 per cent of £105.50 (income above £94.50)
    = £70.42.

This is then used to reduce the amount of tax owed or as an extra payment.
    Once granted the WTFC lasts for six months when it is reassessed.

## Children's Tax Credit

From April 2001 a tax allowance called the Children's Tax Credit is available to parents with at least one child under 16 living with them. There is one credit regardless of the number of children living with the parent(s). The credit will apply to the parent with the highest income.

### Child Tax Credit and Working Tax Credit

From April 2003 there will be radical changes to the tax and benefits system. The tax credits will be operated by the Inland Revenue rather than the Department for Work and Pensions. The Child Tax Credit will replace the amounts currently paid for in most benefits and tax credits (with the exception of child benefit). The Working Tax Credit will replace the Working Families Tax Credit which will be abolished.

### Taxation on separation

A couple are treated as remaining married unless:

1. they are separated under a court order or a deed of separation; or
2. there is no court order or deed but they are in fact separated in such circumstances that the separation is likely to be permanent (see s282 ICTA 1988).

The spouses are then taxed as two separate individuals.

## 16.3 Maintenance payments

There used to be financial relief on maintenance payments. This was an important benefit which was the subject of much income tax legislation and case law. From 6 April 2000 financial relief on maintenance payments (with some exceptions) ceased (except for married couples aged 65 years or more).

Before 6 April 2000 the tax rules were complex. Maintenance orders or agreements set up for the first time since 15 March 1988 were taxed differently from those made before them. For orders or agreements after March 1988 ex-spouses who received maintenance paid no tax on it and the person who paid it received tax relief on their payments up to a given limit (£1,970 in 1999–2000, but restricted to 10 per cent). For orders or agreements made before March 1988 the person paying the maintenance received tax relief which in past years could have been extremely generous.

## 16.4 Inheritance tax

The threshold for inheritance tax is £250,000 for 2002–2003 and charged at 40 per cent.

The following are free from inheritance tax:

1. gifts to a surviving spouse (provided that both spouses are domiciled in the UK – s18 Inheritance Tax Act 1984);
2. transfers made pursuant to a court order on divorce (s10 ITA 1984);
3. maintenance payments (s11 ITA 1984);
4. some wedding gifts, gifts to grandchildren and some small gifts are exempt;
5. gifts up to £3,000 in any one year;
6. gifts made more than seven years before death.

Gifts made within seven years of death attract tax at rates which depend on when the gift was made.

It will be rare for inheritance tax liability to be incurred as a result of divorce.

## 16.5 Capital gains tax

Capital gains tax (CGT) only applies to capital gains of over £7,500 (2002–2003 rates). Above this, starting-rate taxpayers pay capital gains tax at 10 per cent, basic rate taxpayers at 20 per cent and higher rate taxpayers at 40 per cent.

Certain gains are free of CGT:

1. gifts between husband and wife;
2. the disposal of a person's only or main home;
3. maintenance paid to ex-spouses and transfers of property as part of a divorce settlement;
4. gifts for the education, maintenance or training of a child if the child is still in full-time education;
5. annual gifts up to £3,000.

The 2002–2003 rate is 40 per cent.

After divorce there is no longer an exemption for spouses so a transfer of property after divorce may give rise to a CGT liability. The principal private residence exemption will normally still apply for up to two years after one party ceased to reside there. Any sale or transfer after that two-year period may give rise to a CGT liability.

In relation to the main or only home exemption, if the parties separate only one of them will be living in the home. The Inland Revenue operates a concession whereby, if one of the spouses has continued to live in the property, any transfer on separation or divorce to the occupying spouse will be exempt (see ss101–109 Capital Gains Tax 1989 and Inland Revenue practice).

# Index

# Unannotated Cracknell's Statutes for use in Examinations

## New Editions of Cracknell's Statutes

### £11.95 due 2003

Cracknell's Statutes provide a comprehensive series of essential statutory provisions for each subject. Amendments are consolidated, avoiding the need to cross-refer to amending legislation. Unannotated, they are suitable for use in examinations, and provide the precise wording of vital Acts of Parliament for the diligent student.

**Constitutional and Administrative Law**
ISBN: 1 85836 511 2

**Equity and Trusts**
ISBN: 1 85836 508 2

**Contract, Tort and Remedies**
ISBN: 1 85836 507 4

**Land: The Law of Real Property**
ISBN: 1 85836 509 0

**English Legal System**
ISBN: 1 85836 510 4

**Law of International Trade**
ISBN: 1 85836 512 0

For further information on contents or to place an order, please contact:

Mail Order
Old Bailey Press
at Holborn College
Woolwich Road
Charlton
London
SE7 8LN

Telephone No: 020 8317 6039
Fax No: 020 8317 6004
Website: www.oldbaileypress.co.uk

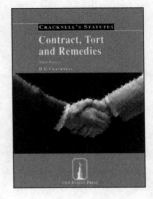

# Suggested Solutions to Past Examination Questions 2001–2002

The Suggested Solutions series provides examples of full answers to the questions regularly set by examiners. Each suggested solution has been broken down into three stages: general comment, skeleton solution and suggested solution. The examination questions included within the text are taken from past examination papers set by the London University. The full opinion answers will undoubtedly assist you with your research and further your understanding and appreciation of the subject in question.

**Only £6.95 due November 2003**

**Company Law**
ISBN: 1 85836 519 8

**Evidence**
ISBN: 1 85836 521 X

**Employment Law**
ISBN: 1 85836 520 1

**Family Law**
ISBN: 1 85836 525 2

**European Union Law**
ISBN: 1 85836 524 4

For further information on contents or to place an order, please contact:

Mail Order
Old Bailey Press
at Holborn College
Woolwich Road
Charlton
London
SE7 8LN

Telephone No: 020 8317 6039
Fax No: 020 8317 6004
Website: www.oldbaileypress.co.uk

Company Law

2001–2002 LLB Examination Questions
and Suggested Solutions

University of London
External Examinations

Solutions by Susan Barber

# Old Bailey Press

The Old Bailey Press integrated student law library is tailor-made to help you at every stage of your studies from the preliminaries of each subject through to the final examination. The series of Textbooks, Revision WorkBooks, 150 Leading Cases and Cracknell's Statutes are interrelated to provide you with a comprehensive set of study materials.

You can buy Old Bailey Press books from your University Bookshop, your local Bookshop, direct using this form, or you can order a free catalogue of our titles from the address shown overleaf.

The following subjects each have a Textbook, 150 Leading Cases/Casebook, Revision WorkBook and Cracknell's Statutes unless otherwise stated.

Administrative Law
Commercial Law
Company Law
Conflict of Laws
Constitutional Law
Conveyancing (Textbook and 150 Leading Cases)
Criminal Law
Criminology (Textbook and Sourcebook)
Employment Law (Textbook and Cracknell's Statutes)
English and European Legal Systems
Equity and Trusts
Evidence
Family Law
Jurisprudence: The Philosophy of Law (Textbook, Sourcebook and
    Revision WorkBook)
Land: The Law of Real Property
Law of International Trade
Law of the European Union
Legal Skills and System
    (Textbook)
Obligations: Contract Law
Obligations: The Law of Tort
Public International Law
Revenue Law (Textbook,
    Revision WorkBook and
    Cracknell's Statutes)
Succession

| Mail order prices: | |
| --- | --- |
| Textbook | £15.95 |
| 150 Leading Cases | £11.95 |
| Revision WorkBook | £9.95 |
| Cracknell's Statutes | £11.95 |
| Suggested Solutions 1999–2000 | £6.95 |
| Suggested Solutions 2000–2001 | £6.95 |
| Suggested Solutions 2001–2002 | £6.95 |
| Law Update 2003 | £10.95 |
| Law Update 2004 | £10.95 |

Please note details and prices are subject to alteration.

**To complete your order, please fill in the form below:**

| Module | Books required | Quantity | Price | Cost |
|--------|----------------|----------|-------|------|
|        |                |          |       |      |
|        |                |          |       |      |
|        |                |          |       |      |
|        |                |          |       |      |
|        |                |          |       |      |
|        |                | Postage  |       |      |
|        |                | TOTAL    |       |      |

For Europe, add 15% postage and packing (£20 maximum).
For the rest of the world, add 40% for airmail.

## ORDERING

**By telephone to Mail Order at 020 8317 6039**, with your credit card to hand.

**By fax to 020 8317 6004** (giving your credit card details).

**Website: www.oldbaileypress.co.uk**

**By post to: Mail Order, Old Bailey Press at Holborn College, Woolwich Road, Charlton, London, SE7 8LN.**

When ordering by post, please enclose full payment by cheque or banker's draft, or complete the credit card details below. You may also order a free catalogue of our complete range of titles from this address.

We aim to despatch your books within 3 working days of receiving your order.

Name

Address

Postcode                                    Telephone

Total value of order, including postage: £

**I enclose a cheque/banker's draft for the above sum, or**

charge my          ☐ Access/Mastercard          ☐ Visa          ☐ American Express
Card number

☐☐☐☐ ☐☐☐☐ ☐☐☐☐ ☐☐☐☐

Expiry date          ☐☐☐☐

Signature: ................................................Date: ..........................................